POETRY
for Students

Advisors

Jayne M. Burton is a teacher of English, a member of the Delta Kappa Gamma International Society for Key Women Educators, and currently a master's degree candidate in the Interdisciplinary Study of Curriculum and Instruction and English at Angelo State University.

Mary Beth Maggio teaches seventh grade language arts in Schaumburg, Illinois.

Tom Shilts is the youth librarian at the Okemos branch of Capital Area District Library in Okemos, Michigan. He holds an MSLS degree from Clarion University of Pennsylvania and an MA in U.S. History from the University of North Dakota.

Amy Spade Silverman has taught at independent schools in California, Texas, Michigan, and New York. She holds a bachelor of arts degree from the University of Michigan and a master of fine arts degree from the University of Houston. She is a member of the National Council of Teachers of English and Teachers and Writers. She is an exam reader for Advanced Placement Literature and Composition. She is also a poet, published in *North American Review*, *Nimrod*, and *Michigan Quarterly Review*, among others.

Mary Turner holds a BS in Secondary Education from East Texas State University and a Master of Education from Western Kentucky University. She teaches English 7 and AP English 12 literature and composition at SBEC in Southaven, Mississippi.

Brian Woerner teaches English at Troy High School in Troy, Ohio. He is also a Program Associate of the Ohio Writing Project at Miami University.

POETRY
for Students

**Presenting Analysis, Context, and Criticism
on Commonly Studied Poetry**

VOLUME 42

Sara Constantakis, Project Editor

Foreword by David J. Kelly

GALE
CENGAGE Learning·

Detroit • New York • San Francisco • New Haven, Conn • Waterville, Maine • London

GALE
CENGAGE Learning®

Poetry for Students, Volume 42

Project Editor: Sara Constantakis

Rights Acquisition and Management:
Sheila Spencer

Composition: Evi Abou-El-Seoud

Manufacturing: Rhonda Dover

Imaging: John Watkins

Product Design: Pamela A. E. Galbreath,
Jennifer Wahi

Digital Content Production: Allie Semperger

Product Manager: Meggin Condino

For product information and technology assistance, contact us at
Gale Customer Support, 1-800-877-4253.
For permission to use material from this text or product,
submit all requests online at **www.cengage.com/permissions.**
Further permissions questions can be emailed to
permissionrequest@cengage.com

While every effort has been made to ensure the reliability of the information presented in this publication, Gale, a part of Cengage Learning, does not guarantee the accuracy of the data contained herein. Gale accepts no payment for listing; and inclusion in the publication of any organization, agency, institution, publication, service, or individual does not imply endorsement of the editors or publisher. Errors brought to the attention of the publisher and verified to the satisfaction of the publisher will be corrected in future editions.

Gale
27500 Drake Rd.
Farmington Hills, MI, 48331-3535

ISBN-13: 978-1-4144-9503-3
ISBN-10: 1-4144-9503-X

ISSN 1094-7019

This title is also available as an e-book.
ISBN-13: 978-1-4144-9276-6
ISBN-10: 1-4144-9276-6
Contact your Gale, a part of Cengage Learning sales representative for ordering information.

Printed in Mexico
1 2 3 4 5 6 7 17 16 15 14 13 12

Table of Contents

Just a Few Lines on a Page

I have often thought that poets have the easiest job in the world. A poem, after all, is just a few lines on a page, usually not even extending margin to margin—how long would that take to write, about five minutes? Maybe ten at the most, if you wanted it to rhyme or have a repeating meter. Why, I could start in the morning and produce a book of poetry by dinnertime. But we all know that it isn't that easy. Anyone can come up with enough words, but the poet's job is about writing the *right* ones. The right words will change lives, making people see the world somewhat differently than they saw it just a few minutes earlier. The right words can make a reader who relies on the dictionary for meanings take a greater responsibility for his or her own personal understanding. A poem that is put on the page correctly can bear any amount of analysis, probing, defining, explaining, and interrogating, and something about it will still feel new the next time you read it.

It would be fine with me if I could talk about poetry without using the word "magical," because that word is overused these days to imply "a really good time," often with a certain sweetness about it, and a lot of poetry is neither of these. But if you stop and think about magic—whether it brings to mind sorcery, witchcraft, or bunnies pulled from top hats—it always seems to involve stretching reality to produce a result greater than the sum of its parts and pulling unexpected results out of thin air. This book provides ample cases where a

few simple words conjure up whole worlds. We do not actually travel to different times and different cultures, but the poems get into our minds, they find what little we know about the places they are talking about, and then they make that little bit blossom into a bouquet of someone else's life. Poets make us think we are following simple, specific events, but then they leave ideas in our heads that cannot be found on the printed page. Abracadabra.

Sometimes when you finish a poem it doesn't feel as if it has left any supernatural effect on you, like it did not have any more to say beyond the actual words that it used. This happens to everybody, but most often to inexperienced readers: regardless of what is often said about young people's infinite capacity to be amazed, you have to understand what usually does happen, and what could have happened instead, if you are going to be moved by what someone has accomplished. In those cases in which you finish a poem with a "So what?" attitude, the information provided in *Poetry for Students* comes in handy. Readers can feel assured that the poems included here actually are potent magic, not just because a few (or a hundred or ten thousand) professors of literature say they are: they're significant because they can withstand close inspection and still amaze the very same people who have just finished taking them apart and seeing how they work. Turn them inside out, and they will still be able to come alive, again and again. *Poetry for Students* gives readers of any age good practice in feeling the ways poems relate to both the reality of the time and place the poet lived in and the reality of our emotions. Practice is just another word for being a student. The information given here helps you understand the way to read poetry; what to look for, what to expect.

With all of this in mind, I really don't think I would actually like to have a poet's job at all. There are too many skills involved, including precision, honesty, taste, courage, linguistics, passion, compassion, and the ability to keep all sorts of people entertained at once. And that is just what they do with one hand, while the other hand pulls some sort of trick that most of us will never fully understand. I can't even pack all that I need for a weekend into one suitcase, so what would be my chances of stuffing so much life into a few lines? With all that *Poetry for Students* tells us about each poem, I am impressed that any poet can finish three or four poems a year. Read the inside stories of these poems, and you won't be able to approach any poem in the same way you did before.

David J. Kelly
College of Lake County

Introduction

Purpose of the Book

The purpose of *Poetry for Students* (*PfS*) is to provide readers with a guide to understanding, enjoying, and studying poems by giving them easy access to information about the work. Part of Gale's "For Students" Literature line, *PfS* is specifically designed to meet the curricular needs of high school and undergraduate college students and their teachers, as well as the interests of general readers and researchers considering specific poems. While each volume contains entries on "classic" poems frequently studied in classrooms, there are also entries containing hard-to-find information on contemporary poems, including works by multicultural, international, and women poets.

The information covered in each entry includes an introduction to the poem and the poem's author; the actual poem text (if possible); a poem summary, to help readers unravel and understand the meaning of the poem; analysis of important themes in the poem; and an explanation of important literary techniques and movements as they are demonstrated in the poem.

In addition to this material, which helps the readers analyze the poem itself, students are also provided with important information on the literary and historical background informing each work. This includes a historical context essay, a box comparing the time or place the poem was written to modern Western culture, a critical overview essay, and excerpts from critical essays on the poem. A unique feature of *PfS* is a specially commissioned critical essay on each poem, targeted toward the student reader.

To further help today's student in studying and enjoying each poem, information on audio recordings and other media adaptations is provided (if available), as well as reading suggestions for works of fiction and nonfiction on similar themes and topics. Classroom aids include ideas for research papers and lists of critical and reference sources that provide additional material on the poem.

Selection Criteria

The titles for each volume of *PfS* are selected by surveying numerous sources on notable literary works and analyzing course curricula for various schools, school districts, and states. Some of the sources surveyed include: high school and undergraduate literature anthologies and textbooks; lists of award-winners, and recommended titles, including the Young Adult Library Services Association (YALSA) list of best books for young adults.

Input solicited from our expert advisory board—consisting of educators and librarians—guides us to maintain a mix of "classic" and contemporary literary works, a mix of challenging and engaging works (including genre titles that are commonly studied) appropriate for different age levels, and a mix of international, multicultural and women authors. These advisors also consult on each volume's entry list, advising on which titles are most studied, most appropriate, and meet the broadest interests across secondary (grades 7–12) curricula and undergraduate literature studies.

How Each Entry Is Organized

Each entry, or chapter, in *PfS* focuses on one poem. Each entry heading lists the full name of the poem, the author's name, and the date of the poem's publication. The following elements are contained in each entry:

Introduction: a brief overview of the poem which provides information about its first appearance, its literary standing, any controversies surrounding the work, and major conflicts or themes within the work.

Author Biography: this section includes basic facts about the poet's life, and focuses on events and times in the author's life that inspired the poem in question.

Poem Text: when permission has been granted, the poem is reprinted, allowing for quick reference when reading the explication of the following section.

Poem Summary: a description of the major events in the poem. Summaries are broken down with subheads that indicate the lines being discussed.

Themes: a thorough overview of how the major topics, themes, and issues are addressed within the poem. Each theme discussed appears in a separate subhead.

Style: this section addresses important style elements of the poem, such as form, meter, and rhyme scheme; important literary devices used, such as imagery, foreshadowing, and symbolism; and, if applicable, genres to which the work might have belonged, such as Gothicism or Romanticism. Literary terms are explained within the entry, but can also be found in the Glossary.

Historical Context: this section outlines the social, political, and cultural climate in which the author lived and the poem was created. This section may include descriptions of related historical events, pertinent aspects of daily life in the culture, and the artistic and literary sensibilities of the time in which the work was written. If the poem is a historical work,

information regarding the time in which the poem is set is also included. Each section is broken down with helpful subheads.

Critical Overview: this section provides background on the critical reputation of the poem, including bannings or any other public controversies surrounding the work. For older works, this section includes a history of how the poem was first received and how perceptions of it may have changed over the years; for more recent poems, direct quotes from early reviews may also be included.

Criticism: an essay commissioned by *PfS* which specifically deals with the poem and is written specifically for the student audience, as well as excerpts from previously published criticism on the work (if available).

Sources: an alphabetical list of critical material quoted in the entry, with full bibliographical information.

Further Reading: an alphabetical list of other critical sources which may prove useful for the student. Includes full bibliographical information and a brief annotation.

Suggested Search Terms: a list of search terms and phrases to jumpstart students' further information seeking. Terms include not just titles and author names but also terms and topics related to the historical and literary context of the works.

In addition, each entry contains the following highlighted sections, set apart from the main text as sidebars:

Media Adaptations: if available, a list of audio recordings as well as any film or television adaptations of the poem, including source information.

Topics for Further Study: a list of potential study questions or research topics dealing with the poem. This section includes questions related to other disciplines the student may be studying, such as American history, world history, science, math, government, business, geography, economics, psychology, etc.

Compare & Contrast: an "at-a-glance" comparison of the cultural and historical differences between the author's time and culture and late twentieth century or early twenty-first century Western culture. This box includes pertinent parallels between the major scientific, political, and cultural movements of the time or place the poem was written, the time or place the poem was set (if a historical work), and modern Western culture. Works written after 1990 may not have this box.

What Do I Read Next?: a list of works that might give a reader points of entry into a classic work (e.g., YA or multicultural titles) and/ or complement the featured poem or serve as a contrast to it. This includes works by the same author and others, works from various genres, YA works, and works from various cultures and eras.

Other Features

PfS includes "Just a Few Lines on a Page," a foreword by David J. Kelly, an adjunct professor of English, College of Lake County, Illinois. This essay provides a straightforward, unpretentious explanation of why poetry should be marveled at and how *PfS* can help teachers show students how to enrich their own reading experiences.

A Cumulative Author/Title Index lists the authors and titles covered in each volume of the *PfS* series.

A Cumulative Nationality/Ethnicity Index breaks down the authors and titles covered in each volume of the *PfS* series by nationality and ethnicity.

A Subject/Theme Index, specific to each volume, provides easy reference for users who may be studying a particular subject or theme rather than a single work. Significant subjects from events to broad themes are included.

A Cumulative Index of First Lines (beginning in Vol. 10) provides easy reference for users who may be familiar with the first line of a poem but may not remember the actual title.

A Cumulative Index of Last Lines (beginning in Vol. 10) provides easy reference for users who may be familiar with the last line of a poem but may not remember the actual title.

Each entry may include illustrations, including photo of the author and other graphics related to the poem.

Citing Poetry for Students

When writing papers, students who quote directly from any volume of *PfS* may use the following general forms. These examples are based on MLA style; teachers may request that students adhere to a different style, so the following examples may be adapted as needed.

When citing text from *PfS* that is not attributed to a particular author (i.e., the Themes, Style, Historical Context sections, etc.), the following format should be used in the bibliography section:

"Angle of Geese." *Poetry for Students*. Ed. Marie Napierkowski and Mary Ruby. Vol. 2. Detroit: Gale, 1998. 8–9.

When quoting the specially commissioned essay from *PfS* (usually the first piece under the "Criticism" subhead), the following format should be used:

Velie, Alan. Critical Essay on "Angle of Geese." *Poetry for Students*. Ed. Marie Napierkowski and Mary Ruby. Vol. 2. Detroit: Gale, 1998. 7–10.

When quoting a journal or newspaper essay that is reprinted in a volume of *PfS*, the following form may be used:

Luscher, Robert M. "An Emersonian Context of Dickinson's 'The Soul Selects Her Own Society'." *ESQ: A Journal of American Renaissance* 30.2 (1984): 111–16. Excerpted and reprinted in *Poetry for Students*. Ed. Marie Napierkowski and Mary Ruby. Vol. 1. Detroit: Gale, 1998. 266–69.

When quoting material reprinted from a book that appears in a volume of *PfS*, the following form may be used:

Mootry, Maria K. "'Tell It Slant': Disguise and Discovery as Revisionist Poetic Discourse in 'The Bean Eaters'." *A Life Distilled: Gwendolyn Brooks, Her Poetry and Fiction*. Ed. Maria K. Mootry and Gary Smith. Urbana: University of Illinois Press, 1987. 177–80, 191. Excerpted and reprinted in *Poetry for Students*. Ed. Marie Napierkowski and Mary Ruby. Vol. 2. Detroit: Gale, 1998. 22–24.

We Welcome Your Suggestions

The editorial staff of *Poetry for Students* welcomes your comments and ideas. Readers who wish to suggest poems to appear in future volumes, or who have other suggestions, are cordially invited to contact the editor. You may contact the editor via E-mail at: **ForStudentsEditors@cengage.com.** Or write to the editor at:

Editor, *Poetry for Students*

Gale

27500 Drake Road

Farmington Hills, MI 48331-3535

Literary Chronology

1304: Francesco Petrarca is born on July 20 in Arezzo, Italy.

1374: Francesco Petrarca's Rime 140 is published.

1374: Francesco Petrarca dies of unknown cuases on July 19 in Arqua Petrarca, Italy.

1612: Anne Dudley Bradstreet is born on about March 20 in Northampton, England.

1678: Anne Bradsteet's "The Author to Her Book" is published in *Several Poems Compiled with Great Variety of Wit and Learning.*

1672: Anne Bradstreet dies of tuberculosis in North Andover in the Massachusetts Bay Colony on September 16.

1809: Edgar Allan Poe is born on January 19 in Boston, Massachusetts.

1830: Emily Dickinson is born on December 10 in Amherst, Massachusetts.

1840: Thomas Hardy is born on June 2 in Higher Bockhampton, Dorset, England.

1849: Edgar Allan Poe's "A Dream within a Dream" is published in *Flag of Our Union.*

1849: Edgar Allan Poe dies of unknown causes on October 7 in Baltimore, Maryland.

1865: William Butler Yeats is born on June 13 in Sandymount, County Dublin, Ireland.

1865: Joseph Rudyard Kipling is born on December 30 in Bombay, India.

1874: Amy Lowell is born on February 9 in Brookline, Massachusetts.

1886: Emily Dickinson dies of prolonged illness on May 15 in Amherst, Massachusetts.

1889: Gabriela Mistral (Lucila Godoy Alcayaga) is born on April 7 in Vicuna, Chile.

1897: Rudyard Kipling's "Recessional" is published in *The Times.*

1903: Countee Cullen is born on March 30. Reputable sources disagree about his place of birth, but Louisville, Kentucky and New York City are the most frequently cited.

1907: Rudyard Kipling is awarded the Nobel Prize in Literature.

1912: Thomas Hardy's "Convergence of the Twain" is published.

1917: William Butler Yeats's "The Wild Swans at Coole" is published in *The Little Review.*

1920: Amy Lowell's "Lilacs" is published in *New York Evening Post.*

1922: Philip Larkin is born on August 9 in Coventry, Warwickshire, England.

1922: Gabriela Mistral's "Serene Words" is published.

1923: William Butler Yeats is awarded the Nobel Prize in Literature.

1923: Denise Levertov is born on October 23 in Ilford, Essex, England.

1925: Countee Cullen's "Incident" is published.

1925: Amy Lowell dies of a stroke on May 12 in Brookline, Massachusetts.

1926: Amy Lowell is awarded the Pulitzer Prize for Poetry for *What's O'Clock*.

1928: Thomas Hardy dies of heart failure on January 11, in Dorchester, England.

1928: Maya Angelou is born on April 4 in St. Louis, Missouri.

1936: Rudyard Kipling dies of natural causes on January 17 in England.

1939: William Butler Yeats dies of natural causes on January 28 in Roquebrune, France.

1941: William James Collins is born on March 22 in New York City.

1943: Nikki Giovanni is born on June 7 in Knoxville, Tennessee.

1945: Emily Dickinson's "Tell all the Truth but tell it slant" is published in *Bolts of Melody: New Poems of Emily Dickinson*.

1945: Gabriela Mistral is awarded the Nobel Prize for literature.

1946: Countee Cullen dies of high blood pressure and uremic poisoning on January 9 in New York City.

1952: Naomi Shihab Nye is born on March 12 in St. Louis, Missouri.

1957: Gabriela Mistral dies of pancreatic cancer on January 10 in Hempstead, New York.

1967: Denise Levertov's "What Were They Like?" is published.

1972: Nikki Giovanni's "The World is Not a Pleasant Place to Be" is published.

1977: Philip Larkin's "Aubade" is published in the *Times Literary Supplement*.

1978: Maya Angelou's "Phenomenal Woman" is published in *And Still I Rise*.

1985: Philip Larkin dies on November 28 of esophageal cancer.

1991: William James Collins's "The History Teacher" is published.

1997: Denise Levertov dies of complications due to lymphoma on December 20 in Seattle, Washington.

2002: Naomi Shihab Nye's "All Things Not Considered" is published in *19 Varieties of Gazelle*.

Acknowledgements

The editors wish to thank the copyright holders of the excerpted criticism included in this volume and the permissions managers of many book and magazine publishing companies for assisting us in securing reproduction rights. We are also grateful to the staffs of the Detroit Public Library, the Library of Congress, the University of Detroit Mercy Library, Wayne State University Purdy/Kresge Library Complex, and the University of Michigan Libraries for making their resources available to us. Following is a list of the copyright holders who have granted us permission to reproduce material in this volume of PfS. Every effort has been made to trace copyright, but if omissions have been made, please let us know.

COPYRIGHTED EXCERPTS IN *PfS*, VOLUME 42, WERE REPRODUCED FROM THE FOLLOWING PERIODICALS:

Alif: Journal of Comparative Poetics, 2007. Reproduced by permission.—*American Poetry Review*, March/April, 2009 for "Dickinson's Stories" by Michael Ryan. Reproduced by permission of the author.—*Atlantic*, May, 1989 for "The Saddest Englishman" by Peter Davison. Reproduced by permission of the Literary Estate of the author.—*Atlantic Monthly*, July 1904.— *Commonweal*, January 11, 2002; September 26, 2008. Copyright © 2002, 2008 Commonweal Publishing Co., Inc. Both reproduced by permission of Commonweal Foundation—*Continent*, Vol. 5, No. 4, January 23, 1884.—*Explicator*, Winter, 2006 for "Bradstreet's 'The Author To Her Book'" by Lisa Day-Lindsey; Summer, 2007 for "Echoes of Eliot's 'The Love Song of J. Alfred Prufrock' in Larkin's 'Aubade'" by Richard Rankin Russell. Both reproduced by permission of Taylor & Francis Group, LLC, http://www.taylorandfrancis.com and the respective authors.—*Gay & Lesbian Review Worldwide*, July/August, 2004. Copyright © 2004, *Gay & Lesbian Review Worldwide*. Reproduced by permission—*Georgia Review*, Spring, 1966. Copyright © 1966 by The University of Georgia. Reproduced by permission.—*History Today*, June, 1997. Reproduced by permission.—*Hollins Critic*, October, 1991; June, 2002. Copyright 1991, 2002 by Hollins College. Both reproduced by permission.—*Horn Book*, September/October, 2002. Copyright 2002 by The Horn Book, Inc., Boston, MA, www.hbook.com. All rights reserved. Reproduced by permission.—*Journal of Negro History*, Summer, 2000. Reproduced by permission.— *Kirkus Reviews*, April 15, 2002. Copyright © 2002 Kirkus Media. All rights reserved. Reproduced by permission.—*London Times Literary Supplement*, March 20, 1919. Reproduced from *The Times Literary Supplement* by permission— *MELUS*, Winter, 2001; Winter, 2006. Copyright MELUS: The Society for the Study of Multi-Ethnic Literature of the United States, 2001, 2006. Both reproduced by permission.—*Modern Age*, Fall, 2000. Reproduced by permission.—*Mother*

Jones, March/April, 2002. © 2002, Foundation for National Progress. Reproduced by permission.— *New Criterion*, September, 2007 for "The Absence of Amy Lowell" by Carl Rollyson. Reproduced by permission of the author.—*New Hibernia Review*, v. 10, Winter, 2006 for "Joyce and Yeats: Easter 1916 and the Great War" by Wayne K. Chapman. Reproduced by permission of the publisher and author.—*New Republic*, January 26, 1974. Copyright © 1974 by The New Republic, Inc. Reproduced by permission of *The New Republic.*— *Opportunity*, January, 1926 for "'Color'—A Review" by Alain Locke. Reproduced by permission of the author.—*Publishers Weekly*, June 28, 1999. Reproduced from *Publishers Weekly*, published by the PWxyz, LLC, by permission.— *Renascence: Essays on Values in Literature*, Summer, 2006. Copyright © 2006, Marquette University Press. Reproduced by permission.—*Revista Hispanica Moderna*, December, 1997. Reproduced by permission.—*Studies in the Literary Imagination*, Spring, 2006. Copyright © 2006 Department of English, Georgia State University. Reproduced by permission.—*Susquehanna University Studies*, June, 1963. © 1963 by Associated University Presses, Inc. Reproduced by permission.— *Twentieth Century Literature*, Fall, 1992. Copyright © 1992 Hofstra University Press. Reproduced by permission.—*Writer*, April, 2006 for "Billy Collins" by Kay Day. Reproduced by permission of the author.

COPYRIGHTED EXCERPTS IN *PfS*, VOLUME 42, WERE REPRODUCED FROM THE FOLLOWING BOOKS:

Collins, Billy. From *Questions about Angels: Poems*. William Morrow and Company, Inc., 1991. Reproduced by permission of Chris Calhoun Agency LLC on behalf of the author.— Giovanni, Nikki. From *My House: Poems by Nikki Giovanni*. William Morrow and Company, Inc., 1972. Copyright © 1972, renewed 2000, by Nikki Giovanni. Reproduced by permission of HarperCollins Publishers Inc.—Hagen, Lyman B. From *Heart of a Woman, Mind of a Writer, and Soul of a Poet: A Critical Analysis of the Writings of Maya Angelou*. University Press of America, 1997. Reproduced by permission.—Keating, Peter. From *Kipling the Poet*. Secker & Warburg, 1994. Reproduced by permission of the author.— Latta, Kimberly. From *Inventing Maternity: Politics, Science, and Literature, 1650-1865*. University of Kentucky Press, 1999. Reproduced by permission of The University Press of Kentucky.—Lerner, Arthur. From *Psychoanalytically Oriented Criticism of Three American Poets: Poe, Whitman, and Aiken*. Fairleigh Dickinson University Press, 1970. Reproduced by permission.—Poe, Edgar Allen. From *Poe: Poetry and Tales*. Penguin, 1969.— Ramsey, Priscilla R. From *A Current Bibliography on African Affairs*, v. 17, 1984-1985. © 1984 Baywood Publishing Co., Inc. Reproduced by permission of Baywood Publishing Co., Inc.— Thackrey, Donald E. From *Emily Dickinson's Approach to Poetry*, 1954.

Contributors

Susan Andersen: Andersen is a writer and teacher with a PhD in literature. Entry on "Serene Words." Original essay on "Serene Words."

Bryan Aubrey: Aubrey holds a PhD in English. Entries on "The Convergence of the Twain" and "What Were They Like?" Original essays on "The Convergence of the Twain" and "What Were They Like?"

Rita M. Brown: Brown is an English professor. Entry on "The History Teacher." Original essay on "The History Teacher."

Catherine Dominic: Dominic is a novelist and a freelance writer and editor. Entries on "A Dream within a Dream" and "Phenomenal Woman." Original essays on "A Dream within a Dream" and "Phenomenal Woman."

Michael Allen Holmes: Holmes is a writer with existential interests. Entries on "Lilacs" and "Tell all the Truth but tell it slant." Original essays on "Lilacs" and "Tell all the Truth but tell it slant."

Sheri Metzger Karmiol: Karmiol teaches literature and drama at the University of New Mexico, where she is an adjunct professor in the University Honors Program. Entry on

"The World Is Not a Pleasant Place to Be." Original essay on "The World Is Not a Pleasant Place to Be."

David Kelly: Kelly is an instructor of creative writing and literature. Entry on "Incident." Original essay on "Incident."

Michael J. O'Neal: O'Neal holds a PhD in English. Entry on "The Author to Her Book." Original essay on "The Author to Her Book."

Rachel Porter: Porter is a freelance writer and editor who holds a bachelor of arts degree in English literature. Entry on "Aubade." Original essay on "Aubade."

Chris D. Russell: Russell is a freelance writer. Entry on "Recessional." Original essay on "Recessional."

Bradley A. Skeen: Skeen is a classicist. Entry on "Rime 140." Original essay on "Rime 140."

Carol Ullman: Ullman is a freelance writer and editor, specializing in literature. Entries on "All Things Not Considered" and "The Wild Swans at Coole." Original essays on "All Things Not Considered" and "The Wild Swans at Coole."

All Things Not Considered

NAOMI SHIHAB NYE

2002

"All Things Not Considered," by Naomi Shihab Nye, is a poem about the innocent casualties of the long-standing Israeli-Palestinian conflict. Nye, an Arab American whose father was part Palestinian, uses her work to argue for peace. She points to the deaths of children as an indication of the irrelevance of the argument that the conflict is justifiable as a religious war. Nye, who worked in public schools for twelve years, writes about and for children and teens, and this poem is no exception. The topic of "All Things Not Considered" is difficult but timely; the collection of Nye's this poem first appeared in, *19 Varieties of Gazelle: Poems about the Middle East*, was released just one year after the terrorist attacks of September 11, 2001, in the United States. Over the next decade, the Israeli-Palestinian conflict continued to escalate, making the need for a peaceful solution greater than ever.

First published in 2002, *19 Varieties of Gazelle* is a collection of sixty poems, approximately half of which are new, about life in the Middle East and about Nye's experiences as an Arab American. This collection drew wide praise from critics for its even treatment of hot-button issues. Nye does not take sides, and her message is always one of peace. The poems in this book will help American students see life in the Middle East from a new—and sometimes familiar—perspective. Nye's *19 Varieties of Gazelle* was a finalist for the National Book Award.

The poem expresses the sorrow of the generations of Arab-Israeli conflict. (© alexmillos / Shutterstock.com)

in 1986. In the 1990s, inspired by her son, Nye began to write for children and to compile anthologies for young adults. The first anthology she edited, *This Same Sky: A Collection of Poems from Around the World* (1992), was a response to anti-Arab sentiment during the Gulf War. The poet also wrote a semiautobiographical novel, *Habibi*, published in 1997. The young-adult poetry collection in which "All Things Not Considered" appears, *19 Varieties of Gazelle*, was published in 2002. In thirty-five years of professional writing, Nye has published more than thirty books, collections, and anthologies.

Nye has received many awards for her writing, including a Guggenheim Fellowship, the Lavan Award from the Academy of American Poets, the Isabella Gardner Poetry Award, and several Pushcart Prizes. She was elected a chancellor of the Academy of American Poets in 2010. As of 2012, Nye lived in San Antonio, Texas, with her family.

AUTHOR BIOGRAPHY

Naomi Shihab was born on March 12, 1952, in St. Louis, Missouri, to Aziz Shihab, a journalist, and Miriam, a teacher. Her father was a Palestinian immigrant who loved to tell Middle Eastern folktales to his children. Her American mother had a fine arts degree in painting. Shihab developed a passion for poetry at an early age, learning to read through the work of the poet Carl Sandburg. She published her first poem in a children's magazine at age seven and continued to publish steadily thereafter.

Shihab and her family lived in Jerusalem, Israel, for a year when she was fourteen. Her father was editor of the *Jerusalem Times*, but the family relocated to San Antonio, Texas, when the Six-Day War broke out in 1967. Shihab attended Trinity University in San Antonio, graduating summa cum laude in 1974 with a bachelor of arts degree in English and world religions.

After graduation, Shihab worked for the Texas Writers in the Schools project while writing and publishing her own poetry on the side. *Hugging the Jukebox*, her second full-length collection, garnered national attention and established her reputation after it was chosen as part of the National Poetry Series.

She married lawyer and photographer Michael Nye in 1978 and had a son, Madison Cloudfeather,

POEM SUMMARY

The text used for this summary is from *19 Varieties of Gazelle*, Greenwillow, 2002, pp. 133–35. A version of the poem can be found on the following web page: http://rinabeana.com/poemoftheday/ index.php/2005/12/04/all-things-not-considered-by-naomi-shihab-nye/.

"All Things Not Considered" is an elegiac poem that describes innocent victims—all children—of the violent strife between Israelis and Palestinians in the Middle East at the turn of the twenty-first century. Generally speaking, the Israelis are Jewish, and the Palestinians are Arab, although there are many combinations of nationality (Israeli, Palestinian), ethnicity (Jewish, Arab), and religion (Jewish, Christian, Muslim), further complicating the conflict.

Section 1
The first section, lines 1–18, establishes the poem's form of lines without rhyme or meter (the pattern of stressed and unstressed syllables), though these eighteen lines appear in couplets. The opening lines give very specific details of domestic scenes that are irreparably ruptured by the deaths of children who are swept up in the conflict between adults over landownership. Lines 1 and 2 describe a dead boy who cannot be brought back to life. The poet uses sewing terminology, eliciting emotions surrounding domesticity and motherly care.

MEDIA ADAPTATIONS

- *Reading Rumi in an Uncertain World* is a two-hour DVD of poetry readings by Naomi Shihab Nye and Robert Bly. They read from the works of Rumi and other Middle Eastern poets, past and present. They also read from their own works, including Nye's recitation of "All Things Not Considered." Recorded in 2004 in front of an audience of five hundred, the readings are underscored with music by David Whetstone and Oliver Rajamani. The DVD was produced by the nonprofit organization Nafas and Farid Mohammadi and is available for purchase from Wings Press.

- *Promises* is a 2001 Emmy Award–winning documentary that follows filmmaker B. Z. Goldberg as he visits Jerusalem and the West Bank from 1995 to 2000, where he meets seven Palestinian and Jewish children, aged nine to thirteen. Directed by Goldberg, Carlos Bolado, and Justine Shapiro, *Promises* was distributed by Cowboy Pictures. The DVD of *Promises* (available from libraries or online retailers) includes a 25-minute follow-up with all seven children four years later.

Lines 3 and 4 describe a brother and sister who are killed by a bomb blast while playing with toys in their bedroom, illustrating a quiet, peaceful scene (line 3) that is blown apart (line 4). Nye's indignant response to these tragic deaths is captured in italics in lines 5 and 6, where the poet firmly declares that the deaths of children can in no way be divinely sanctioned, no matter which religion, identified by language, claims it to be so.

In lines 7–12, Nye describes another two scenarios of innocence, now coupled with bravery. First, two Jewish boys are killed in a cave while playing hooky from school (lines 7–8). The event Nye refers to is the 2001 deaths of thirteen-year-old Yaakov Mandall and fourteen-year-old Yosef Ishran, who went for a hike instead of going to school and were later found bludgeoned

to death in a nearby cave. The community was shaken by their deaths; the boys' murderers were never found.

Next Nye discusses the death of Asel Asleh (lines 9–12), a young Arab Israeli who was an activist and deeply believed in the possibility of a peaceful resolution of the Israeli-Palestinian conflict. Asleh had rescinded his Palestinian nationality and considered himself an Arab Israeli, a controversial stance in troubled times. Nye states in her poem that Asleh was shot to death while bending over to help someone else, another pointless death that robbed the world of its future. Instead of being able to help bring about peace in one of the world's most troubled regions, Asleh was killed, and no one was sure by whose hand. In lines 13 and 14, the poet asks, in italics, for new religions, because the ones the world has must be fundamentally flawed to consider these murders to be sacred.

In lines 15–18, Nye gives more specific examples of the senseless deaths of children as a result of the conflict. First is Mohammed al-Durra, a twelve-year-old boy who, with his father, was caught in cross fire between Israeli and Palestinian forces and died as a result (lines 15–16; his father was injured but lived). Al-Durra's death was caught on film and broadcast worldwide while both sides sought to vilify the other for their carelessness; significant controversy surrounded this incident, including assertions that al-Durra did not die. Nye's position is that al-Durra's death is the ugly reality of violence in general and this conflict in particular.

Lines 17 and 18 describe the incredible pain of an Arab father burying his infant daughter. Iman Hiju's death was reported widely in the media and held up by some Palestinian groups as an example of Israel's brutality. The Palestinian baby died just days before the murder of Mandall and Ishran, and some claimed that the murder of those Jewish boys was a retaliatory action. Hiju's father's anguished response in line 18 underlines the horror of trading blood for blood over the deaths of children.

Section 2
In these seven lines (19–25), set apart from the two-line stanzas of section 1, Nye warns the reader not to assume that these children did not have parents who loved and took care of them. She points out that most parents would endure many hardships for the sake of their children,

including homelessness and hunger; but it is easy to make these assertions from the secure comfort of distant homes, far from the danger and stress of a war-torn country.

Section 3

Lines 26–31 compose the first stanza of the third section. The crux of Nye's point lies in these lines, where she places the blame on no one and on everyone. Using italics to emphasize her idea and to underline that this is her point of view, Nye wonders what might change if both sides were to get together and admit that they are each equally responsible.

Lines 32–43 make up the second stanza of the third section. Nye seeks to give the Israeli and Palestinian combatants an out from the shame of making mistakes. She points out that people have always made mistakes and have always been hurt. Some have been driven by their hurt to take up weapons (lines 35–37), while others have peacefully engaged in schoolwork and scholarship (lines 42–43).

Section 4

In the final section of the poem, lines 44–52, Nye returns to the form of the first section, using short two- and also one-line stanzas to deliver her verse. Her images here are both more abstract and more beautiful. She describes a baby's ear, a bucket of water, an orchard of well-loved trees, and Jewish and Arab women standing together. These are all symbols of life, balancing out the death of section 1. In the final, italicized line of the poem, Nye wonders if people might actually be what make up a holy land, effectively discarding the notion of the physical location of Israel/Palestine as holy and therefore worth fighting for.

THEMES

Death

A dominant theme of Nye's poem is death. She not only points out the finality of death—for example, in the first two lines she writes about a boy without breath whom no amount of work can repair—but also its senseless tragedy. Families such as that of the Arab baby who died, as described in lines 17 and 18, are irrevocably altered. The death of a child is especially tragic because children represent the future of humankind. Within each family a child represents the promise of the future; a child

lost is an entire life's worth of potential forever erased and replaced with grief and speculation on what could have been. As Nye writes in lines 35–43, some survivors in their grief take up arms against those they deem to be enemies, perpetuating the violence. In her perspective, the violence has become absurd, and people who kill children no longer know what they are fighting for.

Nye also uses this poem to mourn for the innocent who have died in the Israeli-Palestinian conflict, pointing to these dead children as an indication of the meaninglessness of what these people are fighting about. The deaths she specifically mentions are all the more poignant because they cannot be linked to specific killers. These deaths of innocents by unknown hands—some of them perhaps accidental—have been appropriated after the fact by the media (line 16) and by political groups to further their own agendas through speculation and historical revision. Meanwhile, families grieve, and combatants continue to kill in the name of their cause, their god, and their doctrine.

If all the children are killed, Nye argues, who will be left to inherit when all is said and done? What will they inherit? The only solution, Nye points out (lines 49–50, 52), is peaceful coexistence between Arabs and Jews.

Innocence

Nye uses the innocence of civilian children fatally caught up in a brutal conflict to underline her frustration with the righteousness of the Israeli and Palestinian combatants. Intimidation of civilians to force an agenda is considered to be terrorism, an accusation leveled against both sides since violence again escalated starting in September 2000, after the failure of the Oslo Accords.

Young children do not understand the nuances of the historical and political context surrounding this conflict, which makes them innocent regardless of their nationality, ethnicity, religion, or indoctrination. The deaths of innocent people for a righteous cause is a terrible tragedy that Nye hopes will inspire people to peaceful action rather than further aggression or revenge. In this poem she acknowledges that although some people have turned to violence for revenge (lines 35–37), others could see similarities with their enemies (lines 32–34) and lay down weapons in favor of a better life for their children, regardless of the difficulty of the task of negotiating peace. To protect the innocence of our children, who will grow up to take

TOPICS FOR FURTHER STUDY

- Research the major events of the Israeli-Palestinian conflict going back to its origins, and create a multimedia presentation with a time line that shows these events in chronological order. In your time line, include links to news stories and nongraphic images, as well as brief descriptions of each event. Share your presentation with your class.

- Choose a country or culture that is part of the Middle East and read about daily life for the people there. What do they eat? What do their clothes look like? What do their homes look like? What holidays do they celebrate? What is the weather like? What kinds of pets do they keep (if any)? What is school like? Using what you have learned in your research, write a poem from the perspective of a child or teenager living in the culture you chose. Make sure you communicate the setting as well as the argument or story of your poem.

- Research and prepare a dish to share from Middle Eastern cuisine (there is a lot of variation, so if you are already familiar with Middle Eastern food, try something you have never had before). Bring your dish to class, and see if your classmates can guess its origins. Be prepared to discuss the distinctions between different Middle Eastern dishes for the benefit of your classmates.

- Research the history of Israel and Palestine and how the conflict of the late twentieth and early twenty-first centuries came about. What kinds of attempts have been made at making peace? Divide into two or more teams and hold a formal debate about what the best solution might be for this troubled region, making reference to what has already been tried and why these solutions have not worked. As Nye does in her poem, resist casting blame entirely on one side or the other.

- Read Elizabeth Laird's novel *A Little Piece of Ground* (2006), about a twelve-year-old Palestinian boy living in occupied Ramallah, a city north of Jerusalem that is considered the base of the Palestinian National Authority. Compare and contrast Laird's novel and Nye's poem. What is the emotional impact of each work? How do their messages differ? Do they have similar themes? Which one do you like better and why? Write a paper presenting your examination of these two works.

- Find out (as accurately as possible) how many people have been killed in the Israeli-Palestinian conflict. You can choose to divide your numbers between civilians and combatants and/or between Israelis and Palestinians or have no divisions. Use these numbers to create a striking visual representation of those who have been killed. Mount your display in your school. Include poetry—yours, Nye's, or someone else's—to encourage people to think of peaceful solutions to problems.

---

care of their parents and the legacy left to them, people must invest in a task more difficult than violence and mere survival; they must talk to each other (lines 28–29).

Righteousness

Righteousness is behavior dictated by divine law or moral standard. One who is righteous believes that what he does is so correct that he is free from guilt or sin. People have done many terrible things to each other throughout human history out of a sense of righteousness, including conquest, torture, and murder. In "All Things Not Considered," Nye vilifies righteous behavior, holding up the tragic, sometimes accidental deaths of children as a reason for why this is *not* moral or divinely sanctioned. In lines 5–6 and lines 13–14, she speaks directly to the reader, asking who could find these acts of violence against children in any way holy. In lines 26 and 27, Nye declares that no one involved is right. In line 52, the final line, Nye suggests that holiness comes from people, which

Military conflicts with religion in the Middle East. (© Attila Jandi | Shutterstock.com)

some could interpret to mean that she believes, in the face of the deaths of these children, that there is no God and therefore no divine law to be righteous about.

STYLE

Free Verse

Free verse is a form of poetry that has no specified meter or rhyme but still maintains a poetic structure, such as through line breaks and stanzas, which differentiate free verse from prose poetry, fiction, or nonfiction. Nye often writes in free verse, such as with "All Things Not Considered." The first section of the poem comprises nine two-line stanzas, each expressing a powerful moment in time. Many of these stanzas concern the death of a child, but several stanzas throughout, set in italics, are the poet speaking directly to the reader. These short stanzas give the reader a quick and painful glimpse at the tragic fallout of this conflict, and the information comes quickly at the reader, like bullets.

The middle of the poem comprises two sections, one with one long stanza (of seven lines) and one with two long stanzas (of six lines and twelve lines). These longer stanzas are the poem's rational center, where the poet argues that no side will win by violence. The reader must dwell longer here and think more deeply on the ideas presented, which are more abstract than the images that preceded them in the first section.

The fourth and final section returns to a format that is similar to the first section, with very short stanzas, of one or two lines. The lines themselves are also shorter, and here Nye presents peaceful, quiet images of life in the Middle East as she guides the reader toward her final, emphatic point in the last, italicized line. Using free verse for this poem allowed the poet to tailor the poem's form to her important message.

Polemic

"All Things Not Considered" is a polemical poem. A *polemic* is a strong argument with scornful overtones. Nye is hypercritical of the violence between Jew and Arab, pointing out that they have taken it so far as to use the deaths of their children as badges of righteousness. For example, after Mohammed al-Durra was accidentally killed in cross fire between Israeli and Palestinian forces in 2000 (lines 15–16), many Palestinians upheld the child as a martyr who died for his people; but the painful reality is that most other people in the world saw him as a scared child in the wrong place at the wrong time who did not willfully die for any cause, as a martyr would do.

Nye's polemic questions the purpose of religion in this conflict and suggests, in lines 13 and 14, that if religion allows children to be murdered for a cause, then perhaps new religions are needed. Ever the optimist and pursuer of peace, Nye suggests an abandonment of arms in favor of discussion (lines 28–29), pointing out that Arabs and Jews are more similar than they are different (lines 33–34 and 49–51). Her final, powerful, and biting commentary, in line 52, suggests that there is no God—or at least no land made holy by God—and people only have each other.

HISTORICAL CONTEXT

Israeli-Palestinian Conflict

Jews have settled in the region known as Palestine—modern Israel, the West Bank, and the Gaza Strip—throughout history, and relations with

Arab Palestinians have often not been easy. This area, especially the city of Jerusalem, has significant religious meaning for Jews, Christians, and Muslims alike, motivating people toward righteous behavior as a way to resolve disputes. The early twentieth century saw a rise in both Zionism, a form of Jewish nationalism, and Arab nationalism, repeatedly bringing the two groups into bloody conflict.

The number of Jewish settlers in Palestine increased dramatically during World War I (1914–1918) and World War II (1939–1945). Especially following the Holocaust of World War II, Jews all over the world sought refuge in a Jewish homeland from the increasing anti-Semitism in Europe sparked by Nazi propaganda. This surge in Jewish immigrants dramatically increased the strife between Arab residents of Palestine and Jewish settlers. Riots broke out in Jerusalem in 1929 over the right to pray at the Western Wall, a site that is sacred to Jewish people. The Western Wall, once part of the Second Temple, is on the western boundary of the Temple Mount, a place that is extremely sacred to Jews, Christians, and Muslims and the site of the Dome of the Rock, an Islamic shrine.

The conflict between Arabs and Jews only intensified after Israel declared sovereign independence from the British Mandate of Palestine in 1948, effectively forming the nation of Israel. The day after this declaration, neighboring Arab states, including Syria, Lebanon, Jordan, and Egypt, began to attack Israel in solidarity with their displaced Palestinian brethren. The Arab-Israel War of 1948 lasted only one year but did not resolve the region's problems for the long term. The Six-Day War broke out in 1967, prompting Nye's parents to move their family back to the United States. In 1973, Egypt and Syria attacked to reclaim disputed territory. Israel, supported by Western countries, was able to successfully defend itself in every war.

In 1987, the First Intifada, or uprising, broke out as Palestinians unified and revolted against Israeli presence in territories known as the Gaza Strip and the West Bank. The First Intifada lasted six years and gave rise to militant political groups such as Hamas and Islamic Jihad. Peace talks between Israeli leaders and the Palestinian Liberation Organization (PLO) in September 1993, known as the Oslo Accords, brought an end to the First Intifada, although tensions were only eased and were far from resolved.

US president Bill Clinton hosted Palestinian leader Yasser Arafat and Israeli prime minister Ehud Barak at Camp David, in Maryland, for the Middle East Peace Summit in July 2000, but these talks were a failure, with both sides blaming each other for lack of compromise. A few months later, in October, riots broke out around the Temple Mount, and this incident marked the beginning of the Second Intifada. The intifada raged on for about five years, with thousands of Palestinian and Israeli casualties. The intifada lost strength after the death of Arafat in late 2004 and is considered to have ended in 2005, although Israeli-Palestinian violence did not cease.

In the winter of 2008–2009, Israel Defense Forces launched an attack on the Gaza Strip, an independent Palestinian state near the border with Egypt. Israel claimed that Palestinians were using Gaza, which is on the coast of the Red Sea and shares a border with Egypt, to import weapons and organize military activities against Israel. Over one thousand Palestinians died in the Gaza War.

No amount of bloodshed in the Middle East has brought either party closer to "winning," and compromise is tenuous. Nye's argument for forgiveness and peaceful coexistence is compelling in light of how unsuccessful militant and terrorist actions have been for either side.

The Persian Gulf War and the Iraq War

Iraq invaded the small, oil-rich Middle Eastern nation of Kuwait, located on the Persian Gulf, in the summer of 1990. Allied forces, led by the United States, came to the aid of Kuwait in January 1991, largely to protect allied oil interests. The allied forces declared victory on February 28. This military event is known as the Gulf War, the Persian Gulf War, or Operation Desert Shield.

The Persian Gulf War severely deteriorated relations between Iraq and the United States. Iraqi leader Saddam Hussein was blamed for the terrorist attack on the World Trade Center in New York City in 1993; when those towers were destroyed in 2001 by Saudi terrorists, US leaders immediately looked to Iraq, again questioning—as they did following the Gulf War—whether or not Hussein was stockpiling weapons of mass destruction. Mounting tensions between Iraq and Western nations led to the US invasion of Iraq in March 2003. The Iraq War was long and devastating to the nation of Iraq, although allied forces were finally able to capture the despotic Hussein in December 2003 and put him on trial for crimes against humanity. (His efforts to exterminate the

Jerusalem, the epicenter of the Arab-Israeli conflict (© Eve81 / Shutterstock.com)

Kurdish minority in Iraq were widely known, among other criminal activities.) Found guilty, Hussein was executed by hanging in December 2006. The Iraq War officially ended in December 2011, although civil strife and political upheaval continued to trouble Iraq. The events of the Persian Gulf War and the Iraq War have had an immense (and some say negative) impact on how Arab Americans are treated in the United States, coloring Nye's experience growing up in a biracial family.

CRITICAL OVERVIEW

The volume that included "All Things Not Considered," *19 Varieties of Gazelle*, was published in 2002, only a year after the September 2001 terrorist attacks in the United States (carried out by Saudi radicals) and shortly before the Iraq War broke out in March 2003. This was a crucial time in the United States, when curiosity about and antagonism toward Arabs and Arab Americans was high. Critics celebrated Nye's volume as an accessible way for American students to examine life in the Middle East, to ponder the struggles faced by people who live there, and to gain greater understanding of the difficulties, including prejudice, faced by Arab Americans.

Hazel Rochman, reviewing the collection for *Booklist*, wrote that "the best poems bring big and small together, personalizing the disasters." Rochman criticizes Nye for overindulging in details but overall celebrates the collection as "timely" and relevant to young people. A critic for *Kirkus Reviews* gave a glowing review, writing, "There are no false steps here—only a feeling of sensory overload," echoing Rochman's sentiment. A *Publishers Weekly* reviewer found *19 Varieties of Gazelle* to be "an excellent way to invite exploration and discussion of events far away and their impact here at home," while Nina Lindsay of *School Library Journal* wrote, "This offering is a celebration of her heritage, and a call for peace."

Catherine Wagner, in a lengthy review for *MELUS*, describes Nye's collection as "elegiac" and goes on to describe how Nye "emphasizes the characters' everyday, ordinary dignity in order to remind us of our shared humanity." Wagner finds fault in Nye's oversimplification of good versus evil, describing how Nye writes about violence as if it were being imposed on those who perpetrate it. "Nye's poems do not represent those victims who turn violent; she restricts herself to representing the wise multitude who abstain from violence," Wagner explains. Nevertheless, this approach may be what makes Nye's work more accessible to young readers.

Jennifer M. Brabander, writing for *Horn Book* magazine, describes Nye's collection as "clear and haunting," pointing out that Nye's purpose is to present a view of the Middle East that is balanced. Craving peace, the poet wishes to steer people away from diametrical opposition and toward seeing people not only as individuals, but also, in most cases, as innocent in the events that unfolded around September 11, 2001.

CRITICISM

Carol Ullmann

Ullmann is a freelance writer and editor, specializing in literature. In the following essay, she examines Nye's message of peace through forgiveness in her poem "All Things Not Considered."

WHAT DO I READ NEXT?

- *There Is No Long Distance Now: Very Short Stories* is a 2011 collection by Nye containing forty stories concerning how to close the mysterious distance that comes between family, friends, enemies, and everyone in between.

- *The House on Mango Street* (1984), by Sandra Cisneros, is a coming-of-age novel told in vignettes narrated by a Hispanic girl who copes with life in a poor district of Chicago by writing stories and poems.

- *Baghdad Diaries: A Woman's Chronicle of War and Exile* is a 2003 book by Nuha al-Radi that recounts the lives of ordinary people living in Baghdad during the Persian Gulf War in 1991, the effects of the Western embargo on Iraq following the war, and al-Radi's own years of living abroad.

- Julia Otsuka's debut novel, *When the Emperor Was Divine* (2003), tells the story of a Japanese American family incarcerated in an internment camp during World War II when suspicion in the United States about Japanese spies was high.

- *American Born Chinese* is a 2006 graphic novel by Gene Luen Yang about Jin Wang, Danny, and the Monkey King, all characters who struggle with alienation and must find a way to help each other. *American Born Chinese* won the 2007 Eisner Award for Best Graphic Album and was the first graphic novel to be nominated for a National Book Award.

- Li-Young Lee's first collection of poetry, *Rose* (1993), made a powerful impact on readers and critics in light of his beautiful use of language and astute handling of poetic technique.

- *Poets on the Edge: An Anthology of Contemporary Hebrew Poetry* (2008), selected and translated by Tsipi Keller, brings together Israel's most prominent poets from the past forty years, including Yehuda Amichai, Dan Pagis, and Shin Shifra.

> POETRY HAS THE ABILITY TO BRING PEOPLE CLOSE, BY HAVING THEM DRAW ON THEIR SHARED HUMANITY."

"All Things Not Considered" is a political poem concerned with the deaths of children brought about by the ongoing strife in Israel, the West Bank, and the Gaza Strip. In this poem, Naomi Shihab Nye argues for peace between Israelis and Palestinians and suggests that bilateral, unconditional forgiveness is the only way to achieve peace. Catherine Wagner, in a review of *19 Varieties of Gazelle* for *MELUS*, remarks that Nye "uses personal details to explain that we are all people, that we must recognize that and stop hurting one another. Nye hopes and trusts that knowledge will bring empathy."

The Middle East has been a troubled region for most of the twentieth century. Known as the cradle of civilization, it is a region rich in history. Several of the world's major religions began in the Middle East, and Jerusalem, the capital city of the modern state of Israel, is especially holy to those religions. Judaism, Islam, and Christianity all have mythical and historical connections to Jerusalem; for example, Jerusalem is home to the Temple Mount, the Dome of the Rock, the Church of the Holy Sepulcher, and the Western Wall—all significant religious sites. The proximity of different religions in such a small area has, for centuries, contributed to the trouble experienced by people living in the Middle East. For example, in October 2000, riots broke out around the Temple Mount following Israeli presidential candidate Ariel Sharon's visit there. The Temple Mount is the holiest religious site for Jews and is also where the Dome of the Rock, an important Islamic shrine, is located.

The early twentieth century saw a sharp rise in conflict between Muslim Arabs and Jews from eastern Europe resettling in Palestine (now Israel, the West Bank, and the Gaza Strip). This conflict reached a crisis when Great Britain gave up its mandate of Palestine and the Jewish state of Israel was declared independent in 1948. Arab Palestinians felt exiled from their homeland, and thus began the modern unrelenting bloody strife between Arab Palestinians and Israelis (who are ethnically and religiously diverse, including Jews as well as Arab Christians and Arab Muslims). This strife has gone on for more than sixty years with no end in sight.

In the context of this conflict, Nye's "All Things Not Considered" is a call to action. Nye is not asking people to fight for a cause; instead she is asking people to stop fighting and take a look at what is happening to their children and to the land they profess to love. Peace in the Middle East has been an elusive goal for most of the twentieth century, as Israelis and Palestinians have fought over relatively small but precious pieces of land. Religious doctrine has been used to support violent behavior as righteous and holy. This righteous behavior includes the murders of innocent children and is a tactic Nye reviles.

Nye's objection to the use of violence is unwavering. Born to a Palestinian father who keenly felt his exile, Nye's intimate perspective nonetheless does not slant her opinion in favor of one side or the other. She takes the high road, calling Jews and Arabs to stand together, to live together, and to see more significance in their similarities than in their differences. For this to work, people have to own up to their culpability (lines 26–27 and 32) and their pain (lines 33–34) and then let go of their mistakes and injuries for the sake of the future and their children. Nye plays to the power of parental love when she writes about how most parents would choose to be with their children rather than have a home (line 19), criticizing the combatants in the Israeli-Palestinian conflict for choosing landownership over children, who are being needlessly sacrificed in the fight for possession.

One way that Nye breaks down the argument for violence in her poem is by rejecting the perspective that the deaths of these children are in any way righteous or holy. She asserts that any religion that sanctifies the deaths of children is no good and needs to be replaced (lines 13–14). She writes of how the unbearable pain of the death of a child is the same regardless of ethnicity (lines 5–6), indicating another kind of shared experience between Israelis and Palestinians. These horrors are balance by the peaceful images at the end of the poem that emphasize life: the beauty of a baby's features; cool, still water; an orchard in the arid climate of the Middle East; and Jewish and Arab women standing side by side.

Samina Najmi's article "Naomi Shihab Nye's Aesthetic of Smallness and the Military Sublime," in *MELUS*, argues that Nye focuses on the daily details of life in an effort to promote compassion: "Nye's poetry connects cultures and countries through emphasis on the small and the ordinary, insisting on the mundane and the everyday to stress human connections." Najmi continues, "A sense of shared humanity enables empathy, which renders violence against one another irrational, homicidal, and self-destructive."

Jews (the ethnic and religious majority in Israel) and Arab Muslims (the ethnic and religious majority in the Palestinian territories) are more similar than they are different. Both religious groups descend from the same ancestor, Abraham, and consider Jerusalem to be a holy city. They eat many of the same foods and have similar religious laws regarding food purity. Religiously observant men and women on both sides often wear black out of modesty, a visual commonality observed by Nye (line 51) in her plea for solidarity and peace. Sephardic Jews (those of Middle Eastern descent) and Arab Muslims often both have dark hair and olive complexions; a BBC News report from 2000 confirms that Jews and Arabs are closely related genetically, despite twenty-five hundred years of Jewish diaspora living outside the holy land.

In a 2009 interview with Kate Long for *World Literature Today*, Nye said, "No matter what one is living through, or where one finds oneself, words help us navigate the place, scene, experience." Nye uses her poetry to communicate her message of mutual forgiveness and peace. "Art and poetry preempt destructive emotions and physical violence," Najmi writes about Nye's work and her message. Words force us to slow down and think, but first one must be willing to read. The poet's ultimate goal of peace can only become a reality if those who are fighting are willing to stop and read or listen, think, and possibly turn their hearts toward forgiveness. The obsession with right and wrong will consume one's life and then the lives of one's children, friends, and neighbors. Righteousness has a voracious appetite that can never be sated and will only be stopped by those who deliberately turn down a different path.

Part of Nye's message is in the title, "All Things Not Considered." The title announces that this poem is about ideas the reader has not been thinking about, such as children killed as part of the Israeli-Palestinian conflict and peace through forgiveness. The poet indicates that, amidst all the debate of how to achieve a resolution and bring both parties to some kind of peace, the politicians and combatants have not fully considered that their bombs are killing babies, schoolchildren, and teenagers. Nye also underlines her idea that the path to peace is by way of forgiveness (lines 26–29) and focusing on cultural commonalities between Jews and Arabs (lines 32–43 and 49–51). For full impact, the poem cannot stand apart from its title, which is not repeated in the text. With this title, the poet is asking the reader: Have you considered *this*?

The pursuit of peace between Israelis and Palestinians cannot be taken lightly. Fueled by religion, combatants on both sides believe that what they are fighting for is greater than individual lives. Meanwhile, the deaths of civilians—and especially children—have touched everyone living in Israel, the West Bank, and the Gaza Strip. Young people like Asel Asleh (lines 9–12) are increasingly seeking peaceful solutions, such as forming bilateral youth discussion groups, taking part in peace rallies, and renouncing allegiance to groups who use force and violence in pursuit of their goals. Drawn to youth's idealism, Nye delivers a powerful message of forgiveness and peace in "All Things Not Considered." It is a poem about young people *for* young people. The youths who read this poem are the future, and they will take the lessons learned as children—whether to pick up a gun or to pick up a pen—and apply them to the problems they face as adults. Giving children a message of forgiveness and peace is potentially the best tool to effect change in a conflict that otherwise appears hopeless.

"Poetry may succeed in healing when all else has failed," wrote Wagner about *19 Varieties of Gazelle*. Poetry, being a form of writing that operates at an emotional level, seems the perfect tool for peace and against violence and the deaths of innocents. Poetry has the ability to bring people close, by having them draw on their shared humanity. Through the carefully chosen words of poetry such as Nye's "All Things Not Considered," people caught in conflict may be able to rediscover the meaning of their lives, see beauty and familiarity in the works of their friends and neighbors, and extend a hand of welcome across the divide.

Source: Carol Ullmann, Critical Essay on "All Things Not Considered," in *Poetry for Students*, Gale, Cengage Learning, 2013.

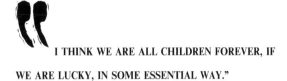

I THINK WE ARE ALL CHILDREN FOREVER, IF WE ARE LUCKY, IN SOME ESSENTIAL WAY."

Sharif S. Elmusa

In the following interview, Elmusa and Nye explore the views of both mothers and children in Nye's poetry that give it such universal appeal.

This interview with poet Naomi Shihab Nye explores how her poems are informed by an inquisitive, child-like spirit and an ever-watchful eye of a mother. Such 'vital attitude' uniquely enables her to write poetry for all ages. It has also propelled her to travel across the United States and five continents, teaching the craft of poetry, and inviting audiences to experience how poems possess the power to connect people, to illuminate the mysteries of things, and to avail us of moments for self-restoration.

INTRODUCTION

I first got acquainted with Naomi Shihab Nye's poetry in the mid 1980s when I was selecting poems with Gregory Orfalea for what would become *Grape Leaves: A Century of Arab-American Poetry*. I was immediately taken by the beauty of the poems, by the direct, almost artless language, fresh images, and deep immersion in the philosophy of everyday life—"impure poetry," advocated by the Chilean poet Pablo Neruda. Both Orfalea and I agreed that she was going to occupy a large space in the anthology.

Since then, Nye—who is also a folksinger—has become a prominent poet in America, invited to read at, among other places, the White House during Bill Clinton's presidency and the Library of Congress. Her books won coveted prizes—including in 1982 the National Poetry Series selection—and many notable and best book citations from the American Library Association. More recently, her anthology *19 Varieties of Gazelle: Poems of the Middle East* (2005) was a National Book Award finalist. She has won the Jane Addams Children's Book Award twice and the Pushcart Prize four times.

Nye is the daughter of an American mother and a Palestinian father, a journalist who immigrated to the United States a short while after the

Palestinian *nakba* (catastrophe) in 1948. Although she lived all her life in the US, Palestine has been one of the major, nourishing arteries of her creativity. Perhaps I would not be off the mark to say that the Palestinian plight is constitutive of the poet's sensibility: empathy with the vulnerable, aversion to loss, and abhorrence of aggression and violence.

Nye published numerous poetry collections, anthologies, and occasional fiction. Her poems are plentiful in quantity and encompassing in scope. It is as if every object, person, and organism she comes across can be molded into a line, a stanza, and, if lucky, a whole poem. What makes for this opulence?

I do not claim to know. The easiest thing to say is that it is a natural gift. And gifted, she is. But there must be something else besides the gift. That something might be found in what the Mexican poet Octavio Paz termed the "vital attitude" of the poet. Nye seems constantly astonished by the mystery of things, fleeting events, or flashes of memory: "Sometimes objects stun me / I touch them carefully / saying, tell what you know." And they have much to divulge: "A man leaves the world / and the streets he lived on / grow a little shorter." And: "The train whistle still wails its ancient sound / but when it goes away, shrinking back / from the walls of the brain / it takes something different with it every time" (*Yellow Glove,* "Trying to Name What Doesn't Change" 1). In Nye's astonishment there is the child who refuses to be repressed.

Yet, she seems never to sleep, keeping one eye open on our imperfect, vulnerable selves: "Each carries a tender spot / something our lives forgot to give us" (*Red Suitcase,* "Jerusalem" 21–22). Still, she looks most after the missing, the hurt, and the maltreated. The bull escaping men with pistols in the street, "could he have gotten away?" (*Yellow Glove,* "The Tunnel of Questions" 10). The fireflies which once captivated her little son prompt the lines, "Lately I looked for you everywhere / but only night's smooth stare gazed back" (*Red Suitcase,* "Fireflies" 71). In Jerusalem the poet grows indignant: "Why are we so monumentally slow! / Soldiers stalk a pharmacy / big guns, little pills. / If you tilt your head just slightly / it's ridiculous" (*Red Suitcase,* "Jerusalem" 21–22). At a dinner party she protests how everyone comments on "texture of meat or herbal aroma," and ignores "the translucence of onion / now limp, now divided /

or its traditionally honorable career: / For the sake of others / disappear" (*Yellow Glove,* "The Thinly Fluted Wings of Stamps" 27). Nye's vigilance is that of a mother.

The offspring are scattered across the Globe: in a classroom, a park, India, Amman, Lima (Peru), Mexico City, Niagara, San Antonio—the mostly Hispanic Texan city where she resides with her husband, Michael Nye, a lawyer and photographer, and her son, Madison Cloud Feather.

This is Nye, child and mother. It is most natural that she also decided to devote herself to writing for, and teaching, young people poetry—becoming a poet for all ages. The last time I saw her read was in the summer of 2006, when she came to Virginia to visit schools and bookstores. At the bookstore where she gave a talk and read poems before an audience of youngsters and adults, she wove a wonderful web of associations and propositions about the "word": how it connected us, gave us power, made us go places, brought out laughter, provided a boulder to scan the landscape, endowed us with depth. If purchasing books was an indicator, the many bags of Nye's books that left the store afterward told of great appreciation.

When *Alif* asked me to do this written interview with Naomi in fall 2006 for this special issue on children, I felt both pleased and honored. I also thought of it as an opportunity to hold a sustained conversation with a longtime friend about her work, something we could not manage before in the fleeting encounters, letters, and e-mails.

SE: You are trying to encourage kids to write poems and to appreciate the value of words and the worlds that words open up for them. When did you start writing poetry?

NSN: I started at age six. I started sending work to children's magazines at age seven.

SE: Modern education has banished memorization, celebrating analysis and so-called critical thinking. Does this stymie poetic creativity? Do you encourage kids to memorize poems?

NSN: I think memorization, of a few short well-loved poems, is a great thing. They become yours forever. I still "own" the poems I memorized in second grade. Yes, I encourage this whenever possible. But I am usually not around long enough to see the results. Last year, some graduate students requested that I add memorization of a beloved poem to our curriculum (I was visiting writer at the Michener Center for

Writers in Austin for one semester—the third time I have done this) and I loved hearing them recite their poems, hearing what they chose.

SE: When my son started listening to rap, the genre was controversial because of the foul language and the violence it seemed to promote. But I encouraged him to listen because I liked the way rappers played with words. Rap seemed like the next-best thing to poetry. Was that bad parenting?

NSN: No, I think it was good parenting. My son also loved rap. He used to make up his own too. I also appreciated the ways rappers played with words. My guess is our sons do not use worse language than others because they listened to rap. We had a few conversations about how saying "bad words" more often made it easier to say them. But my guess is I still use more "bad words" than my son does.

SE: The philosopher Gaston Bachelard was a great advocate of waking up the child in us, of opening the gates of memory and the unconscious to let the dormant child daydream. Do you feel that being in constant touch with children keeps the child within you alive or makes you more conscious of the gap?

NSN: I think being with children keeps our own child-sense alive. I find it waking up very quickly when I am with them. The refreshment of being with children remains one of the most creative uplifts I know. So I tell teenage-kids, if you're having trouble writing something, go babysit.

SE: On the same point, someone, rejecting likening humans to computers, said that the computer was never a child. Do you feel grownups shed away too much of the child in them that it becomes seductive to compare them to computers? Would reading children's books restore some of the lost childhood?

NSN: Yes, we should all read children's books forever. Read and reread. Sometimes I stand back at gatherings of adults and just listen to all the predictable grooves of chit-chat and wish I could run away to a playground. Or a lost woodland trail.

SE: Poetry in modern American history was considered sissy, whereas in the Arab tradition it was more legitimate, sometimes associated with heroism. Does the seeming femininity of poetry affect American boys' interest in it?

NSN: This is where good teachers come in. I think it is all in the presentation. The exposure to good poetry, the relationship of poetry to life, seizes a boy's imagination as quickly as a girl's. But some boys who are not exposed might only have a vague notion of greeting-card, sweetie-pie verse. So how could they feel attracted?

SE: Do you find differences in the reaction of boys and girls to particular types of poems? Do love poems, for example, appeal more to girls than to boys?

NSN: I never used love poems—as in, love between people—in very many classes. I was always trying to extend the notion of what people might write about—and "love poems" was a stereotype for many kids. I used love poems toward things, ideas, cities, animals, objects, more frequently. I would think that traditionally "romantic" poems might appeal more to girls but really do not have the expertise with this.

SE: The poet Federico García Lorca spoke of two kinds of lullaby, the "wounding," Spanish variety and the mild, Anglo-Saxon one. Do you think children's poems should wound?

NSN: I think children are wounded by many things automatically and poetry parallels those painful experiences, or shines light on them, without healing or solving them completely. I was, for example, particularly wounded as a child by how the things/moments/scenes I loved were so finite. They were all going away. We could not save them. Poetry also seemed to me to be describing that experience, so it helped me a great deal. I had an overactive nostalgia for everything, and still do.

SE: Do you assume that children are capable of moral understanding, like, say, Antoine de Saint-Exupery assumes in The Little Prince? *The poems you yourself write for children, and that you select in your anthologies, do they lean one way or the other?*

NSN: At this point, I think children may have more moral understanding than adults do. I am stricken by how adults get "bought out"—by money, power, greed; goodness knows what they want—and children are not yet so "tainted." *The Little Prince* was one of my favorite books when I was growing up. I do not mind moral leanings in poems. I just do not think brazen messages work very well there.

SE: Adults seem confused about how to view children. Do you see children as adults in miniature form? Are they just a bundle of innocence? Is "the child the father of the man"? I'm asking because I suppose an author's initial premise usually affects the kind of things that she chooses to present to children.

NSN: I think we are all children forever, if we are lucky, in some essential way. I think a child's perspective—not yet so filled and guided by others—is fascinating. The receptivity of childhood, the willingness to swerve and bend and laugh and wonder and put things together in odd ways—might serve us all mightily, if we remembered it more often.

SE: How do children respond when you tell them you are Palestinian? Do they show interest in the place? What do they want to know?

NSN: They are interested. They often want to know if I have been there, when, how often, what happened, and how I feel about the most recent news. They often seem sympathetic to the plight of people in exile, what it would mean to be treated as a second-class citizen in one's own home-place. Recently, some students asked me very pointedly if I had ever had negative encounters with Israeli soldiers myself. They wanted to know all the details! Jewish children often want to tell about their own trips to Israel and how the people they met were interacting or not with Palestinian people.

SE: You wrote a novel for young readers entitled Habibi. *Was that not a commercially-risky title, in the sense that the word is not known to the English-reading public? How was it received by readers?*

NSN: My publisher suggested changing the title before the book came out, worried that students would not select a book whose title they did not understand (this is absurd, many books have odd or esoteric titles) and various alternative titles were suggested to me by editor/publisher. But I marched off to a local middle school, told some classes about the book, made a list of possible titles on board without suggesting my own predisposition, and took a survey. Hands-down they voted for *Habibi* as the favored title. So my publisher went with it and I have never been sorry.

SE: Once, when my daughter was six or seven, my wife went to a conference and my little daughter was concerned that I will not be able to do her pony tail. I tried to reassure her that I could; she was not convinced and said: "Moms are different." How are moms different? Does their difference translate, for instance, into more women than men promoting youngsters' literature?

NSN: We care more about domestic details and rituals. At least, in my own house we do. So, kids, who like details, respond to that. I think there are probably quite a few men in my line of work. Kevin Henkes of Wisconsin, for example, not only does what I do, but he also does his brilliant art. Peter Sis, same. I am sure there are many people who do much more than I do, and better.

SE: Are there any particular books of poetry for young people that you would recommend for translation into Arabic?

NSN: A book by William Stafford, I believe it is called *Living in the World*, would be my top pick. Actually, any of William Stafford's books. His voice has guided my life since I was sixteen. He was a pacifist and a brilliant, deeply ethical human being, as well as a great and subtle poet.

SE: I suppose you receive fan-mail from your young audiences. What are some of the most memorable responses you have received?

NSN: One, just a few years ago, was from a twelve-year-old girl in Calgary, Alberta, Canada. I have never been there. She had never been to the Middle East. But she said she read *Habibi* once, fell in love with it, and decided to read it again. She asked her mother to cook only Arabic food for her while she was reading the book the second time. She made a list of all the foods that are mentioned. She said her mother had to go buy a special cookbook. She said: "I will never think about the Middle East in the same way again. It has become a real and human place to me. I care about it now." She also said, most wondrously, that whenever she read the sections of the book that contain Sitti, the grandmother character, she would "place a white cloth on her own head to feel close to her."

This was my favorite letter.

Source: Sharif S. Elmusa, "Vital Attitude of the Poet: Interview with Naomi Shihab Nye," in *Alif: Journal of Comparative Poetics*, No. 27, Annual 2007, pp. 107–14.

Catherine Wagner

In the following review, Wagner compares Nye's poetry in 19 Varieties of Gazelle *with the poetry of new Middle Eastern poet Mohja Kahf.*

Two new books by Arab American poets offer surprisingly different methods of pursuing similar political agendas. *19 Varieties of Gazelle* collects famous Palestinian American poet Naomi Shihab Nye's elegiac poems about the Middle

> THE ANGER KAHF'S POEMS EXPRESS IS MUCH
MORE AGGRESSIVE THAN THE POIGNANT
HOPEFULNESS IN NYE'S WORK."

East for young adult readers (though the book is just as appropriate for adults). *E-mails from Scheherazad*, a first book of poems from Syrian American poet and scholar Mohja Kahf, is probably too racy for children: it is a bold, sexy book that attacks common (and restrictive) wisdom about gender and cultural identity. Both books are political acts that set out to represent, celebrate, and build political capital for a particular group. For Nye, that culture is mostly Palestinian, while Kahf focuses on Middle Eastern women living in America.

Nye's poems amass everyday emotional details of Palestinian lives so that her readers can identify with them, see their humanity and, Nye hopes, recognize their plight. She sees poetry as a powerful tool for peace. One knows what to expect from a Nye poem—a graceful, empathic rendering of characters in pain:

> Even on a sorrowing day
> the little white cups without handles
> would appear
> filled with steaming hot tea
> in a circle on a tray
> and whatever we were able
> to say or not say,
> the tray would be passed,
> we would sip
> in silence,
> it was another way
> lips could be speaking together.... (105)

This poem, like most of Nye's, emphasizes the characters' everyday, ordinary dignity in order to remind us of our shared humanity.

Kahf's poems celebrate humanity too, but they aren't often in pursuit of dignity. They're deadpan or passionate by turns; they present a cast of characters from goddesses to babysitters to painted odalisques, and they are varied formally. Though the bulk of Kahf's poems are casually conversational, her frequent use of anaphora (along with certain images and literary references) invokes traditional Middle Eastern

poetry. Kahf's poems, like Nye's, describe the details of Arab American and Middle Eastern lives, often to similar effect, sparking understanding and compassion in the reader. Kahf's characters feel edgier than Nye's, though. They do not need your empathy, and they expect your respect; they are presented as a welcome threat to conventional American cultural assumptions. Many of Kahf's poems are enjoyably hyperbolic: ancient Middle Eastern goddesses such as Ishtar romp through American cities, raising havoc and hackles as they exercise their confidently sexual, provocatively destructive (and creative) feminine powers. Such poems suggest Kahf's hopes for an expansion of the possibilities available to women, Middle Eastern and otherwise, in America today.

The differences in these poets' works are significant. Nye, who lived in Jerusalem as a teenager, avoids aggressive language entirely, while Kahf's poetry riskily uses violence as a figure for a powerful force in American society that we ignore at our peril—energetic and daring Middle Eastern women. Kahf's stance is complicated. Her poems evidence a strong affection for the American everyday, with a simultaneous strong disdain for American cultural and political ignorance and ethnocentrism. Kahf writes a sex column for a progressive Muslim web site, www.MuslimWakeUp.com, and she sometimes wears the hijab. I told a friend about Kahf's book, adding that the picture of Kahf at the end of *E-mails from Scheherazad* shows the author wearing a headscarf. My friend said, "Don't Muslim progressives want to get rid of that kind of restrictive headgear?" Kahf vigorously combats such assumptions: she's a feminist, she writes sexy and aggressive poems, and she's a Koran scholar who wears a headscarf. If you thought you knew what a feminist was or what a Muslim was, Kahf insists that you think again.

The anger Kahf's poems express is much more aggressive than the poignant hopefulness in Nye's work. Nye's poems frequently try to comfort, to provide by the end of the poem some enlarging image to connect suffering to a larger stability. In her poems as in her eloquent letter "To Any Would-Be Terrorists" (www.arches.uga.edu/~godlas/shihabnye.html), Nye maintains that anger is not the answer; she uses personal details to explain that we are all people, that we must recognize that and stop hurting one another. Nye hopes and trusts that knowledge will bring empathy. Kahf offers us similarly evocative details about Arab American lives, but her poems often simply allow the details to inhabit our minds. "Just another driver on the demographic edge of New Jersey," ends one poem (33). The poems don't often call upon the closing strategy Nye's poems employ: locating some tiny comfort or universality in the difficult situations she describes. In Nye's description of luncheon in a park in a town shredded by war, the characters are still able, gracefully, to make a toast to "you":

> ...who believe true love can find you
> amidst this atlas of tears...
> [P]eople moved here, believing
> and someone with sky and birds in his heart
> said this would be a good place for a park. (37)

Though the poem certainly doesn't suggest that the problems of war can be erased by a brief and generous meeting over lunch in a park, Nye concentrates on the positive.

Whereas Nye's work focuses on the peaceable wisdom her characters have in common, Kahf trusts that we will be attracted to the assertive, jokey energy of her characters, and perhaps hopes that we will be galvanized into taking a stand against sexism and bigotry by their raucous calls to action and rowdy threats. One of Kahf's most daring poems, "Copulation in English," describes an aggressive sexual encounter: the Arabic language speedily seduces the English language, making English "hoarse with the passion we will have taught English to have" (72). The poem ends:

> after this night of intense copulation,
> we may slaughter English in its bed and redeem our
>   honor,
> even while pregnant with English's bastard. (72)

A hyperbolic image, to be sure, but the poem serves both as desire and warning. Kahf is claiming that Arab Americans are part of America—more so every day—and other Americans had better learn to enjoy the ride or get out of the way.

Kahf's language is also confrontational in a way Nye's is not: it calls for audaciousness on the part of progressive Arab Americans, for a move away from conciliation and toward bold self-definition. For example in "Hijab Scene 7" she writes:

> Yes, I speak English
> Yes, I carry explosives
> They're called words
> And if you don't get up
> Off your assumptions
> They're going to blow you away. (39)

Kahf's poems take action from a new and evolving perspective, one that is both threatening and cajoling. When oppression is perceived, Kahf unapologetically counters with aggression. The aggression, of course, is not literally violent; it is embedded in language. Though "Hijab Scene 7" hints that oppression breeds violence, Kahf is not literally calling for violent action. Her poems call for community—for acceptance of different kinds of dress and behavior, and for loving acceptance even of the Arab machismo she occasionally complains of; however, when a loving attitude does not seem an appropriate response, Kahf freely expresses anger.

For Nye, it seems, a loving attitude is invariably an appropriate response, but she can also be critical. In the following poem, she wonders what can be in Israeli soldiers' minds when they abuse Palestinians:

> On the steps of the National Palace Hotel
> soldiers peel oranges
>
> throwing back their heads so the juice
> runs down their throats
>
> This must be their coffee break
> guns slung sideways
>
> They are laughing
> stripping lustily
>
> They know what sweetness lives within
> How can they know this and forget
>
> so many other things? (32–33)

Though Nye is reproaching the soldiers, her approach remains empathic. She wants to understand them emotionally, and though she fails, her attempt to feel what they feel makes her criticism of them sharper. In the preface to *19 Varieties of Gazelle*, Nye says she believes that her beloved dead "wise grandmother" wants her to speak for those the soldiers abuse: "Speak for me too. Say how much I hate it. Say this is not who we are," the grandmother says (xviii). Nye hopes to persuade Americans and Arabs alike that the Arab tradition is not about fundamentalism or terrorism—that Middle Easterners are good people.

Kahf is not interested in persuading anyone of the goodness of Arabs, though she does give us a sense of Arab and Arab American culture's diversity and verve. Her Arabs are everybody: flawed or brilliant, hip or angry, sexist or beautiful. Reading Kahf, I find myself relishing the raffishness of everyday culture. When I read Nye's images of exquisitely patient Palestinians, on the other hand, I worry that they risk depicting an unlikely Palestine that would be entirely perfect and loving if only the horrible wars would go away. Criticisms of Arab society are almost absent in Nye; Kahf, on the other hand, rails against what she sees as Arab men's sexism—while simultaneously confessing respect for and sexual attraction to the same men. The complexity of her relationship to Arab and Arab American culture is best represented in the poem "My Body Is Not Your Battleground," which insists that women's bodies remain independent from those who would use them for political purposes:

> My breasts do not want to lead revolutions...
>   release them
> so I can offer them to my sweet love
> without your flags and banners on them...
> My body is not your battleground...
> Is it your skin that will tear when the head of the new
>   world
> emerges? (59)

Kahf is not inclined to speak politically for others; she does write poems in others' voices, but the poems represent multitudinous difference, not just of background but of attitude.

Central to Nye's vision of the Middle East is a sense that it is always "they"—that is, others—who are violent. "Who made [the bombs]?" she asks. "Do you know anyone who makes them?" (61). When people pick up guns, it is "because guns were given" (134). Violence is imposed on unwilling victims. Nye's poems do not represent those victims who turn violent; she restricts herself to representing the wise multitude who abstain from violence. Her poems thus depict a bifurcated world of evil killers and innocent victims in which violence is an incomprehensible evil and its victims are always wise and good. I cannot help suspecting that the simplicity of Nye's representation of the Middle East is a valiant effort to encourage us all to identify with what she sees as right, an effort that—I think forgivably—ends up tidying messy borders between good and evil. Nye takes seriously her grandmother's urge to her to "speak for" others. She feels responsible to her Palestinian American background and to the millions of Palestinians whose voices have been silenced; she has decided to be their stateswoman here, and in a way her sense of responsibility limits her. Poetry may succeed in healing when all else has failed:

> We will take this word in our arms.
> It will be small and breathing. We will not wish to
>   scare it.
> Pressing lips to the edge of each syllable.
> Nothing else will save us now. (67)

Despite Kahf's punchier attitude, she shares this goal, as the poem "Affirmative Action Sonnet" makes clear:

> Where is the salve? We write.
> We recognize
> —we must——each other...
> or we will die from what we do not know...
> I came across the world to write for you. (92)

Like Nye, Kahf also believes that it is up to language-workers to close the distances between us.

Source: Catherine Wagner, Review of *19 Varieties of Gazelle: Poems of the Middle East* and *E-mails from Scheherazad*, in *MELUS*, Vol. 31, No. 4, Winter 2006, pp. 235–41.

Jennifer M. Brabander

In the following review, Brabander considers Nye's 2002 volume of poetry as reflecting the voices of the characters in her famous novel Habibi.

As with much of Nye's writing, these sixty poems—half of which are new, half of which have been published in her collections for adults—aim in sum to present a balanced yet intimate view of both the Middle East and Arab Americans. Clear and haunting, Nye's poems are accessible to young adults, and the autobiographical element of her poetry makes them even more so, especially for teens who have read her semi-autobiographical novel *Habibi* (rev. 11/97). Those readers who remember *Habibi*'s fourteen-year-old word-passionate Liyana will feel they are reading the grown-up Liyana's poetry (they are, in a way) and will easily recognize people in these poems, especially her beloved Sitti, her grandmother. They'll also be familiar with the point of view that informs the poems, namely Liyana/Naomi's identity as "half-and-half," the daughter of a Palestinian-American father and German-American mother. In her introduction Nye asks us to remember, in the aftermath of September 11, that there are many innocent people in the Middle East, and the poems that follow are an eloquent plea to see people as individuals and to believe in peace. Nye's introduction mentions finding solace in poetry; though readers will find much that is painful here, solace is also here, as simple and sustaining as the bread from Sitti's round oven.

Source: Jennifer M. Brabander, Review of *19 Varieties of Gazelle: Poems of the Middle East*, in *Horn Book*, Vol. 78, No. 5, September/October 2002, pp. 591–92.

Kirkus Reviews

In the following review, a contributor to Kirkus Reviews *commends the collection for bringing together so many subjects vital to the time.*

In a collection as rich as the subject, Nye (*Come With Me*, 2000, etc.) brings together all of her poems about the Middle East, old and new, familiar and unknown. Opening with a poem about a young man just released from prison on the morning of September 11th, she follows with a reflection on what that day has meant for everyone, especially for Arabs and Arab-Americans, who, through Nye, say: "This is not who we are." She follows with exquisitely nuanced images of fig trees, grandmothers, Palestinian children, the loss of "pleasant pauses," and "The Man Who Makes Brooms." Asking "How Long Peace Takes," Nye writes, "As long as the question—what if I / were you?—has two heads," and answers a border guard, "We will eat cabbage rolls, rice with sugar and milk, / crisply sizzled eggplant. When the olives come / sailing past / in their little boat, we will line them on our / plates / like punctuation. What do governments have to do / with such pleasure?" Poem after poem will elicit a gasp of surprise, a nod of the head, a pause to reflect. There are no false steps here—only a feeling of sensory overload and a need to take a deep breath and reread or to find someone to share the intensely felt emotion that springs from the lines. In her closing poem, a musing on what one should have said, she writes, "Say it / as if words count." With this gifted writer, they really do.

Source: Review of *19 Varieties of Gazelle: Poems of the Middle East*, in *Kirkus Reviews*, Vol. 70, No. 8, April 15, 2002, p. 575.

Ibis Gomez-Vega

In the following essay, Gomez-Vega examines the course of Nye's poetical oeuvre prior to 19 Varieties of Gazelle.

When Naomi Shihab Nye says in "For Lost and Found Brothers" that "Facts interest me less than the trailing smoke of stories" (*Words under the Words*), the essence of her work becomes clear. As a poet she is, at heart, a storyteller, one who focuses on the lives of everyday people, especially her own relatives, to understand the world around her. She is neither a "New Formalist" nor a "Language" poet, the terms that define the work of some of the most critically revered contemporary poets. Instead, she writes free verse in what is, by most standards, fairly accessible language. Like most poets, Shihab Nye is enamoured of words, but her free verse poems tell stories which seem to emerge from that "boundary [that] becomes the place from which

> IF ANYTHING, HER WORK AIMS FOR CLARITY AND ACHIEVES IT BECAUSE THE POET HERSELF IS CONSCIOUSLY TRYING TO REACH READERS AND NONREADERS ALIKE, ANYONE WHO CAN MAKE THE TIME TO HEAR A GOOD STORY."

something begins its presencing in a movement not dissimilar to the ambulant, ambivalent articulation of the beyond" that Homi K. Bhabha defines in *The Location of Culture*. Often, the stories become a tool for survival, the only way to make sense of difficult moments in a harsh world, and nowhere is this more evident than in "How Palestinians Keep Warm," a poem about the subtle changes that have taken place in the lives of contemporary Palestinians who huddle together in a war-torn city. The poet says, "I know we need to keep warm here on earth / and when your shawl is as thin as mine is, you tell stories" (*Red Suitcase* 26).

> Often, the stories become a tool for survival, the only way to make sense of difficult moments in a harsh world, . . .

Naomi Shihab Nye's first collection of poems, *Different Ways to Pray* (1980), marks the beginning of her exploration of what will become recurrent themes through the body of her work. Her concern with family connections is the subject of many of her poems because, as she states in *Fuel* (1998), "If you tuck the name of a loved one / under your tongue too long / without speaking it / it becomes blood," so "No one sees / the fuel that feeds you" ("Hidden"). The family must be acknowledged; it must be recognized, but so must the fact that families have been torn asunder by the displacement created by war. For this reason, the sense of loss so prevalent in the work of exile or immigrant writers also runs through Shihab Nye's poetry even though she is herself not an exiled poet.

Born to a Palestinian father and a mother of European ancestry, Naomi Shihab Nye was born and raised on a farm in St. Louis where she learned to love animals and appreciate her father's love for the land. At the age of twelve, she spent a year in Palestine getting to know her father's family, an experience that filled her with a deep sense of belonging and, thereby, displacement. Lisa Suhair Majaj points out that Shihab Nye's poetry "explores the markers of cross-cultural complexity, moving between her Palestinian and American heritages" because Shihab Nye's poems document the differences as well as the similarities between two very divergent peoples, although Suhair Majaj also claims that Shihab Nye "is heir to an Arab essence passed down across generations." Regardless of her "Arab essence," Naomi Shihab Nye's work lies well within the American tradition of story-telling poets like Robert Frost.

Whether she is writing about her father's Palestinian family or her own connections with people in other parts of the world, Shihab Nye's poems are acquainted with the pain of displaced people. In "Brushing Live," she writes about an unexpected meeting between her father and a Palestinian man in Alexandria.

> In a shop so dark he had to blink twice
> an ancient man sunk low on a stool and said,
> 'You talk like the men who lived in the world
> when I was young.' Wouldn't say more,
> till my father mentioned Palestine
> and the gentleman rose, both arms out, streaming
> cheeks. 'I have stopped saying it. So many years.'
> My father held him there, held Palestine, in the dark,
> at the corners of two honking streets.
> He got lost coming back to our hotel.
> (*Red Suitcase*)

The encounter is awkward and casual, but it taps at the pain of the exiled, the displaced, the pain of a people adrift in a violent world. Gregory Orfalea, when asked to discuss the Palestinian connection in Shihab Nye's work, points out that "her work is faithful to the minute, but essential tasks of our lives, the luminous in the ordinary."

Because so much of her work harks back to her memories of the Shihab family home in Palestine, a picture of her Palestinian grandmother, Sitti Khadra, graces the cover and half title page of *Words under the Words*, a volume that brings together three of her early books: *Different Ways to Pray* (1980), *Hugging the Jukebox* (1982), and *Yellow Glove* (1986). The photograph was taken by Michael Nye, Naomi Shihab's Swedish American husband, which seems appropriate because much of Shihab Nye's work focuses on the moments recovered from family connections. She writes in *Never in a Hurry* that when she visits Palestine, "feelings crowd in on" her, and she reasons that "maybe this is what it means to be in your genetic home. That you will feel on fifty levels at once, the immediate as well as the level of blood, the level of uncles, . . . weddings and graves, the babies who didn't make it, level of the secret and unseen." She tells herself that "maybe this is heritage, that deep well that gives us more than we deserve. Each time I write or walk or think, I drop a bucket in."

The influence of the Shihab family on the Palestinian American poet evolves through the years. In "My Father and the Figtree," one learns about the time when the poet, at age six, eats a fig and shrugs, unaware of what the taste of a fig means to her Palestinian father:

> 'That's not what I'm talking about!' he said,
> 'I'm talking about a fig straight from the earth—
> gift of Allah!—on a branch so heavy it touches the
>   ground.
> I'm talking about picking the largest fattest
>   sweetest fig
> in the world and putting it in my mouth.'
> (Here he'd stop and close his eyes.)
> (*Words under the Words*)

The six-year-old child, raised in a country where figs are exotic, not as common as apples or even oranges, fails to understand her Palestinian father's appreciation for the fruit, even if the taste of figs functions in the poem like Proust's madeleine to bring back the past. The father's longing for the memory of the fig's taste reiterates the poet's concern with her father's displacement and her own sense of inadequacy as a Palestinian who does not share her father's memories.

In "The Words under the Words," Shihab Nye remembers her grandmother, Sitti Khadra, who lived north of Jerusalem and impressed her with her silence and wisdom. Because she lives in a war-torn country, "my grandmother's voice says nothing can surprise her. / Take her the shotgun wound and the crippled baby. / She knows the spaces we travel through, / the messages we cannot send" (*Words*). For the grandmother, affected by war, the one constant is Allah. Her "eyes say Allah is everywhere, even in death. . . . / He is her first thought, what she really thinks of His name." The grandmother reminds the poet to

> 'Answer, if you hear the words under the words—
> otherwise it is just a world with a lot of rough edges,
> difficult to get through, and our pockets full of
>   stones.'

Her grandmother's words remind her to look for meaning in life, to look for the words under the words, which is exactly what the life of this poet is about, creating a context for understanding through story telling.

Because meaning can only spring from what she knows, Naomi Shihab Nye also writes about what it means to be "different" in America. Her most poignant poem on this subject is "Blood," published in *Yellow Glove* in 1986. In it, she remembers how

> Years before, a girl knocked,
> wanted to see the Arab.
> I said we didn't have one.
> After that, my father told me who he was,
> 'Shihab'—'shooting star'—
> a good name, borrowed from the sky.
> Once I said, 'When we die, we give it back?'
> He said that's what a true Arab would say.

That she tells the girl that they "didn't have" an Arab in the house reiterates Shihab Nye's own sense of inadequacy. Although she shares her father's Palestinian ancestry, she does not recognize it as a marker.

Although the child in the poem does not know that she does in fact have an Arab in the house, the adult poet refuses to forget him or her own connection to his ancestry. In the same poem, Shihab Nye confronts the disturbing news emerging from the Palestinian struggle for self determination.

> I call my father, we talk around the news.
> It is too much for him,
> neither of his two languages can reach it.
> I drive into the country to find sheep, cows,
> to plead with the air:
> Who calls anyone civilized?
> Where can the crying heart graze?
> What does a true Arab do now?

The Arab American who can see both sides of the story in the Israeli/Palestinian struggle is torn between her desire for justice and her love for her ancestral country. The struggle, however, leads the poet to recognize her ethnicity and her own place as an "other" in America.

In "Speaking Arabic," a short essay in *Never in a Hurry*, Shihab Nye ponders the need for ethnic identity as she wonders why she could not "forget the earnest eyes of the man who said to [her] in Jordan, 'Until you speak Arabic, you will not understand pain.'" She considers his statement "ridiculous" and remembers how he goes on to say "something to do with an Arab carrying sorrow in the back of the skull that only language cracks." As in the case of her father's earlier longing for the taste of figs, the man's

statement leads her to remember yet another man's statement when,

> At a neighborhood fair in Texas, somewhere between the German Oom-pah Sausage stand and the Mexican Gorditas booth, I overheard a young man say to his friend, 'I wish I had a heritage. Sometimes I feel—so lonely for one.' And the tall American trees were dangling their thick branches right down over my head.

Words from a zealot and from someone who has lost his heritage are juxtaposed in an attempt to understand what it means to have a heritage, to come from a place so deeply ingrained in the mind that figs savored in childhood retain their taste forever.

As an Arab American, Naomi Shihab Nye writes in English even as she frets over her inability to understand Arabic as well as she would like.

> I thought pain had no tongue. Or every tongue at once, supreme translator, sieve. I admit my shame. To live on the brink of Arabic, tugging its rich threads without understanding how to weave the rug ... I have no gift. The sound, but not the sense. (*"Arabic," Red Suitcase*)

She associates speaking Arabic with her father and with relatives who live far away, and, probably because she is a poet who values words, she wants the gift of that language.

The power of words to renew and uplift the spirit is another theme that runs through Naomi Shihab Nye's work, and it is manifested in her appreciation for the work of other poets. Through the years, she has written many poems to her mentor and teacher, William Stafford, of whom she says in "Bill's Beans" that "He left the sky over Oregon and fluent trees. / He gave us our lives that were hiding under our feet, / saying, You know what to do" (*Fuel*). Shihab Nye also maintains close relationships with many contemporary poets. In "You Know Who You Are," words from one of these poets sustain her. She claims that "Because sometimes I live in a hurricane of words / and not one of them can save me. / Your poems come in like a raft, logs tied together, / they float." Then, after observing the behavior of fathers and sons together and wandering "uselessly in the streets I claim to love," she feels "the precise body of your poems beneath me, / *like a raft*, I felt words as something portable again, / a cup, a newspaper, a pin" (*Words under the Words*). Words move her, sustain her, connect her to the world in ways that only words can explain, which is why she attempts to teach one of her students in "Valentine for Ernest Mann" that

> poems hide. In the bottoms of our shoes,
> they are sleeping. They are the shadows
> drifting across our ceilings the moment
> before we wake up. What we have to do
> is live in a way that lets us find them. (*Red Suitcase*)

For Naomi Shihab Nye, poems hide everywhere, and her task as a poet has been to write ordinary poems in an accessible language, what Vernon Shetley calls the "colloquial free-verse lyric that occupies the mainstream." There is no "'unreadability'" as "a goal in itself" in Naomi Shihab Nye's poetry. If anything, her work aims for clarity and achieves it because the poet herself is consciously trying to reach readers and nonreaders alike, anyone who can make the time to hear a good story.

Living "in a way that lets us find" the poems suggests that people, as poets or simply as citizens of this world, must live a life committed to other people and all of creation. This is another one of Shihab Nye's themes, and one that speaks volumes for the soul of this poet. In "Kindness," she reminds her readers that

> Before you know what kindness really is
> you must lose things,
> feel the future dissolve in a moment
> like salt in a weakened broth.
> What you held in your hand,
> what you counted and carefully saved,
> all this must go so you know
> how desolate the landscape can be
> between the regions of kindness . . .
>
> Before you know kindness as the deepest thing
>   inside,
> you must know sorrow as the other deepest thing.
> You must wake up with sorrow.
> You must speak to it till your voice
> catches the thread of all sorrows
> and you see the size of the cloth. . .
> (*Words under the Words*)

Kindness emanates from Naomi Shihab Nye's work. The five volumes of her work reveal a deep understanding of our weaknesses, our humanity, as the stories that she creates define her ties to a people who endow her with an appreciation for heritage and a strong sense of what she has lost and what she has gained as she defines her own place in the world.

Source: Ibis Gomez-Vega, "The Art of Telling Stories in the Poetry of Naomi Shihab Nye," in *MELUS*, Vol. 26, No. 4, Winter 2001, pp. 245–52.

SOURCES

Brabander, Jennifer M., Review of *19 Varieties of Gazelle: Poems of the Middle East*, in *Horn Book*, Vol. 78, No. 5, September/October 2002, pp. 591–92.

de Preneuf, Flore, "Asel Is Gone," in *Salon*, October 7, 2000, http://www.salon.com/2000/10/07/asel/singleton/ (accessed March 6, 2012).

Feller, Leslie Chess, "In Search of Peace on Common Ground," in *New York Times*, August 29, 1999, http://www.nytimes.com/1999/08/29/nyregion/in-search-of-peace-on-common-ground.html (accessed March 10, 2012).

"Iraq-U.S. War," in *International Encyclopedia of the Social Sciences*, 2nd ed., Vol. 4, edited by William A. Darity, Jr., Macmillan Reference USA, 2008, pp. 145–48.

"Jews and Arabs Are 'Genetic Brothers,'" in *BBC News*, May 10, 2000, http://news.bbc.co.uk/2/hi/science/nature/742430.stm (accessed March 10, 2012).

Lindsay, Nina, Review of *19 Varieties of Gazelle: Poems of the Middle East*, in *School Library Journal*, Vol. 48, No. 5, May 2002, p. 175.

Long, Kate, "Roots: On Language and Heritage; A Conversation with Naomi Shihab Nye," in *World Literature Today*, Vol. 83, No. 6, 2009, p. 31.

Najmi, Samina, "Naomi Shihab Nye's Aesthetic of Smallness and the Military Sublime," in *MELUS*, Vol. 35, No. 2, Summer 2010, p. 151.

Nye, Naomi Shihab, "All Things Not Considered," in *19 Varieties of Gazelle: Poems of the Middle East*, Greenwillow, 2002, pp. 133–35.

Odenheimer, Alisa, Corky Siemaszko, and Tim Burger, "Palestinian Group Calls It Revenge," in *New York Daily News*, May 10, 2001, http://articles.nydailynews.com/2001-05-10/news/18170251_1_palestinian-girl-palestinian-baby-gaza-refugee-camp (accessed March 5, 2012).

Peretz, Don, "Arab-Israel Conflict," in *Encyclopedia of the Modern Middle East and North Africa*, 2nd ed., Vol. 1, edited by Philip Mattar, Macmillan Reference USA, 2004, pp. 235–39.

"Poetic Expressions (Children's Notes)," in *Publishers Weekly*, Vol. 249, No. 20, May 20, 2002, p. 69.

Rees, Matt, "Mohammed al-Durra," in *Time*, December 25, 2000, http://www.time.com/time/world/article/0,8599,2050464,00.html (accessed March 6, 2012).

Review of *19 Varieties of Gazelle: Poems of the Middle East*, in *Kirkus Reviews*, Vol. 70, No. 8, April 15, 2002, p. 575.

Rochman, Hazel, Review of *19 Varieties of Gazelle: Poems of the Middle East*, in *Booklist*, Vol. 98, No. 15, April 1, 2002, p. 1315.

Wagner, Catherine, Review of *19 Varieties of Gazelle: Poems of the Middle East* and *E-mails from Scheherazad*, in *MELUS*, Vol. 31, No. 4, Winter 2006, p. 235.

FURTHER READING

Hirshfield, Jane, *Nine Gates: Entering the Mind of Poetry*, Harper Perennial, 1998.

> In this book, Hirshfield guides the reader to a deeper understanding of how to read and experience poetry.

Nye, Naomi Shihab, *Habibi*, Simon & Schuster, 1997.

> *Habibi* is a semiautobiographical novel by Nye about a young Arab American girl who moves with her family from St. Louis to Palestine and there meets the paternal side of her family, befriends a Jewish boy, and tries to learn to call this strange place home.

———, *You & Yours*, BOA Editions, 2005.

> This collection of poetry focuses on ordinary people—from inner-city Texas to rural America to Israelis and Palestinians in the Middle East—who are brought to life through Nye's deft use of language.

———, ed., *This Same Sky: A Collection of Poems from Around the World*, Four Winds, 1992.

> This multicultural compilation brings together over 125 poems (some translated into English for the first time) from sixty-eight countries to emphasize human commonalities.

Sacco, Joe, *Palestine*, Fantagraphics Books, 2002.

> *Palestine*, winner of the 1996 American Book Award, is a political and historical account of the West Bank and Gaza Strip (modern Palestinian settlements) told in Sacco's characteristic combination of journalism and comic illustration.

Said, Edward, *Out of Place: A Memoir*, Vintage, 2000.

> In this memoir, Said, an intellectual and a Palestinian American, writes about his life growing up in Palestine, Egypt, Lebanon, and the United States and his confusion about his identity.

SUGGESTED SEARCH TERMS

19 Varieties of Gazelle

"All Things Not Considered"

Arab-Israeli conflict

Arab-Israeli conflict AND poetry

Israeli AND poetry

Naomi Shihab Nye

Naomi Shibab Nye AND political poetry

Naomi Shihab Nye AND peace

Palestinian AND poetry

Aubade

PHILIP LARKIN

1977

Philip Larkin's "Aubade" was published in a 1977 edition of the *Times Literary Supplement*, a journal that had frequently published his work since the 1950s. "Aubade" is one of the last poems that Larkin produced, and it is considered by critics to be one of his greatest. In this lyric poem, the speaker explains to the reader how he feels when he wakes up in the middle of the night with an acute awareness of his own mortality, which gives way to an overwhelming fear of his own impending death. As the sun slowly rises behind the speaker's bedroom curtains, his fear does not wane, though he does become progressively more conscious and analytical.

The title of the poem, "Aubade," is a play on the classical definition of the word. Traditionally an *aubade* is a joyful poem that celebrates the coming of the morning, and aubades are often love poems. Larkin's "Aubade" is the complete opposite of a joyful love poem; to the speaker of this poem, the coming of the morning represents his being one more day closer to death. However, the sun rising outside does provide some relief, as it initiates the start of the workday, which will allow the speaker to be distracted from the horror of his own mortality. A copy of "Aubade" can be found in the anthology *Death, Dying and Bereavement*, which was edited by Donna Dickenson, Malcolm Johnson, and Jeanne Samson Katz and published in 2000.

Philip Larkin (© *Daily Express | Hulton Archive | Getty Images*)

AUTHOR BIOGRAPHY

Larkin was born on August 9, 1922, in Coventry, Warwickshire, England, the youngest child of Sydney Larkin and Eva Emily Day. Sydney Larkin was a successful, self-made man who was outspoken about his love for Nazism as well as his love for literature. The latter undoubtedly had a profound impact on Larkin. His father introduced him to the works of the great modernist writers whom he deeply admired, including Ezra Pound, T. S. Eliot, James Joyce, and D. H. Lawrence.

Larkin's sister Catherine (called Kitty) was ten years his senior, and she and their mother educated Larkin at home until the age of eight. The Larkins were a somewhat peculiar family and never allowed visitors in their home. However, even when Larkin was very young, his parents supported his passions, which included playing jazz music and, of course, writing. Larkin wrote both poetry and prose from a young age. He is said to have produced five novels before he began his university studies, though he destroyed all of them.

Larkin was always interested in school, but he did not do well on his certificate exams at the age of sixteen. Nevertheless, he was allowed to stay at school, and two years later he passed his exams with distinction in English and history. He also passed the entrance exams for St. John's College at Oxford University, where he began studying English in October 1940. It was the year after the start of World War II, but Larkin failed the military medical examination on account of his poor eyesight and was able to continue studying at college.

Through his tutorial partner, Norman Iles, Larkin met Kingsley Amis, a peer who would also go on to become a great writer. Larkin and Amis remained friends for life, and Amis was a constant supporter of Larkin's work. Larkin, Amis, and several other friends at Oxford formed a group called "The Seven," which frequently met to drink, listen to music, and discuss each other's poetry. While at Oxford, Larkin published a poem for the first time: "Ultimatum," in the *Listener*. During this time, he also wrote two novellas under the pseudonym Brunette Coleman. In 1943, Larkin sat for his finals and graduated with a first-class honors degree.

Larkin began working as a librarian at the public library in Wellington, Shropshire, in 1943. It was there that he met his first girlfriend, Ruth Bowman. In 1945, Larkin published his first collection of poems, *The North Ship*, which was well received. In 1946, he was appointed assistant librarian at University College, Leicester. This was the same year that Larkin published his first novel, *Jill*. Larkin's second and last novel, *A Girl in Winter*, was published in 1947. Shortly after his father's death from cancer in 1948, he proposed to Ruth. She accepted, but the couple broke it off in 1950, just before Larkin changed jobs, becoming sublibrarian at Queen's University Belfast. He spent five contented years there, during which he had simultaneous relationships with Monica Jones, a lecturer in English, and Patsy Strang, a woman who was in an open marriage with one of his colleagues.

In 1955, Larkin became university librarian at the University of Hull, where he worked until his death in 1985. It was during this period that Larkin produced his most well-known and acclaimed poetry, despite the fact that the volume of his output was drastically reduced. Following the publication of his 1955 collection *The Less Deceived* and its favorable reviews in both the *Times Literary Supplement* and the London *Times*, critics and general readers alike began to take notice of Larkin's work. *The Whitsun Weddings* (1964) and *High Windows* (1974) were Larkin's last two volumes of poetry. Larkin began writing "Aubade" in 1974 but did not complete it until 1977, when it was published in the *Times Literary Supplement*. It was one of his last poems to be published and certainly one of the last of note.

Larkin never married or had children, although he did have long-standing relationships with many women. Larkin was with Maeve Brennan from 1961 until their split in 1973, at which time Monica Jones became his primary partner. However, in March 1975, while still dating Jones, Larkin rekindled his relationship with Brennan and shortly after began a secret affair with Betty Mackereth, his secretary of twenty-eight years. Larkin's simultaneous relationships continued until 1978, when he and Jones became monogamous.

On June 11, 1985, Larkin was admitted to a hospital to undergo surgery for esophageal cancer, but it was discovered that his cancer had spread and was inoperable. On November 28 of that year, he collapsed and was readmitted to the hospital. Larkin died four days later, on December 2, 1985, at the age of sixty-three and was buried at the Cottingham municipal cemetery near Hull, England.

POEM SUMMARY

The text used for this summary is from *Death, Dying and Bereavement*, Sage Publications, 2000, pp. 68–69. Versions of the poem can be found on the following web pages: http://www.poetryfoundation.org/poem/178058 and http://www.poemhunter.com/best-poems/philip-larkin/aubade/.

Larkin's "Aubade" comprises five stanzas of ten lines each that generally follow an *ababccdeed* rhyme scheme and iambic pentameter rhythm, though there are several modifications to these patterns throughout. In this lyric poem told in the present tense, the unnamed, unidentified speaker clearly and carefully expresses his mental state when he wakes in the middle of the night acutely and terrifyingly aware of his own mortality. The present tense and the methodical detail with which the speaker describes this event give the reader of the poem the impression that this sort of middle-of-the-night realization is something that has happened to the speaker several times, or perhaps regularly, and is not an isolated incident.

Stanza 1

In the first stanza, the speaker describes what is perhaps a typical day in his life: working in the day and drinking at night. The speaker then describes waking up at four in the morning, before the sun begins to rise, with a sudden vivid awareness of the

MEDIA ADAPTATIONS

- *Douglas Dunn and Philip Larkin* is an audio recording issued by Faber & Faber in 1984, which includes a recording of Larkin reading "Aubade" aloud.

fact that he will someday die and is now one day closer to that moment. The speaker notes that this reality is not new, it has always been there, but in these moments it somehow seems more real. To the speaker, this thought is powerfully consuming and utterly horrific. It is as if this realization has seized him, and he cannot think of anything else, despite the fact that he finds the prospect terrifying.

Stanza 2

The speaker then moves past the initial horror and begins to process what exactly is so horrific about death. The speaker concludes that the terribleness that he associates with death has nothing to do with regrets. The speaker is not bothered by thoughts that he could have spent his time more wisely or done more good in the world. The root of the speaker's panic is instead the prospect of nonexistence, of no longer being. The speaker knows that it is inevitable but still finds it horrid. The speaker also takes a moment to reflect on the fact that this reality will be upon him relatively soon.

Stanza 3

The speaker moves into another, more analytical phase in the third stanza. He indirectly comments on the universality of this feeling by discussing what he views as the coping mechanisms of others but concludes that these methods are empty and that to the discerning mind there is no escaping the feelings of horror associated with death. The speaker describes religion as an institution created to delude people into believing that they will never truly die; they will simply pass on to some sort of afterlife. He also disputes claims by existential philosophers that fear of death is irrational because we cannot really experience it. Larkin flips the tables on this claim, pointing out that the lack of experience, the lack of feeling anything ever again, is precisely what he fears.

Stanza 4

In the fourth stanza, the speaker reflects on the practical implications of everything he has discussed thus far. He writes that typically, the awareness of death sits on the horizon of his mind, out of focus and largely unnoticed, until it springs to the forefront in moments such as the one he has described. These moments always happen when the speaker is by himself, without people or alcohol to comfort him. He notes that it does not matter how you react to the fear of death, because nothing you could ever do would change the reality of it. Bravely facing death and the fear of it simply means sparing others the terror that you yourself feel.

Stanza 5

The speaker describes what happens as day breaks. The inevitability of death is still very much at the forefront of the speaker's mind as the day begins, and the day's business is imminent. The speaker thinks of the offices that will soon be buzzing with activity and all of the people who simply go about their day-to-day business without giving a thought to the fact that they will soon die.

THEMES

Fear of Death

The first stanza of "Aubade" makes the reader acutely aware that the fear of death will be a major theme in the poem. In fact, the poem is solely about fear of death, in particular a special, vivid, and all-consuming type of fear, as opposed to a vague and general awareness that one day you will die. The fear of death that Larkin writes about in "Aubade" is one that takes you by surprise in the middle of the night when you are half asleep. It exists in the moment when your mind has achieved an absolutely clear awareness of the reality of mortality. From the first line of the poem to the last, Larkin describes how a mind approaches this reality, grapples with it, refusing to come to terms with it, and then reluctantly moves on, but still does not accept it, even after determining that there is nothing that can

be done. This theme is conveyed through metaphors, diction, and subject matter.

Futility

Another important theme in the work is the notion of futility, specifically that there is absolutely nothing the speaker can do about his fear of death. In a way, this sense of hopelessness, the awareness that no matter what he does he will never be able to escape the thing he so fears, compounds the speaker's fear of death even further. This theme is particularly visible in line 22, in which the speaker acknowledges that there is no way to trick him out of his fear; lines 37–40, in which the speaker acknowledges the futility of being brave in the face of death; and lines 43 and 44, in which the speaker acknowledges that he is not able to accept or escape his fear. It is important to note that although the speaker believes in the futility of his situation, he never resigns himself to it. He cannot except death, and thus the inability to alter his fate leaves him in a state of ceaseless conflict.

Consciousness

The notion of consciousness plays a more significant role in the poem than the reader might initially realize, because the poem depicts a cognitive process that evolves depending on the speaker's level of consciousness. The condition that the speaker describes in the poem, the paralyzing fear of death he experiences, occurs when he wakes in the middle of the night. It is in this special state somewhere between sleeping and waking that he is able to most deeply understand mortality. As the poem progresses and the speaker becomes more fully conscious, his thought processes change as well. When he is in the half-asleep and half-awake state, his cognitive processes are more primal and motivated solely by fear. After he comes into full consciousness, his thoughts become more analytical, as he catalogs the things that he will lose when he dies and struggles to accept that there is no escaping death. As light breaks, and the speaker grows fully awake, the horrors of the night begin to fade even further. The situation has not changed, and the speaker has not and never will be able to find a solution, but with the distractions of daily life, the fear will no longer be at the forefront of his consciousness.

Rationality

Rationality is one of the aesthetic cornerstones of the works of Larkin and the other poets of "the Movement" of the era. They believed that

TOPICS FOR FURTHER STUDY

- Larkin's "Aubade" is not a particularly hopeful or uplifting poem, and it was produced during a time when the British economy was suffering and causing widespread social discontent. Oftentimes, the general social atmosphere of an era is reflected in the work that artists produce. Choose an artistic movement that you enjoy (examples include surrealism, symbolism, and romanticism), and create a multimedia presentation about that movement and the social climate that spawned it. Be sure to include examples of the artwork and information on specific historical events.

- The speaker in Larkin's "Aubade" is convinced that after people die they do not move on to an afterlife but simply cease to exist, though many religions and philosophies hold starkly different views on the matter. In a group with several of your classmates, use the Internet to research a non-Western major world religion such as Islam, Hinduism, Buddhism, or Sikhism, and create a PowerPoint presentation to educate your class on that religion. Be sure to include information on what the followers of the religion believe will happen to them after they die.

- Typically an aubade is a poem that celebrates the coming of the morning. Using the Internet, find an aubade written by a poet other than Larkin, such as "Hymn to the Morning," by Phyllis Wheatley; "Aubade with a Book and a Rattle from a String of Pearls," by Octavio de la Paz; or "Morning Poem," by Mary Oliver. Write an essay comparing and contrasting the poem of your choice to Larkin's "Aubade." Thematically and stylistically, how are they the same and how are they different?

- Peruse the book *Life & Death: A Collection of Classic Poetry and Prose*, an anthology of poetry and prose for young adults edited and introduced by Philip Pullman. Thematically, many of the poems included in this volume are similar to "Aubade." Choose a poem from this book that you enjoy, and using a recording device, record yourself reading the poem aloud. Listen to the poem carefully as you play it back, and take notes on the cadence and rhythm of the work. Then write an essay expanding on your notes and explaining how the style of the poem contributes to its overall meaning.

above all else, poems should be rational and clear in subject matter and traditional in form. This is certainly true of "Aubade." Although the poem is largely centered around the emotion of fear, the fear that the poem deals with is perhaps the most rational one a human could have. The reason the speaker is so deeply terrified of death is that he is indisputably going to experience it; there is no chance he will be able to escape it. In a way, the speaker is more rational during these middle-of-the-night moments of lucidity than he is when he goes about his business during the day. The speaker's tone in the last stanza indicates that he views the act of engaging in the business of daily life as a willing denial of the fact that nothing we do matters very much when you consider that we will all be dead soon.

Existentialism

Though existentialism is not directly addressed in the poem, it is an underlying theme. Existentialism is a philosophy centered around the notion that the universe is indifferent and that the human experience does not have any particular meaning. The speaker of the poem mentions several times that he does not believe in any sort of afterlife, and at the time of his death, he will simply cease to exist. He also describes religion as an invention to help mitigate the fear of death. These notions are rooted in existential thought.

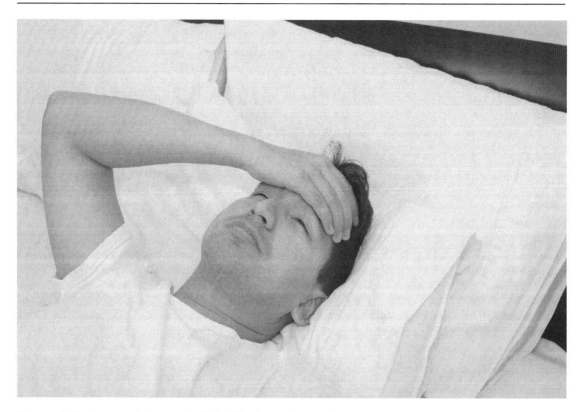

Stanza 1 finds a man lying awake in bed in the early morning. *(© David Castillo Dorr | Shutterstock.com)*

STYLE

"Venus and Adonis" Stanza and Envelope Stanza

As a poet of "the Movement," Larkin was concerned with writing his poems in traditional forms as opposed to free verse. "Aubade" is an excellent example of this characteristic: its five ten-line stanzas are composed of a "Venus and Adonis" stanza and an "envelope" stanza combined. The "Venus and Adonis" stanza is so named because it is the type of stanza William Shakespeare used in his 1593 narrative poem *Venus and Adonis*. This type of stanza has an *ababcc* rhyme scheme, meaning that the last words of the first and third lines rhyme, the last words of the second and fourth lines rhyme, and the last words of the fifth and sixth lines rhyme. In other words, it is the combination of a standard quatrain and couplet written in iambic pentameter. Iambic pentameter features a ten-syllable line of five iambs, where an *iamb* is a metric foot containing an unstressed syllable followed by a stressed syllable.

An envelope stanza is a quatrain that follows an *abba* rhyme scheme, so that the last words of

the first and fourth lines rhyme and the last words of the second and third lines rhyme. Therefore, the stanzas in "Aubade," each of which consist of a "Venus and Adonis" stanza followed by an envelope stanza, follow an *ababccdeed* rhyme scheme. The lines are generally written in iambic pentameter, though there are several exceptions to this meter. Most notably, the ninth line of each stanza, which should have ten syllables, is shortened and consists of five, six, or seven syllables. This creates an interesting effect. Readers typically tend to pause on syllables that complete a rhyme as they invoke a sense of finality. By making the penultimate line of each stanza particularly and unexpectedly short, the reader naturally pauses even longer at the end of those lines. In this way, Larkin emphasizes both the ninth and tenth lines of each stanza. After pausing for a beat on the last syllable of the nine line, the tenth line seems even more potent and more satisfying in its completion of the overall rhyme scheme than it otherwise would.

Conversational Diction

Larkin was known for his love of everyday, common things. He believed that the work of poetry was to capture moments of the everyday

COMPARE & CONTRAST

- **1970s:** The economy of the United Kingdom suffers a terrible slump. Salary caps caused by rampant inflation induces widespread workers' strikes, decreased productivity, and increased unemployment.

  Today: Although the economy in the United Kingdom has enjoyed periods of prosperity within the last three decades, it suffers another major slump in the 2000s and may soon be approaching the catastrophic state of the 1970s once again, according to some forecasters.

- **1970s:** According to the book *Left Shift: Radical Art in 1970s Britain*, by John A. Walker, the cultural shifts of this decade are reflected in its art. Visual art becomes more extravagant, experimental, and obscene. Writers such as Larkin and the other poets of "the Movement" react against this shift, choosing instead to use traditional forms and simple diction.

  Today: The British art scene is expanding geographically rather than thematically. Whereas in the past, Turner Prize winners have typically been from in and around London, the winners of the prize in the past few years have come from Germany, Scotland, and elsewhere. This indicates a significant broadening of the art scene in Britain.

- **1970s:** Although the term originated in the mid-nineteenth century, in the 1970s the term "Continental philosophy" becomes widely used in British universities to collectively describe several branches of Western philosophy (including those that Larkin subscribed to) outside of the analytic movement.

  Today: Continental philosophy is a term that is widely used and understood. Countless American and European universities teach courses in this branch of philosophy.

---

life of an individual. This philosophy is reflected in the casual and conversational diction of the vast majority of his poems, including "Aubade." Though the poem is a lyric, meaning that the speaker of the poem directly shares his or her thoughts with the reader, there are places in the poem (particularly at the beginning) where the tone is so conversational it could be classified as a narrative poem were it not for the first-person speaker. Although Larkin does use many metaphors in the poem, none of them are so complex that they require a great deal of thought to understand. Similarly, the language he uses in the poem is accessible to the general public. There is an absence of obscure vocabulary that would necessitate a dictionary. Larkin rejected modernist poetry by the likes of T. S. Eliot, Ezra Pound, or E. E. Cummings. Modernist poetry was influenced by symbolism and often implemented new and experimental forms. Larkin believed that poetry should be straightforward and easily accessible.

HISTORICAL CONTEXT

"The Movement" in English Literature

"The Movement" was a term invented by J. D. Scott, literary editor of the *Spectator*, in 1954 to describe a group of English writers including Kingsley Amis, Donald Davie, D. J. Enright, John Wain, Elizabeth Jennings, Thom Gunn, Robert Conquest, and Larkin. The Movement came together in the early 1950s. Its members considered themselves to be the true continuation of traditional English poetry. They rejected international influences and instead praised poems written in clear English diction.

The Movement poets were typically considered antiromantic, meaning that they championed rationality and clear, traditional forms. Though romantic elements can be found in some of Larkin's poems, generally his work is very much in line with the style of the other Movement poets. The Movement poets also rejected the work of modernists such as T. S. Eliot, whom Larkin's father

---

Stanza 3 notes feelings at the edges of vision. *(© SVLuma | Shutterstock.com)*

adored. Although Larkin's work was often compared to the work of Eliot, he always denied and resented the comparison. The poems of the Movement were formal, clear, and concise. The Movement poets thought the ideal poem was one that was slow, quietly reflective, and easy to understand rather than hyperemotional and ornate. They believed that their work should capture slices of everyday life and be accessible to common people. Many of their poems were anthologized in two volumes: *New Lines*, published in 1956, and *New Lines II*, published in 1963. By the time of the publication of the second volume, the Movement had largely been succeeded by another school of poets called "the Group."

The Three-Day Week, the Winter of Discontent, and Social Unrest in 1970s Britain

Although the British miners' strikes of 1984 and 1985 are much more well known, there were several strikes and other problems that contributed to social unrest in the 1970s, just prior to the publication of "Aubade." Prime Minister Edward Heath's 1974 implementation of the

"three-day week" was emblematic of these issues. Because of high rates of inflation in the 1970s, the British government put a cap on pay raises. In response, in 1973, the National Union of Mineworkers urged their workers to "work to rule," meaning that they would do only the minimum required of them and meticulously follow every single safety regulation in an attempt to slow down production as much as possible. This in turn caused an energy crisis. Heath's response to that crisis was to limit commercial consumption of energy to no more than three consecutive days in one week. This in turn caused a massive reduction of labor and pay, which made the British public very unhappy. The prohibition of pay raises in an attempt to regulate inflation was also the primary contributing factor to the strikes of the 1978–1979 "Winter of Discontent," which saw widespread social unrest.

The general feelings of anxiety, unease, and unhappiness fueled by Britain's economic crisis likely contributed to the straightforward, no-nonsense poetic style of the decade, which Larkin was very much a part of. The social atmosphere of this decade is reflected in the pervasive sense of fear and unease and the impulse to rage and rebel that is present in "Aubade."

CRITICAL OVERVIEW

Larkin's "Aubade" is one of his most widely read poems and is considered by many to be his greatest, although Larkin himself has had a mixed reception over the years. Larkin first became popular as a poet following the publication of his 1955 collection, *The Less Deceived*. After the collection received highly favorable reviews in both the *Times Literary Supplement* and the London *Times*, critics began to take notice of his work. His popularity steadily grew until he was regarded as one of the greatest poets of his age, although his reputation took a considerable blow nearly a decade after his death with the publication of Anthony Thwaite's *Selected Letters of Philip Larkin* (1992) and Andrew Motion's *Philip Larkin: A Writer's Life* (1993). These two works depicted Larkin as a liar, misogynist, and xenophobe who led a miserable life. After this, critics and academics were more reluctant to praise his work, though it has enjoyed something of a revival in recent years, as several critics have defended Larkin against the earlier attacks.

Of Larkin's works, "Aubade" in particular has received ample praise. In the essay "Larkin's Almost Perfect Poem," *Daily Telegraph* contributor A. N. Wilson lauds, "If I had to name one poem, written in England in my lifetime, of unquestionable greatness, it would be Philip Larkin's 'Aubade.'" Wilson adds, "On one level it is an intensely individual poem, written by a selfish alcoholic bachelor.... But on another level, this poem is universal."

Discussing the poem in her essay in the book *Unnoticed in the Casual Light of Day*, "Rhetorical Strategies II," Tijana Stojkovic also comments on the universality of the poem: "[Larkin's] style of thinking and writing...makes for highly communicative poetry. One of the most common *loci communes*, fear of death, is treated in a common, or more precisely, unspecialized way." Stojkovic expands with two specific points:

First, the speaker bases his main argument about death on the most universal human qualities: sensory, mental, and spiritual faculties.

When imagined, the absence of these strikes us all on some level. Second, the poem has a coherent, reader-friendly structure in the sense that the ideas are put forward with a certain logical development.

Writing on this poem and several others in the *Sewanee Review* essay "Larkin Reconsidered," A. Banerjee comments,

The overall picture of human life that emerges from Larkin's poems is one of ingrained sadness, dullness, and dreariness, consisting of work, the longing for and the failure to lead a meaningful life, and finally the trudge toward extinction. Yet Larkin in his view of the modern man is quite different from modernists such as Kafka, Camus, and Beckett, even though there are similarities.... Larkin's picture of ordinary reality is more accessible and impressive, because his characters and their actions are free of symbolism.

Richard Rankin Russell, a contributor to the *Explicator*, explains how "Aubade" differs from Larkin's other poems: "By the time of the publication of 'Aubade' in the *Times Literary Supplement* on 23 December 1977, Larkin's verse had lost its characteristic vocal balance between the wistful and romantic and the cynical and ironic." Russell continues, "'Aubade' instead wallows in cynicism and even shades toward nihilism, especially in its envisioning of death as an expanse of nothingness and blankness."

Critics almost unanimously agree that "Aubade" is one of Larkin's greatest poems, if not one of the greatest poems of the twentieth century. Its universality and straightforward, logical style are among the most common attributes invoked in this agreement, though it has myriad other points of acclaim.

CRITICISM

Rachel Porter

Porter is a freelance writer and editor who holds a bachelor of arts degree in English literature. In the following essay, she argues that in "Aubade," Larkin uses particular forms of construction and stylistic elements to create an experience for the reader that mirrors the one that the speaker of the poem describes.

In Philip Larkin's "Aubade," an unnamed speaker wakes in the middle of the night to the sudden and sharp realization of his own

WHAT DO I READ NEXT?

- *The Less Deceived*, by Larkin, was first published in 1955, with a recent edition published in 2011. This was the volume of poetry that first catapulted Larkin to popularity. Whereas "Aubade" was one of the last poems Larkin ever published, this work contains poems that he was known for towards the beginning of his career, such as "Toads" and "Maiden Name."

- Larkin's poetry, much to his dismay, was frequently compared to that of modernist poets such as T. S. Eliot, whose work can be read in *The Waste Land and Other Poems: Including the Love Song of J. Alfred Prufrock*, which was edited by Helen Vendler and published in 1998.

- Thomas Hardy, who authored *Tess of the d'Urbervilles*, published in 1891, was a novelist and poet whom Larkin greatly admired. Larkin's mature poetry was often favorably compared with Hardy's. In *Tess of the d'Urbervilles*, Hardy's best-known work, readers will get a sense of his distinctive style.

- In *The Movement Reconsidered: Essays on Larkin, Amis, Gunn, Davie and Their Contemporaries*, published in 2011, author Zachary Leader provides insightful criticism of Larkin's work as well as that of his peers in the Movement.

- *Death before Dying: The Sufi Poems of Sultan Bahu* was written by a Sufi mystical poet called Sultan Bahu, translated by Jamal J. Elias, and published in 1998. In this work, Bahu's poems provide a perspective on death that contrasts with that of Larkin.

- In the young-adult novel *Cures for Heartbreak*, by Margo Rabb, published in 2008, a ninth grader named Mia has to deal with the death of her mother by cancer, immediately followed by her father's hospitalization for heart trouble. Although Mia is confronted by the reality of death earlier than most, she finds her own way to come to terms with it.

---

mortality. Although logically he has always been aware of the fact that he will one day die, something about this state of being half awake and half asleep allows him to feel the reality of it in its most true and vivid form, in a way that he cannot experience during the day when he is distracted by other people and the business of daily life. The sudden sharpness of this reality fills him to the brim with a type of fear that he describes as "special," unlike anything else. It is the horrific combination of two types of being afraid, simultaneously experienced.

The type of fear that is intellectual in nature is easily distinguishable from the type of fear that is primal and instinctual. Animals in the wild, for example, experience only the latter. Instinctual fear is what you might experience when being chased by an angry dog or discovering that you are about to be hit by a car. These are fears that are not deeply thought about; they are more physical and automatic. These types of fears trigger a rush of adrenaline designed to help a person fight for his life. Intellectual fears, on the other hand, are those that are methodically arrived at through careful thought. They occur when one's higher brain deduces that one may suffer negative consequences from something one has either done or is about to do, such as showing up late to an important job interview.

Sometimes, however, intellectual fears can seem so threatening that one's body will interpret them as an immediate threat, and it will trigger the same physical reaction as instinctual fear. Despite the fact that your life is not in immediate danger, you will have the same rush of adrenaline and other physical reactions that

> **BRILLIANTLY, LARKIN RECREATES AT LEAST THE SHADOW OF THIS SENSE OF ALL-CONSUMING FEAR FOR THE READERS OF 'AUBADE' BY SIMULTANEOUSLY APPEALING TO THEIR INTELLECTUAL AND EMOTIONAL FACULTIES THROUGH HIS ANALYTICAL CONSTRUCTION AND STYLISTIC CHOICES, RESPECTIVELY."**

you would have if you were fighting for your life. It is at the intersection of these two types of fear that one can become completely paralyzed and consumed by it, and it is this type of fear that shakes the speaker of "Aubade" awake at four in the morning and fills him with agonizing terror. Brilliantly, Larkin recreates at least the shadow of this sense of all-consuming fear for the readers of "Aubade" by simultaneously appealing to their intellectual and emotional faculties through his analytical construction and stylistic choices, respectively.

It is Larkin's carefully analytical construction that appeals to the reader's higher brain and draws the reader in to the version of reality that the speaker of the poem is experiencing. The poem is constructed to mirror a person's logical thought process. As the poem progresses, it seems that the speaker of "Aubade" is preemptively arguing with the reader. The speaker anticipates the logical objections that the reader might think of to his assertion that death is a terrible and horrifying fate, such as the possible existence of an afterlife or the philosophical arguments against the rationality of fearing death, and negates them before the reader even has a chance to think them up. The religions and philosophies that might mollify the fear of death in some do not work for the speaker. He convincingly proves to the reader that he has thought about this situation from every possible angle and has rationally come to the conclusion that escape is impossible.

On the other hand, Larkin's stylistic choices appeal more to the reader's primal and emotional sense of fear. Through the repetition of certain sounds, words, and phrases and the use of an eerie but conversational tone, Larkin is able to impart a sense of fearfulness or at least uneasiness to his readers without their realizing how or why unless they stop to think about it. Larkin concentrates these stylistic choices towards the ends of his stanzas, which gives the poem a jerky sense of forward-thrusting momentum at regular intervals and also makes the last two lines of each stanza seem particularly poignant and potent.

The last two lines of the first two stanzas provide excellent examples of how Larkin uses sound to manipulate the emotions of the reader. The next-to-last lines in each of these stanzas are dominated by hard, harsh sounds, while the last line is dominated by soft sounds. The fact that the penultimate line of each stanza is dominated by harsh sounds and also ends on a syllable that completes a rhyme compels the reader to pause at the end of the line, lending a sense of false finality. When these lines are followed by lines dominated by soft sounds, such as *sh*, *s*, and *th*, it gives the effect that the last line of the stanza is spoken in a hushed whisper. This "after the fact" whisper that provides the stanza with a second, quieter sense of finality sounds eerie and is almost unsettling when read aloud. It also gives the illusion of sorrowful resignation to a fate that cannot be evaded.

Another way in which Larkin communicates a sense of disquiet to the reader is through his strategic placement of repeated words and phrases that, in combination with his rhyme scheme, make the poem seem chant-like in places. A particular preponderance of repeated phrases occurs in lines 18–20, lines 28–29, and lines 42–43 ("not to be" and "nothing more" are two examples). Depending on the context, chant-like repetition of phrases can evoke anything from nostalgic reminiscence of innocent schoolgirl hand-clap and jump-rope songs to the sinister spells of Shakespeare's witches in *Macbeth*. Either way it is evocative. In a poem about the all-consuming horror of eternal nothingness that the speaker and reader alike are rapidly hurtling toward, the chant-like language undoubtedly has a creepy effect.

It is also important to note that Larkin achieves the previously mentioned jerky sense of momentum that the reader experiences in the last several lines of each stanza through the use of an envelope rhyme scheme (*abba*) and consistently truncating the second-to-last line of the stanza. The combination of these two stylistic choices conjures within the reader the impulse to read quickly and then slow down within the space of four lines. The second and third lines of an envelope stanza are typically read faster because they rhyme, while the first and fourth are read at a slightly slower pace.

In "Aubade," this effect is compounded by the fact that Larkin has made the second-to-last line of each stanza significantly shorter than the rest by three to four syllables on average. This causes the reader to take an even longer pause at the end of this line than one otherwise would. This forcefully speeds the reader up and slows the reader down, emphasizing one of the underlying messages of the poem: time belongs to no one and is no one's to control. We are all constantly being pushed forward closer and closer to death whether or not we want to be.

Lastly, like many of Larkin's other poems "Aubade" is conversational in tone. Larkin believed that poetry should be accessible. He adored the commonplace things of everyday life and believed that the work of poetry was to capture small slices of reality that a lot of people would be able to relate to. He did not believe in using obscure vocabulary and dense metaphors that would appeal only to academics and literary sorts and isolate most other readers from his work. Thus, when reading "Aubade," it is not difficult to tap into the mental state of the speaker; his point of view is clear and accessible. This common, easy-to-understand language somewhat unexpectedly has the effect of compounding the feeling of disquiet that the reader might feel as one moves through "Aubade." Were the poem written in a dialect particular to a specific place or time, or were Larkin to use the lofty, academic language that he was certainly capable of, the reader would easily be able to distance oneself from the speaker. Instead, Larkin writes in plain and standard English that will give the majority of people reading his poem the sense that the narrator is no different from themselves and that, therefore, the dreadful fate of the speaker will also be theirs.

Thus, Larkin directly appeals to his readers' sense of intellect by constructing a rational and logical portrait of a typical human thought process, while indirectly and more subtly appealing to his readers' emotions by using sounds, repetition, and metrical rhythms to instinctively fill readers with uneasiness. In this way, readers are able to understand the speaker's fear on an intellectual and emotional level simultaneously. The speaker of the poem, like death itself, leaves his readers cornered up against a wall with no means of escape or relief save the distractions of day-to-day life.

Source: Rachel Porter, Critical Essay on "Aubade," in *Poetry for Students*, Gale, Cengage Learning, 2013.

John Garvey

In the following essay, Garvey explains why "Aubade" is a favorite of his among Larkin's poems.

Philip Larkin's poem "Aubade" is one of my favorites. It is a formally perfect composition, and its vision of death is chilling. The poem is bitter, dark, and thoroughly unsentimental in its view of death. This is the first of its five stanzas:

> I work all day, and get half-drunk at night. Waking at four to soundless dark, I stare. In time the curtain-edges will grow light. Till then I see what's really always there: Unresting death, a whole day nearer now, Making all thought impossible but how And where and when I shall myself die. Arid interrogation: yet the dread Of dying, and being dead, Flashes afresh to hold and horrify.

Larkin was not a believer (he considered religion a "moth-eaten" trick), nor was he the kind of blithe atheist who says there will be no "you" left to experience death or sorrow for not being. This precisely, he says,

> is what we fear—no sight, no sound, No touch or taste or smell, nothing to think with, / Nothing to love or link with, / The anaesthetic from which none come round.

Like any serious Christian (this comparison would surprise him), Larkin finds death outrageous. We long for life, and know that we will die. He writes, "Most things may never happen: this one will." And he hates it.

"Aubade" may speak to me so strongly because of recent encounters with suffering and death and new life. As a couple of friends struggle to live with chronic, recurring cancer, another young woman gives birth. Two friends, about to marry relatively late in life, experience new depths of life as they are surprised and delighted by their love. Other people live with near constant pain, struggle with depression, work uphill against addictions.

We want to hold on to life, but much of what many of us experience as life is a very mixed bag, and it is impossible to imagine wanting to hold on to this particular kind of life for all eternity. Life as we know it is a limited, partial, wanting thing.

The final stanza offers a vision of an office awaiting its morning occupants. (© *David Asch | Shutterstock.com*)

Christianity inverted the belief of the ancient world that this life is our most vivid time, and that those who have died are shadows of their former selves. In Judaism a belief in resurrection began to take hold, a vindication of Israel's just and a condemnation of the unjust; and in Christianity the belief that Jesus was the firstborn of those who would be resurrected placed resurrection at the center of belief. Paul insisted that life in the resurrected state will be so much more real than what we now experience as life that we are incapable of imagining it.

The best parts of the life we live now are hints of what we are called to. What we know is far from the fullness of what we know is far from the fullness of what we are meant to know; it touches that fullness and makes us yearn for more than what this mortal life offers us. What we really yearn for can't be killed, or know death's destruction.

Of course this seems too good to be true, and believers must try to understand the skepticism of unbelievers sympathetically, because it does seem strange to think of everything we experience as a metaphor for something deeper and

greater, to think of the life we live now as not yet our truest life. This can look like wishful thinking, and belief in God like a child's belief in an imaginary friend.

But the alternative is to believe that evolution has set us up for a kind of cosmic swindle: we love life, see something good in it, want to hold on to that good and experience it in all of what its depths seem to promise us; and at the same time we know that this can never be, that our desire to live will come to nothing, that this will be taken from us, often after a period of great suffering.

Those reductionist atheists who speak of their awe at the beauty of a meaningless universe apparently aren't aware of the near-gnostic implications of their vision: what lies at the base of a universe without purpose is that all of our most beautiful hopes and desires, the things that most define our humanity, are in the end meaningless.

There is a way of learning to live with this, but it means a certain hardening of the heart, a final indifference to things we are meant to love. Christianity finds death outrageous, as Larkin did. "Death is no different whined at than withstood," he wrote, and he was right. The doctrine of resurrection does not say that we can learn to accept and live with death. It says that in Christ what we perceive instinctively as evil in suffering and death has been destroyed, and that we are right to rejoice.

Source: John Garvey, "Outrageous Death: Resurrection or Resignation?," in *Commonweal*, Vol. 135, No. 16, September 26, 2008, p. 6.

Richard Rankin Russell

In the following essay, Russell presents evidence that despite Larkin's denials, T. S. Eliot was indeed an influence on his poetry.

Philip Larkin long eschewed the influence of T. S. Eliot on his verse. One of his most quoted statements has provided sufficient disavowal of Eliot's impact on his poetry to have generally led commentators away from his possible influence: "As a guiding principle I believe that every poem must be its own sole freshly created universe, and therefore have no belief in 'tradition' or a common myth kitty [...]" (qtd. in *Poets of the Nineteen-Fifties* 78). Notwithstanding the rendering of "tradition" in scare quotes, surely meant to criticize Eliot's particular understanding of the term as literary influence in his seminal essay, "Tradition and the Individual Talent," Larkin's poetry itself abounds in this type of tradition, despite a continuing critical strain that views him as a writer who disdained modernist literary predecessors and thus was relatively uninfluenced by them. Whereas Auden, Hardy, Yeats, Dylan Thomas, and Betjeman were acknowledged exemplars in Larkin's introduction to the 1965 reissue of *The North Ship*, Eliot is mentioned only in passing with them and others as one of "the principal poets of the day" ("Introduction to *The North Ship*" 28). Yet research has begun to show Eliot's sway over Larkin's poetry. Raphael Ingelbein's recent essay, for example, demonstrates how Eliot's sequence *The Four Quartets* had a significant impact on Larkin's poems written during and soon after World War II (130–43). The question of influence from Eliot to Larkin may turn out to be chiastic: whereas Eliot's late poetry such as *The Four Quartets* has proven influential for Larkin's early poetry, his early poems seem to have influenced some of Larkin's late poems, particularly in their grim realism expressed through startling images.

Terry Whalen's assessment of Larkin as "a late Imagist poet" sets the context for the present note's elucidation of a key image in Larkin's well-known poem "Aubade." One of the few poems by Eliot that has been briefly argued as an influence on Larkin's poetry is his 1917 work, "The Love Song of J. Alfred Prufrock." Surprisingly, however, no commentator has recognized the influence of one of the poem's most famous images—that of an "evening [...] spread out against the sky / Like a patient etherized upon a table" (*The Complete Poems and Plays 1909–1950* 3; henceforth *CPP*)—on the central image for death in Larkin's "Aubade." Eliot's etherized evening serves as the backdrop for his paralyzed, neurotic figure of J. Alfred Prufrock, a sort of modern-day Hamlet, and presents urban modernity generally as a site of indecision and dehumanization. Despite his long years spent living in the English city of Hull and the enjoyment of the isolation that the city's off-center locale gave him, Larkin shared Eliot's views of the city, seeing it as a site of impersonality and separation. Larkin's perception of the paralyzing effects of the urban is heightened when it is expressed through medical images, as in "Ambulances": "They come to rest at any kerb: / All streets in time are visited" (*Philip Larkin: Collected Poems* 132; henceforth *PL:CP*).

By the time of the publication of "Aubade" in the *Times Literary Supplement* on 23 December 1977, Larkin's verse had lost its characteristic vocal balance between the wistful and romantic and the cynical and ironic. "Aubade" instead wallows in cynicism and even shades toward nihilism, especially in its envisioning of death as an expanse of nothingness and blankness. Gone is the hopeful limitless expanse of "the deep blue air that shows / Nothing, and is nowhere, and is endless" that is featured in the striking conclusion of "High Windows" (*PL:CP* 165). The absence of color abounds in Larkin's picture of death in "Aubade." In particular, death is imaged in line 30 as "[t]he anaesthetic from which none come round" (*PL:CP* 208). In this line, Larkin has clearly borrowed from Eliot's vision of the evening "Like a patient etherized upon a table" in "Prufrock." Confirmation of his employing the synonymic noun *anesthetic* for Eliot's adjectival *etherized*, occurs in Larkin's oblique allusion to Eliot's famous line in a 1978 essay on Andrew Marvell, written a year after he finished "Aubade," the opening of which focuses largely on Eliot's establishment of Marvell's reputation in the early twentieth century. There, Larkin wryly recalls that "Eliot's growing influence [...] was enough to bring Marvell to the attention of the young critics, and in the space of a remarkable few years he became one of the favourite subjects on their dissecting tables" ("The Changing Face of Andrew Marvell" 247). Larkin was undoubtedly thinking of etherized patients, bodies extended, being operated on, and thus used the image from Eliot's "Prufrock" as an ironic comment on critics' rigorous analysis of Marvell after Eliot's reclamation of the metaphysical poet's reputation.

Larkin's line about anesthetic, in the context of the poem's vision of the "uncaring / Intricate rented world" as a vast, impersonal city with workers headed off to "locked-up offices" (*PL:CP* 209) shares Eliot's fear of urban life as a site of impersonality that leads to a sort of intellectual death. Yet the specifically medical connotation of Larkin's line departs from Eliot's construction of the earthly world, symbolized by the city, as deadening and develops an image of the afterlife as a site of numbness.

This medical image, coupled with the famously clinical last line of "Aubade"—"Postmen like doctors go from house to house" (*PL:CP* 210)— suggests our inexorable trajectory toward death just as surely as postmen deliver the mail, a paradoxically personal conclusion for a poem about death as the ultimate state of impersonality. And yet this final image is finally one of utter desolation and separation, unlike Eliot's concluding image of communal drowning at the end of "Prufrock": "We have lingered in the chambers of the sea [. . .] / Till human voices wake us, and we drown" (*CPP* 7). Like the absorbent ambulance in Larkin's "Ambulances" that "dulls to distance all we are" (*PL:CP* 133) and whose patients are delivered to death, Larkin's postmen deliver images of blankness that prefigure death as a state of numbness. Eliot's deadened, dark evening has been elided and replaced by the contrasting focus of Larkin's anti-aubade on bright morning as leading us one step closer to numbing death. Larkin sees death as a permanent state of blinding, insensate nothingness, leading the narrator to realize, "The mind blanks at the glare" (*PL:CP* 208).

Source: Richard Rankin Russell, "Echoes of Eliot's 'The Love Song of J. Alfred Prufrock' in Larkin's 'Aubade,'" in *Explicator*, Vol. 65, No. 4, Summer 2007, pp. 234–37.

Peter Davison

In the following essay, Davison presents editor Anthony Thwaite's Collected Poems *as a good autobiographical representation of Larkin's poetical canon.*

Philip Larkin, perhaps the finest English poet of his generation, died in 1985 at the age of sixty-three, leaving behind him a legion of frustrated admirers. This sardonic, lonely, despondent artist was unique among the English poets after Auden in his power to reach across national boundaries; but after he first attracted a following with his 1955 collection, *The Less Deceived*, he produced only two more collections in thirty years, *The Whitsun Weddings* (1964) and *High Windows* (1974). What Larkin's long-awaited *Collected Poems* reveals is that after 1974 his poetry seems to have surrendered to despair and silence: Anthony Thwaite has found fewer than twenty poems, mainly unpublished, to speak for those last eleven years.

But this book does a tremendous service. Thwaite has carefully arranged all of Larkin's mature poetry in order of its completion, and he has relegated youthful and apprentice work to a separate section, which amply proves that nothing worthwhile is being hidden from us. Thus the reader shares an almost biographical journey through the heartening rise and depressing fall of a writing life. Born in 1922 in Coventry, Larkin showed great precocity as a teenage poet, his muse vibrating to the echoes of Auden. At Oxford, during the Second World War, he was introduced to the work of Yeats by the poet Vernon Watkins, and he embraced it in dozens of imitations. After Oxford, Larkin spent most of his mature life in the ancient but foundering fishing port of Hull, in Yorkshire, where he served as university librarian and where he died. He was unusual among English poets in that he lived out his days in secondary cities, neither dallying in London nor spending any lengthy period of time in the countryside.

However despondent Larkin ultimately became, his poetry, in Thwaite's exemplary edition, reveals a youth that began in Wordsworthian gladness, in "a dream of sea and hay." Those increasingly rare poetic passages that deal with the satisfied senses seem always to evoke grass and the sea. But when Larkin's work ripened, after Oxford, he emerged as the most polished of craftsmen, the most inhibited of personalities, the wittiest of self-depreciators. Yet Larkin discovered disappointment over and over again with an air of ghastly triumph.

> For you would hardly care
> That you were less deceived, out
> on that bed,

Than he was, stumbling up the
breathless stair
To burst into fulfilment's desolate
attic.

Once Larkin's Oxford phase was over, words like failure and loss began to steal into his poetry like recidivist thieves. Failure gradually wound its way, obsessively, into a desolate counterpoint to images of the sea and the fields. The early work, expressing a time when meadow, grove, and stream called out to the poet, began to give way under the pain of some "obscure hurt" like that which afflicted Henry James and which, Larkin's poems intimate, arose from some sexual rebuff. A long poem, "The Dance," never finished, and published here for the first time, seems destined to get to the crux of the matter, but it breaks off in mid-sentence; other poems make mock of his frustrations:

Sexual intercourse began
In nineteen sixty-three
(Which was rather late for me)—
Between the end of the Chatterley
ban
And the Beatles' first LP.

In mid-career Larkin seems to have written with relative copiousness, though spurts of creativity alternated with periods of dormancy. At this stage his work increasingly declared its debt to the poems of Thomas Hardy: formal yet demotic, earthy, aware of society's discontents, ironic, though Larkin's work leans toward self-castigation where Hardy would have taken the road leading to grief and regret. Glimpses of the unfulfilled, distant love appear ("Leaving me desperate to pick out / Your hands, tiny in all that air, applauding") but are shoved aside by animadversions on the decline of England, whether in looking back to 1914 ("Never such innocence, / Never before or since") or, in "Homage to a Government," complaining that "Next year we shall be living in a country / That brought its soldiers home for lack of money," or expressing sardonic outrage at the state of the culture ("Don't read much now:.../...Get stewed: / Books are a load of crap"). Death becomes a second obsession, and age; in one poem, "The View," Larkin seems to be announcing his finish at fifty, even though at fifty Hardy in his poetry was just getting up steam.

At the bottom of this wonderful poet's imagination, however, lies the dominant twentieth-century British vision, one of nostalgia for a glorious past (splendor in the grass) combined with a sour self-criticism:

Truly, though our element is time,
We are not suited to the long
perspectives
Open at each instant of our lives.
They link us to our losses: worse,
They show us what we have as it once
was,
Blindingly undiminished, just as
though
By acting differently we could have
kept it so.

It is tragic to read through the exquisitely wrought, heartbreakingly endearing passages of Larkin's work and find the poet not only predicting his own failure but also fulfilling it, sinking from satire into obscenity, from self-pity into self-hatred, from disgust with society to withdrawal from it. Oh, the journey is illuminated with wit, as in "Administration":

Day by day your estimation clocks up
Who deserves a smile and who a frown,
And girls you have to tell to pull
their socks up
Are those whose pants you'd most like
to pull down.

But the destination rings with pathos. One of Larkin's last public poems, "Aubade," begins, "I work all day and get half-drunk at night...," and another begins, "I never remember holding a full drink." It sounds remarkably like the aftermath of empire, nipping at the chota peg on the bungalow veranda while the native troops march back to their barracks—scenes and feelings all too familiar in the world of *Masterpiece Theatre*.

Perhaps this collective nostalgia has something to do with the reason why Larkin's *Collected Poems* has sold more than 40,000 copies in Britain since October—"Something to do with violence / A long way back, and wrong rewards, / And arrogant eternity." Larkin's poetry rings the knell on the white man's triumph, on the arts and riches of the island kingdom, on a culture of which he regarded himself as one of the last qualified, yet impotent, stewards.

English poetry since Larkin's heyday has turned to deeper, supranational roots in the primitive past, in the work of such poets as Geoffrey Hill and Ted Hughes, and only recently have such younger poets as Tony Harrison and Craig Raine, after a long, grave pause to reflect, begun taking up the instruments that Larkin left them—rhyme, humor, irony—to resume the sort of Little England music that this sweet, sad poet left us. To have this poignant collection of his work in one volume now is a great gift, one of the prizes of the decade.

Source: Peter Davison, "The Saddest Englishman," in *Atlantic*, Vol. 263, No. 5, May 1989, pp. 95–96.

SOURCES

Aldrick, Philip, "UK Economy Could Contract in 2011, Warns Bank of England's Paul Fisher," in *Telegraph*, December 22, 2010, http://www.telegraph.co.uk/finance/economics/8220185/UK-economy-could-contract-in-2011-warns-Bank-of-Englands-Paul-Fisher.html (accessed March 14, 2012).

Banerjee, A., "Larkin Reconsidered," in *Sewanee Review*, Vol. 116, No. 3, Summer 2008, pp. 428–41.

Finch, Peter, "British Poetry since 1945," Peter Finch Archive, http://www.peterfinch.co.uk/enc.htm (accessed March 10, 2012).

Higgins, Charlotte, "The Turner Prize: Artists Kiss Goodbye to London," in *Guardian*, May 6, 2011, http://www.guardian.co.uk/culture/charlottehigginsblog/2011/may/06/art-turnerprize (accessed March 20, 2012).

Larkin, Philip, "Aubade," in *Death, Dying and Bereavement*, edited by Donna Dickenson, Malcolm Johnson, and Jeanne Samson Katz, Sage Publications, 2000, pp. 68–69.

Orwin, James L., "Philip Larkin (1922–1986)," Philip Larkin Society website, http://www.philiplarkin.com/biog.htm (accessed March 10, 2012).

Perkins, David, "In and Out of The Movement," in *A History of Modern Poetry: Modernism and After*, Harvard University Press, 1987, pp. 418–44.

"Philip Larkin," Famous People, http://www.thefamouspeople.com/profiles/philip-larkin-199.php (accessed March 10, 2012).

"Philip Larkin," Poetry Foundation website, http://www.poetryfoundation.org/bio/philip-larkin (accessed March 10, 2012).

Russell, Richard Rankin, "Echoes of Eliot's 'The Love Song of J. Alfred Prufrock' in Larkin's 'Aubade,'" in *Explicator*, Vol. 65, No. 4, Summer 2007, pp. 234–37.

Stojkovic, Tijana, "Rhetorical Strategies II," in *Unnoticed in the Casual Light of Day*, edited by William E. Cain, Routledge, 2006, pp. 119–61.

Walker, John A., "Radical British Art in the 1970s: Art in Crisis during a Decade in Crisis," Scribd, http://www.scribd.com/doc/18181567/Radical-British-Art-in-the-1970s (accessed March 14, 2012).

Watt, Nicholas, "UK Economy 'Lurching Back to the 1970s,' Says Thinktank," in *Guardian*, September 16, 2009, http://www.guardian.co.uk/politics/2009/sep/16/uk-economy-public-spending-thinktank (accessed March 14, 2012).

Wilson, A. N., "Larkin's Almost Perfect Poem," in *Daily Telegraph*, February 4, 2008, p. 23.

FURTHER READING

Coopey, Richard, *Britain in the 1970s: The Troubled Economy*, Palgrave Macmillan, 1996.
Coopey provides a comprehensive portrait of the British economy in the 1970s, the decade in which Larkin produced "Aubade," and the effect of the economy on British culture at the time.

Fagan, Andrew, *Making Sense of Dying and Death*, Rodopi, 2004.
Fagan's book is an interdisciplinary and intercultural study of how humans approach the subject of death and dying. He not only approaches the topic from a psychological angle, as Larkin does in "Aubade," but also analyzes a variety of cultural perspectives and practices regarding the matter.

Motion, Andrew, *Philip Larkin: A Writer's Life*, Noonday Press, 1994.
In this controversial biography, Motion asserts that Larkin's life was much more troubled than people are aware of. Drawing on previously unpublished papers and letters, Motion claims that Larkin was a deceitful, misogynistic, porn-addicted, lonely, and miserable person. Since the publication of this volume, several scholars have stepped forward to debate some of its claims.

Osborne, John, *Larkin, Ideology and Critical Violence: A Case of Wrongful Conviction*, Palgrave Macmillan, 2008.
In this work, Osborne argues that critics of Larkin's writing should cease to approach it from a biographical perspective. Osborne acknowledges that Larkin was a controversial figure but claims that this is totally irrelevant when it comes to analyzing his poetry. Instead, Osborne approaches Larkin's poetry as a body of work independent of its creator and urges others to do the same.

SUGGESTED SEARCH TERMS

Philip Larkin

Larkin AND "Aubade"

Larkin AND poet

Larkin AND the Movement

Larkin AND modernism

Larkin AND Thomas Hardy

Larkin AND death

"Aubade" AND death

"Aubade" AND traditional forms

"Aubade" AND conversational

The Author to Her Book

ANNE BRADSTREET

1678

Anne Bradstreet, a seventeenth-century American poet who was among the earliest settlers of the Massachusetts Bay Colony, wrote "The Author to Her Book," a brief poem in which she addresses her own book of poetry as if it were her child. While still in her teens, Bradstreet left her home in England to live in the New World with her husband, Simon Bradstreet, an official with the Massachusetts Bay Colony. For the next four decades, she made time to write a small but powerful collection of historical poems, intimate lyric poems about her daily family life and its joys and tragedies, and meditative poems about her religious faith. Her earliest poems existed only in manuscript form until 1650, when her brother-in-law John Woolbridge, a minister in Andover, Massachusetts, took them with him to London. There he had fifteen of them printed under the title *The Tenth Muse*—the first book of poetry written in the New World. As an indication of how the norms of entitling books have changed since the seventeenth century, it might be noted that the full title of the book was *The Tenth Muse, lately Sprung up in America, or Several Poems Compiled with Great Variety of Wit and Learning, Full of Delight, Wherein especially is Contained a Complete Discourse and Description of the Four Elements, Constitutions, Ages of Man, Seasons of the Year, together with an exact Epitome of the Four Monarchies, viz., The Assyrian, Persian, Grecian, Roman, Also a Dialogue between Old England and New, concerning the late troubles. With divers*

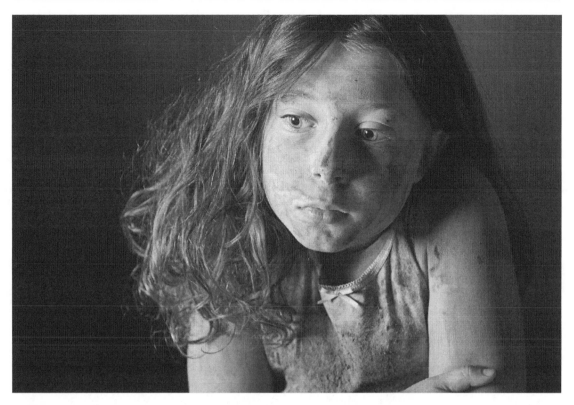

Bradstreet uses a metaphor that her writing is like a dirty child that needs to be cleaned up before publication. (© JPage | Rfphotos | Shutterstock.com)

other pleasant and serious Poems, By a Gentlewoman in those parts.

It remains an open question whether the collection was published with or without Bradstreet's knowledge. The assumption is that Woolbridge acted without her authorization. However, she may have known of Woolbridge's intention but had to pretend not to, for women with literary and intellectual aspirations would have met with harsh censure at the time. By calling the book *The Tenth Muse*—Woolbridge's title, not Bradstreet's—he made the publication of the poetry more acceptable, for at the time it was easier for people to see a woman as a source of inspiration, as a "Muse," than as an author. (The nine Muses in Greek mythology were personifications of inspiration for music, dance, history, poetry, comedy, tragedy, and other forms of art.) The appellation "Tenth Muse" is one that has frequently been applied to female poets, particularly in France.

As a second edition of the collection was under consideration, Bradstreet wrote "The Author to Her Book," probably in about 1666. The poem

was included in a posthumous 1678 edition of her poetry, which was published in America under the title *Several Poems Compiled with Great Variety of Wit and Learning.* This collection included the poems contained in *The Tenth Muse* and a number of new poems. "The Author to Her Book" is widely available. It can be found in *Great Poems by American Women: An Anthology*, edited by Susan L. Rattiner and published in 1998, and online.

AUTHOR BIOGRAPHY

Anne Dudley was born in Northampton, England, in 1612, probably on or about March 20. Her father, Thomas Dudley, was steward to the Earl of Lincoln; that is, he was an estate manager, responsible for such duties as supervising servants, keeping accounts, collecting rents, and serving as his employer's agent. Her mother was Dorothy Yorke, a well-educated woman of noble heritage. Dudley doted on his daughter and did all he could to ensure that she received an education; when she was seven years old, she had as many as eight tutors. At the age of sixteen, she married twenty-five-year-old Simon Bradstreet, a graduate of Cambridge University. Bradstreet, the son of a Puritan minister, had fallen under the Dudleys' care after the death of his father. In the year following the couple's marriage, Simon was appointed to an administrative position with the Massachusetts Bay Company.

In April 1630, the Dudleys and the Bradstreets, including Anne's four siblings, were among three hundred settlers who, along with newly appointed governor John Winthrop, boarded the *Arabella* and set sail for New England and the Massachusetts Bay Colony; the *Arabella* was one in a fleet of ships carrying about a thousand settlers. The journey was arduous, and many of the emigrants died along the way or shortly after the ship arrived at what is now Salem, Massachusetts, in June.

Bradstreet's stay in Salem was brief. She and her family moved first to Charlestown (now part of Boston), then, after a brief stay there, to what would become the city of Boston. Yet another move took the family to Cambridge, Massachusetts (then called Newe Towne or Newtowne, near what would become Harvard Square), where Bradstreet gave birth to the first of her eight children. Later the family moved to Ipswich before finally settling in North Andover. In 1650, her collection of poems *The Tenth Muse* was published in London. Throughout this period, Bradstreet suffered from poor health, including paralysis in her joints, but she sustained herself through her fervent religious beliefs and her deep love for her husband and family. Simon frequently had to travel on colonial business (see her poem "A Letter to Her Husband, Absent upon Public Employment"), but Bradstreet kept herself busy by reading and teaching her children. In 1666, tragedy struck when a fire destroyed their home and all their possessions, but the family recovered, thanks in large part to Simon's high standing in the community. (See her poem "Here Follows Some Verses upon the Burning of Our House July 10th, 1666.") At about the same time, Bradstreet wrote the poem "The Author to Her Book," which was first published in her posthumous 1678 collection, *Several Poems Compiled with Great Variety of Wit and Learning.*

During the last years of her life, Bradstreet's health slowly failed. She contracted tuberculosis, along with other ailments, and died on September 16, 1672, in North Andover, Mass-achusetts. Her place of burial has been lost to posterity.

Several prominent Americans, including authors Oliver Wendell Holmes, Sr., Sarah Orne Jewett, and Tennessee Williams; Supreme Court justices Oliver Wendell Holmes, Jr., and David Souter; President Herbert Hoover; astronaut Alan B. Shepard, the first American to travel in space; and Massachusetts senator (and 2004 presidential candidate) John Kerry are among the many notable descendants of Simon and Anne Dudley Bradstreet.

POEM TEXT

Thou ill-formed offspring of my feeble brain,
Who after birth didst by my side remain,
Till snatched from thence by friends, less wise than true,
Who thee abroad, exposed to public view,
Made thee in rags, halting to th' press to trudge, 5
Where errors were not lessened (all may judge).
At thy return my blushing was not small,
My rambling brat (in print) should mother call,
I cast thee by as one unfit for light,
Thy visage was so irksome in my sight; 10
Yet being mine own, at length affection would
Thy blemishes amend, if so I could:
I washed thy face, but more defects I saw,
And rubbing off a spot still made a flaw.
I stretched thy joints to make thee even feet, 15
Yet still thou run'st more hobbling than is meet;
In better dress to trim thee was my mind,
But nought save homespun cloth i' th' house I find.
In this array 'mongst vulgars may'st thou roam.
In critic's hands beware thou dost not come, 20
And take thy way where yet thou art not known;
If for thy father asked, say thou hadst none;
And for thy mother, she alas is poor,
Which caused her thus to send thee out of door.

POEM SUMMARY

The text used for this summary is from *The Norton Anthology of American Literature,* Vol. 1, edited by Ronald Gottesman, et al., W. W. Norton, 1979, pp. 50–51. Versions of the poem can be found on the following web pages: http://www.poetryfoundation.org/poem/172953 and http://www.annebradstreet.com/the_author_to_ her_book.htm.

Throughout "The Author to Her Book," Bradstreet addresses her collection of poetry, *The Tenth Muse*, as though it were a child to whom she gave birth. She says that the child/ book, the offspring of her own mind, is not very well formed. She notes that her book was taken from her side by friends, who then took it abroad and published it; Bradstreet is referring to her brother-in-law, John Woodbridge, who took her poems to England and had them published, presumably without her knowledge. She imagines her book of poems as being dressed in rags and taken with all its errors to the printing press. When she saw the finished product, she blushed because she was the mother of such an unruly book.

Her initial response was to cast the book/ child aside, partly because it was unfit, partly because she found its very presence annoying. But as a mother, she was unable to disown the book. In time, her affection for it grew, and she was able to overlook the book's imperfections. She tried to clean the book up, presumably by revising the poems, but the more she did that, the more flaws she saw—and she even created new ones. She tried to smooth out the lines, but they remained awkward. She wanted to provide the poems with better dress, but all she could find was homely cloth. She indicates that her book of poems will satisfy common people, but she urges the book to stay away from critics, who might judge it harshly. She then tells the book that if anyone asks who its father is, it is to say that it has no father. Regarding its mother, the book is to say that its mother is poor and that is why she released the book to the public.

THEMES

Humility

In the Puritan New England of the seventeenth century, the primary role of women was to submit to God, the church, and their husbands and care for their families. That Bradstreet, despite poor health, gave birth to eight children and dedicated herself to their upbringing would not have been considered at all unusual. In order to carry out their domestic responsibilities, women were expected to avoid intellectual and imaginative pursuits. The level of education that Thomas Dudley provided for his daughter was highly unorthodox for the time. Thus, the fact that Bradstreet wrote poetry, particularly intellectual poetry about historical topics, was, at least to some extent, outside the norm, but she was able to do so in part because of the close and loving relationship she had with her husband. Nevertheless, a strain of humility or modesty runs through "The Author to Her Book." She refers to her own intellectual capabilities as feeble. She depicts herself as unsuccessful at correcting the errors and flaws in her book of poetry. She tells her book to avoid critics, presumably because they would find further fault with the book. This self-deprecation is part of the poem's rhetorical strategy, enabling her to claim parenthood for the book yet not betray what might have been considered an inordinate amount of pride in her accomplishments as a poet. In this sense, the poem is highly ironic, for Bradstreet was a highly educated, accomplished woman who had nothing to apologize for. The poems were well received in England, and Bradstreet would have known that she scored a hit with their publication.

Mother-Child Relationships

Closely connected to the theme of modesty is that of motherly affection. Again, the principal role of a woman in the Puritan New England of the seventeenth century was that of wife and mother. Women typically had large numbers of children, in part to ensure that at least some survived to adulthood, in part to create souls to glorify God. Fortunately, Bradstreet had a good role model for an affectionate, loving parent in each of her own parents, who provided her with an education that was probably at least the equal of that of any well-educated man at the time. Thus, an important element of Bradstreet's worldview was her affection for her children. In "The Author to Her Book," she sees the published collection of her poetry as one of her children. She recognizes the flaws in it, but just as she would try to correct the flaws in her children, she tries to correct those in her poetry. Ultimately, she develops a fondness for the book, just as she might have developed a fondness for an unruly child whose imperfections were plain to see by all the world.

TOPICS FOR FURTHER STUDY

- Thomas Dudley, Anne Bradstreet's father, was a magistrate at the trial of another famous colonial Anne, Anne Hutchinson, who was ultimately banished from the Massachusetts Bay Colony for religious heresy. Investigate the life and beliefs of Anne Hutchinson. Then write a dialogue in which you imagine the two Annes conversing about some aspect of life in colonial Massachusetts, perhaps their religious beliefs. With a willing partner, perform the dialogue for your classmates.

- In connection with Anne Hutchinson, read the young-adult novel *Trouble's Daughter: The Story of Susanna Hutchinson, Indian Captive*, written by Katherine Kirkpatrick and published in 1998. The novel is a fictionalized account of a true story: Hutchinson's daughter Susanna was the only survivor of an Indian raid in which her mother and her siblings were killed. She was then held captive by the Lenape Indians for several years. After reading the novel, prepare an essay in which you examine relations between the English and the Indian tribes in and around Massachusetts, commenting on whether Kirkpatrick's novel is accurate and realistic.

- Initially, the Massachusetts Bay colonists enjoyed a peaceful relationship with the Indian populations. But in time, frictions arose, and during Bradstreet's first decade in New England, the Pequot War (1636–1638) broke out. Investigate the war, including its causes, the combatants, and the war's major engagements. Then prepare an oral report for your classmates discussing the war and how you think it might have affected Bradstreet and her family.

- What would daily life have been like for the earliest colonists in New England? What did they eat? How did they cook? What did they wear? What kinds of homes did they live in? What were their communities like? Using the Internet, locate images of daily life from that time and place; these could include sketches and drawings created at the time and photographs of artifacts from the period. Assemble your images into a visual presentation for your class using a tool such as Slideshare or Jing.com.

- Bradstreet was the first poet, not to mention the first woman poet, in the New World. Ann Rinaldi's *Hang a Thousand Trees with Ribbons*, published in 2005, is a novel about the first known African American poet in the colonies, Phillis Wheatley, who was transported from Africa to be a slave in the eighteenth century. One came voluntarily; the other came as a prisoner. Write a report in which you speculate on how this fundamental difference might have influenced the two women's poetry. Wheatley's poetry, published in a 1773 collection titled *Poems on Various Subjects, Religious and Moral*, is available in *Phillis Wheatley: Complete Poems*, published in 2001.

- Who were the Puritans? What did they believe? How did they differ from the Pilgrims of Thanksgiving Day fame? What events in England prompted many Puritans to want to settle in the New World? How did Puritanism affect the culture and history of the United States? After you research the topic, develop a multimedia presentation that provides answers to one or more of these questions.

- Write a poem in which you develop a conceit. You could compare any two things or ideas: Growing a garden is like raising a family or owning a pet. Looking at the sky on a clear night is like swimming in the ocean. Flying in a plane is like snowboarding or skateboarding. Writing an English essay is like flying a kite or scrubbing the kitchen floor. Use your imagination and have fun. Share your poem with your classmates on your social networking site and invite them to comment.

Books are like babies; they need to develop.
(© Mavetal | Shutterstock.com)

STYLE

Conceit

Conceit as a literary term is only very loosely related to the modern use of the word to refer to "vanity"; since hundreds of years ago, *conceit* has been a synonym for something like "concept." A conceit is typically a metaphor, or comparison between otherwise dissimilar things. But a conceit differs from a simple metaphor in that it is elaborate, fanciful, ingenious, and sometimes even strained. Further, a conceit differs from a standard metaphor in that the conceit is carried through several lines of a poem, sometimes through the poem as a whole. The conceit was a favored literary device in the poetry of Elizabethan and Jacobean England—that is, during the late sixteenth and early seventeenth centuries (when Queen Elizabeth I and then her successor, King James I—*Jacobus* in Latin—were on the throne of England). Among the most famous poets who regularly relied on conceits in

his poetry during this period was John Donne; he and his fellow metaphysical poets, as they were called, wrote dense, complex poems that often depended on a conceit. Thus, this literary device was "in the air" during the time that Bradstreet was growing up and receiving her education.

The conceit that is sustained throughout "The Author to Her Book" is that Bradstreet's collection of poetry is a child to which she has given birth. Bradstreet sustains the conceit in a number of ingenious ways. As the mother, she gave birth to the child. The child is ragged and unkempt. Its flaws are obvious to any member of the public willing to examine it. As a mother, Bradstreet tries to clean up her child—that is, edit the poems—but all she succeeds in doing is exposing more flaws. The child walks awkwardly, allowing Bradstreet to develop the conceit by referring to the child's "feet"—in this case, the metrical feet found in poetry. She wishes that she could provide her offspring with better dress, but the only fabric that is available to her is homespun cloth.

Heroic Couplet

The metrical form in which "The Author to Her Book" is written is the heroic couplet. A couplet comprises two lines of poetry that rhyme. Almost always the rhyme is a masculine rhyme, and the couplet is almost always end-stopped rather than enjambed. In a heroic couplet, the metrical form of the lines is iambic pentameter.

These terms need definition. First, a masculine rhyme is one in which a single, stressed, final syllable in the lines rhyme; thus, if a pair of lines ends with "dog" and "fog," the rhyme would be masculine. (A feminine rhyme, in contrast, is one that matches two or more syllables, with the final one unstressed; thus, "passion" and "fashion" would form a feminine rhyme.) An end-stopped line is a line that corresponds with a syntactic unit, whether a phrase, a clause, or a sentence; typically, a mark of punctuation will fall at the end of an end-stopped line. The opposite of an end-stopped line is an enjambed line, which breaks a syntactic unit into two or more lines so that a thought flows from one line into the next with no break.

Iambic pentameter refers to the metrical rhythm of the poem. *Iambic* refers to a metrical foot, an iamb, consisting of an unstressed followed by a stressed syllable; *pentameter* means that each line contains five such metrical feet, so the typical line consists of ten syllables. Rarely, though, do poets follow the iambic pentameter form in a rigid, lockstep fashion. Individual lines can vary the rhythm, as Bradstreet does in the line about the awkwardness of her versification, where she adds a syllable that causes the line itself to stumble slightly.

A close examination of "The Author to Her Book" shows that Bradstreet uses the heroic couplet. Each pair of lines rhymes, and the rhymes are consistently masculine. Some of the rhymes seem to be what are called near rhymes or slant rhymes, meaning that the words almost rhyme but not quite, but it must be remembered that differences in pronunciation between now and the seventeenth century can account for some of these apparent inconsistencies. Further, the lines of "The Author to Her Book" are consistently end-stopped rather than enjambed. Thus, each pair of lines becomes an enclosed rhetorical unit.

HISTORICAL CONTEXT

The Puritans were an English Protestant sect that wanted to "purify" the Church of England by, among other things, purging it of ornamentation and lingering pre-Reformation Catholic influences. Puritans were widely persecuted because the established Church of England saw them as a threat to religious orthodoxy. By the 1620s, Puritans had come to believe that they would never enjoy religious freedom in England and that the Church of England was too settled in its ways to admit of reformation. Accordingly, many were willing to abandon their homes and country and settle elsewhere; a number of these joined the Massachusetts Bay Colony in New England. The Puritans of the Massachusetts Bay Colony are not to be confused with the Pilgrims of the Plymouth Colony (memorialized each year on Thanksgiving Day), which predated the Massachusetts Bay Colony. While the Puritans' preference was to remain within the Church of England and reform it, the Pilgrims were "separatists," meaning that they were more willing to break entirely from the Church of England.

The roots of the Massachusetts Bay Colony extended back to 1624, when an organization called the Plymouth Council for New England created a settlement at Cape Ann. This settlement was placed under the supervision of a group of investors called the Dorchester Company, which was organized by John White, a Puritan minister. The Cape Ann settlement, however, failed to turn a profit, so in 1625 the investors in the Dorchester Company withdrew their backing. While most of the settlers abandoned the village, a few moved south and settled near the village of Naumkeag, named after a local Indian tribe. White, though, refused to give up. He rallied a new group of investors, called the New England Company for a Plantation in Massachusetts Bay, and in 1628 the company was issued a land grant by the Earl of Warwick for territory lying between the Merrimack and Charles Rivers. The company elected Matthew Craddock as its London governor and immediately began recruiting settlers. The first contingent of about a hundred, under the leadership of John Endecott, sailed in 1628. They joined the earlier settlers who had migrated to Naumkeag and renamed the settlement Salem, derived from the Hebrew word for "peaceful." The following year another contingent of about three hundred arrived under the leadership of the Reverend Francis Higginson.

Concerns arose about the legality and ability to enforce land claims in the New World. Territories there were unfamiliar to authorities in England, and various land claims overlapped. Accordingly, the company sought a royal charter, which would solidify its claim. King Charles I granted the charter in 1629, although it is not clear whether he knew that the purpose of the colony was as much to support Puritan emigration as it was to serve commercial endeavors. The charter encompassed territories that were or would become portions of the states of Massachusetts, New Hampshire, Maine, Rhode Island, and Connecticut. Oddly, in ceding a horizontal strip of land, the charter theoretically extended all the way west to the Pacific Ocean.

In the years that followed the granting of the royal charter, the Massachusetts Bay Colony enjoyed considerable independence; the governor, for example, was elected by "freemen" in Massachusetts, not appointed by the king. *Freemen* was a term used in colonial New England to refer to an immigrant who acquired full civil rights only after becoming a member in full of a Puritan church and serving an unspecified probationary period under the watchful eyes of Puritan elders; "becoming a member" was an arduous process and not the same thing as merely attending a Puritan church.

COMPARE
&
CONTRAST

- **1666:** The number of people living in Massachusetts, including both the Plymouth Colony and the Massachusetts Bay Colony, is roughly 12,000 to 15,000.

  Today: As of July 2011, the population of the state of Massachusetts (a smaller geographical area than the Plymouth and Massachusetts Bay colonies) is 6.5 million.

- **1666:** Until about 1664, full civil rights were extended to males in the Massachusetts Bay Colony only if they were members in full of a Puritan church.

  Today: No person in Massachusetts or anywhere in the United States is required by law to adhere to any particular religious beliefs, or any religious beliefs at all, to enjoy full civil rights.

- **1666:** The only institution of higher learning in the American colonies is Harvard College, established in 1636 (although the school did not begin construction until 1638). The purpose of the college is primarily to prepare Puritan ministers.

  Today: While the Harvard University Divinity School continues to educate ministers and others interested in religious studies, the university as a whole is secular and makes no religious demands on students. Harvard is considered the most elite university in the United States.

Puritans in England were optimistic about the future of the company, so they made further financial investments in it. In April 1630, a fleet of eleven ships, bearing a total of about a thousand people, made ready for the treacherous journey to the New World. The expedition's flagship was the *Arabella*, among whose passengers were Thomas and Dorothy Dudley and Simon and Anne Bradstreet, as well as the company's newly appointed governor, John Winthrop. The expedition set sail on April 10. The *Arabella* arrived at Salem on June 12, with the remaining ships arriving over the next two weeks. The arrival of the "Winthrop Fleet" marked the beginning of what came to be called the Great Migration (1630–1642), when thousands of English settlers made the voyage to the New World. (Some scholars mark the start of the Great Migration later, perhaps 1634.) It should be noted that not all the settlers were devout Puritans. Some remained loyal to the Church of England, did not join a Puritan church, and did not become freemen, yet they helped the colony achieve its economic, if not its religious, goals.

Despite the hardships and the deaths of hundreds of settlers, the colony survived. Winthrop served as governor on and off for more than a decade (he was the second, sixth, ninth, and twelfth governor) and remained active in colonial affairs until his death in 1649. Meanwhile, the Great Migration ground to a halt in the early 1640s because of the English Civil War—essentially, a series of conflicts between the monarch and Parliament—which led to the deposition, trial, and execution of Charles I in 1649. These wars and the events surrounding them are the "late troubles" referred to in the extended title of Bradstreet's 1650 book of poems, *The Tenth Muse*.

The charter of the Massachusetts Bay Company remained in effect until it was revoked in 1684, primarily because the colony was, in the Crown's view, acting in an insubordinate fashion over such issues as tariffs and trade. In 1686 King James II established the Dominion of New England with the goal of bringing all the New England colonies under royal control. That scheme, however, collapsed when James was deposed in the Glorious Revolution of 1688. In 1691, his successors, William of Orange and his co-regent, Mary, issued a new charter merging the Massachusetts Bay Colony and Plymouth into a single royal colony, the Province of Massachusetts.

Publishing a book is compared to saying goodbye to a child. (© Monkey Business | Shutterstock.com)

CRITICAL OVERVIEW

Bradstreet's critical reputation has waxed and waned over the past three and a half centuries. During the colonial period, she was, perhaps somewhat surprisingly, held in relatively high regard as a poet. In England, Edward Phillips, the nephew of poet John Milton, assembled a poetry anthology published in 1675 under the title *Theatrum Poetarium*. In a section titled "Women among the Moderns Eminent for Poetry," he included an entry on Anne Bradstreet in which he noted that the memory of her poetry "is not yet wholly extinct" (quoted by Robert Hutchinson in *Poems of Anne Bradstreet*). The mere fact that he included her as an "eminent" modern poet suggests that her abilities were respected. The famous Puritan minister Cotton Mather, in a 1702 book titled *Magnalia Christi Americana*, called her a "Crown" to her father and stated that her poems, "divers times Printed, have afforded a grateful Entertainment unto the Ingenious, and a Monument for her

Memory beyond the Statliest *Marbles*" (quoted by Raymond F. Dolle in *Anne Bradstreet: A Reference Guide*).

During the nineteenth century, Bradstreet fell into some disfavor. Typical of the kinds of condescending comments made about her is this one, found in Samuel Kettell's *Specimens of American Poetry*, published in 1829: "The earliest poet of New England, however, was ANNE BRADSTREET.... We must come down to a late period in the literary annals of the country before we find her equal, although her productions are not without the marks of the barbarous taste of the age" (quoted by Elizabeth Wade White in *Anne Bradstreet: "The Tenth Muse."*) Later, in an 1862 book titled *Memorable Women of the Puritan Times*, James Anderson pointed to the "blemishes" of Bradstreet's poetry: "It is often prosaic" and "deficient in melody of versification." Anderson added, "It will not be difficult to find in her poems passages of bad taste and of sheer doggerel." Nevertheless, he also called attention to Bradstreet's "warm heart, a cheerful, debonair disposition, genuine candour, and earnest piety."

In the twentieth century, two poets helped resurrect Bradstreet and her works. The first was modernist poet Conrad Aiken, who published an anthology of American poetry in 1912 and placed her poems at the beginning of it. The second was John Berryman, a Pulitzer Prize–winning poet whose *Homage to Mistress Bradstreet* (1953) is a book-length poetic dialogue with Bradstreet. In the later decades of the twentieth century and beyond, some scholars have attempted to place Bradstreet within a tradition of feminist poetry. Numerous examples could be cited, including Elisa New, who wrote "Feminist Invisibility: The Examples of Anne Bradstreet and Anne Hutchinson" (1993). New claims, for example, that "beneath Bradstreet's blandishments to male patronage" is "a vision of female autonomy." Later in the essay, she claims that "The Author to Her Book" suggests a "palpable and epidemic female unhappiness."

CRITICISM

Michael J. O'Neal

O'Neal holds a PhD in English. In the following essay, he examines the rhetorical strategy behind the diction of "The Author to Her Book."

WHAT DO I READ NEXT?

- One of Bradstreet's most frequently anthologized poems is "To My Dear and Loving Husband," which can be found in a 2000 edition titled *To My Husband and Other Poems*. Readers interested in sampling her devotional poetry will find "Contemplations" in the same volume.

- Alice Morse Earle's illustrated *Home Life in Colonial Days* was first published in 1898 but is available in a 2006 edition. Earle wrote a number of books about colonial America, including *Child Life in Colonial Days, Woman's Life in Colonial Days*, and *Customs and Fashions in Old New England*—all of which are available in modern reprint editions.

- Readers interested in the historical details surrounding the formation of the Massachusetts Bay Colony will find Barbara A. Moe's *The Charter of the Massachusetts Bay Colony: A Primary Source Investigation of the 1629 Charter* (2002) informative. The book was written for young-adult readers.

- One of the nation's most widely read and respected historians is Daniel J. Boorstin, whose book *The Americans: The Colonial Experience* was first published in 1964 and remains a classic examination of the nation's earliest years.

- Laurie Lawlor's young-adult novel *Voyage to a Free Land, 1630* (2001), tells the fictional story of ten-year-old Hannah and her twelve-year-old sister, Abigail, who travel to the New World aboard the *Arabella*, the ship that brought Bradstreet to the New World in 1630.

- A classic young-adult novel about colonial America is Elizabeth George Speare's Newbery Award–winning *The Witch of Blackbird Pond* (1958), which tells the story of a sixteen-year-old girl who leaves her home in Barbados to live with her Puritan relatives in Connecticut—and runs the risk of being perceived as a witch.

- In 1666, the year in which Bradstreet probably composed "The Author to Her Book," Sarah Kemble Knight was born in Boston. Knight's name survives as that of the author of *The Private Journal of a Journey from Boston to New York*, written in 1704–1705. Knight was a different type of woman than Bradstreet: earthy, worldly, humorous, and tough-minded. Her journal is available in a 2009 reproduction of an 1865 edition edited by William Law Learned, whose ancestors lived in Charlestown, Massachusetts, at the time of Bradstreet's arrival in the colony.

- Miriam Bat-Ami is the author of *Two Suns in the Sky* (2001). Set during World War II in 1944, the novel involves a refugee, persecuted for his religion, who joins other refugees in a voyage to a new life in America.

- Just as Bradstreet is thought of as standing at the beginning of American literature, Sor Juana Inés de la Cruz, a nun who wrote during the seventeenth century, is regarded as Mexico's first poet in Spanish. Her poetry and other writings can be found in *Poems, Protest, and a Dream*, translated by Margaret Sayers Peden (1997).

When composing a poem, a writer has to make decisions, perhaps unconscious ones, about the level of diction the poem demands. Some poets want to produce simple, direct, intimate works, so they draw on a vocabulary that is correspondingly concrete and elemental. Other writers want to produce works that are abstract, intellectually challenging, and formal. For this type of writing, a more elaborated vocabulary might be needed, one better suited to expressing the conceptual than the concrete.

Fortunately for poets, English is a rich, democratic, multifaceted language. Its unique history has given poets in English a vocabulary that derives from two complementary sources. Early on, English developed on the British Isles as a separate language among the Germanic tribes that had settled the islands, including the Angles and the Saxons; hence the term Anglo-Saxon. Literacy was not widespread among the Anglo-Saxon tribes—and the few who did read and write did so in Latin—so their vocabulary remained largely restricted to simple, everyday, tangible objects and activities: family relationships, tools, domestic objects, foods, actions such as running and walking, and the like. Most of the Anglo-Saxon words that survive in English tend to be short, often just a syllable or two, rather than polysyllabic, and most reflect the origins of Anglo-Saxon English in everyday life.

The history of English, however, changed in 1066 when England was invaded by the Norman French. For reasons not necessary to explain here, William of Normandy, often called William the Conqueror, crossed the English Channel and subdued the Anglo-Saxon nobles; he and his descendants assumed the throne of England, bringing with them not only the French language but also French customs and culture. But French is a Romance language, not a Germanic one. Along with Spanish and Italian, it evolved from Latin, the language of ancient Rome (and the root of the word *romance*). The result was that in the centuries that followed the Norman Conquest, English developed as a hybrid language, as the Latin-based vocabulary of the Romance languages was grafted onto the native Germanic vocabulary of the Anglo-Saxons.

This process of hybridization was accelerated after the printing press and movable type were developed in the fifteenth century. As books became more widely available, English needed a vocabulary for philosophical, theological, and scientific discourse; the Anglo-Saxon vocabulary would not do. However, the Latinate vocabulary of the Romance languages provided roots for thousands of words, many of them words denoting concepts and abstractions. The result of this intermingling is that English probably has a larger vocabulary than any other language. The vocabulary of French, for example, consists of about a hundred thousand words (although it can be difficult to state with precision what a "word" is). Some scholars estimate the number of English words to be at least a quarter million, possibly three quarters of a million if distinct meanings of the same word are included. The Global Language Monitor organization claims that English added its millionth word on June 10, 2009.

Anne Bradstreet, writing in the seventeenth century, inherited both of these language traditions. On the one hand, according to Ann Stanford in *Anne Bradstreet: The Worldly Puritan*, she would have been familiar with the major poets of the late sixteenth and early seventeenth centuries: Shakespeare, Edmund Spenser, Sir Philip Sidney, John Donne, Robert Southwell, and Robert Herrick among them. Further, she was familiar with a number of historical works, including Sir Walter Raleigh's *The History of the World*. These writers would have expanded her Latinate vocabulary. At the same time, as a devout Puritan, she read the Geneva Bible, first published in 1560; this translation of the Bible, known for its Anglo-Saxon rigor and simplicity, went through 150 editions between 1560 and 1644 and was particularly favored by Puritans. Other Puritan works that Bradstreet undoubtedly read would have included John Foxe's *Actes and Monuments* (1563).

This takes us finally to "The Author to Her Book." The style of the poem is in large part determined by the simplicity of Bradstreet's diction, the plain style that would have been preferred by a devoutly religious Puritan in the seventeenth century—the style of the Geneva Bible. That simplicity derives from her reliance on a basic Anglo-Saxon vocabulary. The poem consists of 206 words in twenty-four lines. Of these, only thirty words consist of two or more syllables, and many of these are simply inflected forms of words; that is, the extra syllable comes from a plural or past-tense ending. Most of the words of two syllables or more are themselves basic Anglo-Saxon words; examples include *mother* and *even*. Only a few, such as *visage* and *defect*, are of Latinate origin. At least four lines consist entirely of single-syllable words, and at least eight lines have just a single multisyllabic word. Only a single word, *affection*, is more than two syllables. With some consistency, Bradstreet chooses the Anglo-Saxon word over the corresponding Latinate word; one example is her use of *irksome* rather than, perhaps, *annoying* or *irritating*.

Bradstreet, then, was able to pull off a neat rhetorical trick in the poem. On the one hand, the poem makes use of a sophisticated conceit, the kind of conceit that might have been found in the poetry of, for example, John Donne or any of the other sophisticated poets of the preceding decades, those who moved in court circles and among well-educated people. Her use of the heroic couplet also elevated her poetry into something resembling an epic sphere. Yet the simplicity of the poem's diction is calculated to give it an intimate, domestic feel. The book of poems is part of the author's "family," where no pretension or pride is allowed to reign. The result is that the poem is highly ironic. It becomes a poem about the process of publication, using the metaphor of giving birth to a child, nurturing that child, cleaning it up, dressing it, and sending it out into the world. These would be the kinds of domestic activities that would have dominated Bradstreet's day-to-day life. By couching the imaginative process of conceiving poetry, writing it, revising it, and bringing it to the attention of the world in simple, domestic terms, Bradstreet is able to have her cake and eat it too: she is able to maintain her status as a stoutly Puritan "goodwife," one who leads a life of domestic simplicity, while at the same time engaging in the same kinds of intellectual pursuits in which men took part. It is this ironic wit that makes "The Author to Her Book" one of Bradstreet's most memorable poems.

Source: Michael J. O'Neal, Critical Essay on "The Author to Her Book," in *Poetry for Students*, Gale, Cengage Learning, 2013.

Lisa Day-Lindsey

In the following essay, Day-Lindsey places the anxiety Bradstreet expresses in the poem in the context of the culture in which Bradstreet lived.

> Thou ill-formed offspring of my feeble brain,
> Who after birth did'st by my side remain,
> Till snatched from thence by friends, less wise than true,
> Who thee abroad, exposed to public view,
> Made thee in rags, halting to th' press to trudge,
> Where errors were not lessened (all may judge).
> At thy return my blushing was not small,
> My rambling brat (in print) should mother call,
> I cast thee by as one unfit for light,
> The visage was so irksome in my sight;
> Yet being mine own, at length affection would
> Thy blemishes amend, if so I could.
> I washed thy face, but more defects I saw,
> And rubbing off a spot still made a flaw.
> I stretched thy joints to make thee even feet,
> Yet still thou run'st more hobbling than is meet;
> In better dress to trim thee was my mind,

> READ AS A POEM ABOUT THE BIRTH OF A CHILD, ANNE BRADSTREET'S 'THE AUTHOR TO HER BOOK' IS FILLED WITH A DEGREE OF SHAME, GUILT, AND FEAR OF REPERCUSSIONS."

> But nought save homespun cloth i' th' house I find.
> In this array 'mongst vulgars may'st thou roam.
> In critic's hands beware thou dost not come,
> And take thy way where yet thou art not known;
> If for thy father asked, say thou hadst none;
> And for thy mother, she alas is poor,
> Which caused her thus to send thee out of door.

This immediate cultural context of Puritan Boston informs Anne Bradstreet's poem "The Author to Her Book." Along with others' interpretations that the poem is Bradstreet's modest claim of authorship along with a justification of the unfinished, private work that her brother-in-law published in England without her consent. As most critics agree, Bradstreet treats her poetry anthropomorphically by comparing it with a child, but the child in the comparison is essential to the milieu of the poem.

To have been a Puritan in colonial America was to agree to a firm set of rules regarding daily life, and to have been a Puritan woman meant that the rules were even more abundant and strict. Anne Bradstreet, whose father was the Massachusetts Bay Company's Deputy Governor John Dudley and whose husband was Chief Administrator Simon Bradstreet, was well aware of Puritan standards and, more important, knew the consequences of every behavior. Governor John Winthrop dealt consistently with infidels of any sort and preferred to conduct civil as well as church trials to use the criminal sinners as examples for the community and the congregation.

Seemingly, one of Winthrop's fascinations was miscarriage, as he discusses several instances in his *Journal*, calling the stillborn fetuses "monsters" and describing them in dramatic, horrific language, as in the case of Mary Dyer's child.

> It had a face, but no head, and the ears stood upon the shoulders and were like an ape's; it had no forehead, but over the eyes four horns, hard and sharp; two of them were above one inch long, the other two shorter; the eyes standing

out, and the mouth also; the nose hooked upward;
all over the breast and back full of sharp pricks
and scales, like a thornback. (141)

He emphasizes shape, directions, and distortions to distinguish the stillbirth from a healthy, full-term newborn. Winthrop deemed it necessary to record these specific details into his *Journal*, which he used for preparing sermons and for recording memorable events in his colony.

Winthrop continues his 2 April 1638, entry by telling of the woman's convulsions during the miscarriage of the "said monster": "The bed whereon the mother lay did shake, and withal there was such a noisome savor as most of the women were taken with extreme vomiting and purging, so as they were forced to depart" (142). Apparently, this "noisome savor," or unpleasant odor, was a sure sign that Satan was responsible. Throughout his *Journal*, Winthrop seems enthralled by Anne Hutchinson's persistent objections to Puritan teachings, and when she miscarries "six weeks before her delivery" while under house arrest for heresy, Winthrop goes into even more grotesque detail with her "monstrous birth":

> I beheld innumerable distinct bodies in the form of a globe, not much unlike the swims of some fish, so confusedly knit together by so many several strings (which I conceive were the beginning of veins and nerves) so that it was impossible either to number the small round pieces in every hump, much less to discern from whence every string did fetch its original, they were so snarled one within another. (147)

Unable to resist a closer investigation, Winthrop says, "The small globes I likewise opened, and perceived the matter of them (setting aside the membrane in which it was involved) to be partly wind and partly water" (147). He confers with a doctor, who gives his clinical description of the fetal tissue: "The lumps were twenty-six or twenty-seven, distinct and not joined together; there came no secundine after them" (Winthrop 147). These traumatic, intimate moments of miscarriage certainly gained an audience of distinguished men. After their examination, the men assume that the only source of these "monsters" is Satan, which meant that the women had to be punished.

As John Winthrop describes in his *Journal*, consequences of misbehavior varied in severity. Some women in the Puritan community were persuaded to conceal the miscarriage and to grant "instruction" by a minister. In some cases,

midwives were accused of witchcraft, therefore causing the pregnancy; apparently no human male could have created such atrocities. After Mary Dyer's miscarriage, her midwife fled the area because it became known that she "practised physic." William and Mary Dyer's minister intervened and made a public apology for both of them, on Winthrop's request (Winthrop 141–43).

The first six lines of Bradstreet's poem call attention to the defects in her book, compared with the features of a deformed newborn. Right away, Bradstreet calls the book her "ill-form'd offspring . . . who after birth did'st by my side remain, / Till snatcht from thence by friends" (1–3). Bradstreet surely had heard reports of John Winthrop and others' treatment of miscarried fetuses and stillbirths taken from their mothers and examined; in fact, Bradstreet's father had presided at the civil and church trials of Anne Hutchinson (Winship 131). In the extended metaphor, Bradstreet says her child's "errors were not lessened (all may judge)" (6), similar to Winthrop's lengthy, graphic descriptions of the births of Mary Dyer and Anne Hutchinson.

In the middle section of the poem, Bradstreet's poem takes a different turn from the dismayed descriptions of birth defects. She describes her futile efforts to make her child more appealing: "I stretcht thy joints to make thee even feet, / Yet still thou run'st more hobbling than is meet" (15–16). In the metaphor, the child has one foot longer than the other, and she stretches its legs so that the child can run more smoothly—and more swiftly away from temptation. On a poetic level, the effort describes her manipulation of metrical feet so that her poems will read more traditionally. There may be another biographical level to these lines, as Bradstreet suffered from "lamenesse" in her joints.

Bradstreet, like Mary Dyer and Anne Hutchinson with their miscarriages, claims responsibility for her child ("being mine own"), and she denies that anyone else was at fault for the deformities. Bradstreet tells the child, "If for thy father askt, say, thou hadst none" (22). In this line Bradstreet exonerates her husband, as she does not want him to be implicated if she is to be punished. With this statement no one can bring charges against Simon Bradstreet, and Bradstreet is careful not to mention any godly or evil influences at the risk of heresy.

Knowing her immediate audience, Bradstreet conveys the anxiety of Puritan women who feared not only an abnormal childbirth, but also the public castigation of her motivations and influences. Read as a poem about the birth of a child, Anne Bradstreet's "The Author to Her Book" is filled with a degree of shame, guilt, and fear of repercussions. In light of her immediate surroundings, Bradstreet certainly could have been charged with heresy for creating something that did not meet with the approval of Puritan elders. Bradstreet surely sensed that her own well-being was in jeopardy as well as the sometimes tenuous reputation of her father with Winthrop and her husband's irregular employment in the colony. In addition to Bradstreet's self-effacing sarcasm in "The Author to Her Book," the poem also contains a culturally significant subtext of anxiety.

Source: Lisa Day-Lindsey, "Bradstreet's 'The Author to Her Book,'" in *Explicator*, Vol. 64, No. 2, Winter 2006, pp. 66–69.

Kimberly Latta

In the following excerpt, Latta examines the domestic, familial, and spiritual bonds in Bradstreet's poetry and argues that the focus on the distinction between the spiritual and the physical expresses a "modern" understanding of the physical universe.

MATERNITY AND PUBLICATION

... The interrelation of spiritual, economic, and genealogical meaning in words used to express Christian bondage suggests that notions about redemption, money, and reproduction were only just beginning to come apart from one another during this period of early merchant capitalism. Bradstreet's use of these terms seems to indicate the beginnings of conceptual divisions between these categories, divisions which were not yet present, for example, in John Donne. The early seventeenth-century poet and Anglican minister connected redemption, money, and reproduction when he preached that Christ came to pay Adam's original debt

> in such money as was lent: in the nature and flesh of man; for man had sinned and man must pay. And then it was lent in such money as was coyned even with the Image of God; man was made according to his Image: that Image being defaced, in a new Mint, in the wombe of the Blessed Virgin, there was new money coyned; The Image of the invisible God ... was imprinted into the humane nature. And then that there might bee *omnis plenitudo*, all fullness, as God, for the paiment of this debt, sent downe the Bullion, and the stamp, that is, God to be conceived in man, and as he provided the Mint, the womb of the Blessed Virgin, so hath he

> 'THE AUTHOR TO HER BOOK' ALSO DIFFERS FROM BRADSTREET'S OTHER POEMS ABOUT PARENTHOOD BECAUSE IN IT THE POET NEITHER LONGS FOR HER OWN DISSOLUTION IN THE SPIRIT NOR SEEKS TO DRAW HER CHILD UP AFTER HER; SHE MERELY ACKNOWLEDGES THE BOOK AS HER PROGENY AND SENDS IT ON ITS WAY."

provided an Exchequer, where this mony is issued; that is his Church.

Donne imagines Christ as appearing on earth in the same "money as was lent." But unlike worthless human currency, the coin that issues from the mint of Mary's womb has miraculous, infinite, and intrinsic value that alone can redeem all of God's human children. Christ's value, mixed with the base metal of human specie, ensures and enables the final return of humanity into its original principle, the heavenly womb of God the Father.

Donne's association of the reproduction of children with money lending was conventional and helps to explain this imagery in Bradstreet's work as well as her uneasiness about her own necessarily fallen generation and spiritual debt. While medieval and Renaissance scholastics accepted what they sometimes called "spiritual usury," which involved the reproduction of children as lawful interest on the loan of life that God had made, they rejected fiscal usury, or moneylending, because it seemed to bring forth illegitimate and indeed blasphemous value from a thing which was perceived to have no intrinsic spiritual value. The antiusury writers looked back to Aristotle, who instructed that money was a barren thing and should not "breed." Money should be used only as a medium of exchange. By the seventeenth century, however, English men and women both at home and in America increasingly accepted modest interest on loans and disapproved only of those who charged exorbitant rates for the sole purpose of enriching themselves. Writing about this topic, John Winthrop distinguished between lending as an act of mercy and lending "by way of commerce," arguing that the former was subject to the biblical injunction to be charitable, whereas "the rule of justice" should govern the latter. He thereby made a categorical separation between the spiritual and the secular in matters of market exchange itself. Anne Bradstreet must have been aware of the debate over interest, since Thomas Dudley worked closely with Winthrop, and her sister's father-in-law, Robert Keayne, was twice censured for taking too much profit. She may also have known that Winthrop considered her father's grain lending usurious.

An early English proponent of interest, James Spottiswood, also contributes to our understanding of Bradstreet's eschatological concerns about poetry as "mites" generated from an inherited or invested talent. Spottiswood rejected the idea that "money begetteth not money" on the grounds that "there is a lawfull increase & gaine made of artificiall things as well as natural as Houses and Shippes." The yield of money through trade was "artificiall" for Spottiswood, because it was value produced through human management. As such, its "increase" was no less real or legitimate than the profit gained from the increase of natural things, such as livestock or land. From a strictly religious viewpoint, Spottiswood's theory that artificial things (things not found in nature, such as money) can increase appropriates for human imagination the power of generation that properly belongs to God alone. To make things that human beings have made yield of themselves seems from this standpoint covetous or self-glorifying, for it is to assert that human-made values can be as real or as legitimate as values which proceed from God alone. From Anne Bradstreet's perspective, poems could participate in spiritual but not worldly usury. As textual productions, or "artificiall things" generated, they should serve only as mediums of exchange, or currency that acknowledges one's obligation to the spirit, and not as things that increase one's own worldly value.

Yet Anne Bradstreet approaches Spottiswood's potentially blasphemous and therefore dangerous view when she manipulates the idea that one legitimately yields interest on the loan of life through the production of children *as well as of writing*. She does this when she refers to her poem as a "mite," which meant both a coin and a child, in "To Her Father with Some Verses," and in one of her devotional poems, "May 11, 1661." She also treads into potentially heretical territory

in her maternal epistles, where she associates the production of children with the production of narrative and seems to imagine her letters to her children giving rise to or "breeding" similar texts. If Bradstreet goes out of her way to emphasize her worthlessness in her poems to her father and her desire to glorify not herself but God in her letters to her children, it may be because she is aware of the danger she courts by imagining her writing as interest. The danger is that she will become a poetic usurer by believing that she has the power to create and to give artificial things the power to generate themselves rather than understanding this power as God's alone. The danger is also that she will set herself up as a creditor in her own right, a source of value and life, to which loans, "notes," and children will return and be redeemed. Finally, the danger is that she will imagine herself as an author in the sense of a person who can generate texts that signify in and of themselves, rather than in the sense of a person whose texts only imperfectly signify higher truths.

The poet contemplates the dangers of generating herself in writing in "The Author to Her Book." It is worth quoting in full:

> Thou ill-formed offspring of my feeble brain,
> Who after birth didst by my side remain,
> Till snatched from thence by friends, less wise than
>   true,
> Who thee abroad, exposed to public view,
> Made thee in rags, halting to th' press to trudge,
> Where errors were not lessened (all may judge).
> At thy return my blushing was not small,
> My rambling brat (in print) should mother call,
> I cast thee by as one unfit for light,
> Thy visage was so irksome in my sight;
> Yet being mine own, at length affection would
> Thy blemishes amend, if so I could:
> I washed thy face, but more defects I saw,
> And rubbing off a spot still made a flaw.
> I stretched thy joints to make thee even feet,
> Yet still thou run'st more hobbling than is meet;
> In better dress to trim thee was my mind,
> But nought save homespun cloth i' th' house I find.
> In this array 'mongst vulgars may'st thou roam.
> In critics hands beware thou dost not come,
> And take thy way where yet thou art not known;
> If for thy father asked, say thou hadst none;
> And for thy mother, she alas is poor,
> Which caused her thus to send thee out of door.

In this poem Bradstreet recounts the history of her manuscript's unauthorized publication in 1650, her initial rejection of the book, and her subsequent editing of the second edition, which appeared posthumously in 1678. She also extends

John Woodbridge's metaphor of her book as an "infant" whose "birth" he helped to force. While it circulated in manuscript form among her friends, Bradstreet imagined it to be by her side, still within the purview of her management and interpretive control, as if still connected to her maternal body. This manuscript was kidnapped and introduced into the world before its mother could dress it properly for public—or divine—view. Regarding this "ill-formed offspring of my feeble brain," the poet also seems to view her book "as one unfit for light," as a monstrous birth. Children born misshapen were thought to express their mother's spiritual deformity. Likewise, as Mack points out, "evil opinions or malicious acts . . . were portrayed as monstrous births, and their authors as monster mothers."

Insofar as Bradstreet's earlier "mites" functioned to praise God for lending her the skills with which to repay the immense loan he had made to her, they served as elaborate demonstrations of a bondage that signaled her readiness for glorification—that final union with the paternal/maternal corpus. John Woodbridge disrupted this poetic economy when he surreptitiously removed Bradstreet's manuscript to public view. I am speculating that Bradstreet regarded the copies of *The Tenth Muse Lately Sprung Up in America* (1650) that found their way back to Massachusetts and into public circulation as a kind of illegitimate interest that increased (because it was published and issued in multiple copies) by itself, beyond her control. The book was also illegitimate because it was born without a father; it proceeded from her, but not through the bonds that tie all of her other interestlike offspring to her Father in heaven. Confronting the prospect of her privately written and privately circulated poems roaming "'mongst vulgars," Bradstreet betrays anxiety about how her art will be understood and received in the world: "In critics hands beware thou dost not come." The book, she instructs, must be careful how it presents itself, lest people who do not understand the soteriological function of her writing fail to see or endeavor to undermine its spiritual creditworthiness. Will the poems in this book still register as symbols of her intent to pay her religious debts if they circulate in the material economy and are exchanged for money rather than for the approval and inspiration of those who have helped to guide her to God? Or does the birth of this misshapen child register her own spiritual bankruptcy?

The idea of repayment corresponds to the Protestant soteriological vision of reunion with the parent in the sense that the true value of the child as bond note is realized only when it is paid, when it finds its way back to the original lender, who makes it "good." To make a loan is to disburse a portion of one's money and allow it to circulate independently, like a child or a book, in the world. In Protestant theology, the loan, child, or book needs to return to its parent, to be reunited with its source, in order to have any real value or meaning. As Bradstreet's contemporary, John Robinson, observed, "Writing is the speech of the absent. . . . Great care is to be taken, and circumspection used in writing of Books; not onely (though specialy for conscience of God); but also because the Author therin exposeth himself to the censure of all men." Just as Bradstreet sought to maintain her bond with her children in order to ensure their acceptability as lawful interest to her heavenly father, she wanted to preserve control over her writing so that it would serve as a sacred offering and legitimate increase on her loan of life and talent from him.

In "The Author to Her Book" Anne Bradstreet makes explicit a problem that is only implicit in her maternal epistles: the problem of maintaining control over one's (re)production. In the maternal epistles she associates writing with children and with the perpetuation of herself by regulating her own sons and daughters, who have gone out into the world but who will give accurate "accounts" of her "travail" to their own offspring. She associates writing with children by conceiving of her book as a child that has entered the world, where it will report about her to (and be reckoned by) strangers. The maternal epistle maintains a spiritual bond, a contract and a link, between mother and child. But Bradstreet's "ill-formed offspring" has broken that connection and wanders without guidance. The poet recognizes with some pain that she cannot shepherd her book in the world (as she can shepherd her children through her maternal epistles) and that the accounts it will give of her "stewardship" will be unreliable. "In better dress to trim thee was my mind," she complains, as if she has been unable to tailor garments for this child that accord with divine dispensations.

Finally, the break that the book makes with its mother launches it into a space that is divorced from the spiritual realm at the center of her maternal epistles. Thus Bradstreet's reluctant acknowledgment of maternity and assumption of responsibility for sending her illegitimate child "out of door" because she is "poor" troubles the spiritual water in which we expect to find all of her work. Has she acknowledged this "rambling" (wandering, sinful) "brat" as her own for worldly or economic, as opposed to spiritual, reasons? Does she want to make money with it? Or does she imagine that its proliferation in print yields upon her own poetic value in the world? She admits that "affection" for her earthly, public child has motivated her to "amend" its "blemishes" and make it more fit to be seen. But if no amount of rubbing can wash this child, is this so because, like the hands of Lady Macbeth, its sins cannot be cleansed? Has this creature of an earthly and not a divine womb been permitted to wander in the world because it will never find its way to heaven? And if so, then what kind of existence or meaning does its mother imagine it having, if not a purely worldly one? "Take thy way where yet thou art not known," Bradstreet counsels her book, seeming to encourage it to circulate and become valuable independently in a public, commercial world not enclosed by the spirit. As in all of Anne Bradstreet's work, earthly images figure divine realities. "The Author to Her Book" registers Bradstreet's nervousness that she and her book may have no legitimate spiritual value. That possibility, though denied, remains present in the poem. The potential for worldly value separates from its spiritual complement even as it is asserted as a thing that the spirit overwhelms. Thus the image of her book as an errant child in the world, which will not be redeemed and dissolved in the spirit, becomes embraceable on its own terms. Not quite "profane," it nonetheless exhibits nonreligious value. Rather than taking us to a higher realm, this figure of the book as child exhibits a possibly secular worthiness through its circulation in the material world, a "worth" that Bradstreet only hints at in her poems to her father and that she begins to articulate in her maternal epistles.

Although recent critics have interpreted Bradstreet's nervousness in this poem as the trepidation of a woman worried about offending patriarchal authority by speaking in public, I see it also as gender-neutral anxiety about autonomous generation, a fear of offending the creator by imitating

him through the generation of worldly value that both male and female writers shared. George Herbert's (1593–1633) presentation of his "writings" as a "special Deed" in "Obedience," Andrew Marvell's (1621–78) meditation on the insignificance of the "wreaths of Fame and Interest" in "The Coronet," or Edward Taylor's (ca. 1642–1729) endless scrutiny of his value in such lines as "Am I thy Gold? Or Purse, Lord, for thy Wealth" in *Preparatory Meditations* I:6, all worry about the dangers of overweening poetic creation in a language of marketplace terms and values. That said, I have also tried to show how, by embracing the role of mother, Anne Bradstreet assumed a spiritual and creative authority and that the problem of generating value was particularly vexed because of the affective bonds she formed with her real and textual children. These bonds conferred a worthiness that seemed to slip past the boundaries of religious culture and that made her children valuable purely because they sprang from her.

Like many early modern writers, Bradstreet attempted to accommodate the worldly to the spiritual. The world of finance, agriculture, and genealogy is both merged and set into conflict with the spirit in the father-poems. The poems on marriage and biological motherhood sketch out further conflicts between worldly and heavenly values but reconcile these oppositions by imagining all realms and all distinctions as things transcended in the spirit. "The Author to Her Book" seems to disrupt this larger spiritual economy in which Bradstreet located all of her work. The book becomes a child adrift in the world where it has a material value but owes no obligation to its mother, its only parent. Completely dissociated from the contractual bonds that originate in God the Father and that are enforced by the mother, such a production can never be redeemed and therefore will not maintain a spiritual connection to its origin. "The Author to Her Book" also differs from Bradstreet's other poems about parenthood because in it the poet neither longs for her own dissolution in the spirit nor seeks to draw her child up after her; she merely acknowledges the book as her progeny and sends it on its way. The bond Bradstreet establishes with her book, then, remains an earthly connection. She finally does not cast it aside as blasphemy, but sets it apart as a thing that exists in a universe parallel, if inferior, to the spiritual realm that encompasses all her other offspring. It is as if the very effort to articulate the spiritual in graphically material terms, to read religious meaning into all worldly experiences, resulted for her in a nascent distinction between spiritual and worldly experience. "The Author to Her Book" records the culmination of a secularizing trend within the poet's essentially spiritual thought, for it demonstrates how the domestic, the economic, and the theological—which Anne Bradstreet understood as interrelated locations of the bond between parents and children—were beginning to come apart for her as separate but analogous realms.

Bradstreet's writing about obligation and restitution between parents and their offspring demonstrates the complex connections between familial, commercial, and sacred aspects of experience in a culture in which it became possible to conceive of value outside of the spiritual canopy that theoretically encompassed all existence. That she rejected nonspiritual values does not mean that she also repudiated the positive power to create things of earthly significance, which she associated with being a poet and a mother. The metaphor of Christian bondage afforded Bradstreet a position of great authority and creativity, not only as a mother-producer and nurturer but also as the fortunate recipient of priceless gifts from God. Finally, and perhaps most important to her, the ineluctability of her bonds promised reunion in heaven for all time with those she loved most: "Where we with joy each other's face shall see / And parted more by death shall never be" ("To the Memory of My... Father," lines 74–75).

Source: Kimberly Latta, "'Such Is My Bond': Maternity and Economy in Anne Bradstreet's Writings," in *Inventing Maternity: Politics, Science, and Literature, 1650–1865*, edited by Susan C. Greenfield and Carol Barash, University of Kentucky Press, 1999, pp. 57–85.

SOURCES

"2010 Census Interactive Population Search," United States Census Bureau website, http://2010.census.gov/2010 census/popmap/ipmtext.php?fl=25 (accessed February 23, 2012).

Anderson, James, "Anne Dudley, Wife of Simon Bradstreet," in *Critical Essays on Anne Bradstreet*, edited by Pattie Cowell and Ann Stanford, G. K. Hall, 1983, p. 23; originally published in *Memorable Women of the Puritan Times*, Vol. 1, Blackie and Son, 1862, pp. 156–84.

"Anne Bradstreet: Biography," Anne Bradstreet website, http://www.annebradstreet.com/anne_bradstreet_bio_001. htm (accessed February 22, 2012).

"Anne Dudley," Church of Jesus Christ of Latter-Day Saints website, http://www.familysearch.org/Eng/search/ AF/individual_record.asp?recid=6883751&frompage=99 (accessed February 22, 2012).

Bradstreet, Anne, "The Author to Her Book," in *The Norton Anthology of American Literature*, Vol. 1, edited by Ronald Gottesman, et al., W. W. Norton, 1979, pp. 50–51.

Deetz, Patricia Scott, J. Eric Deetz, and Christopher Fennell, "Population of Plymouth Town, Colony & County, 1620–1690," Plymouth Colony Archive Project, 2000, http://www.histarch.uiuc.edu/plymouth/townpop. html (accessed February 23, 2012).

Dolle, Raymond F., *Anne Bradstreet: A Reference Guide*, G. K. Hall, 1990, p. 5.

Garraty, John A., *The American Nation: A History of the United States*, 2nd ed., Harper & Row, 1971, pp. 31–33.

Gordon, Charlotte, *Mistress Bradstreet: The Untold Life of America's First Poet*, Little, Brown, 2005, pp. 283–84.

"History of Harvard University," Harvard University website, http://www.harvard.edu/history (accessed February 23, 2012).

Hutchinson, Robert, Introduction to *Poems of Anne Bradstreet*, edited by Robert Hutchinson, Dover, 1969, p. 30.

"Massachusetts: History," in *Columbia Electronic Encyclopedia*, 6th ed., 2007, http://www.infoplease.com/ce6/ us/A0859530.html (accessed February 23, 2012).

New, Elisa, "Feminist Invisibility: The Examples of Anne Bradstreet and Anne Hutchinson," in *Common Knowledge*, Vol. 2, No. 1, 1993, pp. 99–117.

"Number of Words in the English Language," Global Language Monitor, http://www.languagemonitor.com/ no-of-words/ (accessed February 24, 2012).

Sanford, Ann, *Anne Bradstreet: The Worldly Puritan*, Burt Franklin, 1974, pp. 135–44.

"Thomas Dudley, Gov. (1576–1653)," Geni, http://www. geni.com/people/Gov-Thomas-Dudley/60000000010139 32506 (accessed March 2, 2012).

White, Elizabeth Wade, *Anne Bradstreet: "The Tenth Muse,"* Oxford University Press, 1971, p. 373.

FURTHER READING

Hawke, David Freeman, *Everyday Life in Early America*, Harper & Row, 1988.

This relatively compact, illustrated volume provides the reader with a description of day-to-day life in colonial America. Chapter titles include "Settling In," "The Farm," "The House," "War," "Wonders of the Invisible World," and others.

Hayes, Kevin J., ed., *The Oxford Handbook of Early American Literature*, Oxford University Press, 2008.

This volume provides the reader with a broad context for Bradstreet's poetry by examining the literary climate of the colonial period in US history. The book is arranged in parts and includes essays on such topics as literature promoting the colonies, devotional literature, libraries, newspapers, travel narratives, and the voices of native peoples.

Nichols, Heidi L., *Anne Bradstreet: A Guided Tour of the Life and Thought of a Puritan Poet*, P&R Publishing, 2006.
This compact biography not only narrates the facts of Bradstreet's life but also includes information about Puritanism and excerpts from Bradstreet's poetry.

White, Peter, ed., *Puritan Poets and Poetics: Seventeenth-Century American Poetry in Theory and Practice*, Pennsylvania State University Press, 1986.
Readers interested in the subject of Puritan poetry during the early colonial period will find this collection of essays informative. The volume includes essays on individual poets, poetic forms, and the cultural context in which the poems were produced.

Anne Bradstreet

Bradstreet AND "The Author to Her Book"

Bradstreet AND *The Tenth Muse*

colonial American history

colonial American literature

Massachusetts Bay Colony

Pequot War

Plymouth Colony

Puritans

Winthrop Fleet

The Convergence of the Twain

THOMAS HARDY

1912

"The Convergence of the Twain" is a poem by British nineteenth- and twentieth-century poet Thomas Hardy. As the statement that appears below the title in parentheses in reproductions of the poem makes clear, it is a poem about the sinking of the RMS *Titanic*, a luxurious ocean liner that represented the best that modern technology could create. It was thought to be unsinkable, and yet on its maiden voyage in April 1912, from Southampton, England, to New York, it hit an iceberg in the Atlantic Ocean and sank in the early morning of April 15. The death toll was 1,513 people, many of them wealthy, influential people from the upper echelons of society. There were not enough lifeboats onboard, and this increased the loss of life.

Hardy completed "The Convergence of the Twain" just nine days after the disaster. It was first published a month later, in the program of the "Dramatic and Operatic Matinee in Aid of the 'Titanic' Disaster Fund," given at Covent Garden Theatre in London. It was later published in Hardy's *Satires of Circumstance* in 1914. The poem has always been admired for the skillful way it is constructed, and it also well illustrates Hardy's characteristically pessimistic philosophy. It can be found in almost any edition of Hardy's poetry, including *Selected Poems* (1998), edited by Robert Mezey.

Thomas Hardy (© Downey / Getty Images)

AUTHOR BIOGRAPHY

Novelist, poet, and short-story writer Hardy was born on June 2, 1840, in a village near Dorchester in the county of Dorset, England. His father was a master mason who instilled in his son a love of music; his mother was a former maidservant who taught her son to read and write at an early age. Hardy attended local schools, and when he was sixteen, he was apprenticed to an architect. By 1862, he was helping to design church restorations in London. He also began to write poetry. Returning to Dorchester in 1870, he met Emma Gifford, whom he married in 1874. By this time, Hardy had published his first successful novel, *Under the Greenwood Tree* (1872). *Far from the Madding Crowd* followed in 1874 and was an even greater success. Hardy decided to give up architecture and pursue a career as a novelist. His next novels, *The Return of the Native* (1878) and *The Mayor of Casterbridge* (1886) were, like the earlier novels, set in the fictional area he called Wessex, in the south and southwest of England.

Tess of the d'Urbervilles (1891), a novel in which a young woman is seduced by an aristocrat, was considered immoral by some readers and critics, and *Jude the Obscure* (1895) was denounced in some quarters as not only immoral but also coarse. The criticism did not stop the novels from becoming popular, however. Over a century later, these two novels are often regarded as Hardy's finest. Nonetheless, Hardy was stung by the criticism and decided to write no more novels. Instead, he returned to writing poetry. In 1898, he published *Wessex Poems and Other Verses*, a collection of poems he had written over the previous thirty years. *The Dynasts* was a long verse drama about the Napoleonic Wars published in three parts from 1904 to 1908. Other volumes of poetry included *Time's Laughingstocks and Other Verses* (1909), *Satires of Circumstance* (1914), which contains "The Convergence of the Twain," *Collected Poems* (1919), and *Late Lyrics and Earlier with Many Other Poems* (1923). Through these publications Hardy established a reputation as one of the finest twentieth-century poets.

In 1910, Hardy was awarded the Order of Merit. In 1912, Hardy's wife Emma died. In "Poems of 1912–13" (later included in *Satires of Circumstance*), Hardy wrote many elegies of her in which he recalled their happy early years together. He remarried two years later, to Florence Emily Dugdale, an admirer of his writings who was thirty-nine years his junior.

Hardy died on January 11, 1928, of what his doctor described as heart disease contributed to by old age. His ashes were placed in Poets' Corner in Westminster Abbey.

POEM TEXT

I

> In a solitude of the sea
> Deep from human vanity,
> And the Pride of Life that planned her, stilly
>   couches she.

II

> Steel chambers, late the pyres
> Of her salamandrine fires,   5
> Cold currents thrid, and turn to rhythmic tidal
>   lyres.

III

> Over the mirrors meant
> To glass the opulent

The sea-worm crawls—grotesque, slimed,
    dumb, indifferent.

IV

    Jewels in joy designed   10
    To ravish the sensuous mind
    Lie lightless, all their sparkles bleared and
        black and blind.

V

    Dim moon-eyed fishes near
    Gaze at the gilded gear
    And query: 'What does this vaingloriousness
        down here?'   15

VI

    Well: while was fashioning
    This creature of cleaving wing,
    The Immanent Will that stirs and urges
        everything

VII

    Prepared a sinister mate
    For her—so gaily great—   20
    A Shape of Ice, for the time far and dissociate.

VIII

    And as the smart ship grew
    In stature, grace, and hue,
    In shadowy silent distance grew the
        Iceberg too.

IX

    Alien they seemed to be: 25
    No mortal eye could see
    The intimate welding of their later history,

X

    Or sign that they were bent
    By paths coincident
    On being anon twin halves of one august event.   30

XI

    Till the Spinner of the Years
    Said 'Now!' And each one hears,
    And consummation comes, and jars two
        hemispheres.

POEM SUMMARY

The text used for this summary is from *Selected Shorter Poems of Thomas Hardy*, Macmillan, 1969, pp. 45–46. A version of the poem can be found on the following web page: http://rpo.library.utoronto.ca/poems/convergence-twain.

"The Convergence of the Twain" consists of eleven stanzas, each comprising three lines—two short lines followed by one long line.

Stanza 1

As the text and the parenthetical ordinarily appearing beneath the title imply, the poet evokes the *Titanic* after it has sunk to the bottom of the Atlantic Ocean. It lies there in solitude, far from the human world in which it was conceived and built. That human world is presented by the poet as being full of vanity and pride in its accomplishments.

Stanza 2

This stanza and the next two present contrasts in how the ship was when it was afloat and how it appears now, at the bottom of the sea. The first line refers to the *Titanic*'s boilers, in which coal was burned to power the ship. Once the coal was burnt, it left ashes, and this is what the poet refers to in the second part of the line, although the word *pyre* refers to a structure used for a funeral rite—an appropriate word to use since the *Titanic* was the grave of many of its passengers. The second line continues the description of the boilers as they worked when the ship was afloat, before line 3 provides the stark contrast: the boilers are now filled with the cold water of the ocean. The word *thrid* is likely an alternate spelling of "thread."

Stanza 3

This stanza begins by presenting an image of the mirrors on the ship, in which the wealthy passengers could admire themselves. Line 3 brings out the contrast: Now, sea worms cover those same mirrors. In place of the pride and self-regard that characterized the human society on the ship, a primitive form of life that can comprehend nothing has taken over.

Stanza 4

After the mirrors of the previous stanza, the poet focuses in lines 1 and 2 here on the jewels that were delightful to the senses when they were worn by the women on the ship. But now, line 3 explains, they have lost their luster and are covered with the dark slime of the ocean floor.

Stanza 5

Like the previous three stanzas, this one also contrasts the former majesty of the ship with the condition it is now in, but it does so in a slightly different way. It presents a fanciful, personified image of fish staring at the remains of the once-opulent ship. The fish then, in line 3, pose a question about why such a thing is now at the bottom of the ocean. As an expression of the vanity alluded to in stanza 1—an excessive pride on the part of those who constructed it—the ship is obviously out of place.

Stanza 6

Stanza 6 contains the beginning of the answer to the question posed by the fish. It marks the turn in the poem, which is divided roughly into two halves. The first half has described the wreck of the *Titanic*, contrasting its present with its former state; the second half will describe the event that caused its doom. In this stanza, the poet states that while the ship was being created, a fundamental force in the universe, a kind of inscrutable, unknowable will that is responsible for everything that happens, was also stirring.

Stanza 7

This stanza describes the iceberg that was being created by the impersonal will that drives life forward. The iceberg is presented as a kind of groom or companion for the ship, being destined for the function it would fill many years into the future.

Stanza 8

This stanza continues the idea expressed in the previous stanza. Just as the ship was being constructed until it took on its large, elegant final form, so, too, the iceberg grew, at a different time and place.

Stanza 9

The first line of this stanza emphasizes how different the ship and the iceberg were. It seemed as if they had nothing to do with each other. Line 2 builds on this thought. No one could possibly have known how their histories would become entwined.

Stanza 10

Stanza 10 continues the thought expressed in the previous stanza. No one could possibly have discerned the paths that ship and iceberg would take that would result in their fateful meeting.

Stanza 11

This stanza describes the moment the ship and the iceberg meet in their fatal collision. The collision comes as the moment decreed by whatever impersonal force controls all events in the universe, including the human world.

THEMES

Vanity

This is not a poem that conveys any sympathy for the dead. On the contrary, the disaster is used to present the main theme of human vanity, pride, and arrogance. The poet states this clearly in the first stanza and builds on it throughout the first five stanzas, which evoke the former glories of the ship and contrast it with its present sunken condition. The description of the ship emphasizes its luxurious nature and the wealth and self-regard of the passengers. The women wore expensive jewelry, and there were plenty of mirrors in the rooms on the ship for people to gaze admiringly at their finery. The power of the ship is emphasized in stanza 2, with its evocation of the furnaces that powered it. Stanza 6 suggests that the designers and builders of the ship created something that resembled a living thing that could move so gracefully through the waters that it almost seemed as if it were flying.

These descriptions all suggest the pride humans take in their creations, and the belief in this case that the modern technology that created the ship represented a triumph over nature. So mighty and indestructible did the ship seem, so much a testament to human ingenuity and skill, that people seemed to forget that such a mighty craft, loaded with every luxury, was still vulnerable to the even more mighty force of nature.

After just one encounter with a single iceberg—and for this climactic event, in the last two lines the poem switches to the present tense—all the ship's power turns to nothing. The ship that was declared to be unsinkable sinks. Human technology is shown to be a puny, fragile thing when set against the natural perils that lurk on, and under, the open seas. And it is foolishness and pride, the poem suggests, not to recognize this state of affairs. As the old saying goes, "Pride goes before a fall," and in the case of the *Titanic*, at least according to "The Convergence of the Twain," it was ostentatious, boastful human

TOPICS FOR FURTHER STUDY

- Read *Terror on the Titanic* (1996), by Jim Wallace, in the "Bantam Books for Young Readers" series, about the *Titanic* disaster. After reading the book, make a list of the measures that might have been taken to avert the disaster. Who is to blame for the sinking of the *Titanic*? Give a class presentation in which you describe your findings.

- Watch the 1997 movie *Titanic*, rereleased in April 2012 to commemorate the one-hundredth anniversary of the disaster. Although the main characters are fictional, some characters are based on people who really were on the *Titanic*. Using Internet research, examine the extent to which the movie portrayals of Captain Edward J. Smith, Thomas Andrews, Joseph Bruce Ismay, and Molly Brown conform or depart from what is known historically about these characters. Write your comments in your web log and share it with your classmates. Note that this film does contain some sexual material that may not be appropriate for younger viewers.

- Visit the website of the Titanic Historical Society (http://titanichistoricalsociety.org), and explore the site's large content. Click on the "Articles" tab and read the articles that capture your interest. Make notes on any questions that arise as you read, and then post your questions to the "Forum" section, which contains a very active message board. Take part in the discussion.

- Read Hardy's poem "A Plaint to Man," which was written just a few years before "The Convergence of the Twain." How would you describe the philosophy the speaker espouses in this poem? How does it amplify, shed light on, or contradict the philosophy expressed in "The Convergence of the Twain"? Write an essay in which you compare and contrast these two poems. You can find the poem at the following web link: http://www.readbookonline.net/readOnLine/10238/.

pride that was punctured and destroyed by that lurking lump of ice in the cold water of the Atlantic Ocean.

Predestination

The poem strongly suggests that the disaster was predestined. The ship did not merely meet with some ill luck; the iceberg did not just randomly appear. The sinking of the *Titanic* was not, in a metaphysical sense, an accident. The incident reveals more than simply an encounter of humanity versus nature in which humanity gets the worst of it. This in itself would not surprise anyone, since disasters at sea have been going on since humans first created ships. What the poem suggests is something more than the ordinary perils of seafaring, in which man hazards his life by leaving firm ground and taking to water. The poem suggests that behind the phenomena of nature such as icebergs and the course taken by human and natural life, there lies not a benevolent God, as Hardy's Victorian predecessors might have supposed, but something far more disturbing: a kind of divine, impersonal cosmic Will. (Hardy capitalizes the word in the poem.) From the beginning, way back somewhere in the mists of time, this Will appears to have deliberately shaped the tragic outcome. The Will is the impersonal force that stirs all things into activity (as suggested by the last line of stanza 6), and it is a far more potent force than the will of humankind, which is why the iceberg can so easily destroy the ship. It is as if the two were made for each other as a test of strength, although the outcome is a foregone conclusion. Unlike this impersonal Will, no human knowledge, as stanza 9 states, could possibly have foreseen how ship and iceberg would one day come together in a clash that so rocked the human world. The moment of collision is dictated by a force or entity that in stanza 11 Hardy describes simply as that which is responsible for the endless passage of time over years immemorial. Impersonal it may be, but it knows when the moment is right, and it is at that moment when ship and iceberg collide. It is as if everything is preplanned, quite beyond the realm of human knowledge, and certainly not with human happiness in mind. But the overall message of the poem also suggests that humans contributed to the disaster by their refusal to acknowledge the presence of a force greater than anything they could muster, that could in a moment bring all their efforts to naught.

The Titanic *sank on April 15, 1912 after hitting an iceberg in North Atlantic.* *(© Classic Image / Alamy)*

STYLE

Rhythm, Rhyme, and Meter

Each stanza follows the same rhyme scheme and meter. All three lines in each stanza rhyme. The first two lines are iambic trimeter, which means that these lines contain three iambic feet. An *iamb* consists of two syllables; the first one is unstressed and the second one is stressed. The iambic foot is the most common poetic foot in English poetry. The last line of each stanza is much longer, typically containing six iambic feet, known as hexameter.

The poet makes several variations in the meter to create variety. The most frequent variation is in the first foot. In the first foot of the first lines of stanzas 2 and 4, for example, the poet substitutes a trochee for the iamb. A *trochee* is a foot in which the first syllable is stressed and the second syllable is unstressed. Hardy uses the same device in the first feet of stanza 1, line 2; stanza

5, line 2; and stanza 6, line 1. The first foot of stanza 2, line 3, provides an example of another kind of foot, the *spondee*, which consists of two stressed syllables.

Alliteration

Alliteration, the repetition of initial consonants, is a notable device in this poem. Examples can be found in every stanza except stanzas 9 and 10. Notable examples occur in stanza 4, line 1, with its repetition of the letter *j*; in stanza 5, line 2, with its triple repetition of the letter *g*; and stanza 4, line 3, with its triple repetition of the letters *bl*.

Imagery

The ship is described in rich, sensuous imagery that recreates its splendor before it hit the iceberg. The imagery is concentrated in the first six stanzas; the iceberg, which is described in the later stanzas, is presented in more abstract language. Most noticeable is the imagery suggesting marriage or courtship between the ship and iceberg. They are a pair meant for each other. The ship is consistently presented as female; it is as if she is dressed to the nines in all her finery just to meet her bridegroom.

She lies as if in a bed, and the iceberg is described in stanza 7 as being specifically intended as a companion for the ship, as if they are two aspects of one reality (stanza 10). They are destined for an intimate, close relationship (stanza 9). The final line of the poem suggests that in some way their meeting and grotesque kind of union is the fulfillment of the purpose for which they were designed.

HISTORICAL CONTEXT

The Titanic *Voyage Begins*

The dramatic and tragic story of the sinking of the *Titanic* on its maiden voyage has had a strong grip on people's imaginations for over one hundred years, since that fateful night in April 1912 in the icy waters of the Atlantic Ocean. The *Titanic* was thought of as a miracle of modern engineering that could never sink. The ship, which was built by Harland & Woolf in its shipyard in Belfast, Ireland, and operated by the White Star Line, was extremely large, measuring nearly 900 feet in length, 94 feet in width at its widest point, and 175 feet in height. As Walter Lord points out in *A Night to Remember*, his classic account of the sinking of the *Titanic*, this is the equivalent of an eleven-story building stretching for four city blocks. The ship could travel at speeds up to 25 knots. Lord explains why the *Titanic* was thought unsinkable: It was constructed to be watertight.

> She had a double bottom and was divided into 16 watertight compartments.... She could float with any two compartments flooded, and since no one could imagine anything worse than a collision at the juncture of two compartments, she was labeled 'unsinkable.'

For passengers traveling first class, the ship was the ultimate in luxury. The private suites had private promenade decks. The staterooms had splendid wood paneling, with expensive furniture and luxurious carpets. The rooms were furnished in various periods and styles. There was a well-equipped gymnasium, two libraries, a Turkish bath, a heated swimming pool, a squash court, and four restaurants. The Café Parisien offered sumptuous cuisine and was the center of social life for the younger passengers. There were also four electric elevators on the ship.

On its maiden voyage the *Titanic* had 2,224 people on board, including 885 crew members. The passengers included many of the rich and famous of their day, such as millionaire John Jacob Astor IV, industrialist Benjamin Guggenheim, and Isidor Straus, the owner of the department store Macy's, to name only a few. The voyage began at noon on April 10, 1912, at Southampton, England. The ship stopped at Cherbourg, France, and the following day at Queenstown, Ireland, before setting out on the Atlantic Ocean for New York City, where it was scheduled to arrive on April 19.

As the *Titanic* steamed across the Atlantic, it covered more than 500 miles within a twenty-four-hour period. On April 14, the *Titanic* received a succession of warnings about ice in the area. Lord lays out the time line for the day: The first warning came at nine o'clock in the morning, from the Cunard liner *Caronia*. Two more reports were received during the afternoon, one of which placed the ice at 250 miles ahead of the *Titanic*. The ship's senior officers, including the captain, Edward J. Smith, remained unconcerned. They thought they would have little trouble in seeing and avoiding any ice.

The Iceberg Hits

At 7:30 p.m. a warning was received from the *Californian*, which had spotted three icebergs in the area the *Titanic* was approaching. Meanwhile, the temperature began to drop as the *Titanic* moved forward at full speed. At 9:30 p.m. Second Officer Charles Lightoller warned the engine room to keep an eye on the freshwater, which might freeze. He also asked the lookouts on the crow's nest to watch for ice. At 9:40 p.m., the *Mesaba* reported icebergs directly ahead of the *Titanic*. No action was taken. By 10:30 p.m. the temperature of the sea was 31 degrees Fahrenheit. At 11:00 p.m., the *Californian* warned of ice but was cut off before it could give its location. At 11:40 p.m., the *Titanic* collided with an iceberg. Lord described that fatal moment. Lookout Frederick Fleet, in the crow's nest, spotted the iceberg. He rang the crow's nest bell and telephoned the bridge to report it. Fleet and his fellow lookout Reginald Lee watched and waited as the iceberg approached. Lord relates,

> The berg towered wet and glistening far above the forecastle deck, and both men braced themselves for a crash. Then, miraculously, the bow began to swing to port. At the last second, the stem shot into the clear, and the ice glided swiftly by along the starboard side. It looked to Fleet like a very close shave.

COMPARE
&
CONTRAST

- **1910s:** People wanting to cross the Atlantic Ocean travel by sea. Intercontinental air travel has not yet been developed. Large ocean liners like the *Olympic II* and the *Britannic* make the crossings. Like the *Titanic*, these ships are operated by the White Sea Line. The *Olympic II*'s first voyage is in 1911, and it carries 2,500 people. During World War I, the *Olympic* is converted to a troop transport ship.

  Today: Few people make trips from North America to Europe by ship anymore. Air travel is much faster and more convenient. Flight times can be as little as four hours. However, it is still possible to travel by passenger ship. Cunard's *Queen Mary II* is the last of the great ocean liners. Each year between April and October it makes eleven double crossings from Southampton, England, to New York and back.

- **1910s:** The *Titanic* is not the only major shipwreck during this decade. In 1914, the luxury liner *RMS Empress of Ireland*, owned by the Canadian Pacific, is on its way to an Atlantic crossing when it collides with *SS Storstad* in the Saint Lawrence River. The death toll is 1,012. It is Canada's worst maritime disaster. In 1915, during World War I, the liner *Lusitania*, en route from New York to Liverpool, England, is sunk near Ireland by a torpedo fired from a German U-boat. Of 1,959 people onboard, only 764 survive.

  Today: In January 2012, the Italian cruise ship *Costa Concordia* hits a rock in the Tyrrhenian Sea off the western coast of Italy. The rock pierces the ship's hull. Taking in water and listing, the ship manages to reach shallow water, where it capsizes. Over four thousand people are onboard, and all but thirty-three are saved. In a remarkable coincidence, one of the survivors is the granddaughter of a woman who survived the sinking of the *Titanic*. Her great-uncle had also been on the *Titanic* but did not survive.

- **1910s:** In Britain, this decade marks the transition from the last years of the Edwardian era. Britain's King Edward VII dies in 1910, although the era is often extended to either the sinking of the *Titanic* in 1912 or the start of World War I in 1914. A settled social order gives way to a period of more rapid change and the questioning of old values that no longer seem valid. In the United States, this period is known as the Gilded Age, and when it ends after World War I, the United States emerges as a leading world power.

  Today: In Britain and the United States, the 2010s are marked by the lingering effects of the great economic recession of 2008–2009. Both economies struggle to recover, and a period of fiscal austerity begins.

It was, of course, more than a close shave. As told by Robert D. Ballard in his book *The Discovery of the Titanic*, the ship's officers had done what they could after they received the alarm from the lookout. They turned the ship to port and closed the doors to the watertight compartments at the bottom of the ship. But it was too late to avert catastrophe. Just thirty-seven seconds elapsed from the time the iceberg was spotted to when it struck the *Titanic* a fatal blow on the starboard side. People in the ship felt only a slight jolt, and almost no one realized the severity of the situation. After a few minutes the ship's engines stopped.

Captain Edward J. Smith, along with the ship's designer, Thomas Andrews, inspected the damage. Five of the watertight compartments had been breached, and they knew the ship could not survive. Andrews, according to Ballard, said it would sink in an hour or an hour and

An artist's impression of the Titanic *going down* (© *The Print Collector | Alamy*)

a half. Wireless calls for help were made and distress signals fired. The *Carpathia*, fifty-eight miles southeast of the Titanic, responded to the distress call, changing course and heading straight for the stricken ship.

Fifty-five minutes after the collision, the first lifeboat was lowered. However, there were only about half the number of spaces in lifeboats as there were passengers. Some of the lifeboats, which by order contained only women and children as well as crewmen, were not filled to capacity. One lifeboat that could hold forty left with only twelve aboard.

The ship finally sank at 2:20 a.m., two hours and forty minutes after the collision with the iceberg. At 4:10 a.m., the *Carpathia* picked up the first lifeboat and then collected eleven more over the next few hours. There were 711 survivors and 1,513 dead.

In England and the United States, the disaster made sensational news. Some years later, the sinking of the *Titanic* began to take on symbolic significance as signaling the imminent end of an era. As Ballard puts it, it represented the point "when people lost their innocence and their sense of certainty. In those late-Edwardian days, before the carnage of the First World War, people still knew what they believed in."

CRITICAL OVERVIEW

"The Convergence of the Twain" has been discussed by many critics, and the poem is universally admired, often for its poetic technique rather than its philosophical pessimism or determinism. For example, Donald Davie, in *Thomas Hardy and British Poetry*, calls it "one of [Hardy's] most dazzling compositions.... The poem itself is an engine, a sleek and powerful machine; its rhymes slide home like pistons inside cylinders, ground exactly to fractions of a millimeter."

For Richard C. Carpenter in *Thomas Hardy*, the poem is "memorable because of its masterful technique and its absorption of a philosophical idea into images." Carpenter argues that the poem is both atypical and typical of Hardy. It is unusual for Hardy in that he did not often write about specific historical events, preferring to focus on people. However, Carpenter continues, "It is pure Hardy in its stanza pattern and philosophical perspective... while the ironic juxtaposition which forms its backbone is about as characteristic of Hardy's poetic thought as anything we could find." William Buckler, in *The Poetry of Thomas Hardy: A Study in Art and Ideas*, comments on the poetic technique Hardy employs:

> The rhythms maximize the stresses of both poetry and prose; the insistent masculine rhymes pound the message home; and the verse forms (two trimeters, one hexameter) make of each stanza an ominous unity mirroring the whole.

For Samuel Hynes, in *The Pattern of Hardy's Poetry*, the poem is an example of a typical pattern in Hardy's poems. Hynes points out that Hardy often divided his poems into two parts: "In the first part one term is set up, in the second its opposite is set against it, and their mutual antagonisms are ironically, but dispassionately remarked." Hynes sees an example of this in the diction of the poem, which "is of two distinct kinds: the lush, exotic, polysyllabic language of the first part works against the monosyllables of the second."

CRITICISM

Bryan Aubrey

Aubrey holds a PhD in English. In the following essay, he examines why Hardy wrote such a pessimistic, unsympathetic poem about a great tragedy in "The Convergence of the Twain."

The sinking of the *Titanic* was a huge shock to millions of people in the United States and Great Britain. Not only was there great loss of life, but the disaster seemed incomprehensible: the *Titanic*, by all accounts, was the greatest ship ever to set forth on the seas, a miracle of modern engineering that was carrying the rich and the famous on its maiden transatlantic voyage. How could such a ship sink? The disaster proved to be a sobering reminder of the power of nature and the relative frailty of human beings, even when armed with all that modern technology could provide. When news of the disaster reached the United States and Britain, people's compassion was aroused. Many events were held on both sides of the Atlantic to raise money for the families of the survivors. In New York City, famous opera singer Enrico Caruso and the Metropolitan Opera put on special concerts to aid the victims. In England, concerts were held at various venues in London and also in Southampton, the city from which the *Titanic* had begun its voyage. The biggest of these concerts was held on May 14, 1912, at London's Royal Opera House in Covent Garden. It was called "Dramatic and Operatic Matinee in Aid of the 'Titanic' Disaster Fund." A forty-page souvenir program was published to accompany the event, and appearing in it was Hardy's poem "The Convergence of the Twain," which he had written a few weeks before. Those members of the well-off audience at this event who gave Hardy's poem more than a cursory glance (but perhaps knew little of the author's work) might have been expecting to read a sympathetic poem expressing an appropriate amount of grief, perhaps tinged with sentiments akin to those expressed in the hymn "Nearer My God to Thee," which had reportedly been played by the band on the deck of the *Titanic* as it sank. If so, these very first readers of "The Convergence of the Twain" were in for a mighty shock. Even in the face of such an enormous tragedy, the poet is in no mood to assuage or even acknowledge human grief, let alone offer pious thoughts about a benevolent God calling his people home. This was not what Thomas Hardy's work was all about. Instead, he offers a poem that might well be described as merciless, without a shred of human sympathy. The speaker appears to be an objective observer who has no interest in seeing into the sorrows of the human heart and sensing the vastness of its pain. He takes the long view, the distant one, focusing on a process that has unfolded over a span of time as dictated by the Will, the universal pulse of life that drives things on and has no pity for the individual.

Some readers and critics have admired exactly this quality in the poem. This is pointed out by Jahan Ramazani, in *Poetry of Mourning: The Modern Elegy from Hardy to Heaney*, who

WHAT DO I READ NEXT?

- "Drummer Hodge," is a poem by Hardy that memorializes a humble British soldier who was killed in the Boer War of 1899–1902. In its quiet empathy for the fallen drummer, the poem is a sharp contrast to the lack of feeling for the victims shown by the speaker of "The Convergence of the Twain" and suggests how wide and deep Hardy's sympathies actually ran. The poem can be found in Hardy's *Selected Poems* (1998), edited by Robert Mezey.

- Hardy is always thought of as a pessimistic writer, and his poem "To an Unborn Pauper Child" gives plenty of evidence to support such a notion. The speaker addresses a child still in the womb and urges it not to come into the world because the life that awaits it is so cruel. It is better not to be born, the speaker says. But the second part of the poem suggests a more nuanced view. The speaker, in spite of his pessimism about life, nonetheless fervently wishes the child happiness and joy, even though he knows it flies in the face of reason to do so. The poem expresses Hardy's philosophy in a nutshell. This poem can also be found in Hardy's *Selected Poems*, edited by Mezey.

- *Titanic: The Long Night*, by Diane Hoh (1998), is a novel about the *Titanic* disaster written for young readers. The novel follows the stories of five teenagers who are onboard the *Titanic* on that fateful voyage. Two are traveling first class, and when they meet they fall in love. The other three teenagers are traveling third class, all hoping to find a promising future in the United States. Romance emerges for them, too.

- *Titanic: Triumph and Tragedy* (1995), by John P. Eaton and Charles A. Haas, was first published in 1986 and then revised to add material, including color photographs, of the wreckage of the *Titanic*, which the authors personally explored. This comprehensive book examines the history of the *Titanic* from its origins to its demise. Many readers find it the best book yet written about the ship.

- "Wreck of the Hesperus" is a poem by the nineteenth-century American poet Henry Wadsworth Longfellow. It is a grim ballad about the captain of a schooner who takes his young daughter with him on a voyage, just for company. He fears that a hurricane may be on the way, and when it arrives he straps his daughter to the mast to keep her safe. But the strategy fails, and they both die. The ballad can be found in *Henry Wadsworth Longfellow: Poems and Other Writings* (2000), edited by J. D. McClatchy.

- "Shipwreck" is a poem by Emily Dickinson that describes a shipwreck in a way that expresses compassion for those who die as well as the impersonal nature of the ocean that swallows them. The poem can be found in *The Complete Poems of Emily Dickinson* (1976), edited by Thomas H. Johnson.

- *Hurricane Dancers: The First Caribbean Pirate Shipwreck* (2011), by Cuban American author Margarita Engle, is a historical novel in verse for young-adult readers, set in the Caribbean in the early sixteenth century. The young boy Quebrado is taken from his home on present-day Cuba and is enslaved on a pirate ship. When a hurricane destroys the ship, Quebrado manages to escape to dry land, where his life changes for the better.

---

notes that "the cold eye of such poems [by Hardy] became exemplary for modernists such as Auden," who valued (in Auden's own words) the "hawk's vision" they showed, the ability to observe life "from a very great height." Ramazani's own comment that follows, in the context of whether this poem might be considered an elegy, is very apt:

"

EVEN IN THE FACE OF SUCH AN ENORMOUS
TRAGEDY, THE POET IS IN NO MOOD TO ASSUAGE
OR EVEN ACKNOWLEDGE HUMAN GRIEF, LET
ALONE OFFER PIOUS THOUGHTS ABOUT
A BENEVOLENT GOD CALLING HIS PEOPLE HOME."

The dispassionate stare of the Immanent Will
would seem to be anathema to elegy; the genre
had always depended on involvement, its
pathos being born of resistance to death. To
look on loss from a great height and see it as
part of a fated pattern is to reduce mournful
feelings to ironic twinges.

It is this "dispassionate stare," suggestive of
a lack of sympathy for innocent victims of a
recent tragedy, that makes "The Convergence
of the Twain" an unusually stern poem. The
grim notion of an indifferent fate is also linked
to the pattern of imagery, in which the ship and
the iceberg are presented as female and male,
respectively, and their predestined meeting as a
kind of sexual encounter, a marriage for which
they have been preparing, if unconsciously, for
some time. They come together like two halves
of one reality; each is incomplete without the
other, and their fulfillment comes at that instant
in which they touch for the first and only time.
This pattern of imagery gives the poem a grotesque, eerie quality, and Ramazani even finds in it
a kind of "grim humor."

What prompted Hardy to write such an
apparently hard-hearted poem? In his book
*The Poetry of Thomas Hardy: A Handbook and
Commentary*, J. O. Bailey presents an interesting
piece of detective work. He points out that
Hardy would likely have read a news story that
appeared in the *Dorset County Chronicle* on
April 18, 1912, just three days after the disaster.
The story emphasized the great luxury for which
the *Titanic* was renowned, and the wealth of
many of the passengers. The article also reported
a question that one of the surviving passengers,
Mrs. Albert Caldwell, asked of a deckhand
when she boarded the ship: "Is this ship really
unsinkable?" The deckhand replied, "Yes, lady,
God himself could not sink this ship." It is this

comment, Bailey suggests, that stimulated Hardy
to come up with a poem about the *Titanic* in which
the philosophical position that characterizes the
speaker represents, in Bailey's words, "something
like a rebuke to the deck-hand's arrogant quip."
The unfathomable yet powerful Will that the
poem describes then becomes, in Bailey's view,
"like the Greek concept of Fate that rebukes
hubris," implying that "God, working in ways hidden from human sight, will not be mocked."
Hardy might have quibbled with the word
"God" in this context, since he chose another
term, but it does seem from the poem that this
all-powerful Will is not merely the driving force
behind a blind process but has a direct, godlike
purpose and intent. It dictates by sudden decree
(in the last stanza) the exact moment of the fatal
collision, as if man does indeed need to be taught a
lesson about where real power actually lies. Seen
in this light, the poem takes on a traditional cast.
The gods in any religious tradition do not usually
take kindly to being disobeyed or otherwise challenged. They represent forces that humanity
would be well advised to work with rather than
against. Readers may recall that in Greek mythology, Poseidon, the god of the sea (whom the
Romans called Neptune), would regularly punish
those mortals who offended him, including Odysseus, which is why it took Odysseus so many years
to return home after the Trojan War.

However, it must also be noted that Hardy
did not believe that the universe was governed
either by gods or a supreme God. Although he
did famously write at the end of his novel *Tess
of the d'Urbervilles* (1891), after the young
heroine is hanged, that "the President of the
Immortals... had ended his sport with Tess,"
he later clarified that he meant the phrase alle-
gorically, as a personification of all the impersonal forces that were arrayed against her. Tess
falls victim to the implacable Will just as the
victims on the *Titanic* do in "The Convergence
of the Twain." In Hardy's work as a whole,
including his novels, the human characters work
out their tragic destinies in a universe that is
indifferent to whether they succeed or fail, live
or die. There is no loving God, and certainly no
blissful afterlife awaits even the pious believer. It
is a grim picture of life, but Hardy's position was
perhaps not as pessimistic as it might first appear.
He was in fact a meliorist, believing that although
human beings are placed by some unknowable
Fate in conditions of life that lay them open to
suffering and misery, they nonetheless possess

qualities such as kindness and compassion that can help to ease the burden placed upon them. According to this view, humans can improve their lot through their own efforts. Nevertheless, the path will always be a difficult one, and in Hardy's world, as "The Convergence of the Twain" demonstrates, people would do well to remember that there are always forces at work in the universe that will strike down complacency and pride at the most unexpected times.

Source: Bryan Aubrey, Critical Essay on "The Convergence of the Twain," in *Poetry for Students*, Gale, Cengage Learning, 2013.

J. Joseph Edgette

In the following excerpt, Edgette examines "The Convergence of the Twain" in the context of poetry and song lyrics about the sinking of the Titanic.

As of 15 April 2006, only two survivors, both women, from the *Titanic* remained alive. The other 2200-plus passengers died during that terrible maritime disaster or later, after having survived the ordeal. Other than the three dedicated burial plots in Halifax, Nova Scotia, the deceased victims and survivors were interred, entombed, or cremated in several countries crossing vast geographical boundaries. Many of the markers and crypt covers do mention the connection between the individual and *Titanic*; however, it is the site off the Grand Banks on the ocean floor that has been designated internationally as the official gravesite of the *Titanic* and that of its initial victims (Ballard 210). This essay will examine the literature and several other related publications pertinent to this historic event.

The folklorist looks at "legend" as a type of folktale and defines it as an oral account of an event, a person, or a place that actually existed and can be authenticated through documentation as having been a reality. The story of the *Titanic* and of the events surrounding her fateful maiden voyage has become a well-known and circulated legend of the sea. On 15 April 1912, exactly two hours and forty minutes following its collision with an iceberg, the RMS *Titanic* foundered off the Grand Banks in the icy waters of the north Atlantic not far from Newfoundland (Lord 136). Having broken into two pieces at first, she slowly sank to a depth of approximately two-and-a-half miles beneath the water's surface, where three pieces of her hull rest today. The ninety-fourth anniversary on 15 April 2006 of the worst event in the annals of twentieth-century maritime history stirred memories and elicited lore about the tragedy that resulted in the loss of more than 1500 lives. This catastrophe has been perhaps the most chronicled, discussed, and argued about in history. Not only did it remain the focus of news media through newspapers and magazines for nearly two months worldwide, but it also became the genesis of literature and popular culture as well. The impetus of such universal attention was probably the fact that it was *Titanic*'s maiden voyage and that its passenger manifest included some of the wealthiest and most socially elite people of that time. Known by accolades such as: "World's Greatest Ship," "Ship of Dreams," "Wonder Ship," "Queen of the Ocean," "Millionaires' Express," and for the irreverent, "The Ship That God Could Not Sink," her gargantuan size and her grandiose and luxurious accommodations were fitting for those aboard. First class cabins and suites were rivaled by no others provided by competitive shipping lines, second class cabins were also very impressive by their design and appointments, and those among the third class or steerage bookings were not uncomfortable by any means.

Although interest in the *Titanic* has never really waned, periodically a renewed interest or booster shot, if you will, is administered that revitalizes the interest for the next generation. The release of James Cameron's film version of *Titanic* in 1997 is a good illustration of this kind of renewal. Following its box office success and the scheduling of several national exhibits by Titanic, Inc., the research component emerging from Robert Ballard's discovery a little more than a decade earlier, the general public was not only mesmerized by the film but also began to seek as much information as possible to satisfy both an intellectual and popular curiosity. Fast approaching is *Titanic*'s centennial, which will once more cause a resurgence of strong popular interest. That event will surely generate an unequaled popular obsession for the terrible tragedy of 1912. By then, there will most likely be no survivors remaining, and the physical remnants of the ship itself will be no more.

As long as the printed word exists, written narratives and accounts together with scholarly investigations and treatises will continue to keep the story of the RMS *Titanic* from fading and eventually disappearing into the abyss of failing human memory. To prevent such an unfortunate failure of memory, it remains of paramount importance to preserve that which must be kept cogent as a link to the past. We cannot plan for the future unless we connect to our past. The only way to preserve the past is to periodically review it, refresh it, and make it available to others for the future.

SONG LYRICS AND POETRY

. . . The music—both tunes and lyrics—inspired by *Titanic* is often poignant. For this reason music is included in this article. Sheet music produced during the nineteenth and twentieth centuries was another reflection of strong interest in certain events at the time. We know through the study of ethnomusicology that prior to the arrival of radio, sheet music and parlor singing were major and popular forms of entertainment in the home (Bid 139). It was not at all uncommon to see songs, ballads, and laments written on the occasion of a major disaster. The songwriters produced the music and lyrics, and the publishers printed the music for immediate sale to the anxiously waiting consumer.

Housed in the Library of Congress are two boxes full of sheet music written specifically about *Titanic*. Most of it was published from 1912 to 1914, including titles like "The Loss of the *Titanic*," "The Sinking of the *Titanic*," "The Wreck of the *Titanic*," and other variations on the sinking theme. Often, the lyrics captured the emotion and overall sense of the catastrophe. In effect, the musical compositions reflected cultural expressions of grief over the *Titanic* event. For example, E. V. St. Clair wrote the lyrics and composed the music for "The Ship That Will Never Return" shortly after the disaster in 1912:

Mothers they sobbed in prayer
As they parted from loved ones there
Husbands and sons, brave hearted ones,
On the ship that will never return.

An example of the lament/ballad type is "My Sweetheart Went Down with the Ship," which tells of a betrothed woman's loss of her fiancé:

My sweetheart went down with the ship
Down to an ocean grave,
One of the heroes who gave his life,
The women and children to save
Gone but not forgotten,
As the big ship rolled and dipped;
He went to sleep in the mighty deep,
My sweetheart went down with the ship.
My ship. (Lewis and Klickman)

Lyrics such as these memorialize the victims as having been real people with real ties. The loss of each was felt directly by loved ones; the loss of each touched on the sympathy of many. Like the calamity of September 11, 2001, in Manhattan, New York, the loss of those killed was felt by scores of relatives, friends, acquaintances, and neighbors alike. It has often been observed that a profit can be made on tragedy. Such was the case when it came to music. However, in the case of the *Titanic* loss, the music very often bore a disclaimer at the top stating all proceeds would go toward a relief effort or memorial fund.

On the English side of the Atlantic, Paul Pelham and Lawrence Wright wrote and composed "Be British!" to praise the courage and loyalty of the British crew of the *Titanic*. Its chorus went as follows:

Be British! was the cry as the ship went down,
Every man steady at his post,
Captain and crew, when they knew the worst:
Saving the women and children first,
Be British! is the cry to everyone,
And though fate has proved unkind,
Show that you are willing, with a penny or a shilling,
For those they've left behind.

This song lyric suggests the strong stoicism of the British, the maintaining of a stiff-upper-lip attitude and the commitment to loyalty, bravery, and a strong sense of duty in the path of pending danger or doom.

Though many different lyricists wrote moving words about the tragedy, the music for dozens was composed by M. C. Hanford. Two of the more unusual musical selections include "The Sinking of the *Titanic* March" by Lulu Wells and "A Pleasure Ride to Death Symphony: Descriptive of the *Titanic* Disaster" by Carl Scheben. To take advantage of the increasingly popular player devices, sheet music evolved to the next level: piano rolls, then Edison cylinders, large brass disks, and early phonograph disks. The music thus became accessible to an even greater public audience. In contemporary times, sheet music and other formats saw a surge in sales by those wanting to secure the music from the 1997 film. Twenty years ago, Harry Chapin wrote and produced a highly successful album, *Dance Band on the "Titanic,"* inspired by the original dance band that perished that fateful night:

> "There's no way this could happen,"
> I could hear the old Captain curse.
> He ordered lifeboats away; that's when I heard the Chaplain say,
> "Women and children and chaplains first."
> Well, they soon used up all of the lifeboats.
> But there were a lot of us left on board.
> I heard the drummer sayin, "Boys, just keep playin,
> Now we're doin' this gig for the Lord."
> I heard the dance band on the *Titanic*
> Sing Nearer, my God, to Thee. . . .

Chapin recounts the role of the orchestra who voluntarily remained at their stations as the great ship sank. The sixty-four lines of lyrics tell the whole story of their loyalty and bravery that night.

As was the case with songs, musical memorial tributes, and musical funerary dirges, the number of poems produced in the period immediately following the disaster was not exceptionally large; however, it is interesting to note that more poems associated with the *Titanic* were written following the release of Cameron's film version in 1997. The first poem written about *Titanic* was by one of the very men who built her. Built in Belfast, Ireland, at Harland and Wolff Shipyard, the largest ship in the world was the pride of the thousands of workers who had a hand in her construction. After the news filtered through that the *Titanic* had sunk as the result of colliding with an iceberg, a memorial poem was written by an unnamed member of the shipbuilding staff that built *Titanic* shortly after her foundering. Its title, "The Big Boat 4-0-1," referred to the shipyard's official build number during construction (McGookin 2). The date of the poem's public reading was 16 April 1912. The poem provides details about the shipyard's workers who perished, naming the eight comrades known as the *Titanic* Guarantee Group. Most importantly, the poem conveys the grief, pain, and feelings for the men who worked shoulder-to-shoulder as the ship was built. The only known copy of the poem, which is owned by Harland and Wolff, was placed on display in Belfast's City Hall to commemorate the ninety-second anniversary of the sinking in 2004. Verse number four illustrates the love felt for the Harland and Wolff co-workers.

> He sends his ice like morsels—Who
> before it can stand?
> For surely The *Titanic*
> Had the cream of all the land
> We'll talk of our dear workmates
> Not what the great ship cost
> Tom Andrews, our dear Manager
> Rob Knight and Artie Ford

The eight-stanza memorial poem is a moving tribute to those skilled and loyal workers who fulfilled the dream. In the Belfast Shipyard they had a saying: "The sinking of the *Titanic* was a disaster—the building of the great ship was not!" (McGookin 2). It is a saying that is still used today. After a prestigious 151-year history, Harland and Wolff Shipyard closed their gates in May 2004 (*Commutator* 28:167, 134).

After the sinking there followed a sampling of poems that spanned the entire emotional spectrum, from the mourning and memorialization of the victims and thanksgiving for the survivors, to the power of icebergs, might of the sea, action of heroes, power of God, love of man, the ship itself, and reactions of the crew. Among the more notable poems was "Master and Man" by Ben Hecht, which appeared on the front page of the 17 April 1912 *Chicago Journal* newspaper. It presented a scornful *Titanic* disaster poem that emphasized the horror of the disaster just as the news was breaking (Nitschke). Some authorities claim that Hecht's title was a reference to Tolstoy's parable "Master and Man." The *Titanic* version smacked of anti-Capitalistic rhetoric, standard fare for the mainstream press of 1912. The opening and closing lines from the poem will provide a good glimpse at the message:

> The Captain stood where a
> Captain should
> For the Law of the Sea is grim,
> The Owner romped while the ship was
> Swamped
> And no law bothered him . . .
>
> He earned his seaman's pay
> To hold your place in the ghastly face of
> Death on the Sea at Night
> Is a seaman's job.
> But to flee with the mob
> Is an Owner's Right. (Hecht, 1–5, 12–16)

Published in 1912 in the aftermath of the *Titanic*, Thomas Hardy's "Convergence of the Twain" is one of the most well-known *Titanic* poems and is often reprinted in cultural studies of *Titanic* (Nitschke 288). To provide a sense of the aftermath of the foundering, the following excerpt is intended to reveal Hardy's moving and detailed description:

> Steel Chambers, late the pyres
> Of her salmandrine fires,
> Cold currents thrid, and turn to rhythmic tidal lyres.
>
> Over the mirrors meant
> To glass the opulent
> The sea-worm crawls—grotesque, slimed, dumb, indifferent.
>
> Jewels in joy designed
> To ravish the sensuous mind
> Lie Lightless, all their sparkles bleared
>   and black and
> blind. (4–12)

Here we see the power of the sea that has reduced the "Ship of Dreams," the most luxurious ship ever built, to a broken, tattered, and lifeless wreck two-and-a-half miles below the surface of a cold ocean together with the 1500-plus passengers who share her watery grave.

Joyce Kilmer, best known for his "Trees," also wrote on more difficult and worldly themes. Written for Alden March, a friend who perished aboard the *Lusitania*, "The White Ships and the Red" references *Titanic*:

> White as the ice that clove her
> That unforgotten Day,
> Among her pallid sisters
> The grim *Titanic* lay.
> And through the leagues above her
> She looked aghast and said:
> "What is this living ship that comes
> Where every ship is dead?"

Another example was published in 1929 in a collected works volume by British poet Ronald Campbell MacFie. "The *Titanic* (An Ode of Immortality)" was originally published as a thirty-page, stand-alone book in 1912 shortly after the sinking (Nitschke 31). It skillfully blends the historical, romantic, and mundane in one of the more florid presentations of *Titanic*'s final hours. Other significant examples of the poetry generated by the *Titanic* tragedy can be found in Steven Biel's *Down With the Old Canoe: A Cultural History of the Titanic Disaster* published in 1996 by Norton. Throughout this informative and revealing volume, Biel has meticulously sprinkled relevant and meaningful poetic excerpts.

It is interesting to note the inability of some to differentiate between fact and fiction especially when considering matters pertaining to *Titanic*. When visiting the burial plot for the victims at Fairview Lawn Cemetery in Halifax, Nova Scotia,

THE *TITANIC* DISASTER IS TONED BY HARDY'S FAVORITE VOICE, IRONY."

it is always surprising to see the number of grave goods left at the grave of J. Dawson. Yearbook photos, love notes, and poetry abound. These visitors, who probably mean well, do not realize that this "J. Dawson" was Joseph, not Jack of DiCaprio fame (Beed 101). The poems left on Dawson's grave tend to be verses that reflect the love-struck ramblings of an adoring movie fan. . . .

Source: J. Joseph Edgette, "*RMS Titanic*: Memorialized in Popular Literature and Culture," in *Studies in the Literary Imagination*, Vol. 39, No. 1, Spring 2006, pp. 119–43.

Louise Dauner

In the following excerpt, Dauner discusses Hardy's poetry, emphasizing the poet's capacity for lyrical expression of universal emotions.

Five minutes before he died, Thomas Hardy posed his last question to the universe. "What is this?" He had been asking it for most of his 88 years. It epitomizes his lifelong intellectual and spiritual efforts to understand "Life with the sad seared face." The question, with its many variations, like a revolving mirror trained on the human predicament, is treated in his many prose works (14 novels, numerous short stories, essays, and sketches), in his over 800 short lyrics, and in the massive three-part verse drama, *The Dynasts*. The "answers" that Hardy worked out did not make him happy. Indeed, his naturalism, with its bleak philosophy, exposed him to negative, often harsh criticism until nearly the end of his life.

Nevertheless, his death, on January 12, 1928, was an international news event. British literature, said the *London Times*, had been deprived of its "most eminent figure"—a sentiment echoed worldwide. The burial in Westminster Abbey of the ashes of the country boy from the poor county of Dorset was a national rite. The Abbey was crowded with the famous in politics, the arts, education, and society, while crowds waited in pouring rain to file past the open grave in Poet's Corner. He was the first novelist to be buried there since Dickens, in 1870, and the first poet since Tennyson, in 1892. Leading the list of the distinguished participants were the Heads of Magdalene and Queen's Colleges, of Cambridge and Oxford, of which Hardy was an Honorary Fellow, and the pallbearers included Stanley Baldwin, the Prime Minister, Ramsay MacDonald, leader of the Opposition, and six of the most eminent men of letters of the day. Simultaneously, in a "divided funeral," in Stinsford Churchyard, at Hunsford, where Hardy's grandparents, parents, and first wife, Emma, were buried, Hardy's heart was returned to his native earth.

For by then, though he was one of the most controversial writers of his time, this gentle, soft-voiced, self-effacing little man was the acknowledged master of the English novel in his age. He had also become an astounding poet. Born in 1840, he is the third Victorian poet with Browning and Tennyson. And now, in comparison, he seems more comprehensive, more dynamic, technically more original and ingenious, and philosophically more uncompromising.

Hardy's poetry suggests an eclectic landscape, with several varieties of "plants" growing out of differing kinds of soil. First, there was his rural heritage, his detailed knowledge of the flora and fauna of the countryside, its dialect and rustic characters. That gave him not only an authentic voice, but such a keen knowledge of nature that, for example, he was able to identify by their calls not only many species of birds but also their characteristic environs. Then, exceptionally sensitive to music, both instrumental and vocal, he early became an amateur violinist, often accompanying his stone-mason father, Thomas, also a violinist, as a second fiddler at weddings, dances, and other rural occasions. That gave him a sense of rhythm and meter, in poetry. From the age of fifteen, and for a number of years thereafter, he studied and practiced architecture, repairing Gothic churches, an interest he maintained during his life. That gave him a sense of design and structure. At the same time, he was sketching and painting in watercolor. That made him aware of visual patterns and tone color. Meanwhile, financially unable to attend Cambridge, a dream he held for many years, he educated himself, reading in the Greek and Roman classics, English and French literature, and philosophy. Moving to London in 1861, he had access to great paintings, music, and the theater. During these years, he often read in his room from six o'clock in the evening until midnight. In a touching gesture, a few hours after his death the scarlet robe of his

honorary D. Litt. from Cambridge (1913) was fitted over his nightshirt. His favorite Spirit of Irony, of which he was the most eloquent voice of his age, must have smiled.

...I select our final poem not because its subject has captivated the public for 86 years—in the last several years almost to the point of popular hysteria—but because this is an extra-ordinary, even an amazing poem. Hardy titled it, "The Convergence of the Twain," and it was written within two weeks of the catastrophe. It was "made" for him, in its subject, theme, instances of coincidence and irony, and essential tragedy. I refer, of course, to the sinking of the *Titanic*, on April 14, 1912.

I

    In a solitude of the sea
    Deep from human vanity,
And the Pride of Life that planned her,
stilly couches she.

II

    Steel chambers, late the pyres
    Of her salamandrine fires,
Cold currents thrid, and turn to rhythmic
tidal lyres.

III

    Over the mirrors meant
    To glass the opulent
The sea-worm crawls—grotesque, slimed,
dumb, indifferent.

IV

    Jewels in joy designed
    To ravish the sensuous mind
Lie lightless, all their sparkles bleared and
black and blind.

V

    Dim moon-eyed fishes near
    Gaze at the gilded gear
And query: "What does this vain gloriousness down here?"...

VI

    Well: while was fashioning
    This creature of cleaving wing,
The Immanent Will that stirs and urges
everything

VII

    Prepared a sinister mate
    For her—so gaily great—
A Shape of Ice, for the time far and dissociate.

VIII

And as the smart ship grew
In stature, grace, and hue,
In shadowy silent distance grew the Ice-
berg too.

IX

Alien they seemed to be:
No mortal eye could see
The intimate welding of their later history,

X

Or sign that they were bent
By paths coincident
On being anon twin halves of one august
event,

XI

Till the Spinner of the Years
Said "Now!" And each one hears,
And consummation comes, and jars two
hemispheres.

This is an "occasional" poem, one written for a special situation or occasion. Hardy is especially effective with this type of poem, another memorable one being "And There Was a Great Calm," written shortly after the end of World War I, and commemorating Armistice Day, November 11, 1918.

The *Titanic* disaster is toned by Hardy's favorite voice, Irony. The story is one of *hubris,* and Hardy saw in it the spirit of classical tragedy. Historically, this disaster came to symbolize the end of an era—when Victorian smugness and sense of certainty gave way to its opposite, a loss of certainty and confidence which has colored life ever since.

The poem is divided into eleven three-line stanzas, numbered in Roman numerals, suggesting formality and care. Stanzas one through five, and six through ten divide the poem neatly into two parts, with the final stanza acting as a kind of "summary," and stating the critical moment of the action.

The first stanza is itself extraordinary. In twenty words and three lines we are given the setting, the theme, and the situation. In "solitude," 12,460 feet deep in the North Atlantic, far removed from human vanity and pride, "stilly couches she." The inverted syntax puts the (female) subject of the poem and of the long sentence at the end, now calm, and as though she is resting. Contrasting the elegance of the ship and its passengers, "the opulent" with the dark subterranean depths, we meet again this theme of "vain gloriousness." (We remember that this ship was designated "unsinkable.")

In the second five stanzas we begin to sense a growing tension. Thousands of miles away, "a sinister mate for her," "so gaily great," a "Shape of Ice" is slowly developing:

And as the smart ship grew
In stature, grace, and hue,
In shadowy silent distance grew the Ice-
berg too.

Nothing, it would seem, could have been farther apart than these two *dramatis personae*.

Or sign that they were bent
By paths coincident
On being anon twin halves of one august
event.

Here again is Hardy's law of coincidence. And then the climax:

Till the Spinner of the Years
Said "Now!" And each one hears,
And consummation comes, and jars two
hemispheres.

The imagery of the poem, the personification of the ship and the iceberg, She, feminine, "a creature of cleaving wing" half-bird and half-ship and the Shape, presumably masculine, but more effective for not being specifically described, are brought together for the main metaphor of the poem, a "consummation"—a kind of unholy marriage, an "intimate welding." And we know that never again will this ship and this iceberg be sundered.

A marked use of alliteration in the poem can be discerned, for example, in stanza IV:

Jewels in joy designed
To ravish the sensuous mind
Lie lightless, all their sparkles bleared and
black and blind.

The metrical pattern is also interesting: basically iambic, and the accent on the last line falls heavily on "bleared" and "black" and "blind." The first two lines of each stanza are in trimeter, the last line being in hexameter. Twice three is six. It is easy to feel that each of the two short lines suggests one of the actors in this drama, and the last line, the coming together of the two. Also, if you look at the visual pattern of any stanza in the original publication, you see that the lines form an outline of a ship. Here again, Hardy's architectural sense seems to be working.

There is a significant shift in the tone of the poem, from the formal quality of the first half to the more relaxed conversational tone introduced by "Well." Then follows an answer to the question, "What does this vain gloriousness down here?" We note also that the first five stanzas—the first half—are all in the present tense. The next five shift to the past tense, which continues until the "Now!" of the last verse when, at the moment of the "consummation," the present tense comes, making the climax immediate and effective.

The poem is masterly, and a fitting conclusion to our sample consideration of Hardy's poetry. As analyses continue, we will increasingly find Hardy to be the poet he always was, and as he wished to be known.

Hardy is not Shakespeare or Milton or Wordsworth or Yeats, though he may have affinities with each. And in the massive corpus of his poetry there is some inevitable unevenness. Sometimes the polemic of a poem weighs too heavily on the "poetry." Sometimes the technical ingenuity becomes the major focus.

Nevertheless, today Hardy looms like a modern Colossus, bestriding the pages of English poetry, one foot firmly on the nineteenth century, the other on the shores of the twentieth, while beneath, the swirling waters of poetic fashions come and go. As Ezra Pound said of T. S. Eliot, "Read him!" It is a fitting epigraph.

Source: Louise Dauner, "Thomas Hardy, Yet and Again," in *Modern Age*, Vol. 42, No. 4, Fall 2000, pp. 358–71.

SOURCES

Allen, Peter, "'*Titanic* Theme Played in Onboard Restaurant as Doomed Cruise Ship Started to Keel Over,' Claim Swiss Brothers," in *Mail Online*, January 18, 2012, http://www.dailymail.co.uk/news/article-2088361/Costa-Concordia-Titanic-theme-tune-played-onboard-cruise-ship-started-sink.html (accessed January 25, 2012).

Bailey, J. O., *The Poetry of Thomas Hardy: A Handbook and Commentary*, University of North Carolina Press, 1970, pp. 265–66.

Ballard, Robert D., *The Discovery of the Titanic*, Madison Publishing, 1987, p. 10.

Buckler, William, *The Poetry of Thomas Hardy: A Study in Art and Ideas*, New York University Press, 1983, p. 237.

Carpenter, Richard C., *Thomas Hardy*, Twayne Publishers, 1964, pp. 172–73.

Collis, Roger, "Trans-Atlantic Voyages by Cruise Ship or Freighter," in *New York Times*, June 27, 2007, http://intransit.blogs.nytimes.com/2007/06/29/trans-atlantic-voyages-by-cruise-ship-or-freighter/ (accessed January 25, 2012).

Davie, Donald, *Thomas Hardy and British Poetry*, Routledge & Kegan Paul, 1973, p. 17.

Hardy, Thomas, "The Convergence of the Twain," in *Selected Shorter Poems of Thomas Hardy*, edited by John Wain, Macmillan, 1969, pp. 45–46.

———, *Tess of the d'Urbervilles*, edited by Juliet Grindel and Simono Catrell, Oxford University Press, 1988, p. 384.

Hynes, Samuel, *The Pattern of Hardy's Poetry*, University of North Carolina Press, 1961, pp. 45, 47.

Lord, Walter, *A Night to Remember*, Holt, Rinehart and Winston, 1955, pp. 14, 170.

"Lost Liners: *Lusitania*," PBS website, http://www.pbs.org/lostliners/lusitania.html (accessed January 28, 2012).

Murphy, Gavin, "Swallowed in 14 Minutes," in *Encyclopedia Titanica*, June 20, 2001, http://www.encyclopedia-titanica.org/empress-of-ireland.html (accessed January 28, 2012).

Ramazani, Jahan, *Poetry of Mourning: The Modern Elegy from Hardy to Heaney*, University of Chicago Press, 1994, p. 33.

FURTHER READING

Dauner, Louise, "Thomas Hardy, Yet and Again," in *Modern Age*, Vol. 42, No. 4, Fall 2000, pp. 358–71.
  This analysis of six Hardy poems, including "The Convergence of the Twain," examines the poet's themes and his poetic techniques.

Graves, Roy Neil, "Hardy's 'The Convergence of the Twain'," in *Explicator*, Vol. 53, No. 2, Winter 1995, pp. 96–99.
  This is a close reading of the poem in terms of its imagery, tone, and theme.

Kramer, Dale, ed., *The Cambridge Companion to Thomas Hardy*, Cambridge University Press, 1999.
  This collection of twelve essays provides a comprehensive overview of Hardy's work, examining among other things his life, aesthetics, and philosophical ideas. The book includes a chronology and a list of further reading.

Tomalin, Claire, *Thomas Hardy*, Penguin, 2007.
  This is a critically acclaimed biography of Hardy that also includes succinct interpretations of his work, with as much emphasis on the poetry as on the novels. Tomalin gives a sensitive account of Hardy's long first marriage, which began well but later was a cause of bitterness.

SUGGESTED SEARCH TERMS

Thomas Hardy

"The Convergence of the Twain"

Titanic

meliorist

maritime disasters

pessimism

predestination

sin AND pride

A Dream within a Dream

EDGAR ALLAN POE

1849

As a poet and short-story writer, Edgar Allan Poe confronted a number of dark themes, including death, despair, grief, and madness. In the poem "A Dream within a Dream," published late in Poe's life, he questions the nature of reality, wondering whether everything that may be perceived is actually nothing more than a dream. The speaker in the poem, after bidding farewell to a loved one, comments on the loss of hope and his intense feeling of being disconnected from reality. As the poem progresses, the speaker uses language that repeatedly underscores his sense of grief and despair at the inevitable passage of time. The poem closes with the speaker repeating the sentiment of the preceding stanza, asking if the illusion, the dream of life, is really all that exists.

"A Dream within a Dream" was originally published in 1849 in the Boston newspaper *Flag of Our Union*. Two earlier versions of the poem were published, the first in 1827, in the newspaper *Yankee*, under the title "Imitation." A later revision was published in the same paper two years later, under the title "To ———"; the addressee is not identified. The poem in its much altered, final version was published first in *Flag of Our Union* and again in *The Works of the Late Edgar Allan Poe* in 1850. The poem is also found in the 1984 collection *Edgar Allan Poe: Poetry and Tales*.

Edgar Allan Poe (The Library of Congress)

AUTHOR BIOGRAPHY

Poe was born on January 19, 1809, in Boston, Massachusetts, and was orphaned not long after. Poe's father, David Poe, was an actor who abandoned the family in 1810 and is believed to have died shortly afterward. Elizabeth Poe, also an actor, died in 1811. The Poe children were separated following their mother's death. Poe's sister, Rosalie, was taken in by foster parents, while Poe's brother, William, was raised by his paternal grandparents. The wealthy John and Frances Allan, of Richmond, Virginia, became Poe's foster parents. Allan was a wealthy tobacco merchant who provided Poe with a private education and trips abroad; Poe and the Allans lived in Scotland from 1815 to 1820.

In 1826, Poe began studies at the University of Virginia. He briefly excelled but was unable to afford his tuition and fees with the income Allan provided him. Poe began gambling to raise money but soon accrued large debts, which Allan refused to help him pay. After a year, Poe withdrew from the university. Upon discovering that his fiancée,

Elmira Royster, became engaged to someone else in his absence, Poe escaped to Boston and enlisted in the US Army. Poe published his first volume of poetry in 1827, the anonymous *Tamerlane and Other Poems*. Following his foster mother's death in 1829, Poe sought a discharge from the army and applied to West Point Academy not long after. He then published a second volume of poetry, *Al Aaraaf, Tamerlane, and Minor Poems*.

With Allan's assistance, Poe was admitted to West Point. But he attended the military academy for just eight months and was court-martialed in 1831. Poe then relocated to Baltimore, where he moved in with his grandmother, aunt, and young cousin Virginia Clemm. During this time, Poe began selling short stories to a number of magazines. Following his grandmother's death, Poe moved his aunt and cousin to Richmond, Virginia, in 1835, where he had secured a position as the editor of the literary journal *Southern Literary Messenger*. The following year, Poe and his cousin, the thirteen-year-old Virginia, were married.

In 1837, after resigning from the *Messenger*, Poe and his family moved to New York and then Philadelphia, where Poe eventually became the editor of *Burton's Gentleman's Magazine* in 1839. During this tenure, Poe continued to write and publish short stories. The journal changed owners and names, becoming *Graham's Magazine*, while Poe retained the editorship. In *Graham's*, Poe published some of his best-known works, including the short story "The Murders in the Rue Morgue" in 1841.

Poe and his wife returned to New York in 1844, where Poe worked as an editor for the *Evening Mirror*. In this paper, the acclaimed poem "The Raven" was published in 1845. Poe became the editor of the *Broadway Journal* in 1845 and later purchased the paper. Following the collapse of this paper, Poe and his wife left New York City in 1846 and lived in a cottage in the country. Virginia's health was steadily declining. After her death from tuberculosis in 1847, Poe began lecturing, in addition to continuing to write short fiction and poetry. In the aftermath of two failed romances, Poe became engaged to the widowed Elmira Royster Shelton, his former fiancée.

In 1849—the year "A Dream within a Dream" was first published—on his way from Richmond to Philadelphia, where he was pursuing an editorial position, Poe stopped in Baltimore. On October 3, he was found in a semiconscious state. He was taken to Washington College

Hospital and died on October 7, 1849. The cause of death remains a mystery, although it has been speculated that he died of a brain tumor or from rabies. His use and possible abuse of alcohol has also been discussed in connection with his death.

POEM TEXT

Take this kiss upon the brow!
And, in parting from you now,
Thus much let me avow—
You are not wrong, who deem
That my days have been a dream;   5
Yet if Hope has flown away
In a night, or in a day,
In a vision, or in none,
Is it therefore the less *gone*?
All that we see or seem   10
Is but a dream within a dream.

I stand amid the roar
Of a surf-tormented shore,
And I hold within my hand
Grains of the golden sand—   15
How few! yet how they creep
Through my fingers to the deep,
While I weep—while I weep!
O God! can I not grasp
Them with a tighter clasp?   20
O God! can I not save
One from the pitiless wave?
Is *all* that we see or seem
But a dream within a dream?

POEM SUMMARY

The text used for this summary is from *Edgar Allan Poe: Poetry and Tales*, Library of America, 1984, p. 97. A version of the poem can be found on the following web page: http://www.poetry foundation.org/poem/237388.

Stanza 1

"A Dream within a Dream" comprises two stanzas. In the first, the speaker appears to be addressing a lover from whom he is departing. He bestows a kiss on her forehead before leaving. In his good-bye, he claims that those who would describe his life as a dream are right to characterize his existence in this fashion. He then wonders about the nature of hope, questioning whether it can continue to exist even after it flies away, during the dark of night, during daylight,

MEDIA ADAPTATIONS

- Poe's "A Dream within a Dream" is available as a downloadable MP3 recording published by Eternal Classic Audio Books in 2011. The selection is from the collection *The Best of Edgar Allan Poe*, also available for download.

in a vision of the future, or in the absence of such a vision. The first stanza concludes with the contention that everything that can be seen, everything that we seem to perceive, is simply a dream embedded within another dream. In this way, Poe, through the poem's speaker, appears to be questioning both the nature of reality and the nature of existence itself. Not only is what one perceives only a dream, but, according to the speaker's assertion, the dreamer himself is also a part of a dream.

Stanza 2

In the second stanza, the speaker describes himself as standing on a shore, buffeted by the surf. Holding a handful of sand, he marvels at how few of the many grains on the beach he can actually hold within his hand. At the same time, he marvels at the way the grains of sand escape his grasp and return to the waves on the beach, waves that without remorse swallow up the fallen grains. The speaker sees the grains of sand slip though his fingers, and he weeps at his inability to hold onto them.

The grains of sand the speaker describes here are used as a metaphor for all that is fleeting in life, including one's existence, one's time on earth. Grains of sand are commonly used poetic images meant to represent time and its passage. The grains of sand in the speaker's hand slip through his fingers, calling to mind the image of sand slipping out of the uppermost chamber in an hourglass. The speaker's tears underscore his lamentation for the inevitable passage of time, the eventuality of death.

As he goes on, the speaker describes his inability to keep even one grain of sand from slipping back into the ocean; here, his sense of futility is emphasized. In desperation, the speaker cries out to God. Poe here draws attention to the speaker's grief and his desire to seek comfort. Yet the speaker's sense of hopelessness is undeniable, and even his faith is depicted as futile. In the final two lines of the poem, the speaker reiterates the closing two lines of the previous stanza, but instead of using a statement, the speaker closes the poem with a question, which highlights the tone of despair and disbelief.

THEMES

Despair

In the first stanza of "A Dream within a Dream," Poe explores the theme of despair and the related idea of loss. In the opening couplet, the speaker kisses a loved one prior to a parting. As the poem progresses, the reader is led, by the speaker's sense of grief and loss, to the conclusion that this parting is a final one. Whether because the person the speaker kisses has died or because the relationship is over, the speaker describes his time spent with the loved one as a dream.

This dreamlike state is contrasted with what the speaker feels now: the absence of hope. Like the loved one, hope has departed. The speaker describes the way hope has fled, and he contemplates the way hope—linked with the departure of the loved one—can disappear at night, or during the day, or in a dream. Sometimes, it simply vanishes. The speaker goes on to wonder whether or not it matters *how* hope has fled, as one feels its absence just as powerfully no matter how it departs.

Poe returns to the notion of the dream in the final couplet of this stanza. The speaker states that everything that one sees, the reality that appears to exist, is not only a dream, but a dream occurring within yet another dream. This statement underscores the speaker's sense of disconnection, isolation, and disorientation. Having parted from his love, perhaps forever, he feels alone, adrift from an understanding of everything, including reality. His sense of despair becomes even more palpable in the second stanza, as he discusses the futility of trying to slow the ebb of time. Unable to hold on to even a moment of time, the speaker weeps. He cries out repeatedly to God in his anguish.

The second stanza concludes as the first did. The notion of life as a dream is repeated, but it is phrased as a question this time. The fact that the speaker initially *states* that everything exists only as a dream within a dream and later *questions* whether this can in fact be true, further emphasizes the speaker's despair. He is unable to succumb to the bleak view he has outlined. He wonders how this can be, how everything can be a dream conjured by an unnamed dreamer. In his failure to outline an alternate view, he concludes the poem in a state of torment.

Time

Poe spends much of the poem's second stanza exploring the notion of time's passage. The language and imagery Poe uses here underscore the extremely negative state of mind of the speaker regarding the passage of time. The roar of the surf is described as deafening, and the surf itself is depicted as torturing the shoreline with its force. As the stanza progresses, the association between the sand on the shore and the notion of time is established. The speaker holds a fistful of sand, which trickles through his fingers to rejoin waves described as merciless in the way they devour the grains of sand. This image calls to mind an hourglass, a perennial symbol of time and, more specifically, its inevitable passage. As the sand falls through the speaker's grasp he weeps, wailing God's name and wondering why he cannot hold the grains more tightly in his fist. He mourns the fact that he cannot even save a single grain of sand, suggesting his sense of futility at not being able to hold on to just one moment of time.

Overwhelmingly, the passage of time, conveyed by the continued fall of sand into the ocean's cruel waves, is discussed in terms that emphasize the speaker's sense of hopelessness and grief. This further strengthens the notion, developed in the first stanza, that the parting described in the opening couplet is a permanent one. The depth of the speaker's grief imparts the sense that the loved one has died and that the speaker's lament over time's passage is related to

TOPICS FOR FURTHER STUDY

- In "A Dream within a Dream," Poe explores the notion that life, seeming to be nothing more than a dream, is therefore meaningless. This corresponds with the philosophical notion of nihilism, which was also a theme in other romantic works of prose and poetry during the nineteenth century. Using research aids such as the chapter "Romanticism and Nihilism: The Demonic Hero," in Michael Allen Gillespie's *Nihilism before Nietzsche*, study the intersection of romanticism and nihilism in nineteenth-century literature. Write a paper in which you describe the way nihilism was treated by romantic writers of this time period. Be sure to cite all of your sources.

- In many of his works, including the poem "A Dream within a Dream," Poe explores feelings of hopelessness, despair, and loss. He uses a variety of metrical forms and a varied rhyme scheme in this poem. Taking Poe as your inspiration, write your own poem in which you explore feelings of grief, sadness, loss, or despair. Attempt to employ a basic structure that includes a rhyme scheme. Consider incorporating a simple metrical pattern in your lines of verse as well. Lewis Turco's *The Book of Forms: A Handbook of Poetics* or the University of North Carolina Writing Center's "Poetry Explications" (http://writingcenter. unc.edu/resources/handouts-demos/specific-writing-assignments/poetry-explications) may be of assistance in understanding meter (the pattern of stressed and unstressed syllables) and structure. Share your poem with your class through an oral reading.

- Traditional Native American poetry was passed down during the nineteenth century orally, but many works were later written and translated. Many deal with nature, as well as with dreams and dreaming, like Poe's "A Dream within a Dream." Peruse Native American poetry that deals with nature or dreams, such as those poems found in *Native American Songs and Poems: An Anthology*, edited by Brian Swan, or *Earth Always Endures: Native American Poems*, edited by Neil Philip. In what ways do Native Americans in these traditional songs and verses treat the topics of dreams or nature? What imagery is used? Consider as well the tone of the poems you examine. Are the poems mournful, mysterious, or celebratory? Write an essay in which you survey the themes of either nature or dreams in traditional Native American poetry. Narrow your focus by selecting works from a particular Native American culture. Reference specific poems or songs and the cultures from which they emanate. Discuss the form of the works as well as their thematic interests.

- In many ways, "A Dream within a Dream" deals with loss, including the loss of a loved one and the loss of hope. Similarly, the young-adult collection of poetry selected by Naomi Shihab Nye entitled *What Have You Lost?* centers around themes of loss. With a small group, read a selection of poems from Nye's anthology. What types of loss do the poets explore? What types of images are employed in the works you have chosen? Are the poems written in free verse, rhymed verse, or verse that includes rhyme and meter? How do such formal structures, or their absences, contribute to the poems' tone and meaning? Create an online blog that serves as a discussion board for your group. Analyze the poems and share your reactions and responses to the works.

how quickly the speaker's time with his beloved passed. Given that the poem was published two years after the death of Poe's wife, critics such as

Mary Ellen Snodgrass, in the *Encyclopedia of Gothic Literature*, have suggested that the poem refers to the death of his wife, Virginia.

In stanza 1, the couple is parted from each other. *(© Poulsons Photography / Shutterstock.com)*

STYLE

Mixed Meter and Rhyme Scheme

In "A Dream within a Dream," Poe structures his poem into two stanzas in which a variety of metrical forms are employed. In poetry, *meter* is the pattern of accented and unaccented syllables in a line of poetry. The use of such patterns establishes a certain rhythm within the poem. Each grouping of unaccented and accented syllables constitutes a unit, or metrical foot, within a line of poetry, and the number of feet within a line contributes to the poem's rhythm. For example, an unaccented syllable followed by an accented syllable is known as an *iamb*. If there are five iambs in a line of poetry, the line is described as being written in iambic pentameter.

By making use of a variety of metrical patterns in "A Dream within a Dream," Poe creates a rhythm that is perpetually interrupted. At the same time, the variations in meter draw attention to points of emphasis within the poem. Poe's poem incorporates both trimeter (lines with three accented syllables per line) and

tetrameter (lines with four accented syllables per line). Some lines make use of the *trochee*, a metrical foot in which an accented syllable is followed by an unaccented syllable, or a *dactyl*, in which an accented syllable is followed by two unaccented syllables. Others open with an *anapest*, in which two unaccented syllables are followed by an accented syllable. Poe follows these anapestic feet with two iambic feet. Still other lines begin with what is known as a *spondee*, or two accented syllables. The effect of the use of the spondee is jarring; opening a line of poetry with the force of two accented syllables makes the line stand out because it differs from natural speech patterns. Multiple readings of the poem may yield differing interpretations regarding which syllables should be stressed within the poem.

Furthermore, lines that are linked through end-rhyme pattern do not always possess the same metrical structure, further complicating the scansion (or metrical reading) of the poem. The first stanza consists of a rhymed triplet (three lines in which the end words rhyme) followed by four rhymed couplets (two lines in which the end words rhyme). In this stanza, the lines within each couplet or triplet, save for the closing couplet, resemble their mate or mates in terms of metrical structure. However, in the second stanza, Poe varies the patterns further. This stanza opens with two rhymed couplets followed by a triplet and ends with three rhymed couplets. The lines in each of these groupings rarely exhibit the same metrical pattern as the other line or lines within the group. A number of lines both begin and end with stressed syllables, and Poe uses italics to stress syllables that would not have ordinarily been stressed. Rhythmic patterns are interrupted just as quickly as they are established, yet by incorporating rhymed couplets and triplets, Poe creates the illusion of a poem with a more simply structured sense of rhythm. In establishing such a complex structure for the poem, Poe juxtaposes illusion and reality. The control he exhibits over the poem's form is contrasted with the disturbing and incongruous effect of the variations in meter. This complements the poem's tone of confusion and despair.

Language and Imagery

In the first stanza of "A Dream within a Dream," the poet uses little concrete visual imagery. The language of this stanza is largely conceptual, as Poe describes how hope flies away, and reality itself is called into question. Poe wonders if everything, in fact, exists only within the world of dreams. By decoupling his language from concrete imagery, Poe emphasizes the speaker's sense of disorientation brought on by his feeling of hopelessness.

In the second stanza, Poe utilizes the imagery of surf and sand. The speaker is described as standing on the shore while waves rush in. He holds grains of sand that slip through his fingers and rejoin the ocean waves. The emphasis of this stanza is on futility, and this is revealed in the speaker's ineffectual interaction with the world around him and in the imagery Poe uses. No matter how tight the speaker's grasp, the grains of sand still sift through his fingers. As the grains of sand fall into the surf, the speaker describes the waves of the ocean as unforgiving in the way they devour the dropped grains of sand. The speaker weeps and laments the fact that he cannot even save one solitary grain of sand from rejoining the ocean. He calls out in despair to God and wonders once again if

everything that he can see, or that appears to be, is in fact just a dream.

The grains of sand and the ocean waves are the only concrete visual imagery used in the poem. In that the grains of sand call to mind the sand that slips from one chamber of an hourglass into the other, they emphasize in Poe's poem the relentless passage of time. The waves are described as unmerciful in the way they gobble up the sand that falls from the speaker's hand. In this way, the natural world is seen as malevolent and destructive. The waves crash upon the beach, swallow the sand, and draw attention to the speaker's suffering.

HISTORICAL CONTEXT

Mid-Nineteenth-Century American Romanticism

Romanticism was a literary, artistic, and philosophical movement that began in Europe at the close of the eighteenth century and became prominent during the nineteenth century. A movement away from neoclassicism's emphasis on tradition, reason, restraint, and objectivity, romanticism focused on individualism, imagination, and subjectivity, as well as on the beauty and power of the natural world. In mid-nineteenth-century America, the notion of romanticism dovetailed with the burgeoning transcendentalist movement, which centered on an individual's personal experience with the divine through the world of nature. Ralph Waldo Emerson and Henry David Thoreau were transcendentalist authors, and romantics, whose writings focused heavily on man's spiritual experience in nature. William Cullen Bryant is considered one of the first American romantic poets. In his work, Bryant examines the individual's subjective experience in and with nature. In this way, Bryant's poetry exemplifies the American romantic movement in the early to mid-century. As Mary Louise Kete explains in an essay for *The Cambridge Companion to Nineteenth-Century American Poetry*, through the mid-nineteenth century, "Americans continued to value poetry that appealed primarily to feelings and which grounded its authority on the authenticity of the poet's voice."

A number of critics have explored the influence of the British romantic poets, including Lord Byron and Percy Bysshe Shelley, on

COMPARE & CONTRAST

- **1840s:** Poetry written by American writers during this time period is characterized by the influence of romanticism. Romantic poetry features a focus on individual, subjective experience and often explores the natural world or uses nature imagery.

  Today: Twenty-first-century poetry has moved away from romanticism, yet modern free-verse poetry has built upon romantic traditions and conventions in the way it often explores the poet's subjective response to the world.

- **1840s:** The philosophical notion of nihilism is not a widespread mode of thought, but the notion of life's meaninglessness is nevertheless explored by writers such as Poe and by philosophers such as Friedrich Jacobi.

  Today: The idea of nihilism, having been popularized by late-nineteenth-century writers and thinkers, including Ivan Turgenev

  and Friedrich Nietzsche, and later in the twentieth century by Albert Camus and Jean-Paul Sartre, finds its way into twenty-first-century politics, as the concept is used to describe failures to act within political parties or within American culture in general.

- **1840s:** Dreams are a subject of fascination among writers but have not been widely studied in a scientific manner. They form the basis of works of poetry and fiction, and some attempts are made to observe the relationships between sleep, dreaming, and various mental phenomena.

  Today: Twenty-first-century science has exposed the inaccuracies of nineteenth-century and early-twentieth-century dream theories. Although psychoses were once believed to represent the intrusion of the world of dreams into one's waking life, it is now asserted that this connection does not exist.

American romantic poets. Poe's admiration and emulation of Byron is well documented, as Frederick S. Frank and Anthony Magistrale point out in *The Poe Encyclopedia.* Julia Power, in *Shelley in America in the Nineteenth Century: His Relation to American Critical Thought and His Influence,* similarly details Shelley's influence on transcendentalist writers, including Thoreau and Margaret Fuller, as well as on Poe. Power goes on to describe the ways in which Poe was inspired by Shelley's work in both style and poetic theory. Power further demonstrates the influence of British romantic poets such as Byron and William Wordsworth on lesser-known Southern poets, including Edward Coote Pinkney.

Mid-Nineteenth-Century Notions of Dreams and Dreaming

Although it was not until the closing years of the nineteenth century and the early years of the

twentieth century that dreams began to be explored in a systematic, scientific way by psychoanalyst Sigmund Freud, who published his *The Interpretation of Dreams* in German in 1899, the mystery and significance of dreams and dreaming were topics studied by a number of writers. In the early years of the nineteenth century, dreams were regarded as a sleep state, explains Tony James in *Dream, Creativity, and Madness in Nineteenth-Century France.* James traces the development of theories related to dreaming and cites an 1861 French work by Alfred Maury as the most significant precursor to Freud's dream studies. According to James, Maury asserts that sleep and dreaming were associated with hallucinations, mental illness, and various delusions. James notes that in works written in the earlier part of the century, similar associations were made.

Dreams were also the focus of poets and fiction writers and were examined in a variety

In stanza 2, the narrator laments the slipping of grains of sand through his hands. (© johnnychaos / Shutterstock.com)

of ways. As William D. Brewer maintains in *The Mental Anatomies of William Godwin and Mary Shelley*, "A number of Romantic-era writers shared certain beliefs regarding dream phenomena, but there was no 'dream theory' as such that was widely accepted during the period." Brewer identifies British poet Samuel Taylor Coleridge as a "dedicated student of dreams" and finds in Godwin's and Mary Shelley's writings a sustained interest in dreams that builds on the notions of dreams formulated in the eighteenth and early nineteenth centuries. Brewer goes on to discuss the way Charles Darwin's eighteenth-century observations and writings on dreams shaped the perceptions regarding dreams of nineteenth-century writers. In particular, Brewer notes, Darwin comments on both the inconsistency and the vividness of dreams and attempts to correlate the dreamer's posture or position while sleeping with the occurrence of nightmares.

Whereas Darwin's approach to dreams is one rooted in scientific observation, nineteenth-century writers, including Mary Shelley and Poe, characterize dreams in their writings as imaginative and intuitive. As Mary Ellen Snodgrass states

in the *Encyclopedia of Gothic Literature*, dreams were incorporated into the plots of many works of nineteenth-century literature, including narrative poems by Lord Byron and Mary Shelley's *Frankenstein* (1818). Snodgrass studies Poe's continued interest in dreams, beginning with "A Dream" (1827); "Dreams," written the same year and focusing on "mental creations as escapes from reality"; and the haunting lyric "Dream-Land" (1844). In "A Dream within a Dream," Poe continues to explore the dream, this time not as an escape from reality, but perhaps as the *only* reality.

CRITICAL OVERVIEW

During his lifetime, Poe received mixed assessments of his fiction and poetry. He had achieved some critical and popular success by the mid-1840s, as evidenced by his ability to publish his work steadily in a variety of journals. Susan Amper observes in *Critical Insights: The Tales of Edgar Allan Poe* that although modern criticism of Poe "focuses largely on his tales, he was better known as a poet and probably best-known as a magazine editor and critic." Having been omitted from two major poetry anthologies of his day, explains Amper, Poe "complained bitterly." She goes on to note, "It seems that Poe's reputation was high enough that he could reasonably claim unfairness but not so high that editors felt obliged to make more room for him in the first place."

G. R. Thompson notes in an essay on Poe for the *Dictionary of Literary Biography* that Poe was the target of critical attacks. Thompson states, "In January 1846 the *Knickerbocker* [a New York literary journal] viciously attacked not only Poe's poetry and criticism, but also his character." Modern critics, such as Tony Magistrale in the *Student Companion to Edgar Allan Poe*, assess the value of Poe's poetry within the larger framework of his literary career. Magistrale contends, "Poe's poetry is an absolutely critical component to understanding his literary vision." The critic goes on to observe, "In his best poems, Poe's language revolves around vague and indeterminate subjects; surreal vistas are summoned forth through remarkable sound effect and impressive imagery that place the reader in irrational, death-haunted and dreamlike realms."

Poe's later poetry in particular is singled out for praise, by such critics as Thomas Ollive Mabbott, in his introduction to Poe's *Complete Poems.* Mabbot asserts that while Poe sought to use the language of "the ordinary speech of ordinary men" in his later poetry, "What is elaborate is the metrical form; that grew more complex with the years, while Poe's prose tended to be increasingly simple, straightforward, and less ornamented."

In discussing "A Dream within a Dream" in particular, critics focus on the philosophical implications of the work. Frederick I. Carpenter, in *American Literature and the Dream*, maintains that Poe "believed in the world of dream, and in its truth and beauty, more passionately than did either Emerson or Thoreau, but he wholly disbelieved in any possibility of its realization." In *An Introduction to Living Philosophy: A General Introduction to Contemporary Types and Problems*, D. S. Robinson, in examining various types of philosophical idealism, observes that Poe explores the philosophical notion known as solipsism, "the view that the agent or subject doing the thinking and his ideas are the only realities, and that all the outer world is but a dream of the subject." Robinson additionally notes that "for Poe the subject is also a dream." Michael Ferber, in *A Dictionary of Literary Symbols*, stresses, "Poe in part expressed the Romantic view, inherited by psychoanalysis, that dreamers enter a deeper or truer reality than the world of consciousness or reason."

CRITICISM

Catherine Dominic

Dominic is a novelist and a freelance writer and editor. In the following essay, she explores the romantic nihilism Poe exhibits within the poem "A Dream within a Dream."

In "A Dream within a Dream," Edgar Allan Poe conveys an overwhelming sense of despair and sorrow. He first asserts and then questions the notion that everything we see, perceive, and experience is just a dream. Poe's negation of conscious existence, or experiential reality, as evidenced by "A Dream within a Dream," has led him to be described as a romantic nihilist by critics such as Frederick I. Carpenter, in *American Literature and the Dream*. Nihilism, later known as existential nihilism, refers to the philosophical viewpoint that life, or existence, is

> POE'S NIHILISM, EXEMPLIFIED IN 'A DREAM WITHIN A DREAM,' IS TERMED 'ROMANTIC' BECAUSE POE'S FOCUS IS ON THE IMAGINATIVE, SUBJECTIVE SELF AND HIS EXPERIENCE WITHIN A WORLD DEPICTED AS DEVOID OF MEANING."

essentially meaningless. Poe's nihilism, exemplified in "A Dream within a Dream," is termed "romantic" because Poe's focus is on the imaginative, subjective self and his experience within a world depicted as devoid of meaning.

The term *nihilism* came into use in the nineteenth century, when the writer Friedrich Heinrich Jacobi used the word to describe the condition of certain philosophers, particularly contemporaries whose thinking was gaining critical attention, including Immanuel Kant and Friedrich Wilhelm Joseph Schelling. The *Stanford Encyclopedia of Philosophy* explains that according to Jacobi, these philosophers reduced words and concepts to abstraction and in doing so rendered them meaningless. Nihilism increasingly became associated with the notion of life's essential meaninglessness, or alternatively, with the meaninglessness or subjectivity of morality and values. In "A Dream within a Dream," Poe suggests, through the use of metaphor and nature imagery, the nihilistic assertion that life as we perceive it is devoid of meaning.

The poem opens with a couplet depicting a scene of departure, a farewell between the speaker and an unnamed individual. This departure sparks the speaker's journey from his loved one's side and into a state of sustained despair and hopelessness. The third through fifth lines of the poem indicate the bleak direction in which the speaker is headed. He claims that anyone who would characterize his days to this point in his life as a dream would be correct. While the dream the speaker refers to here may possibly be the happy, dreamlike days spent with the person from whom he is now departing, the use of the term *dream* in these lines also foreshadows the darker, more ominous use of the word that occurs repeatedly later in the poem. From the kiss, the good-bye of the first couplet, to the

WHAT DO I READ NEXT?

- Poe's short stories are collected in *Edgar Allan Poe: The Complete Short Story Collection* (2009). His short stories provide students of his poetry a fuller understanding of his work and explore themes such as death, madness, grief, and loss.

- *Edgar Allan Poe's Annotated Poems* (2008), edited and introduced by Andrew Barger, provides a collection of Poe's poetry that includes descriptive annotations elucidating Poe's work and translating foreign words and phrases that Poe incorporated into his verse. Barger's edition further includes poems written to Poe by those with whom he had romantic affairs.

- Margaret Fuller was a contemporary of Poe's and an admirer, like Poe, of British romantic poets. Her essays and poetry explore such transcendentalist themes as nature and spirituality, in addition to feminist and political themes. *The Essential Margaret Fuller* (1992), edited by Jeffrey Steele, contains her most highly regarded essays and poetry.

- In the second half of the nineteenth century, the Spanish American literary movement known as *modernismo*, or modernism, began to take hold as a reaction against the romanticism that had pervaded Spanish American poetry throughout the earlier decades of the nineteenth century. Nicaraguan poet Rubén Darío is said to have initiated the movement. His works are translated by Stanley Appelbaum in *Stories and Poems/ Cuentos y poesías: A Dual-Language Book*, published in 2002.

- Set in Virginia in the 1830s, Ann Rinaldi's 2008 young-adult novel *The Letter Writer* details the history of a time and place familiar to Poe, who lived in Virginia during that decade. Rinaldi's novel captures the trauma and tragedy of slavery and focuses on a famous slave rebellion that occurred in Virginia during this time, the Nat Turner rebellion.

- Robin Mookerjee's 2008 volume *Identity and Society in American Poetry: The American Romantic Tradition* explores nineteenth-century American romanticism and its influence on later literary movements, including modernism and objectivism.

---

somewhat ambiguous description of the speaker's days as a dream, the poem quickly descends toward an absence of concrete imagery and toward the departure first of hope, then of meaning.

In the sixth through ninth lines, the speaker discourses about the nature of hope. Hope is gone, he explains; he describes it as having flown away. The notion of flight is one of the few hints of visual imagery Poe provides in this stanza. The reader can only guess at what this departing hope is linked with. And the reader can only assume that whatever it is the speaker hopes for, it is in some way associated with the person from whom he has just departed. The speaker reveals no other object or subject to whom the notion of hope can refer, or to whom it may be attached.

The speaker then contemplates the ways in which one stops hoping. Hope can desert one in the light of day or in the cover of night. One may perhaps have a vision of what it will be like to experience hopelessness, or one might suddenly find oneself without hope. Through the delineation of all these examples, Poe underscores the void that is left in hope's absence. This void is again emphasized when the speaker wonders, futilely, if it makes any difference *how* hope has vanished. It cannot be any more or less gone once it has evaporated. This absence of hope, suffused with the speaker's sense of grief over the departure that occurs in the first two lines, leads the speaker to state his feeling that everything is, as the title of the poem indicates, a dream within a dream.

In examining the first stanza, the absence of concrete imagery is glaring. Aside from the kiss the speaker places on the brow of an unknown person, the poem is dominated by imprecise language and abstract concepts. Hope flies away. This departure, mirroring and highlighting his own departure from the person he has kissed, is examined in a series of lines whose meaning remains elusive and vague. The closing couplet, concerned with seeing, seeming, and dreaming, is similarly indefinite. Not only does Poe assert that everything exists within a dream—that is, everything is essentially *notreal*—but he goes on to claim that this dream, the one the speaker inhabits, exists within yet *another* dream. Here, the series of abstractions is compounded. Poe then forces the reader to posit an unanswerable question: Who is the dreamer dreaming the dream in which the speaker lives and longs for the hope that has fled?

Poe layers one abstraction upon another, embeds dreams within dreams. In doing so, he reiterates the notion that nothing is real, that life essentially has no meaning. He has, as Jacobi accused his contemporary philosophers of doing, reduced ideas to such abstract states that they have been denuded of meaning. Poe is not suggesting that someone is *literally* dreaming the speaker's life, but rather he is intimating, through the metaphor of the dream, that for a person who lives without hope or exists in a state of grief or in despair, life is devoid of connection, value, and meaning.

As the poem progresses, this sense of grief and despair is intensified, as are the senses of decay, decline, and degeneration associated with romantic nihilism. The speaker metaphorically describes himself as positioned on a shoreline. In describing the way the surf savages the lip of the beach and deafens the speaker, Poe suggests the violent nature of the onslaught of pain the speaker endures. Poe then turns from the broad landscape to the speaker's interaction with it, as the speaker grasps handfuls of sand, only to watch the grains slip through his fingers and into the waves. In four lines, the speaker is shown to be futilely clutching the sand. This image is interrupted by the description of the speaker weeping, a sentiment expressed twice in the same short line. For the next four lines, the speaker again clutches the sand, as he bemoans the fact that he cannot save a single grain from slipping through his fingers.

In the repetition of the images—the speaker clutching the sand, his weeping, and his grasping a handful of sand again, Poe creates a mournful scene. The reader witnesses the speaker on the beach, waves crashing upon the shore, then watches the speaker grasp a fistful of sand, sees him weep, and finds him once again clutching the sand. The stanza captures a glimmer of movement, but not much action—the speaker stands, bends, watches, and weeps—but all is done in vain. He is torn by grief, but his actions are essentially futile. Time, represented by the grains of sand, cannot be held or stopped. The beach will continue to be eroded by the surf, the water will continue to engulf the grains of sand. The speaker is powerless to hold on to something that is *his*—a moment of his own life. He repeats the sentiment expressed in the closing couplet of the previous stanza. This time, however, the speaker phrases his thoughts as a question.

That Poe makes this punctuation change is significant. The fact that the speaker *asks* if everything is just a dream rather than stating that life is only a dream can be read in at least two ways. It is possible the speaker, horrified at what he has taken to be life's meaningless, simply wonders, "But how can this be?" His question may be taken simply as a lament, an expression of both grief and disbelief. Alternatively, the question may indicate the speaker's sense of rebellion at this notion. Poe leaves the reader wondering whether or not the grief-stricken, despairing speaker will defiantly seek meaning in a world that perhaps, as the remainder of the poem indicates, has none.

Throughout the poem, Poe uses abstract concepts and language that together evoke a sense of loss and emptiness. Forcing the reader to question the existence of hope, as well as the nature of existence itself, Poe creates in his reader the same sense of disorientation and disconnection with meaning and understanding that the speaker in the poem experiences. By the poem's second stanza, Poe has prompted the reader to share the speaker's grief and, at the very least, to be emotionally prepared to empathize with the speaker's sense of loss and isolation.

Source: Catherine Dominic, Critical Essay on "A Dream within a Dream," in *Poetry for Students*, Gale, Cengage Learning, 2013.

Stanza 3 begins with a description of violent surf. (© Marco Vittur / Shutterstock.com)

Arthur Lerner

In the following excerpt, Lerner examines psycho-analytical criticism of Poe's poetry, suggesting that the scope of such criticism should cover not just the tragic elements of Poe's life but also his personal philosophy of poetry.

ATTEMPTS TO STUDY POE PSYCHOANALYTICALLY

Edgar Allan Poe's life (1809–1849) was so psychologically complicated that psychoanalytically oriented writers can easily find in it gold mines of information for their theories. Poe's writing includes, among other topics, such themes as love, horror, anxiety, fantasy, and strange conditions of the mind. His material, therefore, is also a "natural" for psychological theories that are concerned with personality aberrations. His life is extremely enticing in this direction and has led critic Vincent Buranelli to make the following comment:

> Edgar Allan Poe is the most complex personality in the entire gallery of American authors. No one else fuses, as he does, such discordant psycholog-ical attributes, or offers to the world an appear-ance so various. No one else stands at the center

of a mystery so profound. Hawthorne, Melville and Faulkner are, by comparison with Poe, easy enough to classify, while Edwards, Cooper and Hemingway emerge with crystal clarity. Poe resists easy interpretation and broad general-ization. Any plausible analysis of his work, like any authentic story of his life, must begin with this primary and essential truth.

Even the simplest of personalities contain complexity that is often misunderstood. And Poe's was no simple personality. With excellent understanding of the personality makeup of an artist like Poe, Buranelli also reminds us:

> It is false to call him little more than an artist of nightmares, hallucinations, insane crimes and weird beauties, little more than an intuitive poetic genius dabbling in pretentious logic when he is not lost in the black forest of pathological psy-chology. Nor is he a frigid allegorist living in an ivory tower safely away from the contamination of the world. Poe is a dreamer (in the widest sense of the term), and that is where an analytical study may properly begin; but it must not end until it has accounted for Poe the rationalist, the scien-tist, the hoaxer, the humorist, and the literary and social critic. (p. 19)

> THE IDEA THAT TRUTH, REALITY, AND A
> MOMENT OF BEAUTY ARE ALL EPHEMERAL FORMS
> IS PUT IN THE FORM OF A QUESTION ABOUT A
> DREAM WITHIN A DREAM."

The fact that Poe's poetic genius was tied to a distorted personal life was bound to affect his feeling and thinking. These ideas and emotions in turn were naturally reflected in his work. But Philip Lindsay exhibits the real dangers of psychoanalytically oriented criticism when he shifts the focus from the work of art to the case history in a passage like the following:

> Son of shiftless parents and at an early age fatherless and motherless, Edgar Poe was born to live in nightmare. His life, almost from birth, might well have been his own creation, following a pattern similar to one of his tales, macabre and frenzied and ending on a note of pointless tragedy. The story, "William Wilson," was largely autobiographical, not only in external details, but in its emotional content. Here, Poe opened his heart and confessed that his own pitiless destroyer was himself. Most men, were they honest, might make a similar confession. Yet with Poe this was not entirely true. He might have destroyed himself but the seeds of that destruction were germinated in childhood. Always haunting him was the thought of death in love, of the death of his mother, then of the death of a woman he loved, then of the death of his foster-mother, and finally of his wife. These four he loved died as though his kiss were lethal. In the grave, surrendered to the conqueror worm, their once quick flesh rotted, and his desires turned naturally from life towards death. Death, the enemy, became the loved one, and he relished more the thought of dissolution than the living body he clasped, feeling always the skull beneath the hair he touched, the small bones moving in the hand he clasped, and the teeth felt under a kiss.

Poe's strange life has been considered in several ways. One of the attempts as early as 1920 to study Poe as an aberrant personality was that made by Lorine Pruette. In addition to relating, along psychoanalytic lines, some of Poe's poetry to some of the early determinants of Poe's life, Pruette is also concerned with the "individual psychology" of Alfred Adler. "The organic inferiority of both lungs and mind, if we follow the theories of Adler, demanded compensation, which the youth found in drawing and in writing stories and poems" (Pruette, p. 375). Poe's "will to power," Pruette believes, "would brook no superior, nor even equal, in either physical or mental pursuits, and it was this intolerance of the claims of mediocrity which brought upon him in later life the enmity of much of the literary world" (p. 375). Pruette also points out that Poe was of the belief "that his absolutely unswerving devotion to truth was responsible for his scathing criticisms" (p. 375). But Poe's own "devotion to truth" was still tied to a personality that was in a constant state of anxiety and unrest. And in her monumental psychoanalytical study of Poe, Marie Bonaparte emphasizes that Poe's achievement could primarily be understood in terms of the pathological trends in Poe's life. Freud made a special point of this when in the Foreword to Bonaparte's work, he wrote: "Thanks to her interpretative effort, we now realize how many of the characteristics of Poe's works were conditioned by his personality, and can see how that personality derived from intense emotional fixations and painful infantile experiences."

PSYCHOANALYTICALLY ORIENTED CRITICISM OF SELECTED POE POETRY

To enlarge our scope of understanding of the psychoanalytically oriented criticism of selected Poe poetry, an important point must be kept in mind. Poe's poetic endeavors were based on a definite belief that he had of poetry. He states his rationale as follows:

> A poem, in my opinion, is opposed to a work of science by having, for its *immediate* object, pleasure, not truth; to romance, by having for its object an *indefinite* instead of a *definite* pleasure, being a poem only so far as this object is attained; romance presenting perceptible images with definite, poetry with *in*definite sensations, to which end music is an *essential*, since the comprehension of sweet sound is our most indefinite conception. Music, when combined with a pleasurable idea, is poetry; music without the idea is simply music; the idea without the music is prose from its very definitiveness.

So strongly was the above view a guiding belief in all of Poe's work that Norman Foerster remarked: "This was Poe's artistic creed, exemplified in nearly all that he wrote: in his poetry, his tales, his essays on literary theory, and his criticism of literature—on nearly every page of his sixteen volumes."

Poe's definition of poetry has been viewed by Pruette in a broader psychoanalytic sense as follows:

> The poems of Poe are songs of sorrow: beauty is in them, most often dead beauty, love is there, most often the love of those who are dead to him, and madness is there, as if the expression of the prophetic powers of his unconscious. Often enough, in moments of extreme depression, under the influence of drugs or in the temporary insanity induced by the use of stimulants, must he himself have felt those "evil things, in robes of sorrow," which "assailed the monarch's high estate." ("A Psycho-Analytical Study of Edgar Allan Poe," p. 384)

> Beauty and pleasure often appear together in dreams.

Frequently these are intertwined with a desire for love fulfillment, and in real life give an impression of happiness, which is often referred to as a dream. That Poe has captured this feeling is indicated in the last eight lines of his poem entitled "Dreams":

> I have been happy, tho' but in a dream.
> I have been happy—and I love the theme:
> Dreams! in their vivid colouring of life
> As in that fleeting, shadowy, misty strife
> Of semblance with reality which brings
> To the delirious eye, more lovely things
> Of Paradise and Love—and all our own!
> Than young Hope in his sunniest hour hath known.

These lines were published when Poe was still a relatively young man. It appears that he felt deeply apart from humanity at this time. Joseph Wood Krutch has stated:

> It was natural that a young man who felt, as Poe did, desperately isolated from the rest of mankind should find his model in the most popular poet of melodramatic isolation and so, though traces of Keats, Shelley, and Coleridge have been found in him, the dominant influence is obviously Byronic.

Based on another poem, entitled "A Dream," the critics give us further insights into Poe's past hopes and his present situation as well as a contrast between the world of reality and the world of fancy, all closely related to dreams, fantasies, day-dreams, and wish-fulfillments.

"A Dream"

> In visions of the dark night
> I have dreamed of joy departed—
> But a waking dream of life and light
> Hath left me broken-hearted.
> Ah! what is not a dream by day
> To him whose eyes are cast
> On things around him with a ray

> Turned back upon the past?
> That holy dream—that holy dream,
> While all the world were chiding,
> Hath cheered me as a lovely beam
> A lonely spirit guiding.
> What though that light, thro' storm and night,
> So trembled from afar—
> What could there be more purely bright
> In Truth's day-star?

In commenting on the above poem, Pruette points out that in "A Dream" one can see Poe in the midst of the experience of "the contrast between what he has and what he has wanted, between the real and the ideal world of fancy" (p. 382). Also, the poem uses such images as "the dark night," "the past," "holy dream," "lonely spirit," and concludes with a resounding statement. The last stanza, while taking into account the reality of the dark side of life, ends in the form of a question expressing a wish. The word "Truth's" in the last line points up something special here. Truth and science are closely related. Both have a way of shaking men out of their dreams. Both have a way of making dreams a reality if the dreams are based on verifiable assumptions. Hence, it is an easy step to go from this "A Dream" to Poe's "Sonnet—To Science." Writing as though he were thoroughly acquainted with psychoanalytical theory, Poe's "Sonnet—To Science" offers some keen insights into reality and dreams.

"Sonnet—To Science"

> Science! true daughter of Old Time thou art!
> Who alterest all things with thy peering eyes.
> Why preyest thou thus upon the poet's heart,
> Vulture, whose wings are dull realities?
> How should he love thee? or how deem thee wise,
> Who wouldst not leave him in his wandering
> To seek for treasure in the jewelled skies,
> Albeit he soared with an undaunted wing?
> Hast thou not dragged Diana from her car?
> And driven the Hamadryad from the wood
> To seek a shelter in some happier star?
> Hast thou not torn the Naiad from her flood,
> The Elfin from the green grass, and from me
> The summer dream beneath the tamarind tree?
> (Stovall, p. 24)

In asking many questions of science, Poe is actually revealing its power, especially in the use of the word "vulture" in the fourth line of the above poem. Poe is reminding science that she has forced the seer, the poet, to come back to reality, and that the Elysian fields of childhood are only dreams. Here we have Freud's concepts of the reality and pleasure principles further emphasized. Dreams may be forms of wish fulfillments, but science with its emphasis on reality and truth forces one to look at himself, into himself, and at the world around him with great honesty. He is saying all this while voicing the objection of the romanticist "that the scientific attitude reduces everything to the most prosaic reality."

Bonaparte argues that Poe looks upon science as a hated father. She also makes it a point to stress the idea that "true daughter of Old Time" in the first line is

> the appanage of Time, thus being identified, in accordance with the process of the unconscious— which in this case troubles itself little about sex— with Time and so the "father." This was another reason why Poe hated science and would hate it, as bitterly, all his life. (*The Life and Works of Edgar Allan Poe: A Psycho-Analytic Interpretation*, p. 56)

In light of Bonaparte's comments, one might be tempted to forget that beauty and truth were of vital concern to Poe. He writes about this while discussing "The Raven," and touches upon beauty and truth in poetry:

> When, indeed, men speak of Beauty, they mean, precisely, not a quality, as is supposed, but an effect—they refer, in short, just to that intense and pure elevation of *soul—not* of intellect, or of heart—upon which I have commented, and which is experienced in consequence of contemplating the "beautiful." Now I designate Beauty as the province of the poem, merely because it is an obvious rule of Art that effects should be made to spring from direct causes—that objects should be attained through means best adapted for their attainment—no one as yet having been weak enough to deny that the peculiar elevation alluded to is *most readily* attained in the poem. Now the object Truth, or the satisfaction of the intellect, and the object Passion, or the excitement of the heart, are, although attainable to a certain extent in poetry, far more readily attainable in prose. Truth, in fact, demands a precision, and passion, a *homeliness* (the truly passionate will comprehend me), which are absolutely antagonistic to that Beauty which, I maintain, is the excitement, or pleasurable elevation of the soul.

Poe goes on to emphasize, in the same text, that passion and truth may be profitably introduced into poetry. For these two phenomena, passion and truth, may be employed when properly used as means of making the poem itself a more effective work of art and beauty.

Beauty, truth, and science also demand a disciplined appreciation. The reality of life, the remembrance of the beautiful, the realization that nature is oblivious to our desires require a high level degree of understanding. In the poem "A Dream Within a Dream" the last stanza reads as follows:

> I stand amid the roar
> Of a surf-tormented shore,
> And I hold within my hand
> Grains of the golden sand—
> How few! yet how they creep
> Through my fingers to the deep,
> While I weep—while I weep!
> O God! can I not grasp
> Them with a tighter clasp?
> O God! can I not save
> *One* from the pitiless wave?
> Is *all* that we see or seem
> But a dream within a dream?
> (Stovall, p. 18)

The idea that truth, reality, and a moment of beauty are all ephemeral forms is put in the form of a question about a dream within a dream. And according to Pruette, "In 'A Dream Within a Dream' we find rebellion against the disappointments of life" ("A Psycho-Analytical Study of Edgar Allan Poe," p. 382). Always then we are confronted in Poe's poetry with questions of truth, beauty, pleasure, reality, and dream, the very essentials of one's involvement with living and the core of modern depth psychology....

Source: Arthur Lerner, "Edgar Allan Poe," in *Psychoanalytically Oriented Criticism of Three American Poets: Poe, Whitman, and Aiken*, Fairleigh Dickinson University Press, 1970, pp. 43–62.

James Lane Allen

In the following essay, Allen explores the preponderance of night imagery in Poe's poetry.

The appearance of an important biography of Poe in France and the preparation of still another in America, the publication of his most widely-read poem with illustrations by Doré, and the prospective unveiling of a memorial tablet to his honor, seem to furnish a fit occasion for inviting attention to a striking but hitherto unnoted characteristic of his poetry. In fact, with the exception of a comparatively few closeted minds, the attention of the world has thus far been riveted upon the overwhelming sorrows of Poe's lot, the mysterious inequalities of his moods, and the phenomenal aspects of his career, rather than devoted to the critical examination of his works. The retributive swing of the human mind, also, naturally bore it first to the rescue of his name and character both from

> **THUS, WHETHER WE EXAMINE HIS POETRY, OR FIX OUR ATTENTION UPON HIS HABITS OF LIFE, HIS METHODS OF COMPOSITION, HIS VIEWS OF THE POETIC PRINCIPLE OR HIS VERY NATURE, OUR MINDS ARE DRAWN IRRESISTIBLY TO THE SAME THING—NIGHT."**

the innumerable legends that grew up around them during his lifetime, and from the blunders and the malignity that overwhelmed them immediately after his death. Thus, criticism, especially in America, has not yet spent its powers upon his literary remains, and thus it seems possible that a brief examination of his poems may serve to exhibit them in a novel and interesting light.

There are poets who claim all hours and all seasons for their own; but an almost constitutional concomitant of the poetry of Poe is night. Of the more than forty pieces that comprise his poetical works a fifth are wholly night scenes, and in the composition of three-fourths the shadow of night fell athwart his mind and supplied it with its favorite imagery. The remaining poems, with the exception of three, do not contain the element of time at all. Two of these mentioned as exceptions were written in his youth, before he had elaborated his views of the "Poetic Principle," or his imagination had assumed its final cast. Thus, among his later poems that contain the element of time, there is only one—"The Haunted Palace"—that may be called a day-scene; and when it is remembered that this poem is designed to describe the overthrow and ruin of a beautiful mind, so that all the imagery introduced throughout merely expresses the contrast between reason and madness, even it will scarcely be regarded as a solitary exception. Leaving it out of consideration, therefore, we may say that all his most beautiful poems, having any relation to time, belong wholly to the night, and from it draw their elements of power and pathos. These, by general consent, are "The Raven"—the night of dying embers and ghostly shadows, of mournful memories and broken hopes; "Lenore"—the night of the bell-tolling for the saintly soul that floats on the Stygian river;

"Helen"—the night of the full-orbed moon and silvery, silken veil of light, of the upturned faces of a thousand roses, of beauty, clad in white, reclining upon a bed of violets; "Ulalume"—the night of sober, ashen skies and crisp, sere leaves in the lonesome October, of dim lakes and ghoul-haunted woodland; "The Bells"—the night of the icy air through which the stars that oversprinkle all the heavens seem to twinkle with crystalline delight; "Annabel Lee"—the night of the wind blowing out of a cloud, chilling and killing his beautiful bride in the Kingdom by the Sea; "The Conqueror Worm"—the gala knight in his lonesome latter years with its angel throng bedight in veils and drowned in tears; and "The Sleeper"—the night of the mystic moon, exhaling from her golden rim an opiate vapor that drips upon the mountain top and steals drowsily and musically into the Universal Valley—the night of nodding rosemary and lolling water-lily—of fog-wrapped ruin and slumber-steeped lake.

If we turn from his poems to the "Poetic Principle," we shall discover the fascination that night exercised over his poetic imagination, strongly affecting his estimates of poetic beauty in others. Thus, among the minor poems selected by him in the exposition of the "Poetic Principle," on the ground that they best suited his own taste or left upon his own fancy the more definite impression, are "The Serenade" of Shelley, a poem by Willis, beginning with a reference to the on-coming night, the poem by Byron beginning "The day of my destiny is over," the "Waif" by Longfellow, beginning "The day is done and the darkness," and two selections from Hood—one beginning with a figure descriptive of the approaching night, the other being the night suicide on the "Bridge of Sighs."

Passing to his enumeration of the simple elements that induce in the poet true poetical effect, we find him mentioning the bright orbs that shine in heaven, the star-mirroring depths of lonely wells, the sighing night wind, and the faint suggestive odor that comes at eventide from our far-distant oceans illimitable and unexplored. If we leave the "Poetic Principle" and take up his reviews of authors, native and foreign, contributed by him to various periodicals during the course of many years, we derive from them evidences greatly multiplied and not less striking of the spell that such hours possessed for his poetic imagination. Again and again will it be found that passages in some way related to night are selected from a poem or a book of poems, emphasized, and made the subject of delicate analysis or graceful comment.

And, finally, if we but glance at—for we do not wish to explore—his prose tales of the imaginative kind, we may detect further examples of the same compositional bent. In "Ligeia," which he regarded his best tale as involving the exercise of the highest imaginative creativeness, the lady Ligeia's death occurs at high noon of night, and the hideous drama of revivication goes on from midnight till gray dawn; in the "Fall of the House of Usher," the catastrophe takes place at an hour when the full, setting, blood-red moon shines through a fissure of the foredoomed and collapsing ruins; in "Metzengerstein," it is at night that the unbonnetted and disordered horseman leapt the moat and the castle wall and disappears in a whirlwind of chaotic fire.

Of this striking peculiarity the evidences are now, perhaps, sufficiently detailed. In connection with it, it will be interesting to consider certain peculiar habits in the poet's life, his habits of composing, his views regarding poetic art, and his essentially gloomy nature. We find the closely related facts in Poe's habit of going nightly for months to the grave of the woman, who by her tender and gracious reception of him while he was a student in Richmond, became the subject of his confiding tenderness during the rest of her lifetime, and in his remaining for hours at her tomb, leaving it most regretfully when the autumnal nights were dreariest with rains and wailing winds; in his frequently escaping from parade, when a student at West Point, that he might indulge his predisposition to loneliness and solitude on the banks of the legend-haunted Hudson; in his habit of walking to High Bridge during his residence at Fordham, and of pacing the pathway, then so solitary, at all hours of the day and night; in his selecting as a favorite seat a rocky ledge to the east of his cottage, where, during starlit nights, he would sit dreaming his wild dreams of the universe; in his habit of arising from his sleepless pillow for weeks after the death of his wife and of keeping tearful, lonely vigils by her grave; in his habit, while writing "Eureka," of walking up and down the porch in front of his cottage even on the coldest nights, engaged in contemplating the stars and in solving until the approach of dawn the august problems of his ever-wakeful brain; and, finally, in the very pertinent special fact that during one

of these nights of restless wandering the occasion was furnished him of writing one of his most beautiful poems.

All these facts show how inexcusable is the ignorance of some of Poe's biographers in stating that he was afraid of the darkness, and was rarely out in it alone. On the contrary, they reveal him as a voluntary student and loving companion of the night, either because it was most soothing to his irritated sensibility or more pleasing to his imagination, or ablest and aptest to excite in him desired or unhoped for trains of thought. The evidence that they furnish relative to his hours and habits of composing seems to throw a welcome light upon the characteristic of his poetry that is under consideration; and this may be supplemented by certain remarkable statements of his own on the subject—statements that have been entirely overlooked by those who should have had the keenest appreciation of their value. At moments of the soul's most intense tranquility, at those mere points of time when the waking world blends with the world of dreams, there arose in his soul, as if the five senses had been supplanted by five myriad others alien to mortality, evanescent visions of a supernal character—psychical impressions marked by the absoluteness of novelty—fancies of exquisite delicacy—the shadows of shadows—which, despite all his extraordinary powers of expression, he yet utterly failed at first, to adapt to language.

By repeated efforts, however, he acquired the power of startling himself from slumber at the moment when these ecstasies supervened, and of thus immediately transferring the attendant impressions to the realm of memory, when for an instant they could be subjected to the eye of analysis; and thus, finally, he so far succeeded in adapting them to language as to be able to give others a shadowy conception of their character. In this way, no doubt, his mind became the storehouse of images drawn from a world little known to common minds, and the events of his inner life seemed better known to him than the occurrences of outer experience. The conclusion to be drawn, however, is that poetic visions arose in the soul of Poe during the stillness of the night, and either involuntarily or deliberately were yielded up to its influence, and partook of its hue and spirit. Along with this strange revelation of his as to his ecstasies and struggles for utterance, there is no positive statement that the precious material thus so laboriously obtained, passed into the composition of his poetry; but evidence to this effect may be found elsewhere in his writings. For, to Poe, who is the true poet? Not he who sings, with whatever glowing enthusiasm or however vivid a truth of description, of the sights and sounds and odors and sentiments that greet him in common with other minds. The naked senses, if they sometimes perceive too little, always perceive too much. Art is the reproduction of what the senses perceive *through the veil of the soul*; and he is the true poet who, with ecstatic prescience of glories beyond the grave, attains by multiform combinations among the things and thoughts of time, brief and indeterminate glimpses of that supernal loveliness—of those divine and rapturous joys—whose very elements appertain to eternity alone. In his poetry, therefore, we expect to find his own ecstatic visions—his own brief and indeterminate glimpses, which, if prolonged, he said would have compressed heaven into earth. And there we find them—manifested, not as things of sharpest outline and most determinate tone, but in the extra terrestrial accent, the mystical atmosphere, the dreamlike haze, the delicate breath of faery, the arch-angelic purity and nebulous softness of rhythmical movement that distinguished his creations from those of every poet, living or dead.

From his habits of life and of composing, we come to speak of the elements of his "Poetic Principle." These elements, as may be ascertained from various portions of his writings, comprised not beauty alone, and always Beauty Uranian, never Dionan, but also Melancholy, Strangeness, Indefiniteness and Originality. Such a theory of poetic art as he accepted would of itself have led him irresistibly to write of those hours that alone bring the human mind under the Supreme influence of the ideas fundamental to the theory itself. It is only at night, when the veil is thrown over the senses, and is lifted from the soul, that Beauty becomes most elevating and Melancholy most intense; that the Commonplace is supplanted by the Strange; that the Definite, suddenly overleaping its bounds, becomes the vague and vast; and that the poetic soul, rightly attuned to such influences, will be likeliest to attain Originality of the highest order. It is scarcely a fanciful phrase to say, that the elements of Poe's "Poetic Principle" were native to the Night, and lurked in its recesses, throwing dark lines upon the bright spectrum of his creative consciousness, and pervading his creations

themselves as the gloom, the chill, the mystery, the dread, the disturbing strangeness, the unexplored recesses of sorrow, that constitute another group of his poetic attributes.

And, now, finally, we come to that which must be final in every investigation of this kind—the peculiarities of the poet's very nature. Of these his many biographers have had much to say, and it seems but necessary for us, in this connection, to note that Poe dwelt in a perpetual Night of the Soul. Rubens, by a single stroke, converted a laughing into a crying child; but no propitious stroke of destiny could ever have converted this gloom-haunted child of poetry and passion into a joyous singer in the sunshine; not sudden wealth, not troops of friends, nor adequate recognition. Of poverty he himself said that the Nine were never so tuneful as when penniless; of adversity in other forms, that what the Man of Genius wanted was moral matter in motion—it made little difference toward what the motion tended, and absolutely no difference what was the matter. We have come to think of him as the offspring of passion and adventure, as at birth ruled over by a spirit of romance, sinister and stormy, as early in life moulded by much that was *outré* and abnormal, and as bearing upon himself, when even a Man, the stamp of indefinable Melancholy.

Thus, whether we examine his poetry, or fix our attention upon his habits of life, his methods of composition, his views of the Poetic Principle or his very nature, our minds are drawn irresistibly to the same thing—night. Beneath this manifold night, however—the night of nature, the night of theories and the night of the soul, his broken but undying song always rose and soared away toward the realms of light—passing the clouds, passing the moon, passing the stars, passing his visions of floating angels—passing even toward the divine and eternal Beauty.

Source: James Lane Allen, "Night Shadows in Poe's Poetry," in *Continent*, Vol. 5, No. 4, January 23, 1884, pp. 102–104.

SOURCES

Amper, Susan, "Introduction to Poe Criticism," in *Critical Insights: The Tales of Edgar Allan Poe*, edited by Steven Frye, Salem Press, 2009, pp. 36–53.

Brewer, William D., "Dreams," in *The Mental Anatomies of William Godwin and Mary Shelley*, Fairleigh Dickinson University Press, 2001, pp. 183–212.

Campbell, Killis, Notes to "A Dream within a Dream," in *The Poems of Edgar Allan Poe*, Ginn, 1917, pp. 26–28.

Carpenter, Frederic I., "The Logic of American Literature," in *American Literature and the Dream*, Philosophical Library, 1955, pp. 199–207.

Chait, Jonathan, "The Rise of Republican Nihilism," in *New Republic*, December 21, 2009, http://www.tnr.com/article/politics/the-rise-republican-nihilism (accessed March 15, 2012).

Copestake, Ian D., "American Romanticism: Approaches and Interpretations," in *Encyclopedia of the Romantic Era, 1760–1850*, Vol. 1, *A–K*, Fitzroy Dearborn, 2004, pp. 17–18.

Cummings, Allison M., "The Subject in Question: Women and the Free Verse Lyric in the 1980s," in *New Definitions of Lyric: Theory, Technology, and Culture*, edited by Mark Jeffreys, Garland Reference Library of the Humanities, 1998, pp. 151–78.

"Debunking a Dream Theory," in *Psychiatric News*, October 6, 2000, http://psychnews.org/pnews/00-10-06/debunking.html (accessed March 15, 2012).

"Edgar Allan Poe Mystery," University of Maryland Medical Center website, September 24, 1996, http://www.umm.edu/news/releases/news-releases-17.htm (accessed March 15, 2012).

Ferber, Michael, "Dream," in *A Dictionary of Literary Symbols*, Cambridge University Press, 1999, pp. 63–65.

Frank, Frederick S., and Anthony Magistrale, "Byron, George Gordon, Lord," in *The Poe Encyclopedia*, Greenwood Press, 1997, pp. 59–60.

"Friedrich Heinrich Jacobi," in *Stanford Encyclopedia of Philosophy*, 2010, http://plato.stanford.edu/entries/friedrich-jacobi/ (accessed March 15, 2012).

Halliwell, Martin, "American Romanticism: Its Literary Legacy," in *Encyclopedia of the Romantic Era, 1760–1850*, Vol. 1, *A–K*, Fitzroy Dearborn, 2004, pp. 18–19.

Harris, Paul, "Fresh Clues Could Solve Mystery of Poe's Death," in *Observer*, October 20, 2007, http://www.guardian.co.uk/world/2007/oct/21/books.books news (accessed March 15, 2012).

James, Tony, Introduction to *Dream, Creativity, and Madness in Nineteenth-Century France*, Clarendon Press, 1995, pp. 1–12.

Kete, Mary Louise, "The Reception of Nineteenth-Century American Poetry," in *The Cambridge Companion to Nineteenth-Century American Poetry*, edited by Kerry Larson, Cambridge University Press, 2011, pp. 15–35.

Mabbott, Thomas Ollive, "Introduction to the Poems," in *Edgar Allan Poe: Complete Poems*, Harvard University Press, 2000, pp. xxiii–xxx.

Magistrale, Tony, "The Art of Poetry," in *Student Companion to Edgar Allan Poe*, Greenwood Press, 2001, pp. 35–50.

Poe, Edgar Allan, "A Dream within a Dream," in *Edgar Allan Poe: Poetry and Tales*, Library of America, 1984, p. 97.

"Poe's Life," Edgar Allan Poe Museum website, http://www.poemuseum.org/life.php (accessed March 15, 2012).

Power, Julia, "New England; Romanticism and Renaissance: Shelley and the New England Transcendentalists," "The South; Southern Shellyans: *The Southern Literary Messenger*," and "The Influence of Shelley on Poe," in *Shelley in America in the Nineteenth Century: His Relation to American Critical Thought and His Influence*, Haskell House, 1964, pp. 9–29, 87–98, and 99–120.

Pratt, Alan, "Nihilism," in *Internet Encyclopedia of Philosophy*, 2005, http://www.iep.utm.edu/nihilism (accessed March 15, 2012).

Robinson, D. S., "What Idealism Is," in *An Introduction to Living Philosophy: A General Introduction to Contemporary Types and Problems*, Thomas Y. Crowell, 1932, pp. 67–76.

Schmitz-Emans, Monika, "Theories of Romanticism: The First Two Hundred Years," in *Nonfictional Romantic Prose: Expanding Borders*, John Benjamins Publishing, 2004, pp. 13–36.

Snodgrass, Mary Ellen, "Dreams and Nightmares," in *Encyclopedia of Gothic Literature*, Facts on File, 2005, pp. 91–94.

Thompson, G. R., "Edgar Allan Poe," in *Dictionary of Literary Biography*, Vol. 248, *Antebellum Writers in the South, Second Series*, edited by Kent Ljungquist, The Gale Group, 2001, pp. 262–319.

FURTHER READING

D'Agostini, Franca, *The Last Fumes: Nihilism and the Nature of Philosophical Concepts*, Davies Group Publishers, 2009.

> D'Agostini provides a thorough examination of the philosophical notion of nihilism, focusing on the work of such philosophers as Friedrich Nietzsche and Georg Hegel.

Hurley, Jennifer, *American Romanticism*, Greenhaven, 2000.

> Hurley's work explores the romantic prose and poetry of Poe, Nathaniel Hawthorne, Ralph Waldo Emerson, and Henry David Thoreau, among others, and details the ways in which the American romantic movement shaped the literature and culture of nineteenth-century America.

Miller, Perry, *The American Transcendentalist: Their Prose and Poetry*, Anchor Books, 1957.

> Miller's collection includes poems and essays by Poe's contemporaries, transcendentalist

writers such as Emerson, Thoreau, Fuller, and Caroline Sturgis Hooper, among others.

Pick, Daniel, and Lyndal Roper, eds., *Dreams and History: The Interpretation of Dreams from Ancient Greece to Modern Psychoanalysis*, Routledge, 2004

This collection of essays examines the ways in which dreams have been regarded and analyzed throughout history and includes chapters on nineteenth-century dream theory and interpretation.

Quinn, Arthur Hobson, *Edgar Allan Poe: A Critical Biography*, D. Appleton, 1941.

Quinn offers a detailed account of Poe's life and an overview and critical assessment of his works.

SUGGESTED SEARCH TERMS

Edgar Allan Poe AND "A Dream within a Dream"

Poe AND nihilism

Poe AND romanticism

Poe AND British romantics

Poe AND transcendentalism

Poe AND dreams

Poe AND death of Virginia Poe

Poe AND meter

Poe AND poetic theory

Poe as literary critic

The History Teacher

BILLY COLLINS

1991

Billy Collins is one of the most popular and accessible poets of modern-day America, qualities that earned him a place as the poet laureate of the United States from 2001 to 2003. "The History Teacher," a poem from his 1991 volume *Questions about Angels*, brings his characteristic humor and irony to bear on the problems of education. Whether or not education makes people good is a perennial question that Collins addresses, in the specific context of the crisis in education that was widely perceived in American culture when the poem was composed in the early 1990s. Collins answers the question, What happens when what the schools are teaching young people is false? Although a thoughtful reading of "The History Teacher" reveals that Collins has a serious message, the surface of the poem is composed of comic echoes of popular culture, from *The Flintstones* to *Leave It to Beaver*. "The History Teacher" was reprinted in 2002 in Collins's retrospective anthology *Sailing Alone around the Room*.

AUTHOR BIOGRAPHY

William James Collins was born on March 22, 1941, in New York City. His father, William, was an electrician, and his mother, Katherine, was a nurse who, as was then customary, stopped working to take care of Collins when

Billy Collins (© *AP Images | Beth A. Keiser*)

he was born. In an interview with Robert Potts for the *Coachella Review*, Collins described the deep impression made by his parents on his writing with his characteristic humor:

> I think what really happened psychologically is that I started off writing in the voice of my father (wise-cracking) and only later did I find a way to admit my mother (generous, empathetic). And I didn't even need long sessions on the couch to figure that out.

After studying at a college-preparatory Catholic high school, Collins earned a BA in English from the College of the Holy Cross in Worcester, Massachusetts, and then an MA and in 1968 a PhD in English from the University of California, Riverside. He wrote his dissertation on the poets of the romantic movement. Collins immediately began teaching at Lehman College, in the Bronx, part of the City University of New York, and continued there into the 2010s. Collins became active in academic publishing, helping to found the *Mid-Atlantic Review* and the *Alaska Quarterly Review*. However, he devoted his own writing to poetry rather than scholarly research.

Collins began publishing poems in obscure literary journals and in privately printed chapbooks, and his reputation grew slowly throughout the 1980s. In 1988, the University of Arkansas Press published his first full collection of poems, *The Apple That Astonished Paris*. It is very unusual for a major poet's first volume of poetry to be published at age forty. Collins's second volume, *Questions about Angels*, which contains "The History Teacher," came out in 1991. His poetry, once it became available to wider audiences in venues like the *New Yorker*, proved immensely popular because of its humorous and accessible character. His popularity increased further when in 1997 he released an album of readings of his poems under the title *The Best Cigarette*, and he soon became a regular guest on the National Public Radio program *A Prairie Home Companion*.

The celebrity gained from projects like these made Collins the most widely known poet in the United States. In 2001 he was appointed the poet laureate of the United States, a largely honorific post within the Library of Congress. Although there are no duties attached to the position, Collins did compose a poem commemorating the terrorist attacks of September 11, 2001, which he, as poet laureate, read before a joint session of Congress in 2002. He would again read the poem, which he refused to allow to be published in any for-profit medium, at the ceremonies for the tenth anniversary of the attacks. In 2004 he was appointed poet laureate for the State of New York. Collins has devoted much of his time to national tours, giving public readings of his poems.

POEM TEXT

Trying to protect his students' innocence
he told them the Ice Age was really just
the Chilly Age, a period of a million years
when everyone had to wear sweaters.

And the Stone Age became the Gravel Age,   5
named after the long driveways of the time.

The Spanish Inquisition was nothing more
than an outbreak of questions such as
"How far is it from here to Madrid?"
"What do you call the matador's hat?"   10

The War of the Roses took place in a garden,
and the Enola Gay dropped one tiny atom
on Japan.

The children would leave his classroom
for the playground to torment the weak   15

and the smart,
mussing up their hair and breaking their
   glasses,

while he gathered up his notes and walked home
past flower beds and white picket fences,
wondering if they would believe that soldiers   20
in the Boer War told long, rambling stories
designed to make the enemy nod off.

POEM SUMMARY

The text used for this summary is from *Questions about Angels: Poems*, William Morrow, 1991, pp. 91–92. Versions of the poem can be found on the following web pages: http://www.billy-collins.com/2005/06/the_history_tea.html and http://writersalmanac.publicradio.org/index.php?date=2002/03/12.

Lines 1–4

The first line of the poem describes a history teacher who decides to lie to his students about anything in history that he fears might disturb their innocence. The majority of the poem, from lines 2 to 12, gives examples of the history he falsifies.

   The Ice Age becomes the Chilly Age, when, for a million years, people had to wear sweaters. In fact, the earth has had several glacial ages over the last two and a half billion years, including the current one, which began about three million years ago. In the current glacial age, there have been a number of glacial and interglacial periods, in which the ice sheets around the north and south poles expand and contract. The current interglacial period began about ten thousand years ago. So the falsification begins with the description of a single Ice Age of a million years (which is probably a common image in the popular imagination), but the history teacher seems to mainly want to spare his students from having to think about extreme cold, which completely misses the historical point that any ice age will see a wide range of temperatures over various parts of the earth. While the poem was written too early to be concerned with global warming denialism, many fundamentalist Christian groups, who wish schoolchildren to be taught that the earth is only six thousand years old, have tried to pressure school boards into presenting their narrative rather than the widely accepted scientific

MEDIA ADAPTATIONS

- Collins's "The History Teacher" was read by Garrison Keillor for American Public Media's radio show *The Writer's Almanac* on March 12, 2002. The reading may be found at http://writersalmanac.public radio.org/index.php?date=2002/03/12.

findings of geology and climatology, which provide the evidence for past ice ages. Such efforts may well be one target of the poem's satire.

Lines 5–6

The history teacher calls the Stone Age the Gravel Age, in reference to the long gravel driveways of the period. The idea of the people of the Stone Age needing driveways recalls the popular cartoon *The Flintstones*, with its human-powered, stone-wheeled vehicles. The term "Stone Age" refers to the period during which humans and human ancestors relied on the use of stone tools, from about two and a half million years ago until the first use of metal around 6500 BCE (although some isolated populations continued at a Stone Age level of technological culture until contact with Western civilization as late as the twentieth century). Again, Collins may be referring in a satirical way to the frequent efforts by fundamentalist Christian organizations to drive scientific ideas about evolution and the age of the earth out of public-school classrooms.

Lines 7–10

The history teacher represents the Spanish Inquisition as nothing more than a series of questions that one might ask as a tourist in Spain. In reality, the Spanish Inquisition was an ecclesiastical court established at the request of the newly unified Spanish crown in 1492. At that time, the Spanish monarchy had ordered all of its Jewish subjects to either convert to Christianity or leave Spain. The main purpose of the Inquisition was to monitor the new converted Christians to make sure that their conversions were sincere and that they did not relapse into Jewish religious or even cultural practices. The Inquisition remained in existence until 1808, when it was abolished by Napoleon during his occupation of Spain. During its later existence, the Inquisition extended its oversight to the faith of Spanish Catholics as a whole, and in particular ruthlessly acted to suppress any influence of the Protestant Reformation in Spain. Inquisitorial courts routinely tortured defendants, using what is today referred to as water-boarding and other techniques. In the Europe of the Enlightenment, the Spanish Inquisition became a scandalous byword for intolerance and injustice. Collins may be commenting here on the all-too-frequent tendency of American history textbooks up until the 1970s to minimize the roles of racism and religious intolerance in the history of the United States.

Lines 11–12

The history teacher tells his students that the War of the Roses is something that took place in a garden. The War of the Roses was a series of civil wars fought in fifteenth-century Britain among various descendants of relatives of King Henry V for succession to the British Crown. The two factions were generally led by the house of Lancaster and the house of York, symbolized by red and white roses, respectively. This is an uncontroversial topic in American education and seems to have been included for the comic effect of its falsification.

However, the history teacher goes on to say that the Enola Gay dropped only a single atom on Japan. He is referring to the atomic bombing of the Japanese city of Hiroshima at the end of World War II, a single attack that killed over one hundred thousand civilians, not including the many who subsequently died of cancer caused by the radiation from the blast. A second atomic bomb was dropped on Nagasaki three days later. The atomic bombing of Japan has always been controversial, on the points of whether it was morally justifiable or militarily necessary. Treatments of the event in American texts, regardless of their content, have often been criticized as propaganda by holders of the opposite view.

Lines 13–15

The poem now takes off in a new direction. The history teacher's students are dismissed from class and go out to recess. They bully other students who are either weaker or smarter than the tormenters.

Lines 16–20

The history teacher himself is evidently unaware of how his students are acting, or at least is unconcerned about it. He goes home to an idyllic suburb described in terms of its flower beds and white picket fences. He mentally prepares his next lecture, about how soldiers in the Boer War would bore their enemies to sleep. This presumably refers to the Second Boer War (1899-1902), in which the population of Dutch settlers in South Africa (Boers) attempted to assert their independence from British colonial authorities. Like many colonial wars, the Boer War involved irregular rebel troops in an asymmetric battle against regular troops. While the Boers could not have stood in a regular military engagement with the British and other imperial troops, the British could not control the small bands of Boer partisans and terrorists. The British turned to policing the civilian population that sheltered the Boer fighters, herding them into what were called for the first time concentration camps. The settlement of the war created the modern state of South Africa, with its apartheid racial policies. Fraught with controversial material as the Boer War is, it has never proved problematic in the American school curriculum, so it may be that it is included primarily for the sake of the pun between *Boer* and *bore*.

THEMES

Postmodernism

There is considerable uncertainty about what Collins is actually satirizing in "The History Teacher." The poem would seem, from the exaggerated material of the satire, to refer to some educational technique that Collins feels falsifies the material taught to the student. It is not necessary that Collins have only a single thing in mind, but one strong possibility as at least a partial answer is postmodernism. The period of the late 1980s and early 1990s was the high point of the influence of postmodernism in American academia. *Postmodernism* is a school of literary techniques and criticism established especially after World War II by French scholars like Roland Barthes and Jacques Derrida. Postmodernism is a reaction against the intellectual

TOPICS FOR FURTHER STUDY

- In the societies of Japan and China, where shaming is an aspect of ordinary culture, bullying is often ignored, if not actively used, by institutions like schools and businesses. Nevertheless, bullying is increasingly recognized as a social problem, largely due to the reception of sociological theorizing from the West. Research bullying in Japan and China (some places to start looking are the *Handbook of Bullying in Schools: An International Perspective* [2009], edited by Shane R. Jimerson, and *The Japanese High School: Silence and Resistance* [1999], edited by Shoko Yoneyama) and report back to your class on the differences and commonalities of bullying in schools in the Far East and the United States.

- As an exercise in versification, rewrite all or part of "The History Teacher" in iambic trimeter. (This is an assignment that Collins often gives to his own students.) English verse is generally iambic, that is, composed of feet or metrical units consisting of an unstressed followed by a stressed syllable. In trimeter, each line consists of three feet.

- In the early 1990s, one of the first trends on the Internet was the circulation of tests administered to students in the nineteenth century (ranging from those for eighth-grade graduates to college-entrance exams) which seemed impossibly difficult to answer for modern, educated adults, let alone students. Some of these are archived on the Internet at http://gfhs.org/local_lore/class_ of_1895.htm and http://www.pbs.org/wgbh/pages/frontline/shows/sats/where/1901.html. While the comparison is not as straight forward as was once assumed, select part of such a test, research the answers, and then administer it to your classmates. Use the experience to promote a class discussion about how education has changed in the last century.

- Read the 1996 young-adult novel *Push*, by Sapphire (the pen name of Romana Lofton). The main character, a sixteen-year-old girl named Precious Jones, is bullied and abused by her peers, teachers, and family. As a result, she is barely literate, has two illegitimate children, and seems to be doomed, among other things, to bullying and manipulating her children just as her parents did to her. But a shift to a new school brings new hope, and Precious finds she is capable of real intellectual growth and accomplishment. Her psychological condition improves, not only as she receives better treatment, but because she is internally strengthened to receive the hard blows that life still has in store for her. In Collins's "The History Teacher," the students are purposefully kept ignorant and proceed to become bullies. Write a blog post on this topic. How does education relate to personal growth? How does personal growth relate to bullying? Why would people whose view of the world is essentially false be quicker to resort to violence? Have your classmates comment on your blog.

---

consensus reached before World War I, which is viewed as discredited by that conflict. One of the most important postmodern ideas in terms of literature is deconstruction. In America, deconstruction became wildly popular in university English departments during the 1980s in a somewhat simplified form. Roughly, the idea is that a text (such as a poem or novel) should not be interpreted with reference to a literary school or historical period, or anything outside the text itself. Moreover, the reader must tear the text apart—deconstruct it—to find out its true meaning in what it does not say. This effectively leaves the reader free to create any meaning one wants. It is only this created meaning that can have any validity. In such a case, objective truth has no meaning or relevance. The teacher cannot tell the student what a text means. Any attempt to do so would be a falsification of the text, since each reader must create one's own meaning out of the text for oneself.

It is easy to see how this kind of reading could be the target of Collins's satire. In "The History Teacher," the teacher takes a known historical event (which could certainly be a *text* for this purpose), such as the Spanish Inquisition or the War of the Roses, and invents some new meaning for it, different from that of the traditional consensus. In this case, the ridiculous interpretations the teacher gives to his texts are examples of *reductio ad absurdum*, finding their humor in burlesques of the possibility of the reader creating the meaning of texts according to deconstruction. The innocence of the pupils is their freedom to find their own meaning in texts, while the violence they do refers to the left-wing, revolutionary political associations of deconstruction and postmodernism generally. This analysis cannot be pressed too far, but it is certainly one that suggests itself, ironically, to a reader familiar with the historical circumstances of Collins's place in American academia in the late 1980s and early 1990s and attempting to interpret the text according to the author's experience.

American Identity

The identity of Americans has always been built on narratives about the history and destiny of the country: Americans are pioneers because their ancestors are pioneers; America is blessed by God because it is a city upon a hill that stands up to godless opponents like Soviet Russia; America has a manifest destiny to dominate the American continent and take a position of world leadership; America is a beacon of freedom to the world. But since these are narratives, they do not correspond very well to reality, which cannot be so simplistically reduced, even if they encapsulate some part of the truth. No one was so adept at exposing the falsifications of such platitudes as Mark Twain. The very title of his novel *The Gilded Age*, set in postbellum America, suggests how the culture itself was hollow. Americans of his era thought of themselves as living in a golden age of economic expansion following the triumph of the Civil War. But Twain saw that it was really only a gilded age—painted on

The teacher walked home past houses with flowers and white picket fences. (© *Jayne Carney / Shutterstock.com*)

the outside to look like gold—driven by greed rather than divine favor, and leaving many times more Americans trapped in desperate poverty than were elevated to new levels of riches. Although not all of the false historical narratives that Collins satirizes in "The History Teacher" are American ones, the final stanza of the poem suggests that Twain's kind of deflation of American myth is something he has in mind. The history teacher spins out new fantasies while walking through a middle-class neighborhood marked by the ubiquitous white picket fence—a symbol of the American myth of the perfect suburban utopia modeled in popular-culture icons like the television show *Leave It to Beaver*, a myth quite incompatible with the America that was being torn apart by the civil rights movement in real life. The history teacher refuses to educate his students about the realities and injustices of history, so, knowing no better in their so-called innocence, they go right on bullying the weak and helpless.

STYLE

Poetics

Poetry and singing began as the same thing. Only once writing became common (in ancient Greece) did people think of reading a line of verse rather than singing it. The first poem in English ("Sumer Is Icumen In," circa 1250) is a song, complete with musical notation. By the time of Geoffrey Chaucer, in the fourteenth century, English poems were being written that were never meant to be sung. But verse in the eras of William Shakespeare to John Keats to Alfred Lord Tennyson was still composed in meter, with each line employing a distinct rhythm of stressed and unstressed syllables, retaining the character of song and even of dance (the parts of a metrical line are called *feet*). But it was becoming increasingly clear that the most important qualities of poetry transcended the sing-song sound of the words. In the twentieth century, these other qualities came entirely to the fore, and the song fell away from poetry. Collins's poetry can no more be set to music than can the ordinary prose of the newspaper. "The History Teacher" is typeset like verse, with the poet choosing where to end each line, but it has no meter. The line length and stanza length are governed by ideas rather than rhythm. What makes the poem poetry is its compositional structure and its unity in expressing a single idea through the repetition of variations of that idea, yet with a larger movement progressing through the whole. If in Greek poetry each line of verse represented a series of dance steps performed by a chorus on a stage, Collins's poetry dances through the intellect. Most of "The History Teacher" is the same idea over and over, each iteration taking a rather colorful phrase out of history, such as the Stone Age or the War of the Roses, and interpreting it in a false and ridiculous fashion. Prose cannot sustain such repetition, but even in a modern poem, readers or hearers look for echoes of the repeated refrains of song.

Satire

Satire is a literary attack against some target in order to make it look laughable and ridiculous. Within Western culture, satire originated in the highly competitive culture of ancient Greece. The satire that Collins uses in "The History Teacher" is remarkably gentle. He gives ridiculous versions of variously colorfully named historical events, such as the Boer War and the Ice Age. Of course, he is not satirizing history (although the reader might at first think so), but rather he is satirizing whoever in his environment falsifies history. Darker humor comes from the students' becoming bigoted little thugs—

objects of scorn themselves. The actual target of the satire is left purposefully unclear, but the American culture of the 1990s had no shortage of groups spinning out false versions of history for their own purposes.

Figurative Language

Figurative language is the use of words that suggest something more than their denotation and is a hallmark of poetry. In "The History Teacher," each one of the false interpretations of history given by the history teacher, whatever its defects as history, summons up a vivid mental image in the reader's mind; one could easily imagine the poem turned into a video. Perhaps the most striking use of figurative language in the poem is the reference to white picket fences, which evokes a whole world of idyllic middle-class suburbia through a simple phrase that has many well-known, even well-worn, associations.

HISTORICAL CONTEXT

Although in "The History Teacher" Collins treats humorously the last hundred thousand years of history, the poem relates to its own historical context in far more subtle and less obvious ways. In each section of the poem, some historical fact is presented in an absurd manner, reinterpreted so ridiculously that it can give no offense to anyone. But what is the point of such *reductio ad absurdum*? In the 1990s, American culture was gripped by fears over what was happening to the American educational system. Numerous books and articles argued that the content of the curriculum as well as the rigor of the grading were being diminished at both the high-school and college level. Paul Trout, in his essay "Student Anti-intellectualism and the Dumbing Down of the University," posits the perceived problem by quoting a colleague who expressed the fear that "most students nowadays are reluctant to learn and to think and resent being awakened from their stupor. I shudder when I consider the future of this country." The problem was often framed as one of a defense of traditional educational rigor against pandering to a declining student population. As Trout puts it, curriculum was viewed as a "war... between those who think that students should adapt to the rigors of higher education, and

COMPARE & CONTRAST

- **1990s:** There is concern that a general dumbing down of the curriculum in the educational system, motivated by a combination of greed—for high grades among students, for high approval ratings among teachers, and for high enrollment among school administrators—and oversensitivity to students' individual failings, is dooming America's future.

  Today: There is concern that George W. Bush's No Child Left Behind Act of 2001, with its focus on teaching to the test, has negatively affected education in America.

- **1990s:** The French deconstructionist Jacques Derrida is the darling of American academia, especially departments of English.

  Today: Derrida's influence is rapidly waning—especially under the assault on his ideas by academic philosophers and their localization of his ideas in his own particular experience, which makes them seem less universal—a transformation marked in several critical obituaries published in 2004.

- **1990s:** Though receiving some attention in mass media, bullying is largely considered a minor problem to be dealt with by individual schools.

  Today: Bullying is recognized as a societal problem, and an increasing number of states have criminalized it, especially in response to the role of bullying in systematic illegal discrimination, for example against gay students.

those who think that higher education should adapt to the declining motivation and intellectual commitment of students."

The educational system seemed to have been reduced to an economic transaction. University administrators wanted school curricula dumbed down so that the largest numbers of students could do as well as possible and thus keep up enrollment and, along with it, school revenues, while many students had no interest in school except insofar as a degree was a necessary condition of future employment. The perceived dumbing down of American education is what Collins is satirizing (or one of the things that Collins is satirizing), with harsh historical realities transformed into trivialities meant to be inoffensive to students' innocence (that is, their preconceived ideas before encountering the educational system). Collins's own commitment to improving American education is not limited to satire but is testified to by his academic career, and especially his interest in enriching secondary education through the

Poetry 180 project he created for the Library of Congress. This evolving collection of 180 poems (one for each day of the school year) by living poets is designed not for instruction, but to stimulate students to, as the Poetry 180 project website states, "think about what it means to be a member of the human race." In other words, it stimulates learning for its own sake, as a tool to improve the person, not to enable the student to pass—which is the surest corrective of the failings of American education perceived in the 1990s and satirized in "The History Teacher."

CRITICAL OVERVIEW

It is a well-known phenomenon for a writer's popularity to be held against him by academic critics, and Collins, one of the most popular poets in America in terms of book sales, is no exception. When, for example, Rachel Hadas in a 2006 issue of *Modernism/Modernity* draws attention to "the accessibility of two popular

In the second half of the poem, the narrator comments on the children on the playground. (© Mat Hayward/
Shutterstock.com)

and accomplished poets whose work is much simpler, and much less demanding, Billy Collins and Sharon Olds," her compliment to Collins is somewhat backhanded. She implies that Collins's work is able to be appreciated by the uneducated masses and, accordingly, need not concern the learned critic to any great degree, using somewhat coded language to read Collins's poems' simplicity as signifying a lack of substance.

However, the same qualities in Collins's work can be given an opposite interpretation. Robert Potts, in an interview with Collins in the *Coachella Review*, praises Collins for not playing games with his readers or leading them astray, but addressing them in a straightforward manner. He suggests that Collins simplifies the world for his readers in such a way as they might experience while surfing the Internet and is serving a sort of aggregating function for contemporary culture. Roger Gilbert, writing in *Contemporary Literature* in 2001 (just prior to Collins's run as poet laureate), notices that Collins exploited a popular trend of renewed interest

in angels, making his book *Questions about Angels* (in which "The History Teacher" was first published) one of twenty-seven poetry anthologies with the word "Angel" in the title published in the United States in the 1990s. Gilbert attributes Collins's popularity not to his simplicity but rather to his gentle, almost reassuring irony.

When *Questions about Angels* was first published in 1991, it was hardly noticed compared to the wide reception Collins's new books have received in the twenty-first century and so was not extensively reviewed. The individual poems in that volume, including "The History Teacher," have yet to receive much attention from a scholarly world that often holds back from analysis of works until time has passed judgment. Jay Boggis, in a review of *Questions about Angels* in the *Harvard Review*, with reference to the poem "Nostalgia" (in which Collins gives his own version of history, attributing modern American social customs to the sixteenth century, in a manner highly reminiscent of the treatment of history in films), regards

Collins's poetry as written in "a code that is usually more interesting than anything it was trying to conceal," suggesting that any deeper meaning in Collins's poems is inferior to their form of expression. David Baker, in his 1992 review essay "Smarts" in *Poetry*, says that "Billy Collins can be downright funny; he's a parodist, a feigning trickster, an ironic, entertaining magician-as-hero." For him, "The History Teacher," with its rewriting of history, becomes part of "a catalog of transformations and discoveries" in *Questions about Angels*.

CRITICISM

Rita M. Brown

Brown is an English professor. In the following essay, she examines different layers of symbolic meaning in Collins's poem "The History Teacher," searching for its political and philosophical significance.

In Billy Collins's poem "The History Teacher," the title character falsifies the material he teaches to his students, in a misguided attempt to preserve their innocence against knowledge of all the unpleasant things that humans have done or experienced in the last million years. Seemingly as a result of this falsification, the students go out on the playground and bully their classmates who are smarter or weaker than themselves. The teacher, meanwhile, is oblivious to what is going on and strolls through a white-picket-fenced vision of the American dream, planning to continue with his present approach to history. The immediate effect of the poem is humorous, with all of the absurd reinterpretations of historical facts, but the reader is brought up short by the bullying and realizes that the humor is used for a serious purpose. It distracts from the blow of some deeper meaning that Collins wishes to impart. Just as the history teacher's lies are meant to direct students *away* from what he considers unpleasant truths, Collins's jokes are meant to direct the reader's attention *toward* unpleasant truths. The rewritings of history in the poem have to be read as symbols to suggest that deeper meaning. Since Collins himself does not explain the symbolic meaning, the reader is left searching, with no guarantee of going down the right path or finding the goal.

> JUST AS THE HISTORY TEACHER'S LIES ARE MEANT TO DIRECT STUDENTS *AWAY* FROM WHAT HE CONSIDERS UNPLEASANT TRUTHS, COLLINS'S JOKES ARE MEANT TO DIRECT THE READER'S ATTENTION *TOWARD* UNPLEASANT TRUTHS."

The falsification of history portrayed in "The History Teacher" can be interpreted in many different ways. The poem is a satire, but the thing being satirized is not clearly defined, nor does it need to be limited to a single target. The first place to look is the real world of education in the 1990s. Were teachers doing something that could form the basis of Collins's comic exaggerations? There were many trends in the 1990s that could have been attacked in this way, including the perceived dumbing down of the curricula in high school and college and the uncertainty of knowledge within the academy promoted by postmodernism. Another possible satirical target is the constant attempts by fundamentalist Christian groups and organizations like the Discovery Institute to introduce creationism into public schools as a substitute for the sciences of biology and geology, in violation of the separation of church and state guaranteed by the US Constitution. According to the creationist version of history, for instance, the ice ages and stone age never even existed, so this could well be the butt of Collins's satire portraying these ages as trivialities.

But whatever specific phenomena Collins might have had in mind, he was responding to a mood in the country that education was under assault from within, by teachers who were consciously falsifying or cheapening their curricula for what they believed to be the benefit of their students. Collins is certainly not the only person to have thought this. The same interpretation of American education led certain parties to push back against educational trends, whether in the form of the No Child Left Behind Act or the physics professor Alan Sokal's publication of a completely hoaxed postmodernist article (consisting of nothing but streams of meaningless jargon) to point out the lack of rigor in that movement. Indeed, Sokal approached the

WHAT DO I READ NEXT?

- Charles J. Sykes's *Dumbing Down Our Kids: Why American Children Feel Good about Themselves but Can't Read, Write, or Add*, first published in 1995, expresses fears common in the United States at the time over the erosion of quality in the educational system.

- Benjamin A. Elman's *A Cultural History of Civil Examinations in Late Imperial China* (2000) gives a detailed history of the famous Chinese civil-service examination, which (rather than wealth or local influence) provided the entrée into the imperial bureaucracy from the integrated perspective of Chinese culture as a whole. Elman describes the decline of the examination system in the later Manchu period and the havoc caused when well-intentioned reformers abolished it at the end of the nineteenth century.

- Barbara Forrest and Paul R. Gross's *Creationism's Trojan Horse: The Wedge of Intelligent Design* describes the attempt by the Discovery Institute (as outlined in their internal memo known as the "Wedge Document") to reshape American life by injecting fundamentalist Christianity into the public-school curriculum under the pseudoscientific guise of intelligent-design creationism. The 2007 edition of this text adds a chapter on the *Kitzmiller v. Dover* trial, which ended

an attempt by the Discovery Institute to implement its policy in collusion with local school-board members.

- Alan Sokal's 2010 volume *Beyond the Hoax: Science, Philosophy and Culture* not only recounts his hoax satirizing the postmodern critique of science but also presents a wealth of new material warning against the threat that pseudoscience increasingly presents to science and the modern civilization that depends on it.

- Collins's 2001 collection *Sailing Alone around the Room: New and Selected Poems* marked his shift to Random House as a publisher, presenting his work to a much larger reading public. This volume allowed him to publish his uncollected poems from that time in addition to a selection of his previous work, a longed-for achievement by any academic poet.

- Charles J. Sykes's *50 Rules Kids Won't Learn in School: Real-World Antidotes to Feel-Good Education*, published in 2007 (but based on an article from the mid-1990s), is the author's advice to high-school students whom he feels have been damaged intellectually in their preparation for work and college by the dumbed-down education system.

---

problem in the same way as Collins, by making fun of it. But Collins sees the threat in more absolute terms than did most of his contemporaries, which is why he does not bother to list real-world specifics in his poem.

The problem that interests Collins is revealed in the fifth stanza. All along, from the beginning of the poem, the history teacher thinks that he is lying to his students in order to protect them. He believes that he is preserving their innocence. But finally the students are released to their own devices, to go out and act on the principles they have been taught, or rather

mistaught. What they do is invade the playground and bully other students who are either smarter or weaker than themselves. This can be understood in a number of ways. Perhaps the teacher has succeeded in preserving their innocence, and it is that innocence that makes them violent and bigoted. However paradoxical this may seem on the surface, there is reason to think that this is one meaning that Collins wishes the reader to take away from "The History Teacher." Because the students are uneducated and ignorant (for which *innocent* is perhaps a euphemism), they have not built up inner resources of wisdom and self-worth and can only relate to others by lashing out with social violence motivated by fear and hatred. They are left childish and immature and act out with destructive tantrums. In society as it actually exists, the same impulses born of ignorance and fear play out in the same kinds of people as intolerance and bigotry.

In the final stanza, the teacher, evidently oblivious to his students' actions, strolls through an idyllic neighborhood marked by its white picket fences. The white picket fence is often used as a symbol of the American dream, the foremost part of a person's property signifying the whole of well-kept middle-class suburban homes and marking the American success story that builds that kind of neighborhood. More particularly, the white picket fence is rich in nostalgia and is often used to represent a past time when life was simpler and better, uncomplicated by all the difficulties and compromises that beset modern life. The nostalgia of the white picket fence suggests more peaceful, prosperous periods of America's past, like the 1950s or 1920s. This is perhaps the innocence that the history teacher is trying to preserve: an idyllic American past. Why, then, does the preserved innocence result in the violence of the strong against the weak, of the ignorant against the civilized? Largely because that innocence is an illusion. The past is idealized not only because of the peace and prosperity of those earlier times, but because America then seemed more homogenous and unified. The picket fence is the beautiful facade of old-time America, but it hides something quite different behind it. The social disruptions that many Americans fear are the results of the integration of women and racial minorities fully into the structure of American society. The picket-fence facade was a front for a society, indeed government institutions and the law, that oppressed women and blacks. The Ku Klux Klan, for instance, was a major political force in the 1920s and again in the 1950s, precisely because its violence, racial hatred, and anti-Semitism were viewed by its supporters as ways of preventing or controlling social change. Even changes such as the extension of greater liberty to all, and the truer application of the ideals of the Constitution to American society, were feared because the extension of freedom was viewed as coming at the cost of the loss of privilege by the few. The forces of repression imagined that they were defending tradition or restoring the virtues of the past, but really their ideals grew from a false understanding of history that was used to support their oppressive politics and repressive violence. The Klan leaders of the 1920s were able to use the slogan "Let's stand behind Old Glory and the church of Jesus Christ," as if the founding ideals of the United States and the message of the Christian gospels had anything to do with the intercommunity violence and oppression that the Klan practiced and stood for. The bigoted violence that Collins witnessed growing up in the 1950s and 1960s during the civil rights era was premised on a falsified reading of America's past, something that must have seemed to his wit as comic as it was tragic.

The genius of Collins's seemingly trivial poem is that its own rather unimposing facade can be peeled away to lay bare many deeper layers of meaning. It addresses anxieties about the decay of the American educational system, while that in turn reveals the violence that has been an inherent part of American society always at odds with the American goals of liberty and justice, a violence that is always based on false idealization of the past, which, of course can only come about through the failure of education. But the core of "The History Teacher" is philosophical. The teacher thinks that he is helping his students by lying to them. He does not realize that lying always harms the people who are lied to. Therefore he is really harming his students and is directly responsible for their becoming bullies. Plato, in the *Republic* (circa 380 BCE), established this principle over two thousand years ago. In this dialogue, the character of Socrates questions one of his colleagues who believes in the traditional Greek wisdom that one ought to harm one's enemies when possible. By careful questioning, Socrates backs him into a corner, where he is forced to qualify his position so that one should only harm enemies that are themselves bad. Continuing, Socrates demonstrates that harming even the wicked is wrong, because "then it must also be admitted . . . that men who are harmed become more unjust." In other words, harming even one's enemies only makes them worse and is not capable of helping even the one doing the harming, but will recoil upon him as his enemies become more unjust. Therefore, when the history teacher injures his students by lying to them, he cannot preserve their innocence but can only make them more unjust. This indeed is the result that Collins

History teachers (© Clipart deSIGN | Shutterstock.com)

shows in the poem. Instead of helping them, as he believes he is doing, the history teacher is harming his students. His lies turn them into the kind of people who willfully harm others and are a threat against all of society. The same is true of real-life demagogues who incite hatred and violence by lying about history and culture. The ones who do the harm through the lies are just as much deceived as their victims. In his seemingly trivial joke of a poem, Collins has embedded the ethics of Martin Luther King, Jr., and Mahatma Gandhi—that one should not harm even one's oppressors, but should try to educate them—for those willing to do the work to find them.

Source: Rita M. Brown, Critical Essay on "The History Teacher," in *Poetry for Students*, Gale, Cengage Learning, 2013.

Kay Day and Billy Collins

In the following interview, Day and Collins discuss his process of writing poetry, including his routines, ideas, and the composition.

One of America's most popular poets, Billy Collins says a central challenge of his genre rests on getting complete strangers interested in your subjective life. How do you engage them in the fact that you looked out the window and saw a climbing vine? Collins' ability to interest readers in subjects like climbing vines and country mice is unsurpassed. His books rank as poetry best-sellers, and his readings are usually sold-out

events. Collins notes the pleasure for both poet and reader that comes from keeping the "playful" part of writing alive. As U.S. poet laureate (2001–2003), Collins returned poetry to the mainstream by writing poems that are accessible yet well-crafted. For 30 years, he has taught at Lehman College, City University of New York, and he has received many fellowships and awards. He lives in Somers, N.Y., with his wife, Diane, an architect.

Credits: Eight poetry collections, including *The Trouble With Poetry*.

Why: Having spent many years learning how to write, I can't stop. Because then it would waste all those years. Once you've gotten over the publication hump and have books out there, the motive isn't to save the world. It's to assure yourself you can still do it.

Routine: How do you go about kissing someone? I don't have any work habits. Writing is spasmodic and happens irregularly. Often the idea comes very much away from the desk. The desk becomes the place of composition. Poetry is not something that is just done at a desk. It merges out of your experience, then you take that initiating line and work with it.

Ideas: I don't know if my mind has had an idea that hasn't been received from somebody else. I'm always looking around for something I can exploit as a way to begin a poem. For example, a friend of mine told me about statues. My friend is from the South, where there are more equestrian statues. So she knew about symbolism, things like the position of the horse's hooves. Another person might throw this away as another piece of trivia. The dream catcher in me sees it as potential; it offered itself as the beginning of a poem ["Statues in the Park"]. I wrote a poem in August, before the hurricane [Katrina]. It just occurred to me one very hot morning, the idea of gratitude for creature comforts. I had running water and electricity; the light worked.

Composition: For me, this is the exciting part. I write the poems straight through in one sitting. It could take 15 minutes or an hour and a half. I get from beginning to middle to end. I go back and look at the poem and make changes, but they're almost never conceptual. Almost all the changes are to meter or sound. It's often a matter of me trying to make the poem skip down the street a little more smoothly, trying to make it as readable as possible. Anyone who's into

American poetry learns that from Whitman—he accelerates the intimacy. One person writes to one other person. I like to make the reader feel she is an acknowledged presence. The reader is half of the engagement; it almost comes down to manners. So many poems I read, the poet just has bad manners. This can mean the poet is not aware of the reader, is not being kind or clear, or respectful of the fact that readers come into poems wanting something.

Voice: I think you find your voice when you quit censoring yourself. It isn't external. It's inside you. The reason the young writer isn't using it is the voice is being suppressed, usually because of some kind of decorum. I ask young writers to examine themselves. What are you keeping out of your writing? Allowing those things into your writing is ultimately how you find your voice.

Advice: There's only one way: reading. The polite way to say it is to write under the influence of other writers or poets. You need to be envious of other poets....Jealously proceed toward finding your own voice by imitating.

Source: Kay Day, "Billy Collins," in *Writer*, Vol. 119, No. 4, April 2006, p. 66.

Harriet Zinnes

In the following review, Zinnes notes a shadow lurking behind the picture of the American dream in the poems chosen for the collection.

What is fascinating about a Poet Laureate is that he is never a Poete Maudit. It was the late nineteenth-century French Symbolist poet Verlaine who asked with particular accuracy, "Is it not true that now and forever the sincere poet sees, feels, knows himself accursed [maudit] by whatever system of self-interest is in power." And as night follows the day the Poet Laureate is chosen "by whatever system of self-interest is in power." Inevitably, therefore, the poet Billy Collins has become Poet Laureate for the year 2001–2002. There is nothing in Billy Collins's poetry that is ever anything but commendable, fluent, and accomplished, but it is also true that there is never anything within the poetry that suggests any divergence from the American dream. We are all apparently comfortably housed, trees appear outside our windows, birds sing, there are roads for cars to drive on, walks through the hills to be taken, malls to buy in, books to read in libraries or from our shelves, and a dog that one loves is always by our side.

What is missing in this happy picture of languishing domesticity is the laughter and cries of children, and though there is an occasional appearance of a wife, that is rare and seemingly irrelevant—and there is no Afghanistan. A perfect American Poet Laureate, therefore.

Yet there is a shadow lurking behind the ease of these poems. It is the shadow of death, for the poet writes it is always "possible company." But even in his celebrated poem "Picnic, Lightning" (from which the last quoted phrase is taken) while the poet shovels compost into a wheelbarrow and contemplates "the instant hand of Death / always ready to burst forth / from the sleeve of his voluminous cloak," he retains his usual sense of throbbing life. He is reminded that "the soil is full of marvels / bits of leaf like flakes off a fresco, / red-brown pine needles, a beetle quick / to burrow back under the loam." Even the wheelbarrow becomes "a wilder blue, / the clouds a brighter white." The shadow of death therefore fades. Life throbs.

With such a sense of continuous life, how can the poet Billy Collins avoid the sentimental? Using poetic rhythms that are never disruptive, there seems no threatening sorrow in the life of this poet, who is also a professor of English at Lehman College of the City University of New York. The death of a beloved mother is sweetly accepted. There may be the fall of a branch but there is the soothing song of a bird and beautiful still lifes in a museum. Yes, in the early book included in this collection, *The Art of Drowning* (the title itself is a giveaway: drowning, that tragedy, can itself be an "art"), there is a revealing poem called "Osso Buco." In the poem, the poet declares that having eaten his "savory" osso buco prepared by his wife, he is now a "creature with a full stomach." But the poet adds with a hardly contained snarl that such a full-stomach creature is "something you don't hear much about in poetry / that sanctuary of hunger and deprivation." So it is off from the bookshelves, you Mandelshtams and Akhmatovas! Here are Billy Collins's *New and Selected Poems*, and when you read them, you will hardly be *Sailing Alone Around the Room*. The popularity of Billy Collins is astonishing. And for American poetry, as readings may increase by the thumbnail as a result of this popularity, that is a very good thing.

Source: Harriet Zinnes, Review of *Sailing Alone around the Room: New and Selected Poems*, in *Hollins Critic*, Vol. 39, No. 3, June 2002, p. 19.

" ONCE YOU BECOME POPULAR AS A POET, OR
AS ANYTHING, YOU'RE A SITTING DUCK."

Laura Secor and Billy Collins
In the following interview, Collins explains to Secor how the reception of his poetry by readers differs from that of critics.

Billy Collins writes poems that make people laugh and that have reached hundreds of thousands of readers. It's a feat that should disqualify him from membership in poetry's inner circles, where high seriousness and insularity often go hand in hand. What to do with someone who uses titles like "Reading an Anthology of Chinese Poems of the Sung Dynasty, I Pause to Admire the Length and Clarity of Their Titles"? Someone who writes poem after poem confessing to a life spent sipping tea, observing his dog, and writing poems about writing poems?

Why, make him poet laureate, of course, as the Library of Congress did last fall. But when the 60-year-old Collins assumed the post, he found himself the subject of both adulation and controversy. Lambasted by critics for his seemingly mundane subject matter, Collins has also been called America's first truly popular poet since Robert Frost. And that was *before* September 11. Americans have since rediscovered an appetite for poetry and Collins' new collection, *Sailing Alone Around the Room*, has practically sailed off bookstore shelves.

Irreverent and playful—"I used to sit in the café of existentialism . . . / contemplating the suicide a tiny Frenchman / might commit by leaping from the rim of my brandy glass"—Collins wants to change the way Americans first encounter poetry. His high-school program, Poetry 180, will have students nationwide reading a poem of Collins' choosing each day of the school year—on the condition that the students not have to analyze them. The first is Collins' own "Introduction to Poetry," in which a professor laments that all his students seem to want to do is torture a confession out of a poem, to beat it "with a hose / to find out what it really means."

Mother Jones spoke with Collins from his home outside of New York City.

[Mother Jones]: What is the job of the poet laureate?

[Billy Collins]: Well, there is always a temptation just to go to Washington and sit in this office and blow smoke rings for a year while I look out at the Capitol. But because of the excessive activism of my predecessors, it seems that an obligation falls my way to get out and light poetry bonfires and to spread the word of poetry. And so I'm doing that through this program for poetry in the high schools. I've described it as a kind of poetry jukebox that we're building from scratch. Eventually there will be 180 tunes on the jukebox. The poems have to be short, clear, and clean. I don't want to give a reactionary administrator an excuse to kill the program because he sees the word *breast* in a poem. But there are lots of good poems out there without breasts in them, or other body parts, or things like that going on.

Your poet laureateship comes at an extraordinary time.

You're telling me.

How has that affected what you do?

My poetry was never written for a nation in crisis, obviously, if you've read any. But my poems and lots of people's poems are unintentional responses to terrorism, in that they honor life. Poems are a preservative for experience, and there would be no reason to preserve experience if one did not feel that there's something special and even sacred about it. So in that sense I would say that any good poem is a sort of anti-death poem, an anti-terrorism poem. Terrorism goes beyond articulation, and it is committed out of a sense of the absolute. Poetry is very much a statement against absolutism. Poetry is a home for ambiguity. It is one of the few places where ambiguity is honored.

After September 11, were there poets you turned to?

It would be poets like Wislawa Szymborska, Czeslaw Milosz, Anna Akhmatova, Osip Mandelstam, Pablo Neruda, William Butler Yeats. The interesting thing about them is that none of them were American. One thing these poets have in common is that they have lived through times when there has been rubble in the streets and soldiers tramping through one's garden. That hasn't happened in America.

Do you think September 11 will change the shape of American poetry?

That's one of those big, lofty, visionary questions. And to all those questions I give a resounding "I don't have a clue." [*Laughs.*] But in a way, I hope not. I don't think poets should feel an obligation to respond to the event in a literal way.

Have you seen any good poems that do literally address what happened?

No. I've seen a lot of bad ones. Poetry doesn't do very well when it tries to express collective feeling. It does much better at expressing individual feeling. That's why most of those poems fail. Richard Hugo's great counsel to poets was, Never write a poem about something that wants to have a poem written about it. When subject matter is crying out to you, that's usually exactly what to avoid.

You're an advocate for the return of humor to poetry. I laughed aloud reading your poem about shoveling snow with Buddha. He's shoveling away within "the generous pocket of his silence." But eventually Buddha speaks, and there's this moment of anticipation where you break the stanza—but what he says is, "After this, can we go inside and play cards?"

Well, Buddha wouldn't say anything lofty! That's a poem that has humor in it, but I think it may be a representative poem because it's not entirely funny. The perfect poem for me to write would be a poem in which the reader couldn't tell at any point whether the poem was serious or humorous. I guess that's just called irony. What I'm doing by aiming at that balancing act is avoiding two character flaws: One is sentimentality, and the other is sarcasm. Poetry for me is a kind of therapeutic attempt to find a balancing point between those two weaknesses.

Is Robert Frost a major influence?

I think Frost would probably roll over in his grave if he knew I was poet laureate, because I'm not a rhymer, and I've been playing pingpong without a net for most of my writing life—not even tennis! But Frost offers many, many values worth imitating. One of them is clarity, and another is a very intense ambiguity. He begins very clearly and he ends very often in mystery. He starts with something simple, like, Here are two roads—which one should I go down? A dozen lines later, we're talking about fate, the impossibility of decisiveness, the future, how do

we know the past, do we invent the past? Like my dog just now, running into a swamp after a squirrel, we step off a ledge into these very large questions.

Has anything about the reception of your new book surprised you?

Two things. First is the mind-blowing number of books sold. It's been three months and 65,000 copies in print. And that's totally off the charts for poetry. The second thing would be the hostility of the critical reception. So it seems you can't have it both ways.

Why do you think that is?

Well, I would like to say it's just the green element, you know—there's some envy involved. Once you become popular as a poet, or as anything, you're a sitting duck. But you know, there's a great deal of fretting about how poetry is neglected. And most of the people who do that kind of fretting are really fretting about the fact that their own poetry is neglected. And there's usually a very good reason for that, and it's almost entirely their fault. [*Laughs.*]

The solitude of writing poetry is such a part of the process, and yet, now, when you give a reading, sometimes you're standing in front of 500 people.

I write the poems, you're quite right, in solitude. Melville called it the mood for composition—a slow, grass-growing state of mind when you're alone and you have time to think about things like, What would it be like to shovel snow with Buddha? [*Laughs.*] I'm always thinking that a poem will be taken in by someone sitting in a room alone. And I am speaking to them quietly. To find that the one person that you've been whispering these poems to has somehow multiplied into 700 people is kind of shocking. And then you have to scramble a little bit more for the solitude. Take now, for example. Right now I could be writing a lovely poem. [*Laughs.*]

Source: Laura Secor, "Billy Collins: Mischievous Laureate," in *Mother Jones*, Vol. 27, No. 2, March–April 2002, pp. 84–85.

Richard Alleva

In the following essay, Alleva acknowledges Collins's status as a minor poet of light, humorous verse but insists that this is a deliberate strategy on the poet's part.

Billy Collins being named poet laureate was good news to me, yet I think the first words that ran through my head, after hearing of the

> ONE IS TEMPTED TO SAY THAT MINOR-NESS IS WHAT HE STRIVES FOR RATHER THAN WHAT HE FALLS BACK INTO FOR WANT OF GREATNESS."

appointment, were, "They've actually had the guts to honor someone who writes light verse? Ogden Nash should have been so lucky!"

Like a lot of first reactions, it was wrong. But, like all first reactions, it had its reasons.

Light verse jingles along within neatly hedged stanzas. It's the interplay between the poet's fantasticality and the precise meters and nimble rhymes that produces the humor of, for instance, Hilaire Belloc's description (in "Matilda") of eager-beaver firemen "saving" a Victorian mansion that isn't really burning: "They ran their ladders through a score / Of windows on the ball room floor / And took peculiar pains to souse / The pictures up and down the house."

Billy Collins doesn't brandish rhyme or meter or pattern that way. His poems can make you laugh, but their sound effects are muted and help achieve a dry whimsicality that brings to mind the comedian Bob Newhart or the cartoonist Charles Schultz rather than any other poet. Collins's recent volume of new and collected verse bears the pleasant title, *Sailing Alone around the Room* (Random House), but *The Button-Down Mind of Billy Collins* might have been just as apt. Perhaps it's my associating Collins with comic entertainers that made me think of him as a maker of light, comic verse. But there's something else.

I often have occasion to read light verse to children, and I get the same pleasure from reciting these little masterpieces the twentieth time as the first. But I never get more. The peculiar joy and the peculiar drawback of good light verse are that it defies time but it never grows with time. The same is true of most of Collins's poems.

Take "Pinup." The opening,

The murkiness of the local garage is not so dense that you cannot make out the calendar of pinup drawings on the wall above a bench of tools.

is typical Collins: a seemingly slouching gait concealing a basically iambic beat; an apparently rhymeless poem that contains the ghost of rhyme ("murkiness" with "dense"); a protagonist addressed in the second person because he could be Everyman (if not Everywoman) but who is actually Billy Collins not shirking the Everyman role.

Our hero flips through a calendar while a mechanic works on his car. Collins captures the coy, unintentionally comic appeal of the pinup girl, Miss March, with a relaxed, unprurient humanity:

One hand is busy keeping her hat down on her head and the other is grasping the little dog's leash, so of course there is no hand left to push down her dress which is billowing up around her waist . . .

Oh, "of course" the poor dear can't help herself! And it is this gallant excuse-making of the onlooker that becomes the source of the poem's comedy. The hero is being protective not only of Miss March's essential innocence but of his own self-esteem. He refuses to think of himself as the . . . creep that all porn, however softcore, tries to turn a man into. He consents to being an admiring observer but not a peeping Tom. And, since he is a Billy Collins hero, the onlooker carries his fantasy of gallantry as far as he can.

You would like to come to her rescue, gather up the little dog in your arms, untangle the leash, lead her to safety, and receive her bottomless gratitude, but

But the mechanic interrupts the reverie to explain that the repair is going to take longer and cost more than expected. Our hero calmly (gladly, we suspect) accepts the verdict and sidles back to the calendar. He may be gallant but he's also hooked. What does Miss April look like?

This is excellent comedy and good poetry. Reading it for the tenth time, I smiled, chuckled, laughed exactly at the parts I smiled, chuckled, laughed during the nine previous readings. Precisely what happens when I reread Nash and Belloc. Precisely what happens when I listen to *The Button-Down Mind of Bob Newhart* for the umpteenth time.

There is another connection to Newhart and other standup comedians. When Newhart asks us to imagine a public relations adviser urging Abe Lincoln to keep the Gettysburg Address the way the boys in the back room drafted it, it is the very situation that starts the listener laughing even before the jokes begin. The same goes for many a Collins poem. While most poets of the last hundred years make readers work their way into the meaning of a poem gingerly, Collins charms and entices right from the start with his provocative setups: "A sentence starts out like a lone traveler / heading into a blizzard at night" ("Winter Syntax"); "In the morning when I found History / snoring on the couch . . ." ("The Lesson"); "Remember the 1340s? / We were doing a dance called the Catapult" ("Nostalgia"); "Trying to protect his students' innocence / he told them the Ice Age was really just / the Chilly Age, a period of a million years / when everyone had to wear sweaters" ("The History Teacher"). Often Collins fulfills the promise of these crowd-pleasing openings, sometimes he doesn't, but he rarely lifts the entire poem to a plane far above the opening. There is much justice in Adam Kirsch's observation (*New Republic*, October 29, 2001): "the very easiness of the joke suggests its limitation. . . . Once we remind ourselves that the target of the joke is merely an expression, the piling up of new details begins to seem a poor use of Collins's wit."

All this is by way of saying that Billy Collins may be merely (merely!) a good minor poet. But I'm also beginning to believe that the most important thing to say about Collins is that he is a *deliberately* minor poet, even a *rebelliously* minor poet, a poet who would reject major status if it were thrust upon him. One is tempted to say that minor-ness is what he strives for rather than what he falls back into for want of greatness.

Nowadays, an American citizen may feel washed up on strange but inevitable beaches by irresistible, Hegelian waves. Who can defy history when your own country is making it? Are we not all cogs in some mysteriously wired machine? Must not a major American poet— like a latter-day Pound or Eliot—have something important to say about the winds of war, the winds of change, and a lot of other portentous winds? Yet how foolish even the best of poets (even a Pound or Eliot? especially a Pound or Eliot!) can sound when he solemnly licks his finger, holds it up in the air, and solemnly prognosticates. At times, one longs, in a time of crisis, for a minor poet who does nothing but explore, thoroughly, entertainingly, and— above all—honestly, the design of his immediate

surroundings and familiar fantasies. The same goes for all the arts: Now and then we need a Lewis Carroll instead of a Dostoyevsky, a Borges rather than a Thomas Mann, an Edward Gorey not an Anselm Kiefer. The major artists reach further and deeper into history, but the minor ones find crevices within history where we may shelter, take a breath, and know ourselves again.

At his best, Billy Collins achieves this minor glory. He is the bard of the emotional oasis and the life-restoring whim-wham; he is the perfect antidote to Hegel. In "Bar Time," he notes that "universal / saloon practice" sets the pub clock "fifteen minutes ahead / of all the clocks in the outside world." This allows the clientele to do "our drinking in the unknown future, / immune from the cares of the present, / safely harbored a quarter of an hour / beyond the woes of the contemporary scene." But, lest you think Collins is writing a sort of metered escapism, note well that in the aforementioned "The History Teacher," the misguidedly compassionate teacher, having mistaught his grammar school students that "The War of the Roses took place in a garden, / and the *Enola Gay* dropped one tiny atom / on Japan," allows the children out on the playground where they "torment the weak / and the smart, / mussing up their hair and breaking their glasses." Collins doesn't want to escape history; he just doesn't want a consciousness of it to crush awareness of those private joys that are timeless.

Collins knows that the major turning points within every life are, in a sense, timeless, especially the final crisis, death. In "Tomes," there is a sarcastic evocation of the sort of all-encompassing historical book, typically titled *The History of the World*, the kind that weighs eleven pounds and that "always has a way of"

> . . . quieting the riotous sort of information
> that foams around my waist
> even though it never mentions
> the silent labors of the poor
> the daydreams of grocers and tailors,
> or the faces of men and women alone in
> single rooms . . .

Collins then describes his mother on her deathbed:

> the bones of her fingers interlocked,
> her sunken eyes staring upward
> beyond all knowledge,
> beyond the tiny figures of history,
> some in uniform, some not,

marching onto the pages of this incredibly heavy book.

If Billy Collins were nothing but an ahistorical jester, jingling the bells on his cap to distract us from the vicissitudes of history, he would be a strange poet laureate indeed for these post–September 11 times. But, though he certainly doesn't spurn the role of jester, he is also more than that. While many men in various kinds of uniform are warning us that they have every right to kill us if we don't march in the historical direction they have decreed correct, Billy Collins's poems remind us that there are places in the mind where the generals and the publicists and the terrorists cannot reach, and that the most stirring of historical admonitions are often a lot less soul-stirring than the faces of men and women alone in single rooms. If a return to normalcy is really the best refutation of terror, then Collins is indeed the poet fit for these tense times, for he is the celebrant of the beauty and comedy that are everywhere around us in everyday life.

Source: Richard Alleva, "A Major Minor Poet," in *Commonweal*, Vol. 129, No. 1, January 11, 2002, pp. 21–22.

SOURCES

Baker, David, "Smarts," in *Poetry*, Vol. 159, No. 5, 1992, pp. 282–98.

Baker, Kelly J., *Gospel according to the Klan: The KKK's Appeal to Protestant America, 1915–1930*, University Press of Kansas, 2011, pp. 1–33.

Boggis, Jay, Review of *Questions about Angels*, in *Harvard Review*, No. 17, Fall 1999, pp. 179–80.

Collins, Billy, "The History Teacher," in *Questions about Angels: Poems*, William Morrow, 1991, pp. 91–92.

———, "Poetry 180," Library of Congress website, http://www.loc.gov/poetry/180/ (accessed April 13, 2012).

Coontz, Stephanie, *The Way We Never Were: American Families and the Nostalgia Trap*, BasicBooks, 2000, pp. 23–41.

Gilbert, Roger, "Awash with Angels: The Religious Turn in Nineties Poetry," in *Contemporary Literature*, Vol. 42, No. 2, Summer 2001, pp. 238–69.

Hadas, Rachel, Review of *How Poets See the World: The Art of Description in Contemporary Poetry*, by Willard Spiegelman, in *Modernism/Modernity*, Vol. 13, No. 3, September 2006, pp. 595–97.

Kay, Alan N., "I Love History...but I Hated It in School!," in "Young Heroes of History" website, 2006,

pp. 46–48, http://www.youngheroesofhistory.com/images/final%20version.pdf (accessed February 17, 2012).

Moore, Leonard J., *Citizen Klansmen: The Ku Klux Klan in Indiana, 1921–1928*, University of North Carolina Press, 1997, pp. 76–106.

Plato, *The Republic*, translated by Paul Shorey, in *The Collected Dialogues of Plato, Including the Letters*, edited by Edith Hamilton and Huntington Cairns, Bollingen Series LXXI, Princeton University Press, 1963, p. 585.

Plimpton, George, "Billy Collins: The Art of Poetry No. 83," in *Paris Review*, No. 159, Fall 2001, http://www.theparisreview.org/interviews/482/the-art-of-poetry-no-83-billy-collins (accessed February 17, 2012).

Potts, Robert, "A Conversation with Billy Collins," in *Coachella Review*, Fall 2009, http://thecoachellareview.com/poetry/interview_billycollins_fall09.html (accessed January 27, 2012).

Scott, Eugenie Carol, and Glenn Branch, *Not in Our Classrooms: Why Intelligent Design Is Wrong for Our Schools*, Beacon Press, 2006, pp. 15–19.

Selden, Raman, ed., *The Cambridge History of Literary Criticism*, Vol. 8, *From Formalism to Poststructuralism*, Cambridge University Press, 1995, pp. 131–96.

Sokal, Alan D., "A Physicist Experiments with Cultural Studies," in *Lingua Franca*, Vol. 4, May 1996, pp. 49–53, http://www.physics.nyu.edu/faculty/sokal/lingua_franca_v4/lingua_franca_v4.html (accessed February 10, 2012).

———, "Transgressing the Boundaries: Towards a Transformative Hermeneutics of Quantum Gravity," in *Social Text*, Vols. 46/47, Spring/Summer 1996, pp. 217–52, http://www.physics.nyu.edu/faculty/sokal/transgress_v2/transgress_v2_singlefile.html (accessed February 10, 2012).

Trout, Paul, "Student Anti-intellectualism and the Dumbing Down of the University," in *Montana Professor*, Vol. 7, No. 2, Spring 1997, http://mtprof.msun.edu/spr1997/TROUT-ST.html (accessed February 12, 2012).

FURTHER READING

Collins, Billy, *Horoscopes for the Dead: Poems*, Random House, 2011.
     This is Collins's most recent collection of new poems.

Gross, Paul R., and Norman Levitt, *Higher Superstition: The Academic Left and Its Quarrels with Science*, Johns Hopkins University Press, 1994.
     Gross and Levitt's book was one of the first attacks against the relativism of postmodernism and its incompatibility with science and the scientific method.

Lebo, Lauri, *The Devil in Dover: An Insider's Story of Dogma v. Darwin in Small-Town America*, New Press, 2008.

As a local newspaper reporter in Dover, Pennsylvania, Lebo covered the *Kitzmiller v. Dover* trial, which reaffirmed a host of Supreme Court rulings that the doctrine of religious creation cannot be taught as science in public schools, and which established as a matter of law that intelligent design is merely another name for creationism. This book is her considered account of the trial.

Washburn, Katharine, and John F. Thornton, eds., *Dumbing Down: Essays on the Strip Mining of American Culture*, W. W. Norton, 1996.

The essays in this volume deal not only with the perceived deterioration of American education, and the subsequent decline in the standard of public knowledge in topics like science, but also with other profit-driven attacks on American culture, such as the commercialization of art as a mass-market product (the Backstreet Boys compared to Aaron Copland) and the rise of the shopping mall as a public space.

SUGGESTED SEARCH TERMS

Billy Collins

"The History Teacher"

satire

dumbing down AND American education

deconstruction

intelligent design creationism

poet laureate of the United States

Poetry 180

Incident

COUNTEE CULLEN

1925

"Incident" is one of the most famous poems written by Countee Cullen, one of the most well-known and important figures in the Harlem Renaissance movement of the 1920s and 1930s. It was published in Cullen's first poetry collection, when he was just twenty-two.

The poem tells the story of two young boys, about the same age, whose eyes lock on each other in a public place: the black child playfully smiles, and the white child seems initially playful too, but then he quickly proves hostile, cutting his counterpart down with a sharp racial epithet. Readers should note that the poem contains a word that is considered offensive, but the language is a product of the racial context of the time period. In a few short lines, Cullen renders a vivid, chilling scene, one that clearly resonated with the poem's speaker for years, into adulthood.

In 1925, the year that this poem was published in his collection *Color*, Cullen became a national figure, winning more awards for writing than any black writer had won before. The respect he earned from the literary establishment helped draw national and international attention to the flourishing artistic scene in Harlem, the section of New York City overwhelmingly occupied by black citizens. For a time, thanks to works like "Incident," white critics and readers who had marginalized the achievements of black artists came to recognize the intellect and talent

Countee Cullen (The Library of Congress)

of artists like Cullen. "Incident" may also be found in *My Soul's High Song: The Collected Writings of Countee Cullen, Voice of the Harlem Renaissance*, published in 1991.

AUTHOR BIOGRAPHY

Not much is known for certain of Cullen's early years—he was secretive about his past and gave different answers about his background at different times in his life. His birth date, May 30, 1903, is generally accepted, but there has always been uncertainty about where he grew up. Some sources have said that he was born in New York City, while others suggest that his early life was spent in Baltimore, Maryland, which is the setting of "Incident." His second wife, who was his strongest and longest relationship, told interviewers after his death that Cullen was born in Louisville, Kentucky. Throughout his early life,

until he was eighteen, Cullen went by his birth name, Countee Leroy Porter.

Regardless of where he was born, by the time he was eleven, Cullen was living in New York City, having been adopted by Carolyn Belle Cullen and the Reverend Frederick Asbury Cullen of the Salem Methodist Episcopal Church in Harlem. He attended DeWitt Clinton High School, where he quickly began building a name for himself as a writer. In his first year there, 1918, one of Cullen's pieces was published in *Modern School*, and soon after that a poem won first prize in a competition by the Federation of Women's Clubs.

At college, his literary reputation quickly flourished. In his first year at New York University in 1922, he had poems published in *Kelly's Magazine* as well as in the *Crisis* and *Opportunity*, the leading publications for black writers at the time. By the following year, he was publishing in nationwide general-circulation magazines. His book *Color*, which contains the poem "Incident," was published in 1925, the year of his graduation from college. It is supposed that most of the poems in his next two volumes, *Copper Sun* and *The Ballad of the Brown Girl*, both published in 1927, were written after he received his master of arts from Harvard University in 1926.

After earning his degrees, Cullen toured Europe and the Middle East and then returned to a position as assistant editor of *Opportunity*. His 1928 marriage to Yolande Du Bois, the daughter of writer W. E. B. Du Bois, was a lavish affair that showed the world the significance of the black literary scene. Within a few months, though, Yolande recognized that their marriage was not a good one, and she filed for divorce. During Cullen's lifetime, there were rumors of his homosexuality, which letters published after his death confirmed. That did not stop him from marrying again in 1940 and having a secure relationship with his second wife, Ida Robertson, until his death.

Although recognized as a major writer in the Harlem Renaissance, Cullen's literary output dwindled after the publication of his poetry collection *The Black Christ and Other Poems* in 1929. In 1932 he published a novel, *One Way to Heaven*, to tepid reviews. In 1935 he took a position teaching French at Frederick Douglass Junior High School in New York. He was working on a play based on a book by Arna Bontemps in 1945 when his blood pressure, always a problem, spiked, sending him to the hospital, where he died on January 9, 1946.

POEM SUMMARY

The text used for this summary is from *My Soul's High Song: The Collected Writings of Countee Cullen, Voice of the Harlem Renaissance*, Anchor Books, 1991, p. 90. Versions of the poem can be found on the following web pages: http://allpoetry.com/poem/8497385-Incident-by-Countee_Cullen and http://www.poemhunter.com/poem/incident/.

Stanza 1

The first line establishes a vague time line, referring to events of the poem as having happened once, with no other point of reference to help readers guess when these events may have occurred. This opening is similar to the beginning of a fairy tale that takes place in an undetermined setting "once upon a time." The end of the first line continues to place this poem in an indistinct setting: it specifies that the incident occurred in Baltimore, Maryland, but mysteriously refers to the city as old, leaving readers to wonder how different the city may have become in the intervening years.

In the second line, Cullen shows the enthusiasm that a boy might have while traveling. Readers do not know who he was or where he was going to or coming from, but they are told that he had glee in the emotional center of his heart and in the intellectual center of his head. With these few words, the poem establishes the child's attitude, showing that he is happy to experience new things. The strangeness of new encounters could be frightening, but that is not the case for this boy.

The first stanza ends by shaking off the poem's fairy-tale mood and getting down to solid, grim reality. The fact that the other boy in the poem is identified as a resident of Baltimore is significant for two reasons. For one thing, it shows that the speaker of the poem has entered into the other boy's territory, indicating the possibility of insecurity and conflict. More important, however, is that Maryland, though it never officially joined the Confederacy during the Civil War, was a state that allowed slavery and aligned itself with the South. In specifying

MEDIA ADAPTATIONS

- "Incident" is included on the recording *To Make a Poem Black: The Best Poems of Countee Cullen*, read by Ruby Dee and Ossie Davis. This recording was released on vinyl record in 1971 by Caedmon and is available on audiocassette and compact disc as well.

- "Incident" is also included on the CD *I Too Sing America: Three Centuries of African American Poetry*. This CD is a companion piece to a 1998 anthology book of the same name, with poems selected by Catherine Clinton. The recording was released in 2000 by Audio Bookshelf.

the background of the other boy, Cullen alludes to the stated and unstated rules for race relations that were unique to the American South in his childhood. The poet is a traveler in Baltimore, and is therefore perhaps unprepared for the open hostility between races that would have been considered normal in the early 1900s. The last line of stanza 1 suggests that hostility, shown in the other boy's stare.

Stanza 2

The poem fills in details about the scene in the second stanza. Line 5 gives the speaker's specific age when this incident occurred, eight. Cullen makes a point of noting that he was small but then immediately notes that the white boy staring at him was almost the same size. He uses an old-fashioned word, *whit*, to describe the almost irrelevant difference in their sizes, making it clear that this incident was not a confrontation in which either boy felt physically intimidated by the other.

Line 7 shows the relationship that developed between these two boys, based just on the one glance between them. The poem's speaker, feeling the similarity between them, smiles to show that they could be friends. The meaning of the other boy's response, sticking out his tongue, is not immediately clear. It could indicate a playful rivalry, a mock seriousness that equals the smile that the speaker has sent his way. It is a childish response, and for a moment it seems that Cullen's point is to show the immaturity of eight-year-olds.

But the innocence of this encounter between two children is shattered in line 8, at the end of the second stanza. Cullen contrasts the childlike gesture of sticking out one's tongue with the other boy's use of a harsh, derogatory racial slur. The word *nigger*—derived from *negro*, Spanish for "black"—was and is a particularly potent word that has been used to belittle people with black skin from the early days of slavery.

In one instant, the common bond between the two boys of similar age and size is shattered by the social reality of how black citizens were viewed by whites in that culture. Although he was almost certainly aware of the social imbalance in an intellectual way, the narrator is made to feel that imbalance in a sharp, painful way.

Stanza 3

In this stanza, the narrator explains that he stayed in Baltimore after that incident for a significant length of time, for several months, allowing him to get to know the town thoroughly. Instead of simply saying that he saw much or all of the town, he expresses his complete knowledge as coming from having seen the *whole* of it. The way this wording suggests a "hole" is almost unavoidable, implying that this incident with this other boy, whom he thought could be a friend, soured him on the entire town. The shift in his attitude is echoed not just in his play on words but in the time frame of his visit, as well: he arrived in springtime, which is traditionally a time of hopeful expectation, and left with the onset of winter, in December, presumably moving back to the North, to the harsher climate of Cullen's New York home.

In the poem's final two lines, the narrator refers obscurely to things that happened in Baltimore. He does not mention any specific events, but the fact that they are not explained serves to drive home the point of the story he is telling. Readers can expect that he might have seen and done things of some lasting significance during a stay of more than half a year, but the sudden, shocking hostility that he encountered overshadowed them all. To the white boy who said it, that one word seems to have been spoken casually, without much thought put into it, but that passing moment struck such a deep chord in the young narrator as to raise the fleeting event to the level of an unforgettable incident.

THEMES

Innocence

"Incident" is a story of how one man lost his innocence at an early age. The first two stanzas give readers a sense of a boy who is young and enthusiastic. He looks out at the world with wonder and anticipation. When he sees another boy, he is even more excited, for he assumes that their ages will give them enough in common to form a relationship. Obviously, the boy was aware of the existence of racism before this incident, or else the racial slur the other boy hurls at him would have had no meaning for him. Still, the moment he hears that one word is a moment of revelation. In an instant, he is aware of the hatred that is always possible in any situation, and that can rise up as a threat to him at any moment. His innocent faith in the world is shattered.

Racism

Because this poem is told in the first person, from the speaker's perspective, it is difficult to guess the degree of racial hatred felt by the boy whom the narrator encounters. He uses a racially offensive word, but there is no way of knowing if he is angry or if he is just following the racist behavior that was standard at that time. The action that precedes the word—poking out his tongue—could be a playful gesture, meant to bring the young narrator in on his game. It could also be read as the angriest gesture that an eight-year-old boy can think of, which would indicate that he uses the hateful word to be as offensive as he can be.

If the white boy thinks he is playing around, then he thinks that race-based hatred is a game. He does not realize how profoundly his racism can affect another person's life, because he has never been at the receiving end of racism. If he is truly angry at the narrator, for no reason other than the color of his skin, then the white boy has learned at an early age to hate and fear people who are different from himself.

TOPICS FOR FURTHER STUDY

- Cullen dedicated this poem to a friend, West Indian writer Eric Walrond. Read some biographical information about Walrond, and write a comparison showing the similarities between his life and Cullen's, focusing particularly on the subjects each author wrote about and their writing styles. Information on Walrond can be found on the Internet or in the book *Winds Can Wake Up the Dead: An Eric Walrond Reader*, published by Wayne State University Press in 1998.

- How might the narrator of this poem have responded to the other boy's taunt? Would he have been in physical danger? Would he have regretted being silent? Write a letter to the young narrator that explains his options. Include some researched material about the history of racial tensions in the United States during the Jim Crow era to give a realistic view of the troubles that might have faced him. Upload your letter to your blog and encourage your classmates to comment on it.

- An incident like the one from the poem could happen today. Write a short story that envisions how such a confrontation would happen in today's world, with a focus on what would be more specific to our time than to Cullen's.

- The documentary *Louder Than a Bomb* covers a spoken-word poetry competition in Chicago that brought together young high-school students from a range of social

classes in different parts of the city to tell their stories. Watch the film (available on DVD from Virgil Films and Entertainment) and use it as a pattern for your own spoken-word competition on the subject of early-life incidents that may have forced or inspired personal growth. Grade your competition using the guidelines mentioned in the film.

- Often, histories of the Harlem Renaissance mention a few key writers without ever noting that there were female writers as well. Select and analyze a poem by one of the Harlem Renaissance's female writers, such as Georgia Douglas Johnson, Angelina Weld Grimké, Anne Spencer, or Gwendolyn Bennett, to name just a few, and write a comparison between that poem and "Incident," pointing out places where you think the writer's gender may be seen as affecting his or her vision.

- Public transportation was one area of social life that was regulated by segregation laws in the early twentieth century: in some states people of different races were forbidden to ride on the same bus or train car. Research which states had the harshest penalties to enforce segregation laws in the 1920s and report to your class on specific cases, including what people were sentenced for and what their sentences were. Use PowerPoint to create a multimedia presentation to aid in your report.

Travel

Cullen is intentionally unclear about the circumstances covered in this poem. In line 1, the boy is riding *in* old Baltimore, not "to" or "from" or "through" it. The fact that he would be staying there for a while does not become clear until line 10, when the poem describes the length of his stay. There is no information given about where

the boy came from, though readers can assume that it must be somewhere in the North, where an eight-year-old white boy like the one in Baltimore would not be as likely to blurt out an offensive word like the one he uses.

The poem relies on the narrator's travels to make its point. Travel can help a person see new places and meet new and interesting people, but

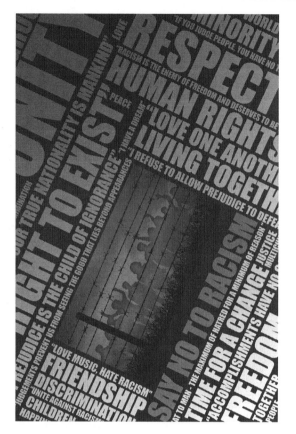

"Incident" is about an incident of racism in Baltimore. (© thomaca | Shutterstock.com)

it can also expose one to the kind of hostility that one would not experience at home. Cullen makes no comment on northern attitudes toward race relations, but he does clearly show that traveling to the brink of the South exposed the narrator to a kind of hostility that he had not previously encountered.

Language

The incident at the center of this poem is actually just a brief, fleeting moment. The young narrator smiles, and the other boy pokes out his tongue. There is only one two-syllable word spoken during their exchange. That word, however, has enough power to change a young man for the rest of his life.

It is natural that Cullen, as a poet, would be sensitive about the power of language and the resonating meanings of words. Here, he presents one particular word, used carelessly by a child, to represent the history of racial tension that evolved from institutional slavery in the United

States. There are other insults that are more graphic, but Cullen frames the epithet in this poem to show that that one word can have more destructive force behind it than many other hateful words and threatening gestures.

STYLE

Hymnal Meter

Hymnal meter is one of the most common forms of ballad meter. It is characterized by four-line stanzas written in iambic meter. The lengths of these lines alternate in hymnal meter, with an eight-syllable line (referred to as "tetrameter") followed by a six-syllable line (referred to as "trimeter"). The most famous example of this style is the hymn "Amazing Grace," which has the exact same syllable count (8-6-8-6) as "Incident." It begins,

> Amazing grace, how sweet the sound
> That saved a wretch like me.
> I once was lost, but now am found,
> Was blind, but now I see.

Cullen's use of hymnal meter allows him to remind his readers of a familiar, reverent experience without actually mentioning religion.

Iambic Feet

One way in which "Incident" conforms to the standards of hymnal meter is in its use of iambic meter, in which an unstressed syllable is followed by a stressed syllable. The two syllables, one unstressed and one stressed, taken together form a poetic unit, or foot, that is called an *iamb*. The poem's eight-syllable lines are said to be presented in iambic tetrameter (four feet) while the six-syllable lines are in iambic trimeter (three feet). Cullen's poem accords with these metrical patterns almost perfectly. In addition to helping the poem conform to the standards of hymnal meter, iambic meter gives the poem a natural, easy flow. Iambic meter is one of the most natural rhythms for English speech.

Rhyme Scheme

In this poem, Cullen follows a consistent *abcb* rhyme scheme, with the last words of the second and fourth lines of each stanza rhyming with each other; meanwhile, the words that end the odd-numbered lines of each stanza stand independent of each other. In the second and third stanzas, the rhymes are feminine, or multisyllabic, with an extra, unaccented syllable added at the end of the line. The overall pattern of rhyming, called a "simple rhyme," gives the poem a playful, sing-song feel, undercutting the horror of the experience that it talks about.

HISTORICAL CONTEXT

The Northern Migration

After the end of the Civil War in 1865, the Thirteenth through Fifteenth Amendments and the period known as Reconstruction, imposed by Congress on the South, helped bring black Americans toward a position of greater social equality. However, when white southerners regained control of their legislatures, they managed to return black Americans to a position of social inequality by passing laws that instituted the segregation of the races. These laws existed until Congress and the Supreme Court made substantial nationwide moves toward full social equality in the 1950s and 1960s.

Much of the problem of segregation stemmed from the traditions that were continued in the South, where slavery based on race had been the norm. After the Civil War ended, many freed former slaves remained in the South for generations: Jeffrey B. Ferguson notes that as late as the 1910s, 90 percent of the black population of the United States still lived in the South. This was despite the fact that much of the South enacted laws to keep races separated, commonly called "Jim Crow" laws (after a comic stereotype black character from minstrel shows). There was a wave of Jim Crow laws enacted in the late 1800s to keep black citizens at a social and financial disadvantage. These laws covered just about every aspect of civic life, restricting where blacks could attend school, where they could live, what public transportation they could take, and so forth. Segregation was deemed to be fair if the treatment of the races was "separate but equal"—a phrase instituted by the 1896 US Supreme Court case *Plessy v. Ferguson*, which found segregation acceptable. But in actuality black Americans would be given less-than-equal treatment until *Plessy* was overruled by *Brown v. Board of Education* in 1954. The situation became even more inhospitable for black citizens in the early part of the twentieth century, when the Ku Klux Klan, a racist terrorist organization that originated in the 1860s, was revived in 1915, to use violence and murder to intimidate blacks who attempted to press for equality.

America's involvement in World War I in 1917 and 1918 helped spur the migration of blacks to the North. The mainly industrial cities of the North were hiring: factories were manufacturing weapons and other war necessities, but many of the white males who had worked in northern factories had been drafted into the military. In addition, the supply of white workers that might have been replenished by immigrants from Europe was cut off because of the war. Ferguson states that around half a million blacks moved to the North between 1915 and 1918, followed by another seven hundred thousand in the early 1920s.

The Harlem Renaissance

Specific communities formed in the northern cities to which rural black families moved in the first decades of the twentieth century. In Chicago, for instance, the South Side became the predominantly black area, while in St. Louis the black community centered in nearby East St. Louis. The black area of New York City was Harlem. Black artists and intellectuals, including Cullen, who lived in Harlem soon gained the attention of critics and publishers, giving them national and international attention, which led to the rise of a movement that was dubbed the Harlem Renaissance.

Following the examples of Booker T. Washington, who founded the Tuskegee Institute (later Tuskegee University) in the 1880s, and W. E. B. Du Bois, author of the influential 1902 collection of essays *The Souls of Black Folk* and a cofounder of the National Association for the Advancement of Colored People, black musicians, poets, and painters asserted their intellectual relevance after the end of World War I. Not all lived in Harlem, but the area became a center of operations for such writers as Jean Toomer, Claude McKay, and Langston Hughes. It also became a convenient way for white writers based in the New York publishing world to characterize the movement. Black journals published in New York, such as the *Crisis* and *Opportunity*, gave writers the visibility they needed to have works published in established national publications.

COMPARE
&
CONTRAST

- **1925:** The Harlem Renaissance art movement is at its height. A young, talented poet like Cullen can draw national attention, though he does it writing in a traditionally white ballad form.

  Today: Traditional versified poetry is seldom found in popular culture, but spoken word, hip-hop and rap lyrics, and slam poetry have captured the public's imagination.

- **1925:** Because of Jim Crow laws, the geographic setting of a racial incident is of vital importance. Maryland is a border state but still supports segregation.

  Today: Laws against racial discrimination have only the minutest differences in different parts of the country. The main result of the civil rights movement of the 1950s and 1960s is that most matters of racial equality are covered under federal law.

- **1925:** Hostility between the races, though a surprise to the young man described in this poem, is common in certain areas of the country.

Today: Mass media has given people much more insight into the lives of others, bringing the country culturally together. Many racist traditions have evaporated. Still, maps of housing taken from census bureau data show that the country is still divided.

- **1925:** A child like the white boy in the poem might think that saying the word "nigger" in a public place is acceptable.

  Today: The word is at times cited in direct quotes but is generally recognized as inappropriate in almost all circumstances. However, many African Americans have co-opted the word for casually addressing and referring to each other, partly defusing its impact as an epithet.

- **1925:** A child who is the victim of a degrading racist slur may be left with the hopeless feeling that his race will always be held against him.

  Today: Barack Obama's achievement of the US presidency has shown that any obstacles due to race can be overcome.

The Offensive Word

The word *nigger* has been used in America for centuries and has been a demeaning insult for much of its long history. Randall Kennedy, who wrote an entire book about the word, titled *Nigger: The Strange Career of a Troublesome Word*, explains that the word—a variation of the Spanish *negro*, deriving from the Latin *niger* (meaning "black")—is in the record of a slave ship bringing Africans to Virginia in 1619. As with many practices during the days of slavery, the word was used as a way of asserting whites' dominant social position over blacks. For instance, in the 1837 book *A Treatise on the Intellectual Character and Civil and Political Condition of the Colored People of the United States: And the*

Prejudice Exercised towards Them, author Hosea Easton, quoted by Kennedy, asserts that the word

> is an opprobrious term, employed to impose contempt upon [blacks] as an inferior race.... The term in itself would be perfectly harmless were it used only to distinguish one class of society from another; but it is not used with that intent.... It flows from the fountain of purpose to injure.

As the years passed, the word retained its function as an insult: though it has taken on many nuanced connotations throughout its long history, its primary function, in Cullen's time and today, is to drive a social wedge between people of different races.

CRITICAL OVERVIEW

In the early 1920s, when Cullen was making a name for himself by publishing poems in black-oriented journals while still in college, the Harlem Renaissance had already begun to take root. Claude McKay opened the way for Cullen among black poets, publishing his influential collection *Harlem Shadows* in 1922, and Jean Toomer's 1923 novel *Cane* was considered an instant American classic upon its publication.

When Cullen published *Color*, the collection that contains "Incident," in 1925, Alain Locke, who had coined the term "the New Negro" as the title of his collection of essays about the growing black intellectualism, could hardly contain his enthusiasm for the young poet. Locke famously pronounced, "Ladies and gentlemen! A genius! Posterity will laugh at us if we do not pronounce him now." Michael L. Lomax, who provides this quote from Locke in "Countee Cullen: A Piece of the Puzzle," also notes that Clement Wood, writing in the *Yale Review*, used *Color* as his justification for going beyond categorizing Cullen only in terms of the black poets of the Harlem Renaissance. Wood placed Cullen in the company of such poetic greats as John Keats, William Shakespeare, and Walt Whitman. While many critics tried to get beyond racial issues by focusing on the universality of the experiences Cullen describes in *Color*, the poet Mark van Doren, also quoted by Lomax, took heed to point out Cullen's use of language, noting that "in this first volume he makes it clear that he has mastered a tune."

Though Cullen was adamant about being categorized as "a poet" and not "a Negro poet," his critical reputation was tied to the Harlem Renaissance, as it has been to this day. He was still a student at New York University when *Color* was published, and it turned out to be his most popular collection. In the latter half of the 1920s he published two more major collections—*Copper Sun* and *The Black Christ and Other Poems*—but the impact of each was less. Little that Cullen did after 1929 gained critical interest.

When *On These I Stand*, a compilation of his poetry, was published in 1947, soon after his death, critics used it as an occasion to look back on the arc of his career, still finding his earliest books to be the most polished. Alan R. Shucard summarizes the critical reviews for this career retrospective: "Though they generally tried to be as gentle to Cullen's memory as possible, the reviews, overall, reflect disappointment that Cullen had not developed adequately, had not fulfilled his early promise."

In spite of his short burst of productivity, Cullen's reputation has not diminished over the decades. Almost a hundred years after his birth, he is still considered to be one of the most influential American poets of the twentieth century. His verse is still read and analyzed in literary circles. Despite having reached the high point of his personal fame during the literary excitement of Harlem in the 1920s, he is not considered to have been a passing fad.

CRITICISM

David Kelly

Kelly is an instructor of creative writing and literature. In the following essay, he examines Cullen's use of different types of verbs in "Incident" and how those choices strengthen the poem's overall message.

It is sometimes said that the truest measure of a poet is their use of verbs, and that makes sense. Nouns are easier to get right because they are always present. They represent objects that everyone can observe, so one expects that the first thing for any writer to develop would be a skill for capturing observed objects with care. And the true art to using adjectives and adverbs is simple: use them sparingly when you have to use them at all. Actions, on the other hand, just slip by in the moment and then disappear. They are more difficult to notice or record properly; they are more difficult than tangible things to capture in words. It takes discipline in a writer to carefully choose the right verbs, and skill for the writer to place them where they will do the most good.

This is the kind of skill that marked Countee Cullen as a stellar talent. A fine example of Cullen's ease with verbs is his early poem "Incident," published in his first collection, when he was still an undergraduate at New York University. The poem is about a racial incident that happened to a child, perhaps to Cullen himself, and the story that it tells contains that potent combination of youthful vulnerability and hostility that draws readers' empathy, which often means that the artist's style is ignored.

WHAT DO I READ NEXT?

- Gordon Parks's novel *The Learning Tree* is considered a classic book for young adults about the problems of growing up in the tense racial atmosphere of Kansas, which, like Maryland, was a border area during the Civil War. The book's young protagonist, Newton, learns to modulate his feelings in a 1920s society that is hostile to black citizens. First published in 1963, the book tells the semiautobiographical experiences of Parks himself, an influential artist and filmmaker.

- Elizabeth Alexander, whose poem "Praise Song for the Day" was read at President Barack Obama's inauguration in 2009, often writes poetry for young adults. Her poem "Race" tells the story of a family member from an earlier generation who passed as white, and how that changed his relationships with his relatives. "Race" was published in Alexander's 1996 collection *Body of Life*.

- The Harlem Renaissance formed around a concept of "the New Negro" that emerged in the 1920s. Noted social philosopher Alaine Locke explained this concept best in his famous essay "The New Negro," first published in 1925. It is available in the 1994 anthology *The Portable Harlem Renaissance Reader* and also at various websites.

- Deborah Ellis and Eric Walters's 2007 novel *Bifocal* looks at modern-day racism, focusing on the perspectives of two high-school students, an academic Muslim student and a popular white football player, and their reactions to a classmate's arrest for supposed terrorist involvement.

- Cullen's poem "Sonnet Dialog" relates a morose discussion between himself and his soul about the subject of his eventual death, showing a different, more internal subject matter than in "Incident" but just as much formal control. It was originally published in the 1935 collection *The Medea and Some Poems* and has been reprinted in other Cullen collections, including *My Soul's High Song: The Collected Writings of Countee Cullen, Voice of the Harlem Renaissance*, edited and introduced by Gerald Early and published in 1991.

- The subtle and overt threats of living in a segregated society are related by those who experienced it in the interviews compiled in *Remembering Jim Crow: African Americans Tell about Life in the Segregated South*, published in 2008. This extensive examination by the Behind the Veil project at Duke University's Center for Documentary Studies brings together the results of hundreds of interviews, allowing participants to speak about what life was like then.

The poem follows its structure with the regularity of a metronome, alternating six-syllable and eight-syllable lines in a smooth iambic rhythm. It has the wit to play with words, filling most of one eight-syllable line with the unusual (but rhythmically precise) five-syllable word *Baltimorean* and bringing the word *whit* out of the distant past to diminish any size difference between offender and victim. But the poem's crowning glory is its poetic use of verbs, handled

with the mastery of an artist much, much older than Cullen was when he wrote it.

A poet must have great self-assurance, for instance, to establish a setting as quickly and as cleanly as he does in "Incident" with just one word, *riding*. Cullen does not tell readers where, specifically, this takes place, leaving them to engage their thought processes right away. It is likely a form of public transportation that both white and black child can be riding,

THAT MOMENT, DANGLING IN THE AIR OF
THE SEVENTH LINE OF TWELVE, IS WHAT THIS POEM
IS ALL ABOUT: THE UNIVERSAL EXPERIENCE OF
WONDERING IF OTHERS WILL ACCEPT OR REJECT
OUR COMMON HUMANITY."

since they are present in the same space for some time; it is also possible that the narrator sees the other boy out a window at a stop. The poem specifically states that Cullen was traveling *in* the city, not to or from it. That would suggest either a bus or a train. Which one? For the purpose of the story Cullen tells, it does not matter, and for the purpose of a tightly written poem that is focused on one brief moment, Cullen does not pretend that it does.

The same sense of economy drives the poem to use the past participle of the verb *fill* to form two compound adjectives, describing the speaker as having both head and heart filled with joyful excitement. Action is implied but not really described in this complex wording. Once more, the immediate situation is described well, but the externals are left off the table, allowing the reader to decide: we are no more told why joy filled his head or heart than we are told on what kind of transportation the narrator was riding, but a smart, involved reader can make an educated guess that will likely be close enough to what Cullen intends.

Still in the first stanza comes Cullen's most interesting verb phrase, and the one that best shows how he can spin a web out of the action in a poem that has just one compelling action. The narrator says that he saw the other boy *keep looking* at him. Putting it this way, working a present-tense verb into his telling, bridges the past when the incident happened with the present when he is telling the story. The action could have been related with just *looking*, or for that matter with *staring* or *gazing* or any number of verbs that would imply the white boy's fascination with his counterpart, but by adding *keep*, Cullen plays with time, breaking the flow of the action for a brief instant.

Although it is a short piece, "Incident" does not keep pushing the action forward. Cullen finds some room for a few passive verbs: the speaker *was* small, the other boy *was* small also. The story Cullen tells must establish a state of existence that is there before the incident occurs. It has to show readers what the norm was: two boys, both small, were put in each other's vicinity, likely on public transportation, and then one opened his mouth and changed the other's worldview. Chronologically, the situation would be established first, then the incident would rise up to change the established situation, but that is not quite the way this poem tells its story.

The initial situation is pushed down, from the beginning to the middle of the poem, to move the actions—riding and staring—up into the first stanza. Though this disrupts the chronology of the story, it is a technique many storytellers use in order to push the more interesting action into the beginning. The frozen, established situation can be caught up with later, as Cullen does here.

A good question would be why he uses passive verbs at all, when he could keep this short, formal poem humming along with lively verb choices. It is questionable, but he seems to have made the proper artistic decision by going with stillness at the start of the second stanza. Doing it this way brings the poem to a quiet, static place right before the shocking climactic moment. After the climactic moment, Cullen retreats back into passive verb territory, with eight months of experience dismissed quickly and casually, as being just what the boy *saw*.

The poem's most important action is, of course, the white child calling the other child the epithet. The most important verb in the poem comes just before that. Cullen's choice of the word *poked* to describe the offending boy's tongue action could not be more sublime. It is a word balanced between playfulness and aggression, and for a moment it is not clear if the white child means it as a recognition of what the two have in common or as a condemnation of the other boy. That moment, dangling in the air of the seventh line of twelve, is what this poem is all about: the universal experience of wondering if others will accept or reject our common humanity. The poem's speaker does not know if he and the other boy are interacting as two boys, or as a black and a white boy. He quickly finds out.

> ALL WAS NOT SORROW IN CULLEN'S RACIAL POEMS FOR SOME JOY AND RACIAL PRIDE ARE EXPRESSED."

A standard rule for writers states that they should generally strive for active verbs over passive verbs, and complex verbs over simple ones. In general, this, like all standard rules, is true. It is also true that an artist knows when to stretch the rules and when to break them. In writing "Incident," Cullen uses just twelve lines to tell a story that reaches into the depths of human existence, a story of faith and betrayal and ultimate surrender to the sadness of the way things simply are. To do so much in such a small space, the author needs to control both the rate and the range of the action, which can be done only with careful verb choice. "Incident" shows its author's skills in several different ways, but none of them is more powerful than the poem's use of verbs.

Source: David Kelly, Critical Essay on "Incident," in *Poetry for Students*, Gale, Cengage Learning, 2013.

Beulah Reimherr

In the following excerpt, Reimherr argues that race is thematically central to Cullen's poetry.

The theme of race consciousness is one of several themes that run through the poetry of Countee Cullen. Nature, classical mythology, love, death, religion, the animals that failed to reach Noah's ark, even cats, captured his pen. Although Cullen stoutly defended his right to deal with any subject that interested him, James Weldon Johnson felt that the best of Cullen's poetry was motivated by race. . . .

In Cullen's poetry, the themes of love and religion hold a place of equal importance with the theme of race consciousness. Cullen was essentially a lyric poet; however, an awareness of color and the difference it made in America influenced his early poetry and ran as an undercurrent of frustration and depression in his later writing. There was a much greater consciousness of race in *Color* than in his subsequent books. One-third of the poems in *Color* have some

reference to race, but only one-seventh of the poems in *Copper Sun* and *The Black Christ* have any racial overtones, and only two poems in *The Medea*.

There was a tension between Cullen's desire to be purely a lyric poet and his feelings of race consciousness. Cullen stated: "Most things I write, I do for the sheer love of the music in them. Somehow or other, however, I find my poetry of itself treating of the Negro, of his joys and his sorrows—mostly of the latter, and of the heights and the depths of emotion which I feel as a Negro."

This was especially true of *Color*, which was impregnated with race consciousness. A reviewer of *Color* stated: "Every bright glancing line abounds in color," the designation used by Cullen for his racial poems [*Crisis*, March, 1926]. This critic pointed out that there are a few poems with no mention of color which any genuine poet, black or white, could have written. These are best exemplified by such poems as "To John Keats, Poet At Spring Time," the numerous epitaphs, and the shorter poems on love, death, and the swift passing of life. A second group of poems have the adjectives "black," "brown" or "ebony" deliberately introduced to show that the author had color in mind. Such poems include "To a Brown Girl," "To a Brown Boy," "Black Magadalens," "A Brown Girl Dead," "Bread and Wine," "Wisdom Cometh with the Years," and "Threnody for a Brown Girl." Others arise with full race consciousness. These include the many poems describing the prejudice of America toward the Negro and his reactions to discrimination. As stated by Owen Dodson, if one were to ask any Negro what he found in Cullen's poetry, he would say: "All my dilemmas are written here—the hurt pride, the indignation, the satirical thrusts, the agony of being black in America ["Countee Cullen," *Phylon*, First Quarter, 1946].

Cullen's first important poem to contain feelings of race consciousness is "The Shroud of Color." Before condemning it for its echoes of Milton and Edna St. Vincent Millay, it should be noted that the poem was written when Cullen was barely twenty. Yet Laurence Stallings considered it the most distinguished poem to appear in *American Mercury* for 1924.

Cullen introduced the poem by describing his joy in the beauty of the world and his idealism that saw in man "a high-perfected glass where loveliness could lie reflected." However, truth taught him that because of his color, man would kill his dreams. His color was "a shroud" that was strangling him, for it prevented others from seeing him as an individual.

> "Lord, being dark," I said, "I cannot bear
> The further touch of earth, the scented air;
> Lord, being dark, forewilled to that despair
> My color shrouds me in, I am as dirt
> Beneath my brother's heel. . . .

In a series of four visions God showed him that struggle, not suicide is the law of life. In the first vision, the struggle of the plant kingdom toward fulfillment was described. Some seeds thrust eager tentacles to sun and rain, climb, yet die; but others burst into triumphant bloom. The second vision revealed the struggle within the animal kingdom for life. In beautiful lines Cullen stated:

> And no thing died that did not give
> A testimony that it longed to live.
> Man, strange composite blend of brute and god,
> Pushed on, nor backward glanced where last he trod.
> He seemed to mount a misty ladder flung
> Pendant from a cloud, yet never gained a rung
> But at his feet another tugged and clung.

But still, his conclusion was that, "those whose flesh is fair" can fight on. The scene shifted to heaven where even God had to struggle to preserve his mastery against the forces of Lucifer. The last scene was a vision of his own people, of their flourishing life of freedom in Africa followed by the dark days of slavery. In spite of having been enslaved, the Negro maintained faith in man. His grief now seemed "puny" in light of the suffering that his people had lived through. The poem thus ended on a note of racial pride, a salient feature of the Negro Renaissance.

> With music all their hopes and hates
> Were changed, not to be downed by all the fates.
> And somehow it was borne upon my brain
> How being dark, and living through the pain
> Of it, is courage more than angels have . . .
> The cries of all dark people near or far
> Were billowed over me, a mighty surge
> Of suffering in which my puny grief must merge
> And lose itself; I had no further claim to urge
> For death. . . .

Some of Cullen's best expressions of race consciousness appear in his sonnets. In an early sonnet, "Yet Do I Marvel," he presented four paradoxes and then "gathering up an infinity of irony, pathos and tragedy in the final couplet"

stated the problem that most vitally concerned him. According to James Weldon Johnson, these are "the two most poignant lines in American literature" [*The Book of American Negro Poetry*, 1931]. When one is oppressed for a difference beyond his control, how can he sing?

> I doubt not God is good, well-meaning, kind,
> And did He stoop to quibble could tell why
> The little buried mole continues blind,
> Why flesh that mirrors Him must some day die,
> Make plain the reason tortured Tantalus
> Is baited by the fickle fruit, declare
> If merely brute caprice dooms Sisyphus
> To struggle up a never-ending stair.
> Inscrutable His ways are, and immune
> To catechism by a mind too strewn
> With petty cares to slightly understand
> What awful brain compels His awful hand.
> Yet do I marvel at this curious thing:
> To make a poet black, and bid him sing!"

Sorrow at the restrictions excluding Negroes from the mainstream of American life deepened in "Hunger" and "The Dark Tower" to a contemplation of suicide in "Mood." In "Hunger" Cullen expressed restlessness with the limited measure alloted him in a world that is "a pageant permeate with bliss." In "The Dark Tower," Cullen cried out against the inferior position accorded Negroes. There was a place for both black and white in creation; surely then God did not intend subjection and sorrow to be the Negroes' eternal lot.

> We shall not always plant while others reap
> The golden increment of bursting fruit,
> Not always countenance, abject and mute,
> That lesser men should hold their brothers cheap;
> Not everlastingly while others sleep
> Shall we beguile their limbs with mellow flute,
> Not always bend to some more subtle brute;
> We were not made eternally to weep.
> The night whose sable breast relieves the stark,
> White stars is no less lovely being dark,
> And there are buds that cannot bloom at all
> In light, but crumple, piteous, and fall;
> So in the dark we hide the heart that bleeds,
> And wait, and tend our agonizing seeds.

In "A Thorn Forever in The Breast," he continued the thought of how far short the actual world was from the ideal world, or for the Negro, the black world from the white. Should he through his writing struggle to bring the actual closer to the ideal? He implied futility when he noted that Christ, the world's greatest idealist, died on a cross.

> A hungry cancer will not let him rest
> Whose heart is loyal to the least of dreams;

There is a thorn forever in his breast
Who cannot take his world for what it seems;
Aloof and lonely must he ever walk,
Plying a strange and unaccustomed tongue,
An alien to the daily round of talk,
Mute when the sordid songs of earth are sung.
This is the certain end his dream achieves:
He sweats his blood and prayers while others sleep,
And shoulders his own coffin up a steep
Immortal mountain, there to meet his doom
Between two wretched dying men, of whom
One doubts, and one for pity's sake believes

All was not sorrow in Cullen's racial poems for some joy and racial pride are expressed. According to Sterling Brown, the complete picture of the Negro in America is not all tragedy. In his words: "I have heard laughter, high spirited enjoyment of living and not always—or mainly, among the lucky few—but rather among the harassed many. The Negro has ability to take it, to endure, and to wring out of life something of joy" [*The Quarterly Review of Higher Education Among Negroes*, July, 1941]. "Harlem Wine," according to Arthur Davis, glorified the "uncontrollable strength of black living, contrasting it by implication with the 'watery' life of the other group" [*Phylon*, Fourth Quarter, 1953].

This is not water running here,
These thick rebellious streams
That hurtle flesh and bone past fear
Down alleyways of dreams.
This is a wine that must flow on
Not caring how not where,
So it has ways to flow upon
Where song is in the air. . . .

An equal picture of joy appeared in "She of the Dancing Feet Sings," in which a girl felt her singing and dancing were out of place in heaven; she would rather join the "wistful angels down in hell."

And what would I do in heaven, pray,
Me with my dancing feet,
And limbs like apple boughs that sway
When the gusty rain winds beat?
And how would I thrive in a perfect place
Where dancing would be sin,
With not a man to love my face
Nor an arm to hold me in?

Racial pride characterized the Negro Renaissance. Instead of trying to submerge their differences, Negro writers gloried in them. In "A Song of Praise" Cullen pictured dark girls as being lovelier and more passionate than white girls.

You have not heard my love's dark throats,
Slow-fluting like a reed,

Release the perfect golden note
She caged there for my need.
Her walk is like the replica
Of some barbaric dance
Wherein the soul of Africa
Is Winged with arrogance. . . .
My love is dark as yours is fair,
Yet lovelier I hold her
Than listless maids with pallid hair,
And blood that's thin and colder . . .

Africa was a source of racial pride. In the Negro's search for a heritage to which he could look with pride, Africa became his dream world. The discovery of ancient Negro sculpture revealed Africa as once the possessor of an advanced civilization. America was discovered as an alien country and Africa pictured as a land of beauty and peace in "Brown Boy to Brown Girl."

. . . in no least wise
Am I uncertain that these alien skies
Do not our whole life measure and confine.
No less, once in a land of scarlet suns
And brooding winds, before the hurricane
Bore down upon us, long before this pain,
We found a place where quiet waters run;
I felt your hand this way upon a hill,
And felt my heart forebear, my pulse grow still.

In this distant heritage there were Negroes who were kings and queens. Thus, Jim the handsome hero of "The Black Christ" was of "imperial breed." The heroine of "The Ballad of The Brown Girl" "comes of kings" and her dagger had once been used by "a dusky queen, in a dusky, dream-lit land." One of Cullen's best sonnets ["Black Majesty"] described the heroic rulers of Haiti who fought for their independence against Napoleon. . . .

Cullen's treatment of Africa was influenced by the twin concepts of primitivism and atavism. For the primitivists, the Negro according to Robert Bone, had an especial appeal as "he represented the unspoiled child of nature, the noble savage—carefree, spontaneous, and sexually uninhibited" [*The Negro Novel in America*]. Atavism, in this context, was the persistence in present civilization of "old remembered ways" from Africa, a concept employed by Vachel Lindsay in "The Congo." A yearning for the African jungles, a desire to dance naked under palm trees, the imagined throbbing of tom-toms, and the feeling of savages were the expressions of atavism.

Several writers exposed the falsity of associating primitivism and atavism with the Negro.

Although Wallace Thurman in his novel *Infants of the Spring* suggested that Alain Locke, Carl Van Vechten, and Countee Cullen favored atavism, he showed its falseness in his satiric description of a literary meeting at which the main writers of the Negro Renaissance debated whether African origins still persist in the American Negro. In this debate (quite the best thing in the entire book) Claude McKay, a poet and novelist of Jamaican background, proved conclusively that African origins do not persist in the American Negro, but that he is a perfect product of the melting pot. Hugh Gloster, in criticizing Van Vechten's novel *Nigger Heaven*, stated that "Van Vechten knows, or should know, that the Negro is no more primitivistic and atavistic than any other racial group that has been transplanted to America. He was merely a literary faddist capitalizing upon a current vogue and a popular demand" [*Infants of the Spring*, 1932]. Yet while the fad lasted, echoes of it appeared in Cullen's writing, especially in *Color*. In "The Shroud of Color" Cullen described the awakening of a chord long impotent in him.

> Now suddenly a strange wild music smote
> A chord long impotent in me; a note
> Of jungles, primitive and subtle, throbbed
> Against my echoing breast, and tom-toms sobbed
> In every pulse-beat of my frame. The din
> A hollow log bound with a python's skin
> Can make wrought every nerve to ecstasy,
> And I was wind and sky again, and sea,
> And all sweet things that flourish, being free.

Here the poet looked with longing to Africa because of the imagined freedom enjoyed there. A fuller statement of atavism is given in Cullen's famous poem, "Heritage." He introduced the poem by asking just what Africa could mean to one three centuries removed. Although the sights and sounds of Africa were forgotten, within the Negro's blood beat the savage rhythm of his "heritage." . . .

In "Atlantic City Waiter," Cullen indulged in the fantasy of a waiter being more dexterous in his footwork because of a heritage of "ten thousand years on jungle clues." The spirit of the jungle flamed through his acquiescent mask.

> Sheer through his acquiescent mask
> Of bland gentility,
> The jungle flames like a copper cask
> Set where the sun strikes free.

To conclude, Cullen knew nothing about Africa save what he had gleaned in the course of his considerable reading. In the words of Arthur Davis, "Africa in his poems is not a place but a symbol; it is an idealized land in which the Negro had once been happy, kingly, and free. . . ."

Source: Beulah Reimherr, "Race Consciousness in Countee Cullen's Poetry," in *Susquehanna University Studies*, Vol. 7, No. 2, June 1963, pp. 65–82.

Alain Locke

In the following review, Locke proclaims Cullen to be a rare talent whose verse is firmly rooted in poetic tradition and in the African American experience.

Ladies and gentlemen! A genius! Posterity will laugh at us if we do not proclaim him now. *Color* transcends all the limiting qualifications that might be brought forward if it were merely a work of talent. It is a first book, but it would be treasurable if it were the last; it is a work of extreme youth and youthfulness over which the author later may care to write the apology of "juvenilia," but it has already the integration of a distinctive and matured style; it is the work of a Negro poet writing for the most part out of the intimate emotional experience of race, but the adjective is for the first time made irrelevant, so thoroughly has he poetized the substance and fused it with the universally human moods of life. Cullen's own Villonesque poetic preface to the contrary, time will not outsing these lyrics.

The authentic lyric gift is rare today for another reason than the rarity of poetic genius, and especially so in contemporary American poetry—for the substance of modern life brings a heavy sediment not easy to filter out in the poetic process. Only a few can distill a clear flowing product, Housman, de la Mare, Sara Teasdale, Edna St. Vincent Millay, one or two more perhaps. Countee Cullen's affinity with these has been instantly recognized. But he has grown in sandier soil and taken up a murkier substance; it has taken a longer tap-root to reach down to the deep tradition upon which great English poetry is nourished, and the achievement is notable. More than a personal temperament flowers, a race experience blooms; more than a reminiscent crop is gathered, a new stalk has sprouted and within the flower are, we believe, the seeds of a new stock, richly parented by two cultures. It is no disparagement to our earlier Negro poets to say this: men do not choose their time, and time is the gardener.

Why argue? Why analyze? The poet himself tells us

Drink while my blood
Colors the wine.

But it is that strange bouquet of the verses themselves that must be mulled to be rightly appreciated. Pour into the vat all the Tennyson, Swinburne, Housman, Patmore, Teasdale you want, and add a dash of Pope for this strange modern skill of sparkling couplets,—and all these I daresay have been intellectually culled and added to the brew, and still there is another evident ingredient, fruit of the Negro inheritance and experience, that has stored up the tropic sun and ripened under the storm and stress of the American transplanting. Out of this clash and final blend of the pagan with the Christian, the sensual with the Puritanically religious, the pariah with the prodigal, has come this strange new thing. The paradoxes of Negro life and feeling that have been sad and plaintive and whimsical in the age of Dunbar and that were rhetorical and troubled, vibrant and accusatory with the Johnsons and MacKay now glow and shine and sing in this poetry of the youngest generation.

This maturing of an ancestral heritage is a constant note in Cullen's poetry. "Fruit of the Flower" states it as a personal experience:

My father is a quiet man
With sober, steady ways;
For simile, a folded fan;
His nights are like his days.

My mother's life is puritan,
No hint of cavalier,
A pool so calm you're sure it can
Have little depth to fear.

And yet my father's eyes can boast
How full his life has been;
There haunts them yet the languid ghost
Of some still sacred sin.

And though my mother chants of God,
And of the mystic river,
I've seen a bit of checkered sod
Set all her flesh aquiver.

Why should he deem it pure mischance
A son of his is fain
To do a naked tribal dance
Each time he hears the rain?

Why should she think it devil's art
That all my songs should be
Of love and lovers, broken heart,
And wild sweet agony?

Who plants a seed begets a bud,
Extract of that same root;
Why marvel at the hectic blood
That flushes this wild fruit?

Better than syllogisms, "Gods" states the same thing racially:

I fast and pray and go to church,
And put my penny in,
But God's not fooled by such slight tricks,
And I'm not saved from sin.

I cannot hide from Him the gods
That revel in my heart,
Nor can I find an easy word
To tell them to depart:

God's alabaster turrets gleam
Too high for me to win,
Unless He turns His face and lets
Me bring my own gods in.

Here as indubitably as in Petrarch or Cellini or Stella, there is the renaissance note. What body of culture would not gladly let it in! In still more conscious conviction we have this message in the "Shroud of Color":

Lord, not for what I saw in flesh or bone
Of fairer men; not raised on faith alone;
Lord, I will live persuaded by mine own.
I cannot play the recreant to these;
My spirit has come home, that sailed the
doubtful seas.

The latter is from one of the two long poems in the volume; both it and "Heritage" are unusual achievements. They prove Mr. Cullen capable of an unusually sustained message. There is in them perhaps a too exuberant or at least too swiftly changing imagery, but nevertheless they have a power and promise unusual in this day of the short poem and the sketchy theme. They suggest the sources of our most classic tradition, and like so much that is most moving in English style seem bred from the Bible. Occasionally one is impressed with the fault of too great verbal facility, as though words were married on the lips rather than mated in the heart and mind, but never is there pathos or sentimentality, and the poetic idea always has taste and significance.

Classic as are the fundamentals of the verse, the overtones are most modernly enlightened:

The earth that writhes eternally with pain
Of birth, and woe of taking back her slain
Laid bare her teeming bosom to my sight,
And all was struggle, gasping breath, and fight.
A blind worm here dug tunnels to the light,
And there a seed, tacked with heroic pain,
Thrust eager tentacles to sun and rain.

Still more scientifically motivated, is:

Who shall declare
My whereabouts;
Say if in the air
My being shouts
Along light ways,
Or if in the sea
Or deep earth stays
The germ of me?

The lilt is that of youth, but the body of thought is most mature. Few lyric poets carry so sane and sober a philosophy. I would sum it up as a beautiful and not too optimistic pantheism, a rare gift to a disillusioned age. Let me quote at the end my favorite poem, one of its best expressions:

"The Wise"

Dead men are wisest, for they know
How far the roots of flowers go,
How long a seed must rot to grow.

Dead men alone bear frost and rain
On throbless heart and heatless brain,
And feel no stir of joy or pain.

Dead men alone are satiate;
They sleep and dream and have no weight,
To curb their rest, of love or hate.

Strange, men should flee their company,
Or think me strange who long to be
Wrapped in their cool immunity.

Source: Alain Locke, "*Color*—A Review," in *Opportunity*, Vol. 4, No. 37, January 1926, pp. 14–15.

SOURCES

Ferguson, Jeffrey B., Introduction to *The Harlem Renaissance: A Brief History with Documents*, Bedford Series in History and Culture, Bedford/St. Martin's, 2008, pp. 1–16.

Gardner, David, "Revealed: The Maps That Show the Racial Breakdown of America's Biggest Cities," in *Mail Online*, September 26, 2010, http://www.dailymail.co.uk/news/article-1315078/Race-maps-America.html (accessed March 4, 2012).

Kennedy, Randall, "Chapter One: The Protean N-Word," in *Nigger: The Strange Career of a Troublesome Word*, Pantheon Books, 2002; reprinted in *Washington Post*, January 11, 2011, http://www.washingtonpost.com/wp-srv/style/longterm/books/chap1/nigger.htm (accessed March 1, 2012).

Lomax, Michael L., "Countee Cullen: A Piece to the Puzzle," in *Harlem Renaissance Re-examined: A Revised & Expanded Edition*, SJK Publishing Industries, 1997, pp. 239–47.

Schwarz, A. B. Christa, *Gay Voices of the Harlem Renaissance*, Indiana University Press, 2003, p. 49.

Shucard, Alan R., "The Critics and Cullen on Cullen," in *Countee Cullen*, Twayne Publishers, 1984, p. 86.

Wagner, Jean, "Countee Cullen," in *Black Poets of the United States: From Paul Laurence Dunbar to Langston Hughes*, University of Illinois Press, 1973, pp. 284–91.

FURTHER READING

Ferguson, Blanche E., *Countee Cullen and the Negro Renaissance*, Dodd, Mead, 1966.
This early study of Cullen's career, one of the few book-length biographies of the poet, was comprehensive for its time, though more information of his life has come to light since then. Speculation about his early years, however, is still as open as it was in Ferguson's day.

Huggins, Nathan Irvin, *Harlem Renaissance*, updated ed., Oxford University Press, 2007.
This study, first published in 1972 and recently reissued with a new introduction, has long been considered a definitive telling of the story of Cullen's time period, weaving together the stories of the various authors and artists whose paths crossed in that small area of Manhattan during those fertile artistic years.

Skotnes, Andor, *A New Deal for All? Race and Class Struggles in Depression-Era Baltimore*, Duke University Press, 2012.
Though the Great Depression was decades after the time Cullen describes in this poem, readers can still glean a sense of the continuing racial divisions that defined the lives of whites and blacks in that border town between the North and the South.

Washington, Shirley Porter, *Countee Cullen's Secret Revealed by Miracle Book: A Biography of His Childhood in New Orleans*, AuthorHouse, 2008.
Though this telling of Cullen's mysterious early life did not gain much critical attention when it was published, the author, Cullen's niece, uses family materials to support her claim that he was born and raised in New Orleans, in contrast to the suppositions of most historians.

Wright, Richard, *The Ethics of Living Jim Crow: An Autobiographical Sketch*, Viking Press, 1937.
Acclaimed writer Richard Wright, best known for his novel *Native Son*, tells of the degradation of living in a segregated society and the strategies that black Americans had to devise

just to survive. He includes a frank discussion of the offensive word that is the focus of Cullen's poem.

SUGGESTED SEARCH TERMS

Countee Cullen AND "Incident"

Cullen AND Color

Cullen AND Harlem Renaissance

Harlem Renaissance AND "the New Negro"

Cullen AND Du Bois

Cullen AND Baltimore

Baltimore AND segregation

transportation AND civil rights

children AND racism

Harlem Renaissance AND racial slur

Lilacs

AMY LOWELL

1920

The American poet Amy Lowell was a force of nature in the poetry scene of the late 1910s and early 1920s, becoming a champion of modernist "new poetry" and especially the imagist movement that found her at the helm. "Lilacs" might be considered her crowning achievement. Although she had literary dreams from an early age, Lowell came onto the poetry scene relatively late in life, after being profoundly moved by a Boston performance by an Italian actress, Eleonora Duse. Then twenty-eight years old, though "as ignorant as anyone could be" about poetry—as she would later write in a letter (cited in Benvenuto)—Lowell "sat down, and with infinite agitation wrote this poem.... It loosed a bolt in my brain and I found out where my true function lay." Still, that ode to Duse remained private (for the time being), and eight more years would pass before she began publishing her verse, made the acquaintance of Ezra Pound in London, and returned to flourish the banner of American imagism.

True to the movement's name, "Lilacs" is a poem overflowing with images, of a wide variety of scenes and settings in which the flowers can be found. The poem is also an ode to the Massachusetts native Lowell's home region of New England. First read aloud to a standing-room-only crowd of over 1,200 at the University of Chicago and first published in the *New York Evening Post* on September 18, 1920, "Lilacs" was an immediate success and would become a

Amy Lowell (© *Hulton Archive | Getty Images*)

hallmark of her readings. If she failed to include the poem in her program, it would inevitably be requested as an encore. She even grew tired of always being obliged to read it—and yet, on the other hand, if it was not requested, she could not help being disappointed. "Lilacs" was included in Lowell's collection *What's O'Clock*, which was published just after her death in 1925 and was awarded the Pulitzer Prize in 1926. The poem also appears in her *Complete Poetical Works*, *Selected Poems of Amy Lowell*, and a number of verse anthologies.

AUTHOR BIOGRAPHY

Lowell was born on February 9, 1874, in Brookline, Massachusetts, as the fifth and last living child of Augustus and Katherine Lowell. Their family on both sides had gained great wealth in generations past through the cotton trade, and Lowell's father continued to succeed in business and industry. As a young girl, Lowell was inclined to make clever remarks and was encouraged by everyone's laughter, gaining a family

nickname as "the Postscript." Lowell's figure became an issue for her early in life, with portraits showing a slightly plump preadolescent; biographers have concluded that she had a glandular condition that Western medicine then had little idea what to do about. Tomboyish to begin with, and at once precocious and resentful of teachers' authority, Lowell in her private elementary schooling naturally fell into the role of, as Jean Gould quotes in her biography, "ringleader in fun and mischief." Consequently, she switched schools often. The more she felt herself hopelessly differentiated from her more feminine female classmates, the more she took after her father and brothers, imitating their demeanors. From the time she began keeping a diary around age fifteen, laments and despair over her figure were not uncommon. In light of her low self-regard, she found solace in books, many of which her father read aloud to her; she readily worked her way through the novels of Sir Walter Scott, James Fenimore Cooper, and Charles Dickens, among others.

Lowell's diary entries from the year 1889 include foreshadowing thoughts like "What I would not give to be a poet!" and "I should like best of anything to be literary." Yet, despite attaining a degree of social comfort through friendships, her crushes remained unrequited, and the schooling itself never agreed with her. She ceased her formal education at seventeen, but she would continue to educate herself through diligent hours in her father's library as well as at the Boston Athenaeum, an old library whose founders included a Lowell. Through the early 1890s, Lowell experimented with writing short stories, novels, and plays—she had a natural talent for acting—but none of these genres proved to suit her. She came very close to marrying; after turning down a couple of uninspiring proposals, she agreed to marry a regular visitor from Boston, with whom she fell in love. But after leaving town for a spell, he wrote a brief letter breaking off the engagement. Heartbroken, Lowell grew determined to improve her fitness; but the dieting fad of the day called for eating nothing but tomatoes and asparagus, on a trip up the Nile, if possible. Lowell attempted this, and of course it made her quite sick; she afterward resolved to never torture herself by dieting again.

Lowell's mother died in 1895, her father in 1899, and at this time she inherited the family's Brookline estate, dubbed Sevenels (for having housed the family's seven Lowells). By now, she was determined to bring her literary dreams to fruition, and having freed herself from the idea of marriage, her circumstances were most conducive to her efforts. In 1902, a performance by the renowned Italian actress Eleonora Duse inspired Lowell to write glowing verse, and she realized that poetry was her calling. But not until eight years later would she publish her first poem, in the *Atlantic Monthly*. In 1912 she produced her first collection, *A Dome of Many-Coloured Glass*, and also made the acquaintance of the actress Ada Dwyer Russell; two years later, Lowell invited Russell to live at Sevenels, and the two would remain intimate companions until Lowell's death. Meanwhile, Lowell was struck by the *imagiste* creed demonstrated by the American poet H.D.—Hilda Doolittle—who had moved to England in 1911, and Lowell traveled to London to confer with Doolittle as well as the poets Richard Aldington and Ezra Pound.

From there, Lowell's life became a whirlwind of activity. She returned to the United States, took up the banner of imagism, and became the most vociferous proponent of the "new poetry" being written by imagists and other modernists. Her 1914 volume *Sword Blades and Poppy Seed* was a critical success, as were the three annual anthologies she edited from 1915 to 1917 under the title *Some Imagist Poets*. She became an extremely controversial figure, being opinionated, domineering, and unyielding and often rubbing people the wrong way. Nonetheless, her poetry, especially as read aloud by her on tour, was extremely popular, and through the early 1920s she brought the public spotlight not only to herself but onto all new poetry. But as her fame and obligations increased, her body grew weary. By 1925, after a joyously well attended "Complimentary Dinner in Honour of Miss Amy Lowell," she had to cancel a trip to England, where she had meant to promote her biography *John Keats*, which was lauded in America, owing to her poor health. On May 12, the day before a scheduled operation, she suffered a stroke, and she died that day. Russell and their friends commemorated Lowell's life by gathering armfuls of lilacs from the Sevenels garden and filling the house with them. "Lilacs" was first published in the *New York Evening Post* in 1920 and was included in Lowell's posthumous volume *What's O'Clock*, which was awarded the Pulitzer Prize in 1926.

POEM SUMMARY

The text used for this summary is from *Selected Poems of Amy Lowell*, Rutgers University Press, 2002, pp. 77–79. Versions of the poem can be found on the following web pages: http://www.poetryfoundation.org/poem/171731, http://www.poemhunter.com/poem/lilacs-5/, and http://users.telenet.be/gaston.d.haese/lowell_lilacs.html.

Stanza 1

"Lilacs" opens with a series of five very short lines that place in the reader's mind simple, unadorned images of lilacs of several colors. Lilacs are ordinarily conceived as being either purple or white, so the initial mention of lilacs being falsely blue suggests how in certain amounts of sunlight or shade, the purple flowers may appear blue to the eye. This speaks at once to Lowell's professed focus on creating or re-creating visual images, which she does from a viewpoint that may be subjective, that is, not absolute but dependent on the one seeing. Line 7 initiates a theme of the poem, the poet's identification with her homeland of New England. After the hint of consonance in line 6, with repeated *f* sounds, lines 9 and 10 include several instances of alliteration, in the *or-*, *b-*, and *so-* sounds. A consummate performer, Lowell gave especially popular readings of her poems, which she consciously wrote to be agreeable to the ear in terms of both letter sounds and rhythms, and these qualities are noticeable throughout this poem.

The first stanza presents a series of scenes in which lilacs appear and to which they contribute aesthetically. Orioles hop around in the leaves of lilac bushes and sing quietly; among the branches, sparrows sit on their eggs and peer out. The next images juxtapose the flowers with human-built dwellings, as lilacs near a door converse with the moon, lilacs by the road watch over an empty house, and lilacs bloom over a dugout cellar. The reference to lilacs in a dooryard is recognized as an allusion to Walt Whitman's poem "When Lilacs Last in the Dooryard Bloom'd," written to honor the recently deceased Abraham Lincoln. Section 3 of that poem is a six-line scene in which the poet admires a lilac bush and its leaves shaped like hearts. The section strongly prefigures the tone of Lowell's "Lilacs," and she presumably included the allusion to acknowledge her poem's forebear.

MEDIA ADAPTATIONS

- "Lilacs" was set to music by E. B. Hill, Harvard's music chair and a friend of the Lowells, as a choral work that was played by the Boston Symphony.

- The American composer Elaine Fine wrote an instrumental setting of "Lilacs" for flute, clarinet, cello, and piano that was performed by Illinois's Arcadia Chamber Players and is available on her blog "Musical Assumptions," (http://musicalassumptions.blogspot.com/) posted November 6, 2007.

- A reading of "Lilacs" by Bellona Times, part of a volume titled *37 American Poems* (2009), is available online from LibriVox as an MP3 download.

Lines 21 and 22 expand on the preceding images by declaring that lilacs are not confined to local scenes but both were and are everywhere. More images follow, now juxtaposing the flowers with human institutions, setting the lilacs outside a church window, along the road to school, on a farm by the cows' pastures, and near a home, where the sight of them seals the domestic happiness of a married woman. Presented next is a commercial institution, a customhouse, in which clerks who are meant only to be cataloging inventory are driven to distraction and the writing of verse by the lilacs' lovely scent. Some thirteen lines are devoted to these clerks. They are depicted as paradoxical persons, imposing a statistical logic even on their reading of the Bible at night (the Song of Solomon being a set of love poems included in the Protestant Old Testament); such a strictly logical approach might be said to detract from the spiritual experience of reading the sacred book.

The next images are from a graveyard, as if the mention of the Bible leads the poet to thoughts of death and what becomes of ghosts. The next two lines, 46 and 47, then place the lilacs just beyond the influence of humanity, by

the sea and over the distant hills. But the images that close the stanza bring the flower back within the sphere of civilization, along a shop-lined street in a town, in a public park, and next to a greenhouse, where the lilacs can commune with their purple (or green) grape friends inside.

Stanza 2

The second stanza begins with the same five lines that began the first, bringing the reader back, after the many preceding flowery scenes, to the pure image of simple lilacs. In lines 58–60 Lowell assigns an Eastern origin to the lilac, with the imagery specifically suggesting the Near East or Turkey. A hint of cultural condescension can be detected in these and the following lines. The women are lent an aura of wild power by the description of their catlike eyes, a description that may be primarily intended to approximate the sense of making eye contact with a person whose face is otherwise entirely concealed (like a cat peering through foliage). This alone is not offensive, but the turban of the *pasha*—a term of Turkish origin for a man of some authority—is seen as imbued with an air of aggression, suggesting undue belligerence, and line 61 implies that the lilac's Eastern origins, in contrast to decent New England society, are somehow indecent, perhaps as deemed uncivilized. Such valuating views of foreign cultures were not uncommon in early twentieth-century America, but from a modern perspective these hinted valuations do not reflect so well on the author.

The lilac is now pictured as passive, honest, and forthright, the perfect visual embellishment for a well-kept doorway or garden, where it might be appreciated by a spectacled person. Whether the lilac or the pair of spectacles—that is, the person wearing them—is the one making the poetry is unclear, but either way, the moonlit lilacs are themselves the inspiration.

Lines 68–74 cite the six New England states in turn, from Maine to Connecticut, as host to lilacs. The flowers compare favorably to apples and tulips, and they are likened to people's souls. They are assigned universal relevance in that their scent fills all summers, while they also represent love and memory. They are even connected to the states' founding institutions, perhaps as if growing around the capitol buildings; also, the purple lilac is New Hampshire's state flower. Lines 84–94 now identify the flower with the month of May, such that the lilac gains all the connotations of that quintessential spring month, such as singing birds, the singular greenness, leaf-filtered sunshine, and southerly breezes. Line 94, as if with a wave of the arm, encompasses all of New England in one line in spanning the land from Canada to Narragansett Bay, which nestles into southeast Rhode Island.

Stanza 3

The last stanza begins with the same five lines as the first two, although now a sense of finality is lent by the fifth line's ending with a period instead of a comma. Again returning to the poem's simplest images, just the lilacs and their colors, these lines give the sense that the poem has returned to its point of origin, having cycled through an all-inclusive range of lilac-tinged circumstances, in humanistic, geographic, and temporal terms alike. Indeed, the lilacs are depicted as ubiquitous throughout New England, and where the poet is a representative of her homeland, she, too, directly identifies with lilacs. She herself is like a lilac bush, rooted in the soil and flowering for the sake of all that lives there. The poet stresses her sense of possession or ownership of the land—presumably not a unique sense but one shared with all who live there—in lines 106 and 109, the last. It is this sense of belonging that leaves the poet feeling both entitled and inspired to sing the praises of her homeland, which, through its lilacs, is what this poem has done.

THEMES

Nature

Most tangibly, this poem is, as the title suggests, a paean to lilacs. In fact, much as Herman Melville's *Moby-Dick* is a fictional tour de force on whales, covering virtually every aspect of the leviathan, Lowell's poem can be characterized as a poetic tour de force on lilacs, so thoroughly expounding upon the subject (as Lowell was known to do) that she has left no lilac unturned, so to speak. This was certainly her aim, and her comprehensive treatment is one of the reasons the poem is so effective. The lilac is so ubiquitous in this poem that it seems it could symbolize nothing but itself; but the collection of images in sum suggests that the lilac is being heralded

TOPICS FOR FURTHER STUDY

- Think of an element of nature—or, if necessary, something made by humans—whose presence you have appreciated in the course of your daily life, or during a particular season, or on special trips, or anytime at all, and write a poem about it. As with Lowell's "Lilacs," use a variety of images to produce a collective sense about what the natural element or object in question signifies for you.

- Analyze the cadence of "Lilacs" by counting out the syllables in each of the 109 lines and also searching for instances of recognizable meter—for example, lines 8 and 10 can both be scanned as trimeter (three poetic feet) consisting of two iambs (two syllables, one unstressed and then one stressed) and one spondee (two stressed syllables). Create a graphic representation of the sequence of syllable counts either by hand or using computer software, and with regard to your findings about meter, either incorporate what you discover into your graphic representation (which may amount to an artistic design) or write a brief paper explaining how the instances of meter shape, enhance, and thematically reflect the poem.

- Read the poems "A Flower" and "Ode to a Flower," found in Frederick Douglas Harper's *Poems for Young People: Inspirational, Educational, and Therapeutic Poetry* (available online at http://www.journalnegroed.org/PoemsforYoungPeople.pdf). Compare and contrast both of these poems with Lowell's "Lilacs," considering factors such as the intended audience, the use of repetition, the emotional context, the nature of the images, and the overall effectiveness of the poems.

- Research the history of northeastern American poetry, and write an essay identifying the major historical figures—be sure to include Walt Whitman, Robert Frost, and Lowell—and discussing themes, styles, and philosophies that are common to or that evolved among these poets.

not only for its intrinsic qualities—its color, its scent—but for the role it plays as a link between humankind and nature.

The lilacs' colors are lauded first and foremost, reflecting the manner in which flowers, by virtue of their bright colors, draw one's gaze. While every inch of nature will be seen as beautiful to the appreciative onlooker, brown tree trunks and green leaves do not demand the attention the way colorful flowers do. In this the lilacs are linked with birds (such as the poem's orioles), who have likewise evolved bright colors to catch the right eyes and ensure the reproduction of the species. (Both birds and bees can spread pollen from flower to flower.) But what value does the mere sight of flowers hold for humans? If this boils down to a question of the value of beauty, the answer may be ineffable. With certain types of beauty, the joy of seeing can be logically explained by identifying the rewards that the sight represents and thus stimulates thoughts of in the mind. In people, perceived beauty may be based on the extent to which the viewer can imagine having rewarding interactions with the person; in a scenic landscape, beauty may be based on the feeling of openness and physical freedom represented by the vista. Works of art, the beauty of which can be more problematic to define, may channel these logical senses of beauty as well as others. Flowers are sometimes considered beautiful in being suggestive of women's intimate parts, and in fact, in some or her poems Lowell unmistakably invokes flowers precisely to conjure their erotic connotations; but considering the prominence of the themes of nature and regionalism here and the lack of romantic undercurrents, "Lilacs" does not seem to be such a poem. The beauty of flowers may also be said to stem from the regular geometric arrangements of the petals, which are not perfectly aligned but are patterned in coordinated ways. In this, flowers can be seen as a visual link between the strict geometric precision of man-made structures, most buildings being delineated by rectangles and corners, and the relative chaos of much of the rest of nature, as the fractal patterns of the shapes of tree limbs and mountainsides and swamps are typically so complex as to be beyond ready analysis. With flowers, the numbers of petals can nearly always be counted, and they have definite shapes, and yet the overall pattern is marked by random proliferation.

Many of Lowell's images in "Lilacs" suggest just such an essential intermediary role, between civilization and nature, for the flower. Found by a doorway, the lilacs visually bridge the squareness of the door and the roundness of the moon. Near a deserted house, the lilacs signify nature's intrusion into, and thus acceptance of, the unused structure, uniting it with nature in the absence of man. In drawing the attention of the churchgoer, the schoolboy, and the housewife, the lilacs perhaps forestall feelings of claustrophobia by contextualizing these people's civilized indoor activities within a natural world that remains within reach. In the customhouse, the lilacs are especially emblematic of nature in starkly opposing the confines of capitalism, as the clerks, trapped within the role of inventory taker, are tantalized by the scent of the flowers— as if they would give anything to simply abandon their monotonous posts and return to the lush world of nature; but they cannot, and so they write poetry instead. Lowell, brought up in an elite Boston family well versed in the nuances of capitalism, confined by the aristocratic demands and stiff mores of upper-class society (which she ultimately flouted) as well as by her limiting physique, perhaps recognized better than the average person the value in the mere sight of nature, in the appreciation of its beauty. She was especially fond of the gardens at their family home, Sevenels. This poem speaks to the value she found in lilacs in particular, and by extension in all flowers and all of nature. Her metaphorization of herself as a lilac at the poem's end can thus be read as figuratively allowing her a unity with nature, a flower's unity with nature, that in reality no human can ever achieve.

Regionalism

The reader cannot fail to grasp that "Lilacs" was written by a poet hailing from New England, as she makes quite clear her affiliation with the land. She refers early on, in line 7, to the intimate connection she feels with the region, which she characterizes as hers. The poem then proceeds to establish, through the cascade of flower-filled images, how intertwined the flower is with the land, and each succeeding image strengthens the bond between them; in sum, the lilacs belong to New England, and New England belongs to the lilacs. Thus, a thematic triangle is being outlined, with New England connected to both the poet and the flower; all that remains is for the flower to be connected to the poet. And this is what

Lowell accomplishes beginning with the middle of the second stanza, where the flowers become the people's overflowing souls, the leaves their hearts. Lilacs even become perhaps the most fundamental human emotion, love. Lowell confirms the links between poet, New England, and flower in the compact, powerful third stanza, where the poet metaphorically becomes both New England and a lilac bush. That the poem is an homage to the region is made clear in the closing lines, where Lowell speaks proudly of singing the praises of her homeland.

As a work of regionalism, Lowell's poem will evoke quite different senses in a reader from within the region compared to one from without. For a New Englander, the listing of the names of the region's several states is likely to successfully call to mind the impressions one has of each state—New England is small enough that anyone from the region is likely to have at least a passing impression of all six states. But Lowell does not describe or even mention specific features of the states, aside from Rhode Island's beaches and the Connecticut River. Thus, for a reader unfamiliar with the region, the listing of the state's names may simply amount to a succession of unevocative proper nouns that do not contribute to the poem's overall content. But this should not be seen as a shortcoming. It is worth noting that "Lilacs" was first published not in a national journal of poetry or literature but in a newspaper, the *New York Evening Post*, and indeed Lowell could have expected an almost explicitly regional readership in such a medium. While contemporary poets with elite literary pretensions, like Ezra Pound, might have shied away from regionalism because it would seem to render a poem less universal for posterity, Lowell, an exceedingly popular poet in her day, believed that poetry was meant to be enjoyed by everyone, not just the literary elite. In addition, she was highly attuned to sounds and rhythms in her work, and the inclusion of the states' names can be justified simply on the basis of their aptly carrying the cadence of the verse. Arguably, Lowell's apparent decision to write this poem with a New England/Northeast audience in mind may make the poem slightly more opaque for the nonlocal reader, but the emotional payoff is amplified for the New England born, and moreover this regionalism does not compromise the quality of the verse itself.

The subject of the poem is lilacs. (© Mazzzur / Shutterstock.com)

STYLE

Second Person

A noticeable surface feature of the style of this poem is the use of the second person in scattered instances throughout. While the second person is used rarely in works of fiction, where it is liable to directly place the reader in the story (a somewhat awkward situation), in poems, as in personal letters, the second person often suggests that the poem was written as addressed to someone in particular. In this case, the lilacs are the ones being addressed as "you." Still, even if the reader knows that the poet is talking not to the reader but to the lilacs, a written work with repeated references to "you" carries the connotation that whoever reads it is the one being addressed. That is, in the reader's mind, the dialogic connotations of "you" will in part override, if only subconsciously, the logical assignment of "you" to the lilacs. The upshot of this is that, just as the poet pronounces for herself an intimate identification with the lilacs—the lilacs are said to be her soul and to be within her, and she speaks of her own roots, leaves, and flowers—the reader, too, is led to identify with the lilacs. Lowell quite boldly impels the reader to accept this identification through her use of the second person, and if the reader has approached the poem with an open mind, the result may be an inspiring expansion of consciousness, a truly felt oneness with the flower and with nature.

Imagism

This poem is recognizable as an imagist work, one that, in short, focuses on presenting the reader with images. But the connotations of imagism are more complex than that, a matter that is cogently explained in the preface to *Some Imagist Poets: An Anthology* (1915), an effort directed by Lowell but carried out as a democratic collaboration (in opposition to Pound's exclusive editorship of his volume *Des Imagistes*). In that preface, which is not assigned specific authorship and speaks in the third person as "we" (said to have been written by contributor Richard Aldington), six principles of imagism are outlined:

1. To use the language of common speech, but to employ always the *exact* word. . . .
2. To create new rhythms—as the expression of new moods . . . . In poetry a new cadence means a new idea.
3. To allow absolute freedom in the choice of subject. . . .
4. To present an image (hence the name: "Imagist"). . . . We believe that poetry should render particulars exactly and not deal in vague generalities, however magnificent and sonorous. . . .
5. To produce poetry that is hard and clear, never blurred nor indefinite.
6. Finally, most of us believe that concentration is of the very essence of poetry.

These principles, of course, will be followed to greater and lesser extents in various imagist poems. In "Lilacs," they are well represented. Point 4 may be considered the foundational imagist principle, and Lowell's poem is indeed a succession of images, some simple, some more elaborate. Although her metaphors become complex, she never veers into the realm of the abstract. The clearness of her images—at no point does she leave the reader guessing about what is being described—provides the fulfillment of point 5. Regarding point 1, Lowell has used not erudite vocabulary but common language to accurately describe common sights. As to point 2, the poem is free verse, with neither rhyme nor consistent meter, but there is a distinct cadence that traces through. Point 3, of course, is fulfilled in any circumstance. Point 6 is perhaps the principle that is least fulfilled in "Lilacs," as instead of providing a more compact poem that concentrates on elaborating a single bountiful image, Lowell has intently fashioned this poem to be

expansive, to figuratively encompass not just one beautiful lilac bush but all the lilacs of New England, even all the lilacs that have ever been.

Cadenced Verse

In *Selected Poems of Amy Lowell*, editors Melissa Bradshaw and Adrienne Munich situate "Lilacs" in a section titled "Cadenced Verse," a term that aptly describes the brand of melodious free verse that Lowell so successfully championed and wrote. While the term *free verse* implies an utter absence of poetic rules, Lowell believed that a finer poetry could be produced through the conscious shaping of lines to the reader's natural speaking rhythm. Quoted at the beginning of the "Cadenced Verse" section is Lowell's own characterization of the aesthetic of her free-verse poems from her preface to her breakthrough collection *Sword Blades and Poppy Seed*:

> They are built upon "organic rhythm," or the rhythm of the speaking voice with its necessity for breathing, rather than upon a strict metrical system. They differ from ordinary prose rhythms by being more curved, and containing more stress.

To imagine what she means by the rhythms' being "more curved," one can think of a poem in ordinary meter—such as strict iambic pentameter, or perhaps alternation between tetrameter and trimeter—as being patterned in a linear or angled way, staying at or consistently returning to discrete amounts. But in the natural cadence of "Lilacs," the syllables of lines increase and decrease at varying rates; some lines match or nearly match each other in succession, while others shift the tone of the poem by stretching longer or ending sooner. In the first eight lines, for instance, the syllable counts are two, two, one, two, five, six, ten, six. Thus, if one were to connect these syllable counts in a visual graph, the result would be not a line or a row of jagged teeth but a gradually swelling and receding curve. The fact that Lowell's poems became less popular after her death attests to the fact that they were best appreciated through her readings, in which she could give voice to the precise cadences she originally felt or designed when she wrote them.

HISTORICAL CONTEXT

The Imagist Movement

Through most of the twentieth century, Lowell was remembered as much for her verse as for her championing the imagist movement in American

COMPARE
&
CONTRAST

- **1920:** In the wake of the nation's collective and successful war effort over the final two years of World War I (1914–1918), Americans feel increased national togetherness as well as greater pride in the country and also their particular regions.

  Today: In light of America's recent controversial military engagement in both the Iraq War and the war in Afghanistan—with the United States coming to be seen as an occupier in both nations—many Americans morally dissociate themselves from the country's military operations and feel less pride in the nation. While the conflicts have been subject to debate, the troops themselves have been supported by the people.

- **1920:** By virtue of Lowell's barnstorming poetry-reading tours and her extensive efforts at both promoting her own work and critically praising that of authors such as Robert Frost, Carl Sandburg, and H.D., the "new poetry" movement stirs unprecedented national interest in verse.

  Today: After the modernists' twentieth-century explorations of the unlimited possi-

bilities of free verse, few twenty-first-century poets have found room to revolutionize the field, and poets such as David Orr, also a *New York Times* columnist, have lamented poetry's underexposure.

- **1920:** Lowell, an upper-class woman whose youthful physique did allow her such accomplishments as a tennis-tournament doubles victory but who suffers from a glandular condition, experiences increasing numbers of health problems related to her weight. These include high blood pressure, heart trouble, pulled muscles, and hernia, the last of which necessitates a second operation early in the year.

  Today: In modern America, the tendency toward obesity has been democratized, as people of all classes are susceptible to the consequences of excessive consumption and inadequate exercise as well as physiological conditions. Some 69 percent of the population is considered overweight, including 36 percent considered obese. Health-care costs are an ever-increasing concern for the government and taxpayers.

---

poetry. Imagism originated across the Atlantic with Hilda Doolittle (known as H.D.), Richard Aldington, and Pound, who actually formulated the more French and pretentious-sounding term *imagisme*. It was in January 1913 that Lowell gained exposure to this group's poetics, after reading a few poems bearing the signature "H.D., *Imagiste*." As E. Claire Healey quotes in her essay on the poet, Lowell reported in an interview,

> I had been writing poetry in accordance with my own inclination and I made the discovery that what I had been writing was Imagist poetry.... New ideas were descending through the air, ready to settle into whatever minds were good soil.

That summer, Lowell visited London intending to make the acquaintances of Pound and the

others and, as Healey quotes, to "put the Imagists on the map."

Indeed, based on their shared interests, Lowell and Pound in particular became friends and allies, and while Lowell returned to America to advocate *imagisme* in literary circles, Pound included Lowell's poem "In a Garden" in his 1914 anthology *Des Imagistes*. Pound alone was responsible for the selection of poems presented in his volume. Lowell returned to London that year, but at a dinner she hosted celebrating the volume, a rift became manifest: the younger Pound found Lowell's use of the word "imagism," which he had coined, to be presumptuous; he intended the movement as an elite one, not a common one that might be wrested away from

In the poem Lowell expresses her affection for New England. (© Christian Delbert | Shutterstock.com)

his control. He was particularly irked by an advertisement for Lowell's *Sword Blades and Poppy Seed* that called her the "foremost member of the 'Imagists'—a group of poets that includes William Butler Yeats, Ezra Pound, Ford Madox Hueffer" (cited in Benvenuto). Also, as it happened, Lowell had declined to contribute five thousand dollars to a project of Pound's.

Lowell was not alone in feeling that in the next anthology, the contributing imagists should be given equal space and permitted to select what they considered their own best work. In fact, she was planning on compiling just such an anthology in 1915, but Pound objected to her use of the term *imagisme*. Lowell would ultimately compromise only by dropping the final *-e* and calling her anthology *Some Imagist Poets*. Included were several poets from among Pound's group who, after that fateful dinner, elected to join Lowell's camp, namely, H.D., Aldington, and F. S. Flint, and also included were John Gould Fletcher and the burgeoning literary master D. H. Lawrence, whom Lowell had befriended in England. Letters written by Pound, quoted by Richard Benvenuto in *Amy Lowell*, make clear his resentment of Lowell's

involvement and intentions with regard to this volume. Pound lamented his imagist school's becoming "a democratic beer-garden" and averred that her usage would "weaken the whole use of the term imagist." He stated in 1917, in a letter to Lowell herself, "You tried to stampede me into accepting as my artistic equals various people whom it would have been rank hypocrisy for me to accept in any such manner. There is no democracy in the arts." Pound, as it happened, would veer into a new school that he was nurturing, dubbed "vorticism," that would never gain the same literary traction as that gained by the imagist school.

Perhaps in light of the more favorable opinions toward democratic undertakings to be found in the United States, Lowell's approach proved pitch-perfect. As the collaborators jointly state in the preface to *Some Imagist Poets*,

> We wish it to be clearly understood that we do not represent an exclusive artistic sect; we publish our work together because of mutual artistic sympathy, and we propose to bring out our cooperative volume each year for a short term of years, until we have made a place for ourselves and our principles such as we desire.

Through this anthology and the two that followed, Lowell indeed put the imagists on the map, and in America, at least, her inheritance of the leadership of the imagists was confirmed. More broadly speaking, Lowell heralded the arrival of the "new poetry," which she discussed in critical essays such as "Is There a National Spirit in 'the New Poetry' of America?" What she found so invigorating about the poetry of her day was precisely that it broke from the confinements of the established poetic tradition, a tradition rooted in and beholden to the poets of Great Britain, to create a new, purely American tradition. Counting Walt Whitman as an originator of this tradition, Lowell found that the new poetry reflected the development of America's independent literary soul and confirmed the status of Americans as not just a nation of people but moreover as a distinct, collective race.

CRITICAL OVERVIEW

Although Lowell was at the forefront of the American poetry scene from the 1914 publication of her second volume of verse until her sudden death in 1925, her literary reputation waned through much of the rest of the twentieth century. Critical biographers have attributed this to a variety of factors, including Lowell's being not a poet of a humble nature like, say, Robert Frost (who supported himself by working in a mill) but rather one from a profoundly wealthy family; her being a willful, assertive, and at times demanding person whose brashness earned her a number of literary enemies during her life; her having been engaged in what informed commentators acknowledge was a romantic relationship with Ada Dwyer Russell, such that discrimination against sexual orientation comes into play; and even her having been an overweight individual, one whose private disparagements of her figure in her diary seemed to leave critics and biographers feeling justified in using various degrading terms in their own descriptions of her physique. All in all, as Melissa Bradshaw notes in her introductory essay in *Selected Poems of Amy Lowell*, "As an independent, outspoken, confident woman who took herself and her career seriously, she posed a serious threat to mid-century ideals of appropriate womanhood." As late as 1999, Mary E. Galvin, in her volume *Queer Poetics: Five*

Modernist Women Writers, had to acknowledge that Lowell "is largely ignored and forgotten today." But in the twenty-first century, in part by virtue of the ever-increasing influence of feminist theorists as well as the field of gay and lesbian studies, Lowell is enjoying a minor renaissance in critical appreciation. Writing in 2002, Bradshaw stated,

> That the difficult and enigmatic Lowell—an imperious, politically conservative, physically imposing lesbian—has not yet made her way back into the spotlight should not surprise us. Thirty years ago we might not have known what to do with Amy Lowell. But today we are ready for her.

"Lilacs" is considered one of Lowell's finest poems. It was published in *What's O'Clock* (1925), which critics affirm contains some of Lowell's finest work and fully deserved the Pulitzer Prize it was awarded the year after her death (a prize that might have been considered bestowed partly in honor of her passing). In her essay "Amy Lowell, Body and Sou-ell," Jane Marcus finds strong echoes of Whitman in the poem and describes it in a way that legitimizes Lowell's status among the vanguard of the nation's "new poetry":

> "Lilacs" is about being transplanted to American soil and *taking*. It is about hybridity and hope, about finding a voice. "Lilacs" is Lowell's claim that her hybrid poetry of free verse and formal orientalism is the voice of the Great American Poet.

The "orientalism" Marcus refers to stemmed from Lowell's study of Japanese and Chinese poetry and her efforts at writing English versions of Chinese poems. These Chinese poems exemplified the sentimental restraint and clarity of image favored by Lowell.

In *Amy Lowell*, Richard Benvenuto remarks that "'Lilacs' represents the best of the familiar Lowell" and goes on to praise the "beautiful final lines." Finding the poem reminiscent of William Wordsworth, Benvenuto admires how

> Lowell's language makes one body, one being, out of the flowers and the people.... As the speaker turns herself into a lilac, thus both personifying the flower and using it as a metaphor for herself, self-discovery and the recognition of a collective, lasting regional identity take place together.

In *Amy: The World of Amy Lowell and the Imagist Movement*, Jean Gould notes that "Lilacs" was an "instant success" in Lowell's first reading. In Gould's assessment,

It is a solid yet heartwarming poem, containing a philosophical truth in the relation between people and their native lands, succinctly tracing the history of Eastern and Western civilization while apparently epitomizing New England. In other words, it is universal, and one of Amy Lowell's happiest creations.

CRITICISM

Michael Allen Holmes

Holmes is a writer with existential interests. In the following essay, he considers the qualities that make "Lilacs" a universal poem.

A key word that has been used to describe Amy Lowell's poem "Lilacs" is "universal." While Jean Gould in particular uses that term in her historical biography *Amy: The World of Amy Lowell and the Imagist Movement*, the remarks of other critics suggest the same concept. For example, Richard Benvenuto, in *Amy Lowell*, speaks of how her poem encompasses lilacs and the people of New England into "one body, one being," that is, a universally shared state. It is worth examining the poem more closely to determine the characteristics that impart its universality.

The most basic way in which the poem is universal is in the language. From the first stanza on, the poem is splashed with words like *everywhere*, *everyone*, and *all*, terms that are universal in scope, even if the sphere in which they are applied is limited; that is, to refer to "everyone in New England" would be less universal than to refer to everyone in the world, but the term is still universal within its scope. Interestingly, while the context of "Lilacs" is established as New England, Lowell rarely makes qualifications when she uses universally inclusive words. In the first stanza, the lilacs are said not only to be present in all springs (a comment that is sealed with a period) but to be everywhere, both in the present and in the past. Furthermore, the indefinite use of the past tense allows the declaration to apply at any given point in the past, stretching back indefinitely—or at least to the time when lilacs first came into existence. Of course, the statements that lilacs are and were everywhere may slightly confound a reader, since obviously one can point to many a spot and observe that no lilac is to be found there. This fairly abstract aspect of the poem's universality will be made clearer later on. Beyond the all-inclusive

WHAT DO I READ NEXT?

- Lowell's collection *Pictures of the Floating World*, which was published in 1919, the year before she wrote "Lilacs," shows influence from the art of painting, with poems sometimes referred to as "word-paintings."

- While it cannot be critically judged in the way that her original poetry can, *Fir-Flower Tablets: Poems Translated from the Chinese* (1921) is noteworthy for allowing insight into Lowell's appreciation for Eastern verse. The poems were first translated by Florence Ayscough, who produced direct literal translations with various options for open-ended words, and then Lowell shaped these raw translations into English-language poems.

- Lowell has been historically appreciated for her extensive correspondence with her friend D. H. Lawrence, the multitalented British author of novels such as *Lady Chatterley's Lover* (1928) and poetry collections such as *Birds Beasts and Flowers* (1923). The correspondence between Lawrence and Lowell is collected in the 1985 volume *The Letters of D. H. Lawrence and Amy Lowell, 1914–1925*, edited by E. Claire Healey and Keith Cushman.

- One of Lowell's fellow imagists was Hilda Doolittle, who was known as H.D. and was included in the anthologies Lowell edited. H.D.'s first published collection of verse was *Sea Garden* (1916). In 1919, she wrote a nonfiction treatise on poetics, *Notes on Thought and Vision*, which was not published until 1982.

- In her critical volume *Tendencies in Modern American Poetry*, Lowell considers verse from Robert Frost's collection *Mountain Interval* (1916), which includes the quintessential Frost poems "The Road Not Taken" and "Birches."

- Liz Rosenberg edited an anthology aimed at young adults titled *Roots and Flowers: Poets and Poems on Family* (2001), in which forty contemporary poets share thoughts about family and provide a few family-focused poems.

terminology, the first stanza also features one word that is actually universally exclusive, the word *nobody*. But even that word is used in such a way as to connote inclusivity, as Lowell speaks of no one being at home in a public park; that is, everyone is a visitor; or perhaps, since the park belongs to no one, it belongs to everyone.

The second stanza begins with the same five lines that began the first, and this repetition also contributes to the universal sense of the poem. These five lines appear a third time, as the reader will discover, at the beginning of the third stanza. It is notable that the lines are presented not two but three times. If these five lines were presented just twice, a single circuit or circle would be suggested. The poem would begin at one spot and eventually return to that spot, and (even if the poem still contains more lines) a sense of closure would be implied by the single return; one passes through one's door in beginning a journey, and the same door is passed through as the journey ends. In "Lilacs," the opening five lines are presented three times, thus suggesting a second circuit, and an open-ended one at that; if another circuit is begun, another beyond that is suggested, and no matter the number of further circuits, a sense of closure will never be surely established. The poem thus figures the repeated, potentially endless cycling through of the lilacs' places in the world.

It is within the second stanza that Lowell begins to fuse the people of New England with the lilacs, as she calls on the flower to represent the souls of New Englanders (the group implied by her use of the word *our*), while the leaves of the lilac bush represent the human heart, the shape of which they bear. In these comparisons, Lowell uses not similes, which place distance between the objects being compared with the words *like* or *as*, but metaphors, which directly link the objects. Literally, the lilacs are said not

to represent the souls of New Englanders but to *be* those souls, and further, the lilacs *are* the love of women and children—who together represent the continuation of the human race. Having earlier attributed lilacs to every spring, Lowell now attributes them to every summer as well. The second stanza ends with repeated formulations of what the month of May is. To begin with, May literally is the lilac, and as such, the ensuing comparisons can all be traced back to the lilac: if May is the lilac, whatever else May is, the lilac is as well. Thus, all the other aspects of nature that one can associate with the sight of lilacs—birds, clouds, trees, leaves, the soil, even the wind—are metaphorically tied to the lilac. As all of these associations collect, the lilac itself becomes ever more loaded with those associations. The reader may not consciously think back to each association as the lilac is mentioned anew, but in the reader's immediate subconscious—which collects impressions for as long as the mind is capable of holding them in case they may prove needed—even with this long poem of 109 lines, every line may be subconsciously remembered through to the end. In the reader's subconscious, the word *lilac* will ring with all the associations it has been assigned. And with this expertly crafted poem, that ringing proves to be fully harmonious, even orchestral or symphonic.

The third and final stanza so effectively unites the notions that have arisen in the course of the poem that it requires little further elucidation. Through the images in these lines, lilacs, New England, and the poet are all united. The poem closes with references in the first person that might seem to diminish the all-inclusiveness established earlier. Indeed, some critics have read these lines as being essentially egotistical; Jane Marcus, for one, in "Amy Lowell, Body and Sou-ell," finds that with the poem's close, "Amy Lowell declares herself the primary poetic voice of her nation and her region. No apologies." But it seems more likely that Lowell did not intend to negate the universality of the poem through these lines. Rather, she, as the poet presenting this verse, is taking herself as a representative of New England, the lilac, and all that the flower has come to stand for. She is referring to herself not in an egotistical sense but in an existential sense, as an individual who not only exists in the reality of New England but also perceives the intimate connections between herself and the land; and in perceiving these connections she finds it her duty, as a poet, to bestow this sense of two-way belonging on any who would wish to share in it by hearing or reading her poem. Indeed, Marcus herself, coming from a family of Irish Catholic immigrants uprooted from their nation and traditions, declares, "This poem was the anthem that led me out of a cultural backwater. It gave me a homeland where I lived, replacing the lost Ireland of family legend." The poem successfully called to Marcus's mind her own childhood memories of playing near lilacs. And so although Lowell's closing first-person statements are individuated and thus might appear exclusive rather than universal, whoever reads the poem or recites it in one's mind is led to take on that first-person identity. As Marcus recalls, "When I said 'I am New England' at sixteen, I cast off centuries of superstition and soggy religion and some, but not all, fear and trembling, guilt and shame." Thus, in lending the reader a sense of identification, even Lowell's use of the first person is an aspect of the poem's universality.

The universality of "Lilacs" runs somewhat deeper than the language alone suggests, as the poem's philosophy and images are rooted in not just literary but also spiritual traditions. One of these traditions is transcendentalism, especially as represented by Walt Whitman and Ralph Waldo Emerson. Whitman's poem "When Lilacs Last in the Dooryard Bloom'd" prefigures Lowell's "Lilacs," and generally speaking, Whitman's poetry is flooded with the impressions inspired by his spiritual relationship with the world, including all of humanity and nature. Lowell's poem also bears echoes of Emerson's essay "Nature," in which he, too, elaborates his relationship with the natural world, one that he idealizes as essentially childlike:

> To speak truly, few adult persons can see nature. Most persons do not see the sun. At least they have a very superficial seeing. The sun illuminates only the eye of the man, but shines into the eye and the heart of the child. The lover of nature is he whose inward and outward senses are still truly adjusted to each other; who has retained the spirit of infancy even into the era of manhood.

Lowell, in "Lilacs," calls to mind just such a childlike appreciation for the world through her mention of lilacs representing children's memories of gardens. Emerson further remarks, "In the woods too, a man casts off his years,... and... is always a child. In the woods, is perpetual youth." If, in that quotation, "woods" were changed

to "garden," and "man" to "woman," it would sound very much like something Lowell would have said. Emerson speaks to Lowell's instinctive appreciation for the lilac itself when he meditates on nature's beauty, the human appreciation of which he does not attempt to logically justify: "Such is the constitution of all things, or such the plastic power of the human eye, that the primary forms, as the sky, the mountain, the tree, the animal, give us a delight *in and for themselves*; a pleasure arising from outline, color, motion, and grouping." Stressing the purposelessness of nature's beauty, Emerson later iterates, "Nature satisfies by its loveliness, and without any mixture of corporeal benefit." Lowell's poem connotes just such a pure appreciation of nature's loveliness in the form of lilacs.

Some scholars have seen fit to downplay Lowell's work because of her intent focus on images, whereby one might suggest that she neglects to find deeper ethical or spiritual meaning in those images. For example, Richard Benvenuto finds that in "Lilacs," Lowell extols the flowers' beauty but "makes no claim for a greater moral wisdom in nature. The lilacs simply oppose their beauty to the pursuit of profit." Even Robert Frost, a poet whom Lowell helped bring to public recognition, had trouble seeing beyond Lowell's images. He remarked in a lecture at Amherst College soon after her death, "Her Imagism lay chiefly in images to the eye. She flung flowers and everything else there. Her poetry was forever a clear resonant calling off of things seen." But as Gould, who quotes Frost's lecture in *Amy*, notes, "His observations, unsentimental but deeply poetic, showed clearly that Robert Frost did not realize the emotional value that flowers and all those 'things seen' had for Amy." One might add that "Lilacs" further reflects an appreciation for the spiritual value of the flowers.

Notably, Lowell highlights Frost's work in her 1917 critical volume *Tendencies in Modern American Poetry*, and her comments there suggest that Frost was something of a model for her in the creation of "Lilacs" (first published in 1920), especially with respect to her identification with New England. She refers to him as being "of the very bone and sinew of New England," which he knew so well because with him, "New England is daily environment....Mr. Frost typifies the New England of to-day in its entirety—a remark which should perhaps be qualified by adding the words 'in the country districts.'" In sum, while other poets may be said to represent New England, "Mr. Robert Frost is New England." In time, Lowell found that she, too, could *be* New England, as she declares in "Lilacs," although Gould qualifies this by noting that "if one had to categorize her, Amy was urban New England." Thus, instead of Frost's rural farms or Emerson's forests, where trees might be said to overshadow the flowers, Lowell has written of gardens and street scenes, where nature nonetheless blesses human activity with its presence, drawing attention away from manmade artifices through eye-catching blooms.

The question as to the philosophical roots of Lowell's aesthetic appreciation of nature is addressed by the poet herself in the preface of *Tendencies in Modern American Poetry*. She states that modern poets, being concerned not with tradition but with truth, "see in the universe a huge symbol, and so absolute has this symbol become to them that they have no need to dwell constantly upon its symbolic meaning." Lowell thus suggests that the reader should realize that modern poetry such as her own, even if focused only on images on the surface, is at heart concerned with the search for universal truth. Lowell's ensuing remarks suggest that this aspect of modern poetry was shaped by the foundation laid by transcendentalists like Whitman and Emerson: "What appear to be pure nature poems are of course so, but in a different way from most nature poems of the older writers; for nature is not now something separate from man, man and nature are recognized as a part of a whole, man being a part of nature, and all falling into a place in the vast plan." Once again, the roots of Lowell's line of thought can be found in "Nature," where Emerson posits just such a universal unity:

> Although the works of nature are innumerable and all different, the result or the expression of them all is similar and single. Nature is a sea of forms radically alike and even unique. A leaf, a sunbeam, a landscape, the ocean, make an analogous impression on the mind. What is common to them all,—that perfectness and harmony, is beauty. The standard of beauty is the entire circuit of natural forms,—the totality of nature.

He concludes, "Nothing is quite beautiful alone; nothing but is beautiful in the whole. A single object is only so far beautiful as it suggests this universal grace." It is just this universal grace, this totality of nature of Emerson's, that Lowell is seeking to grasp through her poetic treatise on the lilac.

By this point, it has become clear that, patently imagist as "Lilacs" may be, Lowell has strayed from one of the principles put forth in the preface of her anthology *Some Imagist Poets*. There, the fourth point reads in part, "We believe that poetry should render particulars exactly and not deal in vague generalities, however magnificent and sonorous. It is for this reason that we oppose the cosmic poet, who seems to us to shirk the real difficulties of his art." "Lilacs" may be a classic imagist poem, but it is also undeniably a sonorous poem with cosmic implications.

There is one more spiritual tradition that is worth mentioning in view of "Lilacs": that of Zen Buddhism. It is possible that Lowell was exposed to the Zen tradition—which evolved as Buddhism worked its way from India through China and on to Japan—given how diligently she absorbed in the course of her self-education whatever happened to interest her, and given that she both studied and recreated Chinese and Japanese poetry, which likely reflected Buddhist schools of thought regardless of whether the religion itself was invoked by name. A few Zen concepts are hinted at in "Lilacs." In his text *Zen Keys*, Thich Nhat Hanh explains how Zen is rooted in the world of being, not that of concepts; and for one to be perfectly attuned to the world of being, the world of concepts must essentially be done away with. In order to dismiss all concepts, one must reach a state of "non-discriminative" wisdom, whereby one does not overlay what one sees and experiences with judgments or valuations; one even loses consciousness of one's own identity. That is, as Nhat Hanh states, "This wisdom . . . is a direct and perfect knowledge of reality, a form of understanding in which one does not distinguish between subject and object." In her poem, Lowell tends toward just such a universal "perfect knowledge" when her consciousness merges with both the place that surrounds her and the lilac itself; she is New England, and she is the lilac.

The Buddhist concept of interbeing is also suggested in "Lilacs." As Nhat Hanh explains, everything in nature is interconnected in that every thing depends on the things around it for its existence, and those things depend upon other things, and so forth. A table, for example, comes into existence thanks to the tree that supplied the wood, the mill that shaped the lumber, the craftsman who made the table, the blacksmith who made the craftsman's tools, and so on. Thus, following this chain indefinitely, in Nhat Hanh's words, "The existence of the table demonstrates the existence of all non-table elements, in fact, of the entire universe." Generalizing this notion, he states, "The presence of one thing implies the presence of all other things. The enlightened man or woman sees each thing not as a separate entity but as a complete manifestation of reality." An anecdote helps illustrate this concept of interbeing—a concept whose echo is found in Emerson's "universal grace." No less a person than the Buddha himself, when the time came in the fifth century BCE to transmit his enlightenment to a disciple who would propagate his teachings, silently held up before a gathering of monks a single flower. At that time, as Nhat Hanh relates, "Everyone in the assembly looked at him, but they did not understand at all. Then one monk looked at the Buddha with sparkling eyes and smiled." That monk "truly saw the flower"—that is, through that flower, he saw the universe, and that sudden perception was his enlightenment. Poetry, of course, being rooted in language, is rooted in the world of concepts, and so a sense of Zen enlightenment can be suggested but not exactly embodied in verse. In her poem, Lowell figuratively holds up a sprig of lilacs and, image by image, demonstrates how those lilacs are connected to each and every aspect of the world around her, in terms of time and space, nature and humanity; and if the reader, in one's imagination, can truly see those lilacs, then through those lilacs one will grasp the universe entire—and for that moment of enlightenment one would have Lowell to thank.

Source: Michael Allen Holmes, Critical Essay on "Lilacs," in *Poetry for Students*, Gale, Cengage Learning, 2013.

Carl E. Rollyson, Jr.

In the following essay, Rollyson contends that Lowell was "the premier platform performer among her generation of poets" and reviews the critical responses to her poetry.

When Amy Lowell died in 1925 at the age of 51, she was at the height of her fame. Her two-volume biography of John Keats, published in the last year of her life, had been greeted in this country with almost universal acclaim. She was

Orioles play about in the lilacs in Lowell's poem.
(© Gerald A. DeBoer / Shutterstock.com)

the premier platform performer among her generation of poets.

In 1926, Lowell's posthumous volume of verse, *What's O'Clock*, was awarded a Pulitzer Prize. She had remained in the public eye ever since the publication of her second book, *Sword Blades and Poppy Seed* (1914). She had wrested the Imagist movement away from Ezra Pound, producing three best-selling anthologies of Imagist verse while publishing a book of her own poetry nearly every year. Pound retaliated, calling her appropriation "Amygism."

The pugnacious Lowell dominated the poetry scene in every sense of the word, supporting journals like *Poetry* and the *Little Review*, and publishing pronunciamentos about the "new poetry." Standing only five feet tall and weighing as much as 250 pounds, she made good copy: The sister of Harvard's president, she smoked big black cigars and cursed. She lived on the family estate in Brookline, Massachusetts, where her seven rambunctious sheep dogs terrorized her guests. She wore a pince nez that made her look—so one biographer

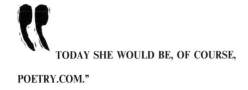

TODAY SHE WOULD BE, OF COURSE, POETRY.COM."

thought—like Theodore Roosevelt. She was even known to say "Bully!" Lowell traveled in a maroon Pierce Arrow, which she shipped to England in 1914 when she decided to look up Pound and seize her piece of the poetry action in London. Pound wanted her monetary support but scorned her verse. When she chose not to play by his rules, he mocked her, parading around a party she was hosting with a tin bathtub on his head—his way of ridiculing her bath poem, written in her patented polyphonic prose:

> Little spots of sunshine lie on the surface of the water and dance, dance, and their reflections wobble deliciously over the ceiling; a stir of my finger sets them whirring, reeling. I move a foot, and the planes of light in the water jar. I lie back and laugh, and let the green-white water, the sun-flawed beryl water, flow over me. The day is almost too bright to bear, the green water covers me from the too bright day. I will lie here awhile and play with the water and the sun spots.

Reading this dithyramb to the Poetry Society of America, Lowell caused an uproar. This was not poetry at all, the conservative membership protested. Another account of this episode mentions titters, as Society members envisioned the elephantine poet at her ablutions—or rather her profanation of what a dignified poet ought to perform.

Lowell went on lecture tours the way rock bands roll from town to town today, with an entourage, a suite at the best hotel, and a gathering of reporters awaiting her latest outrage. On the lecture platform, she would read a poem and then pause, looking out at her audience: "Well, hiss or applaud! But do something!" Almost always she got an ovation—and some hisses. At receptions and dinner parties, she was carefully watched. When would she fight up? She seldom disappointed, although her favored stogie was, in fact, a small brown panatela.

Other women poets—chiefly Elinor Wylie and Edna St. Vincent Millay—also commanded press attention, but none had Amy Lowell's authority.

Publishers deferred to her contractual terms. D. H. Lawrence, Richard Aldington, H. D., and others depended on her largesse and her business sense. She was Poetry, Inc. Today she would be, of course, Poetry.com. T. S. Eliot called her the "demon saleswoman" of modern poetry. Academic critics such as John Livingston Lowes deemed her one of the masters of the sensuous image in English poetry. She helped make the reputations of Edwin Arlington Robinson and Robert Frost.

Of course, Lowell had her detractors, but their views were rarely reflected in reviews of her books. As Norman Mailer said of Marilyn Monroe—Lowell had crashed through a publicity barrier, which meant that no matter what kind of press she got, it all accrued to her benefit. Although she came from a wealthy and staunchly capitalist family and called herself "the last of the barons," it was not her politics but her poetics that captured the public imagination. She was for free verse, or what she called "cadenced verse." Although she would produce sonnets and other sorts of poems with rhyme schemes, she was celebrated for lines of uneven length, a bold, informal voice, and bright, colorful sensory imagery.

Lowell was all surface, her grumbling dissenters alleged, but she always seemed to carry the day by switching modes—from grand historical narratives, to hokkus, to lyrics, to polyphonic prose, to books about contemporary poetry that read as though she had just left the lecture platform to address you, the common reader.

It is not surprising, then, that her enemies—never able to get much traction during her lifetime—should pounce just as soon as the energetic Lowell dropped dead from a stroke. The urge to cut this incubus down to size was irresistible. Clement Wood, a poet and critic who had feuded with Lowell, was first up in 1926, producing a biography systematically dismantling Lowell's reputation as a poet and critic. Lowell had been prolific and prolix, producing in a fifteen-year span an immense and uneven variety of verse and prose that made her an easy target for tendentious criticism. Wood's verdict, in short, was that Lowell was no poet at all. He skirted her lesbianism with references to the "Sapphic fragments" of a "singer of Lesbos." He employed what he called the "new psychology" to suggest her work was wish fulfillment, the product of a desire to be accepted. Lowell's need was pathological, Wood implied, because of her obesity—a word he never used, referring instead to her "immense physique." Wood favored sarcasm, concluding, "All the Harvard pundits and all the claquing men can't set Miss Lowell on a pedestal again." He was chaffing John Livingston Lowes, chair of Harvard's English department, and countless critics who had reviewed her writing positively.

Lowell's next biographer, S. Foster Damon, produced a monumental biography in 1935, noting that Wood's snide attack had not been widely reviewed or credited, but the damage had been done—in part because Wood had played off the epithets of critics like Witter Bynner, who had dubbed Lowell the "hippopoetess," a term Ezra Pound also took up as a way of conflating the person with the poet. Damon, a member of Lowell's inner circle, restored her dignity by detailing her heroic dedication to her writing and to the cause of poetry, but he also unwittingly played Wood's hand by emphasizing the "triumph of the spirit over the tragedy of the body." Poetry, in other words, is what Lowell could do instead of living a full, "normal" life. Damon meant his words as a tribute, but because he did not tell the complete story of Lowell's love life and her working days, he could not recover for readers the Amy Lowell he knew.

Damon's plight raises two issues that plague Lowell biography. Lowell's lover and constant companion, Ada Dwyer Russell, destroyed their letters at Lowell's request. As unfortunate was Lowell's directive to her secretaries that they destroy the drafts of her work each day. Damon could have partly rectified this enormous loss had he candidly described the intimacy between "Peter" (Lowell's nickname for Ada) and the poet. But Russell, who had worked closely with the poet, was also Lowell's executor. Russell lived until 1952, resisting all requests to tell the story of her relationship with Lowell, and thus depriving readers not merely of a love story but of an insight into the poetic process. Damon's reticence made it all too easy for Wood's virulent version of Lowell to metastasize in Horace Gregory's hostile *Amy Lowell: Portrait of the Poet in Her Time* (1958). Employing Wood's vulgar Freudianism, Gregory sketched a view of a masculinized woman who used her bulk as a defense against a hurtful world. Gregory seemed to have no idea that Russell and Lowell had been lovers, although the evidence was rather plain to see, eventually

emerging in Jean Gould's *Amy: The World of Amy Lowell and the Imagist Movement* (1975). Relying on critics such as Glenn Richard Ruilhy, who published in 1957 an edition of Lowell's poetry that emphasized her stunning love poetry, as well as on fresh interviews with Lowell's surviving family and friends, Gould began the work of restoring the person and poet to her full humanity and range.

But Gould was unwilling to confront the full implications of Lowell's subtler poems, in which she carefully disrobed for the world. Gould balked at going "half-way with poets" and feeling "the thing you're out to find," as Lowell wrote in one of her last poems. Gould quoted but did not explore the subtext of her subject's passionate poetry.

Enter C. David Heymann with *American Aristocracy: The Lives and Times of James Russell, Amy, and Robert Lowell* (1980), determined to drag Lowell back to Gregory's procrustean bed. Heymann cut and pasted the work of Lowell's previous biographers, quoted a few published memoirs, and delivered a breezy reprise of the standard brief against Amy Lowell, beginning with Louis Untermeyer's devastating verdict: "Amy Lowell had a genius for everything except the thing she wanted most: permanence as a poet."

Heymann pictures Lowell as "naive, unknowing, and innocent," pronouncing her brashness a cover for a "gigantic inferiority complex" and a "troubled psyche." He delivers his judgments with ex cathedra certainty: "The need to make a kind of technicolor charade of her life was one way of making up for its essential emptiness." And he denies her precisely what recent critics, male and female, have found most valuable in her verse: a deep understanding of love. Instead, he indulges in that most odious of biographical practices: presenting lack of evidence as somehow an occasion for insisting on the validity of what he cannot know. Thus he argues that in the first stanza of Lowell's signature poem "Patterns," "she must have had herself in mind" protesting against "Puritan inhibitions and society's repressive conventions." But Lowell seemed remarkably well adjusted, adroitly negotiating both the high society world of her family and the rarified precincts of poets. It is odd that her aplomb should so often be mistaken for ingenuousness, as if she did not know enough to be embarrassed by her bulk and her fortune.

To be sure, she had her share of self-doubt, but I cannot help but think her air of self-containment nettled those like Pound and Eliot who could find no place for her in the narrative of modernism. Better to think of her as an amateur, a lady poet, and a clubwoman. Hence Heymann guywires her to "Miss Lowell" and "Amy," whereas Pound is never Ezra and Untermeyer is never Mr. Untermeyer.

Heymann calls Lowell's erotic poems "androgynous," born of a close friendship with Ada that was not "necessarily sexual in nature." Why is he so wary of discussing Lowell's sexuality when he is so confident about other aspects of her inner life? It seems that he could not resist joining a long line of male critics who could not envision the body of Amy Lowell in the act of love. Although she did sometimes express anguish and even disgust about her figure ("Look at me," she once said, "I'm a disease"), Lowell wrote poetry that celebrated the bodies of herself, her lover, and other women. Indeed, she often lectured about Whitman and shared his amative nature. Far from suffering from some void in her life, Lowell positively embraced her sexuality.

Modernists like William Carlos Williams could not abide a poet like Lowell, a conservative who refused to apologize for her wealth. Like Pound, he wrote her letters telling her off while asking her for money. Heymann thought it odd that Lowell did not make common cause with feminists given her own "liberated" relationship with Ada Dwyer. That he did not see that he has contradicted himself, providing Lowell with an erotic experience he had previously denied her, is just another index of his unwillingness to see the person and the poet.

Critics like Lillian Faderman and Melissa Bradshaw and poets like Honor Moore, who edited *Amy Lowell: Selected Poems* (The Library of America, 2004), have since become attuned to her bold eroticism, a force that beautifully binds the physical and spiritual, as in these lines from "Absence," Lowell's love poem to Ada Russell:

> My cup is empty to-night,
> Cold and dry are its sides. . . .
> But the cup of the heart is still,
> And cold, and empty.
> When you come it brims
> Red and trembling with blood,
> Heart's blood for your drinking;
> To fill your mouth with love
> And the bitter-sweet taste of a soul.

These were the lines D. H. Lawrence extolled when he expressed his affinity with Lowell, which Lowell herself acknowledged when she quoted back to him his praise for her "insistence on things. My things are always, to my mind, more than themselves." She begins with a cup that is always a cup but is also her heart and then her mouth, just as her lover's coming is both a return and a climax; the literal, the sexual, and the symbolic merge.

Of even greater importance, however, are poems like "The Onlooker" (first published in the *Saturday Review of Literature*, February 1925), which fuses the personal with the historical, espying in an erotic encounter the fate of a civilization:

> Suppose I plant you
> Like wide-eyed Helen
> On the battlements
> Of weary Troy,
> Clutching the parapet with desperate hands.
> She, too, gazes at a battlefield
> Where bright vermillion plumes and metal whiteness
> Shock and sparkle and go down with groans.
> Her glances strike the rocking battle,
> Again— again—
> Recoiling from it
> Like baffled spear-heads fallen from a brazen shield.
> The ancients at her elbow counsel patience and contingencies;
> Such to a woman stretched upon a bed of battle,
> Who bargained for this only in the whispering arras
> Enclosed about a midnight of enchantment.

This Amy Lowell is akin to Constantine Cavafy or Zbigniew Herbert in her reverie over a historic moment, and the conceit that she was no poet seems palpably put-on, part of a master narrative that ought to be annihilated once and for all.

Source: Carl E. Rollyson, Jr., "The Absence of Amy Lowell," in *New Criterion*, Vol. 26, No. 1, September 2007, pp. 77–80.

Diane Ellen Hamer

In the following essay, Hamer explores the effect of Lowell's legacy on the efforts of female poets to break free of conventional sex roles.

When I first discovered the poetry of Amy Lowell, I was so taken with a group of her erotic poems that I suggested to my writer friend Judith that she do a one-woman show as Lowell reading her work. She could use the same sort of

> **"** SHE USED HER REPUTATION AS A CIGAR-SMOKING WOMAN TO ATTRACT PEOPLE TO HER PUBLIC PERFORMANCES, WHICH IN TURN SHE USED TO ADVANCE BOTH HER OWN CAREER AND THOSE OF HER FRIENDS."

props that Lowell herself used when reading, as she did at every opportunity: a bare stage with a chair, a floor lamp, and a table with a glass of water on it. But when I started reading some of the poems aloud, I realized that the lesbian love lyrics were too explicit to be read to the target audience, which I envisioned as a largely college-age crowd of mostly women. One of the most explicit, "The Weather-Cock Points South," was typical of these love poems in its use of flower imagery:

> I put your leaves aside.
> One by one:
> The still broad outer leaves;
> The smaller ones,
> Pleasant to touch, veined with purple;
> The glazed inner leaves
> One by one
> I parted you from your leaves
> Until you stood up like a white flower
> Swaying slightly in the evening wind. [. . .]
>
> Where in all the garden is there such a flower?
>
> The bud is more than the calyx.
> There is nothing to equal a white bud,
> Of no color and of all,
> Burnished by moonlight,
> Thrust upon by a softly-swinging wind.

Flower imagery in erotic lesbian verse already had a long tradition in American women's poetry when Lowell was at work starting in the mid-1910's, so the coded imagery would have been discerned by some of her readers. In a new book, *Amy Lowell, American Modern*, a collection of essays that re-examine her life and work, Lillian Faderman observes: "Lowell landed on the bestseller list, perhaps because many readers refused to understand her metaphor; yet it is not difficult to see the flower image . . . as an evocative and descriptive symbol for female genitalia." Faderman's essay puts the relationship between Amy Lowell and Ada Russell squarely on

display, citing Lowell's own admissions that Russell was in fact "the subject of her love poetry." At any rate, Lowell's use of flower metaphors helped her evade the censors that plagued her colleagues, and she clearly enjoyed the challenge of creating dual layers of meaning in her work.

All told, Lowell wrote nine books of poetry and four books of prose, and edited several anthologies, in the twelve years from age 39 to her death of a stroke at 51. Some of the poetry is exquisite and timeless, some is dreadful and forgettable. Lowell usually wrote in free verse—*vers libre*, as she called it. Her body of work is sufficiently large that most readers will find something of interest, what with subjects ranging from history, war, and the Far East to lesbian love, gardens, and everyday life activities.

Amy Lowell was born in Boston in 1874 to Augustus and Katharine Lawrence Lowell, part of the large Lowell-Lawrence clan. She was the baby sister of the future president of Harvard University, Abbott Lawrence Lowell. She was first educated at home and later at private schools reserved for upper-class girls. She was largely self-educated, though, as she didn't do well in the confines of the classroom. She was a smart, sensitive tomboy caught in a social class and a larger culture that made it very hard for her to find herself. In time she would come to be regarded, quite incorrectly, as a lonely old maid. Her letters and her friends' reminiscences show that she had crushes on girls and women from an early age, and that she understood on some level that making a life with another woman was not socially acceptable. However, upon meeting the actress Ada Dwyer Russell in 1912, she emerged as both a writer and a lesbian.

An earlier significant moment in Lowell's life was when she saw a performance by the Italian actress Eleanora Duse in 1902. Duse had an extraordinary effect on Lowell, as she often had on her audiences, an effect that was documented by other lesbians. For example, Eva Le Gallienne, a noted playwright, actress, and director, wrote that while she was in a sanitarium, "she had clung to Duse's photograph. . . . Duse had ceased to be a woman and had become a god." After seeing Duse perform, Lowell ran home to write a poem and realized this was her calling. She immersed herself in poetry and literature and began to dabble in writing, but it was only after she met and partnered with Ada Russell that she began to write poetry in earnest.

Russell was instrumental in Lowell's success, both as her muse and as her helpmate, tending to Amy's personal and work needs with absolute devotion and care. It's a love story that can only be gleaned from the poetry, which is to say that Lowell chose to be far less obvious about their relationship than did that other lesbian couple of the era, Gertrude Stein and Alice B. Toklas. In a section of *Pictures of the Floating World* (1919), many of the love poems are gathered in a section that Lowell called "Two Speak Together." Most of the poems are short and episodic, or in some cases a series of haiku-like passages stitched together into a longer piece. In "Opal," she writes: "You are ice and fire / The touch of you burns my hands like snow / You are cold and flame." And this in "The Artist": "How pale you would be, and startling / How quiet / But your curves would spring upward / Like a clear jet of flung water / You would quiver like a shot-up spray of water . . . and tremble / and I too should tremble / Watching." Interestingly, some poems that she held back from publishing, considering them too risqué, were published soon after her death by Ada Russell in *Ballads for Sale* (1927).

Lowell's first book of poetry was mostly conventional fare, but after reading a poem by HD (Hilda Doolittle), who called herself an "imagiste," Lowell declared herself to be an imagiste as well. Unfortunately, as she explored the world of the "new poetry," she wound up in a feud with Ezra Pound. Pound was willing to use Lowell for funding and networking, but wasn't above ridiculing her when it suited him. Nor did other authors refrain from disparaging Lowell in their letters and dinner conversation, even while continuing to use their friendship with her to advance their own careers. As shown by Bonnie Kime Scott in her essay in the *American Modern* collection, Lowell was to D.H. Lawrence "a poet, a friend, and a facilitator, rather than a patron, that she was rewarded his dedication of *New Poems* in 1918." However, Lawrence and others sometimes "expressed doubts about her poetry and the very lectures she used to spread their reputations. They worried that they were not always enhanced by her agency." Regardless of the infighting, Amy Lowell and Ada Russell did have a large circle of friends made up of other writers, society people, and family members who frequented their home, often for elaborate dinner parties. Lowell commanded their attention on these occasions but was also capable of genuine concern for her friends and colleagues.

At the height of her notoriety, Lowell was her own best promoter. She believed that marketing oneself was necessary to sell poetry to the general public. She used her reputation as a cigar-smoking woman to attract people to her public performances, which in turn she used to advance both her own career and those of her friends. By traveling and reading her poems before women's clubs and poetry groups, at society teas and small invitational events, she brought her poems to life and managed to market them to literary magazines and anthologies. Her poems were meant to be read aloud, especially those in what she called polyphonic prose. Here the typescript looked like prose, but the cadences and rhymes created a more musical sound, which she likened to the effect of a symphony, with many voices in one. "Only read it aloud. Gentle Reader, I beg, and you will see what you will see," she wrote in the preface to *Men, Women and Ghosts* (1916).

Lowell borrowed from and expanded upon the work of earlier writers to achieve her aural effect. This dependence upon hearing the poems read aloud has undoubtedly limited their appeal. But the main reason that Lowell is barely more than a footnote in literature can be traced to the 20th-century scourges of misogyny, homophobia, and fat phobia (Lowell was far from thin). It didn't help that as an upper-class woman she was often considered a dilettante, and her death at 51 cheated her out of the longevity that might have given her more time to establish herself in American letters. Even with her penchant for entertaining and traveling, she did not develop a cult of personality as, say, Stein and Hemingway did.

Although she won a posthumous Pulitzer Prize, and two of her poems, "Patterns" and "Madonna of the Evening Flowers," are widely published in poetry anthologies, her fame today is confined to a rather small number of devoted readers. Her lasting contribution to modern poetry will probably be the combination of her use of polyphonic prose and her spare images. While she will never be as widely known as Gertrude Stein or Djuna Barnes, she does join them and other innovative writers who blasted into the 20th century with new ways of looking at and writing about the world. In the end, like Stein, Lowell may well be best remembered not for her poetry but for her public persona as a cigar-smoking iconoclast who broke free of conventional sex roles to become an American original.

Source: Diane Ellen Hamer, "Amy Lowell Wasn't Writing About Flowers," in *Gay & Lesbian Review Worldwide*, Vol. 11, No. 4, July/August 2004, pp. 13–14.

SOURCES

Benvenuto, Richard, *Amy Lowell*, Twayne's United States Author Series, Twayne Publishers, 1985, pp. 1–30, 132–33.

Bradshaw, Melissa, "'Let Us Shout It Lustily': Amy Lowell's Career in Context," in *Selected Poems of Amy Lowell*, edited by Melissa Bradshaw and Adrienne Munich, Rutgers University Press, 2002, pp. xv–xxiv.

Emerson, Ralph Waldo, "Nature," in *Selected Writings of Ralph Waldo Emerson*, edited by William H. Gilman, Signet Classic, 1983, pp. 190–200.

Flint, F. Cudworth, *Amy Lowell*, University of Minnesota Press, 1969, p. 35.

Galvin, Mary E., "Imagery and Invisibility: Amy Lowell and the Erotics of Particularity," in *Queer Poetics: Five Modernist Women Writers*, Praeger, 1999, p. 21.

Gould, Jean, *Amy: The World of Amy Lowell and the Imagist Movement*, Dodd, Mead, 1975, pp. 32, 299–300, 349–52.

Healey, E. Claire, "Amy Lowell," in *Dictionary of Literary Biography*, Vol. 54, *American Poets, 1880–1945, Third Series*, edited by Peter Quatermain, Gale Research, 1987, pp. 251–60.

Lowell, Amy, "Is There a National Spirit in 'the New Poetry' of America?," in *Craftsman*, Vol. 30, July 1916, p. 340.

———, "Lilacs," in *Selected Poems of Amy Lowell*, edited by Melissa Bradshaw and Adrienne Munich, Rutgers University Press, 2002, pp. 77–80.

———, *Tendencies in Modern American Poetry*, Houghton Mifflin, 1921, pp. v–xi, 79–90.

Marcus, Jane, "Amy Lowell, Body and Sou-ell," in *Amy Lowell, American Modern*, edited by Adrienne Munich and Melissa Bradshaw, Rutgers University Press, 2004, pp. 186–89.

Nhat Hanh, Thich, *Zen Keys*, Doubleday, 1995, pp. 40–45.

"Overweight and Obesity in the U.S.," Food Research and Action Center website, http://frac.org/initiatives/hunger-and-obesity/obesity-in-the-us/ (accessed March 12, 2012).

Preface to *Some Imagist Poets: An Anthology*, Houghton Mifflin Company, 1915; reprinted in Project Gutenberg, http://www.gutenberg.org/files/30276/30276-h/30276-h.htm (accessed March 10, 2012).

FURTHER READING

Buell, Lawrence, *New England Literary Culture: From Revolution through Renaissance*, Cambridge University Press, 1986.

> This book by a university professor explores the development of a distinct New England literature in the century after the founding of the United States, with reference to Ralph Waldo Emerson, Nathaniel Hawthorne, and Emily Dickinson and various historical circumstances.

Fiala, John L., and Freek Vrugtman, *Lilacs: A Gardener's Encyclopedia*, Timber Press, 2008.

> This reference volume of over 400 pages contains virtually everything one could wish to know about lilacs, from the history of propagation to information on the various species to practical cultivating techniques.

Hughes, Glenn, *Imagism and the Imagists: A Study in Modern Poetry*, Biblo and Tannen, 1960.

> This volume presents the history of the imagist movement and the critical reaction to it as well as portraits of the key imagists, including Aldington, H.D., Lawrence, and Lowell.

Sato, Shozo, and Kasen Yoshimura, *Ikebana: The Art of Arranging Flowers*, C. E. Tuttle, 2008.

> The Japanese have such a fine cultural tradition of artistic flower arrangement that the art itself has a name, *ikebana*; the art form is said to signify the union of nature and humanity. This updated version of Sato's classic text includes instructions for creating a variety of arrangements.

SUGGESTED SEARCH TERMS

Amy Lowell

Amy Lowell AND "Lilacs"

Amy Lowell AND imagism

Amy Lowell AND Ada Dwyer Russell

Amy Lowell AND Ezra Pound

Amy Lowell AND New England

Amy Lowell AND new poetry

imagism AND modernism AND new poetry

Amy Lowell AND criticism

Amy Lowell AND cigars

Phenomenal Woman

MAYA ANGELOU

1978

Award-winning dramatist and poet Maya Angelou published the poem "Phenomenal Woman" in 1978. Angelou is perhaps best known for her autobiographical volume *I Know Why the Caged Bird Sings*, the first in what would become a six-volume autobiography. Like many of Angelou's works, the free-verse poem "Phenomenal Woman" explores notions of female identity. In this poem, the speaker describes her unique appeal to men, noting that in spite of the fact that she does not possess certain qualities associated with traditional notions of beauty, she nevertheless has the power to draw men to her. The poem incorporates a series of lists that itemize the woman's attractive attributes, and a refrain repeated at the close of each stanza highlights the woman's sense of herself as the phenomenal woman of the poem's title.

Critics have explored the poem's focus on positive self-image and have described the work as an examination of African American sisterhood. At the same time, the poem is regarded as a declaration of female beauty and confidence that is both individual and universal. First published in 1978 in *And Still I Rise*, "Phenomenal Woman" has been reprinted in a number of volumes, including *The Complete and Collected Poems of Maya Angelou* (1994) and *Phenomenal Woman: Four Poems Celebrating Women* (1995).

Maya Angelou (© Dave Allocca / Time & Life Pictures / Getty Images)

AUTHOR BIOGRAPHY

Angelou was born Marguerite Johnson on April 4, 1928, in St. Louis, Missouri. She would later change her name to Maya Angelou. Her parents were Bailey and Vivian Baxter Johnson. Angelou and her brother were sent to live in Stamps, Arkansas, after their parents divorced, when Angelou was just three years old. There, the children were raised by their maternal grandmother, who owned a country store. In her autobiographies, Angelou documents the discrimination and racism she experienced during her youth.

When she was eight years old, Angelou visited her mother in St. Louis, and during this stay she was raped by her mother's boyfriend, who was subsequently murdered by her uncles. Following this horrific incident, Angelou stopped talking for approximately five years. She gradually began speaking again and excelled at school.

Angelou completed the eighth grade at the top of her class in 1940, before moving with her mother and brother to San Francisco, where she attended George Washington High School. She also took dance and drama lessons from the California Labor School.

Dropping out of school at the age of fourteen, Angelou went to work as San Francisco's first female African American cable car conductor. At sixteen, Angelou became pregnant, and she gave birth to her son Guy shortly after her 1945 graduation from Mission High School's summer school. After working as a waitress and as a cook, Angelou subsequently moved to San Diego, where she worked at a nightclub. Later, she changed her name, performed regularly at a nightclub as a dancer, and eventually secured a role in the opera *Porgy and Bess*. Angelou toured Europe in 1954 and 1955 as part of the opera's theatrical company. Her career in the performing arts progressed as she studied modern dance under Martha Graham and performed as a singer and dancer on television variety shows. In 1957, she recorded her first album, *Calypso Lady*.

The following year, Angelou moved to New York and joined the Harlem Writers Guild. In New York, she wrote and performed in off-Broadway productions. In 1960, Angelou moved to Cairo, Egypt, and worked for an English-language paper. She later moved to Ghana, where she taught music and drama at the University of Ghana. After returning to the United States in 1964, Angelou was asked by civil rights leader Dr. Martin Luther King, Jr., to work as the Southern Christian Leadership Conference's northern coordinator, a post she accepted.

Angelou continued to write and published her acclaimed autobiography *I Know Why the Caged Bird Sings* in 1970. She worked as a writer in film and television and continued to write both autobiography and poetry as well, publishing the volume *And Still I Rise*, which contains "Phenomenal Woman," in 1978. Angelou has worked as a writer, educator, and speaker. She directed a feature film, *Down in the Delta*, in 1996 and has served on two presidential committees. She was awarded the Presidential Medal of the Arts in 2000 and has received over thirty honorary degrees.

POEM SUMMARY

The text used for this summary is from *Phenomenal Woman: Four Poems Celebrating Women*, Random House, 1995, pp. 1–6. A version of the poem can be found on the following web page: http://www.poetryfoundation.org/poem/178942.

Stanza 1

"Phenomenal Woman" is divided into four stanzas. The first consists of thirteen lines of varying lengths. In this stanza, the poem's speaker claims to have a secret that is wondered about by beautiful women. The speaker asserts that she is neither attractive in a cute way nor the size of a fashion model and states that beautiful women think that she is lying to them when she tells them the secrets of her own appeal. Throughout the remainder of the stanza, the speaker itemizes the particular traits she believes make her uniquely appealing. In discussing her features, including her arms, hips, and lips, the speaker focuses on specific elements pertaining to each physical feature. She states for example, that it is the expanse of her hips and the range of her arms that make her a phenomenal woman, along with the way she walks, and the way her lips curl when she smiles.

Stanza 2

In the second stanza, the speaker describes the confident way she walks into a room and the effect her entrance has upon the men in the room. She maintains that each man in the room either stands or falls to his knees before they all gather around her. She describes the actions of the men as similar to that of honeybees swarming their hive. Next, the speaker again lists her particular qualities that draw the men to her. Included in this list is the spark in her eyes, her flash of white teeth as she smiles, and the gleeful swing in her step as she saunters through the room. As the stanza closes, she repeats the assertion made at the close of the first stanza: she is a phenomenal woman.

Stanza 3

As the third stanza opens, the speaker states that not only have women wondered what makes her so appealing, but the men who are so drawn to her also ask themselves what it is about her that attracts them. The speaker observes how hard the men strive to figure out the mystery of her appeal. She states that when she attempts to

MEDIA ADAPTATIONS

- Angelou's "Phenomenal Woman" is available in an audiocassette recording produced in 1995 by Random House Audio. Angelou reads the poems collected in the 1995 book *Phenomenal Woman: Four Poems Celebrating Women*.

reveal her secret, the men still cannot fathom the mystery she presents to them. The speaker once more itemizes a series of physical attributes that she feels make her so intriguing. This list includes the curve of her back, her happy smile, the movement of her breasts, and her gracefulness. These qualities make her a phenomenal woman, she reiterates.

Stanza 4

In the poem's final stanza, the speaker states that the reader can now understand why she does not bow her head, that is, why she does not carry herself in a shy or ashamed manner. She states that she has no need to draw attention to herself by shouting or jumping or speaking loudly. Rather, when she passes by, she makes people proud, by virtue of her appearance and the way she carries herself. Again, the speaker lists the physical qualities that contribute to her appeal, including the way her heels click on the ground as she walks by and the curl of her hair. She then mentions her hand's palm and the need others have to be cared for by her. She concludes the stanza with the same affirmation that ended the three prior stanzas, asserting that she is a phenomenal woman.

THEMES

Female Identity

Throughout "Phenomenal Woman," Angelou establishes a notion of female identity that is both intensely private and blatantly physical.

TOPICS FOR FURTHER STUDY

- Many of Angelou's poems, with their simple and direct language, create precise images in the reader's mind. For example, Angelou uses the imagery of bees swarming their hive to underscore the effect the speaker in "Phenomenal Woman" has on the men around her. *Words with Wings: A Treasury of African-American Poetry and Art*, edited by Belinda Rochelle, is a poetry anthology aimed at young-adult readers. The work pairs poems by a number of acclaimed African American poets with paintings by African American artists. Study the way the poems and the paintings in the book work together to evoke a mood or tone. Consider the way the poems' language and imagery correlate to the visual images in the paintings with which the poems are paired. Write an essay in which you offer an analysis of one of the poem/painting pairings in the book, describing the poet's use of rhyme, meter, language, and imagery, then assessing the painting it appears with and the way the two art forms complement one another. Do you feel the pairing of the particular painting with the poem you have chosen is an effective, complementary one? Alternatively, write your own poem and create your own sketch or painting to correspond with it. In presenting your poem and artwork to the class, describe the way your words and art work together.

- Cherokee poet Joy Harjo began publishing poetry in the 1970s, just as Angelou did. Her first collection, *The Last Song*, was published in 1975. A later collection, *The Woman Who Fell from the Sky*, explores issues of culture and feminine identity. With a small group, read some of Harjo's poetry from this collection. Consider the ways the themes explored in the collection are similar to those Angelou treats in "Phenomenal Woman." Create an online blog in which you analyze and discuss Harjo's poetry and compare it with Angelou's work. Attend to the issues of form and structure as well as to the themes of the works you have chosen to analyze. Discuss as well your personal responses to the poetry.

- Angelou has repeatedly been identified with feminist themes, and early in her career, when "Phenomenal Woman" was first published, the women's rights movement was a prominent force in American culture and politics. Research the history of the women's rights movement in the twentieth century, tracing how the issues that concerned activists evolved over time. Create a report that can be shared with the class as a web page or summarized as a PowerPoint presentation. Draw attention to the issues the activists addressed and also to prominent figures in the movement.

- Angelou's poem "Phenomenal Woman" describes the body of its protagonist as full and curvaceous and distinctly different from conventional notions of beauty. Using works such as *Recovering the Black Female Body: Self-Representation by African American Women* (2000), edited by Michael Bennett and Vanessa D. Dickerson, study the way African American women have historically described themselves in works of poetry and fiction. Narrow the focus of your research by focusing on a particular time period or author. How is the issue of body image treated? How do various authors represent their own perceptions of their bodies and the responses to their bodies by others? Write a report in which you discuss your findings, and reference particular literary works. Be sure to cite all of your sources. Your report may be created either as a print product or as a web page.

At the onset of the poem, the speaker refers to a secret she possesses. The secret, she suggests, is what makes her appealing to men, and throughout the poem she attempts to describe the particular attributes that make her uniquely attractive. In addition to cataloging her physical qualities, the speaker also references an interior, mysterious part of herself that the men who are drawn to her can never access.

The woman in the poem speaks far more about her exterior qualities than about the mystery she possesses inside of her, yet in the final stanza, she alludes once again to something untouchable and hidden. She proclaims that the reader, at this point in the poem, can now comprehend why she feels no need to bow her head, why she does not need to yell, or draw attention to herself through such dramatic efforts as jumping around, for instance. This undefined thing seems unrelated to the physical qualities she has spent the majority of the poem highlighting and instead seems linked to what she has referred to as being secret and mysterious. The confidence with which she carries herself is perhaps drawn from this mysterious part of herself. Significantly, she cites this inner quality as the source not only of her own pride but also as the reason why others should be proud of her as she passes. She claims to have no need of speaking loudly or drawing attention to herself deliberately, because her sense of self draws others to her, almost magnetically. Her sense of identity appears to be drawn primarily from her physical being, of which she speaks so confidently, but also from something deep within her, at which she only hints.

Near the end of the poem, the speaker refers to a need she inspires in others for her to care for them. Here, the speaker expresses what may be seen as her own desire to be needed by others, which would make this the only glimpse the woman allows the reader of her sense of vulnerability. Her identity as a woman, the speaker demonstrates, is rooted in a physicality freely demonstrated, in private inner strength that remains hidden and guarded, and in her own softly spoken need to be needed by others.

Sexuality

The speaker's sexuality is a primary focus of "Phenomenal Woman." Throughout the poem, Angelou uses language that does more than simply describe the speaker's physical characteristics.

Rather, Angelou's word choice creates a highly sensual tone throughout the poem. In the first stanza, the speaker refers to the way other women—beautiful women, thin women—wonder about her secret. She goes on to insists that she herself is not conventionally beautiful, not in the way a model is. Not only is the speaker emphasizing physical beauty, but she also states that women believe she is lying when she attempts to tell them about her secret.

As she goes on to discuss her attributes, the reader is led to believe that the secret to which she refers is that of her ability to attract men. When she describes her arms, the woman does not discuss them simply in terms of their length or strength but rather describes her arms in terms of how far they reach. Using this vocabulary, in emphasizing *reaching*, the speaker suggests the capacity of her arms to embrace. Her hips are mentioned in terms of their breadth, indicating the speaker's curvaceous stature. Her lips are depicted as curling, perhaps into a smile, an image that seems slow and deliberately sensual. Men are drawn to these features, the speaker assures the reader in the second stanza. They are seemingly hypnotized by her, buzzing about like bees. After describing her fiery eyes and flashing teeth, the speaker discusses her sashaying waist, an image that, coupled with her reference to her hips in the previous stanza, underscores the sensuality of her stature and stride.

Again in the third stanza, the physical descriptions are highly suggestive of the woman's sexual nature, as she comments on her arching back and the sway of her breasts. These images are almost intimate in the way they are detailed and allude in this manner to lovemaking. In the final stanza, the woman speaks of the palm of her hands and the care she can provide, a statement that, given the sexualized remarks of the previous stanzas, may be interpreted as conveying a similarly intimate meaning. Throughout the poem, Angelou sustains an intensely sensual tone that highlights the woman's pride in and enthusiasm for her own sexuality.

STYLE

Rhyme, Repetition, and Rhythm

"Phenomenal Woman" is a poem that includes consistent, if not patterned, end rhymes, and as such may be classified as rhymed verse. (The

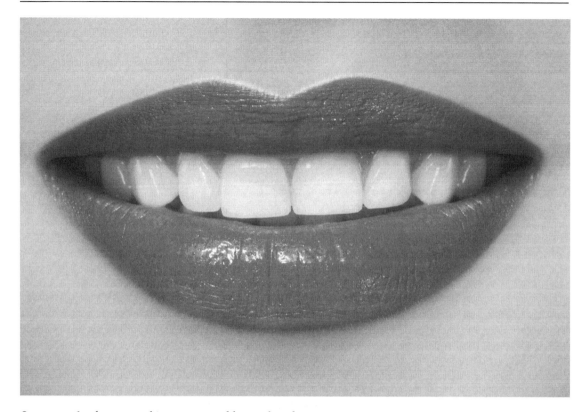

In stanza 1, phenomenal is represented by smiling lips. (© *Ivanova Inga | Shutterstock.com*)

term *end rhyme* refers to the rhyming of the final word or syllable in a line of poetry with the final word or syllable in a subsequent line.) Angelou additionally makes use of word repetition, which produces the same aural effect.

Complementing the rhyming and repetition that occur in the poem is the rhythm produced by the lists that occur in every stanza of the poem, in which the speaker delineates the attributes that make her appealing to men. Each of these lists is structured in the same manner, with each line including a noun followed by a prepositional phrase. The speaker describes, for example, the breadth of her hips and the sparkle in her eyes. The repetition of this line structure, along with the random rhymes that occur throughout the poem, lend the poem as a whole a natural cadence and an almost songlike rhythm.

Additionally, the repetition of the poem's title, "Phenomenal Woman," and the speaker's assertion that she is a phenomenal woman herself both work as refrains to emphasize the anthem-like nature of the work. The rhyme, repetition, and rhythm work together to create the sense that the poem is a declaration, a proclamation of the speaker's beauty and sense of confidence.

Figurative Language

Much of "Phenomenal Woman" is written in straightforward prose that does not make use of figurative language (expressions in which imaginative comparisons are made). Angelou conveys her meaning in a simple manner, stripped of artifice and devoid of the complexities introduced by such figurative devices as similes and metaphors. In many ways, Angelou's candid expression suits the poem's message. The language, like the woman in the poem, derives power from its unadorned simplicity. The speaker does not attribute her appeal with men to her clothes or to any sophisticated airs adopted for the purposes of attracting men. Rather, she describes her appeal as directly related to the simple fact of her being—her hips, her lips, her walk, her smile. In this way, the language of the poem complements and mirrors its subject.

However, Angelou does make use of the figurative device of metaphor when she describes men swarming around the speaker as if she were a beehive. In doing so, Angelou underscores an image of the woman in the poem explored in other stanzas. The speaker is a central figure, a sun around which men orbit. Using the hive/bee imagery, Angelou likens the woman not only to the hive, as she describes herself, but also to what is in the hive—the queen. This further underscores the woman's sense of self-importance and centrality in the poem. Additionally, the comparison to bees reduces men to mindless, swarming insects, motivated by instinct or desire rather than by rational thought. Although Angelou's usage of figurative language is not extensive, the metaphors she employs underscore her characterization of both the female speaker in the poem and the men who surround her.

HISTORICAL CONTEXT

Feminism in the 1970s

Because of the way Angelou explores notions of female empowerment in her poetry and autobiographical works, she is commonly regarded as a feminist writer. In the 1970s, a period of activism known as the "second wave" of feminism was underway, sparked in part by the provocative 1963 work *The Feminine Mystique*, by Betty Friedan. (What later became known as the "first wave" of feminism began in the late nineteenth and early twentieth centuries. This early women's rights movement was focused on securing female suffrage, or women's right to vote.) During the 1970s, the women's movement pursued a political agenda targeted at garnering equal rights for women in the workplace and securing reproductive rights, among other aims.

In examining the history of the women's movement, Barbara Epstein, writing in the *Monthly Review*, argues that the second wave of feminism gradually began to encompass a wide variety of groups, each with their own, targeted agenda. She states, "Unlike first wave feminism, the second wave broadened over time, in its composition and, in important respects, in its perspective." Epstein highlights the groups encompassed by the movement, including lesbian feminists, women of color, and working-class women. She contends that feminists of the second wave ldquo;developed increasing

sensitivity to racial differences, and differences of sexual orientation, within the women's movement."

One of the primary objectives of the women's movement in the 1970s was to get the Equal Rights Amendment passed. The Equal Rights Amendment, or ERA, is a piece of legislation written by women's rights activist Alice Paul in 1923. The legislation was introduced to Congress that year and has been reintroduced into every congressional session since. In 1972, the ERA passed in the Senate and the House of Representatives but was not ratified by the thirty-eight states required for the amendment to become law.

Trends in American Poetry in the 1970s

In the 1970s, particularly toward the end of the decade, American poetry was marked by two distinct trends: formalism and free verse. Formalist poets wrote poetry considered traditional in its adherence to such formal structures as meter (the pattern of stressed and unstressed syllables) and rhyme. Free-verse poets moved away from these structures, seeking freedom of expression in poetry unconstrained by formal concerns. These poets eschewed rhyme and meter and pursued highly subjective and often intensely personal themes.

Although some nineteenth-century poets, such as Walt Whitman, experimented with free verse, as did poets writing in the early decades of the twentieth century, including William Carlos Williams and Ezra Pound, it was the poets associated with the Beat movement of the 1950s, poets such as Allen Ginsberg, Lawrence Ferlinghetti, and Jack Kerouac, who popularized American free-verse poetry. By the 1970s, free-verse poetry had become the dominant mode of American poetry, yet poets Anthony Hecht and Howard Nemerov, among others, continued to adhere to the tenets of formal verse. By the end of the 1970s, formalism began to experience a revival known as "new formalism," which was largely a reaction to the popularity of free verse.

Some popular poets of the 1970s experimented with both free verse and formalism, writing poems that utilized some elements of form—randomly rhymed lines or intermittent meter—but more closely resembled the open nature of free-verse poetry. New formalism later became a firmly established movement in the 1980s. Dana Gioia,

COMPARE
&
CONTRAST

- **1970s:** Feminists are politically active in the women's rights movement and fight for political and economic equality. In 1972, the Equal Rights Amendment (ERA) passes in the Senate and the House of Representatives and is sent to the states for ratification, yet only twenty-two of the required thirty-eight states ratify the amendment. Eight more states ratify in 1973, followed by three more in 1974, one in 1975, none in 1976, and one in 1977. In 1978, women's rights advocates win an extension for ratification of the amendment, until 1982.

  Today: Despite being reintroduced into each congressional session since the ratification extension expired in 1982, the ERA has yet to be ratified by thirty-eight states. In the 2011–2012 congressional session, the ERA is reintroduced, as is a bill that would remove the ratification deadline and would enact the ERA as law upon its ratification by three more states. The states that have not ratified the ERA are Alabama, Arizona, Arkansas, Florida, Georgia, Illinois, Louisiana, Mississippi, Missouri, Nevada, North Carolina, Oklahoma, South Carolina, Utah, and Virginia.

- **1970s:** In American poetry, free verse is a dominant mode of expression. Free-verse poets reject the employment of such structures as rhyme and meter and focus on subjective poetry driven by the poet's response to the world. A reaction against the popularity of free-verse poetry begins to take hold near the end of the decade, as poets later described as "new formalists" begin to once more embrace the structures of rhyme and meter.

  Today: The debate between the perceived value or superiority of either free-verse or formal poetry continues, as evidenced by such essays as James Rother's "The Problems of Prosody," in a 2010 online issue of *Contemporary Poetry Review*. Rother explores the contentiousness between the "Tweeds" (formalists) and the "Sandals" (free-verse poets). The 2007 volume *American Poets in the 21st Century: The New Poetics*, edited by Claudia Rankine and Lisa Sewell, includes a range of representative works, including poetry exemplifying traditional, formalist structures as well as free-verse and experimental poems.

- **1970s:** Conceptions of ideal female body types evolve along with the women's movement, and being thin is equated to being sexually attractive, a notion that developed in the 1960s, in contrast with the more ample female figure lauded as attractive in the 1950s. Some psychiatrists of later decades, including Barbara A. Cohen, will observe that the pursuit of women's rights during the 1960s and 1970s resulted in an ideal body type that was both thin and boyish.

  Today: The notion of an idealized body image is a topic that continues to be debated, as the influence of television, print, and web-based media is pervasive. Health experts insist that children must be taught healthy eating habits and be protected from the vast array of images of sexualized and often extremely thin female bodies.

a poet closely affiliated with the new formalist movement, assessed the history of American verse forms in an essay on new formalism published in *Conversant Essays: Contemporary Poets on Poetry*. In this 1990 essay, Gioia offers a harsh critique of the state of American poetry since 1960, observing that American poets not only have ignored rhyme and meter but have failed to offer innovation in the realms of both metered poetry and free-verse poetry.

In stanza 2, phenomenal means surrounded by men bidding to be by her side. (© darios | Shutterstock.com)

CRITICAL OVERVIEW

Angelou's poetry generally receives less enthusiastic praise than her autobiographical writing. Lyman B. Hagen, in *Heart of a Woman, Mind of a Writer, and Soul of a Poet: A Critical Analysis of the Writings of Maya Angelou*, asserts, "There has been little critical attention given to Angelou's poetry beyond the usual book reviews." After summarizing a series of reviews ranging from negative to lukewarm in their responses to Angelou's poetry, Hagen goes on to state, "Although few critics have found great merit in her poetry, Angelou has acquired a dedicated audience."

Some critics focus on "Phenomenal Woman" specifically. In an essay on Angelou for *Contemporary American Poets: An A-to-Z Guide*, Sandra L. West observes that to Angelou, the "inner strength, self-worth, and acknowledged sexuality of a black sisterhood are extremely important." West cites "Phenomenal Woman" as an example of the significance of these themes in Angelou's work, stating that the narrator of the poem serves as a symbol for "all black women" and that she

"feels gorgeous and blessed with her natural attributes." West goes on to state that this speaker "evokes the chorus of black sisters recognizing a collective as well as a personal phenomenal womanhood." According to West, the poem's popularity is such that it may be regarded as "a national and international poetic anthem for self-actualization, positive self-image, and liberated, courageous womanhood." In summarizing Angelou's reception among critics, West describes the way Angelou, while "appreciated as a 'people's poet' for her clear, plain delivery of everyday issues," is nevertheless "often maligned for this very simplicity and for depicting an unexamined individual experience in her poetry."

Taking another approach to the poem, Andrea Elizabeth Shaw, in *The Embodiment of Disobedience: Fat Black Women's Unruly Political Bodies*, states that in the poem, Angelou addresses the "construction of fatness as repulsive and deserving only of erasure." Shaw notes that in "Phenomenal Woman," Angelou contrasts "fatness and exceptionality" and that in doing so, she "infuses that body's uniqueness with sensuality and the suggestion of expansive strength."

CRITICISM

Catherine Dominic

Dominic is a novelist and a freelance writer and editor. In the following essay, she challenges feminist readings of the poem "Phenomenal Woman" and maintains that the work presents a one-dimensional, sexually objectified speaker who insists upon her superiority to other women.

Maya Angelou has been praised for endorsing a positive female self-image and for engendering a sense of sisterhood among African American women in the poem "Phenomenal Woman." Andrea Elizabeth Shaw, for example, discusses the poem's focus on self-image in *The Embodiment of Disobedience: Fat Black Women's Unruly Political Bodies,* describing the way Angelou's "full-figured narrator...proceeds with a glorified liturgy of her physical attributes that mark her as an exceptional and intriguing woman despite her otherness." Commenting on Angelou's exploration of the notion of African American sisterhood in the poem, Sandra L. West, in *Contemporary American Women Poets: An A-to-Z Guide,* contends, "The speaker of 'Phenomenal Woman' evokes the chorus of black sisters recognizing a collective as well as personal phenomenal womanhood."

The poem is also commonly regarded as a feminist one, and Angelou is often considered as a feminist poet. For example, Cheryl Higashida, in exploring concepts of feminism in her work *Black Internationalist Feminism,* notes that "Angelou is best known through these lenses of liberal feminism and multicultural Americanism." Similarly, Zainab Haruna states in the *Encyclopedia of Feminist Theories* that "the assertive black woman's voice" in Angelou's "Phenomenal Woman" is one characterized by "self-acceptance and triumph over racism and sexism."

In spite of the fact that "Phenomenal Woman" is regarded as feminist in its perspective and is seen as upholding a sense of (black) sisterhood, a close study of the poem reveals that in many ways, it resists such readings. The poem focuses almost exclusively on physicality and sexuality as the sources of the speaker's beauty, and the speaker takes pains to separate herself from other women. She steadfastly stands as an exclusive and oppositional force within the poem.

WHAT DO I READ NEXT?

- Angelou's *I Know Why the Caged Bird Sings* is perhaps her best-known work. The autobiography focuses on Angelou's childhood and young adulthood. Originally published in 1970, it is the first in a series of six autobiographical books by the author. The work was reissued in 2009.

- *Letters to My Daughter,* published by Angelou in 2008, is a series of essays dedicated to the daughter she never had. The essays are emotional explorations of the lessons Angelou has learned throughout the course of her life.

- Like Angelou, Toni Morrison is a prominent African American writer whose career was launched in 1970. Morrison's novel *The Bluest Eye* focuses on a young African American girl growing up in the Midwest and addresses the issues of body image and perception of beauty.

- *Anxiety of Words: Contemporary Poetry by Korean Women,* translated by Don Mee Choi, is a 2006 collection of poetry by female Korean poets. The book includes the poetry of Ch'oe Sung-ja, who in 1979 became the first female Korean poet to publish her work in a literary journal, as well as Korean feminist Yi Yon-ju.

- African American author Rosa Guy published her young-adult novel *Ruby* in 1976. The work, reissued in 2005, explores issues of feminine and sexual identity along with gender roles.

- Catherine Gourley's *Ms. and the Material Girls: Perceptions of Women from the 1970s through the 1990s; Images and Issues of Women in the Twentieth Century,* published in 2007, is a survey of three decades of feminist history. Aimed at a young-adult audience, the work details the major features of the women's rights movement and the culture that surrounded the movement.

From the moment "Phenomenal Woman" opens, the speaker sets herself apart from other women, from those she regards as beautiful in conventional ways. She distinguishes herself in the first few lines by asserting that she is not cute, nor is she the size of a model. These *other* women, the conventionally pretty, fashion-model-sized women, are marked as different from the speaker and seem to understand that she possesses a secret to attracting men, a secret they themselves do not possess. The speaker is certain that the other women therefore wonder about her secret. Furthermore, when the speaker attempts to explain this mystery, the other women believe, according to the speaker, that she is lying to them.

In the first stanza, then, the speaker, having characterized herself as distinct from other women, finds herself able to attract men despite the fact that she lacks the conventional beauty of other women. Her relationship to other women is colored in negative, belittling tones, as evidenced by the speaker's suspicion that the other women believe she is lying to them. In short, the speaker depicts the other women as jealous of her. The speaker goes on to describe her wide hips, the way she walks, and the way her lips curl when she smiles. Her repeated emphasis on her physical presence highlights her body's power to seduce, in a way the conventionally pretty and model-sized (that is, thin) women cannot.

As the poem progresses, the woman exudes a sense of confidence as she relates how, upon walking into a room, men rise from their seats or fall down upon their knees in her presence. With these words, she suggests that men's responses to her physical presence range from respect to worship. Angelou then compares men to bees hovering around the speaker, who represents the hive, or what is in the hive—the queen. Men here are shown to be inferior to the speaker. They are presented as mindless drones, drunk with desire inspired by the speaker's eyes, teeth, and undulating body. Again, the speaker's tone is oppositional, confrontational. This time she sets herself apart from men, regarding herself with the same sense of superiority she demonstrated toward other women—the jealous, pretty, thin women—of the first stanza.

This emphasis on the speaker's distance from men is explored further in the third stanza. The speaker notes that men seem confused by her and by their response to her, as they wonder why they are so attracted to her. Despite their desire for her, the men are unable, the speaker states, to touch that part of herself that she describes as internal and mysterious. This is one of the few places in the poem where the speaker alludes to something about herself that contributes to her ability to attract men but that is distinguished from her outward physical attributes. However, through the speaker, Angelou quickly retreats from this particular personality trait that gives the woman in the poem some dimension. The speaker asserts that when she attempts to reveal some of this mysterious part of her hidden self to men, they fail to see.

The speaker then attempts to draw a connection between this private mystery and her physical being, stating that when the men say they cannot see what is hidden, she tells them that this mysterious "it" can be seen in the curve of her back, in her smile, and in her swaying breasts. In establishing this connection, the speaker dilutes her sense of self, reducing her complete identity to something fractured and entirely physical. When the speaker first mentions this inner and mysterious part of herself, it seems as though she has an opportunity to reveal a deep, meaningful truth about herself, something, perhaps, about her emotions, or her intellect, or her spirituality. Instead, the possibility that this mystery is related to the woman's mind or heart is forcefully and immediately dismissed; the quality in question is instead related to her physical qualities. The mystery of this inner quality, like everything else the speaker has drawn attention to, is connected by the speaker to her body and the way her body moves or performs such actions as walking, smiling, and swaying.

In the poem's final stanza, the speaker asserts that all the physical qualities she has itemized contribute to a sense of pride that she has in herself and that she insists others should have in her as well. Again, she returns to listing her physical traits, asserting that passersby should observe and acknowledge such things as her heels clicking as she walks, the way her hair curls. She then references the palm of her hand and the need others have of her attention. Just as she has stated that the people around her should be proud of her, she similarly asserts that others undoubtedly need her. Her sense of confidence is rooted in others' appreciation of her physical appearance and the need that they have for her attention.

The speaker's emphasis on her physical being, on the sexuality she highlights throughout the poem, seems to run counter to the feminism with which Angelou has been associated. The speaker is sexually confident; she "owns" her sexuality by embracing everything about herself that draws men to her. However, in describing herself almost exclusively in this manner, the woman limits how she is perceived by others. In a very concrete way, she objectifies herself, that is, presents herself to the world as *object* to be sexually desired, rather than as a person to be appreciated for the entirety of her identity. In every stanza of the poem, she deconstructs herself by presenting herself essentially as a list of body parts. The speaker reduces herself to reaching arms, wide hips, curling lips, sparkling eyes, a swinging waist, joyful feet, an arching back, a sunny smile, swaying breasts, clicking heels, curly hair, and the palm of her hand.

The image the speaker portrays of herself is an intensely fragmented one. She is transformed into a series of parts, many of which are described in a way that is highly sensual. Given that the feminist movement of the 1970s was focused on achieving equal rights for women, it seems as though a poem regarded as a feminist one would take more care to present the notion of womanhood as something not entirely sexualized but rather as a unified whole. Angelou reduces the speaker in the poem to one category, one function. The poem's speaker is a physical, sexualized object rather than a multifaceted woman whose intellect, capacity to feel a range of emotions, and spiritual nature all contribute to her sense of identity.

Furthermore, in the way the speaker takes pains to emphasize how different she is from other women and in the way she overstates how much more she appeals to men than do other women, it does not seem that the speaker exemplifies notions of sisterhood. She seems arrogant and disdainful of other women, or at least of the conventionally pretty, thin women. By focusing on physical appearance and sexuality, the speaker objectifies herself and distances herself from other women. The speaker fails to explore the common ground upon which she stands with other women; instead, she distinguishes herself as superior in her ability to attract men. The speaker further characterizes men as mindless creatures, drawn to her because of the physical qualities she has outlined, but unable to comprehend her interior world, perhaps because she keeps it hidden from them.

Repeatedly, the speaker emphasizes and lauds her own uniqueness and in doing so exudes a sense of confidence, which arguably could inspire readers to explore their own unique, desirable qualities. Yet at the same time, the speaker's sense of superiority to other women, and to men, highlighted at several points in the poem, combined with the purely physical and sexual manner in which she describes herself, may be regarded as off-putting to readers seeking a deeper exploration of personal identity and sense of connection to other women or to men.

Source: Catherine Dominic, Critical Essay on "Phenomenal Woman," in *Poetry for Students*, Gale, Cengage Learning, 2013.

Lyman B. Hagen

In the following excerpt, Hagen presents an anatomy of the subject matter of some of Angelou's poetry.

... The titles of Angelou's first four books of poems are attention getters. They are catchy black vernacular expressions. Her first volume, *Just Give Me A Cool Drink of Water* (1971), refers to Angelou's belief that "we as individuals... are still so innocent that we think if we asked our murderer just before he puts the final wrench upon the throat, 'Would you please give me a cool drink of water?' and he would do so. That's innocence. It's lovely."

Angelou covers a wide range of subject matter. In Angelou's writings, poetry or prose, she holds to tradition and makes a special effort to

In stanza 3, phenomenal means mysterious.
(© Innervision Art / Shutterstock.com)

dispel false impressions about African Americans, but does not use this as her sole motivation.

Angelou's poetry belongs in the category of "light" verse. Her poems are entertainments derived from personal experiences and fall into one of two broad subject areas. First, she writes about everyday considerations—the telephone, aging, insomnia—topics that are totally neutral. Second, she writes with deep feeling about a variety of racial themes and concerns.

"The Telephone," for example, exemplifies her universally identifiable reflections on an ordinary subject. She admits in verse that she is dependent on it. Its importance to her daily life is notable by a contrast to its periods of silence.

But she can't stand the quietude long, nor the isolation implied, and so she impatiently demands that the phone ring. This demand follows three structured stanzas: the first physically describes the telephone; the second, its active effect on people's lives; and the third, the effect

of its silence. In the second stanza, she emphasizes the familiar and the feminine by employing a metaphor of sewing, tatting, crocheting, hemming, and darning. The intrinsic themes of black and blue and week-end loneliness are often found in popular blues songs.

Another light general rumination is "On Reaching Forty." In somewhat stuffy language Angelou regrets the passage of time and expresses tongue-in-cheek admiration for those departing this world early and by this bestows upon the poem an unexpected conclusion. She is saddened by the passing of youthful milestones. The years forward will weigh even more heavily.

Inasmuch as Angelou is an accomplished cook, it is not surprising to find that she addresses the appreciation of traditional foods. In "The Health-Food Diner" exotic, faddish health food items are rejected in favor of standard fare such as red meat. In alternating tetrameter and trimeter quatrains, Angelou concludes each stanza with a food preference. Her reader finds life must be sustained by solid values, not notional influences.

Angelou not only has a keen ear for dialogue and dialect but she also evidences a keen psychological understanding of an adolescent girl's romantic concerns and possessiveness. The speaker in "No Loser, No Weeper" expresses in the vernacular a universal sentiment. Again Angelou carefully structures her poem. In each stanza, the speaker notes her reaction to losing something, beginning with childish items and advancing to that of major worth: in the first stanza, a dime; then a doll; then a watch; but especially in the last stanza when she truly hates to lose her boy friend.

The same subject matter—the loss of a boy friend—is expressed in "Poor Girl." The speaker is a teenager who addresses a fickle fellow playing the field. She's afraid there will be another disappointed girl in a long line of disappointed girls, just like her. One girl, she says, will believe the lies but can't be forewarned because of a possible misunderstanding. Eventually the truth will be realized and awareness will set in.

Angelou is a realist. She knows that a married man who sees other women usually returns home to his wife in spite of the attraction and charm of the Other Woman. The speaker in "They Went Home" is aware that she plays a loser's role. While the sentiment is psychologically sound, the lines are prosaic, reflecting the pitiful state of the abandoned.

Sometimes Angelou uses contrasting pairs in her poetry. For example, in "Phenomenal Woman," considered a personal theme-poem, she asserts the special qualities of a particular woman. The woman described is easily matched to the author herself. Angelou is an imposing woman—at least six feet tall. She has a strong personality and a compelling presence as defined in the poem. One can accept the autobiographical details in this poem or extend the reading to infer that all women have qualities that attract attention. Angelou's dramatic presentation of this poem always pleases her audience and is frequently the highlight of her programs.

Angelou pairs this poem with "Men." The speaker is a woman whose experience has taught her the games men play. In this she uses a raw egg metaphor to contrast fragile femininity with dominant masculinity, but the female speaker has perhaps learned to be cautious.

Other contrasting poetic pairs are "America" and "Africa"; "Communication I" and "Communication II"; and "The Thirteens (Black and White)."

In *Gather Together in My Name*, Angelou describes being shown a room full of dope addicts and the impact this picture had on her. In both "A Letter to An Aspiring Junkie" and in "Junkie Monkey Reel" she details the dangerous consequences of using drugs. In both poems the slave master of today is drugs, and the junkie is tied to the habit as if he were the monkey attached to the street vendor's strap. Both poems contain particularly disturbing images.

Angelou uses every opportunity to build African-American pride and in "Ain't That Bad?" she praises black culture, mores, customs, and leaders. Its short lines, its repetition of imperatives, and its repetition of the title help constitute a chant, which categorizes it as a "shouting poem."

In black West African English (Sierra Leone) *i gud baad* means "it's very good." Thus "bad" as used extensively in this poem carries a favorable connotation, meaning to be "very good, extremely good." This meaning has been incorporated into everyday black vernacular and therefore is commonly understood. The last word in the last line of the poem sustains the positive connotations and provides a closure.

As detailed in an earlier chapter, a number of children's activities and responses have been handed down through the years in all cultures and are considered folk materials and light entertainments. This wealth of rhyming folklore, so important in Angelou's childhood, provides an indigenous and unconscious source of much of the style and the flow of both her poetry and prose. It dictates the structure of much of her poetry.

Angelou's second group of meditations is concerned with racial subjects and themes. This group allies poetry with morality by continuing the themes of protest and survival found in her autobiographies. These poems are not excessively polemical; they voice only mild protest.

In this category is Angelou's favorite poem and theme, "Still I Rise," the same title as that of a play she wrote in 1976. The title, Angelou says, refers "to the indominable spirit of the black people." She often quotes this poem in interviews and includes it in public readings. The poem follows Angelou's customary fashion of incremental repetition, and catalogues injustices.

In spite of adversity, dire conditions and circumstances; in spite of racial epithets, scorn, and hostility, Angelou expresses unshakable faith that one will overcome; one will triumph; one will Rise! The lines remind us of the black spiritual "Rise and Shine" as well as other religious hymns that express hope: "Oh, rise and shine, and give God the glory, glory! / Rise and shine, and give God the glory, glory!" In "Our Grandmothers" Angelou voices a similar sentiment contained in another dearly loved spiritual: "Like a tree, down by the riverside, I shall not be moved."

The "I" in "Still I Rise" is designated female by Angelou herself as she numbers this poem as one of the four about women in *Phenomenal Woman*. She speaks not only for herself but also for her gender and race. This extension of self occurs in Angelou's autobiographies and protest poetry. It is in keeping with a traditional practice of black writers to personalize their common racial experiences. Moreover, Angelou implies that the black race will not just endure, but that in the words of Sondra O'Neale, "will triumph with a will of collective consciousness that Western experience cannot extinguish." Angelou's most militant poems are contained in the second section of her first volume of poetry, "Just Before the World Ends." They have "more bite—the anguished and often sardonic expression of a black in a white dominated world," Chad Walsh observes. In her moving address "To a Freedom Fighter," Angelou again as a spokesperson for all blacks acknowledges a debt owed to those who fought earlier civil rights battles. They did more than survive; they endured all indignities for the maintenance of their race.

In "Elegy," the speakers are early black activists, Harriet Tubman and Frederick Douglass, who proudly observe successors to their cause, the torch bearers they spawned.

In their battles for status, African Americans have experienced disappointment with political and social liberals. In her early twenties, Angelou wrote "On Working White Liberals," which expressed the prevailing cynical view of their broken promises. Liberal words have often been empty words, and so the black came to doubt their sincerity. The poem challenges white liberals to an extreme action to prove their racial tolerance. Words are not enough. Angelou has since disavowed the poem's sentiments; she says she was a young "hot-head" at the time she wrote it.

Angelou comes to the defense of Uncle Toms, people censured by black activists because they do not overtly resist unfair treatment. In "When I Think About Myself," Angelou explains why a black woman responds with a simple "Yes, ma'am" for the sake of a job, even to a young white who insults her with the offensive word "girl." The servant does not pity herself and knows she is keeping her race alive. By being servile for an entire lifetime, she has provided sustenance for another generation who may find better conditions. Whenever appropriate, Angelou voices approval of those who endured indignities to feed, shelter, clothe, and educate the family.

Angelou also praises the black slaves who helped build America. In "To a Husband," she reminds readers of this, and that the black man proudly reflects his African roots, while contributing to the physical growth of this country.

Angelou also idealizes black men and enhances their pride in her love poems. Two poems in particular in the first section of *Just Give Me* present admirable images of black men—their color: Black Golden Amber; and their behavior—gentle and grave. In "A Zorro Man" love is found to be exciting; the speaker is delighted that her man is courageous and thrilled with her. "To a Man" admires a man's special qualities: he is Southern, gentle, and always changing. That Angelou dedicated her first book of poems to Amber Sam and the Zorro Man is not at all surprising....

Source: Lyman B. Hagen, "Poetry: Something about Everything," in *Heart of a Woman, Mind of a Writer, and Soul of a Poet: A Critical Analysis of the Writings of Maya Angelou*, University Press of America, 1997, pp. 118–36.

James Robert Saunders

In the following excerpt, Saunders contends that circumstances and Angelou's self-confidence shine through in her poetry.

In his seminal work, *Black Autobiography in America* (1974), Stephen Butterfield establishes the existence of a black autobiographical tradition that has its roots in the American slave narrative, a genre "so powerful, so convincing a testimony of human resource, intelligence, endurance, and love in the face of tyranny, that, in a sense, it sets the tone for most subsequent black American writing." Acknowledging the slave narrative form as an essential base, Butterfield goes on to specify certain characteristics as being consistent across the spectrum of slave narratives and on into the twentieth century, influencing such relatively modern works as Booker T. Washington's *Up From Slavery* (1901) and Richard Wright's *Black Boy* (1945). There is, in all of these works, the initial instance of resistance, a denial of the then existing caste system. Of equal importance is the struggle for education, often in the midst of difficult circumstances. That education is sometimes formal as in the case of Booker T. Washington who attended Hampton Institute. At other times, it

"

THE THERAPY IS SO EFFECTIVE THAT IT MUST HAVE CARRIED OVER INTO THE WRITER'S OWN POETIC CAREER, IN THE PRODUCTION OF SUCH 'ORAL' POEMS AS 'STILL I RISE' AND 'PHENOMENAL WOMAN.'"

is informal as with Frederick Douglass who, in his *Narrative of the Life of Frederick Douglass* (1845), recounts having been secretly tutored by his slavemaster's wife.

It is, furthermore, Butterfield's contention that a physical movement between geographical regions has been part of that literary tradition, a given in slave narratives where virtually all of the authors first had to escape southern slavery and then make their way north before being in a position to record the events of their lives. Such geographical movement has been particularly important in the life and autobiographies of the artist Maya Angelou, described by Butterfield as one who "does not submit tamely to the cage. She is repeatedly thrust into situations where she must act on her own initiative to save herself and thereby learns the strength of self-confidence." Butterfield here makes specific reference to Angelou's first autobiographical installment, *I Know Why the Caged Bird Sings* (1970); however, it actually will be several autobiographical volumes later before the confidence Butterfield refers to evolves into its fullest dimensions.

So much of Angelou's first volume shows her to be the tossed-about victim of circumstance. She was born Marguerite Johnson in 1928, in St. Louis, Missouri. However, at the age of three, she finds herself being shuttled, along with her older brother Bailey, to Stamps, Arkansas, where her paternal grandmother takes up the task of raising her through her formative years. As though it is not enough that she is the offspring of a shattered marriage, she has to live those early years under the tenets of segregation. In *Caged Bird*, the author comments "Stamps, Arkansas, was Chitlin' Switch, Georgia; Hang 'Em High, Alabama; Don't Let the Sun Set on You Here, Nigger, Mississippi; or any other name just as descriptive." The future

writer resides in a place where, as critic Myra McMurry has noted, "the caged condition affects almost everyone in her world."

This first autobiography provides detailed testimony to the daily insults visited upon members of Angelou's extended family as well as neighboring blacks who work hard picking cotton, never to get ahead or even see beyond their debilitating financial situations. While her grandmother is indeed the proud owner of a local general store, even that matriarch suffers insults delivered by young, poor white girls who insist on addressing her by her first name, Annie. That grandmother is further outraged when a dentist, to whom she had lent money when he was in danger of losing his practice, now refuses to examine her granddaughter and adamantly proclaims, "I'd rather stick my hand in a dog's mouth than in a nigger's."

After Marguerite and Bailey have lived in Stamps several years, their father appears one day, giving them the impression that he will take them back with him to California. In actuality, he is merely picking them up for deposit with their mother, Vivian Baxter, who was, at the time, still residing in St. Louis. Whether Angelou was seven years old, as she has maintained in some interviews, or eight, as she provides in the autobiography, she is raped (by her mother's boyfriend) and, as a consequence, lapses into a prolonged silence.

Vivian Baxter had never been very good at parental nurturing, so it is accordingly deemed best that the victimized daughter be returned to the grandmother, who is sensitive enough not to force her grandchild to talk. The silence continues for several years until a teacher, Mrs. Flowers, introduces the young girl to an assortment of literary classics, including the works of Charles Dickens. This educational encounter proves to be a vital turning point, reminding us of an important aspect of American slave narratives. In *Caged Bird*, Angelou explains the sensation of listening to Mrs. Flowers as she read from *A Tale of Two Cities* (1859): "I heard poetry for the first time in my life. . . . Her voice slid in and curved down through and over the words. She was nearly singing." It is Mrs. Flowers who is finally able to get Marguerite to talk, having her read from works that in themselves are demanding recitation. The therapy is so effective that it must have carried over into the writer's own poetic career, in the production of such "oral" poems as "Still I Rise" and "Phenomenal Woman." Lines from the former poem include:

> You may trod me in the very dirt
> But still, like dust, I'll rise....
>
> Did you want to see me broken?
> Bowed head and lowered eyes?
> Shoulders falling down like teardrops,
> Weakened by my soulful cries.
>
> Does my haughtiness offend you?
> Don't you take it awful hard
> 'Cause I laugh like I've got gold mines
> Diggin' in my own back yard.

The following lines make up the other poem's conclusion:

> Now you understand
> Just why my head's not bowed.
> I don't shout or jump about
> Or have to talk real loud.
> When you see me passing
> It ought to make you proud....
> 'Cause I'm a woman
> Phenomenally.
> Phenomenal woman,
> That's me.

Both of those samples are taken from Angelou's third book of poems, *And Still I Rise* (1978), which in general conveys a sense of extreme self-assurance.

However, that is not the condition in which we find Marguerite at the conclusion of *Caged Bird*. Quite the contrary; at the end of this volume, she is sixteen years old and mired in the difficulties of a teenage pregnancy. Having journeyed to California to be finally with her mother, Marguerite had had insecurities about approaching womanhood, thinking it necessary to hurry and get a boyfriend. "A boyfriend," she envisions, "would clarify my position to the world and, even more important, to myself." But a problem is presented: "Understandably the boys of my age and social group were captivated by the yellow- or light-brown-skinned girls, with hairy legs and smooth little lips, and whose hair 'hung down like horses' manes.'" Unfortunately, Marguerite is dark-skinned and six feet tall in a world where the standard of beauty is strict.

So Marguerite must settle for whatever she can get: for instance a one-night stand that, as she puts it, "I not only didn't enjoy..., but my normalcy was still a question." The movement of the young artist in pursuit of adulthood has become a quite prickly affair with limitations seeming to outweigh the possibilities. It was

only fitting that the author should employ a Paul Laurence Dunbar poem as the source for her first volume's title:

> Sympathy
>
> I know what the caged bird feels, alas!
> When the sun is bright on the upland slopes;
> When the wind stirs soft through the springing
>   grass,
> And the river flows like a stream of glass;
> When the first bird sings and the first bud opens,
> And the faint perfume from its chalice steals—
> I know what the caged bird feels!
>
> I know why the caged bird beats his wing
> Till its blood is red on the cruel bars;
> For he must fly back to his perch and cling
> When he fain would be on the bough a-swing;
> And a pain still throbs in the old, old scars
> And they pulse again with a keener sting—
> I know why he beats his wing!
>
> I know why the caged bird sings, ah me,
> When his wing is bruised and his bosom sore,—
> When he beats his bars and he would be free;
> It is not a carol of joy or glee,
> But a prayer that he sends from his heart's deep core,
> But a plea, that upward to Heaven he flings—
> I know why the caged bird sings!

Dunbar's caged bird is a brilliantly wrought metaphor, representing human beings locked away from life's wonders....

Source: James Robert Saunders, "Breaking Out of the Cage: The Autobiographical Writings of Maya Angelou," in *Hollins Critic*, Vol. 28, No. 4, October 1991, pp. 1–11.

Priscilla R. Ramsey

In the following essay, Ramsey argues that Angelou's political and love poetry both acknowledge and transcend despair and unhappiness.

Maya Angelou's physical shifts from Stamps, Arkansas' Lafayette County Public School to the Village Gate's stage in Manhattan and from New York to a teaching podium at Cairo University in Egypt represent an intellectual and psychological voyage of considerable complexity—one of unpredictably erratic cyclic movement. She has chronicled some of this voyage in her three autobiographies.... Additionally she has written three collections of poetry: *Oh Pray My Wings are Gonna Fit Me Well* (1975), *And Still I Rise* (1971), and *Just Give Me a Cool Drink of Water 'fore I Diiie* (1971)....

The public achievements have been many and yet the private motivation out of which her writing generates extends beyond the mere search for words as metaphors for purely private

HER LOVE POETRY...SUGGESTS HER
RELATIONSHIP TO A WORLD WHICH CAN BE
STULTIFYING, MYSTIFYING AND OPPRESSIVE, BUT
ONE SHE WILL NOT ALLOW TO BECOME THESE
THINGS AND OVERWHELM HER."

experience. Her poetry becomes both political and confessional. Significantly, one sees in her autobiographies a role-modeling process—one paradigmatic for other women—while not allowing the didactic to become paramount in either the poetry or the autobiographies.

Her autobiographies and poetry reveal a vital need to transform the elements of a stultifying and destructive personal, social, political and historical milieu into a sensual and physical refuge. Loneliness and human distantiation pervade both her love and political poetry, but are counterposed by a glorification of life and sensuality which produces a transcendence over all which could otherwise destroy and create her despair.

This world of sensuality becomes a fortress against potentially alienating forces, i.e., men, war, oppression of any kind, in the real world. This essay examines the outlines of this transcendence in selected examples from her love and political poetry . . . .

Drawing upon her scholarly and gifted understanding of poetic technique and rhetorical structure in modern Black poetry, Ruth Sheffey explains:

> Genuine rhetoric, indeed all verbal art, coexists with reason, truth, justice. All of the traditions of rational and moral speech are allied to the primitive idea of goodness, to the force of utterance. Because the past is functional in our lives when we neither forget it nor try to return to it, the new Black voices must reach the masses in increasingly communal ways, must penetrate those hidden crevices of our beings only recognizable and reachable by poetry.

Professor Sheffey speaks here to the fundamental meaning and significance Black poetry holds for its private community. Sheffey's remarks could not more appropriately describe

Maya Angelou's poetic voice in terms of motive, content and audience. By way of example consider:

> No No No No
>
> No the two legg'd beasts that walk like men play stink finger in their crusty asses while crackling babies in napalm coats stretch mouths to receive burning tears on splitting tongues
> JUST GIVE ME A COOL DRINK OF WATER 'FORE I DIE . . .

Her metynomic [*sic*] body imagery functions as poetic referent further chronicling and transporting her prophetic message: stop the assault on Black people and recognize their humanness. As prophecy, her succinct assertions for change beginning with napalmed babies, epitomized in hopeful dreams as the poem progresses—disintegrate ironically into the decayed emptiness of an old man's "gaping mouth.". . .

The audience, a Black one, cannot help but understand the universal message this poem imports. It is a collectively oriented statement (the persona's "I" operating synedochically for the group), and one of hope, although a hope which ironically collapses at poem's end.

A similar transcendence becomes the ironically complicated prophetic message in ["The Calling of Names"]:

> He went to being called a Colored man after answering to "hey nigger,"
> Now that's a big jump, anyway you rigger [*sic*],
> Hey, Baby, Watch my smoke.
> From colored man to Negro.
>
> With the "N" in caps was like saying Japanese instead of saying Japs.
>
> I mean, during the war.
> The next big step was change for true
> From Negro in caps to being a Jew.
>
> Now, Sing Yiddish Mama.
>
> Light, Yello, Brown and Dark brown skin, were o.k. colors to describe him then,
>
> He was a bouquet of Roses.
>
> He changed his seasons like an almanac,
> Now you'll get hurt if you don't call him "Black"
>
> Nigguh, I ain't playin' this time.

As significant referents, words are used to recreate a personal reality, but as verbal discourse they remain very close to the writer's understanding of truth. Maya Angelou brings to the audience her own perceptions of historical change and their relationship to a new reality. With the exception of a long ago Phyllis [*sic*] Wheatley, whose poems speak almost exclusively of God, nature and man, few Black artists have focused their poetic gifts outside history, politics and their changing effects upon Black life. Here Maya Angelou engages in this lifelong tradition of speaking to the concerns of a historical and political Black presence in World War II; Voter and Civil Rights legislation of the fifties; finally the Black Power Movement of the sixties—these events name only a few of the historical and political meanings the synedochic [*sic*] imagery of naming has signalled for Blacks in America.

From the ancient African rituals which gave a child a name harmonious with his or her chi to the derogatory epithets coming out of slavery's master-servant relationships—naming has always held a reality redefining importance for black people. It has reached the level contemporarily with the recreation of one's destiny, an incantation signalling control over one's life. Hence the proliferation of African names with significant meanings.

But as the incantation and the structure of the poem's ideas have evolved out of historical and political event, one hears the old degrading epithets merging into new and more positive meanings.

Her title with its article "the" and preposition "of" signal, perhaps, the only formalizing or distancing aesthetic techniques in the poem. Her emphasis is primarily upon the concrete, the substantive movement back to a derogatory black history and a clearly assertive statement about a more positive future. Like many of the poems in this collection this one also works toward the notion of a positive identity, a positive assertion of what and who Black people have decided they will be. Her formal rhyme scheme here is one in which the initial stanzas rhyme the second and fourth lines, a rhyming pattern more constricted than in much of her other political poetry. Less metaphorical transformation and less abstraction appear in this poem, however, and while that makes it aesthetically less pleasing, its meaning speaks more directly to the concrete issues of evolving importance to Afro-American history and politics. The abstractions of metaphor perhaps then do not apply here . . . .

While Maya Angelou's political poetry suggests the irony of emotional distantiation by using bodily imagery as her objective correlative, her love poetry almost equally as often employs this series of patterns to capture an image, an instant, an emotional attitude. Moreover, fantasy often rounds out the missing parts of the human whole when reality fails to explain fully what she sees. Here in the following poem, "To a Man" she explores this mystery, this distantiation from the understanding of a man:

> My man is Black Golden Amber Changing.
> Warm mouths of Brandy Fine
> Cautious sunlight on a patterned rug
> Coughing laughter, rocked on a whirl of French
> tobacco
> Graceful turns on woolen stilts Secretive?
> A cat's eye.
> Southern, Plump and tender with navy bean
> sullenness
> And did I say "Tender?"
> The gentleness
> A big cat stalks through stubborn bush
> And did I mention "Amber"?
> The heatless fire consuming itself.
> Again. Anew. Into ever neverlessness.
> My man is Amber
> Changing
> Always into itself
> New. Now New
> Still itself.
> Still

If indeed this poem talks about a man and not some more hidden and abstract object we cannot define, then "To a Man" explores the mysteries of a baffling and emotionally distant human being through a persona's fantasy, her worshipping recreation of an artifice rather than of any more luminous understanding of his many selves. And while she does not name him in the poem and he could be reminiscent of any of the men she knew, her description of him evokes a picture of Make, a South African freedom fighter and the man who became her second husband. She recounts this marriage and its end in her final autobiography, *The Heart of a Woman.* Whether a husband or not, his mystery constitutes her poem's ostensible statement, through her persona's particular visual gestalt, i.e., approach. The persona's failure to (penetrate) her subject's overpreoccupation with his own personal style as a wall against intimacy becomes a source of the poem's interesting aesthetic and emotional tension. Her subject cannot be captured, i.e., "understood" and he is cut off from the persona's concentrated engagement by this barrier that she creates—his personal style. The word choices she selects to describe or rather, guess at what she comprehends about him are words suggesting the altering and varying nature of his physical and psychic characteristics.

She looks at him seeing only the qualities of an ambiance he creates around himself through the deliberateness of his studied poses. He moves "Cat like." She images his moving dynamism concretely in, "woolen stilts" which both regalize and thrust him backward spatially and temporally to a time when he could have been a royal African chieftain dancing on tall stilts.

She magnificently combines the auditory, tactile and visual into the imagery of his " . . . coughing laughter rocked on a whirl of French tobacco" graphically capturing what we take to be—given all she has said before—still, his moving and elegant dynamism. His sight, sound, smell—even his smoke concretized in French rather than in some ordinary domestic . . . .

Like a musical recitative, she repeats in . . . " To a Man," descriptions framed in rhetorical questions drawing attention all the more to his stolid mystery. In using the repeated rhetorical questions, she counterposes her technique against the traditional way in which modern Black poets use repetition. Modern Black poets use repetitious phrasing for emphasis, clarity and to signal an end to complexity. In Angelou's work the rhetorical questions, increase tension and complexity and build upon his opaque mystery. Why?

Some of the explanation might lie in the fact that writers often repeat the issues and conflicts of their own lives throughout much of the art until either concrete conditions or the art brings insight and resolution. Witness Richard Wright's unending preoccupation with the Communist Party's orthodoxy and demanding control over his work, or Gwendolyn Brooks' mid-career, philosophical redirection after attending the Fisk University Black Writer's Conference. The seeds for a similar obsession lie in her autobiographies and project into Angelou's poetry. She berates herself for her overly romantic ability to place men on pedestals, to create a rose-colored fantasy around them at a distance only to later discover her cognitive error. Her relationships with men in *Caged Bird* and *Gather Together* have this fantasy quality where she overelaborates their personalities in her own mind confusing their concrete behaviors and her day-dream. She does this, sometimes out of her own unconscious desire for their unconditional love— wanting almost a symbiotic object-subject

attachment to them. In the final analysis, each of these men exploits her because all are morally and characterologically flawed in ways her own emotional neediness causes her to miss as her fantasy life recreates their personalities. One lover, temporarily stationed close to her home in San Diego, uses her companionship while his naval assignment lasts then leaves her. He returns to his wife. A fast living "sugar daddy" cons her into prostitution to "help" him with a non-existent gambling debt. Again concrete conditions force her into looking beneath the surface he presents. She finds that her "giving" provided pretty dresses for his wife. Nothing more! Finally, when at last she marries, and her fantasies tell her she has found nirvana in the white picket fenced-cottage she has dreamed of she learns its hidden price: she will become prisoner rather than mistress of the house and husband . . . .

The narcissistic male is always the one most attractive to [Angelou] and the one most mysterious—ultimately he will always turn out to be the man most destructive to her and her capacity to invest too much of her dependency and need in him too quickly. The wonder which underlies her perceptions in "To a Man" are not surprising provided one has read her autobiographies and identified this common psychic pattern she recurringly illustrates. What she identifies as mystery and wonder are part of the guardedness and distance he sustains— keeping her always at a safe length away from himself. One would expect anger from her rather than wonder.

Anger would have been more appropriate toward his self-protection and yet she does not express anger. Perhaps also the absence of anger affirms the passivity Lillian Arensberg has seen in Angelou's writing. We must, however, not overlook another important factor which accounts for what may be occurring here from an aesthetic and artistic rather than a purely psychic point of view. Her persona's opportunity to draw attention to it—rather than to her male subject. Thus, in doing this, she can draw upon her female audience's alleged universal bafflement with the mysterious male psyche. The poem would be better called "To a Woman" in that case, if one accepts this less direct reading of the poem . . . .

While Maya Angelou's poetry may not have taken us into every nook and cranny of her long and complex life starting with the Lafayette County Training School—its various movements and insights have nonetheless helped us understand the themes, the issues even some of the conflicts which have pervaded her inner life. Thus, while we could not share the objective events in all their entirety . . . , her various poetic stances have given us some lead into parts of that subjective voyage. . . .

Her love poetry . . . suggests her relationship to a world which can be stultifying, mystifying and oppressive, but one she will not allow to become these things and overwhelm her. The voyage through her life has not been filled with soft and pliable steps each opening into another opportunity for self acceptance. Her voyage has instead been anything but that and yet she has filled those voids with fantasy, song, hope and the redefinition of her world's view through art.

Source: Priscilla R. Ramsey, "Transcendence: The Poetry of Maya Angelou," in *A Current Bibliography on African Affairs*, Vol. 17, No. 2, 1984–1985, pp. 139–53.

SOURCES

Angelou, Maya, "Phenomenal Woman," in *Phenomenal Woman: Four Poems Celebrating Women*, Random House, 1995, pp. 1–6.

"Biography," Maya Angelou website, http://mayaangelou.com/bio/ (accessed March 14, 2012).

Bloom, Lynn Z., "Maya Angelou," in *Dictionary of Literary Biography*, Vol. 38, *Afro-American Writers after 1955: Dramatists and Prose Writers*, edited by Thadious M. Davis, Gale Research, 1985, pp. 3–12.

"A Brief Guide to New Formalism," Poets.org, http://www.poets.org/viewmedia.php/prmMID/5667 (accessed March 14, 2012).

Cohen, Barbara, "The Psychology of Ideal Body Image as an Oppressive Force in the Lives of Women, Part Two," Center for Healing the Human Spirit Publications, 1984, http://www.healingthehumanspirit.com/pages/body_img2.htm (accessed March 14, 2012).

Derenne, Jennifer L., and Eugene V. Beresin, "Body Image, Media, and Eating Disorders," in *Academic Psychiatry*, Vol. 30, No. 3, 2006, pp. 257–61.

Drury, John, "Beat Poetry," in *The Poetry Dictionary*, F + W Publications, 2006, pp. 35–36.

———, "Free Verse," in *The Poetry Dictionary*, F + W Publications, 2006, pp. 120–21.

Epstein, Barbara, "What Happened to the Women's Movement?," in *Monthly Review*, Vol. 53, No. 1, May 2001, http://monthlyreview.org/2001/05/01/what-happened-to-the-womens-movement (accessed March 14, 2012).

Francis, Roberta W., "The History behind the Equal Rights Amendment," Equal Rights Amendment website, http://www.equalrightsamendment.org/era.htm (accessed March 13, 2012).

———, "Frequently Asked Questions," Equal Rights Amendment website, http://www.equalrightsamendment.org/faq.htm (accessed March 13, 2012).

Gioia, Dana, "Notes on the New Formalism," in *Conversant Essays: Contemporary Poets on Poetry*, Wayne State University Press, 1990, pp. 175–93.

Hagen, Lyman B., "Poetry: Something about Everything," in *Heart of a Woman, Mind of a Writer, and Soul of a Poet: A Critical Analysis of the Writings of Maya Angelou*, University Press of America, 1997, pp. 118–36.

Haruna, Zainab, "Black Women's Literature," in *Encyclopedia of Feminist Theories*, edited by Lorraine Code, Routledge, 2000, pp. 87–88.

Higashida, Cheryl, "Reading Maya Angelou, Reading Black Internationalist Feminism Today," in *Black Internationalist Feminism: Women Writers of the Black Left, 1945–1995*, University of Illinois, 2011, pp. 158–76.

Rother, James, "The Problems of Prosody," in *Contemporary Poetry Review*, July 22, 2010, http://www.cprw.com/the-problems-of-prosody (accessed March 14, 2012).

Shaw, Andrea Elizabeth, "The Anatomy of Unruliness," in *The Embodiment of Disobedience: Fat Black Women's Unruly Political Bodies*, Lexington Books, 2006, pp. 47–76.

West, Sandra L., "Maya Angelou," in *Contemporary American Women Poets: An A-to-Z Guide*, Greenwood Press, 2002, pp. 12–17.

FURTHER READING

Bambara, Toni Cade, *The Black Woman: An Anthology*, Washington Square Press, 2005.
> Originally published in 1970, this work is a collection of poems, essays, and stories by and about African American women. The works explore such issues as race, sexuality, body image, and politics.

Gillespie, Marcia Ann, Rosa Johnson Butler, and Richard A. Long, *Maya Angelou: A Glorious Celebration*, Doubleday, 2008.
> This biography provides, along with a survey of Angelou's life and works, some of Angelou's notes and letters as well as photographs of Angelou and her family and friends.

Guy-Sheftall, Beverly, ed., "Beyond the Margins: Black Women Claiming Feminism," in *Words of Fire: An Anthology of African American Feminist Thought*, The New Press, 1995, pp. 229–358.

This section of Guy-Sheftall's collection of essays focuses on the development of African American feminism during the women's rights movement of the 1960s and 1970s.

Younger, Beth, *Learning Curves: Body Image and Female Sexuality in Young Adult Literature*, Scarecrow Press, 2009.

Younger provides a summary of the way issues of body image and female identity are portrayed and explored in young-adult fiction from the 1970s through the first decade of the twenty-first century.

SUGGESTED SEARCH TERMS

Maya Angelou AND "Phenomenal Woman"

Angelou AND feminism

Angelou AND African American feminism

Angelou AND 1970s poetry

Angelou AND free verse

Angelou AND body image

Angelou AND autobiography

Angelou AND activism

Angelou AND sexuality

Angelou AND *I Know Why the Caged Bird Sings*

Recessional

RUDYARD KIPLING
1897

Rudyard Kipling's "Recessional" stands as a milestone in the famous Anglo-Indian author's career. Written at the turn of the twentieth century in celebration of Queen Victoria's diamond jubilee, "Recessional" represents the peak of both Kipling's career and the global imperialism of the British Empire he adored. Stricken with controversy since its publication in 1897, "Recessional" is arguably the best-known English poem written from the turn of the twentieth century, and its publication placed Kipling in the same canonical field of British poets as William Shakespeare, John Milton, and William Wordsworth. Glorifications of both the monarchy and the imperialistic politics of the era, Kipling's poetry is cherished by some and loathed by others. But the fame of the Anglo-Indian author cannot be denied. His words were published and read almost as fast as he could write them. The poem can be found in *Kipling: Poems,* published in 2007.

AUTHOR BIOGRAPHY

Kipling was born in the Indian city of Bombay (now called Mumbai) on December 30, 1865. Lockwood Kipling and Alice Macdonald, Kipling's parents, were English born but had traveled to India to teach years before the birth of their children. Lockwood was the principal of

Rudyard Kipling

the Jeejeebyhoy School of Art, where he was employed to teach and encourage the production of Indian art. Kipling lived the first six years of his life in Bombay, spending most of his time with the Indian servants in the household. The common practice in Anglo-Indian households during the nineteenth century was to send children back to England to be educated, and the same happened with young Kipling. He and his sister were sent to board with the widow of a sea captain near Portsmouth, where unfortunately he was physically abused by the woman and her son. When he was sent to England, the six-year old Kipling spoke Hindustani more fluently than English; ten years later, at the age of sixteen, Kipling returned to India speaking only English.

From 1878 to 1882, Kipling attended the United Services College, Westward Ho!, in Devon, England. This was a boarding school for the sons of army officers and civil servants and was intended to prepare young men for the life of an army officer. However, Kipling's very poor eyesight and small size kept him from joining the military ranks. Instead, his father helped land him a job as a journalist in Lahore, India, where he became the assistant editor for the *Civil and Military Gazette.*

With his foot in the literary door, the young author became recognized for his bold, conservative, and stubborn opinions. His poetry found a place in issues of the gazette that were thin and needed "scraps" to fill the paper. Over the next few years, Kipling would travel through India on assignment for the gazette. He also gained more creative control with the newspaper, leading to the regular publication of his poetry and fiction in it. Knowing little about life outside of India, Kipling's poetry and fiction at this time was heavily involved in both Indian and Anglo-Indian culture. Though considered satirical and hardheaded, Kipling slowly became the lone voice of Anglo-Indian life and literature (no other serious author had existed in an Anglo-Indian colony before).

As Kipling aged, his writing became less satirical and more mature. By the time he left Lahore in 1889, he was an experienced writer with growing fame throughout the British Empire. Although he would rarely return to India for the rest of his life, Kipling openly regarded his years in India as holding the fondest memories from his past. For twenty years after, Kipling traveled the globe, and it was during these travels that he was able to witness and appreciate the full extent of the British Empire he adored. Within a year of his travels Kipling reached America and met Mark Twain. When he returned to England the following year, he was a celebrity. However, Kipling did not like the treatment he received in London as a result of his fame. He traveled back to America, where he married Caroline "Carrie" Balestier, the sister of his American agent, on January 18, 1892. The couple bought a house in Vermont soon afterward and produced three children. The eldest child, Josephine, died of pneumonia in 1899. Their son, John, was killed in World War I.

During his time in America Kipling continued to write, and his status as a celebrity grew. Although he refused to give lectures and speeches, he met both Theodore Roosevelt and Grover Cleveland during his five years in America. In 1896 Kipling returned to England with his family, though they continued to make trips to America until 1899. He refused many honors, including that of being named poet laureate. However, in celebration of Queen Victoria's diamond jubilee—her sixtieth anniversary as monarch—in 1897, Kipling wrote and published "Recessional."

Kipling became the most famous poet in England during this time, but it was his ability to transcend forms seamlessly that has made him a lasting presence in English literature. He was able to compose poetry, prose, journalism, and children's literature of quality and importance (a trait extremely rare among authors). Three years before "Recessional" was published, Kipling published *The Jungle Book* (1894), which is arguably his most famous work and certainly his most famous work of children's literature.

Political criticism of Kipling's opinionated work began at the turn of the twentieth century, but Kipling was able to remain a large figure in English literature nonetheless. *Kim* (1901), *Just So Stories* (1902), and *Puck of Pook's Hill* (1906) are all famous examples of Kipling's prose. The success of Kipling's collected poetry and prose allowed him to become the youngest and the first English recipient of the Nobel Prize for Literature in 1907. However, following the success of *Rewards and Fairies* in 1910, his reputation began to decline along with British imperialism. He continued to travel, going every year to South Africa, where he had been a correspondent during the Second Boer War. He wrote less frequently during World War I, and by the time of his death on January 12, 1936, he was writing almost nothing at all. In contemporary times Kipling remains controversial, praised for the quality of his writing and reviled for his imperialist opinions.

POEM TEXT

God of our fathers, known of old,
Lord of our far-flung battle-line,
Beneath whose awful Hand we hold
Dominion over palm and pine—
Lord God of Hosts, be with us yet,   5
Lest we forget—lest we forget!

The tumult and the shouting dies:
The captains and the kings depart:
Still stands Thine ancient sacrifice,
An humble and a contrite heart.   10
Lord God of Hosts, be with us yet,
Lest we forget—lest we forget!

Far-called, our navies melt away;
On dune and headland sinks the fire:
Lo, all our pomp of yesterday   15
Is one with Nineveh and Tyre!

Judge of the Nations, spare us yet,
Lest we forget—lest we forget!

If, drunk with sight of power, we loose,
Wild tongues that have not Thee in awe,   20
Such boastings as the Gentiles use,
Or lesser breeds without the Law—
Lord God of Hosts, be with us yet,
Lest we forget—lest we forget!

For heathen heart that puts her trust   25
In reeking tube and iron shard,
All valiant dust that builds on dust,
And guarding, calls not Thee to guard,
For frantic boast and foolish word—
Thy mercy on Thy People, Lord!   30

Amen.

POEM SUMMARY

The text used for this summary is from *Kipling: Poems*, Everyman's Library, 2007, pp. 95–96. A version of the poem can be found on the following web page: http://www.poetryfoundation.org/poem/176152.

"Recessional" was written and published in 1897 in celebration of Queen Victoria's diamond jubilee, the sixtieth anniversary of the English monarch's reign. At the time, Queen Victoria was the first English monarch to celebrate a diamond jubilee, making her the longest-reigning monarch in English history. Although Kipling often refused literary honors (such as with his refusal to be named poet laureate earlier that year), "Recessional" was published for the first time in the *Times* of London on July 17, 1897, "on the same page as a message from Queen Victoria expressing her gratitude for the spontaneous outburst of loyalty and affection that had greeted her sixty years on the throne."

A key aspect of "Recessional" is the influence of the Old Testament, and how the poem reads similar to warnings given by God in Deuteronomy 6:12: "Then beware lest thou forget the Lord, which brought thee out of the land of Egypt, from the house of bondage." Kipling was a strong supporter of the British Empire, and being an English descendant born in India, he felt that the English influence in India was a productive form of social and political salvation. This becomes immediately apparent in stanza 1, lines 1–3 of "Recessional." God reigns over the far-flung reaches of the British Empire, and beneath the Lord's hand the English are doing

MEDIA ADAPTATIONS

- Famous American Opera singer Leonard Warren recorded a singing of Kipling's "Recessional," and the recording can be found on YouTube at http://www.youtube. com/watch?v = aCKY-By4HhY. The song is from the album *Leonard Warren: Prima Voce*, released in 2008 by Nimbus Records.

- To commemorate the memory of fallen World War I veterans, Australia and New Zealand celebrate Anzac Day in late April. Kipling's "Recessional" has become a hymn for the event, and an example of the singing of Kipling's poem in New Zealand in 2007 can be found on YouTube at http://www. youtube.com/watch?v = hVqtdNODTxA. The inclusion of the word "Amen" at the end of Kipling's verse makes the poem a hymn for the people celebrating Anzac Day.

righteous work across the globe. The expansion of the empire is emphasized again in line 4. The palms and pines represent the many differing habitats the English control (pine trees in the north, palm trees in the south). And to finish stanza 1 the speaker asks the Lord to remain by the side of the imperialists. The final phrase of the first four stanzas—*lest we forget*—returns the reader to the line from Deuteronomy: "Then beware lest thou forget the Lord." Kipling meant for this line to stand as a warning to the British to stay holy, and refrain from the temptations of sinful behavior.

In stanza 2 the speaker addresses the mortality of man and the infiniteness of the Lord's existence. In this stanza, wars and arguments begin and end, captains and kings gain power and lose control, but ultimately man must remember to appreciate what the Lord has provided, making sacrifices to remain holy in omnipotent eyes. Again, to end the second stanza, the speaker asks the Lord not to abandon humanity.

In the third stanza, the speaker begins to discuss the possibility of an oncoming decline of the British Empire, creating a large amount of speculation over the title ("Recessional" referring to the final hymn sung at the end of a Christian service). Lines 13–14 address the long distances the Royal Navy has traveled in order to maintain the empire, fighting in such places as dunes and promontories. The rest of the third stanza discusses how the expansion of the British Empire is an example of yesterday's existence, where the English attempted to bring salvation to so-called heathen lands. In terms of biblical symbolism, Nineveh and Tyre in line 16 are examples of large cities that collapsed in the Old Testament. The speaker is warning Great Britain that an empire can fall if it is left without being maintained properly. In line 17 the Lord is addressed as a judge, and the speaker pleads for the Lord's mercy, lest his people forget.

Stanza 4 is written in reference to the boastful, overtly violent, ego-driven mania that accompanied the British imperialistic surge. In this stanza the speaker begs the Lord's forgiveness for the blasphemous behavior of the past, when the English were drunk with power, wild in speech, and boastful. Line 22 is the most controversial line in the poem. The labeling of "lesser breeds" living without order and law has created anger and controversy amongst minorities of all cultures reading Kipling's poem. However, in the vein of interpretation that compares the British Empire with biblical salvation, these "lesser breeds" would simply mean those who have not been saved. Also, many critics believe this line refers almost entirely to the Germans, whom Kipling despised. And yet, even with these interpretations the controversy of the line remains.

The fifth and final stanza of "Recessional" is the only stanza that does not end with the phrase *lest we forget*. In this final stanza the speaker warns that if the political disagreements at home and the unnecessary use of violence against natives abroad continue, they will create a wedge between the people of Great Britain, and then the empire will lose focus, causing it to decline and collapse. The British have succumbed to heathen impulses by taking up weapons in lines 25–26, and they are no longer accepting the Lord the speaker addresses in line 28. In the speaker's mind, this behavior will usher a fall. The final two lines of the poem are a new type of plea. They beg the Lord to ignore the boasts and unwise words spoken by the British. The speaker is now begging for mercy, and it seems that the British people have forgotten the Lord's salvation. Through boastful, heathen behavior, the lands of the British Empire have gone the way of Ninevah and Tyre, the Empire has fallen, in this stern poetic image meant to serve as a warning.

THEMES

British Imperialism

An Anglo-Indian born in Bombay to English parents, Kipling stood as the voice of British imperialism in the East at the turn of the twentieth century. His work dealt almost exclusively with the British Empire, and his opinions always leaned toward the positive aspects of the imperial monarchy. (He believed that the Indians should maintain their own culture, but the industrial development, economical development, and sanitation of the English culture was a productive influence that should be applied to the Indian way of life). "Recessional" was written and published in 1897, just after Kipling returned to England having spent twenty years traveling and witnessing the expanses of the empire. Kipling was regularly disappointed by the disapproval that many English showed toward the expansive empire, especially in London. After spending most of his young life in India, his first journey to Great Britain came as a shock. In India, the Anglo-Indians (including Kipling) saw Britain's foreign policy as the acts of a savior in a land in need of salvation, while in England at the turn of the twentieth century the citizens were beginning to recognize a different justification for expansion (based on economy rather than on humanitarian efforts), and the brutish behavior of the imperial soldiers was becoming unjustified in the minds of many Britons.

A more simplistic way of explaining the dichotomy of opinions regarding the British Empire is to label the two sides by parties. The Conservative Party had control of English Parliament at the time "Recessional" was published. The Conservative Party saw fewer negative aspects regarding the imperialistic pushes of the British government across the world. The Liberal Party, on the other hand, adamantly disagreed with the spreading empire. When "Recessional" was published, the Liberals were fighting to gain political power in England, though they would not do so until

after Victoria's death. In 1897, the British Empire was reaching the peak of the Victorian era, but Kipling recognized that a peak could only be followed by a decline. So while "Recessional" was published in celebration of Queen Victoria's diamond jubilee, it is also a politically driven statement warning against the forthcoming decline, one that began as a disagreement at home and eventually spread throughout the empire. The age of British imperialism, an age of which Kipling stood as the voice, would soon fall apart. Today Kipling stands as a prophet of this change, but when he wrote the poem he was hoping to be an influence of maintenance.

Nationalism

"Recessional" was written in admiration for the queen whose long reign had represented the nationalistic beliefs embodied by Kipling. This is an important theme in the poem, but it is also a complex dichotomy that makes this simple poem difficult to interpret. It cannot be denied that Kipling held affection for Queen Victoria. She was the only queen he had known in his lifetime, and her era on the throne was responsible for much of the expansion of the empire Kipling revered. However, if "Recessional" were simply written in admiration of the queen's reign, it would not hold such complexity. Death coincides with old age, and Victoria was growing old. Only four years after her diamond jubilee, in 1901, she died. Kipling predicted that with Victoria's death, Britain's foreign policies might change. After traveling for many years, Kipling had gathered that British public opinion in 1897 was not always fond of the expanding empire. Kipling, born in a British colony in Bombay, India, could not understand this new way of thinking in Britain. In an almost naive way, he truly believed that British occupation of countries in Africa and Asia was the only way to spread salvation. As George Orwell states in his essay "Rudyard Kipling," "Imperialism as he sees it is a sort of forcible evangelizing." Orwell goes on to say that Kipling simply did not understand that expansion of the empire was primarily an economical conquest. It was Kipling's inability to recognize all the motivations of the empire that allowed him to admire it in such a hopeful manner. "Recessional" was written in admiration during a time of celebration of Queen Victoria, but it was also written in admiration of the public and political thought represented by her era on the throne. "Recessional" served as a warning at a time when pride in Queen Victoria still influenced

TOPICS FOR FURTHER STUDY

- In spite of all the stern and controversial political opinions Kipling held, he never advocated any specific religion. However, the words of "Recessional" are addressed to the Lord of the Old Testament. Why do you think Kipling chose to write the poem using religious language? Remembering the dedication of the poem to the Queen's diamond jubilee, do you think Kipling chose a Christian theme to suit the occasion? Was "Recessional" written as an appeal to the English people not to turn against the empire? Keep in mind that the Church of England is a Christian church and the state church of the United Kingdom. Write an essay explaining your stance.

- Kipling wrote and published "Recessional" during the celebration of Queen Victoria's diamond jubilee. Think of a recent moment in history that seemed as monumental as the diamond jubilee felt to the British in 1897. Did the moment inspire art or poetry? How did the recent moment differ from the diamond jubilee with regard to artistic influence? Drawing on the event you chose, give an oral report explaining why celebrations have changed over time, or defending the idea that they have not changed. Create a PowerPoint presentation to aid your report.

- "Recessional" is a poem about the end of both an empire and an era. Create a blog using "Recessional" as an introduction, and link the themes of Kipling's poem with moments in recent history. Refer specifically to a case of foreign policy where the people living in a nation think differently from the citizens living abroad. How do readers of your blog react to your statements? Tumblr is a free website that can be used for blog space.

- "Recessional" is a poem written with the classical use of rhyme and meter. Using what you have learned regarding poetic feet, write a poem of at least five stanzas following the poetic structure of your choice (iambic pentameter, iambic tetrameter, etcetera). After you finish writing your poem, write a short essay about what you have learned about structured poetry. Do the formulas make poetry more difficult to write? Did you find that the poem produced was better or worse than a free-verse poem without structure? Do you have more appreciation for classical poetry after attempting to follow the format of such poetry?

- Read Kipling's children's book *The Jungle Book*. This book came to be used by the Cub Scout organization as a motivational book. Using the Internet, research the Cub Scouts and, in an essay, tie the moral tone of *The Jungle Book* to the Cub Scouts, explaining why you believe the book was important to this organization.

public and political decisions. It pushed for the restoration of the type of nationalistic pride Kipling thought necessary for the British people to maintain their empire.

Prophecy

Because Kipling wrote "Recessional" as a warning of decline during the peak of the Victorian era, there is a prophetic quality to the verse. In 1897 the fall of the British Empire did not seem as imminent as it would in the early years of the twentieth century.

Therefore, Kipling achieved the status of a prophet, though intending his words to be motivational while celebrating the anniversary of the queen's six-decade reign. In the years that followed the publication of "Recessional" and Queen Victoria's monarchy, the entire world would change in vast ways. So while it is easy for today's reader to dismiss Kipling as the voice of a dying era, it must also be acknowledged that poems like "Recessional" were the author's way of predicting the complicated diplomacy of the approaching twentieth century.

The poem is sung as a hymn in Australia, New Zealand, and Canada. *(© Andrea Danti | Shutterstock.com)*

"Recessional" is a celebration of the long-standing ways of Britain's Victorian era, but it is also a stern glimpse into the coming century of bloody wars and intense political strife. For instance, line 22 is widely understood to be a reference to Germany. Kipling disliked Germany, and he saw them as a future problem. In hindsight, given what the Germans attempted to accomplish in the twentieth century, he was correct. Germany sought a large empire, which frightened Kipling. These prophetic qualities are the major reason why "Recessional" is still studied in contemporary times. Kipling was able to lay a poetic landmark at the peak of the Victorian era.

STYLE

Iambic Tetrameter

The first step in understanding the meter of a poem is to recognize the poetic foot. The poetic foot is the subdivision of the meter with which the speaker delivers a poem to the reader or listener. The meter is the pace with which the poem is meant to be read or spoken, creating emphasis on certain words throughout the lines. The most popular contemporary versions of poetry are songs. Songs with lyrics are sung to a beat. The meter in poetry is identical to the beat in a song with lyrics. The poetic foot is determined by the location of stressed and unstressed syllables within each line of the poem, similar to the drumbeat in a song accenting the delivery of lyrics. Poetry without meter is called free verse, and it exists without these poetic terms. "Recessional" is written in a meter called *iambic tetrameter*: An iamb is a metrical foot consisting of an unstressed syllable followed by a stressed syllable. There are four iambs in each line, so the meter is called tetrameter from the Latin *tetra*, meaning "four." Similar to the way grammar ensures the format of language, poetry written using meter provides a structure with which a reader, without the aid of a speaker, can fully understand the pace of a poem.

Rhyme

All of the rhyming words in "Recessional" are the final words of each individual line. Although this is not the only way rhyme can be utilized in poetry, it is the form Kipling chose for "Recessional." Furthermore, the rhymes follow a pattern of *ababcc*. What this scheme means is that the first line rhymes with the third line, the second with the fourth, and the fifth with the sixth. (Each time a new sound is used, a new letter is assigned.)

This strictly structured poetry exemplifies the culture of tradition in the Victorian era. However, poetic formulas like this rhyme scheme are not the only way poetry can be written. Free-verse poetry (poetry written without structure) has existed as long and has had as much success as structured poetry. If anything, Kipling's use of structure with "Recessional" illuminates his education and desire to follow a format. According to this design, words, like the native peoples in the lands of the British Empire, need a structure to follow, but should not be stripped of their deep, inherent meaning.

HISTORICAL CONTEXT

Victorian Era

"Recessional" was written in celebration of Queen Victoria's diamond jubilee. She was the first British monarch to celebrate such an occasion, making her the longest reigning monarch in British history. But beyond Victoria's ability to remain in power for six decades is the social and political influence a reign like hers had on the British people in both Great Britain and its colonies.

The Victorian era is linked to peace and prosperity in England, artistic progression in both literature and fine art, industrial progress, propriety, gentility, strict social norms, and imperial conquest. Victoria is most synonymous with a growing empire. By 1897, the year of her diamond jubilee and the publication of "Recessional," the expansion of the Empire had slowed, nearly halting, and political opinion in Great Britain began to question the justification and motivation of the empire. It was the violent behavior of the imperial soldiers against natives that had begun to turn people against expansion. As the famous Anglo-Indian author George Orwell wrote, "The mass of the people, in the nineties as now, were anti-militarist, bored by the Empire."

As the nation was celebrating the sixtieth anniversary of their seventy-eight-year-old queen, they were also preparing for the next step in the vast history of Great Britain. Kipling saw that the ongoing use of violence as a manner of maintaining control in conquered lands could only lead to the uprising of the natives. The Second Boer War with the Dutch in Africa was difficult, and creating more enemies could spread the empire thin and lead to a collapse. Queen Victoria died in 1901, and after her death, the empire declined. "Recessional" was left to stand as the final artistic push at the end of an era.

Kipling as Celebrity

Kipling was not a celebrity for his entire writing career. Truthfully, he disdained his celebrity status when he realized it had arrived. His fame first began to rise in the late 1880s, but it was not something Kipling himself recognized until he left India and traveled to London in 1890. From there he continued to travel the globe, and his fame provided him with the pleasure of meeting other famous authors, like his visit with American author Mark Twain. But it was not until the publication of "Recessional" and later "The White Man's Burden" that Kipling noticed his fame. It was the last years of the nineteenth century that solidified Kipling's status as the voice of both Anglo-India and British imperialism, and he would be awarded the Nobel Prize in 1907. He was and is the voice of Victorian nationalism. His work became so important in 1897 that "Recessional" was published in the *Times* just days after he penned the lines. Mark Twain wrote regarding the rapid publication of "Recessional" that Kipling was "the only living person not head of a nation, whose voice is heard around the world the moment it drops a remark." As David Gilmour states in his biography *The Long Recesional*, Kipling was "a national symbol, a one-man embodiment of the Empire."

Unfortunately for Kipling, his rise as the symbol and voice of a generation of thought occurred at a time when that point of view was at its peak. Kipling was not prepared for the next century and the subsequent decline that follows a peak. In the years after the publication of "Recessional," he became a major target for a new, anti-imperialistic political movement throughout Britain. Orwell expressed as much, claiming that Kipling belonged exclusively to the period between 1885 and 1902. Following these years, Kipling no longer knew what to defend, as the nation he adored had

COMPARE
&
CONTRAST

- **1897:** Queen Victoria is the first English monarch to celebrate a diamond jubilee on her sixtieth anniversary as queen.

  Today: In 2012, Queen Elizabeth II becomes the second queen to celebrate the diamond jubilee.

- **1897:** The British Empire is vast and powerful. Because of its powerful navy, Britain has been able to conquer many lands across the world and influence the cultures of each land. The British people are proud of their nation's wide expansion throughout the world. Jingoist imperialism—or aggressive and violent displays of nationalism often influenced by propaganda—is considered a justified foreign policy and encouraged by people like Kipling.

  Today: British influence on the cultures of India and other nations conquered in the age of British imperialism remains; however, the British have dismantled their political con-

trol over India and many other nations once considered a part of the empire. Also, the age of jingo-imperialistic thought has ended in England.

- **1897:** Kipling is regarded as the poetic voice of the empire. Although he does face some critical opposition, for the most part it is agreed that he is a great writer.

  Today: Kipling's works are still appreciated by many, but his staunch political views are often misinterpreted or taken out of context by contemporary readers.

- **1897:** "Recessional" is read as a stern warning against the behavior of the British people and the dangers these behaviors are placing upon the empire.

  Today: After the decline of the British Empire, Kipling's words became prophetic. The poetic decline in "Recessional" intended to be a warning came true.

---

changed its face, its agenda, and its purpose. As Orwell wrote in his essay "Rudyard Kipling," "Kipling spent the later part of his life sulking, and no doubt it was political disappointment rather than literary vanity that accounted for this. Somehow history had not gone according to plan." Kipling's reign as voice and symbol ended with the era he represented.

CRITICAL OVERVIEW

Critical reception of Kipling's "Recessional" can be broadly grouped into two veins of interpretation. The first is the initial reaction from readers while Victoria was alive and at the peak of her reign. At the time, the poem was understood to be a stern warning written by the didactic "true watchman of our Empire," as contemporary

novelist Rider Haggard labeled Kipling, alerting the British public to continue doing what was best for the empire. The second major interpretive lens, read in hindsight after the death of Victoria in 1901 and the subsequent decline in the British Empire, sees Kipling as a prophet predicting this collapse.

Contemporary critical praise for "Recessional" was instantaneous. On July 17, 1897, the day the poem was published in the *Times* of London, it was printed on the same page as a message from Queen Victoria thanking the British public for their support during her diamond jubilee celebration. The British were in a state of joy, and Kipling's poem hit the mark in the minds of the jubilant public. For the next few years the poem would continue to stand as a warning against political change regarding Britain's foreign policies. Harold Begbie's 1899 satirical children's book *The Struwwelpeter Alphabet* includes under

"Recessional" was written for English Queen Victoria's Diamond Jubilee. (The Library of Congress)

the letter *K* an illustration of Kipling alongside Lord Kitchener (the commander in chief of India at the time), and the description beneath the illustration reads, "Lanky sword and stumpy pen, / Doing useful things for men; / When the Empire wants a stitch in her / Send for Kipling and for Kitchener." In the illustration, drawn by Sir. F. Carruthers Gould, short Kipling stands erect next to the much taller Kitchener. Kitchener holds a rifle by his side, and Kipling holds an enlarged pen in the same military-style manner. In the minds of many, including Begbie, Kipling's role was as vital to the British control of India as the military's.

The poem's title (a *recessional* being the final hymn sung at the end of a service) and its use of religious terminology also led to a hymnlike reception, motivating some publications (the Methodist hymnal, for instance) to go so far as to add "Amen" to the end; even later Kipling collections include this final word. But the call-to-arms message of the poem written in Christian terminology also offended some critics. Richard Le Gallienne, offended by Kipling's use of Christian terminology to encourage imperialistic views, took "Recessional" and Kipling's 1899 poem "The White Man's Burden" as exemplifications of the image of "the Englishman as brute."

Following the death of Queen Victoria and the decline of the British Empire as Kipling knew it, "Recessional" began to be seen as a prophecy; Kipling's warning, left unheeded, had come true. T. S. Eliot wrote in an introductory essay to *A Choice of Kipling's Verse*, "It is a poem almost too well known to need to have the reader's attention called to it...something which has the true prophetic inspiration." The poem's fame could not be denied, and Eliot ushered in a new mode of interpreting "Recessional." No longer would Kipling's poem stand as a frightful image of something that could happen. In 1941, in the beginning stages of World War II, Eliot saw the poem as a prophecy. "Recessional" had predicted the turmoil Eliot and the rest of the world faced at the time of his essay.

In line with this new post-Victorian interpretation of "Recessional," Eliot urged readers to remember while reading the poem that it stood as a warning against political change, and only became prophetic after a change had taken place years later. However, in the process of proving his point on the new focus of "Recessional," Eliot explained that Kipling's staunch political beliefs were based on "a sensibility developed and matured in quite different environments: he is discovering and reclaiming a lost inheritance." In short, Eliot meant that the reason Kipling's warning was not heeded was because of his Anglo-Indian birth, and the personality gap his life in India created between the author and the citizens living in Great Britain.

Eliot's essay motivated George Orwell to write "Rudyard Kipling" a year later, in 1942. In his essay, Orwell agrees that Kipling should be read with what he calls a "pre-fascist" mindset, referring to the rise of fascism after the publication of "Recessional." But what Orwell disagrees with in Eliot's essay is the justification of Kipling's opinions based solely on his Anglo-Indian birth (Orwell also being an Anglo-Indian, but holding very different opinions from those of Kipling). Because of Orwell's birth in India, the reader is given an interesting glimpse into the political opposition Kipling warned against in "Recessional." Orwell writes how the "pansy-left circles" laughed at the line "lesser breeds without the law," and how they used the line to create a mental image "of some pukka sahib in a pith helmet kicking a coolie" (*pukka sahib*, in this case, being an Anglo-Indian of incorruptible nature, and a *coolie* being a native of India). In fact, this type of violence against natives is one of the issues Kipling was warning against in "Recessional," but as history shows, the behaviors continued. Ultimately, Orwell dismisses this common interpretation, explaining that the line "refers almost certainly to a German." Nevertheless, Orwell hits on an important point by focusing on the line. It is the most controversial line in the poem—so controversial, in fact, that in 1964 the Methodist hymnal dropped the poem because the line was believed to be a racial slur.

"Recessional" is a poem that should be read through a Victorian lens. When it is read with a post-Victorian lens, the poem is liable to be misunderstood, or seen as prophetic.

CRITICISM

Chris D. Russell

Russell is a freelance writer. In the following essay, he discusses Kipling's fear of an approaching decline of British imperialism and the author's drive to write "Recessional" as a motivational poem meant to prevent such a decline.

One of the many curses an author must carry once a work has left his or her desk is the disregard for authorial intention most critics hold. Some will entertain the notion that an author meant something more than the words on the page, and they will dig up biographical materials, old letters, and such to prove some grand point. But these critics must answer the ultimate question: If the author meant that to be a part of the work, why did they not include it in the work? Interestingly, Kipling did include a small tidbit on an extra note he sent along with "Recessional" to the *Times* on July 16, 1897 (the day before the *Times* first published "Recessional"), in which he wrote, "We've been blowing the Trumpets of the New Moon a little too much for White Men, and it's about time we sobered down." In a letter written around the same time to Rider Haggard, Kipling explained

KIPLING'S WARNING IN 'RECESSIONAL' OF AN ONCOMING DECLINE DID IN FACT PROVE CORRECT, AND IT MADE HIM A PROPHET, THOUGH THAT IS HARDLY WHAT HE DESIRED."

that he meant "Recessional" to say, "Don't gas but be ready to give people snuff," but he had only been able to say the first half of this sentence with the lines in his poem. Both of these sentences are masked with poetic ambiguity, but what do they add to the meaning of "Recessional"?

It is known that Kipling wrote "Recessional" at the same time he was writing "The White Man's Burden" (1899). Perhaps white men were the people Kipling was most relating to at the time. But the line about trumpets and the new moon is a biblical reference to Psalm 81:3. In the King James Version, no doubt the most widely available in Great Britain and all her colonies, Psalm 81:3 reads, "Blow up the trumpet in the new moon, in the time appointed, on our solemn feast day." This line is similar to most other versions of the Christian Bible, but with two variations very different from the others versions. These differences are in the phrase "in the time appointed" and the word "solemn." These variations, if anything, help explain the diligent and serious manner of the British.

What Kipling's note to the *Times* adds to "Recessional" is a small bit of distaste in the author's mind regarding the diamond jubilee celebration. Where Kipling sees an oncoming collapse if the budding problems in the empire are not eradicated immediately, the rest of the nation sees only a time to be jubilant and have fun during Victoria's nationwide party. Perhaps Kipling is frustrated because Victoria's golden jubilee was only ten years before, and to have two parties within a decade is simply irresponsible when there is so much work to be done.

Kipling's letter to Haggard is not as easily defined. In his words, he was able to include the message "don't gas" into "Recessional," and this most certainly is in reference to lines 25–26, with the heathen heart placing trust in a reeking cylinder and iron (smoking gun and sword).

WHAT DO I READ NEXT?

- Kipling's 1895 sequel to *The Jungle Book*, *The Second Jungle Book*, continues with the character Mowgli and in the setting of India. The sequel illustrates Kipling's abilities as a writer of children's literature.

- In 1899, two years after the publication of "Recessional," Kipling wrote the controversial poem "The White Man's Burden," about what he saw as a budding American imperialistic foreign policy at the time of the Spanish-American War. Twenty-one years later, Hubert Harrison wrote a response. "The Black Man's Burden," in the collection *When Africa Awakes*, is an interesting example of Kipling's opinions and verse being disputed by a future generation of authors.

- George Orwell's 1934 novel *Burmese Days* deals with the waning age of British imperialism in India. Orwell, who was born in 1903, is the most noteworthy Anglo-Indian author besides Kipling. Orwell's work has had the same amount of political influence as Kipling's, but the two writers disagree on the subject of imperialism and other political issues. Reading *Burmese Days* will give the reader insight into the next generation of Anglo-Indian thought, which did not coincide with the drive for imperialism that Kipling defended so adamantly.

- William Wordsworth's 1798 poem "Tintern Abbey" is an example of pre-Victorian poetry. Wordsworth was part of the romantic movement, which gave great importance to the influence of nature in art. A reader of Kipling would be interested in reading the

type of poetry that preceded him, as well as catching a glimpse at the poet who was considered the voice of the British people before Kipling. In fact, in his lifetime Kipling was considered a successor to Wordsworth, who had died in 1850.

- Between Wordsworth's time and Kipling's rise to fame, Alfred, Lord Tennyson stood as the poetic voice of Great Britain. Tennyson was also a major influence on Kipling's writing. In 1854, following the Battle of Balaclava during the Crimean War (1854–1856), Tennyson wrote "The Charge of the Light Brigade" (a direct influence on Kipling's 1891 poem "The Last of the Light Brigade"). This poem stands as an example of one of the earliest instances of written correspondence during a war (the poem was written the same year the battle took place).

- Walt Whitman's 1855 poem "Song of Myself" is an example of free-verse poetry. Free-verse poetry is written without the rhyme and meter of traditional poetry and allows the poet to follow a train of thought without being restricted by form.

- Kipling's 1937 autobiography *Something of Myself* is his final work, published after his death. It provides an interesting look into Kipling's mind at the end of his life regarding his past and his works. Editor Thomas Pinney used other autobiographical works from Kipling's collection to fill gaps in the author's original text, giving the reader a more in-depth glimpse into the thoughts that shaped the writer.

With this line Kipling is explaining his largest issue with the empire, and that is an issue with the brutish behavior of the colonial soldiers. He understands that to continue kicking a people will eventually lead to civil unrest. To maintain the empire, Britain must be more intelligent in their domination, with fewer displays of violence

to maintain order. Kipling hits this note by sending the message that it is neither noble nor Christian to be violent when there are other ways to solve the problem. But this line is found in the final stanza of "Recessional." So what Kipling suggested in his letter to Haggard is that an additional stanza would have included a message roughly described as to "be ready to give people snuff." *Snuff*, defined in the *Oxford English Dictionary*, can be both a verb and a noun. The noun is a smokeless form of tobacco. Was Kipling proposing that people should be given tobacco, and that he meant to include that in his poem? Doubtfully. But the verb form of *snuff* is "to stop a small flame from burning," and this seems more likely to be what Kipling meant in his letter to Haggard. When writing to a friend, Kipling was comfortable in saying that it was a bad idea for the colonials to continue with any widespread brutality (gas), but if a small flame should arise the British should not be ashamed in extinguishing it. To do so would not anger the God in "Recessional." The reason Kipling did not include this message in "Recessional" is up for debate. Perhaps he could not find the words he was looking for and decided to publish only the five stanzas he had written. He was working with a deadline: Victoria's diamond jubilee celebration was nearing its end. Nevertheless, it is interesting to ponder over Kipling's almost hypocritical retraction of the message delivered by "Recessional."

Kipling's warning in "Recessional" of an oncoming decline did in fact prove correct, and it made him a prophet, though that is hardly what he desired. What is more fascinating is that these two letters help explain what "Recessional" avoids, and that is the finger of accusation Kipling was vaguely and secretly pointing towards Queen Victoria and those directing the actions and strategies of the British imperialist forces.

Though the letter to Haggard is not written with the Christian terminology used in "Recessional," the note to the *Times* is, and with this poem being very topical of the time it was published, it is a mystery why this reference to Psalm 81:3 was not included in the work. It would have no doubt offended Victoria and those who were celebrating the occasion to be accused of wasting time.

Shifting focus to the use of Christian terminology in "Recessional," it is noteworthy that Kipling was not a practicing Christian. In 1908, he described himself as "a godfearing Christian Atheist," and as biographer Gilmour explains, Kipling "was never, in any real sense, a practicing Christian. Whatever bigotries he may have collected in the course of his life, religious ones were absent." Being born and raised in India—a culture developed long before the British rule of

Kipling's time, with its own spiritual beliefs among many other aspects unique to this grand and highly developed country—no doubt led to Kipling's broad perspective regarding religion.

In the 1973 essay "Rudyard Kipling: Activist and Artist," Vasant A. Shahane reads the use of Christian terminology in "Recessional" as amounting to an activist stance. Shahane believes Jesus was an activist, standing for his beliefs in the face of physical violence from those who disagreed. From this, Shahane deducts that Kipling was a Jesus-like figure of activism, so his use of Christian terminology feels natural in "Recessional." But, as previously noted, Kipling was not a particularly adamant Christian. So why did Kipling use Christian terminology in "Recessional"?

Kipling likely used religious terminology as a motivational tool. The gap between the Britain he knew living in India and the politics of those living in Great Britain was very large. Using Christian terminology, Kipling was able to bridge this gap by appealing to the lowest common denominator. He could hit Britons in their religious beliefs and spark a change with the reminder that their God did not agree with the use of violence. The people in Great Britain did not agree on everything, but by presenting his poetry as a religiously inspired text, Kipling was able to appeal to the members of the Church of England. This may have helped the popular success of "Recessional," but it did not ensure that the procedures Kipling saw as necessary would be followed through with.

If anything, the Christian terminology in "Recessional" gives the poem a biblical sound, ushering its publication in hymnals. It also aids in the post-Victorian interpretation of the poem as a prophecy, but it did not ultimately aid in the Victorian interpretation of the poem as a call to action. The empire fell after Victoria's death.

If Kipling intended the ideas in his letters to the *Times* and Haggard to be in "Recessional," why did he not include them in the poem? Alas, Kipling did not include these messages in "Recessional," but what these lines do give the reader is an added perspective into the motivation behind Kipling's pen. Kipling saw some serious issues that needed to be addressed in 1897, but when he looked to his fellow Britons for help, they were busy partying, or eagerly pulling the trigger on natives they were supposed to be helping. Had he included these messages in "Recessional" he may have been able to prevent the fall of his beloved

**KIPLING WAS NO MERE ACOLYTE
OF BRITANNIA, NO SUPERFICIAL AND LOUD-
MOUTHED CAMP FOLLOWER."**

empire. Kipling's message in "Recessional" did inspire people, but it did not inspire them enough to accomplish what Kipling considered necessary. The empire collapsed, British imperialism declined, and Indians regained political control over India. "Recessional" made Kipling a prophet of British tragedy rather than a hero of victory.

Source: Chris D. Russell, Critical Essay on "Recessional," in *Poetry for Students*, Gale, Cengage Learning, 2013.

Denis Judd

In the following essay, Judd examines "Recessional" and "The White Man's Burden," contending that Kipling was a more sophisticated critic of British and American policies than is generally assumed.

A hundred years ago, between June 19th and 24th, 1897, Britain and the British Empire celebrated the sixtieth anniversary of Queen Victoria's accession to the throne. The Diamond Jubilee celebrations were chiefly staged in order to affirm the achievements of the British people and to glorify the British Empire. During the June festivities the public, both in Britain and throughout the Empire, were able to feast on a rich diet of ceremonial and display, speech-making and official processions, chief of which was the royal procession to St Paul's Cathedral for the Thanksgiving Service in the imperial capital on June 22nd. The festivities were generally marked by an outpouring of over-heated patriotic sentiment, by lavish spending on receptions, balls, street parties and shows, by military and naval displays, and by flags, bunting and glittering illuminations in the streets.

Commenting on the Diamond Jubilee, the *Times* wrote that 'History may be searched, and searched in vain, to discover so wonderful an exhibition of allegiance and brotherhood among so many myriads of men.' Sir Arthur Sullivan composed the 'Jubilee Hymn.' The

Poet Laureate, Alfred Austin, proffered some mediocre, celebratory verse.

The *Daily Graphic* claimed that the Jubilee:

> . . . to the foreigner . . . has been a revelation. He has been enabled to realise for the first time the stability of English institutions, the immensity of the British Empire, and, finally, the strength of the bonds by which the family of nations owing allegiance to the British Crown is united.

In France, *Le Figaro* told its readers that Rome itself had been 'equalled, if not surpassed, by the Power which in Canada, Australia, India, in the China Seas, in Egypt, Central and Southern Africa, in the Atlantic and in the Mediterranean rules the peoples and governs their interests.' From Berlin the *Kreuz Zeitung*, perhaps a shade regretfully, described the Empire as 'practically unassailable.'

Of the sparkling, elaborate and undeniably impressive royal procession of June 22nd, Mark Twain astutely observed that it was Queen Victoria, gravely acknowledging the tumultuous acclamation of her people from her carriage, who was the 'real procession' and 'all the rest . . . embroidery.' G. W. Steevens in the newly-established *Daily Mail*, described the procession lyrically as 'a living gazetteer of the British Empire.' He went on:

> A plain, stupid, uninspired people, they call us, and yet . . . each one of us—you and I, and that man in his shirtsleeves at the corner—is a working part of this world-shaping force. How small you must feel in the face of this stupendous whole, and yet how great to be a unit in it!

Not that the response to the Diamond Jubilee celebrations was uniformly favourable. The Labour politician Keir Hardie, looking ahead to the great royal procession, wrote 'Millions will go out on Tuesday next to see the Queen. What they will see will be an old lady of very commonplace aspect. That of itself will set some a-thinking. Royalty, to be a success, should keep off the streets.' The future Fabian and socialist reformer Beatrice Webb recorded in her diary somewhat disdainfully, 'imperialism in the air, all classes drunk with the sight-seeing and hysterical loyalty.' Among active trade unionists, left-wing Liberals, certain Nonconformist sects, Irish nationalists, pacifists and libertarians could also be found misgivings and, sometimes, downright hostility to the self-congratulatory outpouring of imperial and patriotic sentiment.

Unexpectedly, perhaps, misgivings were also articulated by Rudyard Kipling, one of the most popular and widely-read writers of late-Victorian Britain, but also a man widely regarded as a stalwart imperialist, unshakeably loyal and patriotic.

Kipling had been passed over for the post of Poet Laureate shortly after the formation of Lord Salisbury's Conservative and Unionist government in the summer of 1895. Although both Salisbury and his nephew, Arthur James Balfour, had expressed a strong preference for Kipling, discreet enquiries revealed his antipathy to official recognition. It is also possible that the queen had vetoed his candidature having taken offence at his sprightly, not entirely respectful poem, 'The Widow at Windsor.' At any rate, according to Sir Ian Malcolm's judgement, 'That ass Austin' was named as Poet Laureate on January 1st, 1896, in spite of Salisbury's preference for Kipling, 'though he blows his own trumpet rather loud sometimes.'

Despite Austin's appointment and the common contempt which many felt for the new Laureate's literary powers, Kipling at first resisted a number of suggestions that he should compose an ode to mark the occasion of the Jubilee. The editor of the *Times*, however, persistently lobbied him. As Kipling ruefully recalled: 'the *Times* began sending telegrams so I shut myself in a room . . . I found just one line I liked—"Lest we forget"—and wrote the poem around that.'

On June 22nd, Jubilee Day, Kipling set aside his draft for some new nursery stories, as well as the early version on the 'White Man's Burden,' so that he could work on a poem based on the line 'Lest we forget.' That evening he walked, with has wife Carrie, from their Sussex home to hear the pealing of church bells and to watch the chain of bonfires light up along the south coast, the flames leaping 'on dune and headland' as his poem 'Recessional' was later to put it.

The Jubilee ode had still not been completed by July 16th; indeed a house-guest staying with the Kiplings, Sallie Norton, given permission to rummage through the contents of Kipling's wastepaper basket, pulled out the draft of the poem on the Diamond Jubilee, entitled 'After.' Miss Norton's protest at the notion of destroying the poem were reinforced by others in the household, and eventually Kipling sat down to revise it. He reduced its length from seven to five stanzas, and the final version was dispatched to the *Times'* office that evening by special messenger.

On July 17th the *Times* published the re-titled poem 'Recessional' in its middle pages. The poem was an instant triumph, greeted with a storm of praise, and amply confirming Kipling's reputation as the greatest popular poet of the day. His gratification at his success was compounded a month later when his only son was born, and named John after his grandfather.

Four stanzas of the poem 'Recessional' are worth quoting in full:

> God of our fathers, known of old,
> Lord of our far-flung battle-line,
> Beneath whose awful Hand we hold
> Dominion over palm and pine—
> Lord God of Hosts, be with us yet,
> Lest we forget—lest we forget!
> The tumult and the shouting die;
> The Captains and the Kings depart;
> Still stands thine ancient sacrifice,
> An humble and a contrite heart.
> Lord God of Hosts, be with us yet,
> Lest we forget—lest we forget!
> Far-called, our navies melt away;
> On dune and headland sinks the fire:
> Lo, all our pomp of yesterday
> Is one with Nineveh and Tyre!
> Judge of the Nations, spare us yet,
> Lest we forget—lest we forget!
> If, drunk with sight of power, we loose
> Wild tongues that have not Thee in awe,
> Such boastings as the Gentiles use,
> Or lesser breeds without the Law—
> Lord God of Hosts, be with us yet,
> Lest we forget—lest we forget!

Kipling had used an almost magical formula in the writing of these verses. The lines are stirring yet disturbing, containing a series of measured and sober warnings against patriotic and imperial excess within a framework of thoughtful introspection. Far from indulging in a literary form of imperial and patriotic flag-waving, Kipling plainly identified one of the deep, but barely acknowledged, explanations as to why the nation, and to some extent the Empire, had apparently thrown itself so wholeheartedly into the Jubilee extravaganza.

Behind the bold, brash and frequently self-congratulatory front that the Diamond Jubilee celebrations presented to the world, lurked, in almost unquantifiable measure, pessimism and insecurity. Although many of Britain's leaders and opinion-makers chose not to articulate it, there was a deep-seated anxiety as to what the future held both for the nation and the Empire, especially during the imminent, and unknowable, new century.

Britain seemed beset by a host of problems, pressing in from all sides. On the world stage a revitalised France provided an obstacle, or at least an irritant, in a number of areas of British interest. The arrival on the scene of recently united and now actively colonising nations like Germany and Italy had disturbed the old imperial order and put Britain under new and unwelcome pressures. The serious threat posed to British manufacturing and commercial supremacy by the rapidly expanding capacities of both Germany and the US provided further challenges, highlighting the British failure adequately to modernise and reinvest in their industrial base, and a reminder—to those who chose to see it—that the British economy was only carried into surplus on an annual trading basis by the success of 'invisible' exports.

In addition, the late-Victorians were troubled by a number of challenges, many of them unwelcome, to the old domestic order. From within, British society was faced with a new, more militant, mass trade unionism, with the 'new' man as well as the 'new' woman—who was soon to press for enfranchisement as well as full equality before the law—with the persistence of Irish nationalism, with the perils apparently posed by the growth of domestic socialism and much else besides. Certain 'British' standards, long taken for granted, seemed to be slipping: the public fretted over the adulteration and processing of foodstuffs and the dilution of beer; while such incidents as the conviction of Oscar Wilde in 1895 for homosexual activities had convinced many that the nation, the 'race,' was on the slippery downward slope of decadence and decline.

It was these, and a host of other unformed and barely acknowledged anxieties, that made Kipling's great Jubilee poem appear so relevant and timely. The very real prospect of Britain's loss of its naval supremacy was, by itself, sufficient cause for concern: 'far-called, our navies melt away,' Kipling had written. The apparently irresistible rise of the US as a great naval power, and Imperial Germany's naval ambitions, soon to be made plain by the passing of the 1898 Navy Law in the Reichstag, could only mean that the days of Royal Naval supremacy were, if not numbered, then soon to be seriously challenged. The nightmare of the loss of naval supremacy would return like an unwanted phantom to haunt the British imagination in the years before the outbreak of war in 1914, most painfully

during the 'navy scare' of 1909. It is no accident that this nightmare was soon to be given menacing fictional form in what is commonly regarded as the first British spy novel, Erskine Childers' best-selling *The Riddle of the Sands*, published in 1903.

If Britain failed to respond to these, and similar challenges, then surely chronic and irreversible decline would follow. As Kipling wrote:

> On dune and headland sinks the fire:
> Lo, all our pomp of yesterday
> Is one with Nineveh and Tyre!

The poem contains other strong images. Britain's battle-line is 'far-flung,' her navies are 'far-called.' The anxieties over the stretching of national resources to breaking point were thus strikingly illustrated and reinforced, and were to be promptly addressed shortly after the turn of the century by the Fisher naval reforms, the Anglo-Japanese alliance and the ententes with France and Russia. Until then, however, the bonfires which Kipling and his wife had seen in Sussex blazing on Jubilee Day, might well prove to be temporary and over-optimistic symbols: 'On dune and headland sinks the fire.' The perils of uninhibited and thoughtless celebration, which manifested themselves with such intensity and frequency throughout Britain and the Empire, needed to be put into sharp perspective:

> If, drunk with sight of power, we loose
> Wild tongues that have not Thee in awe,
> Such boastings as the Gentiles use,
> Or lesser breeds without the Law—
> Lord God of Hosts, be with us yet,
> Lest we forget—lest we forget!

Kipling, secure in his reputation as an imperialist and a patriot, had issued 'a call to humility and a warning that the proudest empire is ephemeral as a day's pageant.' The 'lesser breeds without the law' were not necessarily, as was so quickly assumed by critics of the poem, the black or brown citizens of Britain's empire. The poet is surely here referring both to foreigners and to those British citizens and subjects, no matter what their origin or ethnicity, who were unable or unwilling to see what needed to be done in the national interest and what perils and spectres lurked in the shadows. It was not merely the easily distracted, superficially educated and politically immature mass of the British public that Kipling was berating, it was also the 'flannelled fools at the wicket,' and the 'muddied oafs at the goal'—more likely to be the products of the public schools than of the poorly funded and chaotically organised state education system.

Kipling was deluged with praise after the publication of 'Recessional.' His literary agent, A. S. Watt, hastened:

> ... to offer you congratulations on the appearance ... of your magnificent poem. It strikes the right note with regard to the Jubilee Celebration and will recall the nation to the source of its real strength. You are the only rightful heir to the mantles of Shakespeare, Milton, and Tennyson, and the laureate *de facto!* I tried to read 'God of our fathers' aloud this morning at home but I broke down.

His cousin by marriage, J. W. Mackail, an intellectual and a pacifist, wrote ' ... in our household, at least, your poem in the *Times* of this morning was read with tumult of acclaim. I cannot tell you how glad I am of it ... There are all the signs of England saving up for the most tremendous smash ever recorded in history if she does not look to her goings.' In reply, Kipling wrote:

> Seeing what manner of armed barbarians we are surrounded with, we're about the only power with a glimmer of civilisation in us ... This is no ideal world but a nest of burglars, alas; and we must protect ourselves against being burgled. All the same, we have no need to shout and yell and ramp about strength because that is a waste of power, and because other nations can do the advertising better than we can. The big smash is coming one of these days, sure enough, but I think we shall pull through, not without credit. It will be the common people—the 3rd class carriages—that'll save us.

If Britain's need for vigilance and self-renewal, most usefully manifested in the maintenance at whatever cost of her naval supremacy, was one of the great themes of Kipling's poetry as the century drew to a close, there was another one that both commanded attention and fitted neatly, hand in glove, with the first preoccupation.

The year after the publication of 'Recessional,' Kipling had finally composed 'The White Man's Burden.' The message of the poem was apparently straightforward and, at first sight, surprising. It was that the United States should shoulder, with Britain, the responsibility for the spread of Anglo-Saxon civilisation. The United States' comprehensive defeat of Spain during the war of 1898–99 had led to the acquisition of a formal American empire in the Caribbean and the Pacific. Kipling appealed to the American people, as he saw it—the other great half of the English-speaking race and true 'white men' as well—to share Britain's global civilising mission.

The verses were composed 'to the rhythm of a hymn-tune, and the language was again biblical.' The poem was full of striking and unexpected imagery:

> Take up the White man's burden—
> Send forth the best ye breed—
> Go bind your sons to exile
> To serve your captive's need

Americans who, like the British, Kipling took instinctively to understand both the limitations and the benefits of 'the Law' (and among whom, were large numbers of 'gentiles,' on the poet's analysis) were thus encouraged to endure the tribulations of imperial rule and to put up with the ingratitude of their subject peoples. They must:

> ... wait in heavy harness
> On fluttered folk and wild—
> Your new-caught, sullen peoples,
> Half devil and half child.

The drudgery of imperial rule would offer, in Kipling's opinion, little by way of material reward or even any clearly identifiable token of gratitude. It might, moreover, all end in catastrophe, or at least in sterile failure:

> Take up the White Man's burden—
> And reap his old reward:
> The blame of those ye better,
> The hate of those ye guard ...
> And when your goal is nearest
> The end for others sought,
> Watch Sloth and heathen Folly
> Bring all your hope to nought.

Although these inducements were hardly sufficient in themselves to send thousands of young American men in quest of administrative service overseas, leading American statesmen were pleased enough. Theodore Roosevelt, the recently elected governor of New York State and destined to be President, thought the verses 'rather poor poetry, but good sense from the expansionist stand-point.' Henry Cabot Lodge told Roosevelt in turn: 'I like it. I think it is better poetry than you say.'

Taken together, the poems 'Recessional' and 'The White Man's Burden' contained a compelling diagnosis not merely of Britain's current ills but of the possible remedies for the malady. If 'Recessional' had urged sober restraint, introspection and a sensible set of national priorities, 'The White Man's Burden' pointed the way to a resolution of British difficulties through a process of détente and co-operation with the United States—manifestation of the Special Relationship well before the phrase had been invented.

In this respect at least, Britain's policy makers and Rudyard Kipling marched in step. Unwilling to accept the inevitability of its own decline, Britain was making a calculated attempt to bring the New World to the rescue of the Old. During the late 1890s this discreet, sometimes invisible policy was in full swing. It was underpinned by the fact that, overall, Britain's world interests were not seriously in conflict with those of the United States. On those occasions where conflict seemed likely, for example, over the Venezuelan boundary dispute with British Guiana, over the Hay-Pauncefote Panama Canal Treaty and over the demarcation of the Alaskan border with Canada, Britain simply sold out on each occasion to the demands of the United States. This was nothing short of appeasement—on a scale that very few contemporaries were able, or willing, to recognise.

The wheels of Anglo-American co-operation and collaboration were also oiled by the surprisingly substantial level of social interaction between leading British and American families. The most obvious example of this lay in the marriages contracted between high-profile British men and American women—many of them from wealthy US families. It is significant that Kipling was one of those Britons to marry an American, his wife Carrie being the daughter of a well-to-do family based in Vermont in New England. Among contemporary British statesmen who chose American brides were the Liberal Lewis Harcourt, the Duke of Manchester, Lord Randolph Churchill, Lord Curzon and Joseph Chamberlain. Chamberlain had already gone on record in 1887 proclaiming: 'I refuse to think or to speak of the USA as a foreign nation. We are all of the same race and blood ... Our past is theirs— their future is ours ... I urge upon you our common origin, our relationship ... We are branches of one family.' Such sentiments were reinforced by the often complex but enduring connections that linked one side of the Atlantic to the other and involved the commercial spheres of banking, insurance and trade as well as the ready acknowledgement of a shared linguistic, political, cultural and legal inheritance.

Judged, then, on the evidence of the years 1897 to 1899, and chiefly his two poems, 'Recessional'

and 'The White Man's Burden,' an impression of Kipling can be formed sharply at odds with the commonly accepted stereotype of imperial tub-thumper and vulgar patriot. Kipling was a character far more complex, and in some ways perverse, than many suppose. That he composed much bumping, jangling verse mimicking the idiosyncratic and debased English of the common soldier should mislead no one. Kipling was no mere acolyte of Britannia, no superficial and loud-mouthed camp follower. He saw quite clearly the failings of Britain's self-pronounced imperial mission and did not shrink from proposing remedies. His criticisms were, of course, intended to avert disaster and to consolidate and perhaps enhance British global power. His strictures were, in this sense, self-serving. Behind the manifest popularity of much of his work, however, lay a shrewd and accurate analysis of what needed to be done.

Kipling was, indeed, a dangerous enemy of those who either actively wished to destroy the British Empire or were indifferent to its prospective demise, but not in the way that is generally imagined.

Source: Denis Judd, "Diamonds Are Forever? Kipling's Imperialism," in *History Today*, Vol. 47, No. 6, June 1997, pp. 37–43.

Peter Keating

In the following excerpt, Keating discusses Kipling's role as a political spokesman for British imperialism.

... Kipling was now the unchallenged, and unofficial, Poet Laureate of the Empire, pronouncing on international affairs on behalf of the British people, if not the government. When a preferential tariff treaty was signed between Britain and Canada in 1897, he celebrated the event with a poem, "Our Lady of the Snows," in which he not only praised Canadians for going their own way "soberly under the White Man's law," but mocked the objections of other countries as "Gentiles' clamour." Four years later, when the six Australian colonies were united into one commonwealth, he wrote a similar celebratory poem "The Young Queen." A Kipling poem was expected on any important public occasion that involved the Empire or national prestige, and never more so than on the celebrations that marked Queen Victoria's Diamond Jubilee on 21 and 22 June 1897. He was urged by the *Times* to write a special Jubilee poem, and began to do so, but then put the uncompleted

'RECESSIONAL' IS VIRTUALLY A
COMPILATION OF BIBLICAL ALLUSIONS,
QUOTATIONS, AND ECHOES."

draft aside, and spent a fortnight on naval manoeuvres before finishing the poem. "Recessional" (originally called "After") was published in the *Times*, together with an approving editorial, on 17 July. To Kipling's admirers and detractors alike the poem was a surprise. It was not loftily condescending, in the manner of "Our Lady of the Snows," or pugnaciously vulgar, like "Et Dona Ferentes": instead, it took up the solemn strain of "Hymn before Action" and, dropping the veiled threat that that poem contained, called for national humility and responsibility to counterbalance the imperial pomp of the formal Jubilee celebrations. Why exactly Kipling was so long delayed in completing the poem is not known. Carrington points out that Kipling was unhappy with the early draft and also that he always resented any suggestion that his public poems were written to order. Both factors are clearly pertinent. In addition, he may have been temporarily embarrassed by the jingoistic mood in Britain to which he himself in poems throughout the 1890s had substantially contributed. Many years later he described "Recessional" as being "in the nature of a *nuzzur-wattu* (an averter of the Evil Eye)." This is neatly applicable to the poem's central message that if Britain becomes "drunk with sight of power" then the Empire will end up at "one with Nineveh and Tyre," but there is little reason to believe that Kipling himself was at this time the possessor of "an humble and a contrite heart." On 24 June he visited Spithead to see the Jubilee Naval Review and marvelled at the power it represented. "Yesterday I got a chance to see the fleet and went off at once," he wrote to a friend. "Never dreamed that there was anything like it under Heaven. It was beyond words—beyond any description!"

"Recessional" is virtually a compilation of Biblical allusions, quotations, and echoes. Like "The Song of the English," it is based on the assumption that God has made a special covenant with England, but whereas the earlier poem

had centred on the forging of the covenant, "Recessional" points to its possible collapse. The principal text, from which Kipling took the refrain of his poem ("Lest we forget—lest we forget!") is Deuteronomy, 6:12: "Then beware lest thou forget the Lord, which brought thee forth out of the land of Egypt." One of the biblical allusions in particular has been the subject of much controversy. Kipling warns of "Wild tongues that have not Thee in awe," a reference, presumably, to triumphalism within Britain, indulging in:

> Such boastings as the Gentiles use,
> Or lesser breeds without the Law—

The relevant Biblical text is Romans, 2:12–15 where Paul warns: "For as many as have sinned without law shall also perish without law." The "Gentiles" and the "lesser breeds" are, in this context, those people who "have no law" and therefore become "a law unto themselves." Paul acknowledges that such people may have a natural inclination to the law, but God's judgement of them will depend on their actions, whether they "shew the work of the law written in their hearts." As we have just seen, Kipling had recently made a similar reference to "the Gentiles" in "Our Lady of the Snows." In both cases it is likely that he had the Germans primarily in mind, though in "Recessional" he is surely also referring to non-white races. Both are outside the Law, though in different ways. The Germans have turned their backs on it deliberately: the non-white races have still to be shown the benefits of living within the law.

The obliquity of this Biblical allusion and the general humility of "Recessional" are best seen as an indication at this particular moment of Kipling's uncertainty about who exactly could be regarded justifiably as "within" or "without" the law: the evidence of "Recessional" suggests that even England is in danger of losing God's favour. Kipling's concern about international relations and the possible isolation of the Empire reflects the wider frantic diplomatic activity and treaty realignments taking place at the close of the century between the major European countries and the emerging powers, especially America and Japan. The imperial poems published shortly after "Recessional" either celebrate, in a highly patronising manner, the work being done by the Empire in spreading the Law to non-white races ("Pharaoh and the Sergeant" and "Kitchener's School"), or they call for a more solid alliance between the white

Dominions to prepare for possible hostility from the rest of the world. Already in "Et Dona Ferentes" Kipling had presented his symbolic casino brawl as being between two halves of the world, with "the men of half Creation damning half Creation's eyes." Now in his little-known poem "The Houses," first published in the *Navy League Journal*, 28 July 1898, he repeated his conviction that the world was split into two halves, with Britain and the white Dominions defending civilisation against the barbaric threat of the rest:

> By my house and thy house hangs all the world's
> fate,
> On thy house and my house lies half the world's
> hate.
> For my house and thy house no help shall we find
> Save thy house and my house—kin cleaving to kind.

The mood of embattled isolation expressed in this poem, and in others of the time, did not, however, last long. For Kipling at least, it was dispelled in the most sudden, unexpected and spectacular way.

On 25 April 1898, after several months of naval skirmishes, a bloodthirsty press campaign and bitter internal debates between expansionists and non-expansionists, America declared war on Spain. Naval and military activity centred on the Spanish colonies. The war lasted until August and ended with America the decisive victors. Under the Treaty of Paris, drawn up in December, Cuba, Puerto Rico, Guam and the Philippines were ceded to America, and added to Hawaii which the Americans had already annexed. Virtually overnight, the country that had once been a British colony and had developed into one of the British Empire's harshest critics, the country that only a few years earlier was threatening war with Britain over an imperial boundary dispute, had itself become an imperial power, taking over colonies from another country, and committing itself to expansion in the Pacific. Kipling was thrilled. "Haven't your views on matters imperial changed in the last few months?" he asked an American correspondent. "I sit here and chuckle as I read the papers over the water. The land seems to be taking kindly to the White Man's Work." He pursued the theme exultantly in letters to other American friends, calling upon them to support "the White Man's work, the business of introducing a sane and orderly administration to the dark places of the earth that lie to your hand."

To Theodore Roosevelt, who was soon to become President of the United States, he insisted that having "stuck a pickaxe into the foundations of a rotten house" America was "morally bound to build the house over again from the foundations." While a divided America was examining its own conscience on these matters, in September 1898 an Anglo-Egyptian army under Kitchener's command crushed Khalifa Abdullah's dervishes at Omdurman, reoccupied the Sudan, and to public rejoicing in Britain, avenged the death of General Gordon thirteen years earlier. The following month Kipling published another of his oblique political ballads in the *Times*, "The Truce of the Bear," urging that friendly overtures by the Czar of Russia should be ignored, for there could be "no truce with Adam-zad, the Bear that looks like a Man!" Clearly "the white man" was in the ascendant, and it was by no means simply the non-whites who were being excluded. The Russians did not qualify for admission to the Anglo-American Club, nor did the Boers, Germans or Spanish. Most of the Irish were suspect, while the French—always deeply admired by Kipling—were allowed honorary membership, as long as they did not return to their ancient imperial rivalry with Britain. It was in this excited, civilising and missionary mood that on 4 February 1899 Kipling published in the *Times*, and on the following day in several American newspapers, what would come to be regarded as his most infamous poem which pulled together and advanced as a clear statement his thinking as it had developed over the whole decade.

"The White Man's Burden" was first subtitled "An Address to America," though this was later changed to the more descriptive "The United States and the Philippine Islands." In it the imperial process is advanced as a lofty, self-denying mission, a "burden." It demands of America "the best ye breed" who are to "bind" themselves "to exile" so that they can serve their "captives' needs." They must suppress feelings of "pride," develop "patience," and "veil the threat of terror" in order:

> To seek another's profit
> And work another's gain.

In return they can expect ingratitude, hatred, sloth, and "heathen Folly." Like Moses leading the Jews out of Egypt (Exodus 16:2–3; stanza 5), they will be told that the slow path to "the light" is too arduous to bear, and that all the "hosts" they "humour" really desire is an easy return to their "loved Egyptian night." However discouraged, the Americans must persevere, not for their own glory, but for the good of the conquered peoples:

> Take up the White Man's burden—
> The savage wars of peace—
> Fill full the mouth of Famine
> And bid the sickness cease.

Whatever the avowed justification, there can be no doubt that the poem is profoundly racist in sentiment. The "white man" may be a civilising force rather than someone who is simply white, but the "captives" have no choice, no alternative way of life that is worth considering. They are "fluttered folk and wild," "sullen peoples," "half devil and half child." It is precisely the transformation of these qualities that constitutes the "burden" of the white man, and in coming to realise this America enters its period of destiny. *Their* "childish days" are now behind them; no longer can they stand aside from the rest of the world; their "manhood" is about to be tested; they must present themselves for the "judgement" of their "peers." The poem represents Kipling at his highest point of imperial faith and confidence. Immediately, however, it was not America, but Britain and Kipling that were to be tested, and the judgement of their peers was not to prove favourable.

Source: Peter Keating, "The Seven Seas," in *Kipling the Poet*, Seeker & Warburg, 1994, pp. 89–120.

SOURCES

Begbie, Harold, *Struwwelpeter Alphabet*, Richard's Publications, 1899, p. 11.

Eliot, T. S., *A Choice of Kipling's Verse*, Faber and Faber, 1941, pp. 16, 18, 33.

Gilmour, David, *The Long Recessional: The Imperial Life of Rudyard Kipling*, Farrar, Straus and Giroux, 2002, pp. 3–309.

Kelly, Joseph, "Introduction: What Is Poetry?" in *The Seagull Reader: Poems*, W. W. Norton, 2008, pp. xxiii–li.

Kipling, Rudyard, Letter to the Editor of the *Times*, July 16, 1897; reprinted in *The Long Recessional: The Imperial Life of Rudyard Kipling*, by David Gilmour, Farrar, Straus and Giroux, 2002, p. 122.

———, "Recessional," in *Kipling: Poems*, Everyman's Library, 2007, pp. 95–96.

Kipling, Rudyard, and Rider Haggard, *Rudyard Kipling to Rider Haggard*, edited by Cohen Morten, Fairleigh Dickinson University Press, 1975, pp. 34–35.

Le Gallienne, Richard, *Rudyard Kipling: A Criticism*, HP Publishing, 1900, p. 155.

Orwell, George, "Rudyard Kipling," in *A Collection of Essays*, Mariner Books, 1970, pp. 116–31.

Shahane, Vasant A., *Rudyard Kipling: Activist and Artist*, Southern Illinois University Press, 1973, p. 26.

FURTHER READING

Arstein, Walter, *Queen Victoria*, Palgrave Macmillan, 2005.

> Arstein's biography of Queen Victoria helps the reader in understanding the culture of the last half of the nineteenth century under Victoria's monarchy.

Cain, Peter, and Tony Hopkins, *British Imperialism, 1688–2000*, 2nd ed., Longman, 2001.

> Cain and Hopkin's book explores the roots of British imperialism from its beginnings to 2000. Included in this book is the influence of the empire, explaining how the roots of the expansion were based in London and the financial sector of England. It is an interesting read, especially in comparison to the pro-imperialistic work of Kipling.

Longford, Elizabeth, *Queen Victoria*, History Press, 2005.

> Longford is considered by many to have been a top scholar on Queen Victoria, and this concise biography of the queen is a much smaller rendition of the six-hundred-page extensive biography Longford wrote in 1965.

Sen, Sudipta, *A Distant Sovereignty: National Imperialism and the Origins of British India*, Routledge, 2002.

> Sen's book provides a look at the late eighteenth and early nineteenth centuries' British imperialism in India. This is a perfect glimpse into the realities of the world Kipling knew as both a child and a young man. In her book, Sen investigates the social, economical, and political influence of British rule over India, as well as the ways the two cultures affected the identity of each separate nation.

Strachey, Lytton, *Queen Victoria*, Penguin, 2000.

> First published in 1921, Strachey's novel-like biography of Queen Victoria revolutionized the way a biography could be written. Using minor fictional additions based around real facts about the queen's life, Strachey wrote a biography that is both educational and

entertaining. Noteworthy are the relationships included in the biography, which help give the reader a perspective different from the traditional approach to the queen's life.

Wain, John, *The Oxford Anthology of English Poetry*, Vol. 2, *Blake to Heaney*, Oxford University Press, 2003.

This collection of English poetry begins in the nineteenth century, giving examples of the poets who preceded Kipling and even Queen Victoria. From the collection the reader can recognize the type of poetry inspired by Queen Victoria's sixty-three years on the throne as well as the poetry that followed both Kipling and Victoria in the twentieth century.

SUGGESTED SEARCH TERMS

Rudyard Kipling AND "Recessional"

Kipling AND British imperialism

Kipling AND Queen Victoria

Kipling AND George Orwell OR Anglo-Indian authors

British imperialism AND Queen Victoria

Kipling AND poetry

Kipling AND Anglo-Indian culture

Queen Victoria AND diamond jubilee

jingo-imperialism AND England OR Rudyard Kipling

Serene Words

GABRIELA MISTRAL

1922

"Serene Words," by Gabriela Mistral, appears in her first book of collected poems, *Desolación* (Desolation), published in 1922. Mistral was a respected writer in her native Chile, and when Professor Federico de Onís of Columbia University, in New York, read her scattered poetry to his students, they wanted to see more in a book. He gathered her poems and had them published by the Hispanic Institute of New York. Mistral was impressive in her physical presence and in her emotional use of the Spanish language for a poetry of passion. The charisma of her person and book spread her fame to the public and to the diplomatic circles she worked in all over the world as a Chilean consul. Popularly known as the spiritual mother of South America, Mistral made important contributions to Latin American culture as a journalist, poet, diplomat, and human rights activist, winning her Latin America's first Nobel Prize for Literature in 1945.

Mistral initially became famous for her frank portrayal of the emotions of romantic love. Her "Sonnets of Death" were a cry of grief for the death by suicide of her first lover. But the subject of "Serene Words" is her surrender to God, who was an even greater love for the poet. Mistral writes as passionately about her spiritual search as she does about romantic love, nature, motherhood, and children. Because she could have no husband or children, she said,

Gabriela Mistral (© *Leo Rosenthal | Time & Life Images | Getty Images*)

she taught school and wrote tender poems for and about children, loving other people's children as her own. "Serene Words" can be found in several anthologies, including the one translated and edited by her literary executor, Doris Dana, *Selected Poems of Gabriela Mistral: A Bilingual Edition* (1971).

AUTHOR BIOGRAPHY

Mistral was born Lucila Godoy Alcayaga on April 7, 1889, in Vicuña, a small town in the Elqui Valley of the northern Andes Mountains of Chile. She grew up in Monte Grande, a village in that valley, with her mother, Petronila Alcayaga, her father, Juan Gerónimo Godoy Villanueva, and her older half sister, Emilina. The father was a singer, poet, and schoolteacher. He abandoned his family when Lucila was three. She was raised by her mother and Emilina, the poet's first teacher. At the age of eleven she had to return to Vicuña to go to school, but she was miserable there after she was falsely accused of stealing and shunned by the other children.

Mistral was denied entrance to a teacher's college because she had published several poems in local newspapers that were viewed as heretical by the Catholic Church. Thus she educated herself, passed the examinations, and made a successful career for herself as a teacher and principal all over Chile while continuing to publish her poems. In 1914, at the age of twenty-five, she won the greatest poetry prize in Chile for her "Sonnets of Death," recording her grief for the suicide death of her early suitor Romelio Ureta. By 1913 she had changed her name to Gabriela Mistral, combining the names of two poets she admired, Gabrielle D'Annunzio, from Italy, and Frédéric Mistral, from France. She also named herself for the wild mistral wind that blows in France.

In 1922, her poems were gathered and published in New York by her American admirers as *Desolación* (Desolation). This collection contains "Serene Words." The same year she went to Mexico to prepare a curriculum for rural schools after the revolution. In 1924, her second book of poems, *Ternura* (Tenderness), containing children's stories and poems, appeared. Now she began her career as an international journalist, visiting professor, and diplomat, serving as a consul for Chile in Spain, France, Italy, Brazil, and the United States for the next half of her life. She rarely saw Chile again.

In 1938 she published her third book of poems, *Tala* (Felling). Mistral moved around constantly, living with friends in different countries and raising an adopted nephew, Juan Miguel, as her son. In 1943, the boy committed suicide, or was murdered, as Mistral believed, and she was inconsolable. In 1945 she became the first writer from South America to win the Nobel Prize for Literature. In 1951 she received the Chilean National Prize in Literature.

Her last years were spent largely in the United States where she wrote, taught at universities, and served as Chile's representative to the United Nations. *Lagar* (Wine Press) was published in 1954. While living with her friend Doris Dana in New York, she died of pancreatic cancer at Hempstead, New York, on January 10, 1957. She was buried in her beloved Elqui Valley, now a national place of pilgrimage in Chile. Her unfinished epic *Poema de Chile* was published posthumously in 1967.

POEM SUMMARY

The text used for this summary is from *Selected Poems of Gabriela Mistral*, translated by Doris Dana, Johns Hopkins Press, 1971, p. 5. A version of the poem can be found on the following web page: http://teachgoodwriting.blogspot.com/2009/11/life-is-gold-and-sweetness-of-wheat.html.

"Serene Words" originally appeared in the volume of seventy-five poems called *Desolacíon* (1922), which is divided into topics: "Life," "School," "Children," "Sorrow," and "Nature." It is preoccupied, however, with death and tragic love, since it includes Mistral's early poems, including the "Sonnets of Death" that made her famous. "Serene Words" is placed in the section on life, though it is frequently seen as a restatement of "Voto," the wish at the end of the book.

The section "Life" consists of responses to the world around Mistral—the killing of Jews, the death of poet Amado Nervo—but also her feelings about love, faith, and art. In "School" and "Children," Mistral affirms the Christian ethics of love, service, faith, forgiveness, and the sacred duty of the teacher. The children's song "Rounds" is still sung by Chilean schoolchildren. In "Sorrow," the story of the lover's betrayal and death is told. "Nature" includes poems about a second sorrowful love Mistral experienced later. The love stories are not differentiated but blended into one grand loss or desolation. In the book, Mistral uses a variety of forms—sonnets, tercets, quatrains, five-line stanzas, sextains, and ballads. For line lengths, she most often uses the alexandrine, or twelve-syllable line, the hendecasyllabic, or eleven-syllable, line, and the nine-syllable line.

"Serene Words" thus seems to go against the main mood of the book about despair. "Serene Words" transcends the sorrow through the positive influences of art, nature, and faith, here blended into one experience of consolation. The poem has five stanzas in the form of quatrains, or four lines each. In the Spanish, the line endings rhyme in the scheme *abab*. In English, the lines are not rhymed.

Stanza 1

The first stanza contains the whole main point of the poem. In the first two lines, the speaker implies that she is in midlife rather than in youth because she is in the middle of her days.

MEDIA ADAPTATIONS

- Originally for a radio show out of New York City, on WEVD, a taped sound recording was made with Doris Dana and Florence Lennon reading Mistral's work in English and Mistral reading her own poems in Spanish. It was published by the Library of Congress in 1964, OCLC No. 33864882.

Her experiences have brought her a fresh truth that the poem elucidates.

The second two lines say what the truth is: life is sweet because love lasts, while hate fades away. The metaphors she chooses underscore this lesson. Life is compared to the sweetness of golden wheat, and the truth about it comes to her as a fresh and living flower that does not fade, even though she herself is no longer young. The fact that she has gleaned the truth is suggested in the metaphor that implies life is something to be harvested, like wheat. She is picking up the kernels, the essence of life, which is love. She contrasts the duration and size of love with the duration and size of hate, as though they are quantifiable in time and space. Love is huge and unending, while hate is small and brief.

Stanza 2

In the second stanza the speaker likely refers to her own poetry. In the first two lines she says she wants to give up the verse she has been writing, which is full of her bitter heart's blood, for a happier verse. This is an echo of her final apology at the end of the book in "Voto," or "Wish."

The metaphor for this happier poetry is given in line 7, invoking the violets that are opening in the valley and the sweet smell of the wind. Mistral wants to leave behind the dominant impression of desolation and sadness in the book for more uplifting verse, exemplified in this poem. The poem should be like the beauty of nature.

Stanza 3

The third stanza unfolds the poet's new revelation about the goodness of life. In lines 9–10, the speaker says she understands both the man who prays and the man who sings. When one is in sorrow, one prays to God for help. But a happy man feels like singing out for joy. This poem is like the impulse of singing, while her sad love poems were like the man in agony who prays for help.

The last two lines of this stanza affirm life as a struggle through two metaphors: thirst and a steep hillside. Our thirst in life lasts for a long time and seems hard to quench. We are always searching for fulfillment. Life is also like climbing a hill that is twisted with many turns. However, while we climb, we can also be distracted by the sight of a beautiful lily by the wayside, and this is consoling. The hillside twists one way, and the lily takes our attention in the other direction. The poet might also imply, however, that the lily that can ensnare or trap our attention gets the viewer hooked into thinking that life is not so bad. This raises a question as to whether the lily's beauty represents the truth of life or a trick of nature.

Stanza 4

In the first two lines of the fourth stanza, the speaker admits that even if our eyes are heavy from weeping with sorrow, a brook has the power to make us smile. The eyes being heavy is a compressed metaphor for sorrow, combining crying eyes and the heaviness of body that comes from being bowed down. Sorrow is made tangible and given weight, as with love and hate in stanza 1. The brook that can make us smile immediately invokes the sensation of heaviness going off and the feeling of being light while smiling. The brook, like the flower on the hill, goes on pleasantly, despite any human heartache.

Lines 15–16 assert that a song from a skylark can make us forget death. Even though the poem is claiming that life has consolations when we see the beauty of nature before us, the images of the heaviness of human life in this stanza make clear that human distress can be deep. Nature must then be very powerful to lift us up and make us forget even death. So far, though the poet is saying that the good in life outweighs the bad, they seem somewhat equal in terms of the imagery. It is not until the last stanza that the good seems to win out.

Stanza 5

In the fifth stanza, the first two lines make the startling claim that nothing can now hurt the speaker since she has known love. She is at peace. This is an example of Mistral's violent language, however, for she equates peace not with a positive image, but by saying that nothing can pierce her flesh, a metaphor of life as an armed conflict. She does not specify what kind of love has made her peaceful. The kind of romantic love she has been speaking of in other parts of the book left her in torment. She means then that either the old love has raged itself out and purified her, or else she is finding love from a new source.

Lines 19–20 mention two kinds of love: mother's love and divine love. The speaker says that her mother's look can still bring her peace of mind; she feels as if God has put her to sleep. Mistral had a deep and abiding love for her mother, who remained in the Valley of Elqui living close to the earth. The love of her human mother and mother nature blend in her heart. All the beauty and love around her can make her feel that God, like her mother, is taking care of her, perhaps soothing or rocking her to sleep, taking away the memory of the bad. Sleep might also be a metaphor, as dreaming often is, for her poetry. It is a state of quiescence and surrender, opposite to the turmoil of life. God has taken away the pain of life through beauty.

THEMES

Beauty

The poet celebrates the beauty of nature around her, mentioning flowers, the wind, a brook, and a skylark. The flowered valley she describes evokes her paradisal childhood in the Valley of Elqui in the Andes Mountains of Chile, a frequent image in her poetry. In her "Decalogue of the Artist," Mistral gives the poet the commandment to love beauty because it is the likeness of God. Beauty does not dull the senses; it invigorates and makes one glad to be alive. Beauty is of a spiritual nature and makes someone break into song. It uplifts a sorrowful person with the sense of the divine.

Love

Love in all aspects, human and divine, is praised in the poem. Love is eternal and so can outlast hate and suffering, which must come to an end.

TOPICS FOR FURTHER STUDY

- Read *For Whom the Bell Tolls,* by Ernest Hemingway, about the Spanish Civil War (1936–1939). After reading it, give an oral report on the role of Americans in that conflict, using incidents from the novel and film clips from the movie starring Gary Cooper and Ingrid Bergman (1943) to illustrate your main points. Use Internet research to understand the historical background. Why did the conflict galvanize world opinion? Was that civil war comparable in public opinion to any contemporary civil war in another part of the world, such as in Libya?

- Start with the Mapuche International Link (www.mapuche-nation.org) and the Chilean Cultural Heritage Site (www.nuestro.cl/eng/default.htm) on the Internet to learn about the Mapuche Tribe in Chile. Using both print and electronic media for sources, write a paper on the history of this people and their treatment under Spanish colonialism.

- Read "Still I Rise," a poem by Maya Angelou that is appropriate for young adults. Compare and contrast Angelou's poem with Mistral's "Serene Days." In a summary, explain how they both assert triumph after defeat and how lyric poems can lift the spirits. Include this summary on a group web page on lyric poetry of hope, using hyperlinks to highlight favorite poets and poems.

- Using a collaborative research annotation tool like Google Notebook, collect relevant websites on the history of human rights. Include the Universal Declaration of Human Rights, created in 1948 by the United Nations, to which Mistral gave her input. Create a wiki with your comments and conclusions.

- Write a lyric poem about nature, love, or consolation. Set it to music, or ask a friend to do so, and perform it for others.

- Look at Native American poems, prayers, and words of wisdom on the Internet site First People (www.firstpeople.us/FP-Html-Wisdom/poemsidx.html) and/or read *Folk Tales from Chile* (1998), by Brenda Hughes, for poems and tales close to the earth, like the ones that inspired Gabriela Mistral. Give a PowerPoint presentation with slides of nature and nature poems and stories that show nature as sacred or as a source of consolation.

The poet is in the middle of her days, wiser than in youth, when she suffered from the unrequited love of a man. This topic of passionate and tragic love for a man predominates in *Desolacíon.* "Serene Words" comes from a later wisdom that has grown out of those bitter times. She is older and has let go of her anger and disappointment because hatred can only be brief by its very nature. She has learned the truth that once one has truly tasted love, nothing can disturb one's peace again. Love then, is the reality of life.

The love she mentions specifically is her mother's love, and God's love, which she surrealistically blends together in the image of God putting her to sleep. The poem also implies that the suffering she endured with her lover in youth was a purifying rather than a damaging experience. She has transcended that sorrow through the power of love itself, which can never destroy or be destroyed. The last stanza gives a sense of security, with a human mother and a divine parent watching out for her. Mistral's own father had written her cradle songs. The earth, too, is a loving mother who tries to make her smile with birds and brooks. This love is the opposite of the desolation and abandonment she felt from romantic love.

Opposites

Though the poem celebrates what is positive, it implies through contrasts that the nature of life consists of opposites: there is weeping and there is happiness. There is the man who prays in his trouble and the man who sings from joy. As a poet, she writes both verses of gall and smiling verses. The image of the twisted hillside suggests that life is like climbing a crooked mountain path, but the labor of the climb is arrested by seeing the beauty of the lily at one's feet. The skylark's song makes us forget death, but only while it is singing. Are good and evil equally weighted in life, then? There is something greater than these extremes, she seems to say, and that is the point of the poem. The bad can be intense, but there is that which outlasts evil. This is her faith, and that is why she says God is putting her to sleep. God is the one who is the source and ending of all opposites.

Consolation

God putting the speaker to sleep can mean several things. Most obviously, God is soothing her with beauty, like a mother rocking a sad child. The beauty of nature is presented as a consolation for the hardship of life. It also assures the speaker of God's presence in nature, a statement of Mistral's pantheism. The beauty itself is an assurance that life is good, it is divine, it is from God. This poem asserts divine providence, for no matter what nightmares life holds for us, they will not last. The brook and the skylark are not mere amusements; they bolster her faith.

The image of God putting the poet to sleep is an admission that God makes her peaceful after the storms of love and jealousy and grief. Sleep or peace is thus the opposite of passion. The beauty of nature is full of peace. Sleep is also a common image of death. Perhaps she is hinting that now that the passion of youth is past, she walks calmly toward death, beguiled by the song of the skylark that makes her forget her mortality for a moment.

Mistral also says several things about her art in this poem. As a poet, she feels she should exchange her previous verses of pain for verses like this one that make people smile. In "The Decalogue of the Artist" she says that the duty of the artist is to bear witness to God through art. She must console the human heart. This poem fulfills the promise of "Voto" at the end

In stanza 2, violets from heaven scent the valley.
(© Imageman | Shutterstock.com)

of *Desolacíon* to leave off writing of sorrow, and instead to use her poetry to inspire others.

STYLE

Latin American Modernism

Latin American modernism (1888–1916) was a literary movement that occurred earlier than European and North American modernism. The leader was the Nicaraguan poet Rubén Darío, who took Latin American authors away from romantic nationalism to a style that was international in its appeal. He believed in experimentation of form, fusing the formalistic elements of the French symbolists (elegance, musical structure, focus on interior reflection) with the Hispanic tradition of poetry on Spanish themes and landscapes in his landmark collection *Azul* (1888). A poem such as Darío's "Springtime" includes extravagant and classical images in a tropical world. This freedom of style was available as an example for Gabriela Mistral when she began to write poems as a teenager. "Serene Words" can be seen as an offshoot of modernism in its concern with the artist's inner life and artistic medium. She pictures a Chilean landscape but gives it universal appeal, using a musical quatrain but subverting expectations with rougher rhythm, language, and unusual imagery. Mistral is completely aware of herself as an international poet even while she speaks of her beloved homeland. Darío had prepared the way for the next generation of poets to experiment and to write to a larger audience. South American poetry is loved for its beauty, imagination, lyricism, poignant emotion, and outspoken political passion.

Vanguardism

Chilean Vicente Huidobro was a propagator of vanguardism (1920–1960), urging poets to forget tradition and create their own reality in verse (creationism). Vanguardism is one of the postmodern movements in South American literature. It builds on the modernist idea of experimentation and adds the influence of the political passion sweeping South America after the Mexican Revolution (1910–1920). Vanguardism is an avant-garde synthesis, emphasizing the power of the image, experimentation, and political commitment to place and to people and utilizing surrealism. Poetry from Latin America began to flourish worldwide in the 1920s, with such authors from Chile as Gabriela Mistral and Pablo Neruda (1904–1973) part of a founding group of poets in Santiago, breaking from the old modernist models to bring avant-garde freshness to Spanish American poetry. Mistral's prize for "Sonnets of Death" in 1914, her publication of *Desolacíon* in 1922, and Neruda's *Twenty Love Poems and a Song of Despair* (1924), with its daring lack of meter, surrealist imagery, and frank sexual content, were major breakthroughs that made Chilean poets international stars. Mistral was the greatest female writer of Latin America in the first half of the twentieth century. She startled people with her earthy descriptions of female and indigenous experience, her love of the land, her romantic passion, and her lack of adherence to traditional form. Her language is frank and often colloquial, and her imagery is violent and full of pain. She speaks of the abuse of women and Indians, of the cruelty of life. Though religious by impulse, she embraces every contradiction of life in her poems. "Serene Words" is a vanguardist poem, rejecting elegance in favor of plainness. There are no classical images, only images of the earth. Her interior reflections are not in the cool, mannered modernist style but are like uncontrolled feeling that must spill out into irregular lines and oddly juxtaposed images. The music and rhythm are there but are more like the peasant rhythms of folk songs. "Serene Words" says that life is beautiful, but beauty is underscored by blood, entrapment, death, and conflict, a surrealistic or dreamlike mixture of sweetness and doom. She asserts her faith in God but only in powerful images that remind us of struggle.

Lyric Poetry

Lyric poetry is an ancient genre, popular from classical times through the present in almost every culture. *Lyric* means song and was originally a song sung to an accompanying lyre or stringed instrument. A lyric poem is short and musical rather than narrative or dramatic, expressing emotions or thoughts, such as William Wordsworth's "I Wandered Lonely as a Cloud." A personal lyric represents the subjective experience of one speaker on a particular subject, for instance, love, as in the love poems of *Desolacíon*, including "Serene Words." Other topics she treats are women, children, and nature. Latin American literature, until the contemporary novel, was dominated by lyric poetry. Mistral was influenced by the cradle songs her father wrote to her, by the lyric poetry of the Bible, particularly the Psalms, Job, and Ecclesiastes, by the poems of the Indian writer Rabindranath Tagore, by classical poets writing in Spanish, and by the land and people of Chile itself. Like other vanguardists, she uses human speech rather than literary language. She is simple in her expression but uses compressed and surrealist images, and in Spanish is as distinctive in her voice and diction as Emily Dickinson, with whom she is sometimes compared, is in English. Known for fierce passion and the rough effect but moral elevation of her verse, she uses a vocabulary of extremes, from suffering to ecstasy. In terms of metrics, she recasts common lyric forms like the sonnet, the ballad, and the quatrain.

HISTORICAL CONTEXT

The Land of Chile

Chile has a unique landscape that has shaped its people and especially its writers. It is the longest country in the world, 2,700 miles long, on the Pacific coast of South America, and yet only about 110 miles in width because of the barrier of the Andes Mountains, separating Chile from other South American countries on the continent. In the north, between Chile and Peru, is another barrier, the Atacama Desert, the driest place on earth but also the site of mining for nitrates and minerals. Most of the Chilean people live in the green Central Valley, the location of Santiago, the capital. This area is highly cultivated and resembles California. Southern Chile

COMPARE & CONTRAST

- **1922:** The Indigenous people of the Araucanian culture, the Mapuche, are impoverished and living on reservations or in the mountains as the European settlers occupy their fertile ancestral farmland. Mistral champions their cause in her poetry and journalism.

  Today: Indigenous people are beginning to participate in Chile's government, and their demand for fundamental changes in the national constitution to recognize a multiethnic society is being implemented.

- **1922:** Mistral leaves Chile to work abroad, where she finds more recognition and outlets for her talents. Although she loves her country, it is hard for her to stay because it is conservative and geographically isolated from the rest of the world.

  Today: Chile is stable economically and politically, drawing tourists to its beauty, and is itself part of the force for change in the world.

- **1922:** Mistral belongs to the first generation of South American women authors in a male-dominated literary scene.

  Today: South American women authors today include Luisa Valenzuela, Laura Esquivel, and Elena Poniatowska.

---

includes the Lake District, south of the Bio-Bio River, a resort area with volcanos and glaciers and forests. Most of the remaining indigenous people, the Mapuche Indians, live here. Extreme southern Chile has violent storms and ends in Cape Horn, the tip of the continent. Chile also owns Easter Island and the Juan Fernandez Islands in the South Pacific. Gabriela Mistral lived in every part of Chile in her days as a schoolteacher, but she was born in the Valley of Elqui, a high Andean semitropical valley of flowers and fruits in northern Chile, where the poet spent her childhood. She returns to this valley in her poems, referring to it as a paradise. Many believe the valley has a special spiritual influence that shaped Mistral, and spiritual communities have sprung up there since her death.

Ancient Indigenous Civilizations of South America

Powerful native civilizations were already established in South America 3,500 years before the Europeans came. The Mesoamerican or Central American civilizations included the Olmec, Toltec, Mexica (Aztecs), and Maya. The Incas flourished in the South American Andes Mountains. The great Indian empires had the largest city-states in the world, sophisticated calendars, art, mathematics, astronomy, engineering, metalworking, and agriculture. Their road systems and ruined cities, such as the Incan Machu Picchu, in Peru, give evidence of the greatness of their achievements. In the twentieth century, South American writers like Gabriela Mistral, who boasted of some Incan blood, began to see this ancient legacy of the Indians as integral to modern South American identity. Mistral includes portraits of Indians in her poetry as a wise but persecuted people who are close to the earth.

The Spanish Conquest and Wars of Independence

The Spanish conquistador Diego de Almagro came to Chile in 1535 in search of gold. The Mapuche Indians in central Chile fought successfully against the Spanish for years and were not stopped until the 1800s. The Spanish divided up the land into large plantations worked by Indian slaves. Later, the Indians became tenant farmers. In the colonial period, Chile was ruled by a governor answerable to Spanish authority. Spain lost its colonies in the nineteenth century as a result of the wars of independence fought

In stanza 4, a skylark takes away the thought of death. *(© Manamana | Shutterstock.com)*

throughout South America. José de San Martín liberated Chile from Spain in 1818, but civil wars put the Chilean landowners and the Catholic Church in control. It was not until the twentieth century that the working and middle classes had much input in Chile's government or economic life. Mistral was from the working class and part of the new intellectual group that formed modern Chilean culture.

Modernism and Pan-Americanism

Modernism, the poetic movement that lasted in South America from the 1880s to the end of World War I, was a rejection of old traditions and brought Latin American authors a larger recognition in the world. Modernism was a force away from isolated nationalism and gave rise to South American identity as a continent. It was also an impetus for the Pan-American movement advocating cultural ties between North and South America, of which Mistral was a member and proponent. She was upset with the interventionist policy of the United States in South American politics and advocated instead the multicultural tolerance of the Americas as the underlying virtue of the Western Hemisphere.

The Spanish Civil War and World War II

The Spanish Civil War erupted in July 1936 and drew in supporters for both sides of the conflict as a prelude to the full world war that was coming. Fascist Italy and Germany supported the Spanish Nationalists, led by General Francisco Franco, who eventually won the war and became dictator of Spain. Volunteers from other countries such as the United States, Great Britain, and France joined the International Brigades to help the other side, the Spanish Republicans. Many South American writers, like Mistral and Pablo Neruda, were passionate in their support of the Republicans. Franco's forces executed and imprisoned thousands of civilians, some of whom died in German concentration camps. Spanish ethnic groups such as the Basques and the Catalans were persecuted. Basque children were evacuated and sent to other European countries. Mistral, of Basque descent herself, gave her royalties from *Tala* (1938) to the children orphaned in the war.

Mistral had been a consul to Spain until the war broke out. Because of the danger in Europe during World War II, Mistral took her adopted son, Juan Miguel, to Brazil for safety. Mistral was a pacifist, but Brazil soon entered the war, and her Jewish neighbors, Stephan Zweig and his wife, committed suicide out of despair. Shortly afterward, in 1943, Juan Miguel died from suicide or murder, part of the continuing violence that broke Mistral's spirit. She worked as Chilean representative to the United Nations after the war, helping to found UNICEF and giving input to the Universal Declaration of Human Rights (1948).

CRITICAL OVERVIEW

While Mistral was still a Chilean schoolteacher in her twenties, she was published internationally in journals and by the modernist poet Rubén Darío, in his Paris magazine *Elegancias*. As early as 1913, this acceptance made her a serious poet among the well-known intellectual circles of the day. Within Chile, her fame was assured with her first prize in the poetic Floral Games in Santiago in 1914, for her "Sonnets of Death." Another major advance in her reputation came when Columbia professor Federico de Onís gathered Mistral's poems, including "Serene Words," and published her first volume of poetry, *Desolacíon*, in New York in 1922.

Between the world wars, Mistral was admired for her humanitarian journalism. Critic Jonathan Cohen, in "Toward a Common Destiny on the American Continent: The Pan-Americanism of Gabriela Mistral," summarizes her involvement with the Pan-American movement of the 1920s, an early expression of multiculturalism, with her slogan "Dissimilarity without inferiority" (quoted in Cohen). In "'A Wor[l]d Full of Xs and Ks': Parables of Human Rights in the Prose of Gabriela Mistral," Joseph R. Slaughter lauds her defense of human rights for working women, Jews, South American Indians, and children displaced by the Spanish Civil War. Her writing was an "appeal to world conscience."

In 1941 in *Commonweal*, Clarence Finlayson gave an overview of Mistral's writing for English-speaking readers who had probably not heard of her, emphasizing her moral leadership during wartime in her defense of Christian values against totalitarianism. Sidonia Carmen Rosenbaum in *Modern Women Poets of Spanish America* (1945) outlines Mistral's growing fame as an important moral influence in Latin America. This is the same year she became the first Latin American to win the Nobel Prize for Literature.

After Mistral's death in 1957 there was a tendency, especially in South America, to see her as a mystic or saint, as summarized by Sister Rose Aquin Caimano in *Mysticism in Gabriela Mistral* (1969). After comparing Mistral's poetry to that of the great Spanish mystics, Caimano concludes that Mistral "is not a mystic" but rather a visionary poet like Emily Dickinson.

Critics in the 1990s and early twenty-first century de-emphasize the religious aspects of Mistral and see her as a courageous feminist leader for human rights. Marie-Lise Gazarian-Gautier, in her article "Teacher from the Valley of Elqui" (1999), explains that Mistral was singled out for the Nobel Prize as a bright humanitarian light after the darkness of World War II. Elizabeth Horan combats the saintly image of Mistral in "Mirror to the Nation: Posthumous Portraits of Gabriela Mistral" by showing that her image, now on Chilean stamps and money, is used by the state to convey its own messages, "an empty signifier, available for a variety of national projects." Though Mistral herself was not a feminist, Rhina P. Espaillat, in a review for *First Things,* takes a feminist look at a new translation of the "Locas Mujeres," or "Madwomen," poems by Randall Couch, pointing out Mistral's use of masking and ambiguous words to convey more than women could openly say in her time.

CRITICISM

Susan Andersen

Andersen is a writer and teacher with a PhD in literature. In the following essay, she surveys the diverse views on Mistral's poetry and applies these concepts to "Serene Words."

Looking over the place of "Serene Words" in Mistral's body of work, and in the criticism of her poetry for the last fifty years, one is struck by the widely divergent views of Mistral. Before the Nobel Prize in 1945, she was categorized as a tragic love poet, or sometimes dismissed as a children's author because of the many stories

WHAT DO I READ NEXT?

- Mistral was a Catholic who claimed Jewish heritage. *Two Suns in the Sky* (2001), by Miriam Bat-Ami, puts Jews and Catholics together in a young-adult love story involving two fifteen-year-olds: Christine Cook, a Catholic American, and Adam Bornstein, a Jewish Holocaust survivor from Yugoslavia, who fall in love at a refugee shelter in New York.

- Gabriel García Márquez's *Love in the Time of Cholera* (1988) is a love story that is set between the late 1870s and early 1930s in Colombia and illuminates South American culture as it transitions to a modern age; this time period is that of Mistral's generation.

- Pablo Neruda's *One Hundred Love Sonnets* (1959) are earthy love poems to his wife, Matilde Urrutia, with whom he was very happy. They contrast with Mistral's tortured grief over her unrequited love. Mistral thought Neruda the best Chilean poet. The poems are available in a 2007 bilingual edition.

- *Gitanjali* (1910), by Rabindranath Tagore, is a Bengali masterpiece of devotional poems that won the author the Nobel Prize in Literature in 1913. Tagore was a major influence on Gabriela Mistral.

- With photos of people and places, *Cultures of the World: Chile* (2002), by Jane Kohen Winter and Susan Roraff, is an introduction to the culture of Chile including information on races, history, geography, lifestyle, and economy.

- *Madwomen: The "Locas Mujeres" Poems of Gabriela Mistral; A Bilingual Translation* (2009), edited and translated by Randall Couch, includes twenty-six poems of women's experiences, including experiences with war and violence. Some poems in the collection had not previously been published.

MISTRAL'S WORK IS FULL OF THE CONTRADICTIONS OF THE LIFE SHE LED, WRITTEN IN A VOICE PASSIONATE WITH GRIEF OR EXALTATION."

and poems she wrote for children. After her death, she was regarded as something of a saint. Contemporary criticism looks at the political and gender implications, finding a human rights advocate or a woman with lesbian leanings. Some critics praise her for speaking directly without cover, and some insist she speaks through masks. How can a reader approach her with an understanding of her achievement? Mistral's work is full of the contradictions of the life she led, written in a voice passionate with grief or exaltation. Such extremes in thematic material and in her richly nuanced language necessarily give rise to multiple interpretations.

In *Gabriela Mistral: The Poet and Her Work*, Margot Arce de Vazquez asserts that the publication of *Desolacíon* "is one of the important events in the modern history of Hispanic-American poetry" for its "new voice" of "passion, strength, the strange mixture of tenderness and harshness, of delicacy and coarseness." The volume, published in 1922 when she was thirty-three years old, contained her collected work to date. "Serene Words" presents one of Mistral's mystic moods of surrender to the beauty of nature that God has provided for human consolation. This poem does not speak with the same tone as the despairing love poetry that gives *Desolacíon* its name and primary theme.

Behind her lay two failed love affairs and all the grief, jealousy, anger, and feelings of abandonment she experienced, spoken in a naked revelation of human passion. This is the predominant impression the poet left on the public: a woman jilted by men, and by death, unable to become the wife and mother she wanted to be. Arce de Vazquez calls the tragic sections of the book "a strange, tormented landscape" written in words with "the plasticity of clay" for "molding the emotions." The other sections of the book, which praise mothers and are full of parables for children, confirm the idea that Mistral became a teacher and writer as a substitute for her inability to have her own children. Arce de Vazquez says that in the loving poems she wrote about mothers and about ecstasy in nature, Mistral presents "the chaste ardor of a sensuality spiritualized through maternal longing and the religious sense of life" that became her signature.

"Serene Words" represents one answer Mistral found to the desolation of death and the miseries of life. It is a versified version of the "Voto" or wish she placed on the last page of the book, in which she promised to leave off writing of bitterness in the future and instead to write of consolation. To some extent Mistral did just that in her following books, *Ternura* (Tenderness) and *Tala* (Felling). *Lagar* (Wine Press), published in 1954, however, returns to the extreme grief she experienced on the death of her adopted son, Juan Miguel, in such poems as "One Word" and "Mourning." Arce de Vazquez, who knew and lived with Mistral for a time, concludes that the power of her lyricism is in the polarities she presents: "pleasure-pain, maternity-sterility, hope-desolation, life-death."

Because "Serene Words" calls on God's creation as a consoling force, it is important to review Mistral's religion. Though a devout Catholic in her own way, she did not attend Mass. She was in later life a lay member of the Franciscan Order and was influenced by the life of St. Francis and his love of animals. In *Poema de Chile*, she speaks of her mystical relationship with nature as she grew up in the Valley of Elqui in the Andes Mountains, where she communicated with the plants and animals. Margaret Bates, who worked with Mistral on the definitive edition of her poetry, mentions in the introduction to Doris Dana's anthology of Mistral poems that the poet's creed included her experience of a living God in her own heart: "This theme of Divine Immanence is perhaps the most persistent trait of her religious thought." Mistral sees the divine in nature; nature speaks to her as it does to native peoples. Robert Bly, in his important 1980 anthology of poetry for the Sierra Club, *News of the Universe*, includes Gabriela Mistral in "Poems of Twofold Consciousness" that acknowledge nature as having its own presence.

Mistral was denied admission to a normal school for the education of teachers in 1906 because of the pantheism in her poetry; seeing God in nature was against the doctrine of the Catholic Church. Mistral had a dreamy,

contemplative side, which she dated to her childhood communion with the mountain valley. This trait may also have led her to become a Buddhist and to practice Buddhist meditation for a number of years. In later life she returned to the Catholic Church but did not drop her Buddhist beliefs or practice. Mistral was interested in theosophy, which unites aspects of Christianity and Eastern philosophy. In a poem in *Desolacíon* called "My Books," she speaks of the formative influence of the Bible, with its vast panorama and the passionate poetry of the Psalms. Bates asserts that Mistral's tortured language was an attempt to imitate the fire of the Old Testament. In other words, her religion was forged in her heart from many sources. It was not secondhand. Her poems are often born of a spiritual crisis in which she seeks answers from God.

In *Gabriela Mistral's Religious Sensibility*, Martin C. Taylor mentions that the Christ in *Desolacíon* is the tortured Christ on the cross who can share human pain. Bates agrees that for Mistral the suffering portrayed in *Desolacíon* is purifying rather than meaningless. This is perhaps why Mistral implies in "Serene Words" that love can finally redeem human experience. Nothing now can hurt her, she says, after tasting love. Does she mean after tasting human love or divine love? Both were important to her. Both are experienced in the heart.

Fernando Alegría, in "Notes toward a Definition of Gabriela Mistral's Ideology," says that other important influences on her religious beliefs came from the French philosophers Henri Bergson, Pierre Teilhard de Chardin, and Jacques Maritain. Bergson validated the primacy of intuition over reason that is also important in Mistral's work. Teilhard de Chardin spoke of the necessity of spiritual evolution and of an ascent of human consciousness toward God. Though Mistral speaks of personal feelings, she strives to put them into a larger context of faith. Maritain was important in the Christian democratic movement that applied Christian principles to public policy. This idea of active social Christianity, stressing charity, equality, and the common good, was very influential in Latin America and is still important in the politics of Chile. Its compassion and ethics were what brought Mistral back to Christianity.

Far from being a mystic lost in her own world, Mistral was vitally concerned with the people around her. Alegría notes that important social ideas for Mistral included human rights, especially of minorities; social Christianity; antitotalitarianism; pacifism; and pan-Americanism. A poem called "The Mexican Child" celebrates the dark child who came miraculously from the lost Mayans. Mistral claimed Incan blood and also Jewish blood. She created solidarity with Jews during World War II with the poem "The Immigrant Jew." These humanitarian ideals, stressing unity and equality, already apparent in the *Desolacíon* volume of poems in 1922, were especially timely at the end of World War II and led to her winning the Nobel Prize.

Mistral considered the calling of a teacher to be sacred. She gave of herself tirelessly to teach evening classes for workers. In Mexico, she helped to found rural schools for the poor after the revolution. In her prose essays she taught her students and her people to accept all the ethnic groups of Chile with pride and without hatred. Her poems dramatize the life of the people of Chile, especially those close to the earth: the workers, the poor, the Indians, and the farmers. She spoke for those who had no voice, especially women, children, and those marginalized by race, teaching tolerance wherever she went.

Mistral has a mixed reputation as a feminist, however. She dramatizes the abuse of women, as in "Poems of the Saddest Mother" in *Desolacíon*, in which she invokes the mercy of women for the hardships of other women. In her "Crazy Women" portraits in *Lagar*, females are crazed but powerful, feeding the life of the world with their flesh and spirit. Though Mistral advocated education for women, she has often been considered old-fashioned in upholding the traditional female roles of mother and wife advocated by the Catholic Church, a paradox, since she was neither wife nor mother herself.

Elizabeth Marchant states in *Critical Acts: Latin American Women and Cultural Criticism* that Mistral elevates women in her writing but that her later images contradict the motherhood worship in her early poems. Elisa Montesinos, in "Rediscovering Gabriela Mistral," speaks of her sexual ambiguity. Mistral dressed more as a monk than as a woman. She was a large person with a charismatic presence and with such authority that she could represent her nation's government abroad or visit intellectuals and artists in accepted equality. In *A Queer Mother for the Nation: The State and Gabriela Mistral*, Licia Fiol-Matta makes a case for Mistral as a cloaked lesbian.

She sees the motherhood imagery in her poetry as a metaphor for creativity.

Darrell P. Lockhart in his essay "Jewish Issues and Gabriela Mistral" points out that queerness means more than being gay or lesbian; it means anything outside the normal paradigm. Mistral is therefore a "dissident queer, in both sexual and religious terms." Mistral included all sorts of strands in her identity that had not been openly discussed before: she spoke of herself as a mestiza, or person of mixed race, with Indian and Jewish blood. She was from the working class and always lived close to poverty. She had been a bohemian and a spiritual ascetic and had become successful in the artistic and political worlds despite social barriers and persecution. She remained a single woman and a powerful critic of injustice. The characters in her poems, from the poor peasant to the jilted lover, are masks of her own selves, and her poems "challenged the notions of femininity and of patriarchy," says Ivonne Gordon Vailakis in "A Hungry Wolf: The Mask and the Spectacle of Gender in Gabriela Mistral." It was on purpose that Mistral chose the wild and purifying wind of France as her name.

In *Desolacíon* Mistral included her "Decalogue of the Artist," the ten commandments for her art. The artist must bring forth like a mother out of the blood of her own heart, she says, and she must console humans with God's beauty. It is possible that Mistral lived like a nun because of her commitment to her inner spiritual life and to her poetry, which was a sacred duty to her. In "The Flower of Air," Mistral pictures meeting a goddess of poetry in her native mountain valley who commands her to produce invisible flowers, and she must follow this queen of poetry as a servant until she dies. The artist is thus not apart from the divine but a mediator for fellow beings.

Mistral said, "Speech is our second possession, after the soul" (quoted in Dana). She uses her language not to describe but rather, like a native ritual, to bring alive the earth before us. Mistral believed that folk poetry and nursery rhymes were close to the oral poetry that came from the earth. Those are the rhythms she utilizes. Stephen Tapscott, in his introduction to *Twentieth-Century Latin American Poetry: A Bilingual Anthology*, points out that the surrealism of the Latin American vanguardists was not the subconscious associational surrealism of Freudian psychology, but the indigenous surrealism of viewing

Lilies represent the theme of nature in stanza 3. *(© MOSCHEN | Shutterstock.com)*

nature in a sacred manner. That is, Mistral's imagery and rhythms evoke and blend the natural and supernatural together, as in ancient Indian traditions. Margaret Bates concludes that despite her fiery passion, Mistral had a serene core that gave her a balance between the earth and her soul. This is the version of Gabriela Mistral's voice that comes forth in "Serene Words."

Source: Susan Andersen, Critical Essay on "Serene Words," in *Poetry for Students*, Gale, Cengage Learning, 2013.

Maryalice Ryan-Kobler

In the following essay, Ryan-Kobler argues that Mistral's poetry contradicts the accepted, simplified image of Mistral as the saintly mother of Latin America.

The psychoanalyst and feminist Julia Kristeva posits that the speaking subject's unconscious drives persist in the linguistic, psychic and societal orders. These rhythmic drives, or the Semiotic, initially orient the infant towards the body of the mother. When the child passes through the mirror stage and the oedipus complex, this attachment is repressed. Here, the father intervenes, sundering the bond with the mother, but reconciling the child to the estranged mother through the Symbolic medium of language. Kristeva maintains that the maternal Semiotic is not totally repressed after this rupture with the mother, but rather courses the Symbolic order of language in the form of the tone, rhythm, and material properties of language. Other indices of these semiotic drives surface in the text as contradiction, nonsense, disruption, silence and absence. The Semiotic opposes all fixed, transcendental significations of the Symbolic which sustain the bulwarks of patriarchal order and power: God, father, state, order and property. (Kristeva, *Revolution in Poetic Language* 19–106)

Thus, in Kristevan theory, the symbolic and the semiotic are interwoven in language; the dialectic between them determines the discourse as narrative, theory or poetry. A purely semiotic mode of communication, for example, composed of tone, rhythm and sound, is music.

The *power* of the mother in the preverbal order of the Semiotic can not be underestimated.

> NO LONGER CAN MISTRAL BE DISMISSED AS SIMPLY A SAINTLY ICON OF MOTHERHOOD, FOR THE UNDERSIDE OF THAT ICON TEEMS WITH ANGUISH, ALIENATION AND REBELLION."

For that reason, it is repressed or forbidden in the Symbolic. Regression, or reunion with the forbidden maternal produces psychosis, and likewise bars the subject from participating in this order.

Discourses of maternity prevalent in the West (those of religion, science, and certain feminisms) obscure the visceral, primal quality of the semiotic. A pervasive silence surrounds the experience of raw pain as well as the *jouissance* of the semiotic maternal body, undermining its power in society and its affiliation with matrilinearism. Thus, the Symbolic overshadows the Semiotic, preventing it from challenging and undermining the Law of the Father.

Kristeva's icon of the Virgin Mother exemplifies the suppression of the maternal semiotic in the West. (Kristeva, "Stabat Mater" 49–55). The Virgin Mother is the pure vessel, the medium of the Word, or the name of the Father. Emphasis is placed on the Name of the Father who impregnates her, and is displaced from the semiotic body in the maternal processes of pregnancy and birth. This emphasis, according to Kristeva insures paternity and usurps any claims of matrilinear society on the God-child. The Virgin Mother has been domesticated, deprived of her *jouissance*, and as the "mater dolorosa" is only allowed to suffer. The Virgin is the representative of the repressed Semiotic, being only the "silent ear, milk and tears," metaphors of non-speech excluded from the Symbolic (Oliver 51). Unable to contain the semiotic, the Church controls it through the image of the Virgin Mother. By projecting the semiotic onto the symbol of the Virgin, it ceases to be a threat to the paternal order.

Nevertheless, the persistence of the cult of the Virgin affirms matrilinearism and bears witness to those unconscious, primal needs of identification with the mother. Moreover, the whole notion of the feminine is subsumed into the aseptic maternal contained in the icon. Maternity itself is attained in a virginal state. Women identify with the suffering Virgin, the "mater dolorosa," and in this way, dissociated from the semiotic, they remain participants in the realm of the Father without sacrificing their mothers.

Although men fully embrace language because they pass through the oedipal complex that threatens them with castration and forces them to identify with the Father of the Law, women never completely enter language since they identify with their mothers to some degree. For the woman artist this is crucial. The authorial self for the woman writer derives from identifying with their phallic position in the Symbolic. The lure of the maternal semiotic however puts them in danger of returning to that pre-oedipal identification with the mother that results in psychosis. Writing for the woman artist becomes a contest between the symbolic and the semiotic, between the protective phallic shield and the lure of the mother. When not identifying with the Symbolic, they are outside the Law, and according to Kristeva represent "visionaries, dancers who suffer as they speak" (quoted in Oliver, 112).

Longing for the mother and identity with her occurs through childbirth. Thus the process of pregnancy and birth safely renews identity with the mother. Longing for motherhood in the poems we will read, becomes a longing for the lost mother and the semiotic body.

Nearly forty years after her death in 1957, the persona of Gabriela Mistral (1889–1957) as spiritual mother of Latin America overshadows her literary legacy. Critics have cast her as the hieratic mother icon. Indeed, the image of the saintly mother pervades Mistral's work. *Poemas de las madres* (1950) are dedicated to pregnant mothers. *Ternura* (1924) is totally dedicated to children's poems. The poet, speaking of her own intense, if frustrated desire to mother, prays in her prose poem "La oración de la maestra": "Dame el ser más madre que las madres, para poder amar y defender / como ellas lo que no es carne de mi carne" (9–10).

Yet, the image of the mother is an ambiguous one in Mistral's work as I will show in this paper. The poem "Electra en la niebla," discussed at length here, bears witness to the ambiguous mother image in the Mistral opus. I suggest that the reception of the texts of Gabriela

Mistral mimics the drama of the symbolic versus the semiotic dramatized in Kristeva's Virgin Mother, foregrounding the mother icon of the Law and banishing her semiotic counterpart.

A critical conspiracy appears to have existed around Mistral's work that foregrounded the positive and traditional image of the mother, effectively silencing those passages and poems which reveal the conflicted, anguished treatment of the maternal. Mistral complied with critics and accepted her poetic persona. Through a combination of literary artifice and personal diplomacy Mistral inserts herself into the literary order without inviting criticism or ostracism for exposing the raw underside of the maternal in her texts. She manipulates the masks of mother and teacher to both reveal and conceal herself. In several volumes of poems she disappears behind the masks of conformity, encoding her desire in comfortable stereotypes of the feminine. These poems stand as testaments of compliance and repression in the Symbolic. Nevertheless, through the literary artifice of myth and hermeticism, and sometimes alongside the stereotype, the poet crafts her texts to betray an unresolved conflict with the very image of the saintly mother, and ultimately defies the social order she appears to so carefully avoid offending.

Several poems from the poet's opus illustrate my thesis. "La maestra rural," an early poem from *Desolación* (1922) has certainly forged the image of Mistral as exemplary mother-teacher. In "Electra en la niebla," Mistral disguises herself in the folds of the ancient tale of matricide, revealing the writer's anguished relationship to the maternal, and her expulsion from the realm of the Father, undermining her own authorial position. Finally, in her hermetic work "La Fuga" from "Muerte de mi madre" (*Tala*, 1938) Mistral eroticizes the mother and regresses into her embrace.

I propose that beneath the masks of the writer, in the depths of her verses, lie the anguished psyche of the writer and the true complexity of her character. The pious mother and teacher is but a mask that Mistral uses to insert herself into the realm of the Father, the Symbolic. In the drama of her obsession with the mother we see another drama unfold: an unresolved sense of identity that exposes the deconstructive properties of her work. Here, she discloses her ambivalence, her rebellion to the Symbolic order, to the Name of the Father, and

her desire to adhere to, or to return to the semiotic body.

The pious teacher and mother that emerges in the criticism of "La maestra rural" provides a classic example of the way Mistral has been read in the past. The image underscores all that is socially positive in this feminine figure. She is pure and modest, a servant of that God who gives anchor to the patriarchal order:

> La maestra era pura. "Los suaves hortelanos,"
> decía, "de este predio, que es predio de Jesús,
> han de conservar puros los ojos y las manos,
> guardar claros sus óleos, para dar clara luz." (1–4)

Critics have read selectively, privileging positive markers of the feminine stereotype, and dismissing those signs of the anguished woman woven into the description:

> La maestra era alegre. ¡Pobre mujer herida!
> Su sonrisa fue un modo de llorar con bondad.
> Por sobre la sandalia rota y enrojecida,
> era ella la insigne flor de su santidad. (9–12)

The image of the mother-teacher here, is one of anguish, if not rage, as suggested by some critics. (González and Treese 35–38) The mother-teacher is a variant of Kristeva's Virgin Mother, the suffering "mater dolorosa," or the feminine that has survived in the social order, deprived of its raw energy.

In the same poem, Mistral addresses her alienation which she channels into a sense of superiority and a drive for perfection in her station in the rural society. Addressing the mother of one of her students who had unkindly gossiped about her she charges:

> Campesina, ¿recuerdas que alguna vez prendiste
> su nombre a un comentario brutal o baladí?
> Cien veces la miraste, ninguna vez la viste
> ¡y en el solar de tu hijo, de ella hay más que de ti!
> Pasó por él su fina, su delicada esteba,
> abriendo surcos donde alojar perfección
> La albada de virtudes de que lento se nieva
> es suya. Campesina, ¿no le pides perdón? (21–28)

Here, the poetic voice clings to her image as mother-teacher to overcome the pain of rejection or her marginalization by the villager who maligns her. While wearing the mask of virtue, she makes a stunning remark to the campesina, alleging that she, the teacher, is the true mother of the student: "y en el solar de tu hijo, de ella hay más que de ti!" (24). Again, we see the image of the saintly mother, the mask of conformity in dialectical relation to her sense of marginalization and alienation from the social order. The raw energy of the mother, the rage, resides just below the surface, producing an image of a pathetic "mater dolorosa." The dead mother in strophe six, awaiting her daughter from beyond the grave, is an important motif in Mistral's poetry, and describes the longing for the lost mother banished from the order of the Father but surfacing to reclaim what she has lost:

> Daba sombra por una selva su encina hendida
> el día en que la muerte la convidó a partir,
> Pensando en que su madre la esperaba dormida
> a La de Ojos Profundos se dio sin resistir. (29–32)

The writer suggests here that reunion with the mother can only be attained in death. That is, the power of the mother is repressed, yet constantly beckons to the daughter, producing anguish because it must be resisted. Nevertheless, this primal relationship obscures all others, governs all others from beyond the grave, or at least undermines them, leaving the subject alienated from the world around her.

The struggle between the semiotic and the symbolic is less thinly disguised in the poet's later work. The matricidal "Electra en la niebla" dramatizes the poet's ambiguous relationship to the maternal. It demonstrates the constant lure of the forbidden semiotic, thus betraying a troubled alliance with the Father. "Electra en la niebla" recalls the ancient tale of Electra and her brother Orestes who killed Clytemnestra, their mother, to avenge the death of Agamemnon, their father. In the myth, Orestes was driven mad by the Furies as punishment for his unnatural act. For his part, Freud adopted Electra, the woman who kills her mother in order to avenge her father, as the female counterpart of the Oedipal complex, dramatizing in the socialization process the repression of the maternal, or semiotic, in favor of the symbolic.

In rewriting the myth, Mistral privileges Electra's role in her mother's death. Thus, it is Electra who approaches madness as Clytemnestra, her slain mother, surfaces from the semiotic to reclaim her daughter. Symbolically, as Electra abandons herself to the fog-like folds of the mother, she symbolically abandons the fatherland:

> En la niebla marina voy perdida,
> yo, Electra, tanteando mis vestidos
> y el rostro que en horas fue mudado.
> Será tal vez a causa de la niebla
> que así me nombro por reconocerme. (1–5)

The omnipresent fog is the mother surrounding her with her shroud: "La niebla tiene pliegues de sudario / dulce en el palpo, en la boca salobre" (87–88). Yet, this funereal fog also recalls the waters of pre-consciousness, of pre-birth when mother and child are an inseparable dyad.

Electra no longer has a sense of the world about her, the world of the paternal order. The town about her has disappeared, dissolving into the fog:

> Esta niebla salada borra todo
> lo que habla y endulza al pasajero
> rutas, puentes, pueblos, árboles.
> No hay semblante que mire y reconozca
> no más la niebla de mano insistente
> que el rostro nos recorre y los costados. (43–48)

> Ella es quien va pasando y no la niebla
> Era una sola en un solo palacio
> y ahora es niebla-albatrós, niebla-camino
> niebla-mar, niebla-aldea, niebla-barco. (112–115)

Electra identifies with the fog, and thus with the mother as she says: "O yo soy niebla que corre sin verse / o tú niebla que corre sin saberse" (101–102). She knows she must continue to resist her dead mother, or be swallowed up in her embrace and in her revenge: "pero marchar me rinde y necesito / romper la niebla o que me rompa ella" (108–109).

Her relationship to her brother is also a mirror image, suggesting again the regression to the Imaginary stage and transference to a loving Imaginary father (which precedes the stern Father of the Law in the Symbolic). The brother, thus, is the precursor of the Symbolic father, but at this point he simply replaces the mother of the mirror stage. Identity with the male precursor of the Symbolic may well be a vestige of the poetic subject's authorial role in that realm which is now undermined by the surfacing of the semiotic:

> por ser uno lo mismo quisimos
> y cumplimos lo mismo y nos llamamos
> Electra-Orestes, yo, tú Orestes-Electra. (98–100)

In the presence of the fog, of the mother surrounding them, Electra advises her brother that they cannot continue to exist in the realm of the father. The mother's beckoning from beyond the grave is a call to self-immolation:

> Porque ella—tú la oyes—ella llama,
> y siempre va a llamar, y es preferible
> morir los dos sin que nadie nos vea
> de puñal, Orestes, y morir de propia muerte. (80–83)

Union with the mother implies self-destruction, automatic exile from the realm of the Father. In the end, Electra succumbs, alone.

It is significant that her authorial mirror image of the brother disappears. Either mad, or by one mythical account, rescued by Athena to reestablish the patriarchal order, he abandons her. She is left to wander endlessly in the mother, exiled from the fatherland:

> No dejes que yo marche en esta noche
> rumbo al desierto y tanteando en la niebla (70–71)

> Orestes, hermano, te has dormido
> caminando o de nada te acuerdas
> que no respondes. (119–121)

The writer abandons her authorial role in the Symbolic, and is submerged in the maternal semiotic. Thus, we see that Mistral, as Electra, both writes and, at the same time, undermines and rebels against that authorial role.

Finally, the hermetic work "La fuga" from "Muerte de mi Madre" (*Tala*, 1938) laments the death of the mother, and rewrites the myth of Orpheus and Eurydice. Here, a feminine Orpheus descends to the underworld to rescue her mother or mother-substitute ("madre mía"). The writer again abandons the fatherland, this time to wander infernal "paisajes cardenosos," seeking the mother figure. In this journey to recover the mother, participation in the Symbolic is sacrificed for return to the Semiotic:

> Madre mía, en el sueño
> ando por paisajes cardenosos:
> un monte negro que se contornea
> siempre, para alcanzar el otro monte
> y en él que sigue estás tú vagamente,
> pero siempre hay otro monte redondo
> que circundar, para pagar el paso
> al monte de tu gozo y de mi gozo. (1–8)

The anguished voice joyfully anticipates ascending to the mountaintop, a landscape whose physical characteristics are associated with the body of the mother from the child's perspective. The relationship in the semiotic is preverbal, and hence, mother and daughter sense each other's presence; they do not see or speak with each other:

> Vamos los dos sintiéndonos, sabéendonos
> mas no podemos vernos en los ojos
> y no podemos trocarnos palabra. (11–13)

Moreover, the poetic voice eroticizes the mother-daughter union by engaging the myth of Orpheus and Eurydice:

> cual la Eurídice y el Orfeo solos
> las dos cumpliendo un voto o un castigo,
> ambas con pies y con acento rotos. (14–16)

As in the ancient myth, the poetic voice enters the underworld to free Eurydice from death. Here the mother or the mother-lover substitutes for Eurydice. Attempts to return her to life, to the realm of the Father fail.

The conflictive desire of the speaker for the forbidden maternal is demonstrated in the way the speaker carries her mother's remains secretly within her in violation of the Law of the Father. In a futile attempt to reconcile herself with the Father, she presents herself and her mother-lover before the gods, hoping to sanction this forbidden love:

> Pero a veces no vas al lado mío:
> te llevo en mí, en un peso angustioso
> y amoroso a la vez, como pobre hijo
> galeoto a su padre galeoto,
> sin decir el secreto doloroso:
> que yo te llevo hurtada a dioses crueles
> y que vamos a un Dios que es de nosotros. (17–24)

The illicit union with the mother, or mother-substitute is monstrous:

> porque mi cuerpo es uno, el que me diste,
> y tú eres un agua de cien ojos,
> y eres un paisaje de mil brazos,
> nunca mas lo que son los amorosos
> y un pecho vivo sobre un pecho vivo
> nudo de bronce ablandado en sollozo. (31–36)

The mother seeks her with a hundred eyes, and possesses her with a thousand arms, reference to both the unnaturalness of the relationship as well as to its inevitability. It is an impossible love that is condemned to the infernal; outside the realm of the Father, it remains outside the Law.

The poem ends in a hellish vortex of madness as the poetic subject reenters the infernal, womb-like "vórtice rojo" of the mother. Thus she becomes an exile from the realm of the father:

> hasta el momento de la sien ardiendo
> del cascabel de la antigua demencia
> y de la trampa en el vórtice rojo! (50–52)

The poem celebrates the semiotic in a journey through hell. Return to the womb violates all the laws of the Symbolic, of language and society. Return to the mother undermines the very act of writing, and so describes a troubled relation to the Name of the Father. The poem depicts an act of rebellion against the Father, a rejection of a male authorial role and a search for identity with the mother in the Semiotic. Thus the poem becomes a protest against the loss of the mother, and a magnificent attempt to move the Semiotic into the realm of the Father, or simply to bequeath a testament of search for the mother.

In conclusion, the icon of Gabriela Mistral as spiritual mother of Latin America invites us to explore the richness and complexity of a poetry stamped with the image of the maternal but hiding all manner of ambiguity and contradiction within the folds of its verses. Not only is the maternal the earmark of Mistral's poetry, it also is key to her conflicted sense of identity, from her portrayal of herself as the "mater dolorosa" sanctioned by the realm of the Father, to her open rebellion and union with the mother in "Electra en la niebla" and "La fuga." The conflicted and ambiguous relationship toward the maternal demonstrated in these poems gives life and definition to her work. No longer can Mistral be dismissed as simply a saintly icon of motherhood, for the underside of that icon teems with anguish, alienation and rebellion.

Source: Maryalice Ryan-Kobler, "Beyond the Mother Icon: Rereading the Poetry of Gabriela Mistral," in *Revista Hispanica Moderna*, Vol. 50, No. 2, December 1997, pp. 327–34.

SOURCES

Alegría, Fernando, "Notes toward a Definition of Gabriela Mistral's Ideology," in *Women in Hispanic Literature: Icons and Fallen Idols*, edited by Beth Kurti Miller, University of California Press, 1983, p. 219.

Arce de Vazquez, Margot, *Gabriela Mistral: The Poet and Her Work*, New York University Press, 1964, pp. 24, 26–28.

Bates, Margaret, Introduction to *Selected Poems of Gabriela Mistral: A Bilingual Edition*, translated and edited by Doris Dana, Johns Hopkins University Press, pp. xxii, xxiv, xxvi.

Bly, Robert, ed., *News of the Universe: Poems of Twofold Consciousness*, Sierra Club Books, 1980, p. 153.

Caimano, Sister Rose Aquin, *Mysticism in Gabriela Mistral*, Pageant Press International, 1969, pp. 193, 267.

Cohen, Jonathan, "Toward a Common Destiny on the American Continent: The Pan-Americanism of Gabriela Mistral," in *Gabriela Mistral: The Audacious Traveler*, edited by Marjorie Agosín, Ohio University Press, 2003, p. 8.

Daydí-Tolson, Santiago, "Gabriela Mistral," in *Dictionary of Literary Biography*, Volume 331, *Nobel Prize Laureates in Literature*, Bruccoli Clark Layman, Thomson Gale, 2007, pp. 243–56.

Espaillat, Rhina P., Review of *Madwomen: The "Locas Mujeres" Poems of Gabriela Mistral*, translated by Randall Couch, in *First Things: A Monthly Journal of Religion and Public Life*, No. 188, December 2008, p. 48.

Finlayson, Clarence, "Spanish-American Poet: The Life and Ideas of Gabriela Mistral," in *Commonweal*, Vol. 35, No. 7, December 5, 1941, pp. 160–63.

Fiol-Matta, Licia, *A Queer Mother for the Nation: The State and Gabriela Mistral*, University of Minnesota Press, 2002, pp. xiii–xvi, 65.

Franco, Jean, *An Introduction to Spanish-American Literature*, Cambridge University Press, 1969, pp. 3, 16, 28, 39, 119, 123, 162, 256–60.

Gazarian-Gautier, Marie-Lise, "Teacher from the Valley of Elqui: The Legacy of Gabriela Mistral," in *World and I*, Vol. 14, No. 10, October 1999, p. 286.

Horan, Elizabeth, "Mirror to the Nation: Posthumous Portraits of Gabriela Mistral," in *Gabriela Mistral: The Audacious Traveler*, edited by Marjorie Agosín, Ohio University Press, 2003, p. 234.

Lockhart, Darrell B., "Jewish Issues and Gabriela Mistral," in *Gabriela Mistral: The Audacious Traveler*, edited by Marjorie Agosín, Ohio University Press, 2003, p. 98.

Machado, Ana Maria, *Exploration into Latin America*, New Discovery Books, 1995, pp. 9–23, 35–37.

Marchant, Elizabeth A., *Critical Acts: Latin American Women and Cultural Criticism*, University Press of Florida, 1999, pp. 103–106.

Mistral, Gabriela, "Serene Words," in *Selected Poems of Gabriela Mistral: A Bilingual Edition*, translated and edited by Doris Dana, Johns Hopkins University Press, 1971, pp. 5, 121.

———, *Selected Prose and Prose-Poems*, edited by Stephen Tapscott, University of Texas Press, 2002, pp. 163–64.

Montesinos, Elisa, "Rediscovering Gabriela Mistral: A New Trove of the Poet's Papers Promises to Give Researchers Fresh Insights into Latin America's First Recipient of the Nobel Prize in Literature," in *Americas*, Vol. 60, No. 1, January–February 2008, p. 38.

Rosenbaum, Sidonia Carmen, "Gabriela Mistral," in *Modern Women Poets of Spanish America: The Precursors, Delmira Agustini, Gabriela Mistral, Alfonsina Storni, Juana de Ibarbourour*, Hispanic Institute in the United States, 1945, pp. 171–203.

Slaughter, Joseph R., "'A Wor[l]d Full of Xs and Ks': Parables of Human Rights in the Prose of Gabriela Mistral," in *Gabriela Mistral: The Audacious Traveler*, edited by Marjorie Agosín, Ohio University Press, 2003, p. 25.

Tapscott, Stephen, Introduction to *Twentieth-Century Latin American Poetry: A Bilingual Anthology*, edited by Stephen Tapscott, University of Texas Press, 1996, p. 14.

Taylor, Martin C., *Gabriela Mistral's Religious Sensibility*, University of California Press, 1968, pp. 114–17.

Vailakis, Ivonne Gordon, "The Mask and the Spectacle of Gender in Gabriela Mistral," in *Gabriela Mistral: The Audacious Traveler*, edited by Marjorie Agosín, Ohio University Press, 2003, p. 116.

FURTHER READING

Agosín, Marjorie, ed., *Women, Gender and Human Rights: A Global Perspective*, Rutgers University Press, 2001.

Scholars report on conditions and issues for women in various parts of the world—such as the Middle East, South America, and Africa—as well as on general topics such as violence, health, psychology, and public rights. The editor is a Chilean poet, a scholar on Mistral and South American literature, and a social activist who won a United Nations Leadership Award for Human Rights.

Allende, Isabel, *My Invented Country: A Nostalgic Journey through Chile*, translated by Margaret Sayers Peden, HarperCollins, 2003.

The famous novelist and niece of martyred Chilean president Salvador Allende provides a memoir of the land she grew up in, explaining how its magic sparked her literary imagination.

Early, Edwin, *The History Atlas of South America: From the Inca Empire to Today's Rich Diversity*, Macmillan, 1998.

Maps and illustrations show the history of the ancient civilizations in Latin America, the colonial period, the wars of independence, modern growth, the economy, and racial and cultural diversity.

Horan, Elizabeth, and Doris Meyer, eds., *This America of Ours: The Letters of Gabriela Mistral and Victoria Ocampo*, University of Texas Press, 2003.

Translated by the editors, the letters of Gabriela Mistral and Victoria Ocampo, the famous Argentine writer, discuss their impressions of the intellectual and political world scene of the first half of the twentieth century (the Spanish Civil War, World War II, and Latin American politics and writers) in terms of their vision of one united American identity.

Unruh, Vicky, *Latin American Vanguards: The Art of Contentious Encounters*, Latin American Literature and Culture, University of California Press, 1994.

An important study of the vanguard movement of the 1920s and 1930s in South America, this book discusses the writers who influenced Mistral and laid the groundwork for contemporary Latin American writing. They took inspiration from the European avant-garde writers but turned out their own brand of activism through manifestos, performance, and experimental forms.

SUGGESTED SEARCH TERMS

Gabriela Mistral

Desolacíon AND Gabriela Mistral

"Serene Words"

South American Literature

Nobel Prize AND Gabriela Mistral

Chilean poets

history of Chile

South American vanguardists

lyric poetry

human rights AND Gabriela Mistral

Rime 140

FRANCESCO PETRARCH

1374

Francesco Petrarch is one of the most important literary and cultural figures in Western civilization. He is principally responsible for the shift in thought that marks the beginning of the Renaissance as a reaction against the Middle Ages. In his life, he was highly regarded for his classical scholarship and his Latin poetry. Petrarch became the first poet laureate (a title largely of his own invention), beginning a tradition still continued in the appointment of a poet laureate of such countries as the United States. However, today the only works of Petrarch's that are widely read are his poems in Italian, the main subject of which is his love for Laura. In these poems, he created the modern sonnet form, which became a dominant style of verse in English in the works of Shakespeare and many other poets.

The mysterious figure of Laura is a complex mixture of allegory and reality. While she represents poetry and many other abstract concepts to Petrarch, Laura was most likely a real woman whom Petrarch knew only slightly, despite her dominion over his inner life. In Rime (or Sonnet) 140, Petrarch's reason is nearly overcome by desire, but shame before Laura—his ideal vision of Laura—makes love retreat from its attack on his mind.

Petrarch's *Rime sparse* was published after his death in 1374. There have been many Petrarch translations throughout the whole history of

Petrarch *(The Library of Congress)*

English literature, including that by Anthony Mortimer in *Petrarch: Selected Poems* from 1977.

AUTHOR BIOGRAPHY

Petrarch's family belonged to the aristocracy of the city of Florence, but they were exiled by civil strife there. He was born on July 20, 1304, in Arezzo. His given name was Francesco Petrarca, but he is known by convention in English as Petrarch. He trained to be a lawyer, but when his father died in 1326, he abandoned his legal studies and took minor orders in the church.

Cardinal Giovanni Colonna recognized Petrarch's talents and became his patron. He secured a position for him at the papal court in Avignon, which allowed the young scholar to devote all of his time to writing and research. Petrarch worked to recover the lost literature of Roman antiquity, of which many unique examples were to be found languishing unknown in the monasteries of Italy and southern France. He also produced a substantial literature in Latin, which imitated ancient works in style, form, and subject matter. He considered his most important achievement to be the

composition of his epic poem *Africa*, which was based on his own discovery of the historical writings of Livy. Petrarch enjoyed great success throughout his life, and in 1341, he gained the title of poet laureate. Petrarch had a mistress whose identity is entirely lost to history (she was most likely of the lower class and may have been a servant in his household). With her, he had a son and daughter. Petrarch never mentions her in his work. He died on July 19, 1374, in a suburb of Padua, of unknown causes.

In his own estimation, the most momentous event of Petrarch's life happened on April 6, 1327, when he attended Good Friday mass in Avignon and saw his Laura for the first time. She was a young married woman whom Petrarch spent several months or years pestering to have an adulterous affair with him, but without success. Petrarch eventually accepted her rejection and turned his frustration into one of the most significant bodies of poetry in Western civilization, a collection of nearly three hundred sonnets devoted to his love for Laura. The poem under discussion here is the 140th (a draft of which was probably first set down some time between 1327 and 1348) of 366 in Petrarch's anthology of poems written in Italian, which was published after his death by his son-in-law.

Petrarch calls this collection the *Rime sparse* (insubstantial rhymes). The same work is more formally known as the *Canzoniere* (song book), and in the early printed editions of Petrarch's complete works it went by the Latin title *Rerum vulgarium fragmenta* (individual works on various subjects in the vernacular). At some time relatively late in his life, Petrarch collected all of the Italian poems he had written earlier that he wished to keep (there were undoubtedly others that he rejected, which are now lost) and copied them out in a single volume. Thereafter, he added to them from time to time and also edited the earlier items, a process that was not completed at the time of his death. Petrarch himself claimed he considered these works as trifles, because they were not written in Latin, but he nevertheless spent a great deal of time and care on them. Today, they are by far the most widely read of his works.

POEM SUMMARY

The text used for this summary is from *Petrarch: Selected Poems*, translated by Anthony Mortimer, University of Alabama Press, 1977, p. 67.

MEDIA ADAPTATIONS

- The concert pianist and composer Alexander Peskanov wrote a piano piece in 2006 titled *Sonnet 140 of Petrarch: Tribute to Franz Liszt*. It is a tone poem on the meaning of Petrarch's sonnet written in the style of Liszt. It has not yet been professionally recorded, but performances of it can be found on the Internet.

A version of the poem can be found on the following web page: http://www.dorthonion.com/drmcm/english_lit/supplementary/petrarch_mcm.html.

The conceptual framework of the poem is somewhat unclear, partly because the author expects the reader to have read the poem in sequence and partly because of its unusual psychological perspective. The reader should bear in mind that the speaker of the poem is a disembodied self moving freely around the poet's body from his heart to his head and back again, as if it were a separate person moving around a physical place. The speaker is accompanied by personified Love. The female character they both perceive is Laura, whom the poet (including the speaker, his Love, and his body as a unified whole) loves.

Lines 1–4

In the first quatrain (four-line stanza), the speaker of the poem begins as an observer. He reports that Love (i.e., his love for Laura) is living with and ruling over him, keeping his chief residence in the poet's heart, as if he were the king of a country who from time to time toured his dominions but mainly lived in the capital city. However, Love is a warlike ruler who sometimes goes on a military campaign in an attempt to capture the poet's forehead (i.e., his mind), which is not properly part of Love's domain. Love intends to claim this foreign territory as his own, however, by planting his flag there and establishing a military base.

Petrarch is speaking here in a highly allegorical fashion about human psychology. He is talking about reason being overcome by irrational desire when one is in love. Since the romantic period in the early nineteenth century, people in the Western world have thought about love as a benign, tender emotion, but Petrarch here portrays the view of love found in the work of Roman poets like Ovid. For them, love is a kind of insanity that takes over a person like a possessing spirit and is, or can be, cruel, both to the person who suffers the disease of love and to the beloved. The physical aspect of desire is its most prominent characteristic. This is the kind of love that Petrarch describes feeling for Laura in the first part of the poem.

Lines 5–8

In the second quatrain, Laura herself, although she is unnamed, intervenes. She is described as the one who teaches both Petrarch and his personified Love how to love and how to suffer. Teaching is an unexpected idea here. It means that without Laura, Petrarch would not have learned how to love or how to suffer. The suffering comes about from frustration, when Laura does not love him in return. Loving is also an interesting choice of opposite for suffering. Surely it does not mean that he experiences the pleasures of love with Laura; instead he must mean that his experience of desire is at times so intense that he does not notice his suffering.

The desire that Petrarch feels is a flame that burns him and a point that stabs him, so for him, experiencing love is torture. Although Laura is the object of his desire and because it is impossible for his love to be consummated, she inspires Petrarch to rein in Love with reason, shame, and respect. In modern psychological terms, Laura becomes the ego ideal, the part of the mind that checks the irrational impulses of physical desire by mechanisms like repression, which are experienced as feelings of shame. The worshipful attitude toward Laura that Petrarch convinces himself he should feel is the transference of feelings originally held for figures like one's parents, a mechanism that distances Laura emotionally and makes it more difficult for him to desire her as a lover. Laura is not receptive to Petrarch's desire (an experience Petrarch must have had in real life), and he is convincing himself that she rejected him because he did not approach her with the right kind of love.

Lines 9–14

In the sestet (the final six lines of the sonnet), Love is terrified by Laura's rebuff and takes flight—not like the winged boy of mythology, Cupid, but like a defeated general retreating from a battlefield, continuing the military metaphor of the first quatrain. Love abandons his campaign, weeps, and hides in the corner, refusing to come out or face the consequences of his actions. In other words, Love acts like a small, scolded child. This characterization furthers Petrarch's attempt to control his desire by transforming his desire for Laura as a lover into the kind of love felt for one's mother, sister, or friend, something that could be more easily controlled.

In line 12, the speaker finally intrudes himself into the poem. He reveals that he is the slave of Love, referring to the ancient belief that the lover can be enslaved by the love he feels for his beloved. Now that his master Love is defeated, the speaker does not know what else he can do other than loyally stay by Love's side. He does not consider other alternatives, for example, actually using reason to win his freedom from Love, as seems to have been his project earlier in the poem, because then he would no longer feel the pleasure of being in love, however painful it may be. In the final line, he considers that he will die happy because his love is right, that is, according to the accepted traditions of his culture. This seems to suggest that the poet has succeeded in changing his love from something that is adulterous and very much immoral in medieval culture into some kind of maternal or fraternal reverence that he is permitted to feel.

THEMES

Courtly Love

The ideology of courtly love emerged in the twelfth century in the poetry of the troubadours, singers who toured the courts of the nobles of southern France. It is the love of a knight of lower social rank for a lady of higher social rank who is married to another man, usually the knight's lord. When the knight reveals his love to the lady, he is rejected as unworthy but then works to prove himself by excelling in the knightly virtues. Just as the knight is answerable to his lord in the duties of feudal service, in the ethos of courtly love, he must put himself at the service of his lady. The knight's duties to his beloved come close to the Christian requirement to worship God. The literary theme of courtly love spread throughout Europe and is best known in English in Arthurian literature, in the case of Lancelot and Guinevere. To what degree the ideals of courtly love were ever realized in real life is unknowable. However, adultery was commonplace in courtly society because marriages were arranged for political and economic reasons and had nothing to do with the romantic inclinations of the couple. Therefore any ideology that could justify or ennoble adultery would have had some popularity, even if the real situation was quite different.

Petrarch's sonnets present his love for Laura in the character of courtly love and serve as one of the most famous examples of the theme. The standard view of women in the Middle Ages was profoundly misogynistic (showing hatred for or a low opinion of women). According to the Bible, women are debauched temptresses who were responsible for the fall from the garden of Eden. According to Aristotle, they are physically inferior beings who failed to become men because something went wrong in the womb. Although courtly love might seem to idealize women, it is a refinement of misogyny. Because the woman's rejection makes no difference to her lover, her whole autonomy and identity are obliterated. This plays out at several levels in Petrarch's sonnets. The most notable thing is that the reader gains little sense of Laura as a person. Her personality is irrelevant and replaced by what can only be described as idolatry as Petrarch pursues a virtually theological ideal that could not correspond to any actual woman. In Rime 140, for instance, Laura's intervention in the poem takes place entirely in his imagination and may as well be that of an angel. There is no hint in the poem of an actual interaction with a person. This certainly suggests that the ideology of courtly love is an imposition over whatever their real relationship was and not one that Laura would necessarily have recognized.

Modernism

Petrarch is in a unique position as one of the fathers of the Renaissance and hence is a

TOPICS FOR FURTHER STUDY

- There is a long tradition of trying to establish the real-world identity of Petrarch's Laura. In the nineteenth century, the endeavor began to take on a scholarly, rather than a speculative, character, especially with the writings of the Abbe de Sade. Google Books has a rich archive of the articles and scholarly reviews ("Laura de Noves" is a useful search term) in which the matter was debated throughout the nineteenth century, before becoming basically settled in the early twentieth. Read through this literature and write a paper, not about the identity of Laura, but about the evidence gathered, the arguments made, and the scholarly strategies deployed to advance the investigation and how they changed over time.

- Jane Hirschfield translated the works of love poetry by female authors at the medieval Japanese court in her volume *The Ink Dark Moon: Love Poems by Onono Komachi and Izumi Shikibu; Women of the Ancient Court of Japan* (1990). Write a paper comparing these poems with a group of Petrarch's Laura sonnets. Consider how the poems differ because of the poets' genders, as well as because of their cultures. How is adultery viewed in both sets of poems?

- Even before printing, editions of Petrarch's *Rime sparse* were graced with illustrations of Laura, since readers would naturally want to know what this vision of superhuman beauty looked like, even if only in the imagination of the illustrator. A genuine portrait of Laura de Noves still survives, now in the Laurentian Library in Florence. Use the Internet to research the history of Laura illustrations, and if you are artistically inclined, illustrate your own portrait. Present a PowerPoint presentation on the subject to your class.

- Modern adaptations for young adults of medieval literature often tell stories of courtly love. Mary Suttcliff's *Tristan and Iseult* (1971) and T. H. White's *The Once and Future King* (1958) are both examples. What approaches do they take? Do they present information about medieval culture in an instructive way? Are the stories minimized or glossed over? Are details changed to harmonize with modern norms of morality and behavior? Using Petrarch's presentation of courtly love in his sonnets as a baseline, survey these novels and write a paper summarizing and analyzing their techniques.

founder of modernity. He changed the popular conception of his culture's relationship to its past. The humanist tradition he began depended on recovering and imitating classical antiquity. In his work of creation as a poet, however, Petrarch could hardly ignore the medieval present in which he lived. What he achieved was a synthesis of the two worlds, ancient and medieval, to make the modern. He never considered abandoning Christianity for the religion of ancient Rome but incorporated Christianity into his synthesis of ancient culture. One effect of this was introducing the introspective mood of Christianity, represented magnificently in Augustine's *Confessions*, into modern literature. Rime 140 is an outstanding example of this new trend. It is an allegorical exploration of the poet's internal mental process, explaining the conflicting impulses that pain him. There is nothing like this in ancient love poetry. There is nothing like this introspection in, for example, the famous poem *Odi et amo*, by Catullus, in which the poet suffers from feeling two different ways about his lover but is tortured by being unable to understand why.

Petrarch announces in the octave that love has attached itself to his heart. (© Danussa / Shutterstock.com)

STYLE

Sonnet

The sonnet (which means "little song") is a form of poetry that was developed at the brilliant court of the Holy Roman Emperor Frederick II in Sicily during the second quarter of the thirteenth century. It thereafter became popular with Tuscan poets (who effectively spoke a different language from Sicilian) and attained its classic and most influential form with the exiled Florentines Petrarch and his contemporary Dante. Because of the prominence of these poets, the sonnet became a major poetic form throughout Europe, especially in England. The first English sonnets, by Henry Howard and Thomas Wyatt, were translations of Petrarch's (including Rime 140). Sonnets became a standard form of English verse and were written by Sir Philip Sydney, William Shakespeare, Edmund Spenser, John Milton, and John Keats, among others. Even today, the sonnet is a form commonly assigned to poetry students in English. Sonnets are generally described as Petrarchan or Spenserian, depending on their specific form.

A sonnet is composed of fourteen lines of verse divided into an octave, of eight lines (two quatrains), and a sestet, of six lines. Classically, each line has either eleven or twelve syllables, although English sonnets are composed in iambic pentameter, which ideally has ten syllables. (*Meter* is the pattern of stressed and unstressed syllables in poetry, and iambic pentameter has five units of two syllables each: the first unstressed and second stressed.) Rime 140 uses the twelve-syllable alexandrine meter. Rhyme is the property of poetry wherein the endings of different lines share the same stress and sound. For example if the first and third lines of a poem ended in *we* and *thee* and the second and fourth lines ended in *die* and *fly*, those lines would be said to rhyme, and the poem follows the rhyme scheme *abab*. The lines of sonnets rhyme according to a particular scheme; Rime 140's pattern is typical of Petrarch: *abba abba cdc cdc*.

Although sonnets can be written on any topic, thanks to Petrarch the form is most closely associated with courtly love, although the literature of courtly love had been developed up to that time in different poetic forms. Most of the nearly four hundred poems in Petrarch's *Rime sparse* are sonnets describing his devotion to Laura. In Rime 140, the first quatrain describes the attack on the poet's reason by his love for Laura. In the second, these attempts are overwhelmed by her disapproval. The ninth line (beginning of the sestet), as typical in the sonnet, sees the *volta* or swerve, a change of direction in the topic of the poem, to a description of love, wounded by the severity of Laura, sulking back to his heart. The final couplet often makes an ironic or critical comment on the poem; in sonnet 140, this comment is limited to the last line, in which the poet congratulates himself on the quality of his love, regardless of its defeat.

Personification

Personification is a literary device in which something that is not a person is described as if it were a human being. In Rime 140, Petrarch's love for Laura is personified, and his own person is presented as a landscape through which Love moves. Love is a general who camps in the poet's brain, overcoming reason. However, Love's offensive is defeated, and he has to retreat back to the heart. Love is also described as the poet's master, exploiting the common idea of the lover as Love's slave because it impels him to feel and do things he cannot control (e.g., through reason). Note that even though Love is personified, the image that comes to mind from the text would be that of a king or general in glorious military dress, not the naked Cupid of ancient art and literature.

COMPARE
&
CONTRAST

- **1300s:** From what is known of Petrarch's real-life interactions with Laura, after his initial forthright attempts to seduce her are rejected, he brings psychological pressure to bear on her through his unwanted attentions. He relies on courtly hospitality to barge into her house when her husband is away and stare at her until she becomes so nervous she has to ask him to leave. He steals articles of her clothing so that he can talk to her when he returns them (unless even these encounters are entirely Petrarch's fantasy). Petrarch expects his audience to accept these actions as those of an earnest lover.

  Today: Any woman harassed in this way by a man can obtain a court order of protection against him and possibly have him prosecuted for stalking.

- **1300s:** All universities in western Europe are administered by the Catholic Church, and attendance requires taking at least minor orders (a form of ordination short of the full priesthood).

  Today: Many secular universities exist, and education is open to everyone, including women.

- **1300s:** All books have to be copied by hand. Although there is a book trade, it is mostly limited to books used in education. Authors cannot expect to make a living from their works, and indeed their works are usually distributed for free at the expense of the author or his patron. Authorship requires either independent wealth or the support of a patron.

  Today: A large number of authors make a living through their writings from book sales. However, writing and publishing are being rapidly transformed by the Internet and technology.

HISTORICAL CONTEXT

Renaissance Humanism

Petrarch is a crucial figure in the birth of the Renaissance. He helped establish and popularize the idea of the Dark Ages that medieval civilization was fallen and inferior to ancient Roman civilization. This interpretation of history was an innovation based on Petrarch's reading of ancient historians. Ancient thought held that the past began in a golden age, that civilization had been in a continuous decline since then, and that the only way to improve things was to restore the characteristics of the earlier age that had been lost. The historian Theodor Mommsen, in his "An Introduction to Petrarch's Sonnets and Songs," summarizes Petrarch's attitude to history: "He regarded the whole epoch of a thousand years from the fall of the Roman Empire to his own days, as a period of 'darkness.'"

The people of the Middle Ages had not previously viewed their society in this way. For them, antiquity had been the dark age, before the coming of Christ. They believed that history was a triumphal ascent progressing to the return of Christ at the end of time. In the fifth through eighth centuries, western Europe had undergone a catastrophe as a result of internal collapse and invasions by populations from outside the Roman Empire. The population was reduced by half. Cities for the most part ceased to exist. Large towns like Rome or Cologne had only a few thousand people living in ruins. Systems of international trade and education had also collapsed together with the Roman political structure. Probably 90 percent of everything that had been written in Latin before 476 (the political end of the empire) had been lost by 800 (the beginning of the Holy Roman Empire), but a great amount of the most important literature

The relationship has brought pain and suffering, which is evident in the octave. *(© itsmejust | Shutterstock.com)*

remained: poets like Ovid and encyclopedists like the elder Pliny were widely read, and their manuscripts were copied throughout the Middle Ages.

By the year 1300, Western Europe had a larger population and a more prosperous economy than the Roman Empire had ever had, as well as more advanced technology and a more comprehensive education system. Nevertheless, Petrarch succeeded in reframing the perception of history in the way that is still familiar today in popular culture, so that the entire medieval period was viewed as a dark age that could only be ended by restoring classical civilization. For Petrarch, this meant above all what came to be known as humanism (from the distinction in Italian universities of the study of history—human matters—from theology—divine matters). Petrarch worked to discover ancients texts that would show the wisdom of the ancient world.

The first step was to recover an unknown Latin text. This might be a collection of otherwise unknown letters of Cicero that were copied during the ninth century and then shelved away and forgotten in a single monastery, with all other traces of the text lost. The next step was to edit the text to make sure it came as close as possible to what Cicero had actually written. Next, the text would be published by having more copies written out (by hand) and distributed throughout Europe. Finally, the ancient wisdom contained in the text would be used to improve modern life by restoring a little piece of antiquity. Petrarch and his followers over the next two centuries succeeded in recovering a large body of lost Latin literature, including the works of the poet Catullus and the historian Livy and many other of the most important authors.

Petrarch's crowning literary achievement was *Africa*, an epic poem that told the story of the Roman general Scipio's defeat of Hannibal, modeled on Virgil's *Aeneid*. The poem was based on texts of the Roman historian Livy, which Petrarch had recovered and published, and was written in the purest classical style, very different from the Latin of the Middle Ages. The poems in

Petrarch's Italian *Rime sparse* seem at odds with his humanistic program, and for this reason he frequently dismissed them as trifles, but they obviously were of great importance to him because they were written in his native language, and he made certain they would be published after his death. Rime 140 has many superficially classical elements. One source for the conceit of poetry addressed to a mistress is the love poetry of Ovid, while some elements of the psychology of the poem, which was perhaps universal in prescientific times, have good antecedents in Virgil (who himself was copying the Greek poet Homer).

CRITICAL OVERVIEW

Despite the fact that Petrarch is a figure of the first rank in the history of literature, as well as intellectual history and the history of scholarship, surprisingly little has been written about his works in English, probably because so much of the fundamental scholarship in Petrarchan studies has been done in German and Italian. Similarly, translations of Petrarch into English are rarer than one might imagine. Throughout most of the twentieth century, critical analysis of the *Rime sparse* was somewhat limited, addressing only the most obvious meaning that Petrarch places on the surface of the poetry. Morris Bishop, writing in 1963 in *Petrarch and His World*, summarized the Laura poems of the *Rime sparse*:

> It begins with a passionate profane love, seeking its fleshly end. This love, mingling hope and despair, is frustrated by the lady's chastity and is gradually purified by his virtue. The profane love is transformed to the love of the ideal, to the love of God.

Comparatively meaningful analysis has been undertaken in more recent years, for example in Ronald L. Martinez's 2003 article in *Modern Language Notes*, which analyzes the *Rime sparse* in comparison with the Bible. Martinez identifies Petrarch's romantic agony with the suffering of Christ. This is a surprisingly obvious feature of the collection that earlier generations ignored out of a reluctance to discuss theological content. It is possible to view Laura in Rime 140 as a figure of Christian worship overcoming the pagan god Love. Lisa M. Klein, in her 1992 article in *The Work of Dissimilitude*, explains the apparent dichotomy of Laura, who is kind in some sonnets and cruel in others. Klein refers to Rime 140, which reveals that the discrepancy is not in Laura's character, but in Petrarch himself; his response to her is sometimes rational and sometimes irrational.

Rime 140 itself is of particular importance for its relation to English literature, where it was very influential. It was used as source material by the English poet Edmund Spenser and translated twice during the sixteenth century (by Thomas Wyatt and Henry Howard). This kind of reception study is the focus of interest of William J. Kennedy in *Authorizing Petrarch* (1994) and Jonathan V. Crewe in *Trials of Authorship* (1990). For all of the confidence of English literature during the Tudor period, it owed a special debt to Italy and to the sonnet, which became one of the most important English forms.

CRITICISM

Bradley A. Skeen

Skeen is a classicist. In the following essay, he delves into the mystery of Petrarch's Laura, the subject of Rime 140.

The great mystery of Petrarch's poetry and life is the identity of Laura. She is the subject of most of the poems in the *Rime sparse*, but it is unclear from those poems exactly who or what Laura is supposed to be. She is, in the obvious reading of the poems, the woman who animates Petrarch's life and imagination and who inspires in him a desperate love. However, considering Petrarch's identity as a poet, the implications of that love are anything but clear. Usually various possible interpretations of Laura are discussed as alternatives by historians and literary critics, but it seems more likely that Petrarch, as a poet, is purposefully exploiting the many layers of meaning.

Laura is the Italian name of the laurel tree, from the Latin *laurea*. It was as common a given name in medieval Europe as in the English-speaking world today. It is so often chosen for its poetic meaning, and not only because of Petrarch. The laurel was the tree sacred to the god Apollo, who in Greek and Roman myth was responsible for poetic inspiration. Apollo and his followers the Muses were depicted wearing crowns made of laurel twigs. In antiquity, poets honored their divinity by also wearing laurel

WHAT DO I READ NEXT?

- *Petrarch* (1989), in the "Modern Critical Views" series, collects a number of scholarly articles on various aspects of Petrarch's work edited and compiled by the prominent historian of literature Harold Bloom.

- Petrarch's *Africa* was translated from Latin into English in 1977 by Thomas G. Bergin and Alice S. Wilson. This epic poem, which tells the story of the Second Punic War from Roman history, was considered Petrarch's masterpiece by his contemporaries. The work is intended as a successor to Virgil's *Aeneid* and also to illustrate medieval Christian virtues through the famous figures of Roman antiquity.

- One of the largest categories of Petrarch's writings are letters (in Latin), which he collected in three sets: his everyday correspondence, those he wrote in old age, and those written (as literary essays) to ancient Romans. A selection of these were translated by James Harvey Rolfe in 1898 under the title *Petrarch, the First Modern Scholar and Man of Letters.*

- Petrarch's *Trionphi*, his poetic philosophical meditation on Laura (in Italian), was translated into English in 1962 by Ernest Hatch Wilkins under the title *Triumphs.*

- Howard Pyle, in *The Story of Sir Lancelot and His Companions* (originally published in 1907 but still in print), retells some of the Arthurian romances for young-adult readers, including the theme of courtly love as shown by the relationship between Lancelot and Guinevere. Illustrations accompany the stories.

- *The Fashioning of Angels: Partnership as Spiritual Practice*, written by Stephen and Robin Larsen in 2000, present myths and folktales about love from around the world.

during their public readings. To say that a poet is in love with Laura, whatever else it may mean, signifies his devotion to his own art of verse. This is more true of Petrarch than any other poet.

IN THIS SONNET, PETRARCH TRANSFORMS ROMANTIC FAILURE INTO ARTISTIC TRIUMPH."

Petrarch's imperfect knowledge of ancient history led him to the rather strange idea that leading poets such as Virgil and Horace had been rewarded by the Roman state with a laurel crown as a reward for lifetime achievement. The truth is that crowns woven from the leafy twigs of various trees (including the oak and olive as well as the laurel) were worn on both formal and festive occasions by ancient aristocrats, in the same way that white tie and tailcoats are worn today. People who were poets—or aristocrats who fancied themselves to be great poets (which was a much larger category)—would wear laurel crowns on such occasions. It was not a sign of official recognition but simply a sign of their interest in poetry.

Nevertheless, Petrarch, animated by his misunderstanding, lobbied for himself to be crowned a poet with the laurel but, according to his letters, turned down offers to receive such a title from many of the great nobles and rulers of his time. Instead he requested—and was granted—the honor by the town council of the city of Rome, which was a rather modest body concerned with the local government of the city in the absence of its papal ruler in Avignon, but which Petrarch insisted on styling as the Roman senate, as if he were back in the days of the republic. On April 8, 1341, Petrarch received the laurel crown on the Capitoline Hill in Rome, among the ruins of the ancient government offices of the Roman Empire.

Today, many countries around the world (as well as several of the states in the United States) appoint poets laureate in imitation of Petrarch, and recipients of the Nobel Prize, even in the sciences, are called laureates for the same reason. So with this background, there would be every reason to think that the Laura Petrarch loved so dearly was the laurel, symbol of poetry and of his own fame. This might seem to be confirmed by the many puns he makes about his beloved Laura and the laurel in his poems. In fact, even some of Petrarch's closest friends, such as his patron, the Bishop Giacomo Colonna, believed that Laura was nothing other than a symbol of poetry.

A closely related symbolic value of the name Laura comes from the orthography or style of handwriting of the fourteenth century. Modern Italian uses an apostrophe to mark a deleted letter just as English does in words like *don't* or *it's*. Therefore it is easy to distinguish the name Laura from the word *l'aura*, which means the air or the breeze, or even the breath. In Petrarch's poems, however, written out in his own hand in the days before printing was invented, there are neither apostrophes nor capitalizations, so it is impossible to distinguish between the terms, and modern editors have to decide from contexts fraught with puns and double meanings whether the handwritten *LAURA* means *Laura* or *l'aura*. Most agree that the name Laura occurs only four times in the *Rime sparse* compared to hundreds of uses of *l'aura*, but much of the time *l'aura* is a pun on Laura, treating Laura as the source of the poet's inspiration, as if it was *l'aura* or the breath of inspiration breathed into the poet by the Muses. In many instances where *l'aura* is the breath animating the poet's very body, it is especially clear that the breath that sustains him is indistinguishable from his beloved Laura, who again in this case seems to be a symbol for his poetry.

In the sonnets of the *Rime sparse*, Petrarch very clearly presents Laura as a real woman whom he loved without genuinely knowing, whom he met in his youth, and who died in Petrarch's middle age. The Laura sonnets are assigned by modern scholars to two groups, those written during Laura's lifetime and those written after her death. This is based on subject matter, however, and not the time of composition. When any individual poem in the *Rime sparse* was actually written is far from clear, and Petrarch revised and redrafted them right up until the time of his death; but Petrarch says something more about Laura as a real woman in odd places in his writings. Petrarch's personal copy of the ancient Roman epic *Aeneid* of Virgil survives and, because it was the most important book to him, he wrote several personal notes in it, in the way some people do in Bibles today. In one of these notes, he briefly describes his first encounter with Laura and her death (translated by Theodor Mommsen in "An Introduction to Petrarch's Sonnets and Songs"):

> Laura, illustrious by her own virtues and long celebrated in my poems, first appeared to my eyes in the earliest period of my manhood, on the sixth day of April, anno Domini 1327, in the Church of St. Claire, at the morning hour. And in the same city at the same hour of the same day in the same month of April, but in the year 1348, that light was withdrawn from our day.

This reference has allowed historians to infer that Laura was Laura de Noves, who died, almost certainly of the bubonic plague that was devastating Avignon at the time, on the day that Petrarch describes as his Laura's date of death. Two years before Petrarch first saw her, she became the wife of the Count Hugues de Sade (making her the ancestor of the infamous eighteenth-century novelist the Marquis de Sade). Six years younger than Petrarch, she seems to have had an untroubled marriage, and she bore eleven children. Petrarch says something about his actual relationship with Laura, as tenuous as it was, in his *Secretum*, a memoir he composed between about 1342 and 1350, written in the form of a confession to the ancient church father St. Augustine. Petrarch confesses that in regard to Laura (again translated by Mommsen): "Occasionally I wished something dishonourable." At one time, also according to the *Secretum*, he must have made advances to her, despite her marriage, but she was

> not moved by any entreaties nor conquered by any flatteries, she protected her womanly honour and remained impregnable and firm in spite of her youth and mine and in spite of many and various things which ought to have bowed the spirit of even the most adamant.

After Laura rebuffed him, Petrarch remodeled his feelings for her on the tradition of courtly love, which was then a dominant theme in Italian and French vernacular literature. Petrarch's unrealized love for the flesh-and-blood Laura became a force active within him as the inspiration of his poetry. It was this Laura living in his heart that he also describes in the *Secretum* as one who

> does not know earthly cares but burns with heavenly desires. Her appearance truly radiates beams of divine beauty.... Neither her voice nor the force of her eyes nor her gait are those of an ordinary human being.

This Laura was not human at all but rather a divine Muse who was indeed the laurel of the poet's crown. However, Petrarch could not separate the Laura in his imagination from the real woman. In this way, Petrarch's Laura closely recalls the Beatrice of Dante, a Florentine poet who was a friend of Petrarch's father and the

In the final lines of the sonnet, Petrarch announces that love will endure until death. (© Kratka Photography / Shutterstock.com)

author of *The Divine Comedy*, in which the poet searches through the entire cosmos for his dead beloved. Beatrice was for Dante a woman he knew only from afar but who became the very goddess of inspiration in his imagination and verse. Petrarch, however, claimed never to have read Dante, for fear of being influenced, but he could hardly have escaped some familiarity with the most famous poet in Italy during his youth. In any case, Laura also becomes the object of Petrarch's cosmic quest through death and eternity in the *Trionphi*, his other book of Italian verse.

If Petrarch wrote any poetry at the time of his attempt to consummate an actual relationship with Laura, he destroyed it. However, another passage in the *Secretum* gives some information about how he later interpreted that episode. The flesh-and-blood Laura refused to yield to his advances, and the experience brought him back to his senses and to Christian virtue: "The model of her excellence stood before me so that in my own strife for chastity I lacked neither

her example nor her reproach." This is his retrospective view of the matter; at the time one may suppose he let go of shameless desire and then disappointment, over which he later pasted this more philosophical face. In time, he used his rejection to transform his feelings for Laura into a kind of idol worship. He rationalized that it was better to worship her from afar than to have an affair with her once it became clear that that was the way things were going to be.

Laura does not appear by name in Rime 140, but she is the female presence who is the object of Petrarch's love. Some echo of his original love for her as a real woman must be heard in the sonnet. Although she is the obsessive interest of the divine power of Love that takes possession of Petrarch and impels him to metaphorically attack Laura as if he were a general besieging a city, she shames Petrarch for his excessive ardor. Following her example, the poet is able to recover his self-possession and control his passion through reason. This is the same reinterpretation of experience that he describes in the *Secretum*, but put into poetic form. In this sonnet, Petrarch transforms romantic failure into artistic triumph.

Source: Bradley A. Skeen, Critical Essay on Rime 140, in *Poetry for Students*, Gale, Cengage Learning, 2013.

Henry Dwight Sedgwick

In the following excerpt, Sedgwick examines Petrarch's poetry in the context of the importance of his life and history.

. . . Petrarch's renown is so enduring because he is the first master of letters in Europe since the death of Cicero. He was by no means the first modern master of art, even if we pass by Gothic and Moorish art; for in painting, Giotto, in sculpture, Niccola Pisano, in architecture, Arnolfo del Cambio, were a generation ahead of him; in poetry, Dante, born nearly forty years before, was immeasurably greater than he, but Petrarch was the first to make letters as letters the work of his life, and the first to hold the faith that literature is as great a factor in civilization as politics or theology. He was a professional man of letters, and became the first of the great tyrants of European literature; he is more important than his successors—Erasmus, Voltaire, Goethe,—in that he stands at the threshold of modern literature, while it was hesitating which way to turn, while Latin still was the only known classic literature, and national literatures had not yet got out of their leading strings. In contemporary literature what was there? In France, Froissart was a baby; in England, Langland a little boy, Chaucer not born; in Germany and in Spain, only an encyclopadia knows. The *Roman de la Rose*, setting Dante aside, is the one remembered work of letters that existed when Petrarch wrote his sonnets. For the third time in history Italy was about to take her place at the head of Europe, and Petrarch, representing her intellectual life, set his seal on unformed literatures, and stamped an ideal impression.

Poetry is the attempt by man to carry on the divine labor of creation, and make this world more habitable; poets take mere words, and fashion a habitation, whither, when the world of sense grows chill, we may betake ourselves and breathe a richer atmosphere. In another aspect poetry is merely the arrangement of words in a certain order; it is a matter of empirical psychology. Poets are practical psychologists, measuring sensations by measures finer than men yet use in laboratories; and in mastery

> **FROM THIS CENTRAL DOGMA OF THE IDEALISTIC FAITH PROCEED THE DERIVATIVE DOGMAS, THAT ALL LIFE, ALL THINGS GREAT AND LITTLE, ARE NOBLE AND BEAUTIFUL."**

of the fuller knowledge of this psychology Petrarch is perhaps unrivaled. Hundreds of thousands of men have loved as dearly as he; thousands have thought greater thoughts than he, and many poets, English poets at least, have had a nobler instrument; but he had the skill to put his words into the right order, and when we read them we forget everything except love.

The charm of his verses made him famous from the very beginning. Well it might, for his sonnet differs from other sonnets as the song of the bird differs from that of a singing master; the soft Italian syllables unburden all their rapture in the fourteen lines, then close their lips, for they have finished. Italian words are made to be strung in a sonnet. Italian verses rhyme, as if they were lovers—Hero and Leander—calling across the gap between line and line; they melt away in sensuous vowels, they echo melodious in *l's* and *m's* and *r's*.

Perhaps the least objectionable way to deliver a lecture on the Petrarchan sonnet will be to show by example how impossible it is to transport this union of sound and sense across the fatal gap between the *lingua di si* and the *tongue of yes*. I choose the best translation I can readily lay hands upon, out of an attractive little book entitled *Sonnets of Petrarch*, translated by Thomas Wentworth Higginson, which has Italian sounds on pages to the left and English to the right.

> Qual donna attende a gloriosa fama
> Di senno, di valor, di cortesia,
> Miri fiso negli occhi a quella mia
> Nemica, che mia donna il mondo chiama.
> Come s'acquista onor, come Dio s'ama,
> Com' è giunta onestà con leggiadria,
> Ivi s'impara; e qual è dritta via
> Di gir al Ciel, che lei aspetta e brama.
>
> Doth any maiden seek the glorious fame
> Of chastity, of strength, of courtesy?
> Gaze in the eyes of that sweet enemy

Whom all the world doth as my lady name!
How honor grows, and pure devotion's flame,
How truth is joined with graceful dignity,
There thou mayst learn, and what the path may be,
To that high heaven which doth her spirit claim.

To begin the lecture with the first line of the sonnet, in the Italian married women are not excluded from gazing at Madonna Laura, nor, in the second line, does *senno* shrink to *chastity*, nor *valor* to *strength*, even if the *cortesia* of the Italians can be frozen into the *courtesy* of us Americans. The fourth line, *Whom all the world doth as my lady name!* sounds a little like the language of hard-put sonneteers, whereas *che mia donna il mondo chiama* would be said with a bow, hand on heart, from the foot of the Alps to the Strait of Messina. *Come Dio s' ama* and *pure devotion's flame* mark the difference between a religion and our American Sunday-go-to-meeting-isms. *Com'è giunta onestà con leggiadria*—most delightful of meetings! *Onestà*, shy dignity of maidenhood, sweet innocence of motherhood, such as looks out from Raphael's Madonnas; *leggiadria*, the gay, girlish motion of comely youth, the grace of the leaping fawn, the sentiment in Botticelli; how did these most charming of feminine graces meet? At what Golden Gate? Are they corporeal or angelic? How, how and where? "How truth is joined with graceful dignity" is the proper junction of two respectable dames,—a sight that arouses very moderate exhilaration. In the last line of the octave, the Italian heaven, in a heavenly way, waits for Laura, *aspetta e brama*; the English heaven, instinct with Common Law, serving, as it were, a writ from the King's Bench, *claims* her.

We are forced to the conclusion that sense and sound are fatally imprisoned in the Petrarchan sonnet, and must stay there forever; they are stored where time doth not corrupt them, neither can translators break in and steal. But from the days of Wyatt and Surrey to those of Colonel Higginson, men who love poetry have felt ever renewing temptations to translate Petrarch, and to carry home the moonbeams that lie so lovely on water.

The union of sound and sense is very nearly perfect in Petrarch,—he used to test and try and substitute until all the words fell into their true order,—and as this perfection was not of a kind to require special knowledge in order to be enjoyed, his poetry, accredited and sustained by his great reputation as a scholar, quickly passed from mouth to mouth, and so set its seal on the nascent literature of Europe.

His poetry asserted this dogma, that in the only real world, the world of ideas, woman and the love of woman are noble and beautiful. From this central dogma of the idealistic faith proceed the derivative dogmas, that all life, all things great and little, are noble and beautiful. This is the mission of poetry,—to see life as a divine work, to be the priestess of a perpetual revelation, in all things to behold the beauty of God. This is the continuation by man of the divine work of creation, for the Lord rested after six days of labor, before His work was complete, and entrusted the fulfillment of the everlasting task to poets. Petrarch has done his duty. What is Laura? Her corporeal existence has become a myth, but she is a thing of beauty and a joy forever, because Petrarch saw her with the eyes of love and faith. This idealism uplifted all modern literature and constitutes Petrarch's greatness, and not that scholastic excellence by which, according to Mr. John Addington Symonds, he "foresaw a whole new phase of European culture,"—melancholy prospect. The Petrarchan view is set forth in the familiar sonnet of Michelangelo, which says that within the shapeless marble lies beauty imprisoned. So it is with all things: within our rude, rough, shapeless, unpolished selves lies imprisoned something that awaits the liberating eye and hand of faith and love....

Source: Henry Dwight Sedgwick, "Francis Petrarch, 1304–1904," in *Atlantic Monthly*, Vol. 94, No. 61, July 1904, pp. 60–69.

SOURCES

Bishop, Morris, *Petrarch and His World*, Indiana University Press, 1963, pp. 71–83.

Burkhardt, Jacob, *The Civilization of the Renaissance in Italy*, translated by S. G. C. Middlemore, Harper Colophon, 1958, pp. 211–17, 279–352.

Catullus, Gaius Valerius, *Carmina*, translated by Sir Richard Francis Burton, R. F. Burton and L. C. Smithers, 1894, p. 262.

Crewe, Jonathan V., *Trials of Authorship: Anterior Forms and Poetic Reconstruction from Wyatt to Shakespeare*, University of California Press, 1990, pp. 57–59.

Hainsworth, Peter, *Petrarch the Poet: An Introduction to the "Rerum Vulgarium Fragmenta,"* Routledge, 1988, pp. 135–53.

Kennedy, William J., *Authorizing Petrarch*, Cornell University Press, 1994, pp. 5–11.

Klein, Lisa M., "The Petrarchanism of Sir Thomas Wyatt Reconsidered," in *The Work of Dissimilitude: Essays from the Sixth Citadel Conference on Medieval and Renaissance Literature*, edited by David G. Allen and Robert A. White, University of Delaware Press, 1992, pp. 131–47.

Lewis, C. S., *The Allegory of Love: A Study in Medieval Tradition*, Oxford University Press, 1959, pp. 1–43.

Martinez, Ronald L., "Mourning Laura in the 'Canzoniere': Lessons from Lamentations," in *Modern Language Notes*, Vol. 118, No. 1, 2003, pp. 1–45.

Mommsen, Theodor E., "An Introduction to Petrarch's Sonnets and Songs," in *Medieval and Renaissance Studies*, Cornell University Press, 1959, pp. 73–100.

———, "Petrarch's Conception of the 'Dark Ages,'" in *Medieval and Renaissance Studies*, Cornell University Press, 1959, pp. 106–29.

Paterson, Linda, "Women, Property, and the Rise of Courtly Love," in *The Court Reconvenes: Courtly Literature across the Disciplines*, edited by Barbara K. Altmann and Carleton W. Carroll, D. S. Brewer, 2003, pp. 41–55.

Petrarch, "CXL," in *Petrarch: Selected Poems*, translated by Anthony Mortimer, University of Alabama Press, 1977, pp. 66–67.

Rougemont, Denis de, *Love in the Western World*, translated by Montgomery Belgion, Albert Saifer, 1940, pp. 71–78.

FURTHER READING

Cosenza, Mario Emilio, *Francesca Petrarca and the Revolution of Cola di Rienzo*, University of Chicago Press, 1913.

> Rienzo led a popular uprising against the pope as absentee ruler of Rome and the local nobility that acted as his surrogates. Rienzo was able at first to control the Roman mob through his rhetorical skill and his promises to redress their grievances. For a time in the 1340s, he became the virtual dictator of the city, but he was eventually driven out by the powerful Colonna family. Rienzo appealed for justice to Emperor Charles IV but was arrested and surrendered to the pope in Avignon, where he spent many years in prison—until 1353, when the new pope, Innocent VI, released Rienzo and sent him back to Rome because the Colonna were now opposing papal authority.

> However, this time, the mob lynched Rienzo. Cosenza's book gives an account of Petrarch's friendship with and support of Rienzo, whom he imagined was going to restore the Roman Republic and unify Italy, if not the whole of western Europe. Several letters Petrarch wrote to Rienzo survive, as does the ode *Spirito gentil*, which praises the revolutionary. Rienzo became a popular figure in the romantic era, as reflected in, for example, Richard Wagner's 1842 opera *Rienzi, Last of the Tribunes* (Rienzo was his name in the Roman dialect, Rienzi in literary Italian).

Kirkham, Victoria, and Armando Maggi, eds., *Petrarch: A Critical Guide to the Complete Works*, University of Chicago Press, 2009.

> This survey, covering all of Petrarch's Latin and Italian works, deals with the history of scholarship on each book to a greater degree than the works themselves.

Petrarcha, Francesco, *Invectives*, edited and translated by David Marsh, I Tatti Renaissance Library 11, Harvard University Press, 2003.

> These essays by Petrarch are exercises in vitriolic denunciation (severe criticism) in the style of the Roman philosopher and statesman Cicero. In these essays, Petrarch attacks his own ignorance, quacks, rulers without virtue, and the enemies of Italy.

———, *The Secret*, translated by Carol E. Quillen, St. Martin's, 2003.

> This is a modern translation of Petrarch's posthumously published memoir, in which he gives the most detailed discussion about the role of the real Laura in his life.

SUGGESTED SEARCH TERMS

Petrarch

Rime 140

Petrarchan sonnet

Laura de Noves AND Petrarch

Cupid

Renaissance

humanism

courtly love

allegory

Tell all the Truth but tell it slant

EMILY DICKINSON

1945

Little known outside of her circle of admiring acquaintances during her lifetime, the nineteenth-century American poet Emily Dickinson is now recognized as one of history's great literary geniuses, one whose writings stand outside her immediate era in evoking timeless principles of life and human nature. "Tell all the Truth but tell it slant" is a poem that represents the transcendental side of her experience and verse. At the same time, it is frequently cited as an apt formulation of her poetic philosophy, divulging her favored strategy of approaching truth in indirect ways and hinting at her reasons for doing so. The poem follows a metrical pattern that Dickinson commonly used, alternating between lines with four and lines with three stressed beats. While her poems are often sporadic in their adherence to meter, rhyme, and grammatical consistency, leaving the reader obliged to figure out the underlying meanings of disruptions, this poem offers a smooth and clear read. But this is not to say that there is no mystery behind it. Believed to have been written in 1872, the poem was first published in the collection *Bolts of Melody: New Poems of Emily Dickinson*, edited by Mabel Loomis Todd and Millicent Todd Bingham, in 1945. In the numbering offered in Dickinson's *Complete Poems* (1955), edited by Thomas H. Johnson, which has been followed by a majority of critics (and will be used here), "Tell all the Truth but tell it slant" is poem no. 1129. (In the revised canon of her work offered in *The Poems of*

Emily Dickinson (The Library of Congres)

Emily Dickinson: Variorum Edition [1998], by R. W. Franklin, who had better access to Dickinson's original manuscripts and correspondence, the poem is no. 1263.)

AUTHOR BIOGRAPHY

Dickinson was born on December 10, 1830, in Amherst, Massachusetts, where she would live almost her entire life. The family was well established in the area, as her grandfather had a law practice that her father and brother would both join. Her father, Edward Dickinson, would also prove a successful Whig politician, serving twice in the state legislature and for one term as a representative of Massachusetts in the US Congress, from 1852 to 1855. Dickinson was named after her mother, whose maiden name was Norcross. There was a five-year span between Dickinson's older brother, Austin, and her younger sister, Lavinia.

Dickinson attended the town's one-room elementary schoolhouse before proceeding to Amherst Academy, where the general emphasis was on natural sciences. The academy was progressive with regard to offering gender-blind education, and its association with Amherst College allowed students access to advanced studies. Dickinson took to botany, but she did not care for teachers' reduction of the natural world to mere identification and classification. Meanwhile, she gained an appreciation for poetry through the school's principal, Leonard Humphrey. In 1847, Dickinson entered Mount Holyoke Female Seminary, a religious school that classified its students as either observant Christians, those with hope to be such Christians, or those without hope. When Mary Lyon, the school head, once asked all those in Dickinson's class who wished to live as Christians to rise, the future poet was the only one not to stand. She remained in the seminary for just a year, at which point her formal schooling was finished.

Dickinson returned to her father's house in Amherst and was then expected to participate in domestic duties, which she found uninspiring. These duties included receiving and paying social visits, a frequent expectation owing to her father's political prominence. But Dickinson eventually opted out of these visits, preferring instead tasks like gardening and baking bread. She became very fond of a copy of Ralph Waldo Emerson's *Poems* (1847) that she received in 1850. She did travel to Washington, D.C., and Philadelphia in 1855, but otherwise, her life was essentially contained within Amherst. Dickinson began to demonstrate her unique literary sensibility in letters, such as those to her brother, Austin, in the early 1850s. When he returned from Harvard Law School to Amherst and got married, his wife, Susan Gilbert, became one of Dickinson's closest confidantes.

And it was through her confidantes that, during her lifetime, Dickinson's verse became known. She often included poems in letters and asked about their effects, and as she gained confidence, she came to correspond with literary personae such as the *Springfield Republican* editors Samuel Bowles and Josiah Holland. During her lifetime, seven of her poems were anonymously published in that periodical. On paper, Dickinson's relationships with correspondents were very open—she often declared her love for women and men alike—but little is known about her actual romantic interests. She is widely believed to have at least fallen in love, given the insight with which some of her poems address the subject, and a few surviving letters to an unattainable (and anonymous) "Master"—written perhaps to Bowles or the Reverend Charles Wadsworth of Philadelphia, both of whom were married—have spurred much speculation about the recipient's role in her life. Regardless, Dickinson remained solitary almost until her death, dedicating her life to her verse. Sometimes, she declined to receive guests face to face, instead conversing with them from out of sight outside the room. In her spare time, she stitched together favored poems into bound fascicles, but otherwise, she was content to remain unpublished. Nonetheless, the tone of her letters and poems make clear her expectation that her verse would ultimately find a wide audience. The deaths in the 1880s of many people close to Dickinson—including her mother, Charles Wadsworth, her nephew Gilbert, and Judge Otis Lord, her late romantic interest—took a great toll on her. Afflicted by prolonged illness, founded in grief and perhaps hypertension, from 1884 onward, Dickinson died on May 15, 1886. Her surviving friends and family members dutifully saw to the publication of her better poems, and in time, a prolific array of some 1,789 poems would surface.

POEM TEXT

Tell all the Truth but tell it slant—
Success in Circuit lies
Too bright for our infirm Delight
The Truth's superb surprise
As Lightning to the Children eased   5
With explanation kind
The Truth must dazzle gradually
Or every man be blind—

POEM SUMMARY

The text used for this summary is from *Final Harvest: Emily Dickinson's Poems*, Little, Brown, 1964, pp. 248–49. Versions of the poem can be found on the following web pages: http://www.poemhunter.com/poem/tell-all-the-truth/ and http://www.americanpoems.com/poets/emilydickinson/1129.shtml.

"Tell all the Truth but tell it slant," at only eight lines long, is one of Dickinson's shorter

MEDIA ADAPTATIONS

- Among the many audiobooks of Dickinson's poems, *Essential Dickinson*, a CD produced by Caedmon in 2006, read by Julie Harris—who won a Tony Award for portraying Dickinson in *The Belle of Amherst*—includes "Tell all the Truth but tell it slant."

poems and is also less difficult to grasp conceptually than many others. Untitled, like all of her poems, it is referred to by its first line. The opening words, beginning with a subjectless verb, suggest that the reader is being directly addressed. However, the word "you" never appears, as if Dickinson has no particular audience in mind; she is writing not to a person or persons but to a void, or to posterity, and if anyone should happen to read her words, then so be it. Her verse often leaves circumstances or externalities uncertain, and such is the case with this poem. In fact, the poem has no real setting, as it is not a narrative poem but only notions and images; it can be classed as one of her aphoristic poems, consisting of an elaboration of an adage or broader principle.

The first four words are an absolute directive, suggesting that not just some truth but all truth—or perhaps all aspects of a certain truth—should be told. An equivalent idiom used in modern times would be "Honesty is the best policy." But the second half of the line notes that simply telling the truth is inadequate; the truth should be told slantwise, or from an angle, as if straightforward truth is problematic for some reason. The second line supports the end of the first line, assuring now that one will succeed—that is, in effectively communicating the truth—in taking a circuitous, or circular or indirect, approach. The poet has rearranged the syntax of the second line, placing at the very end the verb that would naturally fall after the first word. But this arrangement also allows for the possibility that the third word be read as an adjective, the fourth word as a noun, with *lies* now meaning "falsehoods." This possible reading does not seem to suggest itself as the primary one, but it nonetheless expands the sense of the line to refer to both an indirect approach to truth and an approach to truth through deception. In other words, the strictness of the sense of the word *truth* is partly thrown into question.

The third line characterizes something as producing excessive light, too much to be enjoyed or appreciated by a first-person-plural group in which the poet includes herself. The wording suggests that the poet and others among the implied *we* simply have too weak a capacity for joyful appreciation to take in the brightness in question; this could signal a divide between humanity and the divine. Although the reader might try to connect the brightness with something in the preceding line (since the second line has no end punctuation), the presence of a relevant noun in line 4 makes clear that lines 3 and 4 are grammatically linked. The cadence of the poem also naturally suggests this, as the meter is consistent from couplet to couplet, uniting the two lines within each couplet and creating a natural pause at each couplet's end. What puts off too much light is the truth, or more accurately, the wonderfully surprising nature of the truth. This suggests that not just any truth is being told, but one that is likely to be startling or unexpected when it is at last revealed. Thus, what is likely being posited is some yet-undefined ultimate truth.

Although, once again, no punctuation closes line 4, the reader will readily deduce that line 5 is separate from line 4 and connected with line 6 based on the meter and the grammatical sense. Line 5 introduces the idea of lightning, which ties to the references to brightness and surprise, but the image is cast as metaphorical by the first word in line 5. Together, these two lines state that lightning, being so bright and startling (even prior to the thunder it brings), is easier for children to cope with if they are given some explanation as to how it works. This explanation could be scientific or perhaps mythological; but the suggestion that the explanation is inherently sympathetic or benevolent would seem to rule out one attributing the lightning to an angry or vengeful god.

The metaphor of lines 5–6 ties to the notion that appears in lines 7–8 to conclude the poem. Just as lightning is effectively rendered less fearsome (if not less bright) by an accounting of how

it works (whether that accounting is true or not), the shining truth is made more bearable to the eyes—or perhaps the mind's inner eye—in being revealed in a slow, deliberate fashion. This accords with the indirect or roundabout approach to the truth suggested in lines 1–2. In fact, while the sight of lightning is bright but bearable (unless the strike is extremely close), line 8 asserts that the ultimate truth being referred to is so bright, literally or figuratively, that direct exposure to it could leave anyone and everyone blind.

THEMES

Truth

This poem amounts to the author's most concentrated philosophical consideration of truth, in which the truth is discussed on not a particular but a universal level. Dickinson's body of verse as a whole features such an abundance of key terms that its conceptual density resembles that found in the plays of William Shakespeare; and, as with Shakespeare, there is a reference noting all the instances of all the significant words in Dickinson's poetry, *A Concordance to the Poems of Emily Dickinson*, edited by S. P. Rosenbaum. Thus, one can discover that she wrote some twenty poems mentioning "truth," and these can be consulted to see what she might have meant in referring to an unspecified truth in no. 1129. One other notable poem is "We learned the Whole of Love" (no. 568), which portrays two individuals as somehow divinely ignorant, in a childlike way, which leaves them unable to grasp some great multifaceted truth, one that is described only as something that neither understood. In "He preached upon 'Breadth' till it argued him narrow" (no. 1207), the poet depicts a haranguing minister whose words reveal that what he calls truth is no such thing; while he speaks, truth itself is said to be figuratively silent. Perhaps most relevantly, in "Truth—is as old as God" (no. 836), prefiguring no. 1129, the poet presents a depiction of universal or ultimate truth, as the first line makes clear. "Truth—is as old as God" proceeds to posit truth as God's twin, who will last for the same eternity that God lasts for. The second stanza further tells that truth will perish when God, too, has become lifeless. As to whether this should ever come to pass, the poem is unclear.

TOPICS FOR FURTHER STUDY

- Think of a creed or principle that you live by, or perhaps aspire to live by; it might be associated with your relationships with others, your daily activities, your life goals, or some other aspect of your existence. Write three different poems of at least eight lines each that express and illustrate this principle in different ways—you can try different formulations of the principle, different analogies, and different rhyme and metrical structures. Show the set of poems to your classmates or friends, perhaps by posting online, and request feedback as to which poem people like best and why. Then write a brief reflection paper discussing which poem you think is best and why.

- Find a volume containing Dickinson's complete works (or at least selected poems), and also obtain a copy of S. P. Rosenbaum's *A Concordance to the Poems of Emily Dickinson*. Using the concordance, consult other poems of Dickinson's that refer to one or more of the following words from "Tell all the Truth but tell it slant": *lightning* (along with *light*), *circuit* (and *circumference*), *children*, or *blind*. Identify the other poems most relevant to no. 1129, and write a paper explaining the uses of the term(s) in those poems and how those connotations relate to the meanings in no. 1129.

- Use online resources to collect images of at least ten works of art that depict scenes or images of divine light or lightning. Create a slide-show presentation of these works using the appropriate software, providing commentary for each image on how the work of art can be said to relate to the ideas in Dickinson's poem "Tell all the Truth but tell it slant." You should be able to provide unique commentary for each piece.

- Select a poem from Sara Holbrook's young-adult collection *Walking on the Boundaries of Change* (1998) that contains the word "truth" in it. In an essay, compare and contrast the poem you select with "Tell all the Truth but tell it slant," considering such issues as the sort of truth under discussion, the stated importance of truth, the poet's relationship with truth, the suggested approach to the truth, and others.

- Choose three religious or spiritual traditions and consult the literature to find what the traditions say about honesty and truthful living. For example, in Christianity, the concept of truth arises in the ninth commandment and in the practice of confession, as well as elsewhere. Write a research paper summarizing each tradition's approach to the truth, and draw comparisons between the different traditions. Try to draw a conclusion as to the general spiritual and/or philosophical importance of truthfulness.

These several other poems' commentaries on truth are reflected in "Tell all the Truth but tell it slant." Here, as in no. 568, Dickinson foregrounds a consideration for the degree to which children can grasp truth; the metaphor comparing the truth to lightning places the poem's *we* in the position of children in the face of something fearsome. That is, with respect to this ultimate truth, all people can glean only a child's level of understanding. As in no. 1207, the truth is figured as capable of asserting itself; it has an active quality. And both nos. 836 and 1129 suggest a truth of great permanence, as eternal as the figure of God. In sum, this truth must indeed be the very truth of existence, of the universe—the divine truth of transcendence. This is the breed of truth said to be only accessible to the mystics, those who are born with or develop a capability of coming in direct contact with the divine. This mystic knowledge is the very height of esotericism: as traditions have it, only in knowing this truth can one know it; one can seek it, but if one does not know it, then one does not know it. But Dickinson seems to want this truth to eventually be exposed.

Light

The most striking quality of this poem's mystical truth is its phenomenal brightness. The link between truth, light, and the divine has roots in the Bible—a work of poetic literature that Dickinson highly valued—where God and Christian devotion are associated with both truth and light. For example, John 3:21 reads (in the New International Version), "But whoever lives by the truth comes into the light, so that it may be seen plainly that what they have done has been done in the sight of God." Exodus 34:35 notes that after conferring with the Lord, Moses's face is "radiant." Dickinson was well versed in the Bible but avowedly non-Christian, and so her references to truth and light carry these connotations but should be understood overall on a more expansive, universal level.

In "Tell all the Truth but tell it slant," it seems that, as with the sun, one cannot try to directly perceive this truth, as the result would be blindness. The poem's reference to lightning is actually somewhat deceptive: since the truth is effectively compared to lightning, one may attribute the image of lightning to the image of truth—but in most circumstances lightning, however bright, is not blinding, and Dickinson does not really mean the metaphor this way (although the coincidence of light-based imagery intensifies the poem). Rather, ordinary people's relation to the truth is deemed analogous to children's relation to lightning: that is, both are simply incomprehensible. The electrical explanation of lightning is beyond the intellectual reach of children, just as the explanation of transcendent truth is beyond the intellectual reach of ordinary humans, including the narrator of the poem. But this does not mean that transcendent truth was beyond the reach of Dickinson herself. Universal truth is often said to be graspable, but in nonlogical or irrational ways—in mystical ways—and it is surely not a coincidence that one who grasps the universal truth is considered "enlightened." This poem, then, amounts to a brilliant hint at the mystery of enlightenment: Dickinson suggests that the greatest truth

Blind men cannot see the truth. (© Jef Thompson / Shutterstock.com)

might somehow be grasped, if one only takes an indirect approach and allows oneself time to adjust to the blinding light. But where this truth and light can be found, she cannot or does not say.

STYLE

Hymnal Meter

Dickinson is known to have based the familiar meter of her verse on hymns. Though not proving dogmatically religious herself, she attended religious schooling and church as a child and was regularly exposed to Christian psalms and hymns, particularly those composed by the Congregationalist Isaac Watts. "Tell all the Truth but tell it slant," like many of her poems, can be broken down into couplets, each with a longer line followed by a shorter line. In particular, the odd-numbered lines are in iambic tetrameter, consisting of four metrical feet, each with an unstressed followed by a stressed syllable, while the even-numbered lines are in iambic trimeter, with three feet each. Unlike many of Dickinson's poems, the meter here is perfectly regular, provided the word *gradually* is read smoothly as three syllables. This is interesting because Dickinson's poems often feature a tweaked or curtailed metrical foot that hints at an aspect of the poem's message—a strategy that demonstrates the indirect approach to the truth suggested in

"Tell all the Truth but tell it slant." But in this poem, which posits that very strategy, the steady meter suggests that Dickinson is not simply playing guessing games in her verse; rather, she wants here to straightforwardly communicate that at times the truth—especially the greatest truth—can simply be approached only from an angle.

Rhyme

Rhyme is also common to Dickinson's verse, and as with the meter, its use here is not quite typical. In general, to carry the nuances and subtle messages of her verse, she makes adroit use of imperfect rhyme, including rhyme through repetition, near rhyme (as with *door* and *sure*), eye rhyme (*cost* and *most*), and displaced rhyme, with a rhyming word shifted from its expected location to a different line, perhaps the one before or after. In the present poem, the rhymes in lines 2 and 4 and in lines 6 and 8 are perfect. The end words of odd-numbered lines, in turn, are not necessarily expected to rhyme, but here they do contain similar sounds, as lines 1 and 3 both have an ending -*t* sound, while lines 5 and 7 both feature a long *e* sound. Furthermore, the poem includes numerous instances of consonance and internal rhyme. Line 1 features a profusion of *t* and *l* sounds, while line 2 features many *s* and *c* sounds. In line 3, the second word rhymes with the last, and in line 4, the last two words are alliterative, both starting with *su-*, and also both have internal *p* and *r* sounds. The phonetic features of the last four lines are slightly less pronounced. In line 5, the first half of the word *lightning* resonates with the rhyming words from line 3. And then, in line 7, the sequential disyllables *dazzle gradual-* effectively rhyme while also both containing *d* and *l* sounds. The poem's final two words make for one last instance of alliteration. In sum, for a Dickinson poem, the rhyme is remarkably agreeable, combining with the meter to allow for the smooth, cadenced recitation of the poem even upon first reading. These aspects of the style suggest that however blinding the truth under consideration may be, at heart it is very simple—as simple and steady as sunlight itself—and harmonious, such that one under its influence can write just such simple, steady, and harmonious verse.

Capital Letters

A third feature that distinguishes Dickinson's verse is her frequent use of capital letters not just to begin lines or designate proper nouns but also to enhance the stress or meanings of words. By and large, the words she capitalizes are nouns, along with the occasional verb or adjective. In "Tell all the Truth but tell it slant," the only extra capitalized words (beyond those that open lines) are nouns. The word *truth* is capitalized all three times it appears, and the other capitalized words are readily linked with the universal aspects of the poem. The word *circuit* in Dickinson's verse is often construed as a synonym for *circumference*, a word that can take on existential overtones in referring to the outer limits of the sphere of the universe, or the sphere of human knowledge. Thus, the capitalization of *circuit* can be taken as a hint that she means not just a circuitous approach to the truth but a universal approach, one that encompasses everything within the circumference of the universe; this would have to be in a mystical sense. Similarly, the capitalization of *delight* might suggest that in grasping for this truth, the people would be grasping not for ordinary joy but for the ultimate delight of enlightenment. A last aspect of note is the fact that *children* is capitalized but *man*, in the last line, is not. This might suggest that Dickinson considers a childlike state of mind to be in certain senses superior to the ordinary adult state of mind. This notion can be linked to the mental and emotional evolution back to a childlike state that is often associated with an individual's progress toward enlightenment.

HISTORICAL CONTEXT

The Zeitgeist of the Nineteenth Century

Dickinson's poetry is often viewed as existing outside of time. For one thing, she had little interaction with the historical world around her, never forging a material existence independent from that provided by her family, while her personal life was one of seclusion; many of her relationships were conducted largely through mailed correspondence. As for the verse itself, external circumstances are rarely mentioned and almost never definitively established, and since she never published under her name while alive, an impact on broader society cannot be traced during the span of her life. However, she was at least aware of contemporary national occurrences and philosophical trends owing to her regular exposure to the newspapers and journals

COMPARE
&
CONTRAST

- **1870s:** Through the early part of the decade, the only means to communicate verbally with people outside of one's home (excluding use of the telegraph) is through the writing of letters, and authors such as Dickinson write and receive volumes' worth of personal correspondence. Interpersonal communication is revolutionized in 1876 with Alexander Graham Bell's invention of the telephone.

  Today: Mobile phones and Internet communication services make it possible to communicate by voice with people across the globe at any time, and e-mail and text messaging are popular means of instantly sending written notes. Most younger people never communicate by handwritten letters.

- **1870s:** While the women's rights movement effectively began with the Seneca Falls Convention of 1848, women yet have limited political rights and no suffrage, and women's opinions can be widely subjugated and ignored by male politicians.

  Today: Women have by and large gained equality of rights under the law, and they hold 17 percent of seats in the 112th US

Congress and greater proportions of seats in state legislatures. In the wake of the historic voter turnout inspired in part by Hillary Clinton in the Democratic primaries of 2008, many expect the election of the first woman president to be just around the corner.

- **1870s:** Newspapers and journals are proliferating at a rapid pace; in 1840 there were only 1,600 across the nation, but in 1870 there are 5,870, and by 1880 there will be 11,300. Circulation is mostly local; the number of periodicals in Massachusetts in 1870 is 259. Many of these news sources have political affiliations, and readers can expect the reporting to be slanted from the publisher's angle.

  Today: In the age of the Internet, people in any state can access newspapers from across the world, and many news organizations are abandoning the print format to present news online only. Most news agencies profess to report on politics objectively, but some retain political agendas that go unstated, warping people's perspectives of political circumstances.

---

to which her father subscribed. And she was, as all people are, a product of her times. As such, Dickinson's poetry is readily linked with certain historical trends and literary movements within and beyond the mid-nineteenth century.

Within her own lifetime, Dickinson is most directly connected to the transcendentalism embodied by Ralph Waldo Emerson (1803–1882), whose poems and essays alike are known to have been read and appreciated by Dickinson and who was once a guest at her brother's house (an occasion she missed). Many of her ideas can be connected with ideas presented by Emerson, though not easily in a derivative way; rather, she expounded her own notions through her own

poetic sense. As her letters to her brother Austin reveal, she believed that formulating one's views for oneself, as opposed to borrowing them from others, was a matter of the utmost personal pride—a notion that is in fact traceable to Emerson's "Self-Reliance." Other connections with Emerson's writings, especially with regard to Dickinson's appreciation for nature, her excavation of the self, her intimate relationship with the divine, and her interest in the transcendence of the individual mind, are unmistakable. In these respects, these two writers, both of whom came to reject dogmatic Christianity, reflect the increasing tension between faith and science in the nineteenth century. Sweeping religious revivals, such as the one in Amherst in the early 1850s, were countered by the publication of such seminal works as Charles Darwin's evolutionary treatise *On the Origin of Species* (1859), and the opinions of the religious and scientific minded were diverging. In the middle were spiritualists sans doctrine like Emerson and Dickinson. Part of the creed Emerson developed independent of organized religion was self-honesty, living a wholly truthful life, and this notion suggests one reason that Dickinson might have written her poem urging the reader—in the first four words, at least—to be utterly truthful.

While Dickinson's intellectual sympathy with one man, Emerson, most clearly ties her to her own era in terms of philosophy, the lack of intellectual sympathy extended by another man, Thomas Wentworth Higginson (1823–1911), largely accounted for her disconnection from her era in terms of publication. Higginson, a known political activist and essayist, published in 1862 an article in the *Atlantic Monthly* extolling the art of literature and giving advice to aspiring young writers, expressly including women, about honing their craft. Dickinson was moved to respond, presenting Higginson with several of her poems; but Higginson was left at a loss by Dickinson's singular style—in particular her imperfect rhythms and use of hyphenation—which led him to describe the verse as "spasmodic" and "uncontrolled" (cited in Alfred Gelpi, *The Tenth Muse*). Higginson was not impressed by the likes of Walt Whitman (1819–1892), either, whose experimentation in *Leaves of Grass* (1855) he found too informal and crude to amount to actual art. Whitman is often cited as a foil for Dickinson in that the former, with his scandalous verse of personal exposure, was the poetic epitome of the public self, while the latter, with her personal life of utter seclusion, was the poetic epitome of the private self.

In replying to Dickinson, Higginson informed her that he did not believe her poetry yet worthy of publication. From that point on, she not only neglected to seek out publication but actively resisted it, declining to contribute to at least one anthology because, as Higginson had confirmed, her verse was simply not good enough. And yet Dickinson did not actually cater to Higginson's opinion; at this point she believed in herself as a poet enough to know that she could only

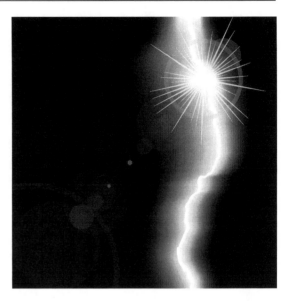

Lightning bolts are associated with clarifying the truth. *(© Daemys / Shutterstock.com)*

follow her inner aesthetic sense, and if anything, Higginson's thoughts confirmed that, in effect, the literary world—at least, the literary world as a patriarchal establishment—was not yet ready for her poems. The scholar Emily Stipes Watts, for one, in *The Poetry of American Women from 1632 to 1945*, invokes "Tell all the Truth but tell it slant" as illustrating the notion that prior to the gaining of greater political rights for women (such as national suffrage in 1920), women could not yet publicly speak or write many truths that men were unwilling or unable to hear.

Dickinson's connections with literary history thus lie largely with the history that came before and after. Certain women poets who preceded her, such as Elizabeth Barrett Browning (1806–1861), are recognized as influences, and Watts notes that Dickinson's verse "represents the culmination of American women's verse to her day." But no woman poet before Dickinson challenged the formal, masculinized poetic tradition in the way that she did, and in the wake of the publication of her verse beginning in the 1890s, many emergent poets, such as Amy Lowell (1874–1925), Gertrude Stein (1874–1946), and Edna St. Vincent Millay (1892–1950), would challenge that tradition in their own ways. In these respects, Dickinson's verse has been characterized as both proto-feminist and proto-modernist.

CRITICAL OVERVIEW

Dickinson is one of the most critically admired poets in American history, and as an emblematic poem, "Tell all the Truth but tell it slant" has inspired significant attention and commentary. Most critics have approached or cited the poem as encapsulating the author's philosophy of poetics. In her encyclopedic *Critical Companion to Emily Dickinson: A Literary Reference to Her Life and Work*, Sharon Leiter cross-references no. 1129 as the poet's "famous tenet" that points toward "the circuitous language of riddle" found elsewhere in her verse. Focusing on the poem's significance as one of her "'metapoems,' or poems about poetry," Leiter describes it as widely deemed "a key statement of her philosophy and way of writing. Ostensibly written as an advice poem, it is really a revelation of herself as a canny, self-aware craftsman and psychologist of the human soul." Joanne Dobson, in *Dickinson and the Strategies of Reticence: The Woman Writer in Nineteenth-Century America*, likewise focuses on the metapoetic aspect, remarking, "This poem seems to posit an aesthetic based on gradual revelation of abstract truth," which is associated with the supreme delight of "all poetry that deals with great and difficult truths." Along the same lines, Ronald Wallace, in *God Be with the Clown: Humor in American Poetry*, notes that in this "uncharacteristically direct poem, Dickinson defines her indirect method of arriving at truth." Contrasting the poet with Whitman, who jolts the reader with bold assertions, the critic finds that Dickinson "preferred to dazzle the reader slyly toward the truth."

Cristanne Miller, in *Emily Dickinson: A Poet's Grammar*, reads the poem as indicative of Dickinson's nineteenth-century female identity. She notes that in general, the author's "cryptically elusive poems baffle even sophisticated readers," with language that is "compressed, disjunctive, at times ungrammatical; its reference is unclear." An exception to "her largely unarticulated decision to write the riddling, elliptical poetry she does," however, comes with "her most famous poem on the subject" of poetic language. Miller suggests that in "Tell all the Truth but tell it slant," the "poet's role becomes implicitly maternal. The thoughtful user of language protects her readers/children from frightening truth by talking around it." In this manner, Dickinson was able to submerge in her verse, for instance, gendered truths with which men might not be sympathetic, as "the poems' linguistic and metaphorical complexity allows Dickinson's readers to see her truths only as they are capable of admitting them."

Gravitating toward the universal dimensions of her work in *The Landscape of Absence: Emily Dickinson's Poetry*, Inder Nath Kher sets out to demonstrate that her verse

> concerns itself with the human predicament and destiny;...that it embodies fully the cosmic theme of life and art as a continuous process; that it contains its own poetics or aesthetic theory; and that it is simultaneously concrete and intangible, present and absent.

In these respects, poem no. 1129 stands out. Kher declares,

> Her poetry embodies a gigantic effort to comprehend reality or truth through the creative process. Dickinson realizes that in order to find truth, as seen through the creative eye of the imagination, one has to live until death in the presence of beauty....Truth and beauty are one in the aesthetic vision.

Highlighting the lucent qualities of poetic truth in "Tell all the Truth but tell it slant," Kher concludes, "The poetic utterance which contains truth in it is the *Mandala* [universal circle] of human consciousness, the dawn of all knowledge."

Other critics have directly addressed Dickinson's veritably mystical understanding of the world. Barton Levi St. Armand, in "Emily Dickinson and the Occult: The Rosicrucian Connection," argues that the poet was one of "a select few" in her era to gain awareness that in the infamous pseudoscience of alchemy, "the quest for the philosopher's stone was an internal process": "Transmutation was, in fact, a profound exaltation of the soul and...the true subject of the alchemical experiment was man." Poem no. 1129 is held to reveal that "she agreed that such a secret must remain a closely guarded one, encoded in a deliberately cryptic language." In his *Introduction to Emily Dickinson*, Henry W. Wells observes that the poet, who "stands in company with the chief poets, seers, mystics, and visionaries" of history, penned verse that is generally "equally rich in the golden ore of mystery and metaphorical implication." In his chapter "The Mystical Way," he cites the many poems that hint at Dickinson's preternatural grasp of the universe, noting, "With strange felicity she describes the mystical experience in terms of light," which makes key appearances in her attempts "to hint at the mystery." Wells holds that mystical knowledge is ultimately to be found "in a transcendent present only," and poems like "Tell all the Truth but tell it slant" thus collectively suggest that the truth of life is "the complete aesthetic experience. Truth and eternity are merely full realization, the soul completely poised."

CRITICISM

Michael Allen Holmes

Holmes is a writer with existential interests. In the following essay, he considers the connections between Dickinson's directive to "Tell all the Truth but tell it slant" and the Zen Buddhist tradition of the koan.

Emily Dickinson's poem "Tell all the Truth but tell it slant" has primarily been considered by critics as a "metapoem" that speaks to the author's aesthetic philosophy, according to which truths are best communicated in a circuitous way, such that the reader becomes involved in the construction of meaning. The poem's first two lines certainly legitimize this reading, quite explicitly stating as much. The metaphor linking light and truth, as well, can easily be taken to represent the difficulty of wrapping one's mind around certain unexpected or dazzling truths. But the poem's last two lines suggest that smaller truths, of the sort that can be effectively communicated a few stanzas at a time, are not at all what this poem is referring to. On the one hand the truth—and each time the term appears, it is with a capital *T*—is delightful, and this accords with the sense of good poetry; on the other hand the truth is potentially blinding, and this accords with the sense of conceptions that pose a threat to the existing social order; but these two sorts of truths would seem to be mutually exclusive. Generally speaking, the delightful and the dangerous cannot coexist in one entity viewed from one coherent perspective (unless the delight is a false delight or the danger an illusory danger— or unless one is a thrill seeker). Furthermore, while the poet may seem to suggest that the truth of her poetry is like lightning, she then speaks of the truth having a gradual effect of illumination, an impossibility with lightning. Thus, the association of both lightning and truth with her verse, however broadly apt,

WHAT DO I READ NEXT?

- Beyond the nearly eighteen hundred poems that Dickinson wrote, her letters, also marked by her distinct style, are of substantial literary interest. A collection of letters to her closest correspondent, her sister-in-law Susan (née Gilbert), is *Open Me Carefully: Emily Dickinson's Intimate Letters to Susan Huntington Dickinson* (1998).

- The earliest forebear of Dickinson's in the history of American women's poetry was Anne Bradstreet, a seventeenth-century Puritan (born in England) whose husband was a colonial governor. During his frequent absences, she wrote verse recording the many hardships of life in colonial New England. Her poems are collected in *The Works of Anne Bradstreet* (1981).

- A half century after Dickinson's death, the poet Genevieve Taggard wrote a highly admiring and perceptive critical biography of her, *The Life and Mind of Emily Dickinson* (1930).

- An accomplished poet whose verse suggests Dickinson's influence is the American modernist Marianne Moore, such as in her well-received collection *What Are Years* (1941).

- In terms of politics and culture, many modern African women are still striving to make their own and other women's voices heard in their native countries. Poems by forty-two poets from eighteen countries are collected in *The Heinemann Book of African Women's Poetry* (1995), compiled by Stella and Frank Chipasula.

- Patrice Vecchione has collected verse dealing with the concept of truth by such famous poets as Denise Levertov, Lucille Clifton, and Gertrude Stein in *Truth and Lies: An Anthology of Poems* (2000), which is aimed at young adults. Dickinson's "Tell all the Truth but tell it slant" is included.

> THE IDEA OF THE KOAN, FOUNDED IN A SKEWED OR PARADOXICAL APPROACH TO THE TRUTH, IS WELL ECHOED IN THE FIRST TWO LINES OF DICKINSON'S POEM."

would seem to be misplaced here; she must be referencing something even greater than her verse, something so bright that it would not just dazzle but would leave one utterly blind. The only entity in physical reality that could carry all of these qualities would be the sun, its warmth life-giving and delightful, the intensity of its light potentially blinding. By analogy, the only human experience that could carry these same qualities would be exposure to the brilliance of the divine, or enlightenment.

The quest for enlightenment is embodied foremost in mystic traditions, which have evolved in a wide number of cultural contexts. As Henry W. Wells notes in discussing Dickinson's mystic intellectual background in his *Introduction to Emily Dickinson*, "Parallels to her thought and phrase occur in virtually all civilized literatures, from China, India, and Persia, to Italy, Germany, France, Spain, and England." These nations and others have been host to the unique mystic traditions of the various religions, from the Kabbalah of Judaism to the Sufism of Islam. Dickinson's own spiritual development came to diverge from the Christianity of her family and town, as she refused to ally herself with any prescribed doctrine. In Wells's words,

> Religion, like truth and beauty, signified the utmost development of the personality. Ultimately, her quest for God was identical with her battle for personal integrity. Her vision even of the divine—perhaps even chiefly of the divine—had to be her own. Indebted to all and enslaved to none, she pursued her quest for eternity.

Hinting at the psychological danger inherent in such a quest, Wells notes, "Needless to add, it proved a voyage perilous."

There is one notable spiritual tradition that centralizes the quest for the divine, for enlightenment, but in the absence of a deistic

formulation of the functioning of the universe: Zen. Rooted in the system of thoughts and practices founded by the Buddha, the fifth-century BCE wellspring of enlightenment, Zen relies on Buddhist conceptions of the universe while declining recourse to identifiable gods or an afterworld. Zen might be called the religion of the present moment, and belief in either a god or an afterlife only serves to displace one from the immediate reality to be experienced on earth.

The Zen tradition accumulated over the course of the centuries during which the Buddhist way of enlightenment migrated east into China and later Japan. A key figure was Bodhidharma, who arrived in China around the sixth century and distilled enlightenment down to the practical essence of meditation. He is said to have gazed at a wall in meditation for some nine years straight. So strictly attuned to present reality was Bodhidharma that he would effectively dismiss questions of doctrine by negating whatever could be formulated. To him, whatever was, was, while whatever could be said was merely words. A legendary dialogue between Bodhidharma and an emperor, cited by Heinrich Dumoulin in *Zen Enlightenment: Origins and Meaning*, has Bodhidharma responding to the question "What is the sacred truth's first principle?" by stating "Vast emptiness, nothing sacred"; while the emperor's question "Who is it that now stands before me?" elicits only "I don't know." In Dumoulin's assessment, this dialogue shows that Bodhidharma "will have nothing to do with a verbalized principle of truth." But this is not to say that he was being untruthful; he simply declined to provide the expected answers, instead offering answers that were true from a certain perspective—how can anyone know *who* anyone is, including oneself?—but which frustrated the expectations of the emperor.

Bodhidharma's mode of interaction, which proved a model for Zen figures for centuries to come, became concretized in the tradition of the koan (in Chinese, *kung-an*), which literally means "public announcement" but might be concisely and more usefully described as an essential paradox. In the formal tradition, a koan consists of a piece of dialogue, an aphoristic formulation of a principle, and poetic commentary on the dialogue and principle. Within the dialogue is contained an exchange that may seem nonsensical, even self-contradictory or paradoxical, but which directs the Zen student toward a truth. The dialogue between Bodhidharma and the emperor, for example, is used as a koan. The koan is fully effective only when given by a master to a disciple, as the master's familiarity with the student's degree of understanding allows him to present a koan that is ideally suited to bringing the student to a higher level of understanding.

Outside the formal tradition, a koan can be represented by a single statement that represents a paradox or unresolvable uncertainty. Perhaps the most famous example of such a koan is "What is the sound of one hand clapping?" Dumoulin describes at length the mental process meant to be inspired by the koan in the Zen practitioner, who "enters a hyperalert state" of concentration in the attempt to resolve it:

> This concentration gives rise to a search—at first for the solution of the koan. Utilizing all his intellectual powers, as he naturally would, the practitioner exerts himself with all his might, but to no avail. The illogical nature of the koan resists logical solution. He then enters into a state of helplessness and runs up against the same wall again and again, like someone locked in a small room. He searches for a way out, and yet the door is open—not where his intellect is aimed, however, for the wall does not give in.

In the end, the practitioner must abandon the search for a logical truth and instead find a deeper, more universal but less tangible, existential truth in the koan. This truth will inevitably be an aspect of the broader truth that amounts to the identity of the divine. (Dickinson unites the ideas of truth and the divine in her poem "Truth—is as old as God.") Dumoulin notes that "The number of accounts, both contemporary and old, that describe an explosive occurrence in the mind as a result of an intense struggle with the koan is not few." As stated by Thich Nhat Hanh in *Zen Keys*—in phrasing that brings the idea of the koan closer to Dickinson's poem "Tell all the Truth but tell it slant"—at the moment of resolution, "'the sound of one hand' can become a sun that dazzles our whole being."

The idea of the koan, founded in a skewed or paradoxical approach to the truth, is well echoed in the first two lines of Dickinson's poem. And as Nhat Hanh confirms, such an oblique approach to the truth can lead to at least a momentary enlightenment, in which one is dazzled as if by a sun—accounting for the third and fourth lines of Dickinson's poem. The fifth and sixth lines stand alone as an apt metaphor for the rational incomprehensibility of enlightenment. But a question remains as to the danger Dickinson seems to suggest, in the last two lines of her poem, to be inherent in an approach to enlightenment—as to how this quasi-solar dazzling can actually leave one blind.

The answer may be said to lie in the psychic risks one may incur in seeking the immersion in the present demanded by Zen. This risk is signified by Bodhidharma's response to the question of who he is: he can honestly state that he does not know. Along with all of one's amassed conceptions of the external world, one's conceptions of one's internal self as well amount to just that: conceptions. To arrive at union with the immediate present, one must dissolve oneself; but the dissolution of the self, if undertaken unguided (such as in the absence of religious dogma), could be tantamount to descent toward insanity. As Dumoulin reports, progress toward enlightenment is even expected to entail disturbing and distressing psychic experiences:

> Zen masters warn against the fascinations of the "devil's realm," which are all the more dangerous the less the student recognizes them for what they are. . . . Sometimes these experiences cast even the zealous Zen disciple into utter despair.

Dumoulin cites a number of recorded instances of psychic distress in Zen disciples and concludes that

> it is absolutely necessary that one entrust himself to a reliable and experienced guide in the practice of Zen. This becomes all the more necessary the further along the student progresses. One should be strongly warned against venturing on his own.

Dumoulin proceeds to cite a number of statements made by Zen disciples who reached enlightenment, and while the descriptions vary widely in their specific content, one common feature is the experience of inundation by light. One man reported, "I was astonished that unnoticeably the Zen hall and I myself were radiant in an absolute light." With a certain woman, "The more fervently she immerses herself in meditation, the vaster the flood of light extends, the deeper it seizes her." One can only guess at the experiences Dickinson went through in her famous seclusion; she is not even definitively known to have been aware of the term *mysticism*. But given the array of similarities to be found

The truth is not always so clear. (© Stephen Coburn / Shutterstock.com)

between "Tell all the Truth and tell it slant" and the Zen tradition of the koan and the quest for the divine, it seems reasonable to conclude that what Dickinson found in her own unique, uncharted quest for the radiant divine truth of the universe was nothing less than enlightenment.

Source: Michael Allen Holmes, Critical Essay on "Tell all the Truth but tell it slant," in *Poetry for Students*, Gale, Cengage Learning, 2013.

Michael Ryan

In the following essay, Ryan proclaims Dickinson to be a master of rhythm, rhetoric, and narrative, as evidenced by reading her poetry aloud.

Dickinson meant her poems to be an experience, to render experience as well as refer to it. "A Book is only the Heart's Portrait—every Page a Pulse—" Dickinson wrote in a letter in 1882, four years before she died. Her very first sentence in her first letter to Higginson is: "Are you too occupied to say if my Verse is alive?"

And she goes on: ". . . Should you think it breathed—and had you leisure to tell me, I should feel quick gratitude." Dickinson raises the intimacy-ante over Yeats's "we should write our poems as in a letter to an intimate friend." For her, the living presence is the poem itself: the poem is not an intermediary between poet and reader; it is the thing alive the reader experiences directly.

Which is why I believe the most articulate thing you can say about a Dickinson poem is to read it aloud. To read it properly, you have to know how the sentences work, how the rhythm works, how the rhetoric works, and how the narrative works—if there is a narrative (by which I mean simply a telling of a story, the telling of events in time). Dickinson was an absolute master of all these: grammar, rhythm, rhetoric, and narrative—and a master of the inextricable, intricate, intimate, and constantly shifting interrelationships among them as they proceed from nanosecond to nanosecond at the

WHAT A CONSUMMATE ARTIST DICKINSON
WAS. THE RANGE OF HER POETIC SKILL IS
UNMATCHED IN MY VIEW BY ANY OTHER POET
EVER."

warp-speed at which the brain processes language. That said, since our focus here is narrative, I'm going to try to describe the narratives of three of my favorite poems.

While you read them, try to exclude everything else from your attention but the story and how it's told. Here's #591:

I heard a Fly buzz—when I died—
The Stillness in the Room
Was like the Stillness in the Air—
Between the Heaves of Storm—

The Eyes around—had wrung them dry—
And Breaths were gathering firm
For that last Onset—when the King
Be witnessed—in the Room—

I willed my Keepsakes—Signed away
What portion of me be
Assignable—and then it was
There interposed a Fly—

With Blue—uncertain—stumbling Buzz—
Between the light—and me—
And then the Windows failed—and then
I could not see to see—
#591F (1863)

"Life is death we're lengthy at, death the hinge to life" she wrote to the Norcross sisters in late May 1863, after their father died. Was she thinking of this poem which she may have just written or was about to write? She was certainly thinking of its subject. In ninety-two words, sixteen lines, and four sentences, she gets as close to that life/death hinge as can be—from both sides of the door. The first line-and-sentence ("I heard a fly buzz—when I died—") hooks us completely, but the suspense doesn't derive from our wanting to know what will happen (it tells us what happened) but from our wanting to know how somebody could tell us what happened when she died. At the moment we finish reading the sentence, the moment-in-the-past being told is distinguished from the moment-in-the-present of telling. The grammatical completion of the sentence coincides with a logical anomaly: We're being spoken to by a dead person. Is this a joke? The meaning of the sentence is clear but we don't know how to understand it. Plus its rhythm is unsettling: the stress on "buzz" comes a syllable too soon. We don't know whether to stress "when" or not. In the warp-speed brainworld in which we're experiencing-processing grammar-rhythm-narrative, we stick on "Fly buzz—." We feel something odd going on. One line-and-sentence into the poem, we're immersed in an is-and-isn't world. Chekhov said never "put a loaded shotgun on the stage if no one is thinking of firing it" before the end of the play. How could someone tell us what happened when she died? is the loaded shotgun—on a stage set at a disorienting angle.

The shotgun does get fired, but not before it's excruciatingly toyed with by the narrator. That we're being told a story by a dead person turns out to be a joke, just as we suspected after reading the first line-and-sentence, but it's not the silly joke we thought it might be. It's a different kind of joke: the sort caused by the uncanny, provoking astonishment not cruelty, fueled as the best jokes are by terror at the inevitable and uncontrollable. The joke, its effects, and its buried assertions finally merge (within a single sentence!) into the compelling story that had been summarized in the first line-and-sentence of the poem.

—and then it was
There interposed a Fly—

With Blue—uncertain—stumbling Buzz—
Between the light—and me—
And then the Windows failed—and then
I could not see to see—

"I heard a Fly buzz—when I died" becomes "I saw a Fly buzz—when I died." The moment initially summarized is translated into visual terms and extended grammatically by the first circumlocution in the poem (and then it was [that] there interposed a Fly with) and by the first triple adjectives (Blue—uncertain—stumbling) in a poem that has almost no adjectives elsewhere, much less triple ones. The sentence's grammar in lines 11–13 interposes between the reader and the forward motion of the narrative (since action is carried through subject-verb-object) just as the fly in the story interposed between the speaker and the light. This gives us the experience of "interposed." The spatial and temporal experience referred to *by* the words is rendered though the sequence *of* the words fixed into form. We're locked into the perspective of the person dying, the character in the story. At the same time, the circumlocution calls our attention to the person "living," the narrator, the teller of the story. "And then there interposed a Fly" would have focused only on what happened, whereas "and then it was [that] there interposed a Fly" hauls the shotgun onto centerstage before the grammar becomes direct and action compressed through the climactic final two words of the poem.

"And then the Windows failed—and then/I could not see to see—" Ka-boom goes the shotgun. The final miraculous move is to turn irony itself on its ear. This ugly annoying fly is the last thing the speaker sensed on earth, and, ironically, it's what appeared while the deathwatchers were expecting the King God to appear. But then "I could not see to *see*—": even this lowly creature provides a great occasion. The assertion buried here is that this great occasion is available to us only while we have physical eyes—only while we're alive for the sacramental act of seeing, only when we're not distracted by doctrine that calls for the appearance of a grandiose God instead of moment-by-moment attention to the humble things of the earth.

But Dickinson isn't preaching, she's practicing. Impossibly, she breaks down the indivisible moment of death into a sequence of smaller moments (And then . . . and then . . . and then): after there interposed a fly, the windows fail. The world acts almost independently of the character-in-the-story while we are inside her point-of-view. Death is something that happens to her, that happens to people. We feel how it feels. We are helpless, on a battlefield or in a bedroom. And this particular death then produces a particular incapacity in this particular person who, up until that last nanosecond, *could* see to see.

Here's another one, whose narrative works very differently.

These—saw Visions—
Latch them softly—
These—held Dimples—
Smooth them slow—
This—addressed departing accents—
Quick—Sweet Mouth—to miss thee so

This—We stroked—
Unnumbered Satin—
These—we held among our own—
Fingers of the Slim Aurora—
Not so arrogant—this Noon—

These—adjust—that ran to meet us—
Pearl—for stocking—Pearl for Shoe—

Paradise—the only Palace
Fit for Her reception—now—
#769 (1863)

What is happening? What's the story? Where is it located? Who are the characters? What are their relationships? All this is implied. We must infer it. The protean links between what the speaker implies and the reader infers are crucial to Dickinson's narratives—as they are to Dickinson's poems in general, and to her letters, and—according to Higginson's reports of his visits with her—to her conversation as well. "Tell all the truth but tell it slant": she was slanting all the time, at every possible angle, in order to get at the truth and to articulate it. We have to infer that the speaker of "These—saw Visions—" is standing over a body, maybe at a wake or funeral (since there are apparently other mourners there whom she addresses with imperatives), and what she says is provoked by her focus on the body from head to toe, from eyes ("These—saw Visions—") to feet ("These—adjust—that ran to meet us—"). She implies information throughout; we have to interpret various kinds of figures for eyes, cheeks, hair, fingers, and feet. It makes us participate. In "I heard a Fly buzz," wherever the speaker is speaking from (and it's certainly not here on earth), she's speaking about her death-bed scene. She's telling the story of the moment of her own death. "These—saw Visions—" makes us infer who the characters are. Who has died and who is speaking about her? Probably a little girl has died ("dimples," "stroked," "ran to meet us"), and certainly the speaker cares deeply about her. A mother, an aunt? We don't know and it doesn't really matter. What's foregrounded is how precious to the speaker the dead child is. We get the emotion unmodified and unqualified. The speaker puts forward another person and thereby the speaker becomes a character the reader values because of her valuing. Puts forward, I mean, both narratively and rhetorically: keeping the other person before the reader's eyes. "These—saw Visions—" is a great example of this—quite literally, because it is such a visual poem. The only singular pronoun in the poem refers to the whole beloved person in the last line at "Her reception," at the speaker's assertion of the tremendous value of this person. (And that "Her" is stressed in this metrical context when it would not be in that same phrase—"fit for her reception"—in ordinary speech.) What we experience of the speaker is her grief and love. The speaker's goodness at being able to feel grief and love for another so profoundly is entirely implicit, but we surely respond to it all the more for that—to this "supposed person" created by her act of speech.

Now for the last of three examples of Dickinson's distinct, ingenious, and utterly embodied narrative techniques. This is #515:

> There is a pain—so utter—
> It swallows substance up—
> Then covers the Abyss with Trance—
> So Memory can step
> Around—across—opon it—
> As one within a Swoon—
> Goes safely—where an open eye—
> Would drop Him—Bone by Bone—
> #515F (1863)

The assertion stated in the first two lines merges into a narrative that ascribes sequence (if not chronology) to human response to utter pain—neither a particular human nor a particular pain, much less Dickinson's personal pain, whatever utter pain may have sparked her writing it. In high contrast to "These saw—Visions—," the narrative is absolutely explicit. There are two characters, Pain and Memory, both personified by their actions. Pain swallows and covers—swallows substance and covers the consequent Abyss it creates; Memory "can step / around—across—opon" the Abyss as "one within a Swoon." A simile—"as" or "like"—always implies the mind of a speaker because a comparison is made by somebody thinking. This speaker's mind is active throughout. We experience her reinterpreting her own words when "swallows" changes from metaphor to dramatic action at the moment the "utter pain . . . *covers* the Abyss with Trance." The compounding of the initial action makes us focus on what such utter pain *does*. And what a sentence the poem is—as complex and clear as a sentence can be, laid across two quatrains, counterpointed by the famous dashes that in her manuscript of this poem are uniform but often are more like dots or diagonals slashed up or down. The One/ Him in the final three lines introduces a human presence, in the conditional mood of the verb, an unnamed character wholly and only within the speculative power of the speaker's mind. He's used to dramatize one consequence of such utter pain (drop Him Bone by Bone), did the utter pain not create its own Trance as survival mechanism. That "covers the Abyss with Trance," paradoxically (and Dickinson loves paradox), is only further testimony of the utterness of the pain, its

power. That power would be less if the pain were only one person's, if it were a first-person speaker's and the poem were a first-person narrative. In contrast to both "I heard a Fly buzz—when I died—" and "These—saw Visions—," all we are asked to infer here is where these actions occur: namely inside the psyche—anyone's psyche who suffers such an "utter pain." The poem lifts trauma from the traumatized and dramatizes it. The location of the story, its time and place, is provided by the person who has felt a pain like this—in other words, everyone: everyone who reads the poem and can follow the grammar of its single sentence. It gives time and place—or at least sequence and location—to a timeless, psychological process. The reader provides the body for its embodiment. The time, characters, and circumstance of the "then" in line 3—between Pain swallowing substance and covering the Abyss it creates—could be and has been the subject of novels. (It is the subject of *Anna Karenina*; all 900 pages of it—although, in that case, Anna finally falls into the Abyss.) Here what constitutes that "then" matters no more than the kinship of the speaker and dead child in "These—saw Visions." In both cases, what does matter is foregrounded. The speaker doesn't tell us what occasioned *her* utter pain, but lets us plug in our own. There is no narrative information in the poem that separates her from us. The poem is made to be an experience instead of referring to one, which is precisely how Dickinson said she knows poetry in her famous remark to Higginson: "If I read a book [and] it makes my whole body so cold no fire ever can warm me I know *that* is poetry. If I feel physically as if the top of my head were taken off, I know *that* is poetry. These are the only way I know it. Is there any other way."

I don't believe there is. I hope you find it as thrilling as I do to hold these three poems up in front of you. They are as good as poetry gets, I think, in every way—including the distinct ways they handle narrative, each one astonishing in itself and essential to the subject, experience, and effects of the poem: explicit first-person narrative in "I heard a Fly buzz," implicit first-person narrative and second-person address in "These—saw Visions," and omniscient third-person narrative in "There is a pain—so utter" with a narrator like Flaubert's "God in the universe, present everywhere and visible nowhere." Each poem would be impossible with any other narrative casting. What a consummate artist

Dickinson was. The range of her poetic skill is unmatched in my view by any other poet ever.

Source: Michael Ryan, "Dickinson's Stories," in *American Poetry Review*, Vol. 38, No. 2, March/April 2009, p. 5.

Paul W. Anderson

In the following essay, Anderson examines comic elements in Dickinson's verse, asserting that Dickinson's subtle humor reflects the profundity, and ambiguity, of her poetry's central themes.

Mirth is the Mail of Anguish—

That Emily Dickinson did, indeed, possess a comic spirit is evident from the remarks by her niece, Martha Dickinson Bianchi, in *Emily Dickinson Face to Face*: "Nothing could be more fatal to knowing Aunt Emily on her own terms than to take her literally when her mood was hyperbolic. Her friend Samuel Bowles rated this quality in her above all others, and called her 'his rascal.' . . . It is the element of drollery in her, the elfin, mischievous strain, that is hardest for those who never knew her to reconcile with her solemn side." This bone is offered to the biographiacs, who have worried (or rejoiced) over Dickinson's reclusive solemnity or who have seen only quaintness or eccentricity in the way of a comic spirit. So much for person. What is the significance of her comic spirit in terms of poetry? In his essay on "Emily Dickinson and Sir Thomas Browne," Herbert Childs touches an aspect of that significance: "Like many great humorists, they (Browne and Dickinson) took a sidelong view of life. . . . In Browne the word is 'asquint' . . . Emily Dickinson used the word 'oblique' . . . The words epitomize their common habit of looking at human affairs indirectly in order to see therein life's ironic pathos and humorous incongruity." George F. Whicher, in his essay on "American Humor," notes the same essential obliqueness: "To grasp the soul at white heat she needed more than ever the tongs that wit supplied. Complete integrity in what lay too deep for tears was possible only by indirection." Tone, as Archibald MacLeish points out ("The Private World"), becomes a highly complex and determinative thing in her poetry. Thought and feeling, seriousness and humor become inseparable: "like our own beloved Robert Frost who has looked long and deeply into the darkness of the world as a man well can, 'their eyes, their ancient glittering eyes' must be gay." T. S. Eliot, too, is aware of this yoking together of

> HUMOR IS OFTEN AT THE HEART OF EMILY DICKINSON'S VISION, IN MANY OF HER BEST POEMS; SHE EXPLOITED THE HUMAN CAPACITY FOR RISIBILITY, WHICH ENABLED HER TO UNITE HER FEELING FOR BOTH A 'A NEARNESS TO TREMENDOUSNESS,' AS ONE POEM PHRASES IT, AND FOR WONDER AT THE FAMILIAR."

disparate sensibilities in one vision. In his essay on Andrew Marvell, working toward a definition of metaphysical poetry, Eliot observes that the wit in "To His Coy Mistress" is "not only combined with, but fused into, the imagination . . . this alliance of levity and seriousness (by which the seriousness is intensified) is a characteristic of the sort of wit we are trying to identify." Tone in metaphysical poetry is often a curious blend of comedy and tragedy, as in many of Donne's songs and sonnets; it is a certain slant of sensibility. Dickinson herself wrote a poem embodying the basic credo for her comic obliquity, number "1129" (poems referred to follow T. H. Johnson's numbering [in *The Poems of Emily Dickinson*]):

> Tell all the Truth but tell it slant—
> Success in Circuit lies
> Too bright for our infirm Delight
> The Truth's superb surprise
> As Lightning to the Children eased
> With explanation kind
> The Truth must dazzle gradually
> Or every man be blind—

The awe of truth can often only be contained within the wide circle of mirth. As William Howard points out in passing, in his essay on "Emily Dickinson's Poetic Vocabulary," this aspect of her work has been generally overlooked or denied. It is this aspect which shall be explored in this paper. The great range of Emily Dickinson's comic spirit, from barely discernible whimsy to obvious satire, renders any neat categorization of her uses of comedy impossible. But an exploration of several facets of her comic spirit, its effect in the poetry, should reveal the decidedly metaphysical nature of her employment of mirth.

Obvious in both its satiric humor and in its metaphysical meshing of the beatific and bestial is the famous "Papa above!" Satire by *reductio ad absurdum* evokes a sinister smile:

Papa above!
Regard a Mouse
O'erpowered by the Cat!
Reserve within thy kingdom
A "Mansion" for the Rat!

Snug in seraphic Cupboards
To nibble all the day,
While unsuspecting Cycles
Wheel solemnly away!

Particularly in the last stanza is there what Whicher calls "that wilfull confounding of scale," that uniting of disparate elements, as Eliot says ("The Metaphysical Poets") which characterizes the tone of metaphysical poetry. The protest in the poem, against orthodoxy's conception of a personal God and a hedonistic heaven, thus is made incisive rather than vindictive. The humor of the juxtaposition places the perspective on the object itself, not on the outraged poet.

On the surface a much simpler poem "The morns are meeker [than they were]" actually contains much subtler implications of the tonic effects of the comic vision:

The morns are meeker than they were—
The nuts are getting brown—
The berry's cheek is plumper—
The Rose is out of town.

The Maple wears a gayer scarf—
The field a scarlet gown—
Lest I should be old fashioned
I'll put a trinket on.

The inevitable and calculated slight shock of the slant rhyme "gown/on" coheres with the tragicomic theme. In the first place, the personification in the poem, characteristic of the majority of Dickinson's nature poems, is a tongue-in-cheek, a comic personification, antipodal to what Ruskin had in mind when he wrote of the "pathetic fallacy." That "the Rose is out of town," that death and decay constitute half the rhythm of life could frequently drive Dickinson to such prosaic, if impassioned statement as

For each ecstatic instant
We must an anguish pay
In keen and quivering ratio
To the ecstasy
("125")

but here, in "The morns," under the control of the comic vision, the poem embodies an essential truth of the human condition, focuses objectively on it, rather than simply megaphoning the agonized message of the writer. Rather than sentimental, the tough reasonableness of the poem resides in the paradox of the last two lines: man's attempts to merge with nature are futile and funny, and yet the "fashion" of fall, of the seasons and what they mean, must be accepted. It could almost be taken as a parody of "Corinna's Going A-Maying." It is certainly as complex in tone.

This tonic complexity by way of a metaphysical kind of mirth permeates much of Dickinson's most serious poetry. The few critics who have recognized this have not investigated its specific effects on poetic technique, particularly use of imagery, and have considered only the psychological function (another form of biographical fallacy) rather than the esthetic. Donald F. Connors, for example ("The Significance of Emily Dickinson"), states that "there are many instances in her poems where her feelings are lodged behind a mask of mirth until the anguish is scarcely perceptible," but he goes no further into the poetics involved. Note, for example, what Dickinson's comic vision does to the "Lotos-Eaters" or death wish theme in number "133," "The Grass so little has to do":

The Grass so little has to do—
. . . . .

And even when it dies—to pass
In Odors so divine—
Like Lowly spices, lain to sleep—
Or spikenards, perishing—

And then, in Sovereign Barns to dwell—
And dream the days away,
The Grass so little has to do
I wish I were a Hay—

This is not a distressing "effort at lightness," not "countrified eccentricity," as Yvor Winters would have it ("Emily Dickinson and the Limits of Judgment"). It is sophisticated poetry: subtle, complex, carefully worded. One may be taken in by the quaint sentiment of the initial "The grass so little has to do," may be lulled into the succulent lethargy of divine odors and lowly spices, but one can only be hoist by his own hay-fork if he fails to detect the deflationary incongruity of "Sovereign Barns"! The poem does deal, and deal seriously, with the malady that Tennyson dramatizes in "Lotos-Eaters," the ennui of existence, of consciousness. But Dickinson does more than dramatize (chiefly in the last line): she also judges the attitude. Through the comic personification of the grass ("stir all day to pretty Tunes," "thread the Dews all night," "hold the Sunshine in its lap") in, typically, incongruously courtly terms, the poem at once warns the reader and sets him up (like the reader traps in *Tale of a Tub*) for a heaven of "Sovereign Barns": a curious blend of satire and sentiment, scorn and remorse, for the comforting old orthodox ideas of heaven and for existence itself. Thus, the last line, "I wish I were a Hay," much more than a wistful or whimsical wish, is, through the tonic complexity of what has gone before, a judgment, a ridiculing of that wish.

By personifying death as a kind of courtly gentleman, Dickinson invades an area of the ineffable shunned by Donne, who also dwelt much on death in his poetry. Donne, however, as in his dealings with the afterlife, nearly always limits himself to *attitudes* towards death. Even in "Death be not proud" Donne is addressing an abstraction rather than a personification. Dickinson confronts death directly, dramatically, often comically:

> I made my soul familiar—with her extremity—
> That at the last, it should not be a novel Agony—
> But she, and Death, acquainted—
> Meet tranquilly, as friends—
> Salute, and pass, without a Hint—
> And thus, the Matter ends—

This, the conclusion to number "412," exemplifies the way in which Dickinson mines material from the ineffable with a mirth that twists with wry humor the old sex/death relationship of Donne's time. Her soul and Death "meet tranquilly, as friends" rather than as the lovers that really are, or were. They "salute, and pass (the soul on its way to heaven?), without a Hint" because their "affair" is over: "And thus, the Matter ends." The pun on "Matter" is obvious. Humor has determined mood, metaphor, tone, but the determinism, the restrictions inherent in the comic vision render her free to use such material as death and the afterlife. Fear, horror, pain, belief are objectified. In the same way she confronts the terrible incomprehensibility of the eternity of the silent dead with a certain slant of language inevitably comic in its distortion:

> Under the Light, yet under,
> Under the Grass and the Dirt,
> Under the Beetle's Cellar
> Under the Clover's Root,
>
> Further than Arm could stretch
> Were it Giant long
> . . . . .

> Further than Guess can gallop
> Further than Riddle ride—
> Oh for a Disc to the Distance
> Between Ourselves and the Dead!

This ["Under the Light, yet under"] is the same sort of comic, cosmic hyperbole that one finds in Donne's love poetry ("The Sunne Rising," "The Relique," for example)—deliberate distortion that fuses pain and poignancy with self-mockery.

In the following poem ("345") emotion is again so muted by mirth that the *attitude* of the poet seems earned, though no logic, no rational construct is involved:

> Funny—to be a Century—
> And see the People—going by—
> I—should die of the Oddity—
> But then—I'm not so staid—as He—
>
> He keeps His Secrets safely—very—
> Were He to tell—extremely sorry
> This Bashful Globe of Ours would be—
> So dainty of Publicity—

Despite the usual "I" in the first stanza, the casually conversationalist lines are too lean for tears: the terrible implacability of time is only intensified by the comic, bemused detachment with which it is observed. Similarly, the image of the dainty bashfulness of this globe at once holds off and evokes the horrors of history with the shield of humor. As MacLeish says, it is characteristic of her unforgettable tone that "it does not clamor at us even when its words are the words of passion or agony."

Charles Anderson's comment (*Emily Dickinson's Poetry*), that "the anthropomorphic conception of deity seemed inadequate, hilariously so to her," is only partially or occasionally true. Her conception of a careless God could also drive her close to despair, and could result in a poem ["Of Course—I prayed—"] in which the comic and tragic visions are juxtaposed rather than fused:

> Of Course—I prayed—
> And did God Care?
> He cared as much as on the Air
> A Bird—had stamped her foot—
> And cried "Give Me"—
> My Reason—Life—
> I had not had—but for Yourself—
> 'Twere better Charity
> To leave me in the Atom's Tomb—
> Merry, and nought, and gay, and numb—
> Than this smart Misery.

The first five lines serve as a comic prelude, a pout from the mouth of a childlike *persona*. They work a kind of comic cajolery, by humorous reduction, to lead the reader into an idea or mood of despair otherwise unapproachable in its shock, its vastness, its heresy. There is a sense of a Miltonic "vast abrupt" between God and the chaotic "smart Misery" of human existence. And yet the comic metaphor of the bird somehow provides deliverance from complete despair by the extreme unction of understatement.

More often, Dickinson's comic spirit finds its way into a poem in subtler fashion. As Whicher so aptly puts it, her "instinct for comedy . . . is woven into the fabric of her poems and cannot easily be separated for analysis. It startles us in an unexpected phrase or epithet and is gone before we know it, as though a bird in flight had slightly lowered an eyelid at us." There is something of the winking bird in the Gothic machinery of "One need not be a Chamber—to be Haunted." Haunted houses, corridors, midnight meetings, a collapsing Abbey—all prepare for the final two stanzas, where the silly and the serious emerge in a complex tone and meaning:

> Ourself behind ourself, concealed—
> Should startle most—
> Assassin hid in our Apartment
> Be Horror's least.
>
> The Body—borrows a Revolver—
> He bolts the Door—
> O'erlooking a superior spectre—
> Or More—

The question, Is it possible, at last, to look around and see your Self? is couched in cartoon language. But the terror of the trap of self-consciousness is felt, dramatized, objectified. Robert Frost's "Desert Places," which treats the same theme, seems flat statement by comparison.

A similar reduction of the Gothic to the absurd is seen in number "861":

> Split the Lark—and you'll find the Music—
> Bulb after Bulb, in Silver rolled—
> Scantily dealt to the Summer Morning
> Saved for your Ear when Lutes be old.
>
> Loose the flood—you shall find it patent—
> Gush after gush, reserved for you—
> Scarlet Experiment! Sceptic Thomas!
> Now, do you doubt that your Bird was true?

Certainly the metaphor of man as lark-splitter is metaphysical in its incongruity. The poem is a serious comment, in comic terms, on the nature of man. Man is the sinister source-seeker, the destroyer of nature and beauty because he cannot simply accept beauty, the way things are.

One of the best of Dickinson's nature poems, "A Narrow Fellow in the Grass," is really another comment on the most elusive aspects of human existence. The tone is typical: polite, wry diffidence, evocative of a very slight, self-mocking smile. Ostensibly a precise rendering of a snake's appearance, the poem is actually a profound perception of the reality of time past, of myth, of the Jungian "collective unconscious." The poem is too well known to be quoted in full. Note, however, the careful preparation for the intensity of tone of the last stanza. In the first stanza, the basal tone is set by immediately calling the snake (never referred to as "snake") "a narrow Fellow," a comic personification the elegant variation of which enforces the theme. (You do not call a snake a snake because, trailing clouds of myth, the snake *is* loathsome.) Also, "his notice sudden is." This underplayed element of surprise, of shock and mystery is carefully built up to prepare for the dramatic, earned emotion in the conclusion. In the second stanza the snake is only glimpsed fleetingly, a "spotted shaft" that opens and closes the grass blades. In the fourth stanza, the startling description of the snake as "a Whip lash / Unbraiding in the Sun" ends with the snake's sudden disappearance: "It wrinkled, and was gone." The warm sociability and familiarity of the fifth stanza, which contrasts the "cordiality" of "several of Nature's People," only intensifies the shock and mystery climaxed in the final stanza:

> But never met this Fellow
> Attended, or alone
> Without a tighter breathing
> And Zero at the Bone—

It evokes a nervous smile, uncertain and self-conscious. A strange truth has been touched here in this half-comic metaphor that gathers together all the threads of the ancient serpent/Satan myth into a fabric of restrained and reality-rooted fear. The conceit of the snake as a "Fellow" is more than quaint. The idea of Satanic embodiment is at least vaguely "there" even in the first line and is reinforced in this last stanza. Further, the reinforcement of the suggestion is accomplished by the reference to Edenic innocence in stanza three, "Yet when a Boy, and Barefoot," and by the "Whip lash" image, suggestive of the scourge of Satan, the punishment of the Fall. Unlike the fantastic "ancient knowledge" Gothicized in Robert Bridge's "Low

Barometer," or some of the highly rhetorical "racial memory" passages in Faulkner, Dickinson's poem presents the perception with precision and convincing reality. The assumed decorum of her comic vision here again achieves vital detachment.

Detachment is inevitably a hard-earned artistic process. Allen Tate believes (*The Man of Letters in the Modern World*) that Dickinson and Donne share the control of detachment: "Their sense of the natural world is not blunted by a too-rigid system of ideas; yet the ideas, the abstractions, their education or their intellectual heritage, are not so weak as to let their purely personal quality, get out of control." That these external aids to artistic control are important is obvious. I should simply like to suggest that in a great many poems Emily Dickinson's primary source of control is her deliberately imposed comic vision. In number "1035," for example, what seems all along to be a homey, personal immersion in nature is undercut suddenly by the revelation of a startling and comic *persona*:

> Bee! I'm expecting you!
> Was saying Yesterday
> To Somebody you know
> That you were due—
>
> The Frogs got Home last Week—
> Are settled, and at work—
> Birds, mostly back
> The Clover warm and thick—
>
> You'll get my Letter by
> The seventeenth; Reply
> Or better, be with me—
> Yours, Fly.

Pure fun, in a kind of comic dramatic monologue, subdues the frenetic, tense anticipation of spring. The mirth, of frogs and flies as harbingers of spring, is metaphysical in its logical entry, its incongruity.

A punch line also punctures a nature-inspired mood of gloom in number "1075":

> The Sky is low—the Clouds are mean.
> A Travelling Flake of Snow
> Across a Barn or through a Rut
> Debates if it will go—
>
> A Narrow Wind complains all day
> How some one treated him
> Nature, like Us is sometimes caught
> Without her Diadem.

In other words, caught with her crown down.

The mercurial quality of her mirth can sometimes take the shape of a comic tableau, as in number "1177," where Dickinson paints a starchy allegorical portrait:

> A prompt—executive Bird is the Jay—
> Bold as a Bailiff's Hymn—
> Brittle and Brief in quality—
> Warrant in every line—
>
> Sitting a Bough like a Brigadier
> Confident and straight—
> Much is the mien of him in March
> As a Magistrate—

The stiff-necked portrait effect is accomplished by using an unusual, for Dickinson, number of adjectives: prompt, executive, bold, brittle, brief, confident, straight. It is a comic comment on the law of nature and the nature of law.

Finally, it should be re-emphasized that Dickinson had the curious ability to avoid sacrificing cosmic implications at the expense of the comic. This will be apparent if two poems of similar circumstance are kept in mind while reading number "1343" below: Gray's "Ode on a Favorite Cat Drowned in a Dish of Gold Fishes" and Freneau's "On a Honey Bee":

> A single Clover Plank
> Was all that saved a Bee
> A Bee I personally knew
> From sinking in the sky—
>
> 'Twixt Firmament above
> And Firmament below
> The Billows of Circumference
> Were sweeping him away—
>
> This harrowing event
> Transpiring in the Grass
> Did not so much as wring from him
> A wandering "Alas"—

The poem can be read as allegory, with bee as man affording obvious comment on the precariousness of human existence, an existence which is swept up in the "Billows of Circumference," the mysterious totality, as Johnson suggests, of "all relationships of man, nature, and spirit." But the poem is richer, more real, more convincing if allegory is not imposed. The poem speaks for itself. The bee exists, and what happens to the bee's existence is important because "I personally knew" that bee. Not only is no *man* an island, but nothing in existence is an island. If this seems an extravagant extraction, note the extravagant scope of imagery, from bees and clover to firmament and circumference. As in most great poetry, especially metaphysical poetry, the question of how to handle the disparate worlds of the concrete and the abstract is asked. What happens to the bee is somehow indicative of the nature of reality. The first three stanzas present the event with comic objectivity. This is what happens: irresponsible "Clover Plank" fails to save a bee from an irresponsible "Freight of Wind," and "Bumble Bee was not." Perfect objectivity. The bee is not brutalized, not murdered, not plotted against. He simply "was not." But with the last stanza the smile becomes very uncertain. What is the nature of reality? How is one to exist? Is one to live with a beelike, stoic acceptance of conscious-less, amoral nature? The first line introduces a value judgment, or so it seems, initiating a curious and complex chain reaction: 1) this is silly, the event is hardly "harrowing"; 2) in the sense of an exemplum of the blind brutishness, the nature of nature, it is, indeed, harrowing; 3) the bee is admirably stoic; 4) the bee is stupidly stolid; 5) which is more real, clover or circumference? No answer is given; as Dickinson says in number "1400" ("What mystery pervades a well"), "nature is a stranger yet." The poem is a comic dislocation of language, syntax, imagery into a new meaning, or a new quest for meaning.

Humor is often at the heart of Emily Dickinson's vision, in many of her best poems; she exploited the human capacity for risibility, which enabled her to unite her feeling for both "a nearness to tremendousness," as one poem phrases it, and for wonder at the familiar. She, too, with Sir Thomas Browne, saw man as "that great and true *Amphibium*, whose nature is disposed to live not only like other creatures in divers elements, but in divided and distinguished worlds." The pain and poignancy of that division she muted and transmuted by a comic spirit that provided sufficient artistic detachment, unity and complexity of tone, a wide range of *materia poetica*, and startling variety in shades of emotion and thought. Of course her metaphysical mirth is not always at work; nor would she or we want it to be. As she said, in what is probably one of her last poems, "The earth has many keys." Her comic spirit is one.

Source: Paul W. Anderson, "The Metaphysical Mirth of Emily Dickinson," in *Georgia Review*, Vol. 20, No. 1, Spring 1966, pp. 72–83.

Donald E. Thackrey

In the following essay, Thackrey considers that, for Emily Dickinson, the writing of poetry was a mystical experience.

From what origin or impulse in the poet does poetry come? An answer to this question necessitates a brief glance at the poet herself. To any reader of her poems or letters, the emotional resources of Emily Dickinson seem boundless. She exhibits the capacity to experience the fullness and variety of an emotional life which the great mystics testify exists beyond the horizons of ordinary experience. . . .

In conjunction with a rich emotional nature can usually be found a highly imaginative life. The letters as well as the poems of Emily Dickinson testify to her imaginative powers. . . .

Two salient characteristics of Emily Dickinson's mind as exhibited in her poems and letters seem to be a result of her abundant emotional and imaginative resources. As we might expect, these characteristics display a typical counterbalance in point of view. There is first of all the supremely intense joy of life. The evidence of this ecstatic joy could be accumulated from innumerable poems and letters. . . .

The second and probably more significant direction taken by her intense emotional and imaginative nature is a thorough awareness of the suffering in life. Suffering seemed to be a basic, unavoidable element of human life, and this fact weighed heavily on a person as capable of profound feeling as Emily Dickinson. . . .

Whatever the cause of suffering, the poems of Emily Dickinson give ample evidence that she had a capacity for experiencing suffering far beyond that of the ordinary person. . . .

One can conclude from the evidence in her poems that Emily Dickinson's emotional and imaginative life was developed to an amazing extent. Joyous ecstasy and the antithetic bleak despair—not to mention the other shades of emotional feeling for which she is noted—possessed her life and gave to it a direction which resulted in a dedication to poetry.

The question which was probably unexpressed but was nevertheless an essential one to Emily Dickinson can now be asked. What course of action was necessary for such a person to achieve some sort of realization of her nature? First of all we must note that history has shown that artists act as if they were under a tremendous compulsion to express whatever vision they have seen. . . .

Thus, for Emily Dickinson, poetry was undoubtedly an unavoidable necessity. Still there were certain rational justifications for turning to poetry....

[In his book *Emily Dickinson*,] Richard Chase maintains that Emily Dickinson regarded poetry as "one of the stratagems by which she was empowered to endure life," and this view is supported by...excerpts from her letters. She strove to raise bloom on the bleakness of her lot, as one of her poems expresses it....

If, however, poetry for Emily Dickinson began as an anodyne for life, it soon developed into something infinitely more important to her—so important in fact, that after Emily Dickinson's maturity, it would scarcely be possible to separate any aspect of her life and personality from her poetry. Poetry became the meaning, the very essence, of life.

Several of her poems speak specifically of poetry. The opening poem in Madame Bianchi's volume is a significant comment.

> This is my letter to the world,
> That never wrote to me,—
> The simple news that Nature told,
> With tender majesty.
>
> Her message is committed
> To hands I cannot see;
> For love of her, sweet countrymen,
> Judge tenderly of me!

Nature's simple news, of course, inspired more than just her so-called nature poems. All her poetry was dependent upon the secrets she thought of as coming from nature. But what, exactly, is poetry? . . .

Emily Dickinson is consistent in regarding the poet as a divine magician, dealing with familiar things, but transforming them into piercing, ravishing "pictures" that so overpower the human imagination that they can only be described in terms of "thunder," "immense attars," and "divine insanity." Words, the mighty, electric elements of poetry, fuse into the incandescent instruments of the divine which one experiences as poetry. It is the use of *words* which effects the magical transformation of existence from "ordinary meanings" into "divine intoxication." But notice also the implication that no one may completely experience poetry, for poetry, like love, has for Emily Dickinson the mystical significance of God. We can prove either love or poetry by the effects they have upon us; yet there remains the awareness

that the essence of love or of poetry, their ultimate potentiality, is forever denied us. Thus poetry, for Emily Dickinson, in spite of the almost illimitable power of words, offers a challenge and a medium by which one can attempt to transcend the normal limits of perception (even highly-developed artistic perception) and enter into the transcendent, mystical awareness that is "intimate with madness." The supreme worth of poetry, consequently, is self-evident....

The position of a poet in relation to the reading public is always interesting and especially so in Emily Dickinson's case because of the unusual manner in which her poems were written, stored away, and finally edited and published. It has often been assumed that Emily Dickinson secluded herself from the world and turned to writing poetry because of an unhappy love affair. To assume that frustrated love was the sole genesis of Emily Dickinson's unusual life and work is, I think, to underestimate her. Emily Dickinson herself suggests that her retirement may have been prompted, in part, by a desire to escape the shallow loquaciousness of ordinary social intercourse....

It may be added, from the general tenor of her work, that the seclusion was not only to avoid certain things but also to gain a positive advantage. Her withdrawal from the world brings to mind again her ever-present tendency toward a mystical view of life. It is well known that mystics are eager to sacrifice their whole lives to a certain object, a certain vision of truth. Such sacrifices are not self-denial in the mystical philosophy, but rather self-fulfillment. Whatever rationale Emily Dickinson conceived for her seclusion, it is certain that this privacy allowed her the time and opportunity to nourish and maintain her poetic genius....

The position of Emily Dickinson as a poet, then, was this: to utilize the tremendous resources of her emotional and imaginative energy to create poetry which in turn provided her with an outlet or an anodyne for this energy which might otherwise have destroyed her sanity. Words, the powerful agents of thought, became the instruments by which she projected herself into first one relationship and then another with the natural world and with that other more elusive world of her mystical intuitions....

Her goal was sometimes obscured, but she nevertheless was determined to approach a complete comprehension of the mysteries of life and death by means of mystical experience recorded and examined through the discipline of the communication of words in the framework of poetic creation. A mystical vision first experienced and then assimilated into her understanding by the expression of it in poetry established the foundation for further exploration of her consciousness which in turn led to new levels of mystical experience. Perhaps her mystical experiences may be thought of as the climb of a giant mountain slope reaching ever upward but interrupted by frequent ledges upon which she paused for orientation, a view of the ground covered, and the gathering of forces for the next ascent. Her ultimate goal will be achieved at death when she becomes the bride of the Father and of the Son and of the Holy Ghost. Until then her position as a poet must reflect the "compound vision" which depends upon the awareness of death.

Source: Donald E. Thackrey, "The Position of the Poet," in *Emily Dickinson's Approach to Poetry*, University of Nebraska Press, 1954, pp. 52–75.

SOURCES

Bennett, Fordyce R., *A Reference Guide to the Bible in Emily Dickinson's Poetry*, Scarecrow Press, 1997, p. 306.

Casper, Scott E., *The Industrial Book, 1840–1880*, University of North Carolina Press, 2007, pp. 224–27.

Crumbley, Paul, *Winds of Will: Emily Dickinson and the Sovereignty of Democratic Thought*, University of Alabama Press, 2010, p. 81.

Dickinson, Emily, "Tell all the Truth but tell it slant," in *Final Harvest: Emily Dickinson's Poems*, Little, Brown, 1964, pp. 248–49.

Dobson, Joanne, *Dickinson and the Strategies of Reticence: The Woman Writer in Nineteenth-Century America*, Indiana University Press, 1989, pp. xi–xvii, 99–105.

Doriani, Beth Maclay, *Emily Dickinson: Daughter of Prophecy*, University of Massachusetts Press, 1996, pp. 116–19.

Dumoulin, Heinrich, *Zen Enlightenment: Origins and Meaning*, translated by John C. Maraldo, Shambhala, 2007, pp. 35–41, 65–76, 139–49.

"Facts on Women in Congress 2011," Center for American Women and Politics, Rutgers University website, http://www.cawp.rutgers.edu/fast_facts/levels_of_office/Congress-CurrentFacts.php (accessed March 20, 2012).

Friedlander, Benjamin, "Devious Truths," in *Emily Dickinson Journal*, Vol. 18, No. 1, 2009, pp. 32–43.

Gelpi, Albert, *The Tenth Muse: The Psyche of the American Poet*, Harvard University Press, 1975, pp. 219–32, 278–96.

Johnson, Thomas H., Introduction to *Final Harvest: Emily Dickinson's Poems*, Little, Brown, 1964, pp. v–xiv.

Juhasz, Suzanne, Cristanne Miller, and Martha Nell Smith, *Comic Power in Emily Dickinson*, University of Texas Press, 1993, pp. 4–7.

Kher, Inder Nath, *The Landscape of Absence: Emily Dickinson's Poetry*, Yale University Press, 1974, pp. 1–6, 129–34.

Leiter, Sharon, *Critical Companion to Emily Dickinson: A Literary Reference to Her Life and Work*, Facts on File, 2007, pp. 52, 68, 84, 92, 180–81, 264.

Miller, Cristanne, *Emily Dickinson: A Poet's Grammar*, Harvard University Press, 1987, pp. 1–19.

Nhat Hanh, Thich, *Zen Keys*, Doubleday, 1995, pp. 49–73.

St. Armand, Barton Levi, "Emily Dickinson and the Occult: The Rosicrucian Connection," in *Prairie Schooner*, Vol. 51, No. 4, Winter 1977/1978, pp. 345–57.

Wallace, Ronald, *God Be with the Clown: Humor in American Poetry*, University of Missouri Press, 1984, pp. 77–83.

Watts, Emily Stipes, *The Poetry of American Women from 1632 to 1945*, University of Texas Press, 1977, pp. 121–36.

Wells, Henry W., *Introduction to Emily Dickinson*, Packard, 1947, pp. xi–xvii, 48–60, 133–64, 208–12, 245–47.

Wider, Sarah Ann, "Emily Dickinson," in *Dictionary of Literary Biography*, Vol. 243, *The American Renaissance in New England, Fourth Series*, edited by Wesley T. Mott, The Gale Group, 2001, pp. 103–28.

FURTHER READING

Fernández-Armesto, Felipe, *Truth: A History and a Guide for the Perplexed*, St. Martin's, 2001.

> The author of this volume, an Oxford University historian, presents a comprehensive treatment of the functioning of truth in society from the earliest civilizations to the present. He opens the preface with a comical discussion on how parents must quash the idea of Santa Claus.

Kapstein, Matthew, ed., *The Presence of Light: Divine Radiance and Religious Experience*, University of Chicago Press, 2004.

> This academic collection of essays, compiled by a Buddhist scholar, treats the role of light in an

array of religious traditions in the interest of drawing universal conclusions.

Miller, Brenda, and Suzanne Paola, *Tell It Slant: Writing and Shaping Creative Nonfiction*, McGraw-Hill, 2004.

> Here the authors use Dickinson's poem as the nominal foundation for an inspirational/instructional guide on presenting truths in compelling ways in nonfiction prose.

Wojcik, Jan, and Raymond-Jean Frontain, *Poetic Prophecy in Western Literature*, Fairleigh Dickinson University Press, 1984.

> This collection of twelve essays discusses how the verse of such authors as Walt Whitman, Mark Twain, and Allen Ginsberg is representative of a literary prophetic tradition.

SUGGESTED SEARCH TERMS

Emily Dickinson AND "Tell all the Truth but tell it slant"

Emily Dickinson AND truth

Emily Dickinson AND light

Emily Dickinson AND nineteenth century AND women's poetry

Emily Dickinson AND Ralph Waldo Emerson

Emily Dickinson AND Amherst

Emily Dickinson AND feminism

Emily Dickinson AND modernism

Emily Dickinson AND mysticism

Emily Dickinson AND eyes

What Were They Like?

DENISE LEVERTOV

1967

"What Were They Like?" is a poem by twentieth-century British-born American poet Denise Levertov. It was first published in her collection *The Sorrow Dance* in 1967, at the height of the Vietnam War, when there was a growing antiwar movement in the United States. Levertov was associated with the antiwar movement, and her poem is one of a number she wrote during the mid- to late 1960s opposing the war. Through the use of two speakers, the poem suggests that Vietnamese culture has been wiped out by the ferocity of the war, and no one can fully remember what it was like. Antiwar activists at the time believed that the methods employed by the US military as it prosecuted the war with ever-growing hi-tech weaponry might indeed, if such methods were to continue for long, annihilate an entire culture in South Vietnam. The poem is notable not only for its unusual structure, in which six numbered questions are followed by six answers numbered as to which question they respond to, but for its evocation of a rich Vietnamese culture. "What Were They Like?" also serves as a testament to the moral conscience aroused in many people in the United States as the Vietnam War continued to escalate through the 1960s with no apparent end in sight.

Denise Levertov (© *AP Images / Associated Press*)

AUTHOR BIOGRAPHY

Levertov was born in Ilford, Essex, England, on October 24, 1923. Her father, Paul Philip Levertoff, was a Russian Jew who converted to Christianity. Her mother, Beatrice Spooner-Jones, was Welsh. Growing up in a bookish household, Levertov and her sister Olga were educated at home by their mother. Both parents regularly read aloud to their children, and Levertov read plenty of poetry for herself. As a child she also attended ballet school. From 1943 to 1945, during World War II, Levertov served as a civilian nurse in a London hospital. Her first book of poetry, *The Double Image*, was published in 1946.

In 1947, Levertov married an American, Mitchell Goodman, and the following year she moved with her husband to New York, where she became friends with the poet William Carlos Williams, who became a mentor to her. She also became a US citizen. During the 1950s she lived for a while in Europe and Mexico before returning to New York in 1959. Her second book, *Here and Now*, was published in 1957, followed by *Overland to the Islands* the following year.

The 1960s proved to be a prolific decade for Levertov, and this was the period in which much of her poetic reputation was forged. Her publications during this period include *The Jacob's Ladder* (1961), *City Psalm* (1964), *O Taste and See: New Poems* (1964), *The Sorrow Dance* (1967)—which contains "What Were They Like?"—*A Tree Telling of Orpheus* (1968), *The Cold Spring and Other Poems* (1968), and *Embroideries* (1969).

During this decade Levertov worked as poetry editor of the *Nation*, received a Guggenheim Fellowship (in 1963), taught poetry seminars at Drew University and City College of New York, and taught at Vassar College in 1966. She and her husband became involved in campus protests against the Vietnam War during this period. She traveled to Moscow in the 1960s and to Hanoi, the capital of North Vietnam, in 1972. In addition to her reputation as a poet, she was noted for being committed to peace and justice from a leftist point of view.

Levertov's significant publications during the 1970s included *Relearning the Alphabet* (1970), *To Stay Alive* (1971), *Footprints* (1972), *The Freeing of the Dust* (1975), *Life in the Forest* (1978), and *The Poet in the World* (1973), a collection of essays. In the 1980s she published, among other works, *Light Up the Cave* (1981), *Candles in Babylon* (1982), *Oblique Prayers: New Poems with 14 Translations from Jean Joubert* (1984), and *A Door in the Hive* (1989).

Levertov taught at Brandeis University, MIT, and Tufts University. From 1982 to 1993 she was a full professor at Stanford University. She moved to Seattle in 1989 and taught part-time at the University of Washington. Her final works were *The Stream and the Sapphire: Selected Poems on Religious Themes* (1997) and *The Life around Us: Selected Poems on Nature* (1997). She died on December 20, 1997, of complications due to lymphoma, at the age of seventy-four. *The Great Unknowing: Last Poems*, was published posthumously in 1999.

POEM SUMMARY

The text used for this summary is from Levertov's *Poems, 1960–67*, New Directions, 1983, p. 234. A version of the poem can be found on the following web page: http://www.nbu.bg/webs/amb/american/5/levertov/they.htm.

"What Were They Like?" is a poem of thirty-one lines written in free verse. It is divided into two sections. In the first section an unidentified (male) speaker asks six numbered questions about the cultural practices of the Vietnamese people. In the second section, a second unidentified speaker answers each question in sequence.

In the first question, the speaker asks about the people of Vietnam, and the kind of lanterns they used. The second question asks whether the Vietnamese held festivals to celebrate the coming of spring. Question 3 is about whether the Vietnamese showed their enjoyment through laughter. Question 4 inquires about what sort of ornaments they used to decorate their homes, naming some precious materials. The fifth question is about Vietnamese literature. The last question is about how they spoke and what their speech sounded like.

The second speaker then answers the questions one by one. She or he addresses the first speaker as *Sir*, indicating that the questioner is a man. The second speaker appears to be someone who is an expert on Vietnamese culture, or is at least regarded as one. The second speaker may or may not be Vietnamese. But she is likely an outsider who has studied the subject and has only limited knowledge of it, as she refers to the Vietnamese in the third, not the first, person.

In response to the first question, the speaker does not at first answer directly, but rather makes a remark implying that the Vietnamese people are or have been enduring a difficult time that has given them heavy hearts. In the next line (line 11 of the poem), the speaker says that no one knows the answer to the first question the man posed. This kind of cultural knowledge is no longer available.

The answer to the second question is a tentative one. The people may, the speaker says, have celebrated the coming of spring at one point in their history, but they no longer do so. There are, figuratively speaking, no more springs in Vietnam because too many children have died violently. This appears to be a direct reference to the Vietnam War, in which civilian casualties were high. In response to the third question, the speaker offers an oblique answer couched in poetic imagery, saying that the people of Vietnam no longer laugh. They have suffered too much; the imagery suggests damage by fire. The answer to the fourth question is equally enigmatic. The

speaker does not know the correct answer but implies that the Vietnamese no longer use such items. The reference in the following line (18) is once again to destruction by fire.

The answer to question 5 is the longest of the six answers. It is similar to the first answer in the passive construction with which it begins, emphasizing that there is no official record of Vietnamese literature. The speaker then adds that most people in Vietnam were peasants and were therefore—it is implied—not likely to develop a written literature. In the lines that follow, the speaker imagines a lost past in which the country was at peace and there was nothing to spoil the beauty of nature. Then, the speaker imagines, people may have related old stories to their children, thus creating, the reader will realize, an oral literature tradition that was passed from generation to generation. But then war came, line 25 clearly states, and all that was lost, to be replaced only by suffering. The coming of war has also had devastating effects on the way the Vietnamese people speak. The speech has lost its former song-like quality. No one now knows what it sounded like, the speaker says, echoing her answers to questions 1 and 5. The use of a poetic image in the penultimate line tries to give some impression of what that speech at one time sounded like. The final line seems to sum up the overall sense conveyed by the speaker's answers to these six questions of an ancient culture destroyed and lost. There are few clues left as to what it was once like.

THEMES

Culture

"What Were They Like?" is about the destruction of a culture that comes about through war. The reference is specifically to Vietnam during the period of the Vietnam War in the 1960s, although it might also be applied more generally to any traditional culture that has been ground down and obliterated by war. The culture is lost, and neither speaker knows exactly what it was like. Both speakers are from outside the culture: the first knows nothing but is curious; the second seems to have accumulated some knowledge, as a reporter or scholar might, but the culture she reports on has vanished in the carnage of war. What it was like can only be partially reconstructed from fragmentary, incomplete memories.

TOPICS FOR FURTHER STUDY

- What was the domino theory (or the expected domino effect), and how did it influence US policy in southeast Asia during the Cold War? Write a short essay in which you explain the history of the concept as applied to US foreign policy at the time. Was the domino theory proved right or wrong?

- Go to Umapper.com and create a map of Vietnam. Show on your map where major battles or important incidents took place during the Vietnam War.

- Read *The Fight for Peace: A History of Antiwar Movements in America* (2006), by Ted Gottfried, which examines for young-adult readers (in grades 8–11) the various antiwar movements in the United States since the Civil War right up to the Iraq War that began in 2003. In particular, read the chapter "The Quagmire," about the Vietnam War, and give a class presentation in which you discuss the main elements of the antiwar movement at that time. Who were the peace activists? What were their methods? What did they achieve?

- What is the value of poetry? Can a poem change anything in the world? In his interview with Levertov in 1971, William Packard quoted W. H. Auden, the twentieth-century British poet, as saying, "I do not think that writing poems will change anything." Levertov disagreed. Who do you agree with, Auden or Levertov? Why? Engage in a class debate in which several students speak in favor of one point of view and several other students argue for the contrary view.

War

It is clear that war is the source of the loss of the traditional culture of the Vietnamese people. The poem mentions that bombs have fallen, children have been killed, and suffering has been immense. The answers to questions 2, 3, 4, and 5 all make this abundantly clear. The war

has not just been fought between two armies; there have been high civilian casualties. Many innocents have died, and a whole way of life that had existed for many generations has been disrupted and destroyed.

Beauty

It is clear from both questions and responses that the Vietnamese had a culture that valued beauty and knew how to create and appreciate art. They also took joy in nature. This is apparent even from the questions asked by the speaker, who knows nothing of Vietnamese culture but who seeks to understand what it was like. The questions are something of a rhetorical device, since if the speaker genuinely knew nothing of the culture, he would not be able to ask such specific questions. The reader is encouraged to believe, even before reading the answers, that the specific things mentioned in these six questions were indeed a prominent part of Vietnamese culture. The Vietnamese cultivated gardens. They used precious stones to create ornaments. They held annual spring festivals to welcome the return of nature's fecundity. It was a refined culture in which people expressed themselves in quiet ways (line 5). They valued tradition, and stories were passed on from one generation to the next.

Loss

In a sense the poem is an elegy for what has been lost and will not return. This is emphasized especially by the answers given by the second speaker, which state that no one now remembers the details of what the culture was like. It has passed out of memory, as if there has been an act of genocide. Genocide is far more than the devastation that war always brings; it refers to the wiping out of an entire people and their culture. This shows that the poem may be set in the future. It is as if the poet has extended her vision to what would happen if present trends in this war were to continue. The weapons of destruction used in such a brutal war, in which one side uses weapons created with modern technology to destroy a peasant culture, will result, the poet seems to be saying, in the absolute annihilation of a people. This gives force to the last line of the poem, which emphasizes silence. No one is left to speak or sing or record history, or carry on the daily tasks of living. The sound of the voices of the Vietnamese people can only be faintly heard by means of a metaphor drawn from nature, according to the last lines. Significantly also,

"What Were They Like" begins with questions about Vietnamese history and culture. *(© beboy /*
Shutterstock.com)

the second speaker, who is supposed to be answering the questions posed by the first speaker, finishes with a question of her own, implying that even what she has heard may not be true since it cannot be verified by anyone.

STYLE

Tone
Although the poem tells of the horrors and destruction of war, including the killing of innocents, the tone of the speakers, especially the second speaker, is detached and objective. The passive construction ("It is not remembered" and "It was reported") in the answer to question 1 (second line), which is used again for answer 5 (first line) and answer 6 (third line), is the most noticeable aspect of this detached tone. The second speaker sounds like a reporter or journalist, commenting on what she has been able to determine about the facts of the matter but remaining disengaged personally. This detached quality is

reinforced by the formality of the numbered questions and answers, as if somebody is formulating a report or preparing a research paper. This cool, detached tone creates a sense of distance between the second speaker and the events she describes. The feeling of distance reinforces the theme of the poem, which is about the wiping out of an entire people and culture. The speaker can only describe it by looking back to what little is known about the past.

Imagery
There is no imagery in the questions the first speaker asks. They are matter-of-fact questions. But images are a feature of the second speaker's responses, and are the means by which she communicates the horrific events that have taken place. While the tone of the second speaker is detached, the intensity of the imagery suggests that she has somehow gained a deeply felt sympathetic understanding of the culture. She immediately transforms the first question about types of lighting to refer not to lamps at all but to the heaviness of hearts crushed by the events of war.

Several images are related to fire, to the burning of flesh and bodies. The speaker ends her answer to question 6, the last question, with a simile to accompany and illustrate the factual statement. The song of the people, now extinguished, was like a beautiful natural phenomenon that anyone can still observe at night—in contrast to the sound of the people singing, which has vanished forever.

HISTORICAL CONTEXT

The Vietnam War

The origins of the Vietnam War lie in the attempt of Vietnam to throw off colonial rule. After World War II, Vietnam was controlled by France. But in 1954, the French were defeated by Vietnam's Communist forces at the battle of Dien Bien Phu. Under the Geneva Accords, Vietnam was then divided into the Communist North and the anti-Communist South. To prevent South Vietnam from falling into Communist hands, the United States offered economic aid and sent military advisers to South Vietnam. This did not stop the North Vietnamese guerrillas, known as the Viet Cong, from increasing their attacks on the South, and gradually the United States was drawn directly into the conflict. The US government alleged that on August 4, 1964, North Vietnamese forces attacked US ships in the Gulf of Tonkin. Three days later, the US Congress passed the Gulf of Tonkin Resolution, which authorized the administration of President Lyndon Johnson to greatly expand American forces in South Vietnam. By the end of 1965, there were nearly 200,000 US combat troops in South Vietnam.

However, the increase in the number of troops did not bring a quick end to the war. Although the US forces possessed superior technology and far greater firepower, this was not effective against an enemy that preferred not to fight pitched battles but favored guerrilla tactics, attacking only in small groups. The United States launched an intense bombing campaign of North Vietnam in 1965, but it did not succeed in bringing the North Vietnamese to the conference table, nor did it stop the Viet Cong from continuing to infiltrate South Vietnam and attack US troops. By the end of 1966, American troop strength had risen to nearly 400,000, and it would rise to nearly half a million by the end of the following year. But there was still

no sign that such a massive force would achieve victory against a determined and elusive enemy. It was estimated that Viet Cong forces in South Vietnam numbered about 300,000, and the Viet Cong also had the support of many Vietnamese civilians in their villages. American efforts to win over the civilian population were less than successful. In January 1968, the Tet offensive began, in which North Vietnamese troops and Viet Cong guerillas attacked South Vietnamese towns, including the capital city, Saigon. This was a setback for US forces, although within days most of the areas attacked by the Viet Cong had been reclaimed. The Johnson administration claimed with some truth that the Tet offensive was a military failure, but nonetheless the American public was becoming increasingly skeptical of the claims made by their political and military leaders. It soon became apparent that the war, to which the United States had committed so much, would prove to be unwinnable.

In 1968, Richard Nixon won the US presidential election with a promise to end the war by strengthening the South Vietnamese army and so reducing the involvement of the US military. However, in 1969, Nixon widened the war to include the secret bombing of neighboring Cambodia to disrupt Viet Cong supply lines, followed in 1970 by an invasion of that country. (US forces withdrew from Cambodia in July 1970.) In 1969, news broke of a massacre of civilians by US forces that had taken place the previous year in the village of My Lai in South Vietnam. The news sent shockwaves through the country and strengthened public opposition to the war.

By 1970, US troop levels had been reduced to 280,000. Peace talks, which had begun in Paris, France, in 1968, eventually bore fruit, and a cease-fire agreement was signed in 1973. American forces withdrew. But by 1974, conflict flared again, and North Vietnamese forces captured Saigon in 1975. The country was formally unified in 1976 as the Socialist Republic of Vietnam. The long US effort to prevent South Vietnam's falling into Communist hands had failed. Total American military deaths in the war were 58,193, according to the National Archives. According to the article "The War's Effect on the Vietnamese Land and People," about 304,000 US military personnel were wounded. On the Vietnamese side, 4 million Vietnamese were killed or wounded on both sides, including as many as 1.3 million civilians in South Vietnam.

COMPARE
&
CONTRAST

- **1960s:** This decade is marked by a strong antiwar movement. In April 1967, over one hundred thousand people march in New York to protest the war. They are addressed by Martin Luther King, Jr., near the United Nations building. Large antiwar protests are held in San Francisco and Washington, D.C., in October. Also in 1967, an antidraft movement springs up that is supported by Levertov and her husband.

  Today: Although the United States has been involved in two wars in the early twenty-first century, in Iraq and Afghanistan, there have been few large public protests against them. This is partly because there is no longer a draft in the United States, the wars being fought by an all-volunteer army, and partly because, in the aftermath of September 11, 2001, the US government has been successful in convincing the public that the wars are necessary in order to combat international terrorism.

- **1960s:** Vietnam is divided into two separate countries, North Vietnam and South Vietnam. North Vietnam is a Communist state and is at war with the US-backed dictatorship of South Vietnam. The war escalates throughout the decade, with heavy casualties on both sides.

  Today: Vietnam is one of the few remaining Communist countries in the world. Over recent decades it has pursued a policy of economic liberalization, and it joined the World Trade Organization in 2007. However, the government still maintains strict control over political expression, and no political parties other than the Communists are permitted.

- **1960s:** This is a turbulent decade in US history. In addition to antiwar protests, a race riot breaks out in Detroit in July 1967 and lasts for four days. There are riots in many American cities following the assassination of Martin Luther King in April 1968. Young people rebel against the values of the earlier generation, giving rise to the hippie or countercultural movement. Important social developments such as the women's movement and the civil rights movement gain momentum.

  Today: The dominant note in the United States is economic austerity. Unemployment is high following the global recession of 2008–2009, and the middle classes experience job insecurity and a fall in income levels. Two different forms of social and political protest emerge. One movement, the Tea Party, channels its energies into supporting right-wing, libertarian candidates for political office under the banner of the Republican Party. Another protest movement, Occupy Wall Street, or the Occupy movement, is more reminiscent of the 1960s. Protesters set up makeshift camps in cities across the nation, protesting growing income inequality and the accumulation of enormous wealth in the hands of the richest 1 percent of the population.

The Antiwar Movement

The anti–Vietnam War movement began almost as soon as the United States sent combat troops to South Vietnam. The protests increased significantly in 1965 as the war escalated. The antiwar movement was centered in colleges and universities, where many students burned their draft cards. As related by Don Lawson in his book *The United States in the Vietnam War*, in a protest in Washington, D.C., at a time when the United States was mounting heavy bombing raids on North Vietnam, twenty thousand protesters assembled outside the White House and chanted, "Hey! Hey! LBJ! How many kids did you kill today?" As the antiwar movement gathered force, it attracted many prominent individuals,

At the end of the poem, Levertov compares the singing of the people with the silent flight of moths at night. *(© Anna Tyukhmeneva | Shutterstock.com)*

including writers such as Norman Mailer, Robert Lowell, and Saul Bellow, as well as the famous pediatrician Dr. Benjamin Spock. In 1967, an organization called RESIST was formed to assist those who were resisting the draft. Both Denise Levertov and her husband, Mitchell Goodman, were involved in that organization. Levertov had been involved in the antiwar movement from its earliest stages. Lawson explains that once college deferments were steadily reduced, among the methods used for draft evasion were "flunking physical examinations by taking drugs, joining religious cults and declaring conscientious objector status, and simply leaving the country."

In August 1968, large antiwar demonstrations outside the Democratic National Convention in Chicago turned violent as police attacked protesters and the protesters fought back. In November 1969, 250,000 demonstrators gathered in Washington, D.C., to protest the war, the largest such gathering in American history. Protests flared again when President Nixon

ordered the invasion of Cambodia in 1970. In one notorious incident at Kent State University, in Ohio, in May 1970, National Guardsmen opened fire on student protesters, killing four people and wounding nine others.

CRITICAL OVERVIEW

As one of the more notable American poems dealing with the Vietnam War, "What Were They Like?" has attracted a fair amount of critical attention. In *Understanding Denise Levertov*, Harry Marten comments that "What Were They Like?," along with other poems in *The Sorrow Dance*, "reveals the nature of human brutalities enacted on behalf of the political state, imagining the thoughts and lives of victims and victimizers alike." Dorothy Nielsen, in "The Dark Wing of Mourning: Grief, Elegy and Time in the Poetry of Denise Levertov," sees the poem as being set in the near future, in which Vietnamese culture has been obliterated by the heavy hand of the US military. The poem is an attempt to portray this "silencing" of Vietnamese culture by a genocidal US war policy. Nielsen argues that the second speaker in the poem, the one who answers the questions, is of Vietnamese descent, but she defends Levertov against a charge of "poetic colonialism, or appropriation of voice," that such might entail. Levertov "borrows another voice in order to demonstrate the horrific implications of casting the North Vietnamese in the role of subhuman enemy," Nielsen writes.

Audrey T. Rodgers, in *Denise Levertov: The Poetry of Engagement*, summarizes the structure of the poem and comments, "The 'answers' ironically pick up the language of the questions, and the perversions of wartime are revealed in the 'distortions' of a once-revered way of life." Rodgers acknowledges that readers might have reservations about the format of the poem, "a pseudo-journalistic and deliberately cold approach to the catastrophe of Vietnam," but added that "the device is reminiscent of the reportage of the Vietnam War in interviews on television." In his essay "Denise Levertov's Political Poetry," Jerome Marzaro points out that "What Were They Like?" has some similarities to Levertov's later political poetry, written in the 1980s, about the conflict in El Salvador.

CRITICISM

Bryan Aubrey

Aubrey holds a PhD in English. In the following essay, he describes the US military's use of Agent Orange and napalm during the Vietnam War, and its relevance for "What Were They Like?"

Written in 1967, at the height of the Vietnam War, "What Were They Like?" presents a nightmarish vision of the future of the Vietnamese people and their culture. Indeed, it is written from the perspective of that future, as if the nightmare has already happened. An entire culture has been destroyed; an act of genocide has taken place. Whereas before there was a rich and civilized peasant culture in which people cultivated the fields, enjoyed the cyclical rhythms of nature, created art, and took a quiet joy in life, now, there is nothing. Vietnam resembles a charnel house. It is as silent as the graveyard. No one can even remember what its culture was like.

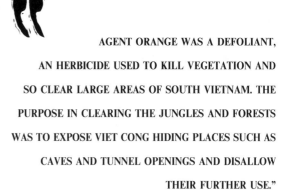

AGENT ORANGE WAS A DEFOLIANT, AN HERBICIDE USED TO KILL VEGETATION AND SO CLEAR LARGE AREAS OF SOUTH VIETNAM. THE PURPOSE IN CLEARING THE JUNGLES AND FORESTS WAS TO EXPOSE VIET CONG HIDING PLACES SUCH AS CAVES AND TUNNEL OPENINGS AND DISALLOW THEIR FURTHER USE."

Acting as a poet-prophet in this turbulent time in American history, Denise Levertov was sounding a warning. She was saying, in effect, that if the United States continued to employ its ruthless and deadly war machine in the same manner, this would be the result. Seen in this light, "What Were They Like?" is a very shocking poem, and it was intended to be so. It is an attempt to wake up a nation, to make its citizens see the destructive, inhuman course it is set upon, all in the name of defeating the enemy.

Levertov had been involved in the antiwar movement, which she referred to in interviews as the peace movement, almost since the beginning. Her conscience was aroused, and as a result, her work took on a political cast. She took the view that the poet had to be involved in society and could not ignore affronts to humanity perpetrated in the name of defending freedom. The view she expressed in "What Were They Like?" was shared by many in the antiwar movement during the 1960s and 1970s. As Dorothy Nielson notes in her essay "The Dark Wing of Mourning: Grief, Elegy and Time in the Poetry of Denise Levertov,"

> anti-War activists were concerned that U.S. military tactics, including napalm spraying, saturation bombing, and defoliation by means of giant bulldozers and agent orange, would annihilate the Vietnamese people if the war went on for too long.

Lest this be seen as an extreme view belonging to those with left-wing sympathies who were automatically opposed to US policies, it should be pointed out that such a view was also expressed by the noted writer, military historian, and anti-Communist Bernard Fall, who supported the US war effort but felt it was doomed to failure. In the

WHAT DO I READ NEXT?

- "Two Variations" is another powerful anti–Vietnam War poem by Levertov, first published in *The Sorrow Dance* in 1967. Like "What Were They Like?" the poem features two speakers. The first speaker addresses an American soldier directly and says that the eyes of a Vietnamese woman whose five children have been killed are watching him. The second speaker is a mother, probably the woman referred to in the first part of the poem, who is mourning the death of her children from a bombing raid. The poem can be found in Levertov's *Poems, 1960–67* (1983).

- Although Levertov was committed to engagement in political matters, much of her best poetry is completely nonpolitical. Many poems simply take joy in the natural world, sensing within it a deep and often mysterious presence. She was a poet who was always alive to the spiritual, transcendental dimension of life. For such reasons, Levertov has often been linked with the romantic poets. Her last published book, *This Great Unknowing: Last Poems* (1999), contains many poems that show this side of her work.

- *Selected Poems* (2003), by Denise Levertov, edited by Paul A. Lacey and with an introduction by Robert Creeley, is a representative selection of Levertov's work over her entire poetic career. The selections are taken from nineteen different books, beginning with *The Double Image* (1946) and ending with *This Great Unknowing: Last Poems* (1999). What emerges is a remarkable picture of the range of the work of one of America's finest post–World War II poets.

- *From Both Sides Now: The Poetry of the Vietnam War and Its Aftermath* (1998), edited by Philip Mahony, is a collection of poetry written by American and Vietnamese poets. Well-known poets such as Allen Ginsberg, Levertov, Sharon Olds, Grace Paley, Hayden Carruth, Philip Levine, James Fenton, and W. S. Merwin are included, but there are many unfamiliar names, too. Some of the poets on both sides were soldiers in the war. The 135 poems are arranged in chronological order, so the reader gets a sense of how the war unfolded.

- *Culture and Customs of Vietnam* (2001), by Mark W. McLeod and Nguyen Thi Dieu, is an introduction to Vietnamese culture. It includes topics such as history, in which the effects of decades of war are discussed, as well as religion, literature, festivals, and the arts.

- *Vietnam War: Battles and Leaders* (2004), by Stuart Murray and Aaron R. Murray, is a history of the Vietnam War for young-adult readers. It outlines the events after World War II in which the French first controlled but were then driven out of Vietnam in the 1950s, paving the way for US involvement in the 1960s. The book describes the most important events in the war and the men who commanded the opposing forces. It includes 150 photographs as well as maps, charts, and a chronology.

- *An Anthology of Vietnamese Poems: From the Eleventh through the Twentieth Centuries* (1996), edited by Sanh Thong Huynh, is a collection of over 300 poems by 150 poets, covering a period of a thousand years. Some of the recent poems cover the relationship between Vietnam and the United States. Explanatory notes help the reader put the poems in context.

---

article "'Losing' the World: American Decline in Perspective, Part I," Noam Chomsky, himself a critic of the Vietnam War at the time and since, noted Fall's prediction that "Vietnam as a cultural and historic entity...is threatened with extinction" as "the countryside literally dies under the blows of the largest military machine ever unleashed on an area of this size."

A brief examination of the use of Agent Orange by the US military in South Vietnam shows why such fears of the annihilation of an entire country were aroused. Agent Orange was a defoliant, an herbicide used to kill vegetation and so clear large areas of South Vietnam. The purpose in clearing the jungles and forests was to expose Viet Cong hiding places such as caves and tunnel openings and disallow their further use. (The herbicide was called Agent Orange because the containers had an orange band around them.) Agent Orange was also used to destroy rice and other food crops that helped the Viet Cong to survive in South Vietnam. This had the additional effect of harming civilians, since their food supply was destroyed, too. During the nine years that Agent Orange was used in Vietnam, the US military sprayed between 3.6 million and 6 million acres with 19 million gallons of the chemical. (Estimates vary; 6 million acres is the equivalent of one-seventh of South Vietnam's land area.) In 1965, 45 percent of Agent Orange use was for destroying crops. This supplies the context for several lines in "What Were They Like?" In her answer to question 3, for example, the second speaker explains that after the war came, nothing grew in the springtime anymore. And in answer to the questioner's fifth question, the speaker evokes a peaceful scene featuring the rice paddies that the Vietnamese people used to rely on in better days. As described in the article "The War's Effect on the Vietnamese Land and People,"

> Before the Vietnam War, the South Vietnamese countryside was lush and green. Farmers tended rice paddies (wet fields where rice is grown) in fertile river valleys. The surrounding hillsides were covered with jungles of trees and plants.

In addition to defoliation by means of Agent Orange, the US military carried out massive bombing campaigns in both North and South Vietnam. The article "The War's Effect on the Vietnamese Land and People" states that the United States dropped more than 14 million tons of explosives during the Vietnam War, which was more than the United States had dropped during the entirety of World War II. Most of the bombs fell on South Vietnam. "The bombing did terrible damage to the land," the article states. The article goes on to say,

> It destroyed many of the dams and canals that the peasants had installed to irrigate their farmland. It also created huge craters in the rice paddies and hillsides. In fact, by the end of the war there were an estimated 21 million bomb craters in South Vietnam.

Also, vast stretches of land, amounting to 1,200 square miles, were simply bulldozed, completely flattened and denuded of whatever had been growing there. The combination of bombing, bulldozing, and defoliation resulted in the destruction of nearly half the crops in South Vietnam. Many people starved to death.

Readers of "What Were They Like?" will notice the allusions to bombing and also to fire. People were burned. This is likely a reference to the use of napalm in the bombs dropped by the US Air Force. Napalm is a thickening agent used in jelling gasoline for use in incendiary devices. It was first developed by the United States in World War II and was used extensively during the Vietnam War. Napalm is a terrifying weapon. As stated by Luca Prono in his article, "Vietnam War," "Napalm inflicts particularly horrible injuries, burning its victims and melting their skin so that the substance remains in their bodies leading to a slow death." The use of napalm in Vietnam enraged the antiwar movement, and much of the anger was focused on Dow Chemical, the company that manufactured it. In his book *The Sixties: Years of Hope, Days of Rage*, Todd Gitlin writes about a demonstration that took place at the University of Wisconsin in October 1967, when Dow Chemical recruiters attempted to visit the campus. In the violent struggle that followed, sixty-five students and seven policeman ended up in the hospital. That fall, according to Gitlin, there were forty large demonstrations on college campuses around the country in protest against the visits of Dow Chemical and military recruiters. In 1972, the horror of napalm bombing was seared into the minds of people all over the globe by a photograph taken on June 8, 1972, in Trang Bang, a village in South Vietnam. The picture, shot by an Associated Press photographer, shows four young children fleeing along a road from a napalm attack. One girl, a nine-year-old named Kim Phuc, has torn off her burning clothes and is naked and crying out in pain as she runs. In the background is the smoking village.

"What Were They Like?," then, is a poem of bitter protest against US military policy in Vietnam. In its mimicking of an objective, journalistic style, juxtaposed with poetically expressed allusions to pain, suffering, and loss, the poem is intended to convey the horror of what was being done to the Vietnamese people, land, and

> DISMISSALS OF LEVERTOV'S 'METAPHYSICS' OR 'AESTHETICS' OF PRESENCE OFTEN HAVE BEEN ACCOMPANIED BY CHARGES (FROM THE SAME CRITICAL QUARTER) THAT HER POETRY ASSUMES TO SPEAK UNIVERSALLY, WITHOUT ATTENDING TO THE MATERIAL AND SOCIAL 'CONSTRUCTION' OF LANGUAGE."

culture. In its attempt to humanize that culture, to give it a face and a form even as its loss and destruction is catalogued, "What Were They Like?" acts as a small counterweight to the attitude that has come to be known as orientalism, by which the West habitually devalues and makes inferior the cultures of the East.

Source: Bryan Aubrey, Critical Essay on "What Were They Like?," in *Poetry for Students*, Gale, Cengage Learning, 2013.

James Dougherty

In the following excerpt, Dougherty examines the phase of Levertov's life during which she wrote The Sorrow Dance.

... With *The Sorrow Dance* (1967) Levertov opened a new phase of her life and poetry that called into question her earlier achievement—but made the oral cast of her work even more evident. Many of its poems seem of a piece with her first five or six books, personal lyric poems shaped by epiphany, presence and the inner voice. But the volume also included "Life at War," a sequence protesting the Vietnam war. Response to these "political" poems, and to later work in the same spirit, opened a critical reassessment of her entire oeuvre.

"Life at War" weighs the human potential for virtue against the horrors of Vietnam—

> the scheduled breaking open of breasts whose milk
> runs out over the entrails of still-alive babies,
> transformation of witnessing eyes to pulp-fragments
>
> ....
>
> our nerve filaments twitch with its presence
> day and night,
> nothing we say has not the husky phlegm of it in the
> saying....

The lines have grown longer, their endings determined by syntactical units; the poem does not seem to pause and listen to an "inner voice." As for their imagery, Cary Nelson wrote dismissively:

> Brutal and accurate as these lines may be, they are essentially clichés of violent war. We can hear in them a history of violence verbalized at a distance, perhaps even specific rhetoric like that of the English reaction to the German invasion of Belgium in the First World War. (163)

Levertov, he continued, was working up her emotions out of "televised images."

Nelson's 1975 critique is akin to Altieri's, published a few years later: they compare the new Levertov unfavorably with the old, and then write off the old as a belated Romantic lyricist, her poems as mimetic recollections of moments of epiphany. They reflect also a then-recent change in critical fashion, according to which her poetry appears to be founded on an illusory "metaphysics of presence." Nelson accuses her of a "mysticism" that shrinks from the actual Vietnam and the actual America (162); Altieri says that "the sensitive eye, which once served to unite the 'I' with the numinous scene, now sees only a demonic version of incarnation.... While she recognizes that the aesthetic of presence no longer suffices, she has only its implicit ethical ideals to work with" (230–32). "[She] has great difficulty constructing specific ethical values or moral images that are more applicable and more general than specific epistemological poses" (237).

In reading these less nuanced, more strident poems, and the hostile criticisms they inspired, it may be helpful to start from remarks that Levertov made in the early 1980s. Confessing that she was no longer wholly dedicated to "the poetry of joy, proclamation, affirmation," she insisted that there could be a poetry which "from literal or deeply imagined experience, depicts and denounces perennial injustice and cruelty in their current forms" (*Essays* 143–44). As precedent, she invoked the Prophets of the Hebrew Testament: "To some extent they had to be poets, or at least persons whose eloquence and oratory could survive being written down, so that it could reach further and be pondered" (148). She said that prophets and poets "transfer over to the listener or reader a parallel experience, a parallel intensity, which impels that person into new attitudes and new actions.... If the prophecy or the poem is the mysterious genuine article and the receiver's sensibility is open to it, some change does take place" (148). These words reveal again Levertov's grasp of the oral quality of her poems. Just as she understood her earlier lyrics as oral colloquy, lover with lover or poet with "heart," she took the protest poem as the written residue of eloquent oratory. As a text, it enjoys the traditional advantages of script and print, namely multiplied distribution (so it may "reach further") and withdrawal from the flow of time (so it may be "pondered"). But for these advantages it pays a price in lost immediacy: its eloquence only "survives" in transcription.

Furthermore, her prophetic poems are governed by principles of rhetoric as much or more than poetics. Walter Ong described the protest poetry of that era as "rhetorical and polemic, in this resembling that of the oral or residually oral culture of the preromantic past" (*Interfaces* 228). They seem designed for oral delivery to an audience gathered to witness on behalf of oppressed peoples in Asia, in Africa, or in the United States. As printed poems, they gesture toward that particular, past moment. When they were delivered, what was present was an audience in sympathy with her anger and her sense of helplessness, and responsive to her words; in print, this audience is present only through its apparent absence. The reader attends not as participant but only as spectator. So positioned, he may be tempted to compare the rhetoric with earlier denunciations of Hunnish atrocities. Nelson was right when he described Levertov's imagery as gleaned from television; but that was the imagery shared by her audience, the burning girls and sidewalk executions on which most dissent from the war was based. In that mediated way, it was present. Further, the protestors' solidarity with war's victims was itself mediated through television; and the televising of their rallies, and of police clashing with them, multiplied and sustained their presence throughout America.

Nelson's indictment of her poems as clichés also arises from his taking them not as the record of rhetorical occasions but as lyric poems in the Romantic tradition, according to which the reader is not an interlocutor but rather one who observes and "overhears." Prior to the rise of Romanticism, says Ong, poems had a stake in rhetoric: the poem "operated within the agonistic framework of real life, of decision and action" (*Interfaces* 222). Levertov sought to restore that

rhetorical context. The reader-spectator, critically detached, may demand "originality" of imagery; but the audience-interlocutor favors invocations of the commonplace, the *loci communes* on which the rhetorician establishes common ground with his/her auditors (*Interfaces* 225, *Presence* 253). The well-known cruelties of technological war are Levertov's bond with those who have come to hear about them, and put a stop to them. As for Altieri's charge that her aesthetics of presence, because subjective, offered no communal platform for ethical outrage (231–32), her reference to the prophets shows that she was on her way to finding such a platform.

Dismissals of Levertov's "metaphysics" or "aesthetics" of presence often have been accompanied by charges (from the same critical quarter) that her poetry assumes to speak universally, without attending to the material and social "construction" of language. Perloff's critique is of this order. But within Charles Altieri's article appears a response to this view. In a note "that should probably be an appendix" (241–44) he singles out the title poem of *Relearning the Alphabet*, the most substantive and intriguing poem in a volume he fairly criticizes as inchoate notebook entries rather than poems. "Relearning the Alphabet" is an alphabetary sequence of twenty-three short poems somewhat in the manner of Psalm 119, except that the governing character is repeated in various places in its poem, not just as the initial letter. In it, says Altieri, following John Searle and J. L. Austin, Levertov discovers language itself as "the repository of fundamental moral instincts, marking and valuing those distinctions and qualities which the culture has found basic to its fundamental human interests" (242). And in language Levertov recognizes a dialogic sense of presence that is not above but within the social matrix of speech. In section "U" she addresses herself: "Relearn the alphabet, / relearn the world, the world / understood anew only in doing." The "Z" poem concludes:

> absence has not become
> the transformed presence the will
> looked for,
> but other: the present,
>
> that which was poised already in the ah! of praise.

"Ah!" was a word in the first poem of the sequence, but there it was linked with knowledge, not with praise. So the alphabet has been re-acquired, and can be said anew, generating new associations for each character. In providing alphabetic cues to a process of meditation, Levertov has given the appearance of controlling spatially the sequence of time—an anomalous act for a poet so committed to the oral; but since the poem's end is its new beginning, it remains thus poised always in the present, as does speech itself. Renouncing a willful search for presence, she discovers an attentiveness to the present . . . .

Source: James Dougherty, "Presence, Silence, and the Holy in Denise Levertov's Poems," in *Renascence: Essays on Values in Literature*, Vol. 58, No. 4, Summer 2006, pp. 305–26.

Keith S. Norris

In the following essay, Norris argues that writing lyric poetry that explores what Levertov calls "resemblances" is important to both the survival and the political development of lyric poetry in the contemporary world.

In "Some Notes on Organic Form" (*PW* 7–13) Denise Levertov asserts the notion of a discoverable form, not proscribed but available to the poet willing to "explore." I want to assert not simply that such exploration is necessary and desirable for contemporary poets but that writing lyric poetries that explore what Levertov calls "resemblances" is crucial to both the survival and the political viability of the lyric poem in the contemporary world. In the post-nuclear age, when worldwide we are reminded of difference and of the inability to communicate beyond the general nastiness of self-assertion, drawing connections to a "form beyond forms" through an individually adaptable lyric makes poetry viable in two ways: first by creating a space where a poet can explore all options, on both the personal and social levels, in order to provide a means of political safe haven, and second by making connections that may help save us from the isolation and separateness that pervade our culture from the streets to the humanities tower, each "department" separated floor by floor.

Levertov redefines Gerald Manley Hopkins's inscape as "the pattern of essential characteristics both in single objects and (what is more interesting) in objects in a state of relation to each other," and of instress as "the experiencing of the perception of inscape, the appreciation of inscape" (*PW* 7). In Levertov's theory, the idea of instress allows the poet to watch herself perceive the essential character of the postmodern environment, an environment often associated

> IN LEVERTOV'S THEORY WE ARE INDIVIDUALLY RESPONSIBLE FOR PURSUING THE UNIVERSAL, NOT PARTICULARLY RESPONSIBLE FOR THE INDIVIDUATION OF ACCEPTED UNIVERSAL TRUTHS."

with a lack of defining form. But it is this constant flux of the contemporary world that a postmodern lyric must reveal and address; Levertov calls this pursuit of conscious poetic evaluation a "fidelity to instress" (10). It is interesting that in her description of inscape, Levertov uses a psychological term, apperception, which she defines as "recognizing what we perceive" (7). Her identification of organic poetry as a "method of apperception" moves the Levertovian idea of organicism beyond the notion of a simple form/content synthesis or a discussion of inherent form to an active poetry, one that can both engage and critique the "postmodern" landscape, external and internal. The idea of fidelity to a process that consciously and continuously attempts to write the structure of a non-structured world celebrates the double bind in which any artist finds herself or himself this late in the twentieth century, rather than suffering under it as I would argue any "new" formalism does.

In his recent *Postmodernism, or the Cultural Logic of Late Capitalism*, Fredric Jameson posits a double role for the required multi-mindedness of the individual in the contemporary world:

> The way in which what I have been calling schizophrenic disjunction or ecriture, when it becomes generalized as a cultural style, ceases to entertain a necessary relationship to the morbid content we associate with terms like schizophrenia and becomes available for more joyous intensities, for precisely that euphoria which we saw displacing the older affects of anxiety and alienation. (29)

This brief passage from a book that effectively shows us how we live and how we respond to living "immersed in the immediate" (400) serves as a definition of a conventional "postmodernism" as it finds its way into poetry. Jameson is responding to the "schizophrenic" nature of language poetry in this context, more specifically to Bob Perelman's poem "China," but I think we can draw an interesting parallel to Levertov's poetic theory here. Language poetry is, in a sense, the extreme example of a connection with the disturbing multitude of images present in the contemporary world; Levertov asserts a poetry that not only can recognize and reproduce that miscellany with a "joyous intensity," but can also achieve a safe place from which to critique such a world. Levertov's poetics offer a way not only of playing the postmodern game but of identifying the postmodern in its historical sequence.

By the time of the Vietnam War, Levertov's poetic theory becomes inseparable from her ideas about the contemporary political scene. In *The Poet in the World* she notes that

> A sense of history must involve a sense of the present, a vivid awareness of change, a response to crisis, a realization that what was appropriate in this or that situation in the past is inadequate to the demands of the present.... We are living our whole lives in a state of emergency which is—for reasons I'm sure I don't have to spell out for you by discussing nuclear and chemical weapons or ecological disasters and threats—unparalleled in all history. (115)

This is the need for a new lyric poetry, one that seeks connections organically while being mobile enough to deal with the postmodern environment. Levertov's "state of emergency" is as good as any starting point for a definition of the postmodern condition; her list of worries, the "demands of the present," marks what is present in almost anyone's definition, the multitude of directions in which the mind is forced to go when considering the larger issues of our culture.

Terry Eagleton's discussion of the Kantian aesthetic is helpful in viewing Levertov's organic lyric as an active creator of political space (as opposed to the purely romantic notion of wished-for space in a poem like Shelley's "Mont Blanc" or the pseudo-modern space of Stevens's "The Idea of Order at Key West"). Eagleton notes:

> Aesthetic judgement is then a kind of pleasurable free-wheeling of our faculties, a kind of parody of conceptual understanding, non-referential pseudo-cognition which does not nail down the object to an identifiable thing. (85)

Eagleton's "non-referential pseudo-cognition" is evasive, yes, but I think evasiveness is precisely

how Levertov's lyric, in its "fidelity to instress," allows for a materialistic critique of evasive post-modern society where, as Inger Christensen points out, the "horrors of war" have separated Levertov from a solely affirmative, religious view of organicism (114–15).

And so a "free-wheeling" organicism is what Levertov eventually adopts, a point of critique that changes with the situation. In her "instress" the subject position of the poet is as flexible as the object content of inscape. Neither subject nor object is constant but they organically change as the need for a new point of view arises. Levertov makes this point clear near the close of "Some Notes on Organic Form" as she recognizes that, while a poem should move immediately from one perception to another, "There must be a place in the poem for rifts too—(never to be stuffed with imported ore). Great gaps between perception and perception which must be leapt across if they are to be crossed at all" (*PW* 13). Here is where the organic lyric poem operates, as do many modern and postmodern narratives—in its ability to move quickly from one perception, or anecdotal narrative we might say, to another, all the while crossing great gaps of meaning, and coming to understanding in how we cross those gaps.

The postmodern lyric poet is fighting against reduction, reification to one point of view with narrative constancy—"fidelity to instress" correctly won't permit a single narrative totality if the poet is alive and "in the world." But, as the deconstructionists have noted, involvement in the postmodern world undermines our ability to assume an Archimedean point and critique it. The shifting, changing nature of the subject/speaker/poet in Levertov's organic poetry moves with the movement of perception and therefore maintains a consistent relationship to it. Levertov calls this the "truth," what she earlier calls "a form in all things," at the conclusion of "Some Notes on Organic Form":

> The X factor, the magic, is when we come to those rifts and make those leaps. A religious devotion to the truth, to the splendor of the authentic, involves the writer in a process rewarding in itself; but when that devotion brings us to undreamed abysses and we find ourselves sailing slowly over them and landing on the other side—that's ecstasy. (*PW* 13)

And so the truth isn't static here, but is the process itself; organicism isn't a form, but a constantly evolving formation. As the lyric poet moves from one anecdotal perception to another she creates narrative connections, which work as a strategy for survival; as Jameson notes in *The Political Unconscious*, narrative can create a "local place" for political freedom, where the individual can return to a world that isn't "compartmentalized" (40). The postmodern lyric, in its organicism, has necessarily adopted a shifting narrative quality that moves with the poet's need to achieve instress.

In the "Prologue: An Interim" section of "Staying Alive" in *To Stay Alive* (1971), Levertov presents the reader with a multitude of voices intimately connected to the present, 1968. We begin in motion, "While the war drags on, always worse, / the soul dwindles sometimes to an ant / rapid upon a cracked surface" (21). This is conventional lyricism, beginning with a situation and noting the condition of the soul in response. But we move on to other voices: a narrator describing various scenes; what we can interpret as the poet responding to language itself; the punctuation of a continuing narrative about an eighteen-year-old fasting war protester; a three-year-old fragment written in Puerto Rico. The whole of these loosely connected fragments is called an "interim," where the poet can bring together the vast collection of perceptions she experiences in both time present and recent history and work toward an evaluation.

In "Great Possessions," an essay originally given as a lecture in 1970, Levertov addresses the idea of writing politically viable poetry:

> But for a poet the attention to things and people, to the passing moments filled to the brim with past, present, and future, to the Great Possessions that are our real life, is inseparable from attention to language and form. And he must recognize not only that poetry is intrinsically revolutionary but that it is so not by virtue of talking about any one subject rather than another (though if he has political concerns they may not be excluded, and not to have political concerns—in the broad and deep sense of the term—is surely impossible to the aware adult in the last quarter of the twentieth century). But whether content in any poem is huge or minuscule, funny or sad, angry or joyful, it can only be deeply and truly revolutionary, only be poetry, "song that suffices our need," by being in its very substance of sound and vision an ecstacy and a giving of life. (*PW* 106)

The poet isn't striving to write about any one thing, but is following the organic movement of the lyric itself; for a poet who is "an aware adult in the last quarter of the twentieth century," that movement includes a move into the realm of revolutionary politics. Some of "Prologue: An Interim" is overtly political as perception takes the poet in that direction, and the sum of the poem is certainly political as it strives toward a language that can still remain viable even as it is used to manipulate understanding, but it is also personally political as it temporarily allows the poet to view, to apperceive, the inscape of the postmodern situation at one point in 1968.

The second stanza of section i describes the soul of the speaker as it moves through its various perceptions: "lightly, grimly, incessantly / it skims the unfathomed clefts where despair / seethes hot and black" (*TSA* 21). This is the poet aware of instress, moving over the gaps she describes in "Some Notes on Organic Form," revealing her purpose to the reader. Levertov reveals connections to us in other, visual ways: the poem is divided into seven sections denoted by small roman numerals; any information about the fasting protester is given in italics; each section works as an independent unit, achieving its own particular movement and meaning. In section ii the first perception the "soul" skims leads the mind of the poet toward the larger inscape her writing is forced to deal with.

> Children in the laundromat waiting while their
>   mothers fold sheets. A five-year-old boy
>   addresses a four-year-old girl. 'When I say,
> Do you want some gum? say yes.' 'Yes . . .' 'Wait!—
>   Now: Do you want some gum?' 'Yes!' 'Well yes
>   means no, so you can't have any.' He chews. He
>   pops a big, delicate bubble at her.
> O language, virtue of man, touchstone worn down
>   by what gross friction . . .
> And,
> '"It became necessary to destroy the town to save it,"
>   A United States major said today. He was talk-
>   ing about the decision by allied commanders to
>   bomb and shell the town regardless of civilian
>   casualties, to rout the Vietcong.'
> O language, mother of thought, are you rejecting us
>   as we reject you?
> Language, coral island accrued from human
>   comprehensions, human dreams,
> you are eroded as war erodes us. (21–22)

The narrator/speaker's initial perception, of the simple manipulation of language by the young boy, leads her both to address language and, by addressing it directly, to deconstruct the relationship language has to the reality created by the boy's substitution of "no" for "yes."

Language as a worn touchstone no longer capable of turning the raw material of words into exactly what is desirable is the result we see in the almost moral corruption of the young boy's speech. The cause, the "gross friction," responsible for this distortion follows with the same "yes for no" construction given by the major to explain the bombing of a Vietnamese village. We return to the speaker's voice in the next stanza as she asks if the connection her apperception has made is true. This is fidelity to instress: following the movement, making connections, allowing the speaker's, or the poet's, voice to intrude in what was moving toward narrative. The speaker answers herself in the affirmative; the connections are valid. The rest of "Prologue: An Interim" follows a course of showing us what we have to do to reclaim language.

Section iii begins, "To repossess our souls . . ." (22), and we follow the development of the speaker's perceptions of her own history (what we suppose is the development of her own language use), the fasting war-resister, and current events both personal and political. We end up, six pages and vast amounts of perceiving later, at the crux of acting on the knowledge of the poem. What is prescribed is a movement which is the movement of organic poetry as Levertov has described it above. The final section reads:

> To expand again, to plunge our dryness into the unwearying source—
> but not to forget. Not to forget but to remember better.
> We float in the blue day darkly. We rest behind half-closed louvers, the hot afternoon clouds up, the palms hold still.
> 'I have a medical problem that can be cured'—Miss Squire said last week when she was removed from the city workhouse to Cincinnati General Hospital, 'I have a medical problem that can be cured only by freedom.' (28)

The assertion that by returning to the source we don't forget the burden of the past and of political experience is precisely what lyric poetry organically adapted to deal with the postmodern world can do for us.

The poem itself is what is left to us, is where we can go to combine the disparate elements of the surrounding culture. Ralph J. Mills has called Levertov's poetry the "poetry of the immediate . . . [which] signifies the complex relationship existing between the poet and the elements that are close at hand in her personal experience" (103–04). We've already seen this in the longer poem "Staying Alive," but this kind of cultural immediacy is also apparent in many of the shorter poems, where a similar personal political space is negotiated, or "mediated" as Jameson would have it (*Political Unconscious* 41–42). In "About Political Action in Which Each Individual Acts from the Heart," from *Candles in Babylon*, Levertov does exactly what the title indicates, shows us the connection between the individual and political action, thereby giving a political resonance both to solitary action and to actions of communion. The poem begins by placing us in a situation, giving us a specific when, a gesture that includes us in the ongoing action and places us in the act of perceiving. We begin when "solitaries draw close," when two individuals "give to each other the roses / of our communion—" (86). The speaker then proceeds to make a connection between the act of two coming together—there is no explicit lovemaking, but the metaphors work together to indicate an intimacy in a fairly confined realm, and political action in the larger world.

> when we taste in small victories sometimes the small, ephemeral yet joyful harvest of our striving,
> great power flows from us, luminous, a promise. Yes! . . . Then
> great energy flows from solitude, and great power from communion. (86)

Organic form works here to bring two together on more than a physical level, to use the "communion" of the two to create a larger connection in the communally political realm. This is lyric revolution, as Julia Kristeva defines the term: "The text is a practice that could be compared to political revolution: the one brings about in the subject what the other introduces into society" (17). The lyric instress creates both political viability and community. The movement of this short lyric, political action beginning with individual intimacy, and the poet discovering the connection through his or her apperception, finds expression in the postmodern lyrics of other contemporary poets as well—in Galway Kinnell's "The Waking," for example, where a couple are able to give change to beggars for breakfast because they have been in bed together.

Less overt in its connections, but perhaps more powerful in its evocation of emotional response to sexual intimacy, is "The Good Dream," from *Footprints* (1972). The poem begins with two lovers rediscovering each other "upon the big bed." This is the only narrative situation in the poem, a brief anecdote. The speaker then finishes the poem with an explication of the situation.

> The joy was not in a narrow sense erotic—not
>   narrow in any sense. It was
> that all impediments, every barrier, of history, of
>   learn'd anxiety, wrong place and wrong time,
> had gone down, vanished. It was the joy
> of two rivers meeting in depths of the sea. (31)

Levertov's organic instress is able to overcome history and present trouble in the most intimate of ways here. The poem is not static in its presentation of the lovers, but active in extending their actions to the world, and in bringing the world to their actions. The poem itself is what enables the speaker to overcome the burden of history and postmodern multiplicity—this is, in its most intimate setting, Levertov's organicism. "The Good Dream" reflects the most direct of Levertov's theoretical statements, from "An Admonition" written in 1970 in response to the manifesto of a little magazine:

> We need a poetry not of direct statement but of direct evocation: a poetry of hieroglyphics, of embodiment, incarnation; in which the personages may be of myth or of Monday, no matter, if they are of the living imagination. (*PW* 61)

To Levertov the poet is constantly breathing in, "openmouthed in the temple of life" (*PW* 8), and while breathing in, is apperceiving the varying structures of those inspired perceptions, and how those structures varyingly connect and identify, at least for a moment, a larger form. In the poetry and in the postmodern environment of the "immediate" such fleeting connections may give us time to save ourselves, may give us opportunity to achieve a moment of political viability, may allow us the presence of mind to act humanely.

Svetlana Boym, in her conclusion to *Death in Quotation Marks*, after analyzing how our main modern critical impulse has been a kind of "necrophilia" that seeks both the literal and figurative death of the poet and of the poet's work, asserts that

> We have to recover a certain kind of nontotalizable and antiauthoritarian ethics that helps to put together the making of poetry, love, and criticism, as well as the making and unmaking of the self. (248)

Perhaps in Levertov's theory we already have this kind of ethics, a fidelity to instress, to constant apperception—toward the end of an organic poetic understanding that creates a safe lyric space in which to write and a viable connection to those around us. In Levertov's theory we are individually responsible for pursuing the universal, not particularly responsible for the individuation of accepted universal truths. As we strive to understand the various violences that surround us at the beginnings of this decade, and to once again reclaim our language from its warmongering worst, the postmodern, post-nuclear lyric is one way we have of not surrendering to a simple transcribing of the babble of the postmodern world. Rather, we can transform that babble into a heteroglossic collection of mini-narratives—postmodern ecstasy.

Source: Keith S. Norris, "Openmouthed in the Temple of Life: Denise Levertov and the Postmodern Lyric," in *Twentieth Century Literature*, Vol. 38, No. 3, Fall 1992, pp. 343–52.

Josephine Jacobsen

In the following review, Jacobsen notes the vehemence with which Levertov speaks for the reach and dignity of poetry in her collection With Eyes at the Back of Our Head.

Fifteen years ago Denise Levertov began her book of poems, *With Eyes at the Back of Our Heads*, with a translation from the Toltec, of which the last two verses run:

> The true artist: draws out all from
> his heart,
> works with delight, makes things
> with calm, with sagacity,
> works like a true Toltec, composes
> his objects, works dextrously,
> invents;
> arranges materials, adorns them,
> makes them adjust
> The carrion artist works at
> random, sneers at the people,
> makes things opaque, brushes
> across the surface of the face of
> things,
> works without care, defrauds
> people, is a thief.

Her own poems have sprung from that concept and the best of them have spoken for it. Her prose is less consistently shaped to all of those considerations. *The Poet in the World* is an interesting, uneven, occasionally exasperating and always sincere collage of essays, criticism, fiction, political statement, articles on teaching and on other poets.

Of its five sections—"Work and Inspiration," "Life At War," "The Untaught Teacher,"

"Perhaps Fiction" and "Other Writers"—by far the most interesting is the first. Miss Levertov can and does, write lucidly of the blunders, prizes and tenacities of the poet sweating out her poem; and her discussion of other writers, (Creeley, Williams and Duncan are those she most admires) though highly subjective, is alive and uncompromising. She is at her most happily typical when she takes on the questions of the nature of poetry and when she describes poetry in terms of a *translation*, a word defined in her 1865 Webster's as "being conveyed from one place to another, remove to heaven without dying." She has some sharply accurate things to say of the flabbiness of much current poetry, of the abuse of the personal pronoun, and of "those wizened off shoots of Williams' zeal for the rhythmic structure of the American language ... who have made the mistake of supposing that he was advocating a process of reproduction, of facile imitation, whereas what he was after was origins, springs of vitality."

Her analysis of the uses of myth in poetry, of the numinous metaphor, is an intelligent discussion of the poverty of urban cynicism. She has a lively and honest belief in the gods: "Personally I cannot bring myself to believe that the gods originate in the mind of man and are merely his way of coping with natural forces or abstract ideas by giving them semi-human personalities and stories. When man describes the gods, he certainly only approximates, and therefore distorts, the reality he intuits, but I fail to see the logic of assuming that therefore they do not exist." While recognizing that "our fear of the high-falutin is related to the salutary dislike of hypocrisy," she joins Roethke, Lawrence and Raine in contempt for the purely egocentric and conversational quoting Lawrence's "There are no gods, and you can please yourself— / go and please yourself— / but leave me alone, leave me alone to myself / and then in the room whose is that presence / that makes the air so still and lovely to me?" and urgently reminds us that *contemplation*" (from 'templum,' temple, a place, a space for observation, marked out by the auger) means not simply to observe and regard, but to do these things in the presence of the god."

But that earlier word "uncompromising" shades uncomfortably in other sections, into the sort of single-mindedness more admirable in a crusader than in a writer. However compassionate or enraged she may be, the difference with which a writer wears her rue must be the evidence of an openness to the unwelcome intrusion of the conditional, to that complexity which is always cutting down the self-indulgence of the simplistic. In Levertov's prose, this problem is mixed up with the absence of that sense of proportion which is humor. Irony, slapstick, self-mockery and wit are temperamentally uncongenial to her. Unwilling to distinguish between that healthy skepticism which ultimately is the protection against cynicism's dry rot, once she quits prosody, her conclusions are often accompanied by a disconcerting overkill. It is impossible not to sympathize with her passionate charge that "the poet is turned away from his impulse to sing, to testify in patterns of words, to the miracle of life, and is drawn will-nilly to warn, to curse, to gnash the teeth of language. It is hard to be an artist in this time because it is hard to be human."

In the section devoted to her trip to North Vietnam, one is at first enchanted by the poet's free and true response to a milieu and locale she has yearned over in an intense indignation and revolt against a brutal and degrading war. The land is seen as beautiful, as green and fresh, with the people miraculously friendly, more tolerant in the face of the savagery of aliens than one could have imagined. But then with dismaying completeness the poet retreats into the lobbyist: the sun is brighter, the people all more beautiful, all institutions benign and effective. As a member of what she describes as the Monster Race, she is understandably abashed by the physical and spiritual beauty she encounters. But alas, in Levertov's pages, the Writers' Union, the Solidarity Committee, the Interpreter, all have the same aura of transfiguration as that of the innocent victims of barbarity. And in her dealing with her own courageous antiwar efforts, there creeps in the unprepossessing inflection of contempt toward any deviants whose similar objectives might lead them to a less spotless confidence. The small piece, "Words From The Elm-tree Theater," releases directly one of the real strengths found in her poetry, the loving and eager expectation of the miracles of becoming. "The seed you take a few minutes to plant now may some day be a branching whispering fountain full of birds." This is part of her honest understanding that "every chink and cranny of nature is full to overflowing. That each instant is crowded full of great events." Like her poetry, her prose is charged with immediate metaphors of her attention to epiphanies. This same sense of a kind of magic expectancy lights up the "Perhaps Fiction" section, and makes one hope that she will write other stories, for these have a luminous dreamlike quality which is genuinely haunting. When she writes of teaching, though she has no revelations for us, her veracity and her empathy with students of any age and background are most appealing.

But what is most impressive in this volume is the vehemence with which Denise Levertov speaks for the reach and dignity of poetry. And if passages of her book seem at times toneless and didactic, without the interest and richness of conclusions forged from the assessing of contradictions, the book always is that of the true; never the carrion; artist. It makes, most movingly, large claims for an art form so often hamstrung in practice by the trivial, the fake and the chic. It is impossible to read this book, to listen to its immediacy, without a quickening. This is the poet who wrote in *O Taste And See*,

> A sense of the present
> rises out of earth and grass,
> enters the feet, ascends
> into the genitals, constricting
> the breast, lightening
> the head—a wisdom
> a shiver, a delight
> that what is passing
> is here, as if
> a snake went by, green in the
> gray leaves.

Source: Josephine Jacobsen, "Hard to Be Human," in *New Republic*, Vol. 170, No. 3081, January 26, 1974, pp. 29–30.

SOURCES

Burrows, E. G., "Politics and the Poet: An Interview with Denise Levertov," in *Conversations with Denise Levertov*, edited by Jewel Spears Brooker, University Press of Mississippi, 1998, pp. 28–34.

Casten, Liane Clorfene, and Paula Anne Ford-Martin, "Agent Orange," in *Environmental Encyclopedia*, Vol. 1, 3rd ed., edited by Marci Bortman, Peter Brimblecombe, and Mary Ann Cunningham, Thomson Gale, 2003, pp. 17–20.

Chomsky, Noam, "'Losing' the World: American Decline in Perspective, Part I," TomDispatch.com, February 14, 2012, http://www.tomdispatch.com/post/175502/tomgram %3A_noam_chomsky%2C_hegemony_and_its_dilemmas/ #more (accessed February 14, 2012).

Dougan, Clark, and Samuel Lipsman, *A Nation Divided*, Boston Publishing, 1984, pp. 98–145.

Gitlin, Todd, *The Sixties: Years of Hope, Days of Rage*, Bantam Books, 1987, p. 254.

Lawson, Don, *The United States in the Vietnam War*, Thomas Y. Crowell, 1981, pp. 70, 72.

Levertov, Denise, "What Were They Like?," in *Poems, 1960–67*, New Directions, 1983, p. 234.

Marten, Harry, *Understanding Denise Levertov*, University of South Carolina Press, 1988, p. 104.

Marzaro, Jerome, "Denise Levertov's Political Poetry," in *Critical Essays on Denise Levertov*, edited by Linda Wagner-Martin, G. K. Hall, 1991, p. 182.

Matalene, Caroline, "Denise Levertov," in *Dictionary of Literary Biography*, Vol. 5, *American Poets since World War II, First Series*, edited by Donald J. Greiner, Gale Research, 1980, pp. 3–9.

Nielsen, Dorothy, "The Dark Wing of Mourning: Grief, Elegy and Time in the Poetry of Denise Levertov," in *Denise Levertov: New Perspectives*, edited by Anne Colclough Little and Susie Paul, Locust Hill Press, 2000, pp. 128–29.

Packard, William, "Craft Interview with Denise Levertov," in *Conversations with Denise Levertov*, edited by Jewel Spears Brooker, University Press of Mississippi, 1998, p. 50.

Prono, Luca, "Vietnam War," in *Encyclopedia of White-Collar and Corporate Crime*, Vol. 2, edited by Lawrence M. Salinger, Sage Reference, 2005, pp. 847–48.

Rodgers, Audrey T., *Denise Levertov: The Poetry of Engagement*, Fairleigh Dickinson University Press, 1993, p. 89.

"Statistical Information about Casualties of the Vietnam War," National Archives website, http://www.archives. gov/research/military/vietnam-war/casualty-statistics.html #branch (accessed February 12, 2012).

"Vietnam," in *CIA: World Fact Book*, CIA website, https://www.cia.gov/library/publications/the-world-fact book/geos/vm.html (accessed February 12, 2012).

"Vietnam Online, Timeline," PBS website, March 29, 2005, http://www.pbs.org/wgbh/amex/vietnam/timeline/ tl3.html#a (accessed February 12, 2012).

"The War's Effect on the Vietnamese Land and People," in *Vietnam War Reference Library*, Vol. 3, UXL, 2001, pp. 187–98.

FURTHER READING

Davidson, Phillip B., *Vietnam at War: The History, 1946–1975*, Presidio Press, 1988.

> This is a book for anyone who wants to understand in detail the origins, course, and outcome of the Vietnam War. Davidson, a retired lieutenant

general, was the chief intelligence officer for General William Westmoreland and for his successor as commander of US forces in Vietnam, General Creighton Abrams. Davidson uses his intimate knowledge of US military operations as well as declassified North Vietnamese documents that give deep insight into North Vietnam's military strategy. The book includes a glossary and an extensive bibliography.

Garfinkle, Adam M., *Telltale Hearts: The Origins and Impact of the Vietnam Antiwar Movement*, St. Martin's Press, 1997.

In this carefully researched and well-argued book, Garfinkle disputes the commonly held idea that that antiwar movement had any effect on the conduct or duration of the Vietnam War. He argues that the tactics of the movement alienated the middle classes, who might otherwise have been more sympathetic, and may even have prolonged rather than shortened the war.

MacGowen, Chrisopher J., ed., *The Letters of Denise Levertov and William Carlos Williams*, New Directions, 1998.

This is a fascinating collection of letters exchanged between two of the most prominent poets of the twentieth century. The exchange began in 1951, when Levertov was a young poet at the beginning of her career. She was much influenced by Williams and told him so. The resulting correspondence and friendship lasted until Williams's death in 1962. MacGowan's introduction and annotations provide context for the letters, which show two poets thinking deeply and exchanging ideas about their craft.

Wagner-Martin, Linda, *Denise Levertov*, Twayne Publishers, 1967.

This is a survey of Levertov's early work up to and including *O Taste and See* (1964). Wagner states that her purpose is to point out the strengths and weaknesses of Levertov's work. She regards Levertov as a major poet on the evidence of the six books published by 1964.

SUGGESTED SEARCH TERMS

Denise Levertov

Vietnam antiwar movement

draft evasion AND Vietnam War

Vietnam War AND poetry

My Lai massacre

Vietnamese culture

Agent Orange

genocide

orientalism

The Wild Swans at Coole

WILLIAM BUTLER YEATS

1917

William Butler Yeats was one of the twentieth century's great English-language poets. "The Wild Swans at Coole," a poem he wrote and published midway through his career, exemplifies his romantic style. In this poem, as in other works, Yeats draws on mythological symbolism and reflects upon his own advancing age and what that might mean for his place in the world, both as a man and as a poet. Although Yeats firmly adhered to traditional metered verse throughout his life, his friendship with modernist poet Ezra Pound influenced his writing. In "The Wild Swans at Coole," for example, the meter (the pattern of stressed and unstressed syllables), while easily detected, is loosely constructed, shifting from line to line with no distinct pattern. This loose metric structure can be considered a transitional form between traditional metered verse and modern free verse.

"The Wild Swans at Coole" was published in *The Little Review* in June 1917 and later collected in the book *The Wild Swans at Coole* in 1917. An expanded edition of *The Wild Swans at Coole* was published in 1919. This poem was written in 1915 or 1916 while Yeats was staying with his friend and sponsor, Lady Gregory, at her estate, Coole Park, in western Ireland, where he often spent summers. Yeats wrote over seventy books of poetry, fiction, drama, essays, and criticism. "The Wild Swans at Coole" is available in most volumes that collect the best of his writing, including the second revised edition of *The*

William Butler Yeats (The Library of Congress)

Collected Poems of W. B. Yeats, edited by Richard J. Finneran and published in 1996.

AUTHOR BIOGRAPHY

Yeats was born in Dublin, Ireland, on June 13, 1865. Yeats's father, Jack, was a talented painter who could not let his work go, plunging his family into poverty. Yeats grew up in Sligo, in northwestern Ireland, where his mother was from; the family also lived at times in Dublin and in London. He hated London and loved Sligo. Yeats's eyesight was weak, and he was a poor student, preferring his own thoughts and wanderings to schoolwork. Under the influence of his father and his father's friends, all painters in the romantic pre-Raphaelite style, Yeats took up reading the poetry of Percy Bysshe Shelley and Edmund Spenser. He began writing poetry at age seventeen and published his first widely distributed book of poems, *The Wanderings of Oisin and Other Poems*, in 1889, when he was twenty-four.

In his thirties, Yeats was deeply involved with the Irish Literary Revival and was a founding member of the Irish National Theatre in 1898 (known as the Abbey Theatre after 1904) along with Lady Gregory, Edward Martyn, and George Moore. Although he is known best for his verse, Yeats also wrote plays, including *The Land of Heart's Desire* (1894) and *Cathleen ní Houlihan* (1902, with Lady Gregory).

Yeats first published "The Wild Swans at Coole" in 1917 (a revised edition followed in 1919), around the time when he finally married at age fifty-two. After decades of fruitlessly pursuing his friend Maud Gonne, an actress and activist, Yeats married Georgiana Hyde-Lees, a woman more than twenty-five years his junior. His good friend and fellow poet Ezra Pound stood as his best man. Yeats and Georgie had a daughter and son together. They were both interested in mysticism (the belief that one can achieve knowledge of spiritual truths through intuition or direct experience), and she helped him experiment with automatic writing, which informed his work in *The Vision* (1925), a nonfiction book that explores astrology, philosophy, history, and poetry.

In 1923, Yeats was awarded the Nobel Prize in Literature, an honor he felt deeply, as Yeats was drawn to elegance and ceremony as much as he was drawn to literature. Chosen to be part of the newly formed Irish Senate in 1922, Yeats was also a dedicated politician at this time in his life. By the late 1920s, high blood pressure and other health concerns began to trouble him. The Yeats family spent winters in the warmer climates of Italy and southern France to help Yeats's health.

After a prolific career as a writer, intellectual, politician, lecturer, and promoter of arts and letters, Yeats passed away at age seventy-three on January 28, 1939, while visiting the French Riviera. Nine years later, his body was removed from France and re-interred with full ceremony in his beloved western Ireland.

POEM TEXT

The trees are in their autumn beauty,
The woodland paths are dry,
Under the October twilight the water
Mirrors a still sky;
Upon the brimming water among the stones   5
Are nine-and-fifty swans.

The nineteenth autumn has come upon me
Since I first made my count;
I saw, before I had well finished,

All suddenly mount   10
And scatter wheeling in great broken rings
Upon their clamorous wings.

I have looked upon those brilliant creatures,
And now my heart is sore.
All's changed since I, hearing at twilight,   15
The first time on this shore,
The bell-beat of their wings above my head,
Trod with a lighter tread.

Unwearied still, lover by lover,
They paddle in the cold   20
Companionable streams or climb the air;
Their hearts have not grown old;
Passion or conquest, wander where they will,
Attend upon them still.

But now they drift on the still water,   25
Mysterious, beautiful;
Among what rushes will they build,
By what lake's edge or pool
Delight men's eyes when I awake some day
To find they have flown away?   30

POEM SUMMARY

The text used for this summary is from *The Collected Poems of W. B. Yeats*, edited by Richard J. Finneran, Collier, 1989, pp. 131–32. Versions of the poem can be found on the following web pages: http://www.poetryfoundation.org/poem/172060 and http://www.bartleby.com/148/1.html.

Stanza 1

In the first stanza of "The Wild Swans at Coole" (lines 1–6), Yeats describes an idyllic autumn scene comprised of trees full of autumn color (line 1), paths through the woods (line 2), and a pond with water that is flat and reflects the sky (line 4). In the last line of the stanza, the poet introduces the swans, of which there are fifty-nine.

This stanza contains many references to myth and magic. First, October is a time of the year when, as the ancient Celts believed, the veil between the living and the dead thins or parts. This belief survives in contemporary times in the traditions of Halloween. Another reference to magic is the twilight setting, a time in Celtic mythology when humans and faeries (who were powerful and dangerous creatures in myth) could more easily pass into each other's realms. Water is also a powerful symbol in Celtic mythology, with the power to transform. One of the

MEDIA ADAPTATIONS

- The British Library maintains online digital recordings of Nobel laureates reading their own work in a collection called "Beautiful Minds," available at http://www.bl.uk/online gallery/features/beautifulminds/sounds.html# yeats. Yeats reading his 1888 poem "The Lake Isle of Innisfree" for the BBC is part of this archive. This reading was originally broadcast on April 10, 1932, and is available in Windows Media Audio (.wma) format.

- The Yeats Society of Sligo (http://www.yeats-sligo.com/poetry) has an approximately eight-minute recording of Yeats talking about his work and his unique reading style and reading several of his poems, including "The Lake Isle of Innisfree" and "Song of the Old Mother." The recordings were made for radio broadcast in 1932, 1934, and 1937.

- *The Great Poets: W. B. Yeats* is an audio-book on compact disc featuring thirty-two of Yeats's poems read by Jim Norton, Denys Hawthorne, Nicholas Boulton, and Marcella Riordan. Produced by Naxos Audio in 2007, this recording includes commentary before each poem to give the listener better context. "The Wild Swans at Coole," "A Prayer for My Daughter," and "Sailing to Byzantium" are among the titles included in this collection.

- Irish actor T. P. McKenna reads for the audio-book *W. B. Yeats: Poems*, released on compact disc in 2006 by HighBridge Classics. This abridged collection includes fifty-two poems by Yeats, including "The Wild Swans at Coole," "The Lake Isle at Innisfree," and "The Fiddler at Dooney."

most prominent deities in ancient Ireland was Manannan mac Lir, who ruled the sea.

Given the reference to Coole in the title, the reader can assume that the poet is observing a scene at Coole Park, the home of his friend Lady Gregory. His references to the aging year, the aging day, and the turning trees are symbolic of the poet's own advancing years. Rather than gaining skill and wisdom, the poet feels as if he is being slowly drained of beauty, creativity, and vitality. Yeats was around fifty years old when "The Wild Swans at Coole" was written. Not only was he feeling the need to get married and have children, he also worried that his best years as a poet may have been behind him.

Stanza 2

In the second stanza (lines 7–12), the poet recalls how nineteen years have passed since he first saw the swans at Coole Park (lines 7–8). The swans taking flight all at once interrupt his reverie of the past (line 10). Their wings are noisy, and in the air, they form loose rings (line 11), echoing the water imagery in line 5 of the first stanza. The broken rings of their flight also symbolize Yeats's failed marriage proposals.

Stanza 3

In stanza 3 (lines 13–18), the poet dwells upon his sorrow and loneliness, heightened by the beauty of the swans (lines 13–14). He thinks about how much he has changed, and not for the better, since the first time he heard the swans take flight above him at twilight (line 15). The poet dwells upon his lost youth, remembering how he once walked with a lighter step, in contrast to the flight of the eternally youthful swans (lines 17–18).

Stanza 4

In stanza 4 (lines 19–24), the poet describes the swans as unflagging and tireless after all these years and all of their lovers (line 19). The swans are part of nature, which is shameless and pure and replicates itself without trouble. In his view, the swans have not aged as the poet has, who is now heartsore and heavy of foot (line 22). Instead they fly, they love, and they travel as much as they ever did, leaving the poet behind, grounded to the earth (lines 23–24).

Stanza 5

In the fifth and final stanza (lines 25–30), the poet regards the swans resting on the water and knows that they will fly away someday and be enjoyed by other men (lines 25 and 27–29). By this, he means he will eventually die and does not himself have the immortality that nature does.

He references the swans building nests along the bank, implying pregnancy and new life (lines 27–28).

THEMES

Aging

Aging is a prominent theme in Yeats's work overall, as seen not only in "The Wild Swans at Coole" but also in poems such as "When You Are Old" and "Sailing to Byzantium." Even as a young man, the poet keenly felt his passing youth, which he equated with a loss of creativity. When "The Wild Swans at Coole" was written, Yeats was middle-aged and unmarried, despite proposing several times over the years to his friend and muse, Maud Gonne; however, less than a year after writing this poem, he finally married Georgie Hyde-Lees and entered the next stage of his life and career.

Aging is a central theme in "The Wild Swans at Coole." The swans represent eternal youth, and in this poem, Yeats contrasts his aging, slowing, even lonely self with the passionate, loving, and beloved swans who are eternally young through the magic of nature's seeming immutability as young swans replace old swans. To draw out the aging theme, Yeats recalls his youthfulness nineteen years earlier, when he first saw the Coole Park swans. Yeats was in his early thirties then and had recently become friends with Lady Gregory, the owner of Coole Park. He describes himself nineteen years before as walking with a lighter step, implying youth's vitality and health. Although he walks with an ever-heavier tread (line 18), the swans fly (lines 10–12). The swans tirelessly love one another (lines 19 and 22), but the poet is heartbroken (line 14). The overall mournful tone of "The Wild Swans at Coole" casts a negative light on the theme of aging, as the author romanticizes youth and disdains the infirmity of old age, a common attitude Yeats brings to his work.

Romanticism

The son of a father who was a pre-Raphaelite painter, Yeats himself valued romantic ideals in his writing. The romantic period is defined as lasting from the middle of the eighteenth century through the early nineteenth century, but romanticism's significant influences on the arts and culture continued to affect writers and artists long

TOPICS FOR FURTHER STUDY

- Yeats wrote in metered verse. Read a few more of his poems, such as "The Lake Isle at Innisfree," "The Song of Wandering Aengus," "The Stolen Child," and "Sailing to Byzantium," then write your own romantic poem in metered verse. A website hosted by the University of North Carolina at Greensboro provides a detailed chart of different types of meter with hyperlinked examples at http://www.uncg.edu/~htkirbys/meters.htm. Your poem does not have to rhyme, but it does need to use stressed and unstressed syllables in a pattern. Read your finished poem aloud to your class.

- In small groups, choose a different poem by Yeats that you like or are interested in and create an audio-video presentation of the poem. Consider using music, animation, acting, and voice-over work. Post your video online and invite the rest of your class to view, rate, and comment on your work. In class, discuss how Yeats's writing style lends itself to video presentation (or not) and how relevant his writing is a hundred years later.

- Yeats expressed his nationalism through a passion for Celtic mythology and folklore. He not only worked as a collector of Irish oral tradition but also imbued his own creative works with references to Irish folk heroes and symbols. In small groups, write a telescript of a story from Irish mythology or folklore and then film your group's performance. With the rest of your class, share your short film with your school by hosting an Irish storytelling event.

- Read *Tyger Tyger: A Goblin Wars Book* (2010) by Kersten Hamilton, a fantasy novel for young adults that blends ancient Irish mythology and the modern world. In this book, a levelheaded seventeen-year-old girl has her world turned upside down when her cousin from Ireland, Finn Mac Cumhaill, comes to stay with her family and mayhem erupts. Write a report about this novel, paying special attention to themes, symbolism, and how the author has connected myth and legend with modern life. Do you see a connection with "The Wild Swans at Coole"? Which work do you like better and why?

after modern movements took hold. Romanticism idealizes nature and values the imagination, emotion, mythology, and symbolism over science, technology, and industry. During the late nineteenth and early twentieth centuries, Irish nationalism favored a literature heavily influenced by Irish mythology. Yeats's romanticism was evident from his earliest publications, including his first collection of poetry, *The Wanderings of Oisin and Other Poems* (1889), whose titular poem is about a legendary Irish poet, dovetailing with Irish nationalism.

"The Wild Swans at Coole" indulges the poet's obsession with himself growing old, and this focus on the self is also a feature of romantic literature. Yeats also dabbled in references to

mythology by setting his poem in October and at twilight (line 3), both of which are times that have significance for travel to and from the faerie realm. The fifty-nine swans (line 6), as Martin Puhvel points out in his *Explicator* article, allude to the fifty-nine silver bells on the bridle of the horse that the faerie queen rode in "Thomas the Rhymer," a seventeenth-century English ballad about a medieval Scottish lord who is seduced into the faerie world for seven years. Thomas was a real person, transformed into a folk hero over the centuries. A concern with medieval history, literature, and aesthetics is also characteristic of romanticism. This allusion to the faerie queen and Thomas the Rhymer colors the understanding of the poet's sorrow, as he would probably

Yeats notes the passage of time in referencing the nineteen seasons he has counted the swans. (© *Samot* / *Shutterstock.com*)

have gladly traveled to the faerie world, where everything is beautiful and eternally young.

Another romantic feature of "The Wild Swans at Coole" is Yeats's near anthropomorphism of the swans. He contrasts his middle age with the vitality of the swans to draw out the theme of aging, but in the process, he discusses the passion of the swans as if they were all young, untroubled lovers (lines 19–24). Of course, because fifty-nine is an odd number, one of the swans does not have a partner, which references the poet's own loneliness. Finally, the sense of timelessness in the last stanza—that the swans will continue on as they always have when he is long gone (lines 27–30)—is a feature of romantic literature.

STYLE

Meter

Meter is the regular—or measured—rhythm of a poem and is a characteristic of the classical poetry that predates modern free verse (poetry without meter). Meter is broken down into smaller portions called feet; a *foot* is a group of syllables that help to create the rhythm. "The Wild Swans at Coole" is written in iambic meter, which is popular in English literature. An *iamb* is a type of foot comprising an unstressed syllable followed by a stressed syllable. A stressed syllable is read with greater emphasis than an unstressed syllable. Yeats does not maintain the same number of iambs per line, and sometimes he breaks the iambic pattern, but this alternating pattern of unstressed and stressed syllables creates a sing-song quality to the verse. Many lines in this poem have three iambs—iambic trimeter—including lines 2, 8, 14, 20, and 28. Less commonly occurring are iambic tetrameter (which has four iambs, such as in line 27) and iambic pentameter (which has five iambs, such as in line 17).

Symbolism

Symbolism is a literary technique in which the author conveys deeper meaning through the use of specific objects or images. The swans of Yeats's poem, for example, are symbolic of youth and passionate, reciprocal love. Yeats uses the vitality and beauty of the swans to contrast with his own advancing age. Other symbols

COMPARE
&
CONTRAST

- **1910s:** The Great War (later known as World War I) begins in 1914 and ends in 1918. According to Professor Keith Jeffery, writing for the BBC, of 210,000 Irish serving in the war, about 35,000 die, mostly from Northern Ireland.

  Today: Ireland does not take part in the Iraq War of 2003, but as a part of the United Nations, it has a small military presence in other areas in the Middle East and parts of Africa. As part of the European Union, Ireland has some Irish soldiers stationed in Somalia and Bosnia-Herzegovina. There are also Irish soldiers in Afghanistan and Kosovo as part of the NATO peacekeeping force.

- **1910s:** In 1911, nearly 90 percent of Irish considered themselves Roman Catholic, with the next largest religious group being the Church of Ireland (including Protestants) at 8 percent.

- **Today:** As of the 2006 census, Catholics in Ireland comprise about 87 percent of the population. The Church of Ireland has dropped to 3 percent of the population, with smaller religious groups taking a larger portion. The Muslim population rises dramatically between 2002 and 2006, taking the position of third-largest religious group in Ireland at 0.8 percent.

- **1910s:** Coole Park, a large and ancient family estate in western Ireland's County Galway near Gort, is the home of Lady Gregory and where Yeats spends his summers writing.

  Today: Coole Park is owned by the National Parks and Wildlife Service and is open to the public. Two trails connect some of the park's more famous features, including the Autograph Tree, the site of the original house (now demolished), and the woodlands that Yeats wrote about in his poem "In the Seven Woods" (1903).

---

in this poem include twilight and autumn, which symbolize middle age (line 3); the broken ring formation of the flying swans, which symbolizes Yeats's failed marriage proposals (line 11); and flight, which is symbolic of freedom (line 23) and youth and contrasts with the poet's own heavy, middle-aged step (line 18).

HISTORICAL CONTEXT

Irish Statehood and the Easter Rising
From the mid-sixteenth century until the eighteenth century, English and Scottish Protestant nobles settled in Ireland, confiscating property from Irish Catholic landholders in order to do so. The native Irish long sought self-sovereignty, resulting in several rebellions. Following a major uprising in 1798, the Act of Union in 1800 created the United Kingdom of Great Britain and Ireland, frustrating Irish nationalists, whose voices were marginalized by the ruling Protestant class.

By the early twentieth century, tensions between Anglo-Irish Protestants and Irish Catholics were not improved, but home rule was quickly becoming a reality. Under home rule, Ireland would self-govern within the United Kingdom but not be an independent nation. Home rule was expected to go into effect in Ireland in 1914, but World War I interrupted the legislative process.

Disgruntled Irish nationalists had little patience for the interruption and lashed out. On April 24, 1916, the day after Easter Sunday, rebellion against English rule broke out in Dublin. Serious communication problems led to a failure to receive a major arms delivery from Germany, and rebel action was suppressed in other parts of Ireland. But rebels seized government buildings in Dublin and proclaimed an

The swans are not old and represent passion to the narrator. *(© Nippel / Shutterstock.com)*

independent Irish Republic. Yeats, lecturing in Scotland at the time, was a little miffed that he had not heard about the secret arrangements for the rebellion since he did have some friends among those who were involved.

The rebellion suffered from poor communication and execution and was ill prepared to fight a modern army. It was squashed six days later, on April 30, and over thirty-five hundred people were arrested by the British government for involvement or suspected involvement. Fifteen men were executed (including Maud Gonne's husband John MacBride). Although the majority of Irish were not in favor of the Easter Rising at the time it happened, the arrests and executions polarized unionist and nationalist feelings, and when the dissidents were released from prison over a year later, they were greeted in Ireland as national heroes. These men formed the center of power in Irish politics for the coming generation, including Eamon de Valera (1882–1975), who was one of Ireland's most prominent political figures for decades and was the nation's first president.

British interests were routed from Irish politics in the general election of 1918. The Irish nationalist party Sinn Féin took a majority of the seats over the Home Rule Party and defiantly refused to go to Westminster in London, instead establishing an Irish parliament, Dáil Éireann, in Dublin. This marked the beginning of Ireland's War of Independence, which raged until July 1921, when the Irish nationalists and British government reached a stalemate and signed the Anglo-Irish Treaty.

Ireland was finally declared an independent state on December 6, 1922, following the signing of the Anglo-Irish Treaty. Yeats was one of the new republic's first senators, serving two terms before his failing health forced him to retire from politics. The county of Ulster in the north, which had a large Anglo-Irish Protestant population, was kept as part of the United Kingdom and became known as Northern Ireland. Strife between Northern Ireland and the Republic of Ireland, known as the Troubles, continued for most of the twentieth century.

CRITICAL OVERVIEW

Yeats began his career as a poet who worked in classic forms, influenced by the romanticism of the previous century. Later influenced by his friend Ezra Pound and other modernists, Yeats let go of rhyme and loosened up his meter. The development of his work from the poems of his first book, *The Wanderings of Oisin and Other Poems*, published in 1889, when he was only twenty-four years old, to the final volume of verse before he died, *Last Poems and Two Plays* (1939), shows Yeats's growth as a poet, belying his concern that growing older negatively affected one's creativity.

"The Wild Swans at Coole," from the collection by the same name, was published in 1917 in the United Kingdom, with a revised and expanded edition of the volume appearing in 1919. An anonymous reviewer for the *Times Literary Supplement* in 1919 celebrated Yeats's midcareer work with an extended analogy to Yeats as a fiddler. "Through all his poetry there is this beauty, a little malign, of desire that has not only failed to find its object but despairs of finding it," wrote the reviewer. A *Guardian* reviewer likewise praised Yeats's new work in 1919, noting that these midcareer poems steered away from the tangible and concrete and toward "a more and more studied evasion of strict form."

Not all critics were enamored with Yeats's work in *The Wild Swans at Coole*. An anonymous *New York Times* critic in 1919 described this collection as "painful"; he conceded that some poems in the collection are still very good, but perhaps not good enough for a poet of Yeats's stature. He drew a parallel between the wild swans and Yeats's creative genius, which this collection illustrated as passing: "In and out of the verses runs the tragedy of a man old in feeling, if not in years."

Eminent British literary critic J. Middleton Murry wrote about Yeats in his 1920 book *Aspects of Literature*, attempting to get at the underlying mythology or phantasmagoria to which Yeats alludes in his poetry. Murry disdained *The Wild Swans at Coole* as a devolution of the poet's career. He states, "Although it has little mysterious and haunting beauty, *The Wild Swans at Coole* is indeed a swan song." Yeats's crucial problem was a lack of true passion that Murry summarized thus: "He has the apparatus

of enchantment, but no potency in his soul." For Murry, *The Wild Swans at Coole* had little substance, and he believed that Yeats "remains an artist by determination, even though he returns downcast and defeated from the great quest of poetry."

CRITICISM

Carol Ullmann

Ullmann is a freelance writer and editor specializing in literature. In the following essay, she examines the theme of transformation in Yeats's poem "The Wild Swans at Coole."

The Wild Swans at Coole (1917; rev. ed., 1919) and its eponymous poem were published at the midpoint of Yeats's career. It was noted by critics in both the United States and Great Britain for a loosening of strict form (rhyme and meter) and for a drawing away from concrete meaning, as Yeats increasingly preferred to be indirect about his allusions and interpretations of his work, the mark of symbolist poetry. All the understanding of "The Wild Swans at Coole," in fact, stems from biographical knowledge of what was happening in Yeats's life just before this volume of poetry was published.

Yeats met Lady Gregory in 1896. She was older than Yeats by about fifteen years, and the two formed a fast and lifelong friendship. According to B. L. Reid in *The Dictionary of Literary Biography*, she offered her home to him to help him work, a great boon to an artist who, though working steadily and even earning acclaim, was far from financially secure. Her sponsorship was not only significant to his financial well-being, but "the snob in Yeats," as described by Reid, was also drawn to the majesty of her old family wealth and aristocratic lifestyle.

Lady Gregory was an ardent supporter of the arts, and for her part, she enjoyed taking care of Yeats and nurturing his career. Yeats spent most of his summers for the next twenty years at Coole Park. He and Lady Gregory not only talked about their work and dreams but also traveled together and collaborated. The inspiring landscape of the grand estate and the engaging friendship of Lady Gregory, as well as the free room and board, enabled Yeats to establish himself as a great poet.

WHAT DO I READ NEXT?

- Irish satirist Jonathan Swift published the amusing and biting tale *Gulliver's Travels* in 1726. The fantastical elements of the story, such as the six-inch-tall Lilliputians, appeal to young readers, while the social commentary engages adult readers.

- Lord Tennyson's famous epic poem "The Lady of Shalott" (1833; rev. ed., 1842) is a romantic poem about a woman imprisoned in a tower, compelled by a curse to not interact with society. The subject is drawn from Arthurian legend and inspired the pre-Raphaelite painters of the Victorian era.

- James Joyce, a contemporary of Yeats's, published a collection of short stories called *The Dubliners* in 1914. This book depicts everyday life in Dublin in the early twentieth century and arose out of Joyce's nationalist feelings.

- T. S. Eliot, born in the United States but naturalized as a British citizen when he was thirty-nine years old, made his name as a poet when he published "The Love Song of J. Alfred Prufrock" in 1915. Like Yeats's poem, Eliot's expresses the loneliness and frustration of a man who has been unlucky in love and possibly in life.

- Yeats's late collection of poetry *The Tower* was published in 1928 and contains twenty-one poems. Included in this volume are famous poems such as "Sailing to Byzantium" and "Leda and the Swan." Like swans, towers were an important symbol in Yeats's writing.

- Seamus Heaney, Ireland's most famous living poet at the beginning of the twenty-first century, published his acclaimed poetry collection *Death of a Naturalist* in 1967. The book deals with Heaney's childhood and the formation of his adult identity.

- *Natural Supernaturalism: Tradition and Revolution in Romantic Literature* (1973), by M. H. Abrams, examines the literary foundation of the romantic age (1789–1835), what was revolutionary about this period, where romanticism stems from, and how it influenced the movements that followed.

- *A Suitcase of Seaweed and Other Poems* (1996), by Janet Wong, is a collection of poetry informed by the author's American, Chinese, and Korean heritage. Wong writes about identity, ethnicity, and family.

- *Paint Me Like I Am: Teen Poems from WritersCorp* is a 2003 collection edited by Bill Aguado and Richard Newirth that captures the diverse voices of at-risk teens in New York City, Washington, D.C., and San Francisco. The young poets write about themselves, their friends, drugs, abuse, and race.

Nevertheless, Yeats was troubled in love. As a young man, he yearned for his beautiful friend Maud Gonne, proposing marriage to her multiple times but each time refused. Gonne, an actress and an activist, eventually married nationalist leader John MacBride in 1903, breaking Yeats's heart. After Gonne's husband was executed for his involvement in the 1916 Easter Rising, Yeats proposed one last time, but Gonne again refused him. Later that year, nineteen years after his first visit to Coole Park, Yeats composed "The Wild Swans at Coole," a poem that expresses the disappointment of a lonely, middle-aged man.

Yeats hated that he was growing old and sought marriage with a determination that bordered on desperation. Spurred by the strong emotions that motivated the writing of "The Wild Swans at Coole," Yeats set out to find a bride because he wanted to have children before he got too much older. Yeats proposed first to Iseult Gonne, Maud's daughter, who refused him, and then he proposed to his friend and

THE POET WISHES HE WERE YOUNG AGAIN,
WISHES HE WERE MARRIED, AND EVEN WISHES HE
COULD BE WHISKED AWAY TO THE FAERIE WORLD."

admirer Georgiana Hyde-Lees, a woman almost half his age. Georgie accepted Yeats, and they were married in October 1917, a year after the composition of this poem and less than a year after its publication.

"The Wild Swans at Coole" is a poem about transformation. The world in this poem is transforming from summer into winter: trees are changing to fall colors, and even the day has grown dark (although it is not night) in order to emphasize the dying year and the aging man. The poet wishes he were young again, wishes he were married, and even wishes he could be whisked away to the faerie world. Heavily influenced by romanticism, Yeats idealizes nature; in this poem, the primary form of that idealization is the perfection of the swans.

He sees the swans as happy companions, eternally youthful, faithful to their species, and working in concert. "Swans," Pooja Dhankhar and Sujata Rana write in an examination of Keats's and Yeats's bird imagery for *Language in India*, "are usually depicted in mythology as pairs, symbolising love and monogamous relationships as well as loyalty and trust in partnership." Yeats's swans live in a peaceful, immutable world all their own that works, without question, argument, or uncertainty. In this poem, Yeats, thwarted in love and fearing his own advancing age, expresses a yearning to have a similar simplicity in his life.

The first personal transformation evident in "The Wild Swans at Coole" is Yeats's desire to be married. When he wrote this poem, his infatuation with Maud Gonne had faded to more of a duty; nevertheless, he desired a wife so that he could have kids before he grew too old to do so. Marriage is a significant rite of passage in a person's life, a transformation, and no less important for men than it is for women. Having children creates a physical legacy beyond that found in one's writing. Children are a future

promise, although one can never know what one's children will ultimately do with their own lives. Perhaps one of Yeats's kids would go on to be a famous poet in the footsteps of their tremendously talented father. (As it happened, his son went into politics, and his daughter became a painter.)

The second transformation was that of Yeats into middle age. Even as a young man, he hated the thought that he was getting older. For him, beauty existed in the vitality of youth, and nature, being able to ever renew herself, was the ultimate source of beauty. In this poem, faced with the prospect of being fifty-one years old and wishing he were married with children, Yeats is dazzled by the perfect beauty of the swans, who represent monogamy, floating on the water, happy and peaceful. Yeats felt that he was slowing down, growing infirm, and losing beauty. He may have also feared losing his creativity along with his youth, a terrifying prospect for a poet.

The third evident transformation is Yeats's desire to become a swan and join the flock. He notes that there are fifty-nine swans—an odd number, significant for creatures who symbolize monogamy. With this number, not far off from his age, although that connection is mysterious, Yeats is providing himself with opportunity. If the circumstances were just right—during the month of October or at twilight, both magical times in Celtic tradition—perhaps he could join them and fill out their ranks. If nothing else, Yeats would then be able to take wing and fly, an exhilarating freedom virtually unknown to humankind in the early twentieth century outside Kitty Hawk, North Carolina. Being able to fly, Yeats could leave the hard earth behind and travel wherever and whenever he pleased. Another interpretation of the odd number of swans is that Yeats, in his youth, was part of this flock and now no longer fits in because of his age. Perhaps his loneliness is echoed by the fifty-ninth swan, who swims with his brethren, unable to fulfill his destiny to procreate, thus the imagery of broken fidelity in line 11.

As noted by Martin Puhvel in the *Explicator*, fifty-nine is also the number of bells on the faerie queen's horse bridle in the ballad "Thomas the Rhymer." This ballad was written down in the seventeenth century but spans back to medieval times, when an actual Scottish laird inspired the composition of this famous poem. In the

The swans represent stability in a world turned upside down. (© *Igor Borodin / Shutterstock.com*)

ballad, Thomas is seduced by the faerie queen to follow her to the faerie world and spend seven years there as her guest. Yeats, in his love for beauty and youth, may wish to be whisked away like Thomas to the faerie world, which is known by many names, including the land of eternal youth. After all, the world of 1916, especially in Ireland, was not an easy one. Much of the world was caught up in the Great War (later known as World War I), and that same year Ireland was the site of a failed and bloody rebellion for independence.

The fourth transformation is alluded to in the last two stanzas. The swans are symbolic not only of youth, as described earlier, but also of Yeats's poetry and therefore his soul. Stéphanie Noirard posits the idea of the swans representing Yeats's poetry let loose in the world in her analysis of "The Wild Swans at Coole" for the *CerclesOccasional Paper Series.* Yeats describes the swans as lovely and enigmatic in lines 25 and 26, a description that can easily apply to his poetry. These swans persist and do not change despite men dying and passing out of their lives: they fly, they love each other, and they have not been

emotionally exhausted (line 22) by all of their companionable joy. The swans (poems) are an eternal fragment of this time and place, which will live on long after he passes from this realm. As Noirard writes:

> Not being heard means death for a poet all the more so as, to refer back to a romantic concept, the work of an author is an edifice that protects him from the worst death of all, oblivion.

Transformation was a rich theme for a poet like Yeats midway through his career, who had as much to draw on from his past works as he had years more of creativity to look forward to.

Source: Carol Ullmann, Critical Essay on "The Wild Swans at Coole," in *Poetry for Students*, Gale, Cengage Learning, 2013.

Wayne K. Chapman

In the following excerpt, Chapman examines the ways in which the Great War and the Easter 1916 insurrection in Ireland informed the works of Yeats.

...Writing in the aftermath of the Easter Rising, and in the midst of the Great War,

Yeats also registered the disturbance of Ireland's Parnellite assertions by "the rude din of this... century," as Joyce had phrased it. Between 1916 and 1918, Yeats wrote several such poems, and of them the best known is the title poem of *The Wild Swans at Coole* (1919). Yeats brought these poems to the attention of English readers in the wartime illustrated papers edited by Clement Shorter, the husband of Dora Sigerson Shorter, and in such pamphlets as *Easter, 1916*, which was privately printed by Clement Shorter in 1917.

Notably, the publication history of these Easter Rising poems coincides with the manuscript history of two of Yeats's four plays for dancers. As Easter plays about betrayal, *The Dreaming of the Bones* and *Calvary* adapt a form of theater that Yeats commended for having arisen "in an age of continual war" in Japan and for having become "a part of the education of soldiers." Hence, during the Easter Rising, the Great War, the Anglo-Irish War, and the Irish Civil War, Yeats published his theatrical experiments in some of the same little magazines that presented his Easter Rising poems. Yeats decided to abandon his effort to write a "fifth" play for dancers which his wife said epitomized the year 1918—the year of the General Election, of the first Sinn Féin Dáil, and the Irish declaration of independence. Even so, a connection exists between this "lost" fifth Noh play and Yeats's political poems of the same period.

In his study of the making of *The Wild Swans at Coole*, Stephen Parrish was right to infer that Yeats "entertained the bold scheme of opening his collection with a commemoration of the Easter Rising and closing it with a dismissal of the war raging in Europe." That is, Yeats must have planned to open with "Easter, 1916," close with the epigram "On Being Asked for a War Poem," and confer prominence to elegies of the group. Prudence demanded substitution of "The Wild Swans at Coole" for "Easter, 1916" and redesign of the 1917 volume, thus giving the displaced lyric to Shorter's private printing on the anniversary of the 1916 Easter Rising. But more was involved in Yeats's reaction to wars real and as he imagined them.

Several of Yeats's patriotic verses, especially "Sixteen Dead Men," were stimulated by his complex feelings as an Irishman and old friend of Dora Sigerson Shorter, whose painful death by cancer was kept from her last poems *Love of*

Ireland and *The Tricolour*, published in America as *Sixteen Dead Men*. After Easter, 1918, and Dora Shorter's death, Yeats wrote frequently to her husband, Clement, who brought out in October a private edition of Yeats's *Nine Poems*. Yeats's "Easter, 1916" circulated discreetly in manuscript and in private printing beside the likes of Dora Shorter's militant *Poems of the Irish Rebellion 1916*. Yeats requested in May, 1918, a set of Shorter's "privately printed rebellion poems" and her new book, *The Sad Years* (1918). Taken together, these constituted in Yeats's words, "all the work she wrote in stress of illness & technically... her best." On the next day, May 7, 1918, de Valéra, the president of the first Dáil, and other Sinn Féin leaders were arrested, after which matters began to escalate until a war with British forces in Ireland broke out later in 1918. "The Wild Swans at Coole," a major poem in an important phase of Yeats's work, appeared in this context.

"The Wild Swans at Coole" found dissimilar company in its first printing in *The Sphere* on June 23, 1917. There, the poem appeared sandwiched between two prose works designed to give expression to moments of sudden discovery accompanied by emotion. A personal essay by E. V. Lucas, "On Finding Things," starts a chain reaction of associations that seems, for the reader, to continue into Yeats's meditative poem. An associational response to the coveted "nine and fifty swans," "The Wild Swans at Coole" enfolds past and present experience in a reflection almost as "mysterious" and "beautiful" as they are, leading to the disillusionment of the next essay. Moving from "The Wild Swans at Coole," the reader of *The Sphere* encounters a prose sketch called "Whither" (by "M. D."), the reflections of a bivouacked officer. The "lost illusions" of 1914 play in the soldier's mind with gramophone music and the "unmelodious" facts of trench warfare collide with them in free association—facts that are pictorially graphic on accompanying pages of the magazine: "Lost illusions have their savour, but sweeter far are the dreams of what may be in the future."

We should not imagine "The Wild Swans at Coole" to be a war poem, though Yeats gave it to be published first in a paper brimming with images and accounts of the war in Europe and elsewhere. However, this context did inspire his reordering of the stanzas, which was, in Parrish's words, "as brilliant a single revision as Yeats ever made." The layout of the poem on the printed page of *The Sphere* directs the reader's attention to the third stanza's enigmatic question, the sustaining balance between actuality and dream:

> Among what rushes will they [the swans] build,
> By what lake's edge or pool
> Delight men's eyes when I awake some day
> To find they have flown away?

Consequently, Yeats effected dramatic improvement in the lyric by shifting the whole stanza to the end of the poem in all printings after this one. But was there, implicitly, a political element in the symbolism, of a disturbance of tranquility in the Irish scene considering the violence of modernity, the filthy modern tide of history in wartime? If so, Yeats guarded this particular secret . . . .

Source: Wayne K. Chapman, "Joyce and Yeats: Easter 1916 and the Great War," in *New Hibernia Review*, Vol. 10, No. 4, Winter 2006, pp. 137–51.

London Times Literary Supplement

In the following review, a contributor praises Yeats's masterful use of sound and suggests that Yeats emphasizes both ephemeral and malignant themes in The Wild Swans at Coole.

Mr. Yeats is like a fiddler taking down his old dust-covered violin and lazily playing an old tune on it; or it seems an old tune at first that he is taking liberties with. How often one has heard it; and yet, suddenly, it is as new as the sunrise—or the moonlight. Go on, go on, we cry. No one can play like that; and then he ceases carelessly, and puts the fiddle away, and talks of other things. All through this book he has the effect of remembering old tunes and playing them over again and making them new. There are some players who possess you with the sense of their mastery by the way they look over the fiddle before they sound a note; and he has this power with the first words of a song. But he likes best to begin with the variation upon an old tune, the tune being implicit in the variation and fading a way out of it into a last line, that seems to stop lazily as if it were just capriciously tired of itself. So in "The Wild Swans at Coole," we are tantalized; he seems to love the mere sound of his fiddle that only he can draw from it and then to grow weary as if all tunes were played and stale.

He himself is aware of this mood and even makes poetry out of it:—

> I am worn out with dreams:
> A weather-worn, marble triton
> Among the streams;
> And all day long I look
> Upon this lady's beauty
> As though I had found in book
> A pictured beauty,
> Pleased to have filled the eyes
> Or the discerning ears,
> Delighted to be but wise,
> For men improve with the years;
> And yet and yet
> Is this my dream, or the truth?
> O would that we had met
> When I had my burning youth;
> But I grow old among dreams,
> A weather-worn, marble triton
> Among the streams.

There he seems to be living on memories and to resent some malignancy in the nature of things which has made of him a work of art incompatible with artless reality. It is this sense of a malignance in things which makes Irish writers themselves so often seem malicious. It is in Synge, and even in Mr. Shaw; they whisper malice about men because to them there is malice in reality. In the second verse of another poem Mr. Yeats says:—

> I would find by the edge of that water
> The collar-bone of a hare
> Worn thin by the lapping of water,
> And pierce it through with a gimlet and stare
> At the old bitter world where they marry in churches,
> And laugh over the untroubled water
> At all who marry in churches,
> Through the white thin bone of a hare.

Irish writers do seem to look at reality through the white thin bone of a hare, through some magic and isolating medium of their own, which makes reality to them far off, absurd, meaningless. And the world of meaning which they desire, for them is not. Hence their malice. They would put us out of conceit with the reality that is at least real to us, because they are out of conceit with it; and Mr. Yeats wanders lost, unable to find that universe which is yet real to him because he so much desires it.

Through all his poetry there is this beauty, a little malign, of desire that has not only failed to find its object but despairs of finding it. That is why he picks up his fiddle so lazily and plays us such short, sweet, tantalizing tunes on it. Stray things suggest to him that state of being he can never find, like the wild swans at Coole themselves:—

The trees are in their autumn beauty,
The woodland paths are dry,
Under the October twilight the water
Mirrors a still sky;
Upon the brimming water among the stones
Are nine and fifty swans.

And the poem ends:—

But now they drift on the still water
Mysterious, beautiful;
Among what rushes will they build,
By what lake's edge or pool
Delight men's eyes when I awake some day
To find they have flow away?

Because they are so beautiful they are to him
visitants and have the transitoriness of his own
delight in them. In his music he seems to inhabit
a world that will tremble away at a touch like
reflections in still water. Even in the beautiful
poem in memory of Major Gregory, full of concrete things and characters, he says:—

Always we'd have the new friend meet the old
And we are hurt if either friend seem cold,
And there is salt to lengthen out the smart
In the affections of our heart,
And quarrels are blown up upon that head;
But not a friend that I would bring
This night can set us quarrelling,
For all that come into my mind are dead.

Friends too, and even friendships are like
the wild swans at Coole. But how good the
poem is; both racy and passionate, like the
poetry of Donne, and like that, without imitation, in its very turns of speech. While we analyse
the poet's mind and seem to judge it, we are
fidgeting away from the real matter, the beauty
of his poetry. That justifies his mind and all its
moods; and in *The Wild Swans at Coole* there are
many beautiful poems, some more homely than
Mr. Yeats is wont to write. Every one can enjoy
the "Two Songs of a Fool," or "The Cat and the
Moon," which is a miracle of things exactly said
that seemed unsayable; and there is a truth most
delicately captured in "An Irish airman foresees
his death":—

I know that I shall meet my fate
Somewhere among the clouds above;
Those that I fight I do not hate,
Those that I guard I do not love;
My country is Kiltartan Cross
My countrymen Kiltartan's poor,
No likely end could bring them loss
Or leave them happier than before.

There he fiddles to an old tune, but what a
new surprise of meaning he gets out of his easy,
lazy, masterly fiddling. And we can only listen
and be grateful.

Source: "Tunes Old and New," Review of *The Wild
Swans at Coole*, in *London Times Literary Supplement*,
No. 896, March 20, 1919, p. 149.

SOURCES

"Census 2006: Volume 13—Religion," Ireland Central
Statistics Office website, November 2007, http://www.
cso.ie/en/media/csoie/census/census2006results/volume13/
volume_13_religion.pdf (accessed March 20, 2012).

Daly, Mary E., "Easter Rising," in *Europe since 1914:
Encyclopedia of the Age of War and Reconstruction*,
Vol. 2, edited by John Merriman and Jay Winter, Charles
Scribner's Sons, 2006, pp. 911–14.

———, "Ireland," in *Europe since 1914: Encyclopedia of
the Age of War and Reconstruction*, Vol. 3, edited by John
Merriman and Jay Winter, Charles Scribner's Sons, 2006,
pp. 1445–53.

Dhankhar, Pooja, and Sujata Rana, "Bird Imagery in
Keats's 'Ode to a Nightingale' and Yeats's 'The Wild
Swans at Coole': A Comparative Study," in *Language in
India*, Vol. 11, No. 12, December 2011, p. 508.

Hopkinson, Michael A., "Struggle for Independence
from 1916 to 1921," in *Encyclopedia of Irish History and
Culture*, Vol. 2, edited by James S. Donnelly, Jr., Macmillan Reference USA, 2004, pp. 683–86.

Jeffery, Keith, "Ireland and World War One," BBC History, http://www.bbc.co.uk/history/british/britain_wwone/
ireland_wwone_01.shtml (accessed March 20, 2012).

"Mr. Yeats's Ardent New Poems," Review of *The Wild
Swans at Coole*, in *Guardian*, April 6, 1919, p. 36.

Murry, J. Middleton, "Mr. Yeats's Swan Song," in
Aspects of Literature, W. Collins Sons, 1920, pp. 39–45.

Noirard, Stéphanie, "'The Wild Swans at Coole': Poem
Analysis," in *Cercles Occasional Paper Series*, 2009,
pp. 233–41.

Puhvel, Martin, "Yeats's 'The Wild Swans at Coole,'" in
Explicator, Vol. 45, No. 1, Fall 1986, pp. 29–30.

Reid, B. L., "William Butler Yeats," in *Dictionary of
Literary Biography*, Vol. 332, *Nobel Prize Laureates in
Literature, Part 4*, edited by Edward L. Bishop, Thomson
Gale, 2007, pp. 507–33.

"Tunes Old and New," Review of *The Wild Swans at
Coole*, in *Times Literary Supplement*, No. 896, March
20, 1919, p. 149.

"With Irish Bards Old and New," Review of *The Wild
Swans at Coole*, in *New York Times*, September 21, 1919,
p. 92.

Yeats, William Butler, "The Wild Swans at Coole," in
The Collected Poems of W. B. Yeats: A New Edition,
edited by Richard J. Finneran, Collier, 1989, pp. 131–32.

FURTHER READING

Frost, Robert, "After Apple-Picking," in *The Poetry of Robert Frost*, edited by Edward Connery Lathem, Owl Books, 1969, pp. 68–69.

This poem, published in 1914 by American poet laureate Frost, has themes of aging and death similar to those in "The Wild Swans at Coole" and also uses nature symbolism.

McGarry, Fearghal, *The Rising; Ireland: Easter 1916*, Oxford University Press, 2010.

Yeats's poem was written around the same time as the 1916 Easter Rising in Ireland. McGarry's critical study of this pivotal point in Irish history is based on seventeen hundred eyewitness accounts never before taken into consideration.

O'Neill, Michael, ed., *The Poems of W. B. Yeats: A Sourcebook*, Routledge, 2004.

O'Neill collects in one volume the significant criticism on Yeats's poetry, published both during his lifetime and after his death. He also reprints over forty of Yeats's key poems, including "The Wild Swans at Coole."

Smith, Stan, *W. B. Yeats: A Critical Introduction*, Rowman & Littlefield, 1990.

Smith's book provides a biographical sketch, twenty-two chapters on themes and motifs in Yeats's work, a guide to further reading, and indexes for poems and names.

Yeats, William Butler, *The Collected Works of W. B. Yeats*, Vol. 3, *Autobiographies*, Touchstone, 1999.

This book collects six autobiographical works that Yeats published in the last decade of his life and includes details about his childhood, his involvement with the founding of the Abbey Theatre, and winning the Nobel Prize in Literature.

———, ed., *Fairy and Folk Tales of the Irish Peasantry*, Dover, 2011.

Yeats collected, annotated, and wrote the introduction to this classic collection of stories about faeries, druids, giants, and priests, originally published in 1888.

SUGGESTED SEARCH TERMS

"The Wild Swans at Coole"

William Butler Yeats

Yeats AND aging

Yeats AND Coole Park

Yeats AND poetry

Yeats AND pre-Raphaelites

Yeats AND romanticism

Yeats AND swans AND symbolism

The World Is Not a Pleasant Place to Be

NIKKI GIOVANNI

1972

Nikki Giovanni's poem "The World Is Not a Pleasant Place to Be" was first included in her collection of poems about love, home, and family titled *My House*, published in 1972. "The World Is Not a Pleasant Place to Be" appears in a section labeled "The Rooms Inside." Its placement in this section suggests that Giovanni intends for the poem to be linked to home and safety. At the time that Giovanni was writing the poem, the Vietnam War was still three years from ending. The late 1960s and early 1970s had been years of tumultuous protests over the war, amid demands for civil rights for all Americans. Focusing on the need for love, the poem is a counter to the turmoil that was occurring outside the home and is a reminder of the importance of love and home as a place of sanctuary.

"The World Is Not a Pleasant Place to Be" is a thirteen-line, four-stanza, free-verse poem with no punctuation or rhyme scheme. Since Giovanni eschews periods, commas, and other forms of punctuation, there are no pauses or places for the reader to stop and catch a breath, which contributes to the natural songlike quality that is true of much of her poetry. Here, Giovanni uses metaphors from nature to illustrate the need for love. The central theme in this short poem is that without love and someone to love, life would be lonely; to be held by another makes the world a safer and happier place in which to live. "The World Is Not a Pleasant Place to Be" is included in *The Collected Poetry of Nikki Giovanni* (2003).

Nikki Giovanni (© Mike Simons / Getty Images)

AUTHOR BIOGRAPHY

Yolande Cornelia Giovanni, named after her mother, was born on June 7, 1943, and grew up in Lincoln Heights, a predominantly African American suburb of Cincinnati, Ohio, although she frequently visited Knoxville, Tennessee, the city of her birth and the home of her grandparents. Her older sister gave her the nickname "Nikki." Giovanni enrolled at Fisk University after her junior year at Austin High School under an early-admission policy, but she was expelled at the end of her first semester when she left campus to visit her grandparents over Thanksgiving. After a new dean of women replaced the one who had expelled her, Giovanni returned to Fisk. She graduated with honors in

1967, with a degree in history. Afterward, Giovanni moved back to Cincinnati. When her grandmother died only a month later, Giovanni began to write poetry as a way to deal with her grief. Many of the poems that she wrote during this period of mourning were published in her first collection, *Black Feeling, Black Talk*, in 1967. Giovanni received a grant from the National Endowment for the Arts and was able to move to New York City, where she continued writing poetry while enrolled at Columbia University's School of Fine Arts; however, she dropped out of their MFA program during the first year. A second collection of poetry, *Black Judgement*, was published in 1968.

Giovanni began teaching, first at Queens College and later at Rutgers University, and then gave birth to her only child, Thomas Watson Giovanni, in 1970. *Re: Creation*, published in 1970, was the third and last of Giovanni's books featuring a revolutionary tone and advocating militant change for the African American community. After she became a mother, the tone of her poetry shifted, becoming less militant, and she also began writing poetry for children. The following year, Giovanni's first collection of poems for children, *Spin a Soft Black Song*, was published, as was a lengthy autobiographical essay, *Gemini*. Also in 1971, Giovanni recorded a spoken album, *Truth Is on Its Way*, with the New York Community Choir. This bestselling album received the National Association of Television and Radio Announcers Award for Best Spoken Word Album.

In 1972, Giovanni's collection of poems about family and home, *My House* (which includes "The World Is Not a Pleasant Place to Be"), was published. A second children's poetry collection, *Ego-Tripping and Other Poems for Young People*, was published in 1973, and *Cotton Candy on a Rainy Day* was published five years later. Although she published only a couple of volumes in the 1980s, Giovanni wrote and published steadily through the 1990s and 2000s. A children's book of African American song lyrics, *On My Journey Now: Looking at African-American History through the Spirituals*, was published in 2007. Giovanni has continued to publish additional collections of poetry in recent years, including *Acolytes* (2007) and *Bicycles: Love Poems* (2009).

Giovanni has received a number of awards, such as being honored as woman of the year by several magazines, including *Ebony* (1970), *Mademoiselle* (1971), and *Ladies' Home Journal* (1972). She was named to the Ohio Women's

Hall of Fame (1985) and received Governor's Awards from both Tennessee (1996 and 1998) and Virginia (2000). Giovanni was awarded the Langston Hughes Medal for her literary accomplishments as an African American (1996) and the Rosa L. Parks Woman of Courage Award (2002). Giovanni's children's book about Rosa Parks, *Rosa* (2005), was selected as a Caldecott Honor Book. Since she began publishing in 1968, Giovanni has had more than two dozen books published, as well as many essays and individual poems. She is a prolific writer and also a teacher. Giovanni has been a professor at Virginia Polytechnic Institute and State University, or Virginia Tech, since 1987 and in 1999 was given the title of University Distinguished Professor, the highest recognition given to university faculty. She resides in Virginia.

POEM TEXT

the world is not a pleasant place
to be without
someone to hold and be held by

a river would stop
its flow if only   5
a stream were there
to receive it

an ocean would never laugh
if clouds weren't there
to kiss her tears   10

the world is not
a pleasant place to be without
someone

POEM SUMMARY

The text used for this summary is from *My House*, William Morrow, 1972, p. 15. Versions of the poem can be found on the following web pages: http://poetry365.tumblr.com/post/374184041/the-world-is-not-a-pleasant-place-to-be-nikki-giovanni and http://poetryforchildren.blogspot.com/2007/04/poems-comfort-and-nikki-giovanni.html.

Stanza 1

The first stanza of "The World Is Not a Pleasant Place to Be" is a three-line statement that love is necessary for the world to be a pleasant place. It is also necessary for the world to be a safe place. More than loving another, though, it is necessary that love be reciprocated. It is not enough for only

MEDIA ADAPTATIONS

- *Legacies: The Poetry of Nikki Giovanni* (1976) is an audio CD from Smithsonian Folkways. "The World Is Not a Pleasant Place to Be" is on this audio CD, which includes twenty poems.

- *Like a Ripple on a Pond* (1993), by Atlantic Records, includes poems from *My House*. Although "The World Is Not a Pleasant Place to Be" is not included on this audio CD, the New York Community Choir joins Giovanni in reading and singing the poems, which adds to the collection's appeal. The CD was reissued by Collectables in 1993.

- Giovanni reads her poetry on *The Nikki Giovanni Poetry Collection* (2002). This two-hour CD was issued by Caedmon.

- *Only the Best of Nikki Giovanni* (2009) is a five-disc audiobook in which the poet reads poetry from several of her collections. Although she does not read "The World Is Not a Pleasant Place to Be," this audio CD provides the opportunity to hear Giovanni read sixty-eight of her poems.

- Giovanni's spoken album *Truth Is on Its Way*, which was recorded with the New York Community Choir in 1971, was reissued by Collectables in 1993. Many of this album's poems are included in her collection *Ego-Tripping and Other Poems for Young People*.

one person to love another. Giovanni makes clear that for love to truly make the world a pleasant place, two people must freely love one another. In addition, it is the act of holding a loved one who returns the embrace that is of most value. The world is a place filled with danger and risk, but giving and receiving affection offers sanctuary and protection from the outside world. These feelings of safety are found in one another's arms.

The poet places this poem in the section of *My House* that is described as "The Rooms Inside." Shared love offers a sanctuary from the outside.

The unpleasantness that is found outside, whether it be racism, civil discord, war, or other unnamed dangers, can be placed in abeyance because there is strength and protection in shared love.

Stanza 2

The second stanza is the only four-line stanza in the poem. This stanza contains a metaphor that reinforces the sentiments of the first stanza. In that feelings are invisible, Giovanni compares a life without love to a river that has no ready outlet for all its power. Both the river and love need a place to go to be fully realized and to be at their most powerful. In this second stanza, a river that flows only into a stream would have no place to empty its reserves of water. The melting snows of winter would fill the river, and with the stream just not large enough to hold all the power of the river and with no place to go, the river would overflow its shores. The flow of water in the river would move without direction in spilling its banks; its smooth flow would simply cease without an outlet able to accept what the river gives so willingly.

If the river is forced to stop because it cannot empty into the needed outlet, the movement of the water would also cease, and without movement, it might well become stagnant. In a way, this is what happens to love when it is not returned and begins to lose life and become stale. The dormant river requires an outlet to continue to live, just as love turns lifeless when it has no one with whom to share life. From the first stanza, the reader knows that the poet views shared love as a refuge from the world outside. This second stanza reaffirms the idea that there is a power in reciprocity that sets people and nature apart and protects them from all that might go wrong in the world.

Stanza 3

In the third stanza, the poet returns to the three-line format and turns her attention to the ocean, which is the rightful outlet for the river's outpouring of power. In this stanza, it is the clouds who work most forcefully with the ocean. The water vapor present in clouds later falls to the earth as rain. The heat of the sun causes water on earth to evaporate into the air, and when it reaches a high enough elevation, the vapor cools again, forming clouds, which eventually release the vapor held within as rain. The rain can be thought of as the ocean's tears, but because the clouds are there to take away the ocean's tears, the ocean is given the freedom to laugh. The analogy of clouds kissing away tears is a reminder that a shared love is there

through happiness and sadness; to kiss away tears is a lovely gift between lovers. The poet uses the feminine gender to describe the ocean's tears, which is in keeping with the tradition of describing nature as feminine, since nature is often depicted as nurturing.

The idea of an ocean laughing creates an image of huge waves rising up from the ocean in an effort to reach up to the clouds. This image once again reinforces the notion of reciprocity that is captured in both of the first two stanzas. The ocean reaches up to the clouds, where the clouds take away the ocean's tears, and thus the cycle of rain is perpetuated and the earth is nurtured through rain. Each element of nature needs the other for it to work properly. This is true of human beings, too, who need one another to feel happy and protected.

Stanza 4

The poem's final stanza essentially repeats the first stanza with small but significant changes. The poet again uses the three-line format, as she did in the first stanza, but this time the placement of words changes. Once again the poet reminds readers that the world is made better, safer, more welcoming with someone to share both the pain and happiness of life. What changes between the first and fourth stanzas is that now the poet leaves out the requirement that being held and holding someone else makes the world easier to bear. The requirement of reciprocity is lessened, but because it was so clearly stated in the first three stanzas, readers should not assume that reciprocity is no longer needed. Rather the poet acknowledges that the point has been made and thus there is no need to restate the obvious. Instead, readers are presented with a simple, but shortened affirmation that the world is made better with someone else with whom to share life. The loneliness of the world is assuaged with a partner who shares the burdens and fears that so often crop up in a world where the daily news carries stories of crime, war, and natural disaster. Just as nature operates more efficiently with the help of others, whether rivers, oceans, clouds, or rain, people are happiest when there is someone to share our lives.

THEMES

Love

In "The World Is Not a Pleasant Place to Be," the poet suggests that love is a refuge from the world outside the home. Because this poem is

TOPICS FOR FURTHER STUDY

- *For Love of Ivy* is a 1968 film starring Sidney Poitier. Watch this film and then compare the message of the film with what Giovanni is saying about the importance of love in "The World Is Not a Pleasant Place to Be." Write an essay in which you compare these two messages and their respective formats— film and poem—and explain which format you think delivers the message most clearly and why you think that one particular format is more successful than the other.

- "The World Is Not a Pleasant Place to Be" uses metaphors to create images about how important it is to love and be loved. Use the first and last stanzas of Giovanni's poem in a poem that you will create. Write at least three new middle stanzas to compare how you feel about loving and being loved. Like Giovanni, you can use comparisons with nature as a way to explain your feelings, but you might also use other metaphors, perhaps even technology, as a way to explain how you feel about love.

- Langston Hughes is considered one of the most important African American poets of the twentieth century. Like Giovanni, Hughes was considered a revolutionary poet who wrote about inequality and oppression in African American life. Hughes also wrote poetry for children. Research Hughes's life and read at least six of his poems from *The Dream Keeper and Other Poems* (1932), a collection of children's poems. In addition, read at least six of Giovanni's poems from her collection *My House*. Write an essay in which you discuss Hughes's poetry of the first half of the twentieth century and compare it to Giovanni's poetry from the last half of the same century. Host a class

discussion and compare poetic style, choice of topics, tone, and content.

- Arnold Adoff writes many poems for children and young adults. In Adoff's poetry collection *Slow Dance Heartbreak Blues* (1995), he focuses on poetry about teenagers and their concerns. Read one of Adoff's poems for teenagers and consider how effective his poetry is in exploring adolescent problems. Consider how Adoff's poetry differs in tone and content from Giovanni's poetry. Prepare an evaluation of the differences that you note and present your findings as a poster presentation to your classmates.

- *My Black Me: A Beginning Book of Black Poetry* (1994) contains fifty poems for young children by Lucille Clifton, Sam Cornish, Langston Hughes, Sonia Sanchez, and Giovanni as well as several other authors. Choose two of the poems from this book to study in more detail. Be sure that you choose poems by two different authors. With at least one other student partner from your class, prepare a multimedia presentation of the poems that you have chosen. Your presentation should include an oral component, in which you either download an audio recording of the poets reading their poems or, if that is not available, you or your partner read the two poems aloud. You should also prepare several PowerPoint slides in which you present what you have learned about the poems that you chose and what you have learned about the kind of poetry these poets are writing. This might mean that your slides will include information about poetic styles, including meter, tone, stanzas, rhyme, imagery, allegory, metaphor, or parallelism, as well as line-by-line comparisons.

---

included within "The Rooms Inside," a subsection of *My House*, readers know that Giovanni intended for the poem to be read as offering a

place where the outside world cannot infringe. As long as love is reciprocated, love will provide a refuge from the rest of the world. In this sense, love both isolates and protects from the world. Outside the home is a world filled with civil strife, racism, war, and economic disruptions in the form of oil embargoes and inflation. But the privacy of home offers a sanctuary. The important point, though, is having someone with whom to share the home and safety. The poem points out that the unpleasant world outside is made more tolerable by the loving presence of another person. The gender, age, and relationship of the loved one is not specified, and indeed, the protection of love can be with anyone. Because Giovanni does not specify that the loved one be a romantic partner, it is possible to consider that the poem is equally reflective of the love between a mother and child or between siblings or even friends.

Poetry that focuses on the love between two people touches the emotions of the reader, and Giovanni's "The World Is Not a Pleasant Place to Be" illustrates that a love poem need not be lengthy to be an effective vehicle for depicting emotions that speak to the reader. Giovanni uses only six short lines in stanzas 1 and 4 to create an image of shared love. Only the first and last stanza directly point to the need for someone to share a home and a life with, but even the second and third stanzas, with their emphasis on nature, suggest that nature is also dependent on sharing to function most effectively.

"The World Is Not a Pleasant Place to Be" begins by noting that being alone is negative.
(© Anneka | Shutterstock.com)

Nature

Like the shared love between human beings, nature can also represent the necessity of reciprocity and even the exchange of affection, as Giovanni defines it. Nature's power is not always depicted in as positive a manner as it is in this poem, but Giovanni envisions nature as a cooperative force in which each part of nature mutually benefits from the other. Moreover, the power of nature is made equal with the power of love, as Giovanni makes clear in this poem. For instance, the interaction between the ocean and clouds demonstrates the need for unity and reciprocity. The ocean for all its power still needs the clouds, which gather moisture, which in turn becomes rain, which in the cyclic manner of nature is again returned to the ocean, where it will once again rise into the clouds as rain. Giovanni depicts this interdependence as a shared kiss between two elements of nature.

The nature in Giovanni's poem is so powerful that it needs an outlet. The river would cease to flow if there were no outlet. This is because the melting snows of winter create a torrent of flow, and if only a stream were present as an outlet for the force of the water, the river would overflow its banks and flood the neighboring land and towns. Nature is a force, then, that requires cooperation. Like human beings, nature needs a partner. The river needs either a larger river or the ocean into which to empty its flowing water. Oceans need to share their wealth with clouds. It is this interaction that makes nature so powerful. Whether it is analogous to love, as Giovanni suggests, or simply a force that provides for crops, which in turn feed a population, is not something that Giovanni explores in this poem. However, what she does make clear is that neither rivers, nor oceans, nor people function independently of one another. There is strength in unity and reciprocity.

STYLE

Allegory

In poetry, an allegory is an extended metaphor in which objects in the poem are provided meaning outside of the narrative. In "The World Is Not a Pleasant Place to Be," the need for reciprocated love is illustrated through the mention of water in various forms. The object in an allegory also has meaning beyond its name. Thus, the river is not simply a reference to the power of water but also refers to the power of love. The river is as powerful as love, and like the river, which requires an ocean into which it can empty its flow, love is at its strongest when it is reciprocated. The use of allegory in poetry is often confused with that of a symbol. In poetry, a symbol is a word that stands for something else; for example, water often symbolizes rebirth. The words *symbol* and *allegory* are often used interchangeably with *metaphor*, in which one object is compared with another. All of this can be confusing, and even scholars debate the different means of how these terms should be used.

Tenor and Vehicle

Tenor and vehicle are terms used by I. A. Richards, a twentieth-century literary critic, in *A Handbook to Literature* to describe two parts of a metaphor. The tenor is the subject, and the vehicle is the object used for comparison. It is necessary for a metaphor to have both a tenor and a vehicle. If both are not present, then no metaphor exists and a sentence is just a sentence. The vehicle makes the tenor, an idea that might be obscure, clear to the reader. In "The World Is Not a Pleasant Place to Be," the river is the vehicle. Readers can visualize a river flowing toward a destination. The tenor is the less visible idea, a love so great that it must find an outlet large enough to receive it. The stream is too small to hold so much love, which requires an ocean to fill.

Figurative Language

Giovanni employs figurative language to create images that are not necessarily intended to be taken literally. Figurative language allows the poet and the reader to use their imaginations to see the world differently, often through the use of simile or metaphor. In figurative language the poet departs from customary meanings of words to help the reader understand a concept. For instance, when the poet writes of clouds kissed by tears, the image is not intended to be literal. The image created by these words is more imaginative than the more literal descriptions. Figurative language

brings new life and imagination to this action. Giovanni's poem can be enjoyed just for its imaginative use of language, but on a deeper level, there are some complex links between ideas that, if understood, create more enjoyment of the poem.

Free Verse

Free verse is poetry that is free of rules of structure, rhyme, or meter. In using free verse the poet is not restricted by the need to shape the poem to a particular meter, which allows the poet to create poetry of complex rhythm and syntax. Free verse is most often associated with modern poetry, but poets have been trying to create poetry free of rhyme and meter for several hundred years, and so while free verse is often associated with modern poetry, it is actually much older. There is no pattern of rhyme or meter to "The World Is Not a Pleasant Place to Be." Some lines are four syllables, some are five, and others are six. The lines have no rhyme scheme, and there is no punctuation. However, free verse is never totally free of poetry styles and conventions. Giovanni does use a loose stanza pattern, and she does rely on some basic repetition of phrasing, but in general, the poem is free of conventional rules of meter or rhyme.

Lyric Poetry

Lyric poetry describes poems that are strongly inflected with emotion, imagination, and a song-like resonance, especially as associated with an individual speaker or narrator. Lyrical poetry emerged during the Archaic Age in Greece. These poems were shorter than the previous narrative poetry of Homer or the didactic poetry of Hesiod. Since lyric poetry is so very individual and emotional in its content, it is by its very nature also subjective. The subjective part reveals the poet's feelings about a subject. Lyrical poetry is the most common form of poetry, especially since its attributes are also common to many other forms of poetry. Giovanni's poem combines many of the attributes of lyrical poetry, especially in its melodic sounds, which suggest it could almost be set to music.

HISTORICAL CONTEXT

A Decade of Turbulence

The late 1960s were a period marked by protests—protests against the Vietnam War, protests for equal rights for African Americans, and protests

COMPARE
&
CONTRAST

- **1970s:** In May 1970, an antiwar demonstration at Kent State University results in the deaths of four students after Ohio national guardsmen fire on demonstrators, who are protesting the escalation of the Vietnam War into Cambodia.

  Today: The United States has been engaged in fighting a war in Afghanistan, while troops have just returned from combat in Iraq. As was the case in Vietnam, public protests against both the Iraq and Afghanistan wars increased the longer the wars lasted. Since the end of hostilities in Iraq, public attention has turned to Afghanistan, with an emphasis on ending the war in that country.

- **1970s:** Much of the opposition to the Vietnam War is led by religious leaders. Both Protestant ministers and Roman Catholic priests take an active role in opposing the war. Church leaders also take an active role in pushing the US government to take action to combat poverty and racial discrimination.

  Today: Religious leaders today are active partners with politicians in political discourse. Much of the discussion in recent years, however, has focused on religious extremists and terrorism and the threats they pose to peace.

- **1970s:** In 1967 the Supreme Court ruled in *Loving v. Virginia* that antimiscegenation laws, which made it illegal for people of different races to marry, were unconstitutional. At the time, seventeen states were still enforcing such laws. In 1970, less than 1 percent of all marriages in the U.S. are interracial. South Carolina (in 1998) and Alabama (in 2000) will become the last states to formally repeal miscegenation laws.

  Today: In 2009 a justice of the peace in Louisiana refuses to officiate at the civil marriage of an interracial couple. Negative publicity results in the forced resignation of this justice of the peace. By 2010, about 15 percent of all new marriages in the U.S. are interracial.

- **1970s:** The median age for marriage is twenty-one for women and twenty-three for men.

  Today: The median age for marriage is twenty-six for women and twenty-eight for men.

- **1970s:** The Black Arts movement represents a period of literary and artistic development for African Americans. This is an effort to create a populist art that would be identified with black culture, through African American publishers, theater groups, and literature. This movement asserts that black experiences, through art and literature, are different from other groups.

  Today: Although officially the Black Arts movement ended nearly thirty years ago, its legacy is (at the least) twofold. Academic studies of this movement flourish at college campuses around the United States, where students study the proponents of this movement and the art and literature that trace their origins to the Black Arts movement. Another legacy has been the tradition of literature by writers like Alice Walker, Toni Morrison, and Giovanni, whose work appeals to readers of all ethnic and racial groups.

---

demanding equal treatment for women. However, the 1970s brought a change in the tenor of these protests, and the change was one of greater violence during the first years of the decade. This was first seen in anti–Vietnam War protests, when protesters turned to bombs to make their point. In one example showing the consequences of this change, three young radical Vietnam War protesters blew themselves up while building a bomb in a house in Manhattan in March 1970. Then in August 1970, four students protesting government research at the University of Wisconsin blew up a campus building at the university campus in Madison, killing a graduate student. In another incident, Brandeis University students protesting the war decided to rob a Boston bank, killing a policeman during the robbery. These uses of explosives and guns and the resulting deaths made clear that the demonstrations against the war had taken on an increasingly violent color.

A decade that began with violence continued with more turbulence in the economy. In 1973 the Organization of Petroleum Exporting Countries (OPEC) became powerful when they raised the price of oil by more than 200 percent. OPEC's move led to gasoline shortages and gas rationing, with outbursts of occasional violence, but that was not the only problem. Inflation was also high, as was unemployment. The economy was stagnant, and it appeared as if all the giddiness of the 1960s had died by the middle of the 1970s. President Richard Nixon resigned in disgrace, amid scandal and rumors of hush money, cover-up, and government corruption. The hopefulness of the 1960s protests for equal rights seemed to collapse under the violence of antibusing protests in the mid-1970s. Hopes for the desegregation of schools and greater access to equal education were never realized. In fact, the number of African American children attending segregated schools decreased by less than half a percentage point during the 1970s. It is no wonder that Giovanni chose to celebrate the importance of home and love, as antidotes to the turmoil on the streets and in the nightly news.

Love and Family on Television
Historically, early films and television showed black people as janitors, maids, cooks, and in other roles defined primarily as service jobs. That finally changed in 1965 with the television program *I Spy*, which paired two espionage agents, one white and one black. *Mission Impossible* debuted in 1966, with one black secret agent. But *I Spy* and *Mission Impossible* were definitely not typical of television programming. *Julia*, in which a single black mother worked as a nurse to raise her young son, debuted in 1968. However, neither *Julia*, *I Spy*, nor *Mission Impossible* depicted racism or bias directed against blacks. *Julia*, in particular, came under attack for being patronizing and unrealistic. There were still no black families, who would not appear on television until the following decade.

Even more change was to occur in the 1970s. With so much violence and threatening activity on the streets, it is unsurprising that television responded with programming, especially situation comedies, that celebrated home and family. Of course, fictional television homes and families were sometimes unconventional. *The Jeffersons*, whose family had finally risen to become an upper-class success story, and *Good Times*, in which a family lived in a ghetto, presented two very different portraits of African American families. Although these were family comedies, *The Jeffersons* contained many racial stereotypes, with characters who were loud, overbearing, and often obnoxious. It was not until 1984 that a serious show about black families finally found its way to television, in the form of Bill Cosby and *The Cosby Show*. Before that time, black families were forced to look inward to their own homes to find a depiction of black family life that was free of bias and negativity.

The Counterculture
Culturally, the 1970s were a decade of disco music, tie-dyed clothing, and love-ins. The 1970s were also defined by rebellion against what was perceived to be the rigidity of the past. In the late 1960s, young people rejected traditional Anglo-American values, including the pursuit of money and the racism that had divided society. In their place, young people substituted communal living, alternative religions, and the power of love. During the 1970s the countercultural lifestyle that had begun in California at the end of the 1960s spread across the United States. Many of these young people adopted the identifier "hippie" to refer to themselves as hip to the latest trends. Communes were established in rural areas as separate societies in which people could live without the conventions of marriage and traditional jobs. As alternatives to conventional Judeo-Christian religious practice, young people explored Eastern religions and tried yoga and meditation as ways to find greater meaning in their existence. The poet Allen Ginsberg coined the phrase "flower power" to define the hippie opposition to the Vietnam War. The rebellion of the 1960s had focused on changing the world. That decade had ended with protests against the war and against racism, which were continued in the 1970s with bell-bottom pants, peace signs, and flower power.

Giovanni compares loneliness to a river without a source of water. *(© elfart | Shutterstock.com)*

CRITICAL OVERVIEW

Giovanni emerged as a poet during the Black Arts movement, which lasted for roughly a decade from the mid-1960s to the mid-1970s. Her early poetry often depicted the injustices and oppression endured by African Americans. As has been the case with many poets, Giovanni's poetry has not always been reviewed by book critics, especially her earlier books. There are ways, however, to evaluate the impact that her work has had on her readers. In 1967 and 1968, Giovanni self-published her first two books of poetry, *Black Feeling, Black Talk* and *Black Judgement*. Her second book sold 6,000 copies within the first six months, with Giovanni distributing the book in a limited area. In a 1973 essay that focuses on Giovanni's poetry, "Fascinating Woman," Lorraine Dusky notes that "publishing houses consider a poetry book to be doing well if it sells 2,500 copies in a year." In self-publishing her books, Giovanni had only limited distribution contacts, and so her success in selling so many books, several times more than were typically sold, was a remarkable achievement that suggests that she had already found a supportive audience. In *Racism 101*, Giovanni writes that she self-published her first books because she feared rejection; however, rejection would not prove to be a problem for the poet. By the time she published *My House* in

1972, Giovanni was already a popular and best-selling author.

Although poetry books are only rarely reviewed in the press, *My House* did find at least one reviewer, who took note of the book's many strengths. In a review of *My House* that appeared in the *Cresset*, writer and professor Jill Baumgaertner describes the poetry included in this collection as removed from the ideology of Giovanni's earlier political poems. As a result, readers "finally can like her poems rather than fight her politics." After labeling Giovanni's poetry as unique, Baumgaertner finds these poems appealing because Giovanni's talent is both "childlike" and "quite firm." The reviewer also claims that these are poems that mostly succeed in their simplicity, with only occasional lapses into the simplistic. Although Baumgaertner is not enthusiastic about every poem in *My House*, she does find that most of them "are delightful touches of whimsy." Baumgaertner concludes her review by pointing out that "Giovanni is profoundly human in these poems—not black human or white human, but woman and poet," which should lead to a greater audience discovering her talents.

It is not just Giovanni's written word that captivates poetry readers. Her readings of her poetry are also enormously popular. In the 2002 article "Giovanni's World," Samiya Bashir states that Giovanni's live readings of her poetry "rivaled the popularity of Amiri Baraka," the iconic poet and dramatist of the 1950s and 1960s. Giovanni's collection *My House*, according to Bashir, "was a watershed with an unheard of 50,000 copies, an unprecedented printing for a black poet at the time." In 1973, Giovanni staged a celebration at New York's Philharmonic Hall to celebrate her thirtieth birthday. With a combination of poetry readings and music, Giovanni entertained a sold-out audience.

Although there are no reviews that specifically mention "The World Is Not a Pleasant Place to Be" and few reviews for the poetry collection in which it appears, *My House*, it is possible to judge Giovanni's legacy as a poet by looking at the reviews of *Acolytes*, published in 2007. Elizabeth Lund states in the *Christian Science Monitor* that Giovanni is both a cultural icon and a poet of the people, but that her reputation as a household name can sometimes outshine her poems. Nonetheless, Lund finds much to like in her 2007 collection. Many of the poems in *Acolytes* deal with ordinary things, which Lund finds "refreshing" and "a wonderful balance to some of the grittier topics she revisits." Lund also suggests that Giovanni's fans will not be disappointed in this collection, which provides a "good reason for fans to continue their journey with the poet." When the *New York Times* asked several writers to write about the books they were currently reading, Haitian novelist and short-story writer Edwidge Danticat noted that she was reading Giovanni's *Acolytes*. Danticat claims that "the fire, eloquence and lyricism in these poems show why Giovanni was able to turn tears into cheers at an April 17 convocation following the Virginia Tech massacre" of April 2007. Danticat also refers to Giovanni as one of her favorite contemporary poets. Like Lund, Danticat finds much to admire in Giovanni's poetry. The reviews of *Acolytes*, in which Giovanni is labeled an icon whose poetry should be celebrated, suggest that her poetic legacy will continue to be celebrated.

CRITICISM

Sheri Metzger Karmiol

Karmiol teaches literature and drama at the University of New Mexico, where she is an adjunct professor in the University Honors Program. In the following essay, she examines Giovanni's shift

> IN DEPICTING LOVE IN THE PRIVATE SPHERE, GIOVANNI HAS NOT ABANDONED HER CONCERNS FOR THE LARGER BLACK COMMUNITY; RATHER, SHE HAS DETERMINED THAT CREATING LOVE WITHIN WILL, SHE HOPES, LEAD TO GREATER LOVE AND CHANGE OUTSIDE THE HOME."

from writing poetry about the need for a black revolution to writing poetry about love and the safety of home, as seen in "The World Is Not a Pleasant Place to Be."

In Nikki Giovanni's poem "The World Is Not a Pleasant Place to Be," the poet describes a scene in which the ocean is kissed by clouds. This touch is a caress, a kiss the expression of love. In this way, Giovanni links the public sphere of nature, with its many images of rivers, streams, oceans, and clouds, with the more intimate personal image of love between two individuals. This conjoined image of public and private love represents a move from the public-protest poetry of Giovanni's earlier collections, such as *Black Feeling, Black Talk* and *Black Judgement*, which were published by 1968, to the love poetry of *My House*, which was published only four years later, in 1972. In the latter volume, rather than reflecting reality, as she does in her political poetry, Giovanni embraces poetry that can create reality. In depicting love in the private sphere, Giovanni has not abandoned her concerns for the larger black community; rather, she has determined that creating love within will, she hopes, lead to greater love and change outside the home.

Instead of writing political or revolutionary poetry as she did throughout the 1960s, in the early 1970s Giovanni turned to writing love poems. The poetry in *My House* reflects this trend. In a 1975 interview with Lynne Domash and Suzanne Juhasz, Giovanni talks about her shift from writing political poetry to writing love poems. Politics deserve prose, Giovanni says, because poetry allows too much interpretation, "too much space," in which a reader can argue that a poet intends a different meaning. Prose

WHAT DO I READ NEXT?

- Giovanni's first collections of poetry, *Black Feeling, Black Talk* and *Black Judgement*, were published in 1967 and 1968. They are representative of her early revolutionary writing.

- Giovanni's *Gemini* (1971) is a lengthy autobiographical essay on her first twenty-five years. The tone of the book is a philosophical discussion of her childhood and her responses to racism and the civil rights movement.

- Giovanni's edited volume *Grand Mothers: Poems, Reminiscences, and Short Stories about the Keepers of Our Traditions* (1996) is a book designed for adolescents. Giovanni has collected a large number of stories by and about grandmothers, including stories from Asian and African writers and stories from the Civil War.

- Giovanni's *Love Poems* (1997) is a collection of poems that celebrate the love between people. These beautiful poems can be enjoyed by people of all ages and in all types of relationships.

- *Poems to Dream Together/Poemas para soñar juntos* (2005), by Francisco X. Alarcón and Paula Barragán, is a collection of poetry for young children. This is a collection of bilingual verses that focus on the objects and people that children love in their homes, neighborhoods, and schools.

- Nikki Grimes's *Hopscotch Love: A Family Treasury of Love Poems* (1999) is a collection of poetry for adolescents that focuses on love between family members, friends, and even teenage crushes.

- *Partly Cloudy: Poems of Love and Longing* (2009), by Gary Soto, is a collection of love poems with narrators of different ethnicities, genders, and ages. The audience is intended to be teenagers, and although Soto is well known as a Hispanic writer, these poems about heartache and love will appeal to all groups of teenagers.

- Naomi Shihab Nye has compiled over one hundred poems from around the world into a single anthology, *The Same Sky: A Collection of Poems from Around the World* (1996). The poems are about childhood, about the love between parents and child, and about home and nature. There are poems from the Middle East, Asia, Africa, India, South and Central America, Sweden, and many other parts of the world.

- At Giovanni's personal website, the author provides audio files of some of her poetry readings, as well as links to other websites with additional biographical information: http://nikki-giovanni.com/index.shtml.

makes meanings very clear, according to Giovanni, and thus prose is now her preferred genre for political writing. In turn, poetry is her preferred genre for love, family, home, and the concerns of the individual. Her more personal love poems, Giovanni says, "have a story to tell," and like all stories have a clear beginning and end. This unity of flow and topic are seen in the comparisons revealed in "The World Is Not a Pleasant Place to Be," in which the reader can understand that love and home offer a

connection as important for survival as the connections in nature between river, ocean, and clouds.

Juhasz again turns to Giovanni's poetry in *Naked and Fiery Forms: Modern American Poetry by Women, a New Tradition*. In examining the transition that Giovanni undertakes in moving from protest or political poetry to love poetry, Juhasz states that Giovanni's decision to write poems that "are not meant to incite anybody to any kind of revolution" reflects the poet's desire to celebrate the individual. These more personal poems reflect a move away from her previous role as a political poet. In her new role embracing the individual, Giovanni's "love poems are private" and are not about social issues like feminism or equality for women or blacks, but are instead about what each person can offer to the other, as an individual and not via the community. These poems are about the exchange of love in the private sphere, not the public. According to Juhasz, Giovanni is doing just this in her poetry collection *My House*. In the poems in *My House*, the poet is doing what women do in dreaming dreams that embrace the private individual. Juhasz claims that Giovanni is "integrating private and public," making each as important as the other by intertwining the two. As a result, for Giovanni love poems become as important as political poems as a mechanism to transform society, with each kind of poem having a role in the world.

"The World Is Not a Pleasant Place to Be" is the ninth of twenty-three poems contained within the first section of *My House*. This collection of poetry is divided into two subsections, "The Rooms Inside," and "The Rooms Outside." The poems on the inside focus on the individual relationships within the house. However, whether the rooms are inside or outside, the house remains the center of this poetry collection, which is bound by the need for love and home. "The World Is Not a Pleasant Place to Be" bridges both the rooms inside and the rooms outside. However, its inclusion in the first section, "The Rooms Inside," suggests that readers are intended to view this poem as predominantly about the love within the house. In the foreword written expressly for *My House*, Ida Lewis writes about Giovanni's love of family as the core of a productive and happy community. For Giovanni, it is the connection between the private individual and the larger community that is important. According to Lewis, Giovanni believes that "family is love: love is family." The love of family, though private, does in turn create a loving community and, ultimately, a loving nation. Lewis notes that Giovanni has moved toward the individual, the private sphere, and away from the image of the poet as a spokesperson for the black community. It is not that Giovanni is no longer interested in the black revolution, but she has found in the individual a way to create change in the outside world through love and family within the house.

It is important to note that Giovanni's shift to love poetry does not signal an abandonment of her concerns for social equality and justice. Love poetry written by black writers is often concerned with depicting black reality, according to Francis S. Foster. In her essay "Changing Concepts of the Black Woman," Foster writes that black art is "an attempt to communicate realities" which, in turn, will give black men and women "the strength and vision to bring about the necessary changes in their existence." Foster describes the artistic beauty in black poetry as fulfilling a distinct purpose that is utilitarian, as well as having an aesthetic purpose. Both of these are fulfilled, writes Foster, "by the accomplishment of its purpose of expressing reality." Giovanni's desire to focus on love as an alternative to revolution recognizes that domestic love is in itself a protection from the world outside. Alluding to the sanctuary of the home, "The World Is Not a Pleasant Place to Be" celebrates the love and safety inherent in being held by and in holding another human being. This willingness to offer and to accept love are in themselves a reality that all readers can understand, whether black or white. In this way, Giovanni embraces the humaneness of all love, thus reaffirming that all men and women are equal.

Juhasz, Lewis, and Foster are not alone in noticing Giovanni's shift to focusing on love, family, and home in her poetry. In his essay "Sweet Soft Essence of Possibility: The Poetry of Nikki Giovanni," William J. Harris also notes Giovanni's movement from the revolutionary writing of the 1960s toward what he calls "the second stage of her career." Harris claims that rather than writing poetry about the need for revolution and civil rights, Giovanni turns to writing poems about love, especially the desire for "domestic love." Harris refers to this shift in focus as "Giovanni's desire to retreat into domestic comforts in the face of a disappointing world." However, Harris is wrong in arguing that Giovanni is simply escaping to safety in her love poetry. Nor is she abandoning the need for revolution and equality. Indeed, rather than abandoning her desire for revolution and equality, she has found a different way to argue for equality by appealing to the universal need for love and home. For Giovanni, this transformation in poetry signals a different approach to combatting the same old injustices. The desire for revolution does not end, but instead, Giovanni replaces her earlier focus on the more contentious and dangerous public sphere with an increased emphasis on the private sphere and the possibilities for love and safety within the sanctuary of home. Not only do readers feel less threatened by this shift from revolution to love, which increases her readership, but readers can also understand the appeal of love and family that Giovanni embraces in the poetry of *My House*.

Giovanni's movement away from writing revolutionary poetry toward an embrace of love poetry is more complex than a simple desire to create a new truth reflecting the black experience. In "The World Is Not a Pleasant Place to Be," love is an equal relationship between two people. Each one holds and protects the other. One is not subservient to the other, which is also true of the relationships that Giovanni depicts in nature. The river is not more important than the stream. They are simply different, with different functions. This is also true of the relationship between ocean and clouds, which are also equal but different. In each of these relationships, one complements the other without dominating the other. Similar, too, is the love between a man and woman. Although Giovanni's earlier poetry focuses on inequities in black life, her poetry about love is based more solidly on equality. As Foster notes in her essay, black poetry creates a new reality, which in turn replaces the view of women as subservient "with a humanism which respects the worth of each individual." This is the truth that Foster says is the defining and "ultimate criterion for Black literature." It is not important whether Giovanni writes love poetry or a call to revolution. What is important is that she depicts the truth of the black experience.

In a brief article by Denene Millner, Giovanni is quoted as saying, "I think it's nice to love. I recommend it." Millner's article, "'Love' in Her Lines of Work: Poet Nikki Giovanni Cooks Up Some Simple, Stirring Truths," focuses on a 1997 collection of Giovanni's poetry, *Love Poems*, in which she includes more than fifty love poems for her readers to enjoy. Millner acknowledges that Giovanni's love poems are not unduly complex; instead, for Giovanni, love is simple. In *Love Poems*, the pinnacle of love is cooking for someone, living with someone, sharing a life with someone. In writing about love and home as a sanctuary from the outside world, Giovanni simply redirects her gaze from the public to the private life and to a home filled with love.

A home is filled with "the rooms inside," which in turn are filled with love and safety from

FURTHERMORE, DOVE'S USE OF SOUTHERN BLACK DIALECT SUCCESSFULLY ADDS PERSONALITY TO THE HISTORICAL CHARACTERS SHE SHAPES POETRY AROUND."

the outside world. In her essay "Homeplace," bell hooks writes that a home is more than a place to live. A home is where black women return after working and where they "make life happen." A home is that private sphere "where all that truly mattered in life took place." This is where people are sheltered and comforted and where the soul is nourished. This is where love is exchanged. A home, according to hooks, is also where "our love for one another was necessary resistance" against the world outside. More salient than simply the exchange of love is the idea that love is its own resistance. While it may not always be possible to change the larger world outside, Giovanni's love poetry and her poem "The World Is Not a Pleasant Place to Be" reaffirm the notion that love within a home is one way to resist the threatening forces outside the home.

Source: Sheri Metzger Karmiol, Critical Essay on "The World Is Not a Pleasant Place to Be," in *Poetry for Students*, Gale, Cengage Learning, 2013.

Jennifer Walters

In the following essay, Walters compares the backgrounds of Giovanni and Rita Dove, reflecting on their contributions to literature and how they are reshaping African American history.

Throughout the centuries, African-American women have acted as agents in their own history, and in doing so defined themselves, for themselves, their communities, and the larger society. Nowhere has this been more apparent than in literature, where experiences, analyses, and understandings are put on paper. And through these stories, African-American women continue the tradition of recording history and the changing times with perspectives that reflect the struggles and survival of African-Americans. Their unique contribution to American poetry brought black women power and a voice—a voice that began with such poets as Phillis Wheatley and thrives today.

Being alone is like an ocean without clouds to feed it rain. (© *Marty Metcalf | Shutterstock.com*)

Nikki Giovanni and Rita Dove, two contemporary poets of great distinction, are examples of self-defined African-American women who found a voice through writing. Their poems are written in very different styles but involve similar themes. Giovanni's and Dove's successes are comparable and their paths similar, although they worked at different periods in contemporary literature. Both poets clearly possess a true passion and voice for writing, making their lives and works worthy of attention and discussion. This essay will compare the backgrounds of Nikki Giovanni and Rita Dove and their contributions to literature and, in doing so, reveal how they as poets help to reshape African-American history.

In Nikki Giovanni's signature and perhaps most popular poem, "Nikki-Rosa," she writes that, although she was poor, "Black love is Black wealth," and while whites may only see the poverty she experienced they would

> "...never understand that
> all the while I was quite happy."

These lines, often the most quoted of the poem, serve as a theme throughout all of Giovanni's poetry, whether writing about the Black Revolution or about being a woman, or remembering her childhood and family.

She was born Yolande Cornelia Giovanni, Jr., on June 7, 1943, and nicknamed Nikki-Rosa by her older sister, Gary. Her family moved less than a month after her birth from their home in Knoxville, Tennessee to Cincinnati, Ohio. Despite better job opportunities in Ohio, Giovanni's family lived in relative poverty. But as the poem "Nikki-Rosa" suggests, there was a richness of family life in the Giovanni home while her parents instilled the importance of education and determination in life.

Giovanni practiced these values as she excelled in school, and later tested as performing at a genius level. The struggle of Giovanni's father against poverty took its toll, and he became fairly abusive. She decided, on her own, to escape the tensions between her mother and father by moving back to Knoxville and living with her grandparents, Louvenia and John Brown Watson. In doing so she practiced the self-determination her parents had taught her.

Giovanni's grandmother Louvenia proved to be a great influence in Nikki's life. A clubwoman of the older generation, Louvenia engaged in many political and social activities, instilling in Nikki a definite sense of responsibility for her community, an awareness of racism in society, and the need to stand up against that which is morally wrong.

In high school, Giovanni's English teacher, Miss Alfreda Delaney, challenged her and set her young student on a course of reading the works of various African-American writers. It was through writing about these books that Giovanni's own talent for writing came through. Another teacher, Miss Emma Stokes, helped Giovanni apply for early admittance to Fisk University.

Entering at age 17, Giovanni proved her intellectual capabilities and continued to exercise her own individualism. This sense of autonomy angered the dean of women, and Giovanni was expelled from Fisk one semester later in 1961 because she went home to visit her grandparents without obtaining proper permission. Three years later, the new dean of women recognized the triviality of her predecessor's decision and asked Giovanni back. This dean, Blanche McConnell Cowan, proved to be another woman of great influence in Giovanni's life. Her nurturing led Giovanni to reestablish the Student Nonviolent Coordinating Committee (SNCC) on campus, edit a political journal, and work with such important people in the Black Arts Movement as poet Amiri Baraka (LeRoi Jones) and novelist John O. Killens.

Giovanni's grandmother, wanting to live long enough to see her favorite granddaughter graduate from Fisk, died two months after Giovannni's graduation in 1966. The death of Louvenia prompted Giovanni to delve into her work to handle the grief she was experiencing. She wrote several poems, creating what was to be the bulk of her first book, *Black Feeling, Black Talk*; became the editor of a Black revolutionary magazine entitled *Conversation*; organized Cincinnati's first Black Arts Festival; and became closely involved with the Black Arts and Black Power Movements. She believed her poetry and other arts were the instrument for "revolution" and did not promote violence, "convinced that progress at the cost of human lives was not progress at all."

Throughout the 1970's Giovanni's poetry began to include other non-revolutionary subjects.

With this evoultion, Giovanni found not only her work but also her personal life attacked by the male leaders of the Black Arts and the Black Power Movement. Giovanni refused to allow her art to be dictated by anyone's ideology and believed that had she not been a successful woman, no one would have argued against her.

Giovanni found herself, like many other black women participants of the Civil Rights Movement, in a complicated predicament. In the beginning years of the movements, black men and women shared a common cause; but as the movements lessened in energy, male chauvinism increased, and black women found themselves speaking out against the sexism. Although black women still wanted to fight the battle of racism, they were forced to fight for their own positions and respect within the movements. Giovanni's strength in speaking out against sexism cost her the acceptance of leaders and critics across the country.

Despite harsh criticisms from within the movements and from poetry critics across the country, Giovanni gained remarkable fame. Continuing the oral tradition of poetry, she released several recordings of her works, and travelled extensively on the college circuit performing them. She published more than fifteen books, including her latest, *Racism 101*. This collection of essays serves largely as a "survival guide" for black students on predominantly white campuses, but includes other essays touching issues ranging from Toni Morrison to "Star Trek." Besides being a prolific writer, she holds honorary doctorates from several universities, numerous awards, and a permanent position as Professor of English at Virginia Polytechnic Institute and State University.

Rita Dove's childhood, although perhaps more sheltered than Giovanni's, provided a basis for education and inspiration much like Giovanni's. Born nine years later, in 1952, she and her family also lived in Ohio, in Akron, where her parents were the first in their family to succeed in the professional world. Her father was a chemist, and her mother was a housewife, and Dove grew up in a middle-class neighborhood, with two younger sisters and an older brother. Dove describes herself as growing up "protected, in a loving, supportive, but stern environment." Although she never held any aspirations to be a writer, she was a voracious reader and began writing short stories as a little girl. Much like Giovanni, Dove was inspired by a teacher, Miss Oeschsner, who took her to a book signing while in high school. This event, and Miss Oeschsner's encouragement, helped Dove realize that writing was a viable profession.

Like Giovanni, Dove excelled in school, graduating as one of the highest nationally ranked high school students in 1970. Although she planned to become a lawyer, in response to her parents' expectations, she was increasingly drawn to creative writing classes and eventually graduated from Miami University of Ohio with a bachelor's degree in English. While Giovanni was involved with the Black Arts Movement and the Black Power Movement, Dove excelled in the world of academia. She studied in Germany, helping to perfect her own German, and then enrolled at the Iowa Writer's Workshop, one of the most acclaimed writing programs in America. Dove went on to publish her first volume, entitled *Ten Poems*, in 1977, followed by several other works, including the short story collection *Fifth Sunday* (1985) and a 1992 novel, *Through the Ivory Gate*.

Throughout the publication of all ten of her books, Dove continued to attend competitive writers' conferences around the world. She soon gained international attention with *Thomas and Beulah*, a collection of poems to be read in sequence that traced the lives of her grandparents in the industrial Midwest. This collection, in fact, served as a collective account of the lives of African-Americans and the great migration from the South to Northern industrial cities. The impressive volume earned her the Pulitzer Prize in poetry in 1987, making her the second African-American to hold the honor, following Gwendolyn Brooks in 1950.

Dove attained one of the highest honors awarded to poets when she was named the United States Poet Laureate in May 1993. She is the first African-American to hold the position and, at age 40, also the youngest. Besides her duties as Poet Laureate, she is Commonwealth Professor of English at the University of Virginia and also a wife and mother.

Though both Giovanni and Dove have earned some of the highest honors bestowed on poets, Dove's critical acceptance has been a constant throughout her career. Giovanni, however, was both ignored and berated by her contemporaries and critics. Like most of the women

writers in the Black Arts Movement, Giovanni's work was overshadowed by the more dominating and influential male poets such as Haki Madhubuti (Don L. Lee) and Amiri Baraka. Giovanni fought this neglect by publishing and distributing her first volumes completely on her own. *Black Feeling, Black Talk* gained the attention of the leaders of the Black Arts Movement. As Giovanni's ideas regarding Black identity and "revolution" evolved, so did her poetry. Because she involved personal issues and poems in her next volumes, leaders of the movement accused her of "selling out," and Haki Madhubuti even stated "she lacked the sophistication of thought demanded of one with pretensions of a 'political see.'" Across the board, critics seemed to condescend to her instead of critique her poetry, saying her words lacked substance, style and maturity.

Much of this negativity Giovanni receives may be because of her popularity as a poet. Though the literary establishment seems to have little interest in her, the public, those ordinary people for whom poetry is intended, constantly affirm the appeal and importance of Giovanni's work. It is her refusal to write for anyone but herself that has allowed her poetry to move through different phases, in reaction to different times. And as she changes, the public stays with her. She is a popular poet whose works are known across class, gender, and racial lines. Only recently have critics been able to recognize and appreciate her unfaltering independence, and therefore reevaluated her works accordingly.

Giovanni's role in the Black Arts Movement helped to shape Black identity on the whole, and also in African-American literature. Dove, nine years younger, entered into the niche Giovanni helped to carve for African-American women poets. Dove herself credits the Black Arts Movement with creating the free and open artistic environment of today. So, although Giovanni's reputation as a serious poet was hurt by the sexism of the Black Arts Movement and the racism of the literary establishment, she remained intolerant of both, and in doing so she paved the way for younger Black women poets, such as Dove and many others.

It is within this more open environment that Dove's poems were perhaps, more readily accepted by the literary establishment. Also, because she writes in a more traditional style about the lives of ordinary folk, her poetry appeals to both critics and popular America. Ironically, the same versatility of subject matter that brought Giovanni criticism now brings Dove praise.

While Giovanni struggled against the ignorance of her critics, Dove has strived to use her acceptance as a way to destroy the popular fears surrounding poetry; fears such as the seemingly incomprehensible nature of poetry and its appeal to only intellectuals. Dove's goal as Poet Laureate is to make poetry more accessible and appealing to the general public. She understands the battle in America between watching television and reading a book and hopes to "show people the pleasure of reading, and that is something continual and deepening—not a quick bite." Dove's steps to this goal include participating in the Library of Congress' poetry and literature programs, consulting on its literature collections and audio-video tape archives, and introducing poets into its series of public readings and lectures.

Both Giovanni and Dove help reinstate poetry as a popular art by writing about timely and touching subjects, namely those stories and issues concerning the richness of African-American heritage and culture, from the watchful and perceptive point of view of Black women in America. As Giovanni grappled with Black identity in her earlier works, she came to discover her own identity as an African-American woman and as a poet. The late 1960's demanded that writers like Giovanni sound a wake-up call to white America and a call to arms for defiance and pride for African-Americans.

Ultimately, Giovanni's refusal to be dictated to by the male leaders of the Black Arts Movement or the Black Power Movement pushed her into discovering a female identity as well as a Black identity. From personal poems juxtaposed with violent and militant works about "killing" the white values imposed on Black America, Giovanni soon began to explore the rites of womanhood. It was not that Giovanni completely and suddenly abandoned the racist war being waged against Blacks in America, rather, she realized that she must find her own identity and her own poetic voice in order to fight this war successfully.

Working with these insights, she published such books as *Re: Creation* and *The Women and the Men* which explored Black female identity both in personal and reflective poems and works about other women. In several poems, Giovanni pays tribute to famous singers and artists such as Lena Horne, whose independence and success, Giovanni asserts, inspired attacks from Black men.

Giovanni recognized the courage of ordinary African-American women in poems about women such as her grandmother and concluded, "We Black women are the single group in the West intact. We are...the only group that derives its identity from itself."

Giovanni witnessed her own self-definition as she explored the theme of motherhood after the birth of her son, a profound event which

"defined my nature
and gave me a new name (mommy)
which supersedes all others."

Within this new role of motherhood, Giovanni continued to defy convention, this time within her personal life, by not marrying or revealing the name of the child's father.

This defiance of categorization and labeling is more thoroughly explored in Giovanni's later work *Cotton Candy on a Rainy Day*, especially in "A Poem off Center," where she writes:

"if you write a political poem
you're anti-semitic
if you write a domestic poem
you're foolish
...of course the only real poem
to write
is the go to hell writing establishment poem ..."

Besides defying the literary establishment and confronting issues of racism in her poetry, Giovanni today tackles current problems in her collections of essays. In *Racism 101*, Giovanni offers advice to the next generation of African-Americans, whose encounters with racism are different from her own, but who can benefit from Giovanni's insight, wisdom, and wit.

Like Giovanni, Dove resists ideology in all its guises, preferring that the individual mind discover truth and meaning within poetry, instead of trying to shape it. Dove took a dramatic turn away from what she saw as the loose form and domineering intentions of the revolutionary poets that came a half-generation before her. Dove, much like Giovanni after her departure from the movements, views poetry as a function of the writer, and she has a profound respect for the future and place of poetry in the everyday lives of ordinary people. Although Dove's poetry is reflective of the African-American experience, she is more accepted by the literary establishment than Giovanni, perhaps due to her rejection of the loose style of the revolutionary poets that came before her.

Where Giovanni is more subjective in her highly personal poems, Dove is a historical poet, writing of black experience through the lives of "ordinary" people in a very objective way. In her volume *The Yellow House*, one group of poems is devoted to themes of slavery and freedom. In the poem "The Abduction" Dove accounts with simple and poignant clarity Solomon Northrup's recapture after his escape to freedom:

"I floated on water I could not drink. Though the pillow
was stone, I climbed no ladder in that sleep.
I woke and found myself alone, in darkness and in chains."

By distancing herself, Dove gives voice to the people she writes about, and when dealing with the psychological terrors of slavery, she is lending a voice to people who often did not have one.

Dove lends her voice to her maternal grandparents in *Thomas and Beulah*, and both tell their stories of being African-American in the twentieth century. Though both characters are deeply involved with one another, their perceptions and reactions to events in their lives are very different. Not only does this narrative serve as a voice for African-Americans in history, it also tells of the manipulation of history. The story twice-told depends on the reactions rather than actions of the characters involved. However, it is clear that even two characters deeply involved with one another tell very different stories. This speaks to a larger picture of our own interpretations of history presented to future generations. Dove makes one wonder what historical truth is if everyone possesses a different perspective of the same event. This sort of historical manipulation serves as the reason for the exclusion of accurate African-American history in textbooks and classrooms across the nation.

Dove tackles issues of racism in contemporary society, as well as in the past, through autobiographical poems such as "Genetic Expedition." She writes of her own interracial marriage, and the curious, often veiled nature of racism in today's society. Dove writes:

"...My child has
her father's hips, his hair
like the miller's daughter, combed gold.
Though her lips are mine, housewives
Stare when we cross the parking lot
because of that ghostly profusion."

Her poems that deal with racism are written in a highly personal yet probing manner, in a way which explores the issue uniquely.

Whether writing about the contemporary or Historical Black Experience, Dove sends a clear message: there are many kinds of American traditions. As an African-American woman, her poetry exists in the context of those facts in the history that she understands, but she hopes to break new ground for African-American writers in a literary tradition that tends to label and pigeon-hole black poetry into one genre. As Arnold Rampersad, an African-American educator and critic, said in reference to Dove's poetry, "...one finds an eagerness [in her poetry], perhaps even an anxiety, to transcend—if not actually repudiate—black cultural nationalism in the name of a more inclusive sensibility."

In escaping the "confining image of [a] long-suffering commitment to Black people," and writing about her international relationship, Dove has joined the ranks of many contemporary African-American women writers, such as Audre Lorde and June Jordan, who have violated several taboos, and in doing so created "another safe space where Black women can articulate a self-defined standpoint." Giovanni also participated in creating this "safe space" using her words as a "form of activism." Both Giovanni and Dove succeeded in breaking new ground as African-American poets but both maintained a decidedly rich style of verse, thick with the voices and styles of African-American heritage, including music and dialects.

In a very literal way Giovanni has used music to enhance her poetry. Her 1971 recording of *Truth Is On Its Way* placed her recitation of poems against the back drop of gospel music—a combination she found perfectly logical, and the public found remarkably powerful. Giovanni also refers to music quite often in her work, whether in homage to such musical giants as Aretha Franklin in "Revolutionary Dreams" where she "dreams of being a natural woman," or in poems where she intentionally styles the words in the blues and soul tradition. Her poetry often mimics a free jazz style as in,

"I wish I could be a melody...like a
    damp...gray...feline
fog...staccatoing...stealthily...over the city..."

Dove also creates musical textures and believes rhythm within a poem to be an extremely important element. This rhythm, she insists, is "the way our entire body gets involved in the language being spoken. And even if we are reading the poem silently, those rhythms exist." It is not surprising that Dove filters her poetry through melody and rhythm, considering her love of music and her skills as a cellist. Some poems are so melodic they seem to become music, as in "Summit Beach, 1921" where she writes,

> "She could wait, she was gold.
> When the right man smiled it would be
> music skittering up her calf
> like a chuckle."

Furthermore, Dove's use of southern black dialect successfully adds personality to the historical characters she shapes poetry around. Giovanni effectively used black forms during the 1960's, in ways that added to the poem, whereas other poets' use of slang and dialect often tended to detract from the point of the poem. In controlling the language within her verse, Giovanni's own personality emerged on the page, purely individualistic and at times even humorous.

Both Nikki Giovanni and Rita Dove are true individuals with clearly different poetic styles. Nonetheless, both have created poems that have touched a multitude of people and in doing so they have helped re-define African-Americans and particularly African-American women's identity in history. They are political in their messages but hold true to their own ideologies and are artistic in the beauty they create with words. Perhaps most important, however, is the invaluable contribution they have made to literature with voices that are telling and true.

Source: Jennifer Walters, "Nikki Giovanni and Rita Dove: Poets Redefining," in *Journal of Negro History*, Vol. 85, No. 3, Summer 2000, p. 210.

Calvin Reid

In the following interview, Reid asks Giovanni about being a poet and her conversational poetry style.

Sitting opposite *PW* at a midtown coffee shop, Nikki Giovanni wears a gray-green pants suit, sharply tailored and threaded with silvery fibers that make the material sparkle every time she moves. Her blue tie, printed with little tumbling champagne bottles ("perfect for a celebration" says Giovanni), also twinkles, increasing the incandescent effect of the ensemble.

"When you're a poet, nobody ever cares what you have on," Giovanni says, "nobody pays attention. But I love this suit." In a few

> GIOVANNI TELLS *PW* THAT SHE LIKES TO
> WRITE AT HER HOME—A HOUSE WITHOUT ANY
> [INTERIOR] DOORS."

hours, Giovanni, along with a host of student poets, will perform at a lunchtime reading in New York City's Bryant Park marking her 30th anniversary as a writer and social activist.

Since the late 1960s Giovanni has written poems of social indignation, mitigated and enriched by a down-to-earth sensibility and empathy. Her poems are aimed at African-Americans and derived from African-American urban and folk traditions; but her work has managed to reach and touch an audience of ordinary Americans regardless of race.

She's published eight volumes of poetry and five books of essays with Morrow (including separate books dedicated to conversations with novelist James Baldwin and poet Margaret Walker) that have combined sales of more than 500,000 copies. Her most recent collection, *Love Poems*, dedicated to the late rapper Tupac Shakur whose streak of defiance and unrealized creative potential continues to inspire Giovanni, sold more than 70,000 copies, an extraordinary number for a serious poet. She's published six books (both poetry and prose works) for kids and young adults with Henry Holt and Scholastic.

Giovanni's blunt, funny and passionate writing established her early on as a voice of black women's political militancy. Morrow placed her under contract in 1970 after she sold 10,000 copies of her self-published first volume of poetry, *Black Feeling Black Talk*, in 1968. In the years since, she has continued to speak her mind in her poetry, making her hallmark a funky, truculent clarity.

Given the changes in her own life in the last 30 years, Giovanni has maintained a remarkably unforced consonance in her poetic concerns. "There *has* been an amazing consistency" she admits. "I'm edgy and I've always been edgy. You know, I'm not a coward. I just keep trying to push the limit. I never like to back down. But I'm not stubborn, you know. I learn things."

Giovanni is so fiercely outspoken, her voice always the voice of youthful rebellion, that it's somewhat disconcerting to hear her talk of growing older, the more so since she has always looked young as well. In the 1960s her pixieish face, surrounded by a massive Afro, seemed to contradict her powerful, soaring poetic voice. These were the years she published such poems as "Great Pax Whitie" (1968), with its intermingling of classical history, irony and anti-racist outrage, and "Woman Poem," which considered the social and sexual limits imposed on black women. Surveying a succession of her book jacket photographs, you can watch as her giant afro becomes smaller (these days it's short and blonde) as the image of the firebrand black militant presented on the cover of her first book, gives way to a gentle, smiling face capable of lyrical, measured candor as well as great bursts of incendiary emotion.

LIFE OF A POET

Born in Knoxville, Tenn., 56 years ago, Giovanni grew up in Cincinnati. Now, in addition to being a poet, she's a college professor and the mother of an adult son. She's also a cancer survivor who lost part of her lung to surgery. She has just published a new book of poems, *Blues for All the Changes* (Morrow), as well as a new young adult book, *Grandfathers* (Holt). Like Langston Hughes and Margaret Walker—two eminent black poets Giovanni admires—she has become something of an American institution, showered with accolades, writing awards and honorary degrees.

Her authority as a poet stems in part from her years of political and artistic activism. While an undergraduate at Fisk University in 1964, she organized a local chapter of the Student Nonviolent Coordinating Committee, a key civil rights organization. Her poems record the racial confrontations and the violence of the late 1960s, and react to the Vietnam war. She recorded a hit spoken-word album, *Truth Is on Its Way*, with the New York Community Gospel Choir in the 1970s; traveled across Africa; and lectured and read her poetry to audiences and students from one end of this country to other. She joined the faculty at Virginia Polytechnic and State University in Blacksburg, Va., in 1987, where she still teaches literature and writing. Giovanni also holds off-campus workshops for high school students and, as she puts it, for her "little old ladies" in a workshop at a retirement center near her home in Virginia.

In the high schools, she's interested in reaching out to "ordinary kids. I don't want to talk to only the talented kids; they go to the NBA, or they go to college, they do whatever their talent demands. I want to talk to ordinary kids because you and I, we're ordinary people, we have to serve our brain, because that's going to keep us out of the toilet."

A diehard sports fan, she's quick to refer to athletes and games of all kinds. She wrote the poem "Iverson's Posse," for Allan Iverson, the gifted and troubled young basketball player for the Philadelphia 76ers. Giovanni, who doesn't know Iverson personally, tells *PW* that the poem urges the young man to "make sure that the people around you are independent of you so they can give you the advice you need,"—advice she also dispenses to her high school students. "I tell them, 'If you're the smartest person you know, you have a problem.'"

When Giovanni was a guest speaker at this year's BookExpo America in L.A., another author asked her, "Do you have to teach?" She says her first thought was, "What does that mean?" Writing poetry, she says, "is a lonely profession but if you're a poet you *are* trying to teach. I think being in a classroom keeps you up to date. I think that you'd miss a lot if all you did was meet other writers; if you never saw another generation." And teaching, she points out, is not simply one-way. "I'm sure that part of my love for Tupac Shakur comes from the fact that the students brought him to me."

But the perspective of her older students is just as valuable. "Younger people keep you edgy," Giovanni says, "but older people, you know, give you comfort." Her retirement home workshop is 10 years old and has only one drawback, says Giovanni. "Right now our oldest writer is 96 and we tend to lose people." Nevertheless several years ago, one of the women came to her and said, "we want to write a book, you know, with an ISBN," Giovanni says, laughing at the memory. So the group found a regional publisher that was interested and the ladies eventually published a book called *Appalachian Elders* published by Pocohantas Press.

CONVERSATIONAL POETRY

Many of Giovanni's new poems are conversational expressions of her state of mind, roaming across the day's events and all manner of pop cultural material. The poems focus on politics, race and, as in one poem in *Blues*, "The President's Penis." She ruminates on urban life and on rural living; Pete Sampras and her own tennis playing; Jackie Robinson and the soul singer Regina Belle.

She describes *Blues for All the Changes* as "my environmental piece," and there are impressions of the land around her home in Virginia, but this collection also salutes the late blues singer Alberta Hunter; it reveals her love of sports as well as her love of Betty Shabazz; jazz riffs mingle with memories of going to the ballpark with her father to see the Cincinnati Reds.

In the poem "Road Rage," her appreciation of the countryside collides poetically with her unconcealed loathing of a local real estate maven ("It is a sincere, legitimate hatred," says Giovanni). It's one of several poems in *Blues* that target, in no uncertain terms, a developer whom she baldly calls R. Kneck Kracker, whose large endeavors near her home are diverting streams and disrupting the land and wildlife. "Road Rage" shows how frustration can build into a moment of rage and violence when she almost runs down a construction worker. This moment, Giovanni tells *PW*, is really "about everything else that went wrong," in that day.

The poem "Me and Mrs. Robin" deals with Giovanni's convalescence from cancer surgery and the family of robins she observed with delight and sympathy from her window. Yet this gentle poem also revisits R. Kneck Kracker, who, the poem notes, has destroyed trees and "confused the birds and murdered the possum and groundhog." It's a poem that Giovanni describes as "very depressing. I don't read it because it just makes me so sad." As she identifies with an injured robin, Giovanni's language invokes a gnostic cosmogony: God who takes care of individuals, Mother Nature wreaks havoc left and right. "No one ever says 'Mother Nature have mercy.' Mother nature don't give a damn," Giovanni says, "that's why God is so important."

Giovanni tells *PW* that she likes to write at her home—a house without any [interior] doors. "I just took them down. A lesson I learned from my father. It's not a door that people respect, its the privacy of the people in the room."

She doesn't have a writing routine. "I write sporadically, always have." She's a "morning person. I like the birds, especially in the spring."

She has also abandoned her electric typewriter for a computer. "I get a line here and an idea there. I used to put them up on a corkboard, in the age of the typewriter—Jill Krementz has picture of me at the writer's desk—but now of course I have a file just called notes. It just gets dumped into the computer."

Of her three-decade relationship with Morrow she says, "It's been a good match. I've had two really good editors, Will Schwalbe and Doris Cooper. For a poet I think moving around is not a good idea. Maybe it's good for novelists because there's a lot of money. But again, there's a consistency and that's important. I didn't get as lost as I maybe would've if I'd been jumping around to look for another $5000."

She describes her children's book writing as an opportunity to "share a bit of the past with children. Black kids deserve to hear their history. My kids books are serious but not dour." Her editor at Holt, Marc Aronson, calls her "an intergenerational influence. The people she inspired in college have kids now and they want to pass her on to the next generation."

That kind of cultural responsibility suits Giovanni just fine. "Right now there isn't anybody like me," she says, "and if that's the case, I have obligations. To history. To black Americans. I say this to the kids all time. You have to decide who you answer to, and unfortunately or fortunately I'm a poet so I don't answer to the bestseller Gods or to the big literary prize gods, but I answer to the ancestral Gods, and the people whose work means the most to me came in here in 1619," the year that the first African slaves arrived in the future United States. "That's going to put you out on the edge."

Source: Calvin Reid, "Nikki Giovanni: Three Decades on the Edge," in *Publishers Weekly*, Vol. 246, No. 26, June 28, 1999, pp. 46–47.

SOURCES

Barringer, Mark, "The Anti-War Movement in the United States," in *Encyclopedia of the Vietnam War: A Political, Social, and Military History*, edited by Spencer C. Tucker, ABC-CLIO, 1998, http://www.english.illinois.edu/maps/vietnam/antiwar.html (accessed February 13, 2012).

Bashir, Samiya, "Giovanni's World," in *Black Issues Book Review*, Vol. 4, No. 6, November–December 2002, pp. 32–36.

Baumgaertner, Jill, Review of *My House*, in *Cresset*, Vol. 38, No. 10, 1975, p. 26.

Courtenay-Thompson, Fiona, and Kate Phelps, eds., *The 20th Century Year by Year*, Barnes & Noble, 1998, pp. 256–71, 280–81.

Cummings, Melbourne S., "The Changing Image of the Black Family on Television," in *Journal of Popular Culture*, Vol. 22, No. 2, Fall 1988, pp. 75–85.

Danticat, Edwidge, "Read Any Good Books Lately?," in *New York Times*, June 3, 2007, p. 8.

Domash, Lynne, and Suzanne Juhasz, "A Talk with Nikki Giovanni," in *Frontiers: A Journal of Women Studies*, Vol. 1, No. 1, Fall 1975, pp. 147–50.

Douglas, Susan J., "1970–1979: Watching the World on TV," in *National Geographic Eyewitness to the 20th Century*, National Geographic Society, 1998, pp. 277–82.

Dusky, Lorraine, "Fascinating Woman," in *Conversations with Nikki Giovanni*, edited by Virginia C. Fowler, University Press of Mississippi, 1992, pp. 49–60; originally published in *Ingenue*, February 1973, pp. 20–24, 81, 83.

Fowler, Virginia C., "And This Poem Recognizes That: Embracing Contrarieties in the Poetry of Nikki Giovanni," in *Her Words: Diverse Voices in Contemporary Appalachian Women's Poetry*, edited by Felicia Mitchell, University of Tennessee Press, 2002, pp. 112–35.

Giovanni, Nikki, *Racism 101*, William Morrow, 1994, pp. 140–41.

———, "The World Is Not a Pleasant Place to Be," in *My House*, William Morrow, 1972, p. 15.

Harmon, William, *A Handbook to Literature*, 11th ed., Pearson Prentice Hall, 2009, pp. 14, 241, 324–25, 340–41, 547.

Harris, William, "Sweet Soft Essence of Possibility: The Poetry of Nikki Giovanni," in *Black Women Writers (1950–1980): A Critical Evaluation*, edited by Mari Evans, Anchor Books, 1984, pp. 218–29.

Henig, Robin Marantz, "What Is It about 20-Somethings? Why Are So Many People in Their 20s Taking So Long to Grow Up?," in *New York Times Magazine*, August 18, 2010, http://www.nytimes.com/2010/08/22/magazine/22Adulthood-t.html?_r=2&pagewanted=all (accessed February 14, 2012).

hooks, bell, "Homeplace," in *The Woman That I Am: The Literature and Culture of Contemporary Women of Color*, edited by D. Soyini Madison, St. Martin's Press, 1994, pp. 448–54.

Jennings, Peter, and Todd Brewster, "Years of Doubt, 1969–1981," in *The Century*, Doubleday, 1998, pp. 424–63.

Juhasz, Suzanne, "'A Sweet Inspiration...of My People': The Poetry of Gwendolyn Brooks and Nikki Giovanni," in *Naked and Fiery Forms: Modern American Poetry by Women, a New Tradition*, Harper Colophon, 1976, pp. 140–76.

Lenz, Günter H., "The Politics of African American Literary and Cultural Critique: From the Black Arts/Black Aesthetic Movement to a Black Postmodern Multiculturalism," in *Black Liberation in the Americas*, edited by Fritz Gysin and Christopher Mulvey, Lit Verlag, 2001, pp. 203–18.

Lewis, Ida, Foreword to *My House*, William Morrow, 1972, pp. ix–xv.

Lund, Elizabeth, "Nikki Giovanni and Charles Bukowski: New Collections from Poetry's Icons," Review of *Acolytes*, in *Christian Science Monitor*, April 17, 2007, p. 13.

Millner, Denene, "'Love' in Her Lines of Work: Poet Nikki Giovanni Cooks Up Some Simple, Stirring Truth," in *New York Daily News*, February 11, 1997.

Taylor, Paul, Cary Funk, and Peyton Craighill, "Guess Who's Coming to Dinner?," Pew Research Center website, March 14, 2006, http://pewsocialtrends.org/files/2010/10/Interracial.pdf (accessed February 16, 2012).

Trager, James, *The People's Chronology: A Year-by-Year Record of Human Events from Prehistory to the Present*, Henry Holt, 1992, pp. 1027, 1043.

Wang, Wendy, "The Rise of Intermarriage," Pew Research Center website, February 16, 2012, http://www.pewsocialtrends.org/2012/02/16/the-rise-of-intermarriage/ (accessed February 16, 2012).

FURTHER READING

Adams, Michael Henry, *Style and Grace: African Americans at Home*, Bulfinch Press, 2006.

This book focuses on African American style and decor, as represented in the homes of more than twenty notable African American celebrities, professionals, and entertainers. The photographs are accompanied by essays that also describe how the owners define what home means to each of them.

Jago, Carol, *Nikki Giovanni in the Classroom: "The Same Ol Danger but a Brand New Pleasure,"* National Council of Teachers of English, 1999.

This book provides a number of suggestions for how to use Giovanni's poetry in the classroom, presenting samples of her verse and excerpts from several of her essays, along with suggestions about how to get students immersed and involved in Giovanni's poetry.

Josephson, Judith Pinkerton, *Nikki Giovanni: Poet of the People*, Enslow, 2000.

This biography is designed for middle-school students. The author provides information about Giovanni's life, from her childhood to her life as an established poet. Several of Giovanni's poems are also included.

Nikuradse, Tamara, ed., *African-American Wedding Readings*, Dutton, 1998.

This book is an anthology of poetry, prose, and song that is intended to function as a resource for proposals, engagement toasts, weddings, and anniversary celebrations. The selections are taken from biblical text, published love letters, and published love poetry and prose.

Patton, Sharon F., *African-American Art*, Oxford University Press, 1998.

> This book includes information about the artistic achievements of black Americans, including art from the 1800s and 1900s created by both slaves and freemen.

Smith, Taigi, ed., *Sometimes Rhythm, Sometimes Blues: Young African Americans on Love, Relationships, Sex, and the Search for Mr. Right*, Seal Press, 2003.

> Smith has compiled a selection of essays that explore the relationships between African American men and women and how they balance education, careers, love, and marriage. The essays are from women's perspectives.

SUGGESTED SEARCH TERMS

Nikki Giovanni

Nikki Giovanni AND *My House*

Nikki Giovanni AND poetry

Nikki Giovanni AND biography

"The World Is Not a Pleasant Place to Be"

Nikki Giovanni AND protest poetry

black women poets

Nikki Giovanni AND love poems

Glossary of Literary Terms

A

Abstract: Used as a noun, the term refers to a short summary or outline of a longer work. As an adjective applied to writing or literary works, abstract refers to words or phrases that name things not knowable through the five senses.

Accent: The emphasis or stress placed on a syllable in poetry. Traditional poetry commonly uses patterns of accented and unaccented syllables (known as feet) that create distinct rhythms. Much modern poetry uses less formal arrangements that create a sense of freedom and spontaneity.

Aestheticism: A literary and artistic movement of the nineteenth century. Followers of the movement believed that art should not be mixed with social, political, or moral teaching. The statement "art for art's sake" is a good summary of aestheticism. The movement had its roots in France, but it gained widespread importance in England in the last half of the nineteenth century, where it helped change the Victorian practice of including moral lessons in literature.

Affective Fallacy: An error in judging the merits or faults of a work of literature. The "error" results from stressing the importance of the work's effect upon the reader—that is, how it makes a reader "feel" emotionally, what it does as a literary work—instead of stressing its inner qualities as a created object, or what it "is."

Age of Johnson: The period in English literature between 1750 and 1798, named after the most prominent literary figure of the age, Samuel Johnson. Works written during this time are noted for their emphasis on "sensibility," or emotional quality. These works formed a transition between the rational works of the Age of Reason, or Neoclassical period, and the emphasis on individual feelings and responses of the Romantic period.

Age of Reason: See *Neoclassicism*

Age of Sensibility: See *Age of Johnson*

Agrarians: A group of Southern American writers of the 1930s and 1940s who fostered an economic and cultural program for the South based on agriculture, in opposition to the industrial society of the North. The term can refer to any group that promotes the value of farm life and agricultural society.

Alexandrine Meter: See *Meter*

Allegory: A narrative technique in which characters representing things or abstract ideas are used to convey a message or teach a lesson. Allegory is typically used to teach moral, ethical, or religious lessons but is sometimes used for satiric or political purposes.

Alliteration: A poetic device where the first consonant sounds or any vowel sounds in words or syllables are repeated.

Allusion: A reference to a familiar literary or historical person or event, used to make an idea more easily understood.

Amerind Literature: The writing and oral traditions of Native Americans. Native American literature was originally passed on by word of mouth, so it consisted largely of stories and events that were easily memorized. Amerind prose is often rhythmic like poetry because it was recited to the beat of a ceremonial drum.

Analogy: A comparison of two things made to explain something unfamiliar through its similarities to something familiar, or to prove one point based on the acceptedness of another. Similes and metaphors are types of analogies.

Anapest: See *Foot*

Angry Young Men: A group of British writers of the 1950s whose work expressed bitterness and disillusionment with society. Common to their work is an anti-hero who rebels against a corrupt social order and strives for personal integrity.

Anthropomorphism: The presentation of animals or objects in human shape or with human characteristics. The term is derived from the Greek word for "human form."

Antimasque: See *Masque*

Antithesis: The antithesis of something is its direct opposite. In literature, the use of antithesis as a figure of speech results in two statements that show a contrast through the balancing of two opposite ideas. Technically, it is the second portion of the statement that is defined as the "antithesis"; the first portion is the "thesis."

Apocrypha: Writings tentatively attributed to an author but not proven or universally accepted to be their works. The term was originally applied to certain books of the Bible that were not considered inspired and so were not included in the "sacred canon."

Apollonian and Dionysian: The two impulses believed to guide authors of dramatic tragedy. The Apollonian impulse is named after Apollo, the Greek god of light and beauty and the symbol of intellectual order. The Dionysian impulse is named after Dionysus, the Greek god of wine and the symbol of the unrestrained forces of nature. The Apollonian impulse is to create a rational, harmonious world, while the Dionysian is to express the irrational forces of personality.

Apostrophe: A statement, question, or request addressed to an inanimate object or concept or to a nonexistent or absent person.

Archetype: The word archetype is commonly used to describe an original pattern or model from which all other things of the same kind are made. This term was introduced to literary criticism from the psychology of Carl Jung. It expresses Jung's theory that behind every person's "unconscious," or repressed memories of the past, lies the "collective unconscious" of the human race: memories of the countless typical experiences of our ancestors. These memories are said to prompt illogical associations that trigger powerful emotions in the reader. Often, the emotional process is primitive, even primordial. Archetypes are the literary images that grow out of the "collective unconscious." They appear in literature as incidents and plots that repeat basic patterns of life. They may also appear as stereotyped characters.

Argument: The argument of a work is the author's subject matter or principal idea.

Art for Art's Sake: See *Aestheticism*

Assonance: The repetition of similar vowel sounds in poetry.

Audience: The people for whom a piece of literature is written. Authors usually write with a certain audience in mind, for example, children, members of a religious or ethnic group, or colleagues in a professional field. The term "audience" also applies to the people who gather to see or hear any performance, including plays, poetry readings, speeches, and concerts.

Automatic Writing: Writing carried out without a preconceived plan in an effort to capture every random thought. Authors who engage in automatic writing typically do not revise their work, preferring instead to preserve the revealed truth and beauty of spontaneous expression.

Avant-garde: A French term meaning "vanguard." It is used in literary criticism to describe new writing that rejects traditional approaches to literature in favor of innovations in style or content.

B

Ballad: A short poem that tells a simple story and has a repeated refrain. Ballads were originally intended to be sung. Early ballads, known as folk ballads, were passed down through generations, so their authors are often unknown. Later ballads composed by known authors are called literary ballads.

Baroque: A term used in literary criticism to describe literature that is complex or ornate in style or diction. Baroque works typically express tension, anxiety, and violent emotion. The term "Baroque Age" designates a period in Western European literature beginning in the late sixteenth century and ending about one hundred years later. Works of this period often mirror the qualities of works more generally associated with the label "baroque" and sometimes feature elaborate conceits.

Baroque Age: See *Baroque*

Baroque Period: See *Baroque*

Beat Generation: See *Beat Movement*

Beat Movement: A period featuring a group of American poets and novelists of the 1950s and 1960s—including Jack Kerouac, Allen Ginsberg, Gregory Corso, William S. Burroughs, and Lawrence Ferlinghetti—who rejected established social and literary values. Using such techniques as stream of consciousness writing and jazz-influenced free verse and focusing on unusual or abnormal states of mind—generated by religious ecstasy or the use of drugs—the Beat writers aimed to create works that were unconventional in both form and subject matter.

Beat Poets: See *Beat Movement*

Beats, The: See *Beat Movement*

Belles-lettres: A French term meaning "fine letters" or "beautiful writing." It is often used as a synonym for literature, typically referring to imaginative and artistic rather than scientific or expository writing. Current usage sometimes restricts the meaning to light or humorous writing and appreciative essays about literature.

Black Aesthetic Movement: A period of artistic and literary development among African Americans in the 1960s and early 1970s. This was the first major African-American artistic movement since the Harlem Renaissance and was closely paralleled by the civil rights and black power movements. The black aesthetic writers attempted to produce works of art that would be meaningful to the black masses. Key

figures in black aesthetics included one of its founders, poet and playwright Amiri Baraka, formerly known as LeRoi Jones; poet and essayist Haki R. Madhubuti, formerly Don L. Lee; poet and playwright Sonia Sanchez; and dramatist Ed Bullins.

Black Arts Movement: See *Black Aesthetic Movement*

Black Comedy: See *Black Humor*

Black Humor: Writing that places grotesque elements side by side with humorous ones in an attempt to shock the reader, forcing him or her to laugh at the horrifying reality of a disordered world.

Black Mountain School: Black Mountain College and three of its instructors—Robert Creeley, Robert Duncan, and Charles Olson—were all influential in projective verse, so poets working in projective verse are now referred as members of the Black Mountain school.

Blank Verse: Loosely, any unrhymed poetry, but more generally, unrhymed iambic pentameter verse (composed of lines of five two-syllable feet with the first syllable accented, the second unaccented). Blank verse has been used by poets since the Renaissance for its flexibility and its graceful, dignified tone.

Bloomsbury Group: A group of English writers, artists, and intellectuals who held informal artistic and philosophical discussions in Bloomsbury, a district of London, from around 1907 to the early 1930s. The Bloomsbury Group held no uniform philosophical beliefs but did commonly express an aversion to moral prudery and a desire for greater social tolerance.

Bon Mot: A French term meaning "good word." A *bon mot* is a witty remark or clever observation.

Breath Verse: See *Projective Verse*

Burlesque: Any literary work that uses exaggeration to make its subject appear ridiculous, either by treating a trivial subject with profound seriousness or by treating a dignified subject frivolously. The word "burlesque" may also be used as an adjective, as in "burlesque show," to mean "striptease act."

C

Cadence: The natural rhythm of language caused by the alternation of accented and unaccented syllables. Much modern poetry—notably free verse—deliberately manipulates cadence to create complex rhythmic effects.

Caesura: A pause in a line of poetry, usually occurring near the middle. It typically corresponds to a break in the natural rhythm or sense of the line but is sometimes shifted to create special meanings or rhythmic effects.

Canzone: A short Italian or Provencal lyric poem, commonly about love and often set to music. The *canzone* has no set form but typically contains five or six stanzas made up of seven to twenty lines of eleven syllables each. A shorter, five- to ten-line "envoy," or concluding stanza, completes the poem.

Carpe Diem: A Latin term meaning "seize the day." This is a traditional theme of poetry, especially lyrics. A *carpe diem* poem advises the reader or the person it addresses to live for today and enjoy the pleasures of the moment.

Catharsis: The release or purging of unwanted emotions—specifically fear and pity— brought about by exposure to art. The term was first used by the Greek philosopher Aristotle in his *Poetics* to refer to the desired effect of tragedy on spectators.

Celtic Renaissance: A period of Irish literary and cultural history at the end of the nineteenth century. Followers of the movement aimed to create a romantic vision of Celtic myth and legend. The most significant works of the Celtic Renaissance typically present a dreamy, unreal world, usually in reaction against the reality of contemporary problems.

Celtic Twilight: See *Celtic Renaissance*

Character: Broadly speaking, a person in a literary work. The actions of characters are what constitute the plot of a story, novel, or poem. There are numerous types of characters, ranging from simple, stereotypical figures to intricate, multifaceted ones. In the techniques of anthropomorphism and personification, animals—and even places or things—can assume aspects of character. "Characterization" is the process by which an author creates vivid, believable characters in a work of art. This may be done in a variety of ways, including (1) direct description of the character by the narrator; (2) the direct presentation of the speech, thoughts, or actions of the character; and (3) the responses of other characters to the character. The term "character" also refers to a form originated by the ancient Greek writer Theophrastus that later became popular in the seventeenth and eighteenth centuries. It is a short essay or sketch of a person who prominently displays a specific attribute or quality, such as miserliness or ambition.

Characterization: See *Character*

Classical: In its strictest definition in literary criticism, classicism refers to works of ancient Greek or Roman literature. The term may also be used to describe a literary work of recognized importance (a "classic") from any time period or literature that exhibits the traits of classicism.

Classicism: A term used in literary criticism to describe critical doctrines that have their roots in ancient Greek and Roman literature, philosophy, and art. Works associated with classicism typically exhibit restraint on the part of the author, unity of design and purpose, clarity, simplicity, logical organization, and respect for tradition.

Colloquialism: A word, phrase, or form of pronunciation that is acceptable in casual conversation but not in formal, written communication. It is considered more acceptable than slang.

Complaint: A lyric poem, popular in the Renaissance, in which the speaker expresses sorrow about his or her condition. Typically, the speaker's sadness is caused by an unresponsive lover, but some complaints cite other sources of unhappiness, such as poverty or fate.

Conceit: A clever and fanciful metaphor, usually expressed through elaborate and extended comparison, that presents a striking parallel between two seemingly dissimilar things— for example, elaborately comparing a beautiful woman to an object like a garden or the sun. The conceit was a popular device throughout the Elizabethan Age and Baroque Age and was the principal technique of the seventeenth-century English metaphysical poets. This usage of the word conceit is unrelated to the best-known definition of conceit as an arrogant attitude or behavior.

Concrete: Concrete is the opposite of abstract, and refers to a thing that actually exists or a description that allows the reader to experience an object or concept with the senses.

Concrete Poetry: Poetry in which visual elements play a large part in the poetic effect. Punctuation marks, letters, or words are arranged on a page to form a visual design: a cross, for example, or a bumblebee.

Confessional Poetry: A form of poetry in which the poet reveals very personal, intimate, sometimes shocking information about himself or herself.

Connotation: The impression that a word gives beyond its defined meaning. Connotations may be universally understood or may be significant only to a certain group.

Consonance: Consonance occurs in poetry when words appearing at the ends of two or more verses have similar final consonant sounds but have final vowel sounds that differ, as with "stuff" and "off."

Convention: Any widely accepted literary device, style, or form.

Corrido: A Mexican ballad.

Couplet: Two lines of poetry with the same rhyme and meter, often expressing a complete and self-contained thought.

Criticism: The systematic study and evaluation of literary works, usually based on a specific method or set of principles. An important part of literary studies since ancient times, the practice of criticism has given rise to numerous theories, methods, and "schools," sometimes producing conflicting, even contradictory, interpretations of literature in general as well as of individual works. Even such basic issues as what constitutes a poem or a novel have been the subject of much criticism over the centuries.

D

Dactyl: See *Foot*

Dadaism: A protest movement in art and literature founded by Tristan Tzara in 1916. Followers of the movement expressed their outrage at the destruction brought about by World War I by revolting against numerous forms of social convention. The Dadaists presented works marked by calculated madness and flamboyant nonsense. They stressed total freedom of expression, commonly through primitive displays of emotion and illogical, often senseless, poetry. The movement ended shortly after the war, when it was replaced by surrealism.

Decadent: See *Decadents*

Decadents: The followers of a nineteenth-century literary movement that had its beginnings in French aestheticism. Decadent literature displays a fascination with perverse and morbid states; a search for novelty and sensation—the "new thrill"; a preoccupation with mysticism; and a belief in the senselessness of human existence. The movement is closely associated with the doctrine Art for Art's Sake. The term "decadence" is sometimes used to denote a decline in the quality of art or literature following a period of greatness.

Deconstruction: A method of literary criticism developed by Jacques Derrida and characterized by multiple conflicting interpretations of a given work. Deconstructionists consider the impact of the language of a work and suggest that the true meaning of the work is not necessarily the meaning that the author intended.

Deduction: The process of reaching a conclusion through reasoning from general premises to a specific premise.

Denotation: The definition of a word, apart from the impressions or feelings it creates in the reader.

Diction: The selection and arrangement of words in a literary work. Either or both may vary depending on the desired effect. There are four general types of diction: "formal," used in scholarly or lofty writing; "informal," used in relaxed but educated conversation; "colloquial," used in everyday speech; and "slang," containing newly coined words and other terms not accepted in formal usage.

Didactic: A term used to describe works of literature that aim to teach some moral, religious, political, or practical lesson. Although didactic elements are often found in artistically pleasing works, the term "didactic" usually refers to literature in which the message is more important than the form. The term may also be used to criticize a work that the critic finds "overly didactic," that is, heavy-handed in its delivery of a lesson.

Dimeter: See *Meter*

Dionysian: See *Apollonian and Dionysian*

Discordia concours: A Latin phrase meaning "discord in harmony." The term was coined by the eighteenth-century English writer Samuel Johnson to describe "a combination of dissimilar images or discovery of occult resemblances in things apparently unlike." Johnson created the expression by reversing a phrase by the Latin poet Horace.

Dissonance: A combination of harsh or jarring sounds, especially in poetry. Although such combinations may be accidental, poets sometimes intentionally make them to achieve particular effects. Dissonance is also sometimes used to refer to close but not identical rhymes. When this is the case, the word functions as a synonym for consonance.

Double Entendre: A corruption of a French phrase meaning "double meaning." The term is used to indicate a word or phrase that is deliberately ambiguous, especially when one of the meanings is risque or improper.

Draft: Any preliminary version of a written work. An author may write dozens of drafts which are revised to form the final work, or he or she may write only one, with few or no revisions.

Dramatic Monologue: See *Monologue*

Dramatic Poetry: Any lyric work that employs elements of drama such as dialogue, conflict, or characterization, but excluding works that are intended for stage presentation.

Dream Allegory: See *Dream Vision*

Dream Vision: A literary convention, chiefly of the Middle Ages. In a dream vision a story is presented as a literal dream of the narrator. This device was commonly used to teach moral and religious lessons.

E

Eclogue: In classical literature, a poem featuring rural themes and structured as a dialogue among shepherds. Eclogues often took specific poetic forms, such as elegies or love poems. Some were written as the soliloquy of a shepherd. In later centuries, "eclogue" came to refer to any poem that was in the pastoral tradition or that had a dialogue or monologue structure.

Edwardian: Describes cultural conventions identified with the period of the reign of Edward VII of England (1901-1910). Writers of the Edwardian Age typically displayed a strong reaction against the propriety and conservatism of the Victorian Age. Their work often exhibits distrust of authority in religion, politics, and art and expresses strong doubts about the soundness of conventional values.

Edwardian Age: See *Edwardian*

Electra Complex: A daughter's amorous obsession with her father.

Elegy: A lyric poem that laments the death of a person or the eventual death of all people. In a conventional elegy, set in a classical world, the poet and subject are spoken of as shepherds. In modern criticism, the word elegy is often used to refer to a poem that is melancholy or mournfully contemplative.

Elizabethan Age: A period of great economic growth, religious controversy, and nationalism closely associated with the reign of Elizabeth I of England (1558-1603). The Elizabethan Age is considered a part of the general renaissance—that is, the flowering of arts and literature—that took place in Europe during the fourteenth through sixteenth centuries. The era is considered the golden age of English literature. The most important dramas in English and a great deal of lyric poetry were produced during this period, and modern English criticism began around this time.

Empathy: A sense of shared experience, including emotional and physical feelings, with someone or something other than oneself. Empathy is often used to describe the response of a reader to a literary character.

English Sonnet: See *Sonnet*

Enjambment: The running over of the sense and structure of a line of verse or a couplet into the following verse or couplet.

Enlightenment, The: An eighteenth-century philosophical movement. It began in France but had a wide impact throughout Europe and America. Thinkers of the Enlightenment valued reason and believed that both the individual and society could achieve a state of perfection. Corresponding to this essentially humanist vision was a resistance to religious authority.

Epic: A long narrative poem about the adventures of a hero of great historic or legendary importance. The setting is vast and the action is often given cosmic significance through the intervention of supernatural forces such as gods, angels, or demons. Epics are typically written in a classical style of grand simplicity with elaborate metaphors and allusions that enhance the symbolic importance of a hero's adventures.

Epic Simile: See *Homeric Simile*

Epigram: A saying that makes the speaker's point quickly and concisely.

Epilogue: A concluding statement or section of a literary work. In dramas, particularly those of the seventeenth and eighteenth centuries, the epilogue is a closing speech, often in verse, delivered by an actor at the end of a play and spoken directly to the audience.

Epiphany: A sudden revelation of truth inspired by a seemingly trivial incident.

Epitaph: An inscription on a tomb or tombstone, or a verse written on the occasion of a person's death. Epitaphs may be serious or humorous.

Epithalamion: A song or poem written to honor and commemorate a marriage ceremony.

Epithalamium: See *Epithalamion*

Epithet: A word or phrase, often disparaging or abusive, that expresses a character trait of someone or something.

Erziehungsroman: See *Bildungsroman*

Essay: A prose composition with a focused subject of discussion. The term was coined by Michel de Montaigne to describe his 1580 collection of brief, informal reflections on himself and on various topics relating to human nature. An essay can also be a long, systematic discourse.

Existentialism: A predominantly twentieth-century philosophy concerned with the nature and perception of human existence. There are two major strains of existentialist thought: atheistic and Christian. Followers of atheistic existentialism believe that the individual is alone in a godless universe and that the basic human condition is one of suffering and loneliness. Nevertheless, because there are no fixed values, individuals can create their own characters—indeed, they can shape themselves—through the exercise of free will. The atheistic strain culminates in and is popularly associated with the works of Jean-Paul Sartre. The Christian existentialists, on the other hand, believe that only in God may people find freedom from life's

anguish. The two strains hold certain beliefs in common: that existence cannot be fully understood or described through empirical effort; that anguish is a universal element of life; that individuals must bear responsibility for their actions; and that there is no common standard of behavior or perception for religious and ethical matters.

Expatriates: See *Expatriatism*

Expatriatism: The practice of leaving one's country to live for an extended period in another country.

Exposition: Writing intended to explain the nature of an idea, thing, or theme. Expository writing is often combined with description, narration, or argument. In dramatic writing, the exposition is the introductory material which presents the characters, setting, and tone of the play.

Expressionism: An indistinct literary term, originally used to describe an early twentieth-century school of German painting. The term applies to almost any mode of unconventional, highly subjective writing that distorts reality in some way.

Extended Monologue: See *Monologue*

F

Feet: See *Foot*

Feminine Rhyme: See *Rhyme*

Fiction: Any story that is the product of imagination rather than a documentation of fact. Characters and events in such narratives may be based in real life but their ultimate form and configuration is a creation of the author.

Figurative Language: A technique in writing in which the author temporarily interrupts the order, construction, or meaning of the writing for a particular effect. This interruption takes the form of one or more figures of speech such as hyperbole, irony, or simile. Figurative language is the opposite of literal language, in which every word is truthful, accurate, and free of exaggeration or embellishment.

Figures of Speech: Writing that differs from customary conventions for construction, meaning, order, or significance for the purpose of a special meaning or effect. There are two major types of figures of speech: rhetorical figures, which do not make changes in the meaning of the words, and tropes, which do.

Fin de siecle: A French term meaning "end of the century." The term is used to denote the last decade of the nineteenth century, a transition period when writers and other artists abandoned old conventions and looked for new techniques and objectives.

First Person: See *Point of View*

Folk Ballad: See *Ballad*

Folklore: Traditions and myths preserved in a culture or group of people. Typically, these are passed on by word of mouth in various forms—such as legends, songs, and proverbs—or preserved in customs and ceremonies. This term was first used by W. J. Thoms in 1846.

Folktale: A story originating in oral tradition. Folktales fall into a variety of categories, including legends, ghost stories, fairy tales, fables, and anecdotes based on historical figures and events.

Foot: The smallest unit of rhythm in a line of poetry. In English-language poetry, a foot is typically one accented syllable combined with one or two unaccented syllables.

Form: The pattern or construction of a work which identifies its genre and distinguishes it from other genres.

Formalism: In literary criticism, the belief that literature should follow prescribed rules of construction, such as those that govern the sonnet form.

Fourteener Meter: See *Meter*

Free Verse: Poetry that lacks regular metrical and rhyme patterns but that tries to capture the cadences of everyday speech. The form allows a poet to exploit a variety of rhythmical effects within a single poem.

Futurism: A flamboyant literary and artistic movement that developed in France, Italy, and Russia from 1908 through the 1920s. Futurist theater and poetry abandoned traditional literary forms. In their place, followers of the movement attempted to achieve total freedom of expression through bizarre imagery and deformed or newly invented words. The Futurists were self-consciously modern artists who attempted to incorporate the appearances and sounds of modern life into their work.

G

Genre: A category of literary work. In critical theory, genre may refer to both the content of a given work—tragedy, comedy, pastoral—and to its form, such as poetry, novel, or drama.

Genteel Tradition: A term coined by critic George Santayana to describe the literary practice of certain late nineteenth-century American writers, especially New Englanders. Followers of the Genteel Tradition emphasized conventionality in social, religious, moral, and literary standards.

Georgian Age: See *Georgian Poets*

Georgian Period: See *Georgian Poets*

Georgian Poets: A loose grouping of English poets during the years 1912-1922. The Georgians reacted against certain literary schools and practices, especially Victorian wordiness, turn-of-the-century aestheticism, and contemporary urban realism. In their place, the Georgians embraced the nineteenth-century poetic practices of William Wordsworth and the other Lake Poets.

Georgic: A poem about farming and the farmer's way of life, named from Virgil's *Georgics*.

Gilded Age: A period in American history during the 1870s characterized by political corruption and materialism. A number of important novels of social and political criticism were written during this time.

Gothic: See *Gothicism*

Gothicism: In literary criticism, works characterized by a taste for the medieval or morbidly attractive. A gothic novel prominently features elements of horror, the supernatural, gloom, and violence: clanking chains, terror, charnel houses, ghosts, medieval castles, and mysteriously slamming doors. The term "gothic novel" is also applied to novels that lack elements of the traditional Gothic setting but that create a similar atmosphere of terror or dread.

Graveyard School: A group of eighteenth-century English poets who wrote long, picturesque meditations on death. Their works were designed to cause the reader to ponder immortality.

Great Chain of Being: The belief that all things and creatures in nature are organized in a hierarchy from inanimate objects at the bottom to God at the top. This system of belief was popular in the seventeenth and eighteenth centuries.

Grotesque: In literary criticism, the subject matter of a work or a style of expression characterized by exaggeration, deformity, freakishness, and disorder. The grotesque often includes an element of comic absurdity.

H

Haiku: The shortest form of Japanese poetry, constructed in three lines of five, seven, and five syllables respectively. The message of a *haiku* poem usually centers on some aspect of spirituality and provokes an emotional response in the reader.

Half Rhyme: See *Consonance*

Harlem Renaissance: The Harlem Renaissance of the 1920s is generally considered the first significant movement of black writers and artists in the United States. During this period, new and established black writers published more fiction and poetry than ever before, the first influential black literary journals were established, and black authors and artists received their first widespread recognition and serious critical appraisal. Among the major writers associated with this period are Claude McKay, Jean Toomer, Countee Cullen, Langston Hughes, Arna Bontemps, Nella Larsen, and Zora Neale Hurston.

Hellenism: Imitation of ancient Greek thought or styles. Also, an approach to life that focuses on the growth and development of the intellect. "Hellenism" is sometimes used to refer to the belief that reason can be applied to examine all human experience.

Heptameter: See *Meter*

Hero/Heroine: The principal sympathetic character (male or female) in a literary work. Heroes and heroines typically exhibit admirable traits: idealism, courage, and integrity, for example.

Heroic Couplet: A rhyming couplet written in iambic pentameter (a verse with five iambic feet).

Heroic Line: The meter and length of a line of verse in epic or heroic poetry. This varies by language and time period.

Heroine: See *Hero/Heroine*

Hexameter: See *Meter*

Historical Criticism: The study of a work based on its impact on the world of the time period in which it was written.

Hokku: See *Haiku*

Holocaust: See *Holocaust Literature*

Holocaust Literature: Literature influenced by or written about the Holocaust of World War II. Such literature includes true stories of survival in concentration camps, escape, and life after the war, as well as fictional works and poetry.

Homeric Simile: An elaborate, detailed comparison written as a simile many lines in length.

Horatian Satire: See *Satire*

Humanism: A philosophy that places faith in the dignity of humankind and rejects the medieval perception of the individual as a weak, fallen creature. "Humanists" typically believe in the perfectibility of human nature and view reason and education as the means to that end.

Humors: Mentions of the humors refer to the ancient Greek theory that a person's health and personality were determined by the balance of four basic fluids in the body: blood, phlegm, yellow bile, and black bile. A dominance of any fluid would cause extremes in behavior. An excess of blood created a sanguine person who was joyful, aggressive, and passionate; a phlegmatic person was shy, fearful, and sluggish; too much yellow bile led to a choleric temperament characterized by impatience, anger, bitterness, and stubbornness; and excessive black bile created melancholy, a state of laziness, gluttony, and lack of motivation.

Humours: See *Humors*

Hyperbole: In literary criticism, deliberate exaggeration used to achieve an effect.

I

Iamb: See *Foot*

Idiom: A word construction or verbal expression closely associated with a given language.

Image: A concrete representation of an object or sensory experience. Typically, such a representation helps evoke the feelings associated with the object or experience itself. Images are either "literal" or "figurative." Literal images are especially concrete and involve little or no extension of the obvious meaning of the words used to express them. Figurative images do not follow the literal meaning of the words exactly. Images in literature are usually visual, but the term "image" can also refer to the representation of any sensory experience.

Imagery: The array of images in a literary work. Also, figurative language.

Imagism: An English and American poetry movement that flourished between 1908 and 1917. The Imagists used precise, clearly presented images in their works. They also used common, everyday speech and aimed for conciseness, concrete imagery, and the creation of new rhythms.

In medias res: A Latin term meaning "in the middle of things." It refers to the technique of beginning a story at its midpoint and then using various flashback devices to reveal previous action.

Induction: The process of reaching a conclusion by reasoning from specific premises to form a general premise. Also, an introductory portion of a work of literature, especially a play.

Intentional Fallacy: The belief that judgments of a literary work based solely on an author's stated or implied intentions are false and misleading. Critics who believe in the concept of the intentional fallacy typically argue that the work itself is sufficient matter for interpretation, even though they may concede that an author's statement of purpose can be useful.

Interior Monologue: A narrative technique in which characters' thoughts are revealed in a way that appears to be uncontrolled by the author. The interior monologue typically aims to reveal the inner self of a character. It portrays emotional experiences as they occur at both a conscious and unconscious level. Images are often used to represent sensations or emotions.

Internal Rhyme: Rhyme that occurs within a single line of verse.

Irish Literary Renaissance: A late nineteenth- and early twentieth-century movement in Irish literature. Members of the movement aimed to reduce the influence of British culture in Ireland and create an Irish national literature.

Irony: In literary criticism, the effect of language in which the intended meaning is the opposite of what is stated.

Italian Sonnet: See *Sonnet*

J

Jacobean Age: The period of the reign of James I of England (1603-1625). The early literature of this period reflected the worldview of the Elizabethan Age, but a darker, more cynical attitude steadily grew in the art and literature of the Jacobean Age. This was an important time for English drama and poetry.

Jargon: Language that is used or understood only by a select group of people. Jargon may refer to terminology used in a certain profession, such as computer jargon, or it may refer to any nonsensical language that is not understood by most people.

Journalism: Writing intended for publication in a newspaper or magazine, or for broadcast on a radio or television program featuring news, sports, entertainment, or other timely material.

K

Knickerbocker Group: A somewhat indistinct group of New York writers of the first half of the nineteenth century. Members of the group were linked only by location and a common theme: New York life.

Kunstlerroman: See *Bildungsroman*

L

Lais: See *Lay*

Lake Poets: See *Lake School*

Lake School: These poets all lived in the Lake District of England at the turn of the nineteenth century. As a group, they followed no single "school" of thought or literary practice, although their works were uniformly disparaged by the *Edinburgh Review*.

Lay: A song or simple narrative poem. The form originated in medieval France. Early French *lais* were often based on the Celtic legends and other tales sung by Breton minstrels—thus the name of the "Breton lay." In fourteenth-century England, the term "lay" was used to describe short narratives written in imitation of the Breton lays.

Leitmotiv: See *Motif*

Literal Language: An author uses literal language when he or she writes without exaggerating or embellishing the subject matter and without any tools of figurative language.

Literary Ballad: See *Ballad*

Literature: Literature is broadly defined as any written or spoken material, but the term most often refers to creative works.

Lost Generation: A term first used by Gertrude Stein to describe the post-World War I generation of American writers: men and women haunted by a sense of betrayal and emptiness brought about by the destructiveness of the war.

Lyric Poetry: A poem expressing the subjective feelings and personal emotions of the poet. Such poetry is melodic, since it was originally accompanied by a lyre in recitals. Most Western poetry in the twentieth century may be classified as lyrical.

M

Mannerism: Exaggerated, artificial adherence to a literary manner or style. Also, a popular style of the visual arts of late sixteenth-century Europe that was marked by elongation of the human form and by intentional spatial distortion. Literary works that are self-consciously high-toned and artistic are often said to be "mannered."

Masculine Rhyme: See *Rhyme*

Measure: The foot, verse, or time sequence used in a literary work, especially a poem. Measure is often used somewhat incorrectly as a synonym for meter.

Metaphor: A figure of speech that expresses an idea through the image of another object. Metaphors suggest the essence of the first object by identifying it with certain qualities of the second object.

Metaphysical Conceit: See *Conceit*

Metaphysical Poetry: The body of poetry produced by a group of seventeenth-century English writers called the "Metaphysical Poets." The group includes John Donne and Andrew Marvell. The Metaphysical Poets made use of everyday speech, intellectual analysis, and unique imagery. They aimed to portray the ordinary conflicts and contradictions of life. Their poems often took the form of an argument, and many of them emphasize physical and religious love as well as the fleeting nature of life. Elaborate conceits are typical in metaphysical poetry.

Metaphysical Poets: See *Metaphysical Poetry*

Meter: In literary criticism, the repetition of sound patterns that creates a rhythm in poetry. The patterns are based on the number of syllables and the presence and absence of accents. The unit of rhythm in a line is called a foot. Types of meter are classified according to the number of feet in a line. These are the standard English lines: Monometer, one foot; Dimeter, two feet; Trimeter, three feet; Tetrameter, four feet; Pentameter, five feet; Hexameter, six feet (also called the Alexandrine); Heptameter, seven feet (also called the "Fourteener" when the feet are iambic).

Modernism: Modern literary practices. Also, the principles of a literary school that lasted from roughly the beginning of the twentieth century until the end of World War II. Modernism is defined by its rejection of the literary conventions of the nineteenth century and by its opposition to conventional morality, taste, traditions, and economic values.

Monologue: A composition, written or oral, by a single individual. More specifically, a speech given by a single individual in a drama or other public entertainment. It has no set length, although it is usually several or more lines long.

Monometer: See *Meter*

Mood: The prevailing emotions of a work or of the author in his or her creation of the work. The mood of a work is not always what might be expected based on its subject matter.

Motif: A theme, character type, image, metaphor, or other verbal element that recurs throughout a single work of literature or occurs in a number of different works over a period of time.

Motiv: See *Motif*

Muckrakers: An early twentieth-century group of American writers. Typically, their works exposed the wrongdoings of big business and government in the United States.

Muses: Nine Greek mythological goddesses, the daughters of Zeus and Mnemosyne (Memory). Each muse patronized a specific area of the liberal arts and sciences. Calliope presided over epic poetry, Clio over history, Erato over love poetry, Euterpe over music or lyric poetry, Melpomene over tragedy, Polyhymnia over hymns to the gods, Terpsichore over dance, Thalia over comedy, and Urania over astronomy. Poets and writers traditionally made appeals to the Muses for inspiration in their work.

Myth: An anonymous tale emerging from the traditional beliefs of a culture or social unit. Myths use supernatural explanations for natural phenomena. They may also explain cosmic issues like creation and death. Collections of myths, known as mythologies, are common to all cultures and nations, but the best-known myths belong to the Norse, Roman, and Greek mythologies.

N

Narration: The telling of a series of events, real or invented. A narration may be either a simple narrative, in which the events are recounted chronologically, or a narrative with a plot, in which the account is given in a style reflecting the author's artistic concept of the story. Narration is sometimes used as a synonym for "storyline."

Narrative: A verse or prose accounting of an event or sequence of events, real or invented. The term is also used as an adjective in the sense "method of narration." For example, in literary criticism, the expression "narrative technique" usually refers to the way the author structures and presents his or her story.

Narrative Poetry: A nondramatic poem in which the author tells a story. Such poems may be of any length or level of complexity.

Narrator: The teller of a story. The narrator may be the author or a character in the story through whom the author speaks.

Naturalism: A literary movement of the late nineteenth and early twentieth centuries. The movement's major theorist, French novelist Emile Zola, envisioned a type of fiction that would examine human life with the objectivity of scientific inquiry. The Naturalists typically viewed human beings as either the products of "biological determinism," ruled by hereditary instincts and engaged in an endless struggle for survival, or as the products of "socioeconomic determinism," ruled by social and economic forces beyond their control. In their works, the Naturalists generally ignored the highest levels of society and focused on degradation: poverty, alcoholism, prostitution, insanity, and disease.

Negritude: A literary movement based on the concept of a shared cultural bond on the part of black Africans, wherever they may be in the world. It traces its origins to the former French colonies of Africa and the Caribbean. Negritude poets, novelists, and essayists generally stress four points in their writings: One, black alienation from traditional African culture can lead to feelings of inferiority. Two, European colonialism and Western education should be resisted. Three, black Africans should seek to affirm and define their own identity. Four, African culture can and should be reclaimed. Many Negritude writers also claim that blacks can make unique contributions to the world, based on a heightened appreciation of nature, rhythm, and human emotions—aspects of life they say are not so highly valued in the materialistic and rationalistic West.

Negro Renaissance: See *Harlem Renaissance*

Neoclassical Period: See *Neoclassicism*

Neoclassicism: In literary criticism, this term refers to the revival of the attitudes and styles of expression of classical literature. It is generally used to describe a period in European history beginning in the late seventeenth century and lasting until about 1800. In its purest form, Neoclassicism marked a return to order, proportion, restraint, logic, accuracy, and decorum. In England, where Neoclassicism perhaps was most popular, it reflected the influence of seventeenth-century French writers, especially dramatists. Neoclassical writers typically reacted against the intensity and enthusiasm of the Renaissance period. They wrote works that appealed to the intellect, using elevated language and classical literary forms such as satire and the ode. Neoclassical works were often governed by the classical goal of instruction.

Neoclassicists: See *Neoclassicism*

New Criticism: A movement in literary criticism, dating from the late 1920s, that stressed close textual analysis in the interpretation of works of literature. The New Critics saw little merit in historical and biographical analysis. Rather, they aimed to examine the text alone, free from the question of how external events—biographical or otherwise—may have helped shape it.

New Journalism: A type of writing in which the journalist presents factual information in a form usually used in fiction. New journalism emphasizes description, narration, and character development to bring readers closer to the human element of the story, and is often used in personality profiles and in-depth feature articles. It is not compatible with "straight" or "hard" newswriting, which is generally composed in a brief, fact-based style.

New Journalists: See *New Journalism*

New Negro Movement: See *Harlem Renaissance*

Noble Savage: The idea that primitive man is noble and good but becomes evil and corrupted as he becomes civilized. The concept of the noble savage originated in the Renaissance period but is more closely identified with such later writers as Jean-Jacques Rousseau and Aphra Behn.

O

Objective Correlative: An outward set of objects, a situation, or a chain of events corresponding to an inward experience and evoking this experience in the reader. The term frequently appears in modern criticism in discussions of authors' intended effects on the emotional responses of readers.

Objectivity: A quality in writing characterized by the absence of the author's opinion or feeling about the subject matter. Objectivity is an important factor in criticism.

Occasional Verse: poetry written on the occasion of a significant historical or personal event. *Vers de societe* is sometimes called occasional verse although it is of a less serious nature.

Octave: A poem or stanza composed of eight lines. The term octave most often represents the first eight lines of a Petrarchan sonnet.

Ode: Name given to an extended lyric poem characterized by exalted emotion and dignified style. An ode usually concerns a single, serious theme. Most odes, but not all, are addressed to an object or individual. Odes are distinguished from other lyric poetic forms by their complex rhythmic and stanzaic patterns.

Oedipus Complex: A son's amorous obsession with his mother. The phrase is derived from the story of the ancient Theban hero Oedipus, who unknowingly killed his father and married his mother.

Omniscience: See *Point of View*

Onomatopoeia: The use of words whose sounds express or suggest their meaning. In its simplest sense, onomatopoeia may be represented by words that mimic the sounds they denote such as "hiss" or "meow." At a more subtle level, the pattern and rhythm of sounds and rhymes of a line or poem may be onomatopoeic.

Oral Tradition: See *Oral Transmission*

Oral Transmission: A process by which songs, ballads, folklore, and other material are transmitted by word of mouth. The tradition of oral transmission predates the written record systems of literate society. Oral transmission preserves material sometimes over generations, although often with variations. Memory plays a large part in the recitation and preservation of orally transmitted material.

Ottava Rima: An eight-line stanza of poetry composed in iambic pentameter (a five-foot line in which each foot consists of an unaccented syllable followed by an accented syllable), following the abababcc rhyme scheme.

Oxymoron: A phrase combining two contradictory terms. Oxymorons may be intentional or unintentional.

P

Pantheism: The idea that all things are both a manifestation or revelation of God and a part of God at the same time. Pantheism was a common attitude in the early societies of Egypt, India, and Greece—the term derives from the Greek *pan* meaning "all" and *theos* meaning "deity." It later became a significant part of the Christian faith.

Parable: A story intended to teach a moral lesson or answer an ethical question.

Paradox: A statement that appears illogical or contradictory at first, but may actually point to an underlying truth.

Parallelism: A method of comparison of two ideas in which each is developed in the same grammatical structure.

Parnassianism: A mid nineteenth-century movement in French literature. Followers of the movement stressed adherence to well-defined artistic forms as a reaction against the often chaotic expression of the artist's ego that dominated the work of the Romantics. The Parnassians also rejected the moral, ethical, and social themes exhibited in the works of French Romantics such as Victor Hugo. The aesthetic doctrines of the Parnassians strongly influenced the later symbolist and decadent movements.

Parody: In literary criticism, this term refers to an imitation of a serious literary work or the signature style of a particular author in a ridiculous manner. A typical parody adopts the style of the original and applies it to an inappropriate subject for humorous effect. Parody is a form of satire and could be considered the literary equivalent of a caricature or cartoon.

Pastoral: A term derived from the Latin word "pastor," meaning shepherd. A pastoral is a literary composition on a rural theme. The conventions of the pastoral were originated by the third-century Greek poet Theocritus, who wrote about the experiences, love affairs, and pastimes of Sicilian shepherds. In a pastoral, characters and language of a courtly nature are often placed in a simple setting. The term pastoral is also used to classify dramas, elegies, and lyrics that exhibit the use of country settings and shepherd characters.

Pathetic Fallacy: A term coined by English critic John Ruskin to identify writing that falsely endows nonhuman things with human intentions and feelings, such as "angry clouds" and "sad trees."

Pen Name: See *Pseudonym*

Pentameter: See *Meter*

Persona: A Latin term meaning "mask." *Personae* are the characters in a fictional work of literature. The *persona* generally functions as a mask through which the author tells a story in a voice other than his or her own. A *persona* is usually either a character in a story who acts as a narrator or an "implied author," a voice created by the author to act as the narrator for himself or herself.

Personae: See *Persona*

Personal Point of View: See *Point of View*

Personification: A figure of speech that gives human qualities to abstract ideas, animals, and inanimate objects.

Petrarchan Sonnet: See *Sonnet*

Phenomenology: A method of literary criticism based on the belief that things have no existence outside of human consciousness or awareness. Proponents of this theory believe that art is a process that takes place in the mind of the observer as he or she contemplates an object rather than a quality of the object itself.

Plagiarism: Claiming another person's written material as one's own. Plagiarism can take the form of direct, word-for-word copying or the theft of the substance or idea of the work.

Platonic Criticism: A form of criticism that stresses an artistic work's usefulness as an agent of social engineering rather than any quality or value of the work itself.

Platonism: The embracing of the doctrines of the philosopher Plato, popular among the poets of the Renaissance and the Romantic period. Platonism is more flexible than Aristotelian Criticism and places more emphasis on the supernatural and unknown aspects of life.

Plot: In literary criticism, this term refers to the pattern of events in a narrative or drama. In its simplest sense, the plot guides the author in composing the work and helps the reader follow the work. Typically, plots exhibit causality and unity and have a beginning, a middle, and an end. Sometimes, however, a plot may consist of a series of disconnected events, in which case it is known as an "episodic plot."

Poem: In its broadest sense, a composition utilizing rhyme, meter, concrete detail, and expressive language to create a literary experience with emotional and aesthetic appeal.

Poet: An author who writes poetry or verse. The term is also used to refer to an artist or writer who has an exceptional gift for expression, imagination, and energy in the making of art in any form.

Poete maudit: A term derived from Paul Verlaine's *Les poetes maudits* (*The Accursed Poets*), a collection of essays on the French symbolist writers Stephane Mallarme, Arthur Rimbaud, and Tristan Corbiere. In the sense intended by Verlaine, the poet is "accursed" for choosing to explore extremes of human experience outside of middle-class society.

Poetic Fallacy: See *Pathetic Fallacy*

Poetic Justice: An outcome in a literary work, not necessarily a poem, in which the good are rewarded and the evil are punished, especially in ways that particularly fit their virtues or crimes.

Poetic License: Distortions of fact and literary convention made by a writer—not always a poet—for the sake of the effect gained. Poetic license is closely related to the concept of "artistic freedom."

Poetics: This term has two closely related meanings. It denotes (1) an aesthetic theory in literary criticism about the essence of poetry or (2) rules prescribing the proper methods, content, style, or diction of poetry. The term poetics may also refer to theories about literature in general, not just poetry.

Poetry: In its broadest sense, writing that aims to present ideas and evoke an emotional experience in the reader through the use of meter, imagery, connotative and concrete words, and a carefully constructed structure based on rhythmic patterns. Poetry typically relies on words and expressions that have several layers of meaning. It also makes use of the effects of regular rhythm on the ear and may make a strong appeal to the senses through the use of imagery.

Point of View: The narrative perspective from which a literary work is presented to the reader. There are four traditional points of view. The "third person omniscient" gives the reader a "godlike" perspective, unrestricted by time or place, from which to see actions and look into the minds of characters. This allows the author to comment openly on characters and events in the work. The "third person" point of view presents the events of the story from outside of any single character's perception, much like the omniscient point of view, but the reader must understand the action as it takes place and without any special insight into characters' minds or motivations. The "first person" or "personal" point of view relates events as they are perceived by a single character. The main character "tells" the story and may offer opinions about the action and characters which differ from those of the author. Much less common than omniscient, third person, and first person is the "second person" point of view, wherein the author tells the story as if it is happening to the reader.

Polemic: A work in which the author takes a stand on a controversial subject, such as abortion or religion. Such works are often extremely argumentative or provocative.

Pornography: Writing intended to provoke feelings of lust in the reader. Such works are often condemned by critics and teachers, but those which can be shown to have literary value are viewed less harshly.

Post-Aesthetic Movement: An artistic response made by African Americans to the black aesthetic movement of the 1960s and early '70s. Writers since that time have adopted a somewhat different tone in their work, with less emphasis placed on the disparity between black and white in the United States. In the words of post-aesthetic authors such as Toni Morrison, John Edgar Wideman, and Kristin Hunter, African Americans are portrayed as looking inward for answers to their own questions, rather than always looking to the outside world.

Postmodernism: Writing from the 1960s forward characterized by experimentation and continuing to apply some of the fundamentals of modernism, which included existentialism and alienation. Postmodernists have gone a step further in the rejection of tradition begun with the modernists by also rejecting traditional forms, preferring the anti-novel over the novel and the anti-hero over the hero.

Pre-Raphaelites: A circle of writers and artists in mid nineteenth-century England. Valuing the pre-Renaissance artistic qualities of religious symbolism, lavish pictorialism, and natural sensuousness, the Pre-Raphaelites cultivated a sense of mystery and melancholy that influenced later writers associated with the Symbolist and Decadent movements.

Primitivism: The belief that primitive peoples were nobler and less flawed than civilized peoples because they had not been subjected to the tainting influence of society.

Projective Verse: A form of free verse in which the poet's breathing pattern determines the lines of the poem. Poets who advocate projective verse are against all formal structures in writing, including meter and form.

Prologue: An introductory section of a literary work. It often contains information establishing the situation of the characters or presents information about the setting, time period, or action. In drama, the prologue is spoken by a chorus or by one of the principal characters.

Prose: A literary medium that attempts to mirror the language of everyday speech. It is distinguished from poetry by its use of unmetered, unrhymed language consisting of logically related sentences. Prose is usually grouped into paragraphs that form a cohesive whole such as an essay or a novel.

Prosopopoeia: See *Personification*

Protagonist: The central character of a story who serves as a focus for its themes and incidents and as the principal rationale for its development. The protagonist is sometimes referred to in discussions of modern literature as the hero or anti-hero.

Proverb: A brief, sage saying that expresses a truth about life in a striking manner.

Pseudonym: A name assumed by a writer, most often intended to prevent his or her identification as the author of a work. Two or more authors may work together under one pseudonym, or an author may use a different name for each genre he or she publishes in. Some publishing companies maintain "house pseudonyms," under which any number of authors may write installations in a series. Some authors also choose a pseudonym over their real names the way an actor may use a stage name.

Pun: A play on words that have similar sounds but different meanings.

Pure Poetry: poetry written without instructional intent or moral purpose that aims only to please a reader by its imagery or musical flow. The term pure poetry is used as the antonym of the term "didacticism."

Q
Quatrain: A four-line stanza of a poem or an entire poem consisting of four lines.

R
Realism: A nineteenth-century European literary movement that sought to portray familiar characters, situations, and settings in a realistic manner. This was done primarily by using an objective narrative point of view and through the buildup of accurate detail. The standard for success of any realistic work depends on how faithfully it transfers common experience into fictional forms. The realistic method may be altered or extended, as in stream of consciousness writing, to record highly subjective experience.

Refrain: A phrase repeated at intervals throughout a poem. A refrain may appear at the end of each stanza or at less regular intervals. It may be altered slightly at each appearance.

Renaissance: The period in European history that marked the end of the Middle Ages. It began in Italy in the late fourteenth century. In broad terms, it is usually seen as spanning the fourteenth, fifteenth, and sixteenth centuries, although it did not reach Great Britain, for example, until the 1480s or so. The Renaissance saw an awakening in almost every sphere of human activity, especially science, philosophy, and the arts. The period is best defined by the emergence of a general philosophy that emphasized the importance of the intellect, the individual, and world affairs. It contrasts strongly with the medieval worldview, characterized by the dominant concerns of faith, the social collective, and spiritual salvation.

Repartee: Conversation featuring snappy retorts and witticisms.

Restoration: See *Restoration Age*

Restoration Age: A period in English literature beginning with the crowning of Charles II in 1660 and running to about 1700. The era, which was characterized by a reaction against Puritanism, was the first great age of the comedy of manners. The finest literature of the era is typically witty and urbane, and often lewd.

Rhetoric: In literary criticism, this term denotes the art of ethical persuasion. In its strictest sense, rhetoric adheres to various principles developed since classical times for arranging facts and ideas in a clear, persuasive, appealing manner. The term is also used to refer to effective prose in general and theories of or methods for composing effective prose.

Rhetorical Question: A question intended to provoke thought, but not an expressed answer, in the reader. It is most commonly used in oratory and other persuasive genres.

Rhyme: When used as a noun in literary criticism, this term generally refers to a poem in which words sound identical or very similar and appear in parallel positions in two or more lines. Rhymes are classified into different types according to where they fall in a line or stanza or according to the degree of similarity they exhibit in their spellings and sounds. Some major types of rhyme are "masculine" rhyme, "feminine" rhyme, and "triple" rhyme. In a masculine rhyme, the rhyming sound falls in a single accented syllable, as with "heat" and "eat." Feminine rhyme is a rhyme of two syllables, one stressed and one unstressed, as with "merry" and "tarry." Triple rhyme matches the sound of the accented syllable and the two unaccented syllables that follow: "narrative" and "declarative."

Rhyme Royal: A stanza of seven lines composed in iambic pentameter and rhymed *ababbcc*. The name is said to be a tribute to King James I of Scotland, who made much use of the form in his poetry.

Rhyme Scheme: See *Rhyme*

Rhythm: A regular pattern of sound, time intervals, or events occurring in writing, most often and most discernably in poetry. Regular, reliable rhythm is known to be soothing to humans, while interrupted, unpredictable, or rapidly changing rhythm is disturbing. These effects are known to authors, who use them to produce a desired reaction in the reader.

Rococo: A style of European architecture that flourished in the eighteenth century, especially in France. The most notable features of *rococo* are its extensive use of ornamentation and its themes of lightness, gaiety, and intimacy. In literary criticism, the term is often used disparagingly to refer to a decadent or over-ornamental style.

Romance: A broad term, usually denoting a narrative with exotic, exaggerated, often idealized characters, scenes, and themes.

Romantic Age: See *Romanticism*

Romanticism: This term has two widely accepted meanings. In historical criticism, it refers to a European intellectual and artistic movement of the late eighteenth and early nineteenth centuries that sought greater freedom of personal expression than that allowed by the strict rules of literary form and logic of the eighteenth-century neoclassicists. The Romantics preferred emotional and imaginative expression to rational analysis. They considered the individual to be at the center of all experience and so placed him or her at the center of their art. The Romantics believed that the creative imagination reveals nobler truths—unique feelings and attitudes—than those that could be discovered by logic or by scientific examination. Both the natural world and the state of childhood were important sources for revelations of "eternal truths." "Romanticism" is also used as a general term to refer to a type of sensibility found in all periods of literary history and usually considered to be in opposition to the principles of classicism. In this sense, Romanticism signifies any work or philosophy in which the exotic or dreamlike figure strongly, or that is devoted to individualistic expression, self-analysis, or a pursuit of a higher realm of knowledge than can be discovered by human reason.

Romantics: See *Romanticism*

Russian Symbolism: A Russian poetic movement, derived from French symbolism, that flourished between 1894 and 1910. While some Russian Symbolists continued in the French tradition, stressing aestheticism and the importance of suggestion above didactic intent, others saw their craft as a form of mystical worship, and themselves as mediators between the supernatural and the mundane.

S

Satire: A work that uses ridicule, humor, and wit to criticize and provoke change in human nature and institutions. There are two major types of satire: "formal" or "direct" satire speaks directly to the reader or to a character in the work; "indirect" satire relies upon the ridiculous behavior of its characters to make its point. Formal satire is further divided into two manners: the "Horatian," which ridicules gently, and the

"Juvenalian," which derides its subjects harshly and bitterly.

Scansion: The analysis or "scanning" of a poem to determine its meter and often its rhyme scheme. The most common system of scansion uses accents (slanted lines drawn above syllables) to show stressed syllables, breves (curved lines drawn above syllables) to show unstressed syllables, and vertical lines to separate each foot.

Second Person: See *Point of View*

Semiotics: The study of how literary forms and conventions affect the meaning of language.

Sestet: Any six-line poem or stanza.

Setting: The time, place, and culture in which the action of a narrative takes place. The elements of setting may include geographic location, characters' physical and mental environments, prevailing cultural attitudes, or the historical time in which the action takes place.

Shakespearean Sonnet: See *Sonnet*

Signifying Monkey: A popular trickster figure in black folklore, with hundreds of tales about this character documented since the 19th century.

Simile: A comparison, usually using "like" or "as," of two essentially dissimilar things, as in "coffee as cold as ice" or "He sounded like a broken record."

Slang: A type of informal verbal communication that is generally unacceptable for formal writing. Slang words and phrases are often colorful exaggerations used to emphasize the speaker's point; they may also be shortened versions of an often-used word or phrase.

Slant Rhyme: See *Consonance*

Slave Narrative: Autobiographical accounts of American slave life as told by escaped slaves. These works first appeared during the abolition movement of the 1830s through the 1850s.

Social Realism: See *Socialist Realism*

Socialist Realism: The Socialist Realism school of literary theory was proposed by Maxim Gorky and established as a dogma by the first Soviet Congress of Writers. It demanded adherence to a communist worldview in works of literature. Its doctrines required an objective viewpoint comprehensible to the working classes and themes of social struggle featuring strong proletarian heroes.

Soliloquy: A monologue in a drama used to give the audience information and to develop the speaker's character. It is typically a projection of the speaker's innermost thoughts. Usually delivered while the speaker is alone on stage, a soliloquy is intended to present an illusion of unspoken reflection.

Sonnet: A fourteen-line poem, usually composed in iambic pentameter, employing one of several rhyme schemes. There are three major types of sonnets, upon which all other variations of the form are based: the "Petrarchan" or "Italian" sonnet, the "Shakespearean" or "English" sonnet, and the "Spenserian" sonnet. A Petrarchan sonnet consists of an octave rhymed *abbaabba* and a "sestet" rhymed either *cdecde, cdccdc,* or *cdedce.* The octave poses a question or problem, relates a narrative, or puts forth a proposition; the sestet presents a solution to the problem, comments upon the narrative, or applies the proposition put forth in the octave. The Shakespearean sonnet is divided into three quatrains and a couplet rhymed *abab cdcd efef gg.* The couplet provides an epigrammatic comment on the narrative or problem put forth in the quatrains. The Spenserian sonnet uses three quatrains and a couplet like the Shakespearean, but links their three rhyme schemes in this way: *abab bcbc cdcd ee.* The Spenserian sonnet develops its theme in two parts like the Petrarchan, its final six lines resolving a problem, analyzing a narrative, or applying a proposition put forth in its first eight lines.

Spenserian Sonnet: See *Sonnet*

Spenserian Stanza: A nine-line stanza having eight verses in iambic pentameter, its ninth verse in iambic hexameter, and the rhyme scheme ababbcbcc.

Spondee: In poetry meter, a foot consisting of two long or stressed syllables occurring together. This form is quite rare in English verse, and is usually composed of two monosyllabic words.

Sprung Rhythm: Versification using a specific number of accented syllables per line but disregarding the number of unaccented syllables that fall in each line, producing an irregular rhythm in the poem.

Stanza: A subdivision of a poem consisting of lines grouped together, often in recurring patterns of rhyme, line length, and meter. Stanzas may also serve as units of thought in a poem much like paragraphs in prose.

Stereotype: A stereotype was originally the name for a duplication made during the printing process; this led to its modern definition as a person or thing that is (or is assumed to be) the same as all others of its type.

Stream of Consciousness: A narrative technique for rendering the inward experience of a character. This technique is designed to give the impression of an ever-changing series of thoughts, emotions, images, and memories in the spontaneous and seemingly illogical order that they occur in life.

Structuralism: A twentieth-century movement in literary criticism that examines how literary texts arrive at their meanings, rather than the meanings themselves. There are two major types of structuralist analysis: one examines the way patterns of linguistic structures unify a specific text and emphasize certain elements of that text, and the other interprets the way literary forms and conventions affect the meaning of language itself.

Structure: The form taken by a piece of literature. The structure may be made obvious for ease of understanding, as in nonfiction works, or may obscured for artistic purposes, as in some poetry or seemingly "unstructured" prose.

Sturm und Drang: A German term meaning "storm and stress." It refers to a German literary movement of the 1770s and 1780s that reacted against the order and rationalism of the enlightenment, focusing instead on the intense experience of extraordinary individuals.

Style: A writer's distinctive manner of arranging words to suit his or her ideas and purpose in writing. The unique imprint of the author's personality upon his or her writing, style is the product of an author's way of arranging ideas and his or her use of diction, different sentence structures, rhythm, figures of speech, rhetorical principles, and other elements of composition.

Subject: The person, event, or theme at the center of a work of literature. A work may have one or more subjects of each type, with shorter works tending to have fewer and longer works tending to have more.

Subjectivity: Writing that expresses the author's personal feelings about his subject, and which may or may not include factual information about the subject.

Surrealism: A term introduced to criticism by Guillaume Apollinaire and later adopted by Andre Breton. It refers to a French literary and artistic movement founded in the 1920s. The Surrealists sought to express unconscious thoughts and feelings in their works. The best-known technique used for achieving this aim was automatic writing—transcriptions of spontaneous outpourings from the unconscious. The Surrealists proposed to unify the contrary levels of conscious and unconscious, dream and reality, objectivity and subjectivity into a new level of "super-realism."

Suspense: A literary device in which the author maintains the audience's attention through the buildup of events, the outcome of which will soon be revealed.

Syllogism: A method of presenting a logical argument. In its most basic form, the syllogism consists of a major premise, a minor premise, and a conclusion.

Symbol: Something that suggests or stands for something else without losing its original identity. In literature, symbols combine their literal meaning with the suggestion of an abstract concept. Literary symbols are of two types: those that carry complex associations of meaning no matter what their contexts, and those that derive their suggestive meaning from their functions in specific literary works.

Symbolism: This term has two widely accepted meanings. In historical criticism, it denotes an early modernist literary movement initiated in France during the nineteenth century that reacted against the prevailing standards of realism. Writers in this movement aimed to evoke, indirectly and symbolically, an order of being beyond the material world of the five senses. Poetic expression of personal emotion figured strongly in the movement, typically by means of a private set of symbols uniquely identifiable with the individual poet. The principal aim of the Symbolists was to express in words the highly complex feelings that grew out of everyday contact with the world. In a broader sense, the term "symbolism" refers to the use of one object to represent another.

Symbolist: See *Symbolism*

Symbolist Movement: See *Symbolism*

Sympathetic Fallacy: See *Affective Fallacy*

T

Tanka: A form of Japanese poetry similar to *haiku*. A *tanka* is five lines long, with the lines containing five, seven, five, seven, and seven syllables respectively.

Terza Rima: A three-line stanza form in poetry in which the rhymes are made on the last word of each line in the following manner: the first and third lines of the first stanza, then the second line of the first stanza and the first and third lines of the second stanza, and so on with the middle line of any stanza rhyming with the first and third lines of the following stanza.

Tetrameter: See *Meter*

Textual Criticism: A branch of literary criticism that seeks to establish the authoritative text of a literary work. Textual critics typically compare all known manuscripts or printings of a single work in order to assess the meanings of differences and revisions. This procedure allows them to arrive at a definitive version that (supposedly) corresponds to the author's original intention.

Theme: The main point of a work of literature. The term is used interchangeably with thesis.

Thesis: A thesis is both an essay and the point argued in the essay. Thesis novels and thesis plays share the quality of containing a thesis which is supported through the action of the story.

Third Person: See *Point of View*

Tone: The author's attitude toward his or her audience may be deduced from the tone of the work. A formal tone may create distance or convey politeness, while an informal tone may encourage a friendly, intimate, or intrusive feeling in the reader. The author's attitude toward his or her subject matter may also be deduced from the tone of the words he or she uses in discussing it.

Tragedy: A drama in prose or poetry about a noble, courageous hero of excellent charac-

ter who, because of some tragic character flaw or *hamartia*, brings ruin upon him- or herself. Tragedy treats its subjects in a dignified and serious manner, using poetic language to help evoke pity and fear and bring about catharsis, a purging of these emotions. The tragic form was practiced extensively by the ancient Greeks. In the Middle Ages, when classical works were virtually unknown, tragedy came to denote any works about the fall of persons from exalted to low conditions due to any reason: fate, vice, weakness, etc. According to the classical definition of tragedy, such works present the "pathetic"—that which evokes pity— rather than the tragic. The classical form of tragedy was revived in the sixteenth century; it flourished especially on the Elizabethan stage. In modern times, dramatists have attempted to adapt the form to the needs of modern society by drawing their heroes from the ranks of ordinary men and women and defining the nobility of these heroes in terms of spirit rather than exalted social standing.

Tragic Flaw: In a tragedy, the quality within the hero or heroine which leads to his or her downfall.

Transcendentalism: An American philosophical and religious movement, based in New England from around 1835 until the Civil War. Transcendentalism was a form of American romanticism that had its roots abroad in the works of Thomas Carlyle, Samuel Coleridge, and Johann Wolfgang von Goethe. The Transcendentalists stressed the importance of intuition and subjective experience in communication with God. They rejected religious dogma and texts in favor of mysticism and scientific naturalism. They pursued truths that lie beyond the "colorless" realms perceived by reason and the senses and were active social reformers in public education, women's rights, and the abolition of slavery.

Trickster: A character or figure common in Native American and African literature who uses his ingenuity to defeat enemies and escape difficult situations. Tricksters are most often animals, such as the spider, hare, or coyote, although they may take the form of humans as well.

Trimeter: See *Meter*

Triple Rhyme: See *Rhyme*

Trochee: See *Foot*

U

Understatement: See *Irony*

Unities: Strict rules of dramatic structure, formulated by Italian and French critics of the Renaissance and based loosely on the principles of drama discussed by Aristotle in his *Poetics*. Foremost among these rules were the three unities of action, time, and place that compelled a dramatist to: (1) construct a single plot with a beginning, middle, and end that details the causal relationships of action and character; (2) restrict the action to the events of a single day; and (3) limit the scene to a single place or city. The unities were observed faithfully by continental European writers until the Romantic Age, but they were never regularly observed in English drama. Modern dramatists are typically more concerned with a unity of impression or emotional effect than with any of the classical unities.

Urban Realism: A branch of realist writing that attempts to accurately reflect the often harsh facts of modern urban existence.

Utopia: A fictional perfect place, such as "paradise" or "heaven."

Utopian: See *Utopia*

Utopianism: See *Utopia*

V

Verisimilitude: Literally, the appearance of truth. In literary criticism, the term refers to aspects of a work of literature that seem true to the reader.

Vers de societe: See *Occasional Verse*

Vers libre: See *Free Verse*

Verse: A line of metered language, a line of a poem, or any work written in verse.

Versification: The writing of verse. Versification may also refer to the meter, rhyme, and other mechanical components of a poem.

Victorian: Refers broadly to the reign of Queen Victoria of England (1837-1901) and to anything with qualities typical of that era. For example, the qualities of smug narrowmindedness, bourgeois materialism, faith in social progress, and priggish morality are often considered Victorian. This stereotype is contradicted by such dramatic intellectual developments as the theories of Charles Darwin, Karl Marx, and Sigmund Freud (which stirred strong debates in England) and the critical attitudes of serious Victorian writers like Charles Dickens and George Eliot. In literature, the Victorian Period was the great age of the English novel, and the latter part of the era saw the rise of movements such as decadence and symbolism.

Victorian Age: See *Victorian*

Victorian Period: See *Victorian*

W

Weltanschauung: A German term referring to a person's worldview or philosophy.

Weltschmerz: A German term meaning "world pain." It describes a sense of anguish about the nature of existence, usually associated with a melancholy, pessimistic attitude.

Z

Zarzuela: A type of Spanish operetta.

Zeitgeist: A German term meaning "spirit of the time." It refers to the moral and intellectual trends of a given era.

Cumulative Author/Title Index

Cumulative
Nationality/Ethnicity Index

Cumulative Nationality/Ethnicity Index

Ghanaian

Du Bois, W. E. B.
The Song of the Smoke: V13

Greek

Cavafy, C. P.
Ithaka: V19
Sappho
Fragment 16: V38
Fragment 2: V31
Hymn to Aphrodite: V20

Hispanic American

Alvarez, Julia
Exile: V39
Baca, Jimmy Santiago
Who Understands Me But Me: V40
Castillo, Ana
While I Was Gone a War Began:
V21
Cervantes, Lorna Dee
Freeway 280: V30
Cruz, Victor Hernandez
Business: V16
Espada, Martín
Colibrí: V16
Mora, Pat
Elena: V33
Legal Alien: V40
Uncoiling: V35
Ortiz Cofer, Judith
The Latin Deli: An Ars Poetica:
V37
Sapia, Yvonne
Defining the Grateful Gesture: V40
Walcott, Derek
Sea Canes: V39
Williams, William Carlos
Overture to a Dance of
Locomotives: V11
Queen-Ann's-Lace: V6
The Red Wheelbarrow: V1
This Is Just to Say: V34

Indian

Divakaruni, Chitra Banerjee
My Mother Combs My Hair: V34
Mirabai
All I Was Doing Was Breathing:
V24
Ramanujan, A. K.
Waterfalls in a Bank: V27
Shahid Ali, Agha
Country Without a Post Office:
V18
Tagore, Rabindranath
60: V18
Vazirani, Reetika
Daughter-Mother-Maya-Seeta:
V25

Indonesian

Lee, Li-Young
Early in the Morning: V17
For a New Citizen of These United
States: V15
The Gift: V37
The Weight of Sweetness: V11

Iranian

Farrokhzaad, Faroogh
A Rebirth: V21

Iraqi

Youssef, Saadi
America, America: V29

Irish

Boland, Eavan
Anorexic: V12
Domestic Violence: V39
It's a Woman's World: V22
Outside History: V31
Carson, Ciaran
The War Correspondent: V26
Grennan, Eamon
Station: V21
Hartnett, Michael
A Farewell to English: V10
Heaney, Seamus
Digging: V5
A Drink of Water: V8
Follower: V30
The Forge: V41
Midnight: V2
The Singer's House: V17
Muldoon, Paul
Meeting the British: V7
Pineapples and Pomegranates: V22
Swift, Jonathan
A Description of the Morning: V37
A Satirical Elegy on the Death of a
Late Famous General: V27
Yeats, William Butler
Easter 1916: V5
An Irish Airman Foresees His
Death: V1
The Lake Isle of Innisfree: V15
Leda and the Swan: V13
Sailing to Byzantium: V2
The Second Coming: V7
The Stolen Child: V34
The Wild Swans at Coole: V42

Israeli

Amichai, Yehuda
Not like a Cypress: V24
Seven Laments for the War-Dead:
V39
Ravikovitch, Dahlia
Pride: V38

Italian

Apollinaire, Guillaume
Always: V24
Montale, Eugenio
On the Threshold: V22
Pavese, Cesare
Two Poems for T.: V20
Petrarch, Francesco
Rime 140: V42
Ungaretti, Giuseppe
Variations on Nothing: V20

Jamaican

Goodison, Lorna
The River Mumma Wants Out: V25
McKay, Claude
The Tropics in New York: V4
Simpson, Louis
In the Suburbs: V14

Japanese

Ai
Reunions with a Ghost: V16
Bashō, Matsuo
Falling Upon Earth: V2
The Moon Glows the Same: V7
Temple Bells Die Out: V18

Jewish

Amichai, Yehuda
Not like a Cypress: V24
Seven Laments for the War-Dead:
V39
Bell, Marvin
View: V25
Blumenthal, Michael
Inventors: V7
Brodsky, Joseph
Odysseus to Telemachus: V35
Espada, Martín
Colibrí: V16
We Live by What We See at Night:
V13
HaNagid, Shmuel
Two Eclipses: V33
Heine, Heinrich
The Lorelei: V37
Hirsch, Edward
Omen: V22
Pastan, Linda
The Cossacks: V25
Ethics: V8
Grudnow: V32
I Am Learning to Abandon the
World: V40
Piercy, Marge
Apple sauce for Eve: V22
Barbie Doll: V9
For the Young Who Want to: V40
To Be of Use: V32

Ravikovitch, Dahlia
  Pride: V38
Sachs, Nelly
  *But Perhaps God Needs the
    Longing:* V20
Shapiro, Karl
  Auto Wreck: V3
Stern, Gerald
  One of the Smallest: V26

Jewish American

Lazarus, Emma
  The New Colossus: V37

Kiowa

Momaday, N. Scott
  Angle of Geese: V2
  New World: V41
  A Simile: V37
  *To a Child Running With
    Outstretched Arms in Canyon de
    Chelly:* V11

Korean

Pak Tu-Jin
  River of August: V35

Lithuanian

Milosz, Czeslaw
  From the Rising of the Sun: V29
  In Music: V35
  Song of a Citizen: V16

Malaysian

Lim, Shirley Geok-lin
  Pantoun for Chinese Women: V29

Mexican

Paz, Octavio
  Duration: V18
  Sunstone: V30
  Two Bodies: V38
Soto, Gary
  Oranges: V30
  Small Town with One Road: V7

Native American

Ai
  Reunions with a Ghost: V16
Alexie, Sherman
  *The Powwow at the End of the
    World:* V39
Baca, Jimmy Santiago
  Who Understands Me But Me:
    V40
Bruchac, Joseph
  Birdfoot's Grampa: V36
Erdrich, Louise
  Bidwell Ghost: V14

Harjo, Joy
  Anniversary: V15
  Remember: V32
Momaday, N. Scott
  Angle of Geese: V2
  New World: V41
  A Simile: V37
  *To a Child Running With
    Outstretched Arms in Canyon de
    Chelly:* V11
Ortiz, Simon
  Hunger in New York City: V4
  My Father's Song: V16
Revard, Carter
  Birch Canoe: V5
Rose, Wendy
  *For the White poets who would be
    Indian:* V13
Silko, Leslie Marmon
  Four Mountain Wolves: V9
  Story from Bear Country: V16

Nigerian

Soyinka, Wole
  Civilian and Soldier: V40
  Telephone Conversation: V27

Osage

Revard, Carter
  Birch Canoe: V5

Peruvian

Vallejo, César
  The Black Heralds: V26

Philippine

Barot, Rick
  Bonnard's Garden: V25

Polish

Herbert, Zbigniew
  Why The Classics: V22
Milosz, Czeslaw
  From the Rising of the Sun: V29
  In Music: V35
  Song of a Citizen: V16
Swir, Anna
  Maternity: V21
Szymborska, Wisława
  Astonishment: V15
  Conversation with a Stone: V27
  The End and the Beginning: V41
  Possibilities: V34
  Some People Like Poetry: V31
Zagajewski, Adam
  Self-Portrait: V25

Roman

Ovid (Naso, Publius Ovidius)
  Metamorphoses: V22

Romanian

Celan, Paul
  Late and Deep: V21

Russian

Akhmatova, Anna
  Everything is Plundered: V32
  *I Am Not One of Those Who Left
    the Land:* V36
  Midnight Verses: V18
  Requiem: V27
Brodsky, Joseph
  Odysseus to Telemachus: V35
Merriam, Eve
  Onomatopoeia: V6
  Two People I Want to Be Like: V37
Pushkin, Alexander
  The Bridegroom: V34
  The Bronze Horseman: V28
Shapiro, Karl
  Auto Wreck: V3
Solzhenitsyn, Alexander
  A Storm in the Mountains: V38
Tsvetaeva, Marina
  An Attempt at Jealousy: V29
Yevtushenko, Yevgeny
  Babii Yar: V29

St. Lucian

Walcott, Derek
  A Far Cry from Africa: V6
  Midsummer, Tobago: V34

Scottish

Burns, Robert
  A Red, Red Rose: V8
Duffy, Carol Ann
  Originally: V25
MacBeth, George
  Bedtime Story: V8

Senegalese

Senghor, Léopold Sédar
  Prayer to the Masks: V36
Wheatley, Phillis
  An Hymn to the Evening: V36
  *On Being Brought from Africa to
    America:* V29
  *To His Excellency General
    Washington:* V13

Serbian

Lazić, Radmila
  Death Sentences: V22

Spanish

García Lorca, Federico
  Gacela of the Dark Death: V20
  The Guitar: V38

Subject/Theme Index

Subject/Theme Index

Cumulative
Index of First Lines

Get up, get up for shame, the
Blooming Morne (Corinna's
Going A-Maying) V39:2

Glory be to God for dappled
things— (Pied Beauty) V26:161

Go, and catch a falling star, (Song)
V35:237

Go down, Moses (Go Down, Moses)
V11:42

God of our fathers, known of old,
(Recessional) V42:183

God save America, (America,
America) V29:2

Grandmothers who wring the necks
(Classic Ballroom Dances)
V33:3

Gray mist wolf (Four Mountain
Wolves) V9:131

Grown too big for his skin, (Fable
for When There's No Way Out)
V38:42

H

"Had he and I but met (The Man He
Killed) V3:167

Had we but world enough, and time
(To His Coy Mistress) V5:276

Hail to thee, blithe Spirit! (To a Sky-
Lark) V32:251

Half a league, half a league (The
Charge of the Light Brigade)
V1:2

Having a Coke with You (Having a
Coke with You) V12:105

He clasps the crag with crooked
hands (The Eagle) V11:30

He was found by the Bureau of
Statistics to be (The Unknown
Citizen) V3:302

He was seen, surrounded by rifles,
(The Crime Was in Granada)
V23:55–56

Hear the sledges with the bells—
(The Bells) V3:46

Heart, you bully, you punk, I'm
wrecked, I'm shocked (One Is
One) V24:158

Her body is not so white as (Queen-
Ann's-Lace) V6:179

Her eyes the glow-worm lend thee;
(The Night Piece: To Julia)
V29:206

Her eyes were coins of porter and her
West (A Farewell to English)
V10:126

Here, above, (The Man-Moth)
V27:135

Here, she said, *put this on your head.*
(Flounder) V39:58

Here they are. The soft eyes open
(The Heaven of Animals) V6:75

His Grace! impossible! what dead! (A
Satirical Elegy on the Death of
a Late Famous General)
V27:216

His speed and strength, which is the
strength of ten (His Speed and
Strength) V19:96

Hog Butcher for the World
(Chicago) V3:61

Hold fast to dreams (Dream
Variations) V15:42

Hope is a tattered flag and a dream
out of time. (Hope is a Tattered
Flag) V12:120

"Hope" is the thing with feathers—
("Hope" Is the Thing with
Feathers) V3:123

How do I love thee? Let me count the
ways (Sonnet 43) V2:236

How is your life with the other one,
(An Attempt at Jealousy) V29:23

How shall we adorn (Angle of Geese)
V2:2

How soon hath Time, the subtle thief
of youth, (On His Having
Arrived at the Age of Twenty-
Three) V17:159

How would it be if you took yourself
off (Landscape with Tractor)
V10:182

Hunger crawls into you (Hunger in
New York City) V4:79

I

I am fourteen (Hanging Fire) V32:93

I am not a painter, I am a poet (Why
I Am Not a Painter) V8:258

I am not with those who abandoned
their land (I Am Not One of
Those Who Left the Land)
V36:91

I am silver and exact. I have no
preconceptions (Mirror) V1:116

I am the Smoke King (The Song of
the Smoke) V13:196

I am trying to pry open your casket
(Dear Reader) V10:85

I became a creature of light (The
Mystery) V15:137

I Built My Hut beside a Traveled
Road (I Built My Hut beside a
Traveled Road) V36:119

I cannot love the Brothers Wright
(Reactionary Essay on Applied
Science) V9:199

I caught a tremendous fish (The
Fish) V31:44

I, being born a woman and distressed
(I, being born a woman and
distressed (Sonnet XVIII))
V41:203

I died for Beauty—but was scarce (I
Died for Beauty) V28:174

I don't mean to make you cry.
(Monologue for an Onion)
V24:120–121

I don't want my daughter (Fear)
V37:71

I do not know what it means that
(The Lorelei) V37:145

I felt a Funeral, in my Brain, (I felt a
Funeral in my Brain) V13:137

I gave birth to life. (Maternity)
V21:142–143

I have been one acquainted with the
night. (Acquainted with the
Night) V35:3

I have eaten (This Is Just to Say)
V34:240

I have just come down from my
father (The Hospital Window)
V11:58

I have met them at close of day
(Easter 1916) V5:91

I have sown beside all waters in my
day. (A Black Man Talks of
Reaping) V32:20

I haven't the heart to say (To an
Unknown Poet) V18:221

I hear America singing, the varied
carols I hear (I Hear America
Singing) V3:152

I heard a Fly buzz—when I died— (I
Heard a Fly Buzz— When I
Died—) V5:140

I know that I shall meet my fate (An
Irish Airman Foresees His
Death) V1:76

I know what the caged bird feels,
alas! (Sympathy) V33:203

I leant upon a coppice gate (The
Darkling Thrush) V18:74

I lie down on my side in the moist
grass (Omen) v22:107

I looked in my heart while the wild
swans went over. (Wild Swans)
V17:221

I love to go out in late September
(Blackberry Eating) V35:23

I met a traveller from an antique land
(Ozymandias) V27:173

I placed a jar in Tennessee,
(Anecdote of the Jar) V41:3

I prove a theorem and the house
expands: (Geometry) V15:68

I saw that a star had broken its rope
(Witness) V26:285

I see them standing at the formal
gates of their colleges, (I go
Back to May 1937) V17:112

I shall die, but that is all that I shall
do for Death. (Conscientious
Objector) V34:46

Cumulative
Index of Last Lines

That's the word. (Black Zodiac)
  V10:47

The benediction of the air. (Snow-
  Bound) V36:248–254

the bigger it gets. (Smart and Final
  Iris) V15:183

The bosom of his Father and his God
  (Elegy Written in a Country
  Churchyard) V9:74

the bow toward torrents of *veyz mir*.
  (Three To's and an Oi) V24:264

The crime was in Granada, his
  Granada. (The Crime Was in
  Granada) V23:55–56

The dance is sure (Overture to a
  Dance of Locomotives)
  V11:143

The eyes turn topaz. (Hugh Selwyn
  Mauberley) V16:30

the flames? (Another Night in the
  Ruins) V26:13

The frolic architecture of the snow.
  (The Snow-Storm) V34:196

The garland briefer than a girl's (To
  an Athlete Dying Young)
  V7:230

The Grasshopper's among some
  grassy hills. (On the
  Grasshopper and the Cricket)
  V32:161

The guidon flags flutter gayly in the
  wind. (Cavalry Crossing a
  Ford) V13:50

The hands gripped hard on the desert
  (At the Bomb Testing Site) V8:3

The holy melodies of love arise. (The
  Arsenal at Springfield) V17:3

the knife at the throat, the death in
  the metronome (Music
  Lessons) V8:117

The Lady of Shalott." (The Lady of
  Shalott) V15:97

The lightning and the gale! (Old
  Ironsides) V9:172

The lone and level sands stretch far
  away. (Ozymandias) V27:173

the long, perfect loveliness of sow
  (Saint Francis and the Sow)
  V9:222

The Lord survives the rainbow of
  His will (The Quaker
  Graveyard in Nantucket)
  V6:159

The man I was when I was part of it
  (Beware of Ruins) V8:43

the quilts sing on (My Mother Pieced
  Quilts) V12:169

The red rose and the brier (Barbara
  Allan) V7:11

The self-same Power that brought
  me there brought you. (The
  Rhodora) V17:191

The shaft we raise to them and thee
  (Concord Hymn) V4:30

the skin of another, what I have made
  is a curse. (Curse) V26:75

The sky became a still and woven blue.
  (Merlin Enthralled) V16:73

The song of the Lorelei. (The
  Lorelei) V37:146

The spirit of this place (To a Child
  Running With Outstretched
  Arms in Canyon de Chelly)
  V11:173

The town again, trailing your legs
  and crying! (Wild Swans)
  V17:221

the unremitting space of your
  rebellion (Lost Sister) V5:217

The woman won (Oysters) V4:91

The world should listen then—as I
  am listening now. (To a Sky-
  Lark) V32:252

their dinnerware. (Portrait of a
  Couple at Century's End)
  V24:214–215

their guts or their brains?
  (Southbound on the Freeway)
  V16:158

Then chiefly lives. (Virtue) V25:263

There are blows in life, so hard . . . I
  just don't know! (The Black
  Heralds) V26:47

There is the trap that catches noblest
  spirits, that caught— they say—
  God, when he walked on earth
  (Shine, Perishing Republic)
  V4:162

there was light (Vancouver Lights)
  V8:246

They also serve who only stand and
  wait." ([On His Blindness]
  Sonnet 16) V3:262

They also serve who only stand and
  wait." (When I Consider
  (Sonnet XIX)) V37:302

They are going to some point true
  and unproven. (Geometry)
  V15:68

They have not sown, and feed on
  bitter fruit. (A Black Man Talks
  of Reaping) V32:21

They rise, they walk again (The
  Heaven of Animals) V6:76

They say a child with two mouths is
  no good. (Pantoun for Chinese
  Women) V29:242

They think I lost. I think I won
  (Harlem Hopscotch) V2:93

They'd eaten every one." (The
  Walrus and the Carpenter)
  V30:258–259

This is my page for English B (Theme
  for English B) V6:194

This Love (In Memory of Radio)
  V9:145

Tho' it were ten thousand mile!
  (A Red, Red Rose) V8:152

Though I sang in my chains like the
  sea (Fern Hill) V3:92

Till human voices wake us, and we
  drown (The Love Song of J.
  Alfred Prufrock) V1:99

Till Love and Fame to nothingness
  do sink (When I Have Fears
  that I May Cease to Be) V2:295

Till the gossamer thread you fling
  catch somewhere, O my soul.
  (A Noiseless Patient Spider)
  V31:190–91

To an admiring Bog! (I'm Nobody!
  Who Are You?) V35:83

To be a queen! (Fear) V37:71

To beat real iron out, to work the
  bellows. (The Forge) V41:158

To every woman a happy ending
  (Barbie Doll) V9:33

To find they have flown away? (The
  Wild Swans at Coole) V42:287

to float in the space between. (The
  Idea of Ancestry) V36:138

to glow at midnight. (The Blue Rim
  of Memory) V17:39

to its owner or what horror has
  befallen the other shoe (A Piéd)
  V3:16

To live with thee and be thy love.
  (The Nymph's Reply to the
  Shepherd) V14:241

To mock the riddled corpses round
  Bapaume. ("Blighters") V28:3

To see the cherry hung with snow.
  (Loveliest of Trees, the Cherry
  Now) V40:160

To strengthen whilst one stands."
  (Goblin Market) V27:96

To strive, to seek, to find, and not to
  yield (Ulysses) V2:279

To the moaning and the groaning of
  the bells (The Bells) V3:47

To the temple, singing. (In the
  Suburbs) V14:201

To wound myself upon the sharp
  edges of the night? (The Taxi)
  V30:211–212

too. (Birdfoot's Grampa) V36:21

torn from a wedding brocade. (My
  Mother Combs My Hair)
  V34:133

they *touch* you. They fill you like
  music. (What Are Friends For)
  V41:305

Turned to that dirt from whence he
  sprung. (A Satirical Elegy on
  the Death of a Late Famous
  General) V27:216

U

Undeniable selves, into your days, and beyond. (The Continuous Life) V18:51

under each man's eyelid. (Camouflaging the Chimera) V37:21

unexpectedly. (Fragment 16) V38:62

until at last I lift you up and wrap you within me. (It's like This) V23:138–139

Until Eternity. (The Bustle in a House) V10:62

unusual conservation (Chocolates) V11:17

Uttering cries that are almost human (American Poetry) V7:2

W

War is kind (War Is Kind) V9:253

watching to see how it's done. (I Stop Writing the Poem) V16:58

water. (Poem in Which My Legs Are Accepted) V29:262

We are satisfied, if you are; but why did I die?" (Losses) V31:167–68

we tread upon, forgetting. Truth be told. (Native Guard) V29:185

We wear the mask! (We Wear the Mask) V40:256

Went home and put a bullet through his head (Richard Cory) V4:117

Were not the one dead, turned to their affairs. (Out, Out—) V10:213

Were toward Eternity— (Because I Could Not Stop for Death) V2:27

What will survive of us is love. (An Arundel Tomb) V12:18

When I died they washed me out of the turret with a hose (The Death of the Ball Turret Gunner) V2:41

When locked up, bear down. (Fable for When There's No Way Out) V38:43

When the plunging hoofs were gone. (The Listeners) V39:136

when they untie them in the evening. (Early in the Morning) V17:75

when you are at a party. (Social Life) V19:251

When you have both (Toads) V4:244

Where deep in the night I hear a voice (Butcher Shop) V7:43

Where ignorant armies clash by night (Dover Beach) V2:52

Which caused her thus to send thee out of door. (The Author to Her Book) V42:42

Which Claus of Innsbruck cast in bronze for me! (My Last Duchess) V1:166

Which for all you know is the life you've chosen. (The God Who Loves You) V20:88

which is not going to go wasted on me which is why I'm telling you about it (Having a Coke with You) V12:106

which only looks like an *l*, and is silent. (Trompe l'Oeil) V22:216

whirring into her raw skin like stars (Uncoiling) V35:277

white ash amid funereal cypresses (Helen) V6:92

Who are you and what is your purpose? (The Mystery) V15:138

Who toss and sigh and cannot rest. (The Moon at the Fortified Pass) V40:180

who understands me when I say this is beautiful? (Who Understands Me But Me) V40:278

Why am I not as they? (Lineage) V31:145–46

Wi' the Scots lords at his feit (Sir Patrick Spens) V4:177

Will always be ready to bless the day (Morning Walk) V21:167

will be easy, my rancor less bitter . . . (On the Threshold) V22:128

Will hear of as a god." (How we Heard the Name) V10:167

Wind, like the dodo's (Bedtime Story) V8:33

windowpanes. (View) V25:246–247

With courage to endure! (Old Stoic) V33:144

With gold unfading, WASHINGTON! be thine. (To His Excellency General Washington) V13:213

with my eyes closed. (We Live by What We See at Night) V13:240

With silence and tears. (When We Two Parted) V29:297

with the door closed. (Hanging Fire) V32:93

With the slow smokeless burning of decay (The Wood-Pile) V6:252

With what they had to go on. (The Conquerors) V13:67

Without cease or doubt sew the sweet sad earth. (The Satyr's Heart) V22:187

Would scarcely know that we were gone. (There Will Come Soft Rains) V14:301

Wrapped in a larger. (Words are the Diminution of All Things) V35:316

Y

Ye know on earth, and all ye need to know (Ode on a Grecian Urn) V1:180

Yea, beds for all who come. (Up-Hill) V34:280

You live in this, and dwell in lovers' eyes (Sonnet 55) V5:246

You may for ever tarry. (To the Virgins, to Make Much of Time) V13:226

you who raised me? (The Gold Lily) V5:127

You're all that I can call my own. (Woman Work) V33:289

you'll have understood by then what these Ithakas mean. (Ithaka) V19:114